Communications
in Computer and Information Science   2109

Rationale

The CCIS series is devoted to the publication of proceedings of computer science conferences. Its aim is to efficiently disseminate original research results in informatics in printed and electronic form. While the focus is on publication of peer-reviewed full papers presenting mature work, inclusion of reviewed short papers reporting on work in progress is welcome, too. Besides globally relevant meetings with internationally representative program committees guaranteeing a strict peer-reviewing and paper selection process, conferences run by societies or of high regional or national relevance are also considered for publication.

Topics

The topical scope of CCIS spans the entire spectrum of informatics ranging from foundational topics in the theory of computing to information and communications science and technology and a broad variety of interdisciplinary application fields.

Information for Volume Editors and Authors

Publication in CCIS is free of charge. No royalties are paid, however, we offer registered conference participants temporary free access to the online version of the conference proceedings on SpringerLink (http://link.springer.com) by means of an http referrer from the conference website and/or a number of complimentary printed copies, as specified in the official acceptance email of the event.

CCIS proceedings can be published in time for distribution at conferences or as post-proceedings, and delivered in the form of printed books and/or electronically as USBs and/or e-content licenses for accessing proceedings at SpringerLink. Furthermore, CCIS proceedings are included in the CCIS electronic book series hosted in the SpringerLink digital library at http://link.springer.com/bookseries/7899. Conferences publishing in CCIS are allowed to use Online Conference Service (OCS) for managing the whole proceedings lifecycle (from submission and reviewing to preparing for publication) free of charge.

Publication process

The language of publication is exclusively English. Authors publishing in CCIS have to sign the Springer CCIS copyright transfer form, however, they are free to use their material published in CCIS for substantially changed, more elaborate subsequent publications elsewhere. For the preparation of the camera-ready papers/files, authors have to strictly adhere to the Springer CCIS Authors' Instructions and are strongly encouraged to use the CCIS LaTeX style files or templates.

Abstracting/Indexing

CCIS is abstracted/indexed in DBLP, Google Scholar, EI-Compendex, Mathematical Reviews, SCImago, Scopus. CCIS volumes are also submitted for the inclusion in ISI Proceedings.

How to start

To start the evaluation of your proposal for inclusion in the CCIS series, please send an e-mail to ccis@springer.com.

Frank Phillipson · Gerald Eichler ·
Christian Erfurth · Günter Fahrnberger
Editors

Innovations for Community Services

24th International Conference, I4CS 2024
Maastricht, The Netherlands, June 12–14, 2024
Proceedings

 Springer

Editors
Frank Phillipson 🆔
Maastricht University
Maastricht, The Netherlands

Gerald Eichler 🆔
Deutsche Telekom Technology & Innovation
Darmstadt, Germany

Christian Erfurth 🆔
University of Applied Sciences Jena
Jena, Germany

Günter Fahrnberger 🆔
University of Hagen
Hagen, Germany

ISSN 1865-0929   ISSN 1865-0937 (electronic)
Communications in Computer and Information Science
ISBN 978-3-031-60432-4   ISBN 978-3-031-60433-1 (eBook)
https://doi.org/10.1007/978-3-031-60433-1

This Springer imprint is published by the registered company Springer Nature Switzerland AG
The registered company address is: Gewerbestrasse 11, 6330 Cham, Switzerland

If disposing of this product, please recycle the paper.

Foreword

The International Conference on Innovations for Community Services (I4CS) celebrated its 24th edition in 2024, occurring for the second time in The Netherlands after 2022. We were pleased to meet many fellow attendees at Maastricht University in person again.

Twenty-three years ago, at Ilmenau University of Technology, Germany, Herwig Unger and Thomas Böhme called for the Workshop on Innovative Internet Community Systems (IICS) as a platform for project result publication. It continued its success story under its revised name I2CS, then I4CS since 2014. It published its first proceedings in books of the Springer Lecture Notes in Computer Science series (LNCS) until 2005, followed by Gesellschaft für Informatik (GI) in Köllen Verlag, and Verein Deutscher Ingenieure (VDI) in 2013. I4CS commenced with the Institute of Electrical and Electronics Engineers (IEEE) before it switched back to Springer's Communications in Computer and Information Science (CCIS) series in 2016 and created a permanent partnership in 2018. The unique combination of printed proceedings and the SpringerLink online edition generates high interest among external readers, with more than 4,300 accesses last year from https://link.springer.com/conference/i4cs.

The selection of conference locations reflects the conference concept: These are the members of the Program Committee (PC) who offer suitable locations to live out our passion as a scientific community. For 2024, the I4CS Steering Committee had the honor to hand over the organizational responsibility to Frank Phillipson and to accept his invitation to his second affiliation after Delft two years ago. Located on the banks of the River Maas and representing an important location for Europe's history with the Maastricht Treaties, we were near the Belgian and German borders, successfully embodying this year's motto, "Crossing Digital Borders".

We were proud to offer a good selection of scientific presentations, combined with a keynote, two invited talks, and a great social conference program to strengthen the cultural community spirit. The proceedings of I4CS 2024 comprise seven sessions that cover a selection of 17 full papers and five short papers out of 44 submissions received from authors in 13 countries. Interdisciplinary thinking is a key success factor for any community. Hence, I4CS 2024 covered several revised scientific, academic, social, and industrial topics, clustered into our three long-lasting and well-known key areas: Technology, Applications, and Socialization.

Technology: Distributed Architectures and Frameworks

- Data architectures and enablers for community services,
- Cryptography and decentralized secure computation,
- 5G/6G technologies and ad hoc mobile networks,
- Data models, artificial intelligence, and big data analytics,
- Distributed and hybrid quantum computing.

Applications: Communities on the Move

- Social networks, news, and mobile work,
- Open collaboration and eLearning didactics,
- Recommender solutions and context awareness,
- VR/AR, robotics, and location-based gaming,
- Intelligent transportation, logistics, and connected cars.

Socialization: Ambient Work and Living

- Remote work challenges and eHealth-assisted living,
- Chat bots and open AI models,
- Smart home, energy control, city, and infrastructure,
- Internet of things and sensor networks,
- Cybersecurity and privacy concerns.

Many thanks go to the 26 members of the Program Committee for 2024, representing 13 countries worldwide, for their 174 worthwhile reviews. Special thanks go to conference chairman Christian Erfurth, this year's program chair Frank Phillipson, and finally to our publication chair, Günter Fahrnberger, who facilitated a very successful cooperation with the Springer publishing board to maintain the high reputation of I4CS, rated C-level at CORE.

Following the alternation rule, the 25th I4CS will take place in Germany around June 2025. Please regularly check the permanent conference URL at http://www.i4cs-confer ence.org/ for upcoming details.

Proposals on new emerging topics, as well as applications from prospective Program Committee members and potential conference hosts and locations, are kindly welcome to request@i4cs-conference.org.

Kind regards on behalf of the entire Steering Committee and the Editors' Board.

I4CS Innovations for Community Services

June 2024   Gerald Eichler

Preface

Welcome to the proceedings of the 24th International Conference on Innovations for Community Services (I4CS), themed "Crossing Digital Borders", held during June 12–14, 2024, at Maastricht University in the city of Maastricht, The Netherlands. It is with great pleasure that I, as Conference Chair, introduce this CCIS volume, featuring cutting-edge research and insights into the dynamic field of digital innovation.

In today's interconnected world, the significance of innovations in community services cannot be overstated. These innovations encompass a broad spectrum of technologies and methodologies aimed at improving the well-being and quality of life for individuals and communities alike. From healthcare and education to transportation and public safety, community services play a vital role in shaping the fabric of society and fostering inclusivity and equity.

The choice of Maastricht as the venue for this year's conference holds special significance. Maastricht, a city steeped in history, is renowned for its role in shaping the European Union through the Maastricht Treaty, signed here in 1992. This treaty laid the foundation for closer European integration, emphasizing cooperation and unity across national borders. In a similar vein, our conference theme, "Crossing Digital Borders", underscores the importance of transcending traditional boundaries in the digital realm, whether they are geographical, technological, or societal.

In this volume, you will find a diverse array of contributions spanning distributed architectures, software frameworks, machine learning, cryptography, and services fostering digital communities and smart mobility. Following a thorough single-blind review procedure by at least three reviewers for each submission, the Program Committee of the I4CS conference compiled an interesting scientific program. It included 17 full papers and five short papers out of 44 submissions. Our esteemed keynote and invited speakers, Anna Wilbik, Klaus-Dieter Rest, and Rob van der Mei, have delved into topics at the forefront of technological advancement, offering insights into responsibility and explainability in automated systems, decision support for home healthcare services in urban regions, and for ambulance services. These topics not only cover the proper use of what ICT can offer us but also show how we as researchers can follow the path to proper valorization of the research into startups and tooling.

Maastricht University, with its reputation for excellence in research and innovation, provided an inspiring backdrop for our discussions and deliberations. The university's commitment to interdisciplinary collaboration mirrors the ethos of our conference, where academia, industry, and government converge to address the multifaceted challenges of our digital age.

I extend my heartfelt gratitude to all members of the Program Committee and external reviewers for their diligent efforts in ensuring the quality and rigor of the conference proceedings. I am also deeply appreciative of the authors, speakers, and participants whose contributions enriched our discussions and fostered new ideas and collaborations. Special thanks are due to Maastricht University for graciously hosting our conference and to all those involved in its organization and execution. Last but not least, we acknowledge the support of the EasyChair conference system and express our gratitude to its management team, which always serves the digital community in an altruistic way. Furthermore, we thank Springer for their technical support and excellent management of our CCIS publishing project.

As we navigate the ever-changing landscape of digital technology, let us remain steadfast in our commitment to exploring new frontiers, transcending boundaries, and harnessing the power of innovation for the betterment of our communities and societies, bringing together research from universities, universities of applied sciences, and industry.

June 2024   Frank Phillipson

Organization

Program Committee

Sebastian Apel	Technical University of Applied Sciences Ingolstadt, Germany
Gerald Eichler	Deutsche Telekom, Germany
Christian Erfurth	University of Applied Sciences Jena, Germany
Günter Fahrnberger	University of Hagen, Germany
Hacène Fouchal	University of Reims Champagne-Ardenne, France
Sapna Ponaraseri Gopinathan	i.k.val Softwares LLP Coimbatore, India
Michal Hodoň	University of Žilina, Slovakia
Mikael Johansson	CSC - IT Center for Science, Finland
Kathrin Kirchner	Technical University of Denmark, Denmark
Udo Krieger	University of Bamberg, Germany
Peter Kropf	University of Neuchâtel, Switzerland
Ulrike Lechner	Bundeswehr University Munich, Germany
Andreas Lommatzsch	Technical University of Berlin, Germany
Karl-Heinz Lüke	Ostfalia University of Applied Sciences, Germany
Kushagra Mishra	Nutanix, USA
Raja Natarajan	Tata Institute of Fundamental Research, India
Deveeshree Nayak	University of Washington Tacoma, USA
Dana Petcu	West University of Timisoara, Romania
Frank Phillipson	Netherlands Organisation for Applied Scientific Work, Netherlands
Siddharth Rautaray	Kalinga Institute of Industrial Technology, India
Jörg Roth	Nuremberg Institute of Technology, Germany
Amardeo Sarma	Trust in Digital Life Association, Belgium
Pranav Kumar Singh	Indian Institute of Technology Guwahati and Central Institute of Technology Kokrajhar, India
Julian Szymanski	Gdansk University of Technology, Poland
Rob van der Mei	National Research Institute for Mathematics and Computer Science Amsterdam, Netherlands
Leendert W. M. Wienhofen	City of Trondheim, Norway

Additional Reviewers

de Kok, Willem
Großmann, Marcel
Vennesland, Auduns

Invited Talks

Decision Support for Home Health Care Services in Urban Regions

Klaus-Dieter Rest🆔

University of Natural Resources and Life Sciences, Vienna, Austria
klausdieter.rest@boku.ac.at

Abstract. Home Health Care (HHC) services enable elderly and frail individuals to maintain independence in their familiar surroundings while receiving professional assistance. This work is grounded in my dissertation and practical insights gained from developing a commercial decision support tool used by a major HHC service provider in Vienna. The tool addresses the growing demand for HHC services and aids in day-to-day operations and disaster management. Vulnerability analyses were conducted to understand the intricate HHC system and its susceptibility to various disasters, visualized through Causal-Loop Diagrams to identify cascading effects and feedback loops. To assist HHC nurses' daily planning in routine and crisis situations, a new mixed-integer linear program and Tabu Search metaheuristics were developed. Unlike previous research focused on rural areas, this work concentrates on urban settings. The algorithms published cater to the requirements of two major HHC service providers in Vienna, encompassing diverse aspects of HHC nurse routing, including working time regulations, flexible breaks, care consistency, workload distribution, and synchronization. Unique features such as time-dependent public transportation usage are incorporated. The developed decision support system is highly adaptable, allowing adjustment of planning based on dispatcher needs and preferences, capable of solving real-world instances swiftly. Extensive numerical studies with real-world data demonstrate substantial savings in travel and wait times, as well as reduced need for second shifts. Scenario analyses were conducted to ascertain operational limits during disasters.

Keywords: Decision support system · Disaster management · Home health care · Metaheuristic · Multimodality · Public transportation · Vehicle routing problem

Saving Lives with Mathematics

The Bumpy Road from Mathematical Modeling to a Successful Company

Rob van der Mei

National Research Institute for Mathematics and Computer Science, Amsterdam, The Netherlands
rob.van.der.mei@cwi.nl

Abstract. In serious, life-threatening situations where every second counts, the timely presence of emergency services can mean the difference between survival and death. In the Netherlands, at least 95% of high-emergency calls should have a response time of less than 15 minutes. In practice, this requirement is often not met. Moreover, due to the aging population, we observe a steady growth in demand, while at the same time, the tight job market makes it hard to find sufficient ambulance personnel. These developments put a tremendous burden on the already-strained ambulance system.

A powerful means to boost the response-time performance of ambulance services is to implement so-called Dynamic Ambulance Management (DAM). Basically, DAM consists of two parts: (1) dynamic dispatching, and (2) proactive relocation. Dynamic dispatching involves deciding which ambulance(s) to dispatch to a newly incoming incident call, depending on the locations and status of the available ambulance vehicles. Proactive relocation involves determining where and when to move ambulance vehicles to achieve desired coverage levels in real-time.

In the context of DAM, we have developed several scalable heuristics to provide real-time decision support for both dispatching and relocation decisions. For the acceptance of DAM in practice, there are several practical constraints: (1) the number of relocations is limited, (2) relocations should not be enforced on personnel just before the end of their shift, and (3) the response-time performance should be significantly better by implementing DAM compared to the classical static and reactive way of working.

To meet all these requirements, we have started a real-life pilot with an ambulance provider in the Netherlands and fine-tuned the model based on feedback from practitioners, such as call center agents, drivers, and emergency medical specialists. In doing so, we have included a limitation on the expected number of relocations per day and a parameter that indicates the timeframe over which an ambulance is not relocated just before the end of a shift. Last but not least, our results showed a great improvement in response-time performance in terms of the fraction of late arrivals, with a strong reduction in late arrivals ultimately saving lives.

As a next step, we have transformed our proof-of-concept DAM software into a stable, fully functional planning software package to be used by ambulance providers via a licensing agreement. The methods are currently exploited by a spin-off company named Stokhos Emergency Mathematics, which is operational in a large number of safety regions in the Netherlands and abroad.

Keywords: Ambulance planning · Dynamic ambulance management · Response-time performance · Spin-off company

Contents

Graphs and Routing

Secure Applications

Information Security in Supply Chains

Blockchain and Digital Sovereignty

Invited Paper

Responsibility and Explainability in Using Intelligent Systems

Anna Wilbik[1,2(✉)] 🆔 and Paul Grefen[3,4] 🆔

[1] Department of Advanced Computing Sciences, Maastricht University,
Maastricht, The Netherlands
a.wilbik@maastrichtuniversity.nl
[2] Brightlands Institute for Smart Society, Maastricht University,
Maastricht, The Netherlands
[3] Department of Industrial Engineering and Innovation Sciences,
Eindhoven University of Technology, Eindhoven, The Netherlands
p.w.p.j.grefen@tue.nl
[4] Eviden Digital Transformation Consulting, Amstelveen, The Netherlands
paul.grefen@eviden.com

Abstract. Recent developments in digital technology domains like Artificial Intelligence and Internet of Things lead to possibilities for more autonomous systems that more directly interact with their business or social environment. This poses new but often implicit questions with respect to the responsibility for decisions made by these systems and the effects of these decisions on their environment. Requirements embedded in design considerations like security constraints, privacy regulations, and traceability demands, however, imply explicit questions with respect to responsibility in information processing. Responsibility may be expected from four different classes of actors: the system itself, the system designer, the system user, and the party whose data is managed by the system, i.e., the object of the system. This paper presents the questions regarding the allocation of responsibility with the development and deployment of autonomous systems, based on requirements imposed by their application context. The discussion of the effect of explainability of decisions on the allocation of responsibility is an essential ingredient here. We provide the necessary concepts and models to make a first analysis and design of the allocation of responsibility.

Keywords: Responsibility · Explainability · Autonomous system

1 Introduction

Recent advancements in technology domains like Artificial Intelligence (AI) and Internet-of-Things (IoT) open new opportunities for a wider use of autonomous systems. These technologies allow digital systems to take decisions by themselves and directly interact with their physical environment. According to a Goldman Sachs report [7], two-thirds of US occupations are exposed to some degree of

© The Author(s), under exclusive license to Springer Nature Switzerland AG 2024
F. Phillipson et al. (Eds.): I4CS 2024, CCIS 2109, pp. 3–14, 2024.
https://doi.org/10.1007/978-3-031-60433-1_1

automation by AI. This automation is expected to be highest in the administrative and legal working domain. It will increasingly affect other domains as well, however.

These developments will also affect community services. For instance, administrative processes in city administration, such as granting parking permits or building permits, can be sped up by the use of AI. As another example, urban safety could benefit from a system analyzing recordings from all cameras in a city to automatically assess whether police intervention is needed. One can imagine also the benefits of using an e-health system that monitors patients and helps them solve minor issues or refill their prescriptions.

There are many benefits of automation, such as increased productivity, shorter processing time, reduced errors, just to name a few [13]. However, there are also risks involved in the automation of tasks that require decisions, as an automated system can take a wrong decision. For instance, in an administrative process a parking permit is denied to someone eligible, or a building permit is issued against the regulations. An urban safety system could unnecessarily dispatch a police unit, and spend unnecessary effort, or send it too late, and as a result not prevent an act of violence. An e-health system could give a wrong advice to a patient, which in turn could have a negative effect on his or her health. When things go wrong, the questions of responsibility [3] and explainability [2] arise.

The concept of responsibility can have several different interpretations, generally trying to answer the question who is to blame when a harm occurs. For instance, responsibility (or accountability) can be understood as the extent to which individuals who develop, distribute and use Autonomous Information Systems (AISs) have responsibility within social and legal systems of a society [15]. However, we should make clear that responsibility is not the same as liability, as responsibility is also viewed as a moral and ethical issue while liability is focused primarily on the legal dimension.

The responsibility attribution in scenarios including autonomous systems is a complex issue [3]. One should consider several aspects, such as autonomy and control level, e.g., task autonomy, conditional autonomy, high autonomy (human supervision) and full autonomy. Additionally, one should deal also with the so-called "problem of many hands", a situation in which, due to complexity and number of actors involved, it is impossible or difficult to hold an actor responsible for a problem at hand [14].

Explainability can be interpreted as the extent to which the operations of a system are intelligible or understandable for stakeholders [15]. It is often combined with the concept of explanation, meant as the means to make a decision (of a system) comprehensible to humans [2]. The concept of explainability is closely related to other concepts such as transparency, interpretability and understandability. Transparency addresses understanding of the reasoning mechanisms of the model. Interpretability is the ability to assign meaning to model elements [10]. Understandability seems to be the most important concept, as it measures the degree to which a human can understand a decision made by a model [2]. Explainability increases the understandability of actions of an autonomous system, hence increasing the awareness which is needed for the allocation of responsibility [3].

In a digitizing society, it is therefore important to keep discussing the issues of responsibility and explainability. To facilitate these discussions, we have designed models that can guide these discussions. They help to understand the complex intricacies. Human awareness or literacy [6] is another aspect in discussing these intricacies with involved stakeholders. In this paper we present these models, as well as their example applications in the domains of healthcare and smart mobility.

2 Basic Model: The Responsibility Triangle

Our initial model to facilitate the discussion about responsibility in the use of autonomous digital systems includes three main responsibility actors: the system designer, the system user and the system itself, as shown in Fig. 1. They are modeled as the vertices of a triangle, which we call the Responsibility Triangle. The edges of the triangle represent the interactions between the actors, along which responsibility can be distributed.

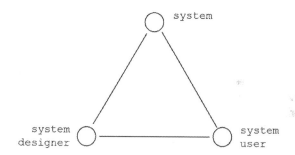

Fig. 1. Responsibility triangle

By the system designer we denote all stakeholders involved in the creation process of the system (like software engineers and system architects), as well its implementation with the system users (like system integerators). The responsibility of the system designers for its creation is mentioned by several organizations. For example, the ACM Code of Ethics [5] lists professional responsibilities, such as: "strive to achieve high quality in both the processes and products of professional work", or "design and implement systems that are robustly and usably secure". The use of AI adds an additional complexity and responsibility level for this class of stakeholders, as mentioned in the so-called Asilomar AI principles [4]. Principle 9 concerns responsibility, stating that: "designers and builders of advanced AI systems are stakeholders in the moral implications of their use, misuse, and actions, with a responsibility and opportunity to shape those implications".

Another important actor is naturally the system user, i.e., the party that operationally uses the system in its way of working. The responsibility with the system user implies that it is up to the user to make all final decisions, from a strategic decision to implement the system until an operational decision to follow or reject the recommendation made by the system. Having a user checking the recommendation of a system is in line with the so-called human-in-the-loop principle [12], in which the user retains control over the machine. Releasing all control to the machine is a decision too, of course, which implies responsibility.

Last, but not least, the third actor in this model is the system. Even though responsibility is ultimately attributed to humans, the autonomous system is represented as a stakeholder, because often in colloquial speech and practical reasoning it is treated as an explicit entity in the execution of processes.

Responsibility of an autonomous system could be guaranteed only if the methods used to develop such a system could make responsibility a non-functional attribute of this system (i.e., a quality characteristic). It would require the development of a method to measure or assess the responsibility of a system. Currently, some aspects of a responsible system are reflected in the quality attributes such as privacy, security, safety, transparency, sustainability, accessibility, fairness, non-discrimination and integrity (accurate data and free from bias). When discussing the responsibility of a system, two perspectives are important to consider: (1) a narrower one focusing on situations when a system malfunctions or delivers incorrect results and (2) a broader one that also takes into account situations when a system fulfills its primary objective, but using the system may have negative consequences.

Automated explanations by the system of its decisions can shift the responsibility in this model. First of all, with explanations, the system is becoming more transparent and to its user it is becoming easier to understand why certain decisions were made. This enables the user (if having sufficient digital literacy [6]) to take more control for the decisions. Therefore, explainability shifts the responsibility more towards the system user. At the same time, explanations will enable the system designers to test the system better, as they can also check the reasoning behind certain decisions, and find the potential mistakes in the system [8]. As a consequence, the system will become more reliable and less responsibility risks will exist for its user.

2.1 The Smart Mobility Case

Smart mobility is a societal application domain that is developing fast under the influence of new digital technology and that has its challenges [11]. A typical characteristic of this domain is the fact that it involves many stakeholders that have different, possibly conflicting, objectives. Processes in this domain have direct impact on the lives of people, both in the private and business contexts. If things go wrong (if people do not arrive at planned times at specific locations, if people cannot arrive at all, or even worse, they have traffic accidents), the question who is to blame and hence responsibility comes into play. Explainability of decisions is core in this respect. Apart from this, there is also responsibility with respect to the privacy of the travelers, i.e., the way their personal and traveling data are handled in involved systems.

In our smart mobility case, we take a smart mobility ecosystem in which advises are created for traveling by private and public transportation to specific locations, like events [16]. These advises are created by a travel advisor organization, which sends them to travellers. This organization uses an automated smart travel planning system. This system uses intelligent algorithms to construct travel advises. The system is designed by a system designer that selects and parameterizes these algorithms.

The basic configuration of this ecosystem can be shown in the responsibility triangle of Fig. 1, resulting in Fig. 2. It includes the designer of the smart travel planning system, the system itself, and the travel advisor organization as the user of the system. In creating and executing a mobility plan, all actors have a responsibility.

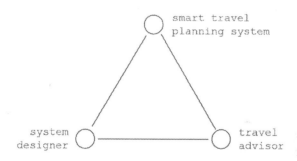

Fig. 2. Responsibility triangle for the smart mobility case

2.2   The Healthcare Case

Healthcare is an important application domain of community services. Automation offers many opportunities for improving or expanding healthcare services. For instance, wearables and IoT technology enables continuous monitoring of patients and timely interventions [1]. Surgical robots are supporting doctors during complicated procedures, enabling the doctors to operate with greater precision [17]. Computer vision systems can process scanned images of patients and diagnose these [9].

In this latter case, a patient with a cancer suspicion will get a scan (for instance an ultrasound) of the related suspicious change to his or her body. The system autonomously can automatically enhance and segment the image, and detect and classify the change. The doctor can give his own diagnosis based on the original images as well as the system recommendation. However, mistakes can be made. For instance, a benign change could be automatically classified as a malicious one, and a patient could suffer from an unnecessary stress and undergo an unnecessary treatment like a biopsy or a surgery. An even worse outcome is, if a cancer is missed and detected too late, at the stage when a successful treatment is no longer possible. The basic configuration of this ecosystem is shown in Fig. 3. In this case, the responsibility is shared between all three actors.

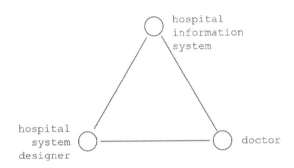

Fig. 3. Responsibility triangle for the healthcare case

If the computer vision system next to the diagnosis also provides an explanation of why it thinks the patient has a specific cancer type, a doctor can better understand the reasoning of the machine and verify it. Therefore, the doctor will have more options then just to accept or reject system recommendation - and consequently has to accept a higher level of responsibility. Moreover, feedback from the doctors about the explanations and possible mistakes allows the system designers to improve the system.

3   Extended Model: The Responsibility Quadrangle

In the triangle model presented in the previous section, we describe direct actors in an ecosystem. But often, there are parties whose data is not actively handled by themselves, but by other parties (who are direct actors). These subjects of data (or owners of data) bear some responsibility too in data processing, as they allow other parties to process their data. This observation leads to an extended responsibility model in which we include data owners. This extends the Responsibility Triangle model into a Responsibility Quadrangle model, shown in Fig. 4.

Of course, we can only expect data owners to actively bear responsibility if they understand what the implications are of having their data processed by other parties, or in other words, if the data owners have a sufficient level of digital literacy, i.e., at the level of digital awareness [6].

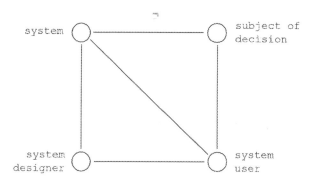

Fig. 4. Responsibility quadrangle

3.1   The Smart Mobility Case

In the smart mobility ecosystem discussed in the previous section, the traveler does not have an explicit role. The traveler does bear responsibility though, in choosing to use the services of the travel advisor and in interpreting these advises. Hence, we can add this party to the ecosystem shown in Fig. 2 to arrive at the ecosystem of Fig. 5.

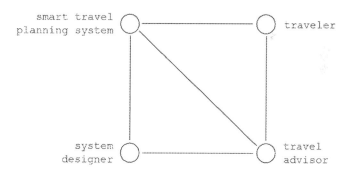

Fig. 5. Responsibility quadrangle for the smart mobility case

This figure illustrates why there is only one diagonal relation in the quadrangle: the traveler is in a direct responsibility relation with the travel advisor (who sends the advise) and the smart travel planning system (which creates the advise based on the data provided by the traveler to the travel advisor), but not with the system designer. Probably, the traveler is not even aware of who created the system used by the advisor.

3.2   The Healthcare Case

The patient is an important role in a healthcare ecosystem. Even though the patient is not directly deciding about a diagnosis regarding himself or herself, he or she provides necessary information to the doctor regarding the symptoms. Moreover, the patient may request a second opinion of another doctor if he or she doesn't trust the first diagnosis. Therefore the patient bears some responsibility. Moreover, the treatment options, expected outcomes, advantages and risks are always discussed with the patient and the patient has to agree with the treatment plan.

Let us consider again the cancer diagnosis system introduced in Subsect. 2.2. The model shown in Fig. 6 includes a patient, next to the doctor and hospital information system (of which the cancer diagnosis system is a part). The patient agrees to certain diagnostic tests using the autonomous systems, as well as interacts with the doctor, who explains the diagnosis (possibly using a diagnosis made by the system).

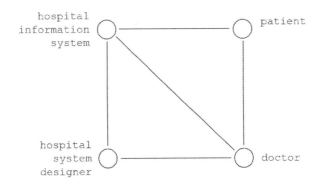

Fig. 6. Responsibility quadrangle for the healthcare case

The explanations of the diagnostic system may not only help the doctor to make a better diagnosis, but also if communicated properly to the patient, may increase his or her acceptance of the diagnosis.

4   Quadrangle with Direct and Proxy Actors

In the models presented so far, systems are treated as actors. A system, however, is not a legal entity in most jurisdictions, so cannot formally be held responsible for decisions they make. From the legal perspective, the system typically is the operational proxy for the owner (or operator) of the system. For this reason, we extend the Responsibility Quadrangle model of Fig. 4 with the owner of a system to arrive at the model in Fig. 7. We discuss this model in the context of our two running case studies.

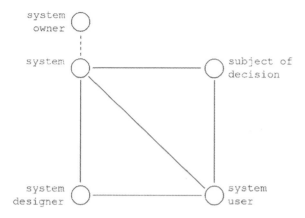

Fig. 7. Responsibility quadrangle with direct and proxy actors

4.1   The Smart Mobility Case

In the smart mobility ecosystem discussed in the previous section, the smart travel planning system generates the travel advises in an intelligent, autonomous fashion. If something goes wrong for a traveler when using these advises (e.g., the traveler does not arrive in time at an important event), the traveler may hold the travel advisor organization responsible for this. The travel advisor organization generated the travel advise by using the smart travel planning system, so may hold the system responsible - for example to request a compensation.

As we have seen above, however, often the system cannot be legally held responsible and we have to turn to its owner. In the smart mobility ecosystem, this owner may be a smart travel planning cloud service provider organization,

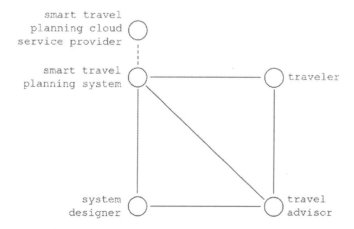

Fig. 8. Responsibility quadrangle with direct and proxy actors for the smart mobility case

which offers the system's functionality to travel advisor organizations (e.g., on a per-advise fee basis). This responsibility configuration is shown in Fig. 8.

4.2   The Healthcare Case

In the healthcare case discussed in the previous sections, the hospital is the owner of the system. It is the hospital who decides to buy and install certain systems to store patient data and have these systems support the doctors in their job. Therefore in this case, the hospital bares some responsibility for the recommendations made by the system, and keeping the system operational. This brings us to the model shown in Fig. 9.

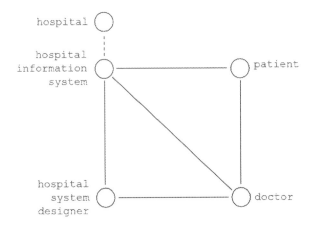

Fig. 9. Responsibility quadrangle with direct and proxy actors for the healthcare case

5   Conclusions

Responsibility in general is important in the interaction between stakeholders in both business and societal settings, especially when things go wrong. In complex ecosystems, it is especially difficult to clearly allocate the responsibility among the stakeholders in the ecosystems.

Autonomous systems are nowadays operating in complex ecosystem with many actors - and their use will very probably further increase in years to come. Given their impact on many situations, it is crucial to discuss the issues of responsibility in the use of autonomous systems in advance. For this purpose, we have presented several models that can facilitate this discussion, from a simple Responsibility Triangle model to an Extended Responsibility Quadrangle model.

We have also shown that explainability can shift responsibility, or the perception of responsibility, towards the user of an autonomous system and the subject of the decisions by that system. The better actors are informed about the reasoning behind (automated) decisions, the more they can be held responsible for (not) accepting these decisions. As discussed, digital literacy (of system users but also of decision subjects) plays an important role in this [6].

The discussion about responsibility can be put in a broader context, e.g., using the concept of trust between stakeholders in settings involving automated systems [12]. More discussion is urgently needed on the topic of responsibility in a world where the application of AI is moving forward faster than many can comprehend. This discussion has to take place in both the realms of the creators or such systems (i.e., the worlds of computer science and data science) and of the users of the systems (i.e., the worlds of sociology, psychology, business science and law).

References

1. Amin, T., Mobbs, R.J., Mostafa, N., Sy, L.W., Choy, W.J.: Wearable devices for patient monitoring in the early postoperative period: a literature review. Mhealth **7** (2021)
2. Explainable artificial intelligence (XAI): Concepts, taxonomies, opportunities and challenges toward responsible AI. Information fusion **58**, 82–115 (2020)
3. Coeckelbergh, M.: Artificial intelligence, responsibility attribution, and a relational justification of explainability. Sci. Eng. Ethics **26**(4), 2051–2068 (2020)
4. Future of Life Institute: The Asilomar AI principles (2017). https://futureoflife.org/open-letter/ai-principles/
5. Gotterbarn, D., et al.: ACM code of ethics and professional conduct (2018). https://www.acm.org/code-of-ethics
6. Grefen, P.: Digital literacy and electronic business. Encyclopedia **1**(3), 934–941 (2021)
7. Hatzius, J., Briggs, J., Kodnani, D., Pierdomenico, G.: The potentially large effects of artificial intelligence on economic growth (2023). https://www.gspublishing.com/content/research/en/reports/2023/03/27/d64e052b-0f6e-45d7-967b-d7be35fabd16.html
8. Kampel, L., Simos, D.E., Kuhn, D.R., Kacker, R.N.: An exploration of combinatorial testing-based approaches to fault localization for explainable AI. Ann. Math. Artif. Intell. **90**, 951–964 (2022). https://doi.org/10.1007/s10472-021-09772-0
9. Lee, H., Chen, Y.P.P.: Image based computer aided diagnosis system for cancer detection. Expert Syst. Appl. **42**(12), 5356–5365 (2015)
10. Lipton, Z.C.: The mythos of model interpretability: in machine learning, the concept of interpretability is both important and slippery. Queue **16**(3), 31–57 (2018)
11. Lu, M., Turetken, O., Adali, O.E., Castells, J., Blokpoel, R., Grefen, P.: C-ITS (cooperative intelligent transport systems) deployment in Europe: challenges and key findings. In: 25th ITS World Congress, Copenhagen, Denmark, pp. 17–21 (2018)
12. Nahavandi, S.: Trusted autonomy between humans and robots: toward human-on-the-loop in robotics and autonomous systems. IEEE Syst. Man Cybern. Mag. **3**(1), 10–17 (2017)
13. Ng, K.K., Chen, C.H., Lee, C., Jiao, J.R., Yang, Z.X.: A systematic literature review on intelligent automation: aligning concepts from theory, practice, and future perspectives. Adv. Eng. Inform. **47**, 101246 (2021)

14. Nissenbaum, H.: Accountability in a computerized society. Sci. Eng. Ethics **2**, 25–42 (1996)
15. Schoenherr, J.R.: Ethical Artificial Intelligence from Popular to Cognitive Science: Trust in the Age of Entanglement, Routledge (2022)
16. Turetken, O., Grefen, P., Gilsing, R., Adali, O.E.: Service-dominant business model design for digital innovation in smart mobility. Bus. Inf. Syst. Eng. **61**, 9–29 (2019)
17. Zemmar, A., Lozano, A.M., Nelson, B.J.: The rise of robots in surgical environments during COVID-19. Nat. Mach. Intell. **2**(10), 566–572 (2020)

Quantum Computing

QUBO Formulation for Sparse Sensor Placement for Classification

Melanie R. van Dommelen[1] and Frank Phillipson[1,2](✉) (iD)

[1] Maastricht University, Maastricht, The Netherlands
[2] TNO, The Hague, The Netherlands
f.phillipson@maastrichtuniversity.nl

Abstract. The demand for facial recognition technology has grown in various sectors over the past decade, but the need for efficient feature selection methods is crucial due to high-dimensional data complexity. This paper explores the potential of quantum computing for Sparse Sensor Placement optimisation (SSPO) in facial image classification. It studies a well known Filter Approach, based on statistical measures like Pearson correlation and Mutual Information, as it offers computational simplicity and speed. The proposed Quadratic Unconstrained Binary optimisation (QUBO) formulation for SSPO, inspired by the Quadratic Programming Feature Selection approach, aims to select a sparse set of relevant features while minimising redundancy. QUBO formulations can be solved by simulated annealing and by quantum annealing. Two experiments were conducted to compare the QUBO with a machine learning (ML) approach. The results showed that the QUBO approach, utilising simulated annealing, achieved an accuracy between random placed sensors and ML based sensors. The ML algorithm outperformed the QUBO approach, likely due to its ability to capture relevant features more effectively. The QUBO approach's advantage lies in its much shorter running time. The study suggests potential improvements by using Mutual Information instead of Pearson correlation as a measure of feature relevance. Additionally, it highlights the limitations of quantum annealers' current connectivity and the need for further advancements in quantum hardware.

Keywords: Hybrid quantum computing · Facial recognition · Sparse sensor placement · Classification

1 Introduction

The demand for facial recognition has experienced a significant increase over the past decade, owing to its simplicity and high accuracy in establishing the identities of individuals. Numerous sectors have already integrated facial recognition into their everyday practices. For instance, fields like law enforcement and the aviation industry use facial recognition for quick identification of people of interest. Other sectors such as the online banking industry or businesses also use

© The Author(s), under exclusive license to Springer Nature Switzerland AG 2024
F. Phillipson et al. (Eds.): I4CS 2024, CCIS 2109, pp. 17–35, 2024.
https://doi.org/10.1007/978-3-031-60433-1_2

facial recognition for quick authentication, to grant individuals access to secure applications or data. Even the retail industry is planning to introduce'pay-by-face', which would enable payments through facial recognition technology [34].

Facial recognition requires images from the individuals of interest, but these images are costly. A good quality picture requires a high amount of pixels, where each pixel has a value that corresponds to a specific brightness. Thus, an image can be seen as a high-dimensional state, where each dimension corresponds to one pixel. High-dimensional data is problematic since it requires a vast amount of storage. Moreover, it is difficult to perform computations on high-dimensional data, due to the presence of irrelevant, redundant, and noisy features. These features can negatively impact the learning performance of an algorithm, as well as the accuracy and computational cost. Fortunately, most high-dimensional states have a low-dimensional representation. By selecting a subset of relevant features (e.g. pixels) as sensors from an image, we obtain a sparse (low-dimensional) representation that captures all information necessary for classification.

Sparse sensor placement is a form of feature selection that holds immense significance in research [1,20]. Especially in the context of machine learning, where high-dimensional data is more prevalent, feature selection becomes essential. Sparse sensor placement has many applications, such as classification of human faces, cancer types and environmental monitoring. Therefore many algorithms have already been developed for feature selection. The main frameworks for feature selection can be summarised into three approaches [3]: the (1) Filter Approach, (2) Wrapper Approach, and (3) Embedded Approach.

Sparse Sensor Placement optimisation is an intractable brute force search among all combinatorial possibilities of choosing p sensors from n features, that is $\binom{n}{p} = \frac{n!}{(n-p)!p!}$ possible choices [1]. Moreover as shown by Chen et al. (1995), the selection of a minimum feature subset is NP-hard [4]. Therefore, optimal sensors are often chosen according to heuristics or intuition. However, the introduction of Quantum Computing in general and specifically Quantum Annealing a few years ago might offer a solution. It is widely believed that the Quantum Annealer has the potential to efficiently compute high-quality solutions to NP-hard problems [33]. By mapping the problem to physical qubits on a quantum chip and performing a process called quantum annealing, quantum computing aims to efficiently search the solution space and find the optimal solution. For mapping the problem to the qubits, in general a Quadratic Unconstrained Binary Optimisation (QUBO) problem formulation is used, with is equivalent to the Ising formulation. This QUBO formulation will be used in this paper.

This work will follow a Filter Approach known as Maximum Relevancy Minimum Redundancy from Nguyen et al. (2014) [25] and creates a QUBO problem formulation to solve the Sparse Sensor Placement problem with quantum/simulated annealing. We will look at the question whether quantum annealing has the potential to perform Sparse Sensor Placement optimisation and makes several contributions in the field of Sparse Sensor Placement optimisation for classification applied to facial images. Firstly, it provides a new QUBO model for sparse sensor placement that can be used for classification and secondly, it gives the comparison of the QUBO model's performance with that of the existing sparse sensor placement algorithms for classification.

The rest of the paper is organised as follows. Section 2 provides an overview of prior research in the field of feature selection to guide the choice of an appropriate framework for the QUBO problem formulation. Section 3 describes the development of the QUBO formulation and briefly introduces the Sparse Sensor Placement optimisation algorithm that is used as a benchmark. Also, a short explanation is provided on the classifier algorithm utilised in the subsequent section. Section 4 starts by introducing the data, followed by two experiments that assess the performance of the QUBO compared to that of the benchmark algorithm. The section concludes with a discussion of the experiment outcomes. Finally, Sect. 5 summarises the key findings and the implications of this study.

2   Related Work

This section focuses on giving an overview of the literature on Feature Selection and Sparse Sensor Placement. The three most common approaches to feature selection are the (1) Wrapper Approach, (2) Embedded Approach, and (3) Filter Approach [3]. The Wrapper Approach uses the classification algorithm to measure the importance of features. Thus, the selected features are optimised based on the classifier method, often resulting in good performance. However, since each considered feature set needs to be evaluated with the classifier algorithm, the computational complexity and computation time quickly increase with the size of the problem, making it quickly too expensive for high-dimensional data sets [15]. Evaluating all 2^n possible subsets is an NP-hard problem [15] and therefore heuristic search algorithms are employed, such as sequential search, genetic algorithms, and particle swarm optimisation. For example, Jadhav [14] implemented a genetic algorithm wrapper feature selection for credit rating, and Inza [13] performed gene selection by a sequential search Wrapper Approach for cancer classification.

Next is the Embedded Approach, which incorporates the feature selection as part of the training process. Unlike the Wrapper Approach, it does not evaluate each considered feature set with the classifier algorithm; this reduces the computation time, but it is still computationally expensive since it uses the classification algorithm to measure the performance of features [3].

Last is the Filter Approach, which selects features on the basis of statistical measures. The features are scored according to a suitable ranking criterion (statistic measure) and the highest- scoring features are then selected to form the sparse subset of features. This ranking criterion is also referred to as feature relevance and it indicates the features' contribution to the model prediction such as classification. Many different measures exist for feature relevance, such as variance, entropy, mutual information, Pearson correlation, etc. [17,36] The performance of the Wrapper and Embedded Approach is usually better when using the classifier algorithm. However, the advantage of not needing the classifier algorithm during the process of feature selection, is that it makes the algorithm computationally simpler, faster, and more scalable [15], unlike the other approaches. Many feature selection approaches have been developed using the Filter Approach [32], such as the one by Brunton et al. [1]. They combine machine learning methods like Singular Value Decomposition and Linear Discriminant Analysis (LDA) with an l_1-norm minimisation problem to find a sparse set of features for different classification tasks, such as facial recognition and cancer classification.

The simplest way to create a sparse subset with the Filter Approach is to select the first x features in the ranking. However, this only maximises the total relevance of the features. In many cases, multiple features with a high relevance score share a lot of the same information, what is called redundancy. Therefore, the Maximum Relevancy Minimum Redundancy (MRMR) framework was introduced by Peng et al. [26] in 2005, which, as the name suggests, maximises relevancy while simultaneously minimising redundancy among selected features. MRMR can be performed incrementally, by greedily selecting features one by one, but this method is prone to suboptimal decisions as features cannot be deselected at a later stage [25]. Therefore, Nguyen et al. [25] created their Quadratic Programming Feature Selection (QPFS) approach which poses feature selection as a global optimisation problem, making a global decision on which subset to select that considers the interaction between all features at the same time. This work forms a suitable framework for the QUBO that is developed in the next section. During our research, the work of [22] was published, that present a comparable approach. However, we focus on the Sparse Sensor Placement Optimisation problem for facial recognition. They recommend to try Pearson's correlation as alternative measure, which is exactly what we do in this work.

3   Methodology

This section describes and justifies the methodology used throughout the rest of this work. To start, an explanation of the model is provided to establish the mathematical notation of the problem. Then follows an introduction to the QUBO problem formulation and quantum annealing, followed by the first approach, which uses the principles of Maximum Relevancy Minimum Redundancy (MRMR) to create a QUBO formulation that finds the optimal features through either quantum or simulated annealing. The second approach is a well-established sparse sensor placement algorithm from Brunton et al. [1] that uses machine-learning methods to find sensors. Last, an explanation is provided of the LDA-classifier algorithm.

3.1   The Model

The sparse sensor placement problem takes as input a high-dimensional data set $X \in \mathbb{R}^{n \times m}$, where n is the number of features (e.g. pixels) and m is the number of samples (e.g. images). In the case of facial recognition, each column of X corresponds to an image $x \in \mathbb{R}^n$. The image x is obtained through reformatting the original image by stacking all the columns of the original image. The entries of X range from 0 to 255 representing the brightness of each pixel.

The full data set X is split into a training set X_{train} and a test set X_{test}. The images selected for the training set are used to train the feature selection algorithm. The images selected for the test set are used to test the performance of the selected sensors.

The objective of sparse sensor placement is finding the best subset of features of all available features n that can correctly classify an image. The optimal subset of features is also referred to as the optimal sensor placement $\Phi \in \{0,1\}^{p \times n}$, where p is the chosen number of sensors. Matrix Φ has p rows and n columns, where

$$\Phi_{i,j} = \begin{cases} 1 & \text{if feature } j \text{ has been selected as sensor } i, \\ 0 & \text{otherwise.} \end{cases} \tag{1}$$

The sum of each row is equal to one so that each sensor corresponds to exactly one feature (e.g. pixel). Given Φ, it is easy to obtain a low-rank representation $y \in \mathbb{R}^p$ of x, or $Y \in \mathbb{R}^{p \times m}$ of X by left-multiplying Φ with x and X respectively. Thus, $y = \Phi x$ is the measurement vector of x, containing only the selected subset of features in Φ.

3.2   Quantum Annealing and QUBO Formulation

Quantum annealing exploits the principles of quantum mechanics that govern the behaviour of subatomic particles [35]. A crucial aspect involves superposition, where quantum bits (qubits) can exist in multiple states simultaneously, and entanglement, where the state of one qubit can be correlated with another, even across great distances. This specialised quantum computing technique aims to solve discrete optimisation problems prevalent in various fields, including finance [10], material science [2], logistics [8,24,28,29], smart city planning [5], telecommunications [27], healthcare [18,23], energy networks [6] and many more.

The objective of quantum annealing is to identify the lowest-energy state of the qubit system. This is achieved by formulating the optimisation problem in a way that associates the energy of a state with the quantity to be minimised. The Hamiltonian, describing the energy of all quantum states, encodes the optimisation problem, and the optimal solution corresponds to the lowest-energy state. Qubits are manipulated in accordance with a predefined schedule or annealing process to minimise the system's energy. This exploration of the solution space seeks to identify the global minimum. D-Wave Systems, a prominent company in quantum annealing, has developed quantum annealers accessible to researchers and organisations exploring quantum computing for optimisation problems.

Quantum annealing processes involve the Quadratic Unconstrained Binary Optimisation (QUBO) problem formulations and equivalent Ising formulations. QUBO is a mathematical framework representing optimisation problems as quadratic functions of binary variables. The first step in creating a QUBO problem formulation involves defining a set of binary variables, representing decisions or choices in the optimisation problem. For instance, in a sparse sensor optimisation problem, each binary variable may denote whether a specific pixel is included (1) or not (0) as sensor.

The subsequent step is to define the objective function, a mathematical expression that needs optimisation and is typically a function of the binary variables. The aim is to find the combination of binary variable values that minimise or maximises this objective function. Constraints from the original optimisation problem can be incorporated into the QUBO model through penalty terms within the objective function. These terms, when constraints are met, should be zero; when constraints are not met, the terms provide values working against the optimisation direction. This ensures that most solutions adhere to the problem constraints.

In mathematical terms, the QUBO problem is expressed as follows:

$$\min_{\boldsymbol{x}\in\{0,1\}^n} \boldsymbol{x}^T Q \boldsymbol{x}, \tag{2}$$

where $\boldsymbol{x}$ is an n-dimensional binary vector, and Q represents the objective function translated into an $n \times n$ matrix. For many problems the QUBO or Ising formulation is known [11,19].

3.3   A Quantum Annealing Approach to Feature Selection

To make sparse sensor placement (SSP) suitable for quantum annealing, it was proposed in Sect. 2 to translate the SSP problem into a MRMR representation. The MRMR framework focuses on finding a minimal-optimal subset of features that has maximum relevance with respect to the target variable, but minimum redundancy with respect to the other selected features. To start, the first subsection will explain an existing MRMR approach by Nguyen [25] who formulated it as a Quadratic Program. Then, the next section will focus on translating this Quadratic Program into a QUBO formulation. Last, a suitable measure for relevancy and redundancy is incorporated into the QUBO formulation.

Quadratic Programming Feature Selection. The QUBO for sparse sensor placement optimisation will be based on the Quadratic Programming Feature Selection (QPFS) approach from [25]. The QPFS approach builds upon the MRMR framework of [26]. Thus, selecting the features that bring the most information, but share the least amount of information with other selected features. QPFS reformulates MRMR as a global optimisation problem,

$$QPFS : \min_{\boldsymbol{x}}\{\alpha \boldsymbol{x}^T H \boldsymbol{x} - \boldsymbol{x}^T f\} \text{ s.t. } \sum_{i=1}^{n} x_i = 1, \; x_i \geq 0, \tag{3}$$

where $f = (f_n)$ is the vector of feature relevancy, $H_{n \times n}$ is the matrix of pairwise redundancy, α is the weighting factor that balances relevancy and redundancy, and $\boldsymbol{x} = (x_n)$ represents the relative feature weights. The relative feature weights can be used to rank the features. Then a feature selection of p sensors can be obtained by selecting the first p features in the ranking. The chosen measure for relevancy f and redundancy H was mutual information for the QPFS. However, any measure for relevancy and redundancy can be used for f and H.

From QPFS to QUBO. Since QUBOs are quadratic, binary, and unconstrained, some adjustments need to be made to the QPFS approach. As can be seen in (3), the QPFS is already quadratic, but the relative feature weights (i.e. x_i) are real numbers between 0 and 1. Moreover, the QPFS has a constraint to ensure that the sum of relative feature weights (i.e. x_i) is equal to 1. However, with some simple alterations, the QPFS can be transformed into a QUBO.

First, the variables are transformed into binary variables. The QPFS formulation uses real-valued variables since the variables are used to make a feature ranking. Nevertheless, a feature ranking is not required when the number of desired features is given. In that case, binary variables can be used to indicate if a sensor is selected or not. Hence, x_i will now be equal to 1 if the feature i is selected and 0 if it is not. By deciding that the relative feature weights are now binary, no adjustments need to be made in terms of QUBO formulation.

Second, we have to get rid of the constraints. The current constraint stating that the sum of relative feature weights should equal 1, has become redundant due to the previous step. However, as mentioned shortly before, the QUBO does not create a ranking but selects the best sensors based on a given requirement for the number of sensors. Therefore, a new constraint is introduced, where the sum of selected sensors should equal the number of desired features p, i.e. $x^T e = p$, where e the vector of all ones. Given this new constraint, a still a second alteration is required since QUBO formulations are unconstrained. Leveraging the fact that quantum annealers always attempt to find the lowest energy (i.e. objective value), the constraint can be incorporated into the objective such that a violation of the constraint increases the objective's values, thereby increasing to probability of a feasible solution. The new constraint, $x^T e = p$, ensures that the number of selected features should equal the number of desired features. Consequently, the objective should increase when the number of selected features is more and when it is less than the desired amount. In other words, the objective should increase if $x^T e - p > 0$ and if $x^T e - p < 0$. By squaring the deviation from the desired amount, the function will be equal to zero if the constraint is satisfied, but a positive number whenever the constraint is violated. Next, $(x^T e - p)^2$ is multiplied by a scalar penalty value, λ, to obtain the penalty term

$$\lambda \left(x^T e - p \right)^2. \tag{4}$$

The penalty term needs to be sufficiently large for infeasible solutions to decrease to probability of obtaining an infeasible solution. This is achieved by choosing a suitable scalar penalty value λ that is sufficiently large, but not larger than necessary, where quantum annealing is sensible for larger values [30]. Last, the penalty term is added to the objective function. After applying the transformations to the QPFS approach, the following quadratic model is obtained,

$$QUBO : \min_{x} \left\{ \alpha x^T H x - x^T f + \lambda \left(x^T e - p \right)^2 \right\} \text{ s.t. } x_i \in \{0,1\}, \quad (5)$$

which can be transformed to the QUBO formulation as expressed in (2).

Feature Relevancy Vector f and Redundancy Matrix H. The values for the feature relevancy vector f and redundancy matrix H are crucial for the performance of the feature selection approach. Following the MRMR framework, the selected features should bring the most information, while simultaneously sharing the least amount of information with other selected features. As mentioned in Sect. 2, a good measure of feature relevance and redundancy is correlation. Hence, the feature relevancy and redundancy will be based on Pearson correlation. The Pearson correlation between two variables x_i and x_j for a sample is usually calculated as follows:

$$\rho_{ij} = \frac{\sum_{k=1}^{N}(x_{ki} - \bar{x}_i)(x_{kj} - \bar{x}_j)}{\sqrt{\sum_{k=1}^{N}(x_{ki} - \bar{x}_i)^2 \sum_{k=1}^{N}(x_{kj} - \bar{x}_j)^2}}. \quad (6)$$

where x_{ki} are the values of variable x_i in sample k and $\bar{x}_i$ is the mean of variable x_i. An alternative method to obtain the Pearson correlations for a data matrix X is to first standardise the data, then multiply X with its transpose, and last divide everything by $(n-1)$, i.e. $PC = \frac{XX^T}{(n-1)}$. Now, the Pearson correlation matrix can be used to determine the redundancy and relevancy of all features.

Starting with the pairwise redundancy, which is measured by $x^T H x$ in the QUBO formulation. Each entry (i,j) of matrix H, corresponds to an entry in the Pearson correlation matrix and thus represents the correlation between feature i and feature j. The diagonal entries of H are set to zero, since there is no interest in measuring self-redundancy. Then, the redundancy in the QUBO, $x^T H x$, is the sum of all absolute values of the pairwise correlations of the selected features.

Next, is the feature relevancy, which is measured by $x^T f$ in the QUBO formulation. The feature with the highest relevancy has the highest overall correlation with all other features. Hence, the relevancy of feature i is measured by summing up all the pairwise correlations between feature i and any other feature j, i.e. $f_i = \sum_{j=1}^{n} H_{ij}$, giving $f = He$. With this, for the current choices, (5) can be rewritten as:

$$QUBO : \min_{x} \left\{ x^T H(\alpha x - e) + \lambda \left(x^T e - p \right)^2 \right\} \text{ s.t. } x_i \in \{0,1\}. \quad (7)$$

3.4   Machine Learning Approach to SSPO by Brunton et al.

Brunton et al. [1] developed a machine learning approach for SSPO that combines Principal Component Analysis (PCA) with Linear Discriminant Analysis (LDA) to find optimal sensor locations. They choose this framework since PCA-LDA is a standard approach in machine learning [9], that can be used for a wide range of problems due to its simplicity and effectiveness.

The PCA starts with performing Singular Value Decomposition on the training set X_{train} to obtain feature basis Ψ. The feature basis Ψ is then truncated into Ψ_r by selecting the first r columns of Ψ. The columns of Ψ become less informative, going from the first to the last column, and so the first r columns contain the most information on the features. Next, the data from the full measurement space is projected into the r-dimensional PCA space using the feature basis Ψ_r, so each image x_i is expressed in terms of the r-dimensional feature coefficients a_i (where $a_i = \Psi_r^T x_i$). In turn the full data set X is expressed as A (where $A = \Psi_r^T X$). Then, the classifier technique LDA is applied to the r-dimensional feature space. LDA aims to find a set of directions into feature space w, where the between-class variance is maximised and within-class variance is minimised as shown in (8),

$$w = \underset{w'}{\mathrm{argmax}}\, \frac{w'^T S_B w'}{w'^T S_W w'}.$$ (8)

Here, S_W is the within-class scatter matrix and S_B is the between-class scatter matrix. In (9) and (10), μ_j is the mean of class j, and μ is the mean of observations in A. The number of classes or the number of different people for facial recognition is denoted by c and N_j is the number of observation for class j.

$$S_W = \sum_{j=1}^{c} \sum_{i \in C_j} (a_i - \mu_j)(a_i - \mu_j)^T$$ (9)

$$S_B = \sum_{j=1}^{c} N_j (\mu_j - \mu)(\mu_j - \mu)^T$$ (10)

Once the set of directions into feature space w is obtained, the sensor locations can be found by solving (11). The equation solves for columns of $s \in \mathbb{R}^{n \times (c-1)}$ simultaneously, where each column of s projects to a column of w.

Here, v is a column vector of $(c-1)$ ones and λ is the value of the coupling weight and can be used to increase of decrease the selected number of sensors. When $\lambda = 0$ the most sensors are obtained. When λ goes to infinity the lowest amount of sensors are selected. As lambda increases the number of nonzero rows should decrease. The equation aims to find the best reconstruction of w while penalizing the total number of nonzero rows of s (i.e. more sensors).

$$s = \underset{s'}{\mathrm{argmin}}\{||s'||_1 + \lambda||s'v||_1\}$$
$$\text{subject to } ||\Psi_r^T s' - w||_F \le \epsilon$$ (11)

Each row of s corresponds to a feature, so the matrix s can be used to select the sensors. Originally, each row with a non-zero value is selected as a sensor. However, in practice when the number of classes (e.g. number of people) increases, most rows of s have non-zero values. Therefore, this work will use matrix s to create a ranking of the sensors by calculating the row sums and using these to score the features. The higher the row sum of the feature the higher the ranking. The sensor locations are then represented as matrix Φ.

3.5   LDA Classifier Algorithm

After obtaining the sensor locations Φ from both approaches as explained in Subsects. 3.3 and 3.4, a new classifier is learned using only the sparsely measured data $Y = \Phi X$. This is done by repeating LDA as shown in Subsect. 3.4 with the sparsely measured data Y.

$$w = \underset{w'}{\operatorname{argmax}} \frac{w'^T S_B w'}{w'^T S_W w'} \tag{12}$$

where S_W is still the within-class scatter matrix and S_B is the between-class scatter matrix. In (13) and (14), μ_j is the mean of all y_i in class j, and μ is the mean of all observations in Y.

$$S_W = \sum_{j=1}^{c} \sum_{i \in C_j} (\hat{y}_i - \mu_j)(\hat{y}_i - \mu_j)^T \tag{13}$$

$$S_B = \sum_{j=1}^{c} N_j (\mu_j - \mu)(\mu_j - \mu)^T \tag{14}$$

Then using the new learned classifier w, Brunton et al. (2016) applies the Nearest Centroid (NC) method to classify the test images. The NC method assigns test image $y_{test} = \Phi x_{test}$ to category j, where the distance between $w^T y_{test}$ and $w^T \mu_j$ is minimized,

$$j = \underset{j'}{\operatorname{argmin}} |w^T y_{test} - w^T \mu_{j'}|. \tag{15}$$

4   Results and Discussion

This section focuses on implementing the QUBO and machine learning (ML) SSPOC algorithm from Brunton et al. [1] by performing Sparse Sensor Placement on human facial images from the extended Yale B database. A short explanation of this database is provided in the first subsection. The second subsection performs experiments to compare the quality of the sensors from the different algorithms. Then, the last subsection further discusses the results obtained from the experiments.

4.1   Extended Yale B Database

The extended Yale B database consists of 2,414 grayscale frontal-face images of 38 individuals. For each subject, (about) 64 pictures were taken under different lighting conditions, see Fig. 1. All pictures for the same individual are taken in a two-second time frame, to ensure the subject has the same facial expression in each picture. The images are cropped and aligned so that the main facial features will have similar placements for all pictures.

Each picture has 192×168 pixels. Each pixel has a value between 0 and 255 that represents the brightness, where 0 corresponds to black and 255 to white. Hence, each picture can be represented as a matrix with 192 rows and 168 columns, where the entries are pixel values. For convenience, the 192×168 matrix is rearranged into a $32{,}256 \times 1$ matrix, by stacking all the columns under each other. Moreover, we can represent the entire database as a $32{,}256 \times 2414$ matrix, where each column represents an image. This will be useful for later procedures such as the proper orthogonal decomposition and calculating the Pearson correlation.

However, performing computations on a matrix of dimension $32{,}256 \times 2414$ can be time-consuming, and in some cases even impossible. For example, calculating the Pearson correlation of this matrix is not possible on a normal computer. Therefore, the decision was made to resize the images from 192×168 pixels to 32×32 pixels. Then following the same steps, an image can be rearranged into a 1024×1 matrix by stacking the columns, and the entire database can be represented by a 1024×2414 matrix, where each column represents an image.

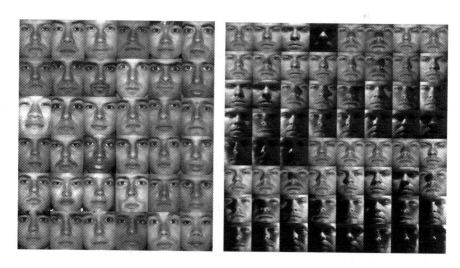

Fig. 1. (left) One image of each person and (right) all images for one person

The database will serve as the foundation for training sensors and assessing prediction accuracy. In order to do so, the database is split into a training set and a testing set. The training set will be used by the QUBO and ML algorithm to learn sensors. Subsequently, the testing set will be used to generate predictions based on the chosen sensors. Finally, the accuracy of these predictions will be evaluated by measuring the frequency of correct outcomes in the preceding step.

For the training set, 48 random images are selected from each of the 38 individuals, leaving the remaining 16 images for the testing set. This results in a training set containing 75% of the original data. Moreover, selecting the same amount of images from each individual for the training set ensures that no features of one individual are favored over another.

4.2   Experiments and Results

Two experiments were conducted to see how the QUBO approach performs relative to the ML approach. The first experiment focuses on the Sparse Sensor Placement itself, by visually comparing the placement of selected sensors from the two methods. The second experiment compares the prediction quality for classification based on the sensors selected both by the QUBO and by the ML approach, as well as random sensors to form a baseline.

Both experiments employed Simulated Annealing for solving the QUBO, using the default settings of D-Wave's SA solution, see [7] as based on [16]. Quantum Annealing is still limited in the problem sizes it can solve. Some tests were conducted on resized images of 10 by 10 pixels, but the resolution of these images was so low, that there was no point anymore to perform sparse sensor placement. Hence, simulated annealing forms a good alternative as it can handle larger problem sizes while still showing the potential of the QUBO to be solved on a Quantum Annealer in the future [12, 21]. The penalty term λ was set manually for every different value of p as low as possible, providing feasible solutions, and the relevancy weight α was set equal to one, implying equal importance for relevancy and redundancy.

Experiment 1: Sparse Sensor Placement Comparison of Feature Selection Models. The first experiment focuses on learning the sensors using the QUBO and the machine learning algorithm. Then follows a visualisation of the sparse sensor placement to compare the QUBO and ML (machine learning) sensors.

During the training process, the machine learning algorithm ranks all sensors. Hence, to obtain a sparse sensor placement of p sensors, one simply selects the first p sensors in the ranking. Conversely, the QUBO is trained with a predefined number of sensors to identify the optimal combination of sensors. Thus, to achieve a sparse sensor placement with a different number of sensors p, one must re-optimise the QUBO for all different values of p. Though the ranking obtained from the machine learning algorithm can be reused for different numbers of sensors, it is important to note that this algorithm has a much higher running time than solving the QUBO problem. Where the ML learning algorithm takes around 7–8 minutes to find a sensor ranking, the proposed QUBO-based approach takes less than half a minute to find a sensor placement. The QUBO-based approach takes around 2 s to calculate the Pearson correlations and then requires an additional 20 s to perform simulated annealing. Selecting random sensors is trivial and takes less than a millisecond. Figure 2 provides a visualisation of the sparse sensor placement for 50, 100, 150, and 200 sensors, which respectively corresponds to around 5%, 10%, 15%, and 20% of the total.

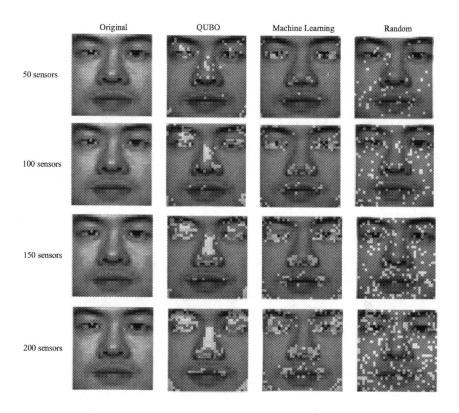

Fig. 2. Sparse sensor placement for QUBO, Brunton, and random sensors

The sparse sensors, found by the ML algorithm from Brunton et al. [1], cluster at major facial features: the eyes, the nose, the mouth, and the jawline. A similar observation can be made for the sensors selected by the QUBO. The biggest difference between the two algorithms is the concentration of sensors around the nose and the mouth. As can be seen in Fig. 2 the QUBO has a much higher concentration of sensors around the nose, whereas the machine learning algorithm has fewer sensors there, mainly focused on the bottom of the nose. Moreover, the QUBO has a much lower concentration of sensors around the mouth, only focusing on the corners of the lips, whereas the machine learning algorithm has more sensors that are evenly spread out over the lips. Both algorithms have a similar concentration and placement of sensors around the eyes, as well as, the jawline.

Interestingly, the QUBO and the machine learning algorithm favor the same features as the human gaze. In 1967, Yarbus [37] conducted experiments where he tracked eye movements of people when looking at a human face. He discovered that people mainly pay attention to the eyes, the lips, and the nose.

Experiment 2: Accuracy Comparison of Feature Selection Models for Classification. The quality of the QUBO sensors is determined by comparing the classification accuracy obtained from the QUBO sensors to that of the ML sensors, as well as random sensors. This experiment will focus on the predictions (i.e. identifying a face) made based on the sensors found after training, more specifically the accuracy of those predictions.

After obtaining the QUBO and ML sensors from training, predictions are made using the sensor-based LDA classifier as explained in Subsect. 3.5. Then the accuracy is determined based on the number of correct predictions. To see how the accuracy improves with more sensors, predictions are made based on a different number of sensors. As explained in the previous subsection the machine learning sensors are trained once to obtain a ranking of sensors. Then the first p sensors are selected from the ranking to make predictions based on p sensors. The QUBO sensors, on the other hand, need to be retrained for every different number of sensors p.

For this experiment, the number of sensors ranges from 20 up to 200, which respectively corresponds to 2% and 20% of the total amount. The accuracy is determined for the number of sensors in increments of 10 and for each number of sensors, tests were repeated 50 times with different training sets to account for randomness in results. The averages of the tests are reported in Fig. 3.

Several observations can be made from Fig. 3. Firstly, it can be seen that the QUBO consistently outperforms the random sensors for all numbers of sensors. Nevertheless, the ML algorithm still gives a higher accuracy than the QUBO for all sensors.

Secondly, the graph exhibits a similar shape for all approaches. The graph follows a logarithmic growth curve marked by rapid initial improvements that gradually diminish as the number of sensors increases. This pattern aligns with the nature of feature selection since an additional sensor can yield significant gains when there are currently few sensors available, but the marginal information gain diminishes as the number of sensors grows higher.

Lastly, the difference between the three approaches is relatively small. As can be seen in the graph, the difference between the machine learning sensors and the random sensors has about a 10% gap at the start which continuously decreases as the number of sensors grows. The QUBO sensors fluctuate between the other two, with a slight tendency toward the machine learning sensors.

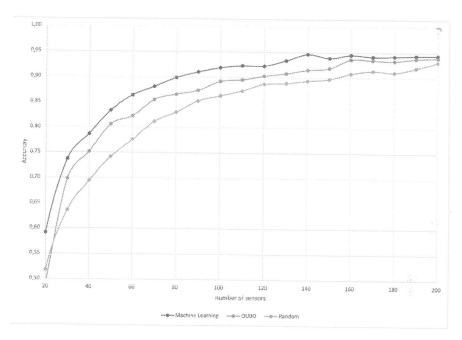

Fig. 3. Prediction accuracy of QUBO, Brunton, and random sensors. The accuracy is on the vertical axis and ranges from 0.5 to 1.0. The horizontal axis has the number of sensors ranging from 20 to 200.

4.3 Discussion

It is clear from the experiments that the QUBO formulation cannot reproduce the results from the ML algorithm. In Fig. 3 from Experiment 2 it can be seen that the accuracy obtained from the QUBO approach is in between that of random sensors and machine learning sensors. Figure 2 from Experiment 1 provides a possible explanation, as both algorithms place sensors on the same facial features (e.g. eyes, nose, etc.) but in different concentrations. The QUBO approach, for example, assigns more sensors to the nose, and the ML algorithm assigns more features to the mouth.

Considering the higher accuracy of the ML sensors, the ML algorithm employs a more effective method for recognising relevant features. As discussed in Subsect. 3.4, the ML algorithm identifies a sparse set of sensors such that the between-class variance is maximised (relevancy) and the within-class variance is minimised (redundancy). Conversely, the QUBO formulation maximises the correlation between a selected sensor and all other features, while minimising correlations between selected sensors. The QUBO method does not account for the fact that images belong to distinct classes and operates on the entire dataset without such discrimination.

Furthermore, a different measure for feature relevance and redundancy could improve the performance of the QUBO approach. This work employed Pearson correlation as its measure of feature relevance and redundancy. This decision was based on its reputation as a reliable means to measure similarity [31]. Moreover, it is favoured for its simplicity and has demonstrated effectiveness across various feature selection techniques. Nevertheless, it is worth considering whether Mutual Information (MI) might be a better measure of relevance due to its ability to capture nonlinear relationships. Rodriguez et al. [31] performed Quadratic Programming Feature Selection (QPFS) with two different measures for relevancy and redundancy: Pearson correlation and Mutual Information (MI). From their experiments, it followed that the QPFS with MI always outperformed the QPFS with Pearson correlation. Therefore, the QUBO (inspired by QPFS) might yield better results by adopting MI instead of Pearson correlation. For example, Mücke et al. [22] have also shown good results using Mutual Information for MRMR-based feature selection.

Additionally, it should be mentioned that there is a large disparity between the running times of different methods for obtaining sensors. As said before, the ML algorithm from Brunton takes around 7 min, the QUBO takes around 20 s, and finding random sensors takes less than a millisecond. This disparity is also reflected in the results, where a longer running time corresponds to a higher accuracy. Therefore, there exists a trade-off between solution quality and the running time.

If the QUBO approach would yield better results by employing Mutual Information and achieve comparable results to that of the ML algorithm, then the QUBO could have a significant advantage over ML since the running time is about much quicker. The current running time is based on simulated annealing, so quantum annealing is expected to give even more of an advantage (with enough qubits/couplers) since the annealing process (excluding finding a minor embedding) only takes milliseconds.

5   Conclusion

This study has determined that the MRMR framework is a suitable choice for the QUBO formulation for facial recognition. MRMR is a filter-based approach, making it computationally efficient as it does not depend on classifier algorithms for feature selection. Initially, Pearson Correlation was used to measure feature relevance and redundancy, but Mutual Information (MI) was considered as a potentially better alternative, as it can capture non-linear relationships, which Pearson correlation cannot. The QUBO formulation in this research is based on the Quadratic Programming Feature Selection (QPFS) approach introduced by Nguyen et al. [25]. QPFS ranks features using real-valued variables and introduces binary constraints to achieve the desired number of selected features. The QUBO approach aims to maximise the relevance and minimise redundancy of selected features. The fully connected QUBO, though theoretically sound, may pose challenges when implemented on current quantum hardware due to limited connectivity. Despite hardware limitations, the QUBO approach remains suitable for simulated annealing, which does not rely on quantum hardware.

To evaluate the QUBO approach's performance relative to a well-established machine learning approach, the study compared the positions and accuracy of selected sensors. Both the QUBO and the machine learning algorithm tend to favour similar facial features such as the eyes, nose, mouth, and jawline. While the machine learning algorithm outperforms the QUBO in terms of accuracy, the QUBO consistently outperforms random sensor selection. There is a significant difference in the running time, with the QUBO approach, even using Simulated Annealing, being much faster than the machine learning approach. The potential for improved QUBO results exists, possibly by using Mutual Information as a measure of feature relevance.

This means that we can conclude that, considering the current state of quantum hardware, SSPO cannot be effectively performed using quantum annealing yet. The limited connectivity of quantum annealers and the fully connected QUBO make it challenging to find embeddings for problems that require SSPO without feature compression, which can lead to a loss of relevant information.

Nonetheless, the results achieved with simulated annealing are promising, as the QUBO consistently outperforms random sensor placement. While it may not match the performance of the machine learning approach for SSPO, the QUBO's advantage lies in its significantly shorter runtime.

Looking ahead, there is potential for improving the QUBO formulation by replacing Pearson correlation with Mutual Information, which could yield better results. Therefore, as quantum hardware continues to evolve, there is potential for quantum computing to perform SSPO effectively, especially if qubit count and connectivity in quantum annealers improve in the coming years.

References

1. Brunton, B.W., Brunton, S.L., Proctor, J.L., Kutz, J.N.: Sparse sensor placement optimization for classification. SIAM J. Appl. Math. **76**(5), 2099–2122 (2016)
2. Camino, B., Buckeridge, J., Warburton, P., Kendon, V., Woodley, S.: Quantum computing and materials science: a practical guide to applying quantum annealing to the configurational analysis of materials. J. Appl. Phy. **133**(22) (2023)
3. Chandrashekar, G., Sahin, F.: A survey on feature selection methods. Comput. Electr. Eng. **40**(1), 16–28 (2014)
4. Chen, B., Hong, J., Wang, Y.: The minimum feature subset selection problem. J. Comput. Sci. Technol. **12**, 145–153 (1997)
5. Zhong, J., Ma, C., Zhou, J., Wang, W.: PDPNN: modeling user personal dynamic preference for next point-of-interest recommendation. In: Krzhizhanovskaya, V.V. (ed.) ICCS 2020. LNCS, vol. 12142, pp. 45–57. Springer, Cham (2020). https://doi.org/10.1007/978-3-030-50433-5_4
6. Colucci, G., Linde, S., Phillipson, F.: Power network optimization: a quantum approach. IEEE Access **11**, 98926–98938 (2023). https://doi.org/10.1109/ACCESS.2023.3312997
7. D-Wave System Documentation: Neal documentation (2022). https://docs.ocean.dwavesys.com/projects/neal/en/latest/index.html [Accessed: 01 Mar 2024]
8. Domino, K., Koniorczyk, M., Krawiec, K., Jałowiecki, K., Deffner, S., Gardas, B.: Quantum annealing in the NISQ era: railway conflict management. Entropy **25**(2), 191 (2023)

9. Duda, R.O., Hart, P.E., et al.: Pattern classification. John Wiley and Sons (2006)
10. Egger, D.J., et al.: Quantum computing for finance: state-of-the-art and future prospects. IEEE Trans. Quantum Eng. **1**, 1–24 (2020)
11. Glover, F., Kochenberger, G., Hennig, R., Du, Y.: Quantum bridge analytics I: a tutorial on formulating and using QUBO models. Ann. Oper. Res. 1–43 (2022). https://doi.org/10.1007/s10479-022-04634-2
12. Heim, B., Rønnow, T.F., Isakov, S.V., Troyer, M.: Quantum versus classical annealing of ising spin glasses. Science **348**(6231), 215–217 (2015)
13. Inza, I., Sierra, B., Blanco, R., Larrañaga, P.: Gene selection by sequential search wrapper approaches in microarray cancer class prediction. J. Intell. Fuzzy Syst. **12**(1), 25–33 (2002)
14. Jadhav, S., He, H., Jenkins, K.: Information gain directed genetic algorithm wrapper feature selection for credit rating. Appl. Soft Comput. **69**, 541–553 (2018)
15. Karegowda, A.G., Jayaram, M., Manjunath, A.: Feature subset selection problem using wrapper approach in supervised learning. Int. J. Comput. Appl. **1**(7), 13–17 (2010)
16. Kirkpatrick, S., Gelatt, C.D., Jr., Vecchi, M.P.: Optim. Simulated Annealing. Sci. **220**(4598), 671–680 (1983)
17. König, G., Molnar, C., Bischl, B., Grosse-Wentrup, M.: Relative feature importance. In: 2020 25th International Conference on Pattern Recognition (ICPR), pp. 9318–9325. IEEE (2021)
18. Lin, M.M., Shu, Y.C., Lu, B.Z., Fang, P.S.: Nurse scheduling problem via PyQUBO. arXiv preprint arXiv:2302.09459 (2023)
19. Lucas, A.: Ising formulations of many NP problems. Frontiers in physics, p .74887 (2) (2014)
20. Manohar, K., Brunton, B.W., Kutz, J.N., Brunton, S.L.: Data-driven sparse sensor placement for reconstruction: demonstrating the benefits of exploiting known patterns. IEEE Control Syst. Mag. **38**(3), 63–86 (2018)
21. Morita, S., Nishimori, H.: Mathematical foundation of quantum annealing. J. Math. Phy. **49**(12) (2008)
22. Mücke, S., Heese, R., Müller, S., Wolter, M., Piatkowski, N.: Feature selection on quantum computers. Quantum Mach. Intell. **5**(1), 11 (2023)
23. Nazareth, D.P., Spaans, J.D.: First application of quantum annealing to IMRT beamlet intensity optimization. Phy. Med. Biol. **60**(10), 4137 (2015)
24. Neukart, F., Compostella, G., Seidel, C., Von Dollen, D., Yarkoni, S., Parney, B.: Traffic flow optimization using a quantum annealer. Frontiers in ICT **4**, 29 (2017)
25. Nguyen, V., Chan, J., Romano, S., Bailey, J.: Effective global approaches for mutual information based feature selection. In: Proceedings of the ACM SIGKDD International Conference on Knowledge Discovery and Data Mining, pp .512–521 (2014). https://doi.org/10.1145/2623330.2623611
26. Peng, H., Long, F., Ding, C.: Feature selection based on mutual information criteria of max-dependency, max-relevance, and min-redundancy. IEEE Trans. Pattern Anal. Mach. Intell. **27**(8), 1226–1238 (2005)
27. Phillipson, F.: Quantum Comput. Telecommun. Surv. Math. **11**(15), 3423 (2023)
28. Phillipson, F.: Quantum computing in logistics and supply chain management-an overview. arXiv preprint. arXiv:2402.17520 (2024)
29. Phillipson, F., Chiscop, I.: Multimodal container planning: a QUBO formulation and implementation on a quantum annealer. In: Paszynski, M., Kranzlmüller, D., Krzhizhanovskaya, V.V., Dongarra, J.J., Sloot, P.M.A. (eds.) ICCS 2021. LNCS, vol. 12747, pp. 30–44. Springer, Cham (2021). https://doi.org/10.1007/978-3-030-77980-1_3

30. Roch, C., Ratke, D., Nüßlein, J., Gabor, T., Feld, S.: The effect of penalty factors of constrained hamiltonians on the eigenspectrum in quantum annealing. ACM Trans. Quantum Comput. **4**(2), 1–18 (2023)

31. Rodriguez-Lujan, I., Huerta, R., Elkan, C., Cruz, C.S.: Quadratic programming feature selection. J. Mach. Learn. Res. **11**, 1491–1516 (2010)

32. Sánchez-Maroño, N., Alonso-Betanzos, A., Tombilla-Sanromán, M.: Filter methods for feature selection – a comparative study. In: Yin, H., Tino, P., Corchado, E., Byrne, W., Yao, X. (eds.) IDEAL 2007. LNCS, vol. 4881, pp. 178–187. Springer, Heidelberg (2007). https://doi.org/10.1007/978-3-540-77226-2_19

33. Symons, B.C., Galvin, D., Sahin, E., Alexandrov, V., Mensa, S.: A practitioner's guide to quantum algorithms for optimisation problems. J. Phys. A: Math. Theor. **56**(45), 453001 (2023)

34. Thales Group: Facial recognition: top 7 trends (tech, vendors, use cases). https://www.thalesgroup.com/en/markets/digital-identity-and-security/government/biometrics/facial-recognition

35. Venegas-Andraca, S.E., Cruz-Santos, W., McGeoch, C., Lanzagorta, M.: A cross-disciplinary introduction to quantum annealing-based algorithms. Contemp. Phys. **59**(2), 174–197 (2018)

36. Wang, Y., Li, X., Ruiz, R.: Feature selection with maximal relevance and minimal supervised redundancy. IEEE Trans. Cybern. **53**(2), 707–717 (2022)

37. Yarbus, A.L.: Eye movements and vision. Springer,New York (2013). https://doi.org/10.1007/978-1-4899-5379-7

Leveraging Quantum Technology to Enhance Community Services and Supportive ICT Infrastructure

Frank Phillipson[1,2]([envelope]) [ORCID]

[1] Maastricht University, Maastricht, The Netherlands
`f.phillipson@maastrichtuniversity.nl`
[2] TNO, The Hague, The Netherlands

Abstract. This article explores the transformative potential of quantum technology in community services, emphasising quantum sensing, quantum computing algorithms, and quantum communication. Community services, spanning healthcare, education, and environmental conservation, are crucial for resident well-being. Quantum technology, rooted in principles like superposition and entanglement, is presented as a game-changer. Quantum sensing offers unparalleled precision, benefiting environmental monitoring, traffic management, and healthcare diagnostics. Quantum computing algorithms, leveraging qubits, promise breakthroughs in resource allocation, data analysis, and telecommunications optimisation. Quantum communication, particularly quantum key distribution, ensures secure data transmission, safeguarding sensitive information in fields like finance and healthcare. The article envisions a future where quantum technology optimises community services, fostering data accuracy, speed, and privacy. The collaborative incorporation of quantum technology into ICT infrastructure is crucial for realising these advancements and enhancing community well-being. The recommendations stress enhancing ICT infrastructure for seamless quantum technology integration. Quantum-safe encryption, high-speed communication networks, and quantum-ready data centres are crucial. Collaboration among stakeholders is deemed essential for identifying applications and ensuring comprehensive integration.

Keywords: Quantum technology · Community services · Quantum sensing · Quantum computing algorithms · Quantum communication

1 Introduction

Community services encompass a wide range of programs and initiatives aimed at improving the well-being, quality of life, and social support within a community. These services are vital for fostering social cohesion and addressing the needs of residents, covering areas like healthcare, education, recreation, environmental conservation, and more. To enhance these services, technology has played a

F. Phillipson et al. (Eds.): I4CS 2024, CCIS 2109, pp. 36–47, 2024.
https://doi.org/10.1007/978-3-031-60433-1_3

pivotal role in improving efficiency, accessibility, and the quality of service delivery. This technological advancement has led to the use of IoT, AI/ML, smart infrastructure, mobile apps, and various other solutions to address community needs. Quantum technology is an upcoming field with the potential to bring about transformative changes in how we approach and improve community services. Quantum technology encompasses quantum sensing, quantum computing, quantum communication, and quantum cryptography. These quantum technologies offer unique advantages, particularly in terms of processing power and data security, which can be harnessed to address challenges in community services and the underlying ICT infrastructure.

In this paper we give an overview of the use of quantum technology in the future of community services and their supportive ICT Infrastructures. First, in Sect. 2 an introduction to quantum technology is given. This is followed by a systematic overview for each of the three sub-areas, quantum sensing, quantum computing and quantum communication and quantum cryptography, in the Sects. 3 to 5. The purpose of this paper is by no means to provide a complete overview. We want to give the reader an overview of a selection of state of the art developments within this playing field and references for further research. We will conclude with some recommendations in Sect. 6.

2   Introduction to Quantum Technology

Quantum technology is a revolutionary field of science and engineering that leverages the principles of quantum mechanics to create powerful tools and applications. In this introduction, the fundamental concepts of quantum technology, such as qubits, superposition, and entanglement, which underpin these advancements, are explored.

At the heart of quantum technology is the qubit, short for "quantum bit." In classical computing, information is processed using bits, which can be either 0 or 1. However, qubits take advantage of quantum superposition to exist in a state that is simultaneously 0 and 1. The distinctive characteristic of qubits enables them to simultaneously carry out numerous calculations, resulting in a quantum computer's exponentially enhanced power for particular tasks.

Entanglement is another intriguing quantum property where two or more particles or qubits become correlated in such a way that the state of one particle depends on the state of another, even when separated by vast distances. This seemingly instantaneous connection, described by Einstein as "spooky action at a distance" [9], has profound implications for quantum sensing and cryptography. It enables secure communication through quantum key distribution and can enhance the sensitivity of quantum sensors.

Quantum technology's roots can be traced back to the early 20th century with the emergence of quantum mechanics. Pioneers like Max Planck, Albert Einstein, Niels Bohr, and Werner Heisenberg laid the foundation for understanding the quantum world. In 1900, Max Planck introduced the concept of quantisation, which explained the discrete nature of energy levels in atomic systems. This marked the birth of quantum physics. Albert Einstein's work on the photoelectric effect in 1905, which described how light behaved as discrete packets of energy called photons, further solidified quantum theory.

In the 1920 s, quantum mechanics was developed into a comprehensive framework by scientists like Niels Bohr, Werner Heisenberg, Erwin Schrödinger, and Paul Dirac. Their work led to the famous Schrödinger equation, which describes the behaviour of quantum systems. Quantum mechanics was applied to various fields, including atomic and molecular physics, solid-state physics, and quantum electrodynamics. This laid the groundwork for technological applications in the future.

During the years 1950–1980, quantum technologies began to emerge. The development of nuclear magnetic resonance (NMR) spectroscopy and electron paramagnetic resonance (EPR) spectroscopy were early applications of quantum principles in sensing and imaging. The invention of the laser in 1960 by Theodore Maiman [48] was another significant milestone, as lasers are essential tools in various quantum technologies.

In the 1980 s and 1990 s, the field of quantum information science took shape. Physicist Richard Feynman [17] proposed the idea of using quantum systems to simulate quantum processes more efficiently than classical computers. In 1994–1996, Peter Shor [52] and Lov Grover [21] developed quantum algorithms that demonstrated the potential of quantum computers to solve problems like factoring large numbers and searching unsorted databases faster than classical computers.

The 21st century saw a surge in quantum technology research and development. Quantum cryptography systems, based on quantum key distribution, were developed to provide ultra-secure communication and Quantum sensors, like atomic clocks and gravimeters, achieved remarkable levels of precision and sensitivity.

3   Quantum Sensing

Quantum sensing is an interesting field of investigation, at the intersection of quantum mechanics and sensor technology, harnessing the unique properties of quantum systems to achieve unprecedented levels of precision and sensitivity in measuring physical quantities [12]. It represents a paradigm shift in the way we observe and interact with the world, offering remarkable opportunities for scientific research, industrial applications, and even the enhancement of community services. At the core of quantum sensing we will need quantum states and their ability to be in superposition. This property enables quantum sensors to process and analyse data in a fundamentally different way from classical sensors, allowing for measurements with exquisite accuracy, precision and long term stability. Entanglement plays a minor role in quantum sensing. Quantum sensing has already found applications in various domains. For instance, it has been employed to detect magnetic fields at nanoscale resolutions [49], enabling advancements in materials science [18], the energy industry [14] and medical diagnostics [37]. Quantum sensors can also detect minute changes in gravity, making them invaluable tools for geophysical exploration [54] and even potentially helping to predict natural disasters like earthquakes [56]. The ability to detect these minute changes in gravity and magnetic field enables also new forms of navigation, completely independent of GPS, i.e. these techniques will also work indoor, underground and underwater.

In community services, quantum sensing holds the potential to revolutionise environmental monitoring, healthcare diagnostics, traffic management, and disaster prediction. Its extraordinary precision can enhance the data needed to make informed decisions and optimise resource allocation. As quantum technology continues to advance, it is poised to play a pivotal role in shaping the future of sensing technologies and, in turn, the improvement of community well-being. In environmental monitoring, quantum sensors can be employed to enhance the monitoring of air quality, soil conditions, water quality [59] and intruder detection [38]. The data from these monitoring activities is crucial for environmental initiatives within the community, such as sustainability efforts and pollution control. Also, quantum sensors on satellites could collect accurate data on levels of groundwater, methane and other gasses [6]. In traffic management, quantum sensors can provide real-time data on traffic flows [31], allowing for optimised traffic management and reduced congestion, thereby improving transportation services within the community and improve the safety of air-traffic control [6]. In healthcare, quantum sensors can be used for highly accurate medical diagnostics and early disease detection [13], improving healthcare services and outcomes for residents. For emergency response services, quantum sensors can enhance the precision of earthquake and disaster prediction [22], enable GPS-free navigation [29] and cameras that can see through fog and around corners [6], improving emergency response plans and ensuring the safety and security of community members. Lastly, in smart infrastructure, quantum sensing can play a role in monitoring and optimising the performance of smart infrastructure systems, such as energy-efficient buildings [14], ultimately improving community development.

4   Quantum Computing Algorithms

Quantum computing algorithms represent a groundbreaking approach to solving complex problems that classical computers struggle with. Unlike classical computers, which rely on bits to process information, quantum computers employ qubits as presented before. This unique ability allows quantum algorithms to explore vast solution spaces, enabling them to tackle problems of immense complexity and significance.

At the heart of quantum computing algorithms is the concept of quantum parallelism. Instead of sequentially evaluating potential solutions, as classical algorithms do, quantum algorithms can simultaneously assess multiple possibilities and join them together in the end constructively. This parallel processing capability offers a significant advantage, particularly when dealing with optimisation problems, data analysis, and simulations.

Quantum computing algorithms have demonstrated exceptional promise in numerous fields, including cryptography, materials science, and healthcare. For example, Shor's algorithm [52], one of the pioneering quantum algorithms, poses a potential threat to classical encryption methods by efficiently factoring large numbers. Conversely, Grover's algorithm [21] accelerates the search for unsorted data, which could have profound implications for database searches and cyber-security. The rise of quantum computing also comes with a demand for quantum computing software stack [8,46].

Quantum algorithms have the potential to revolutionise community services by addressing challenges such as resource allocation, data analysis, and disaster prediction. Their expected capacity to swiftly process vast datasets, identify patterns, and optimise decision-making can significantly enhance the efficiency and quality of community support systems. As quantum computing technology continues to advance, it holds the promise of enabling breakthroughs in numerous community-focused applications, ultimately contributing to improved well-being and quality of life for residents.

The ICT basis of community services relies heavily on the telecommunication infrastructure. The significance of quantum computing in the realm of telecommunications, next to quantum communication and cryptography, is widely acknowledged. It has been underscored in the study by Martin et al. [33], where also the European Commission recognises quantum computing as a pivotal technological advancement [1]. Quantum computing holds the promise of resolving intricate computational challenges encountered in the planning and operation of both current and future telecommunication networks.

The work by Martin [33] specifically points out that a substantial portion of optimisation problems within the telecommunications and ICT domain are presently addressed using algorithms that yield suboptimal solutions. This limitation is primarily due to the prohibitive costs associated with finding optimal solutions. These optimisation challenges encompass a wide array of functions, including but not limited to radio channel estimation, data detection, synchronisation, and data centre optimisation.

Especially in the context of forthcoming mobile communication networks, such as 5G and beyond, the demand for robust computational capabilities to manage and strategise network operations is particularly pronounced [10,60]. As Henrique et al. emphasise in their research [25], the development of a 6G Radio must prioritise qualities like cognitive capabilities, rapid event prediction, and incident prevention. To achieve these objectives, the integration of artificial intelligence, machine learning [45], and the computational power of quantum computers is deemed essential to efficiently process and harness the vast volumes of data. This integration aims to improve service level agreements (SLAs) and the quality of experience (QoE) for users.

For comprehensive insights into the current state and potential applications of quantum computing in telecommunications, overviews are available in the works of Nawaz et al. and Suriya et al. [39,55]. Nawaz et al. delve into the emerging paradigms of machine learning, quantum computing, and quantum machine learning, highlighting their synergistic relationship with communication networks as core enablers for 6G technology. They provide an overview of application areas, though without an in-depth examination of ongoing research. Similarly, Suriya et al. offer a high-level perspective on the field, introducing various relevant topics without extensive analysis. A recent overview of quantum computing applications can be found in [43].

Other examples for the use of quantum computing in the community services environment can be found in Data Analytics. Quantum algorithms will be able to process vast datasets much faster than classical computers in the future [40]. This enables more in-depth data analysis and insights for decision-making in areas like healthcare [27,57], driving AI based educational performance enhancement [15], and urban planning and smart transportation [11,20,44,58] and delivery [34]. Also, quantum computing can optimise the allocation of resources for community services, ensuring more efficient distribution of funding and support where it is needed most.

There will also be applications in crisis management. Quantum algorithms can improve disaster response times by quickly processing large volumes of data and providing real-time solutions for crisis management, as the tasks they need [7] are close to the sweet spots of quantum computing. It will help to minimise incident response times [50], help in drug discovery during pandemics [35], post-disaster restoration [19] and disaster forecasting, such as earthquake, flood, land sliding [41] and by mapping the deep subsurface [16]. Also ambulance real time dispatching could be translated to optimisation problems that can be solved by quantum computers [24,26].

A last example is the use of quantum computation in the area of healthcare. The work by [47,57] gives an overview of potential applications in molecular simulations, precision medicines and clinical trials, diagnosis assistance, radio-therapy (optimisation), drug research and recovery, and risk analysis.

5   Quantum Communication

Quantum communication represents a revolutionary approach to secure data transmission, leveraging the fundamental principles of quantum mechanics to protect information against eavesdropping and interception. At its core, quantum communication ensures the integrity and confidentiality of data through the use of quantum properties superposition and entanglement again, offering an unprecedented level of security. The most prominent application of quantum communication is quantum key distribution (QKD). QKD enables the exchange of cryptographic keys between two parties with the assurance that any interception would be immediately detectable, making it a cornerstone of secure communication.

Quantum Key Distribution (QKD) involves aspects of both entanglement and superposition, depending on the specific protocol used. The most common and well-known implementations of QKD, such as the BBM92 (Bennett-Brassard-Mermin 1992 [5]) protocol, primarily rely on the concept of entanglement. In

QKD, entangled particles (typically photons) are distributed between two parties, often referred to as Alice and Bob. These particles are entangled in such a way that the state of one particle is directly related to the state of the other, regardless of the distance between them. If an eavesdropper, often referred to as Eve, tries to intercept or measure the entangled particles, the entanglement is disturbed, and Alice and Bob can detect this intrusion. The security of QKD relies on the principles of quantum entanglement to ensure the detection of any unauthorised attempts to gain information about the quantum key.

The BB84 (Bennett-Brassard 1984 [4]) protocol, another well-known QKD protocol, is based on the principle of quantum superposition rather than entanglement. In the BB84 protocol, Alice prepares a sequence of qubits in one of two conjugate bases (rectilinear basis or diagonal basis). Each qubit exists in a superposition of the two possible bases. She then sends these qubits to Bob through a quantum channel. Bob randomly chooses to measure each qubit in one of the two bases. The uncertainty introduced by the superposition principle ensures that, in the absence of eavesdropping, Bob has a 50% chance of measuring the qubit in the correct basis. After the measurements, Alice and Bob publicly communicate which bases they used for each qubit but not the specific measurement outcomes. To create a secure key, Alice and Bob discard the measurements where they used different bases. The remaining measurements, where the bases match, form the raw key. By comparing a subset of this raw key (used for error checking) over a classical communication channel, Alice and Bob can detect the presence of an eavesdropper. If the error rate is below a certain threshold, they can perform privacy amplification to distill a shorter, but secure, final key.

Quantum entanglement offers a unique avenue for communication, leveraging the special correlations between entangled qubits. Through entangled qubits, we can establish immediate consensus on information across extensive distances. Although quantum entanglement does not enable communication faster than the speed of light, the capability for instantaneous agreement holds promise for applications such as High-Performance Computing (HPC) and highly secure communication. Quantum networks can facilitate entanglement over substantial distances. In the future, a fully realised quantum internet could provide Entanglement as a Service (EaaS) on a global scale, connecting individuals worldwide with access to entanglement. This technology holds significant potential. For instance, entanglement can be harnessed to construct vastly more powerful (networks of) quantum computers, unlocking novel applications in areas like drug discovery and machine learning.

The implications of quantum communication for security are profound. It addresses long-standing challenges in securing sensitive data and communications, particularly in fields like finance, healthcare, and government, where the consequences of breaches can be catastrophic. It also holds the potential to revolutionise secure community services, ensuring the confidentiality of critical information in areas such as emergency response, healthcare, and data exchange between public services.

As quantum communication technology advances, it promises to offer robust security solutions that protect against ever-evolving cyber threats. Quantum-secure communication systems have the potential to reshape how we approach data privacy and security, ensuring that sensitive community information remains confidential, ultimately enhancing the trust, efficiency, and effectiveness of community services.

This technology can enhance data exchange in community services in multiple ways. In health care, for secure data exchange and medical sensor communication [3, 28, 32, 42, 53], quantum communication can ensure the secure transmission of sensitive healthcare data, such as medical records, ensuring data privacy and enhancing healthcare services. Quantum cryptography can also secure communication networks used by emergency services, ensuring that critical information remains confidential during disaster response and public safety initiatives, for example using UAVs (Unmanned Aerial Vehicles) [51].

6   Recommendations and Conclusions

Improving the underlying ICT infrastructure is essential for the effective implementation of quantum technology in community services. As quantum computers advance, they pose a potential threat to classical encryption methods. Therefore, implementing quantum-safe encryption methods within the ICT infrastructure is essential to protect sensitive community data [2, 23, 30, 36]. Developing high-speed (quantum) communication networks can enhance data exchange for community services, ensuring secure and efficient communication between service providers, government agencies, and community members. Quantum computing can benefit from data centres designed to accommodate the unique requirements of quantum algorithms. These data centres can process and store large volumes of data for community services. Lastly, integrating quantum sensors and devices into the Internet of Things (IoT) infrastructure can provide more precise and secure data collection for various community service applications.

Quantum technology is most effective when integrated into the broader technology ecosystem that supports community services. Collaboration among government agencies, non-profit organisations, technology innovators, and community stakeholders is essential for identifying the most relevant applications of quantum technology. This collaboration can lead to a more efficient, secure, and data-driven approach to community services.

In conclusion, quantum technology holds immense promise for enhancing community services, its ICT infrastructure, and its data security. Quantum sensing, quantum computing algorithms, quantum communication, and quantum cryptography can significantly improve data accuracy, processing speed, and data privacy, ensuring that community services are more efficient, accessible, and secure. These advances, when combined with other technology solutions, have the potential to foster a higher quality of life, social well-being, and resource optimisation within communities. Therefore, a collaborative and integrative approach that incorporates quantum technology into the existing ICT infrastructure is essential to unlock these opportunities fully.

References

1. Acín, A., Bloch, I., et al.: The quantum technologies roadmap: a European community view. New J. Phys. **20**(8), 080201 (2018)
2. Attema, T., Diogo Duarte, J., et al.: The PQC migration handbook. Tech. rep, Dutch National Cryptostrategy (NCS) (2023)
3. Azzaoui, A.E., Sharma, P.K., Park, J.H.: Blockchain-based delegated quantum cloud architecture for medical big data security. J. Netw. Comput. Appl. **198**, 103304 (2022)
4. Bennett, C.H., Brassard, G.: Quantum cryptography: Public key distribution and coin tossing. In: Proc. IEEE International Conference on Computers Systems and Signal Processing, pp. 175–179 (1984)
5. Bennett, C.H., Brassard, G., Mermin, N.D.: Quantum cryptography without Bell's theorem. Phys. Rev. Lett. **68**(5), 557 (1992)
6. Bongs, K., Bennett, S., Lohmann, A.: Quantum sensors will start a revolution-if we deploy them right. Nature **617**(7962), 672–675 (2023)
7. Bouzidi, Z., Boudries, A., Amad, M.: Enhancing crisis management because of deep learning, big data and parallel computing environment: survey. In: 2021 International Conference on Electrical Communication, and Comparative. Engineering, pp. 1–7. IEEE (2021)
8. Van den Brink, R., Phillipson, F., Neumann, N.M.: Vision on next level quantum software tooling. Computation Tools (2019)
9. Chakrabarti, K.: Is There Any Spooky Action at a Distance? In: Maji, A.K., Saha, G., Das, S., Basu, S., Tavares, J.R.S. (eds.) Proceedings of the International Conference on Computing and Communication Systems. LNNS, vol. 170, pp. 669–682. Springer, Singapore (2021). https://doi.org/10.1007/978-981-33-4084-8_65
10. Chiani, M., Paolini, E., Callegati, F.: Open issues and beyond 5G. 5G Italy White eBook: from Research to Market, pp. 01–11 (2018)
11. Chiscop, I., Nauta, J., Veerman, B., Phillipson, F.: A hybrid solution method for the multi-service location set covering problem. In: Krzhizhanovskaya, V.V. (ed.) ICCS 2020. LNCS, vol. 12142, pp. 531–545. Springer, Cham (2020). https://doi.org/10.1007/978-3-030-50433-5_41
12. Choi, C.Q., Fairley, P., et al.: Sensors: a guide to the quantum-sensor boom: atomic scale bolsters sensing revolutions in medicine, tech, and engineering. IEEE Spectr. **59**(6), 5–13 (2022)
13. Chugh, V., Basu, A., Kaushik, A., Basu, A.K.: Progression in quantum sensing/biosensing technologies for healthcare. ECS Sens. Plus **2**(1), 015001 (2023)
14. Crawford, S.E., Shugayev, R.A., et al.: Quantum sensing for energy applications: review and perspective. Adv. Quantum Technol. **4**(8), 2100049 (2021)
15. Dimitriadou, E., Lanitis, A.: A critical evaluation, challenges, and future perspectives of using artificial intelligence and emerging technologies in smart classrooms. Smart Learn. Environ. **10**(1), 1–26 (2023)
16. Dukalski, M., Rovetta, D., et al.: Quantum computer-assisted global optimization in geophysics illustrated with stack-power maximization for refraction residual statics estimation. Geophysics **88**(2), V75–V91 (2023)
17. Feynman, R.P., et al.: Simulating physics with computers. Int. J. Theor. Phys **21**(6/7) (2018)
18. Foy, C., Zhang, L., et al.: Wide-field magnetic field and temperature imaging using nanoscale quantum sensors. ACS Appl. Mater. Interfaces. **12**(23), 26525–26533 (2020)

19. Fu, W., Xie, H., et al.: Coordinated post-disaster restoration for resilient urban distribution systems: a hybrid quantum-classical approach. Energy, p. 129314 (2023)
20. Giraldo-Quintero, A., Lalinde-Pulido, J.G., et al.: Using quantum computing to solve the maximal covering location problem. Comp. Urban Sci. **2**(1), 43 (2022)
21. Grover, L.K.: A fast quantum mechanical algorithm for database search. In: Proceedings of the 28th ACM Symposium on Theory of Computing, pp. 212–219 (1996)
22. Gupta, B.M., Dhawan, S.M., Mamdapur, G.M.N.: Quantum sensing research: a scientometric assessment of global publications during 1991-2020. Available at SSRN 4343681 (2022)
23. Hasan, K.F., et al.: Migrating to post-quantum cryptography: a framework using security dependency analysis. arXiv preprint. arXiv:2307.06520 (2023)
24. Hemici, M., Zouache, D., Brahmi, B., Got, A., Drias, H.: A decomposition-based multiobjective evolutionary algorithm using simulated annealing for the ambulance dispatching and relocation problem during COVID-19. Appl. Soft Comput. **141**, 110282 (2023)
25. Henrique, P.S.R., Prasad, R.: Quantum mechanics for the future 6G cognitive ran. J. Mobile Multimedia, pp. 291–310 (2023)
26. Jagtenberg, C.J., Bhulai, S., van der Mei, R.D.: An efficient heuristic for real-time ambulance redeployment. Oper. Res. Health Care **4**, 27–35 (2015)
27. Jayanthi, P., Rai, B.K., Muralikrishna, I.: The potential of quantum computing in healthcare. In: Technology Road Mapping for Quantum Computing and Engineering, pp. 81–101. IGI Global (2022)
28. Kalaivani, V., et al.: Enhanced BB84 quantum cryptography protocol for secure communication in wireless body sensor networks for medical applications. Pers. Ubiquit. Comput. **27**(3), 875 (2023)
29. Kantsepolsky, B., Aviv, I., Weitzfeld, R., Bordo, E.: Exploring quantum sensing potential for systems applications. IEEE Access, 11 (2023)
30. Kong, I., Janssen, M., Bharosa, N.: Challenges in the transition towards a quantum-safe government. In: DG. O 2022: The 23rd Annual International Conference on Digital Government Research, pp. 282–292 (2022)
31. Kumar, A., de Jesus Pacheco, D.A., Kaushik, K., Rodrigues, J.J.: Futuristic view of the internet of quantum drones: review, challenges and research agenda. Veh. Communi. **36**, 100487 (2022)
32. Kumar, B., Prasad, S.B., Pal, P.R., Pathak, P.: Quantum security for IoT to secure healthcare applications and their data. In: Research Anthology on Securing Medical Systems and Records, pp. 685–705. IGI Global (2022)
33. Martin, V., Brito, J.P., et al.: Quantum technologies in the telecommunications industry. EPJ Quantum Technol. **8**(1), 19 (2021)
34. Masuda, K., Tsuyumine, Y., Kitada, T., Hachikawa, T., Haga, T.: Optimization of delivery plan by quantum computing. Optimization **85**, 1 (2023)
35. Mehraeen, M., Dadkhah, M., Mehraeen, A.: Investigating the capabilities of information technologies to support policymaking in COVID-19 crisis management. European J. Clin. Investig. **50**(11) (2020)
36. Muller, F., van Heesch, M.: Migration to quantum-safe cryptography: about making decisions on when, what and how to migrate to a quantum-safe situation (2020)
37. Murzin, D., Mapps, D.J., et al.: Ultrasensitive magnetic field sensors for biomedical applications. Sensors **20**(6), 1569 (2020)

38. Nagy, M., Nagy, N.: Intrusion detect. Quantum Sens. Network. Sens. **22**(21), 8092 (2022)
39. Nawaz, S.J., Sharma, S.K., et al.: Quantum machine learning for 6G communication networks: state-of-the-art and vision for the future. IEEE Access **7**, 46317–46350 (2019)
40. Neumann, N., Phillipson, F., Versluis, R.: Machine learning in the quantum era. Digitale Welt **3**, 24–29 (2019)
41. Nivelkar, M., Bhirud, S.: Optimized machine learning: training and classification performance using quantum computing. In: 2021 IEEE 6th International. Conference. on Computing Communication and Automation (ICCCA), pp. 8–13. IEEE (2021)
42. Perumal, A.M., Nadar, E.R.S.: Architectural framework and simulation of quantum key optimization techniques in healthcare networks for data security. J. Ambient. Intell. Humaniz. Comput. **12**, 7173–7180 (2021)
43. Phillipson, F.: Quantum computing in telecommunication - a survey. Mathematics **11**(15), 3423 (2023)
44. Phillipson, F., Chiscop, I.: Multimodal Container Planning: A QUBO Formulation and Implementation on a Quantum Annealer. In: Paszynski, M., Kranzlmüller, D., Krzhizhanovskaya, V.V., Dongarra, J.J., Sloot, P.M.A. (eds.) ICCS 2021. LNCS, vol. 12747, pp. 30–44. Springer, Cham (2021). https://doi.org/10.1007/978-3-030-77980-1_3
45. Phillipson, F., Wezeman, R.S., Chiscop, I.: Indoor-outdoor detection in mobile networks using quantum machine learning approaches. Computers **10**(6), 71 (2021)
46. Piattini, M., Peterssen, G., et al.: The talavera manifesto for quantum software engineering and programming. In: QANSWER, pp. 1–5 (2020)
47. Pulipeti, S., Kumar, A.: Secure quantum computing for healthcare sector: a short analysis. Secu. Priv. **6**(5), e293 (2023)
48. Rawicz, A.H.: Theodore Harold Maiman and the invention of laser. In: Photonics, Devices, and Systems IV. vol. 7138, pp. 39–46. SPIE (2008)
49. Schmitt, S., Gefen, T., et al.: Submillihertz magnetic spectroscopy performed with a nanoscale quantum sensor. Science **356**(6340), 832–837 (2017)
50. Serrano, M.A., et al.: Minimizing incident response time in real-world scenarios using quantum computing. Softw. Qual. J. **1**(32), 1–30 (2023)
51. Sharma, J., Mehra, P.S.: Secure communication in IOT-based UAV networks: a systematic survey. Internet of Things, p. 100883 (2023)
52. Shor, P.W.: Polynomial-time algorithms for prime factorization and discrete logarithms on a quantum computer. SIAM Rev. **41**(2), 303–332 (1999)
53. Shyry, P., et al.: Enhanced security protocols for data protection in the internet of healthcare things using quantum key distribution. Preprint (2023)
54. Stray, B., Lamb, A., et al.: Quantum sensing for gravity cartography. Nature **602**(7898), 590–594 (2022)
55. Suriya, M.: Machine learning and quantum computing for 5G/6G communication networks-a survey. Int. J. Intell. Network (2022)
56. Tang, H., Sun, W.: Theories and applications of earthquake-induced gravity variation: advances and perspectives. Earthq. Sci. **36**, 1–40 (2023)
57. Ur Rasool, R., Ahmad, H.F., et al.: Quantum computing for healthcare: a review. Future Internet **15**(3), 94 (2023)

58. Wang, S., Pei, Z., Wang, C., Wu, J.: Shaping the future of the application of quantum computing in intelligent transportation system. Intell. Converged Networks **2**(4), 259–276 (2021)
59. Zhang, J.: Quantum sensing applications with integrated lithium niobate photonic circuits. Ph.D. thesis, Stevens Inst. Technol. (2023)
60. Zhang, Z., Xiao, Y., et al.: 6G wireless networks: Vision, requirements, architecture, and key technologies. IEEE Veh. Technol. Mag. **14**(3), 28–41 (2019)

SATQUBOLIB: A Python Framework for Creating and Benchmarking (Max-)3SAT QUBOs

Sebastian Zielinski[1][(✉)] [iD], Magdalena Benkard[1] [iD], Jonas Nüßlein[1],
Claudia Linnhoff-Popien[1] [iD], and Sebastian Feld[2] [iD]

[1] Institute for Informatics, LMU Munich, 80538 Munich, Germany
sebastian.zielinski@ifi.lmu.de
[2] Quantum and Computer Engineering, Delft University of Technology,
2628 CD Delft, The Netherlands

Abstract. In this paper, we present an open-source Python framework, called satqubolib. This framework aims to provide all necessary tools for solving (MAX)-3SAT problems on quantum hardware systems via Quadratic Unconstrained Binary Optimization (QUBO). Our framework solves two major issues when solving (MAX)-3SAT instances in the context of quantum computing. Firstly, a common way of solving satisfiability instances with quantum methods is, to transform these instances into instances of QUBO, as QUBO is the input format for quantum annealers and the Quantum Approximate Optimization Algorithm (QAOA) on quantum gate systems. Studies have shown, that the choice of this transformation can significantly impact the solution quality of quantum hardware systems. Thus, our framework provides thousands of usable QUBO transformations for satisfiability problems. Doing so also enables practitioners from any domain to immediately explore and use quantum techniques as a potential solver for their domain-specific problems, as long as they can be encoded as satisfiability problems. As a second contribution, we created a dataset of 6000 practically hard and satisfiable SAT instances that are also small enough to be solved with current quantum(-hybrid) methods. This dataset enables meaningful benchmarking of new quantum, quantum-hybrid, and classical methods for solving satisfiability problems.

Keywords: 3-satisfiability · Optimization · QUBO transformation · Software framework

1 Introduction

Satisfiability problems play a central role in computer science. They have been among the first problems for which NP-completeness has been shown [9] and are often used to prove a given problem's hardness. Besides their use in theoretical computer science, they lie at the heart of many real-world application

F. Phillipson et al. (Eds.): I4CS 2024, CCIS 2109, pp. 48–66, 2024.
https://doi.org/10.1007/978-3-031-60433-1_4

domains, like circuit design and verification [20], error diagnosis in software systems [16], planning [25], configuration planning in wireless sensor networks [10], scheduling [5], solving problems in social networks [23], dependency resolution (e.g. in package managers of many operating systems) [2] and many more. For some domains, leveraging the advanced capabilities of contemporary SAT solvers, which are programs designed to solve satisfiability problems, proves to be an efficient, cost-effective, and maintainable approach for solving domain-specific problems. This is achieved by reformulating these domain-specific problems into satisfiability problems and then applying a modern SAT solver for resolution [13,17,24].

Despite significant research efforts over several decades, the satisfiability problem remains intractable. Thus, finding better methods of solving this problem is still an ongoing field of research. New methods of solving satisfiability problems employ AI techniques, such as artificial neuronal networks, to assist established methods in searching for correct solutions or creating new SAT solvers. Our paper primarily concerns solving satisfiability problems through quantum computing, which has gained much attention in the last decade.

With quantum computers' increased availability and capabilities in recent years, quantum computing has evolved from a mere theoretical domain to a field of practical interest. The proof that specific algorithms for quantum computers, like Shor's algorithm [27], theoretically provide exponential speedup for a classically intractable problem fuels the interest of researchers of different domains to find quantum algorithms for their domain-specific problems. However, some significant obstacles must be overcome to yield the full potential that theoretical findings in quantum computing promise. While many of these obstacles concern the physical manufacturing of quantum computers and their components, we only focus on software and application development challenges for quantum computers.

The first challenge related to the application of quantum computing we want to address is the input format of quantum computers and algorithms. An established practical method of solving satisfiability problems on quantum hardware includes transforming a satisfiability problem into an instance of Quadratic Unconstrained Binary Optimization (QUBO). These transformations are often highly technical, while software implementations are often unavailable. Furthermore, studies have shown that the choice of a transformation from a satisfiability instance to a QUBO instance can impact the solution quality significantly [18,31]. To leverage the full capabilities of currently available quantum hardware, it is thus insufficient to implement an arbitrary transformation from satisfiability problems to instances of QUBO. Several different transformations should be implemented and compared to get the best results. Practitioners of a non-quantum field thus need to read, understand, and implement several QUBO transformation methods only to be able to employ quantum methods to solve their domain-specific problems. Another challenge concerns the benchmarking of quantum and quantum-hybrid algorithms. Quantum hardware has been too small in the past decade to meaningfully compare its outputs to that of classical solvers. However, this slowly begins to change. The main benefit of quantum computers is the potential to solve problem instances that currently cannot be solved efficiently by available classical methods. Thus, to receive a meaningful estimation of the capabilities of quantum and quantum-hybrid methods, they should be benchmarked on a set of problem instances that are hard for classical solvers. However, due to the limited size of current quantum computers, often, there is no dataset consisting of problem instances that are practically hard to solve for currently available classical solvers while also being small enough to be able to be solved on currently available quantum hardware using quantum or quantum-hybrid methods. To address these challenges, we present an open-source Python framework called *satqubolib*. The main contributions of satqubolib are:

1. Ready to use Python implementations for thousands of transformations from satisfiability instances to instances of QUBO.
2. A dataset consisting of 6000 practically hard-to-solve satisfiability instances, which are also small enough to be solved on currently available quantum hardware through quantum or quantum-hybrid methods.
3. Implementation of two methods to quickly create practically hard-to-solve satisfiability instances of arbitrary sizes.
4. Example implementations for closely related questions (like a direct comparison of quantum-based SAT solvers vs. state-of-the-artclassical SAT solvers).

The main goals of our framework are to facilitate the use of QUBO-based quantum methods for practitioners of quantum and non-quantum domains alike and to increase the reproducibility of studies concerned with solving satisfiability problems through quantum computing.

The remainder of this paper is structured as follows. Section 2 introduces the necessary foundations of satisfiability and QUBO problems. In Sect. 3, we provide an overview of related work. Section 4 describes our framework's core architecture and most important usage scenarios. In Sect. 5, we conclude the paper and state future work.

2   Foundations

In this chapter, we will introduce the necessary definitions that are used throughout the remainder of this paper.

2.1   Satisfiability Problems

Satisfiability problems are concerned with the satisfiability of Boolean formulae. Thus, we will first define a Boolean formula:

Definition 1 (Boolean formula [3]). Let $x_1, ..., x_n$ be Boolean variables. A *Boolean formula* consists of the variables $x_1, ..., x_n$ and the logical operators AND($\wedge$), OR($\vee$), NOT($\neg$). Let $z \in \{0, 1\}^n$ be a vector of Boolean values. We identify the value 1 as TRUE and the value 0 as FALSE. The vector z is also called an *assignment*, as it assigns truth values to the Boolean variables $x_1, ..., x_n$ as follows: $x_i = z_i$, where z_i is the $i - th$ component of z. If ϕ is a Boolean formula, and $z \in \{0, 1\}^n$ is an assignment, then $\phi(z)$ is the evaluation of ϕ when the variable x_i is assigned the Boolean value z_i. If there exists a $z \in \{0, 1\}^n$, such that $\phi(z)$ is TRUE, we call ϕ satisfiable. Otherwise, we call ϕ unsatisfiable [3].

Satisfiability problems are often given in conjunctive normal form, which we will define next:

Definition 2 (Conjunctive Normal Form [3]). A Boolean formula over variables $x_1, ..., x_n$ is in *Conjunctive Normal Form (CNF)* if it is of the following structure:

$$\bigwedge_i \left(\bigvee_j y_{i_j} \right)$$

Each y_{i_j} is either a variable x_k or its negation $\neg x_k$. The y_{i_j} are called the *literals* of the formula. The terms $(\vee_j y_{i_j})$ are called the *clauses* of the formula. A kCNF is a CNF formula, in which all clauses contain at most k literals. [3]

Given a Boolean formula ϕ in kCNF, the satisfiability problem is the task of determining whether kCNF is satisfiable or not. This problem was one of the first problems for which NP-completeness has been shown. [9]. In this paper, we will especially consider 3CNF problems, which we will refer to as 3SAT problems.

Solving satisfiability problems on a quantum annealer or through special algorithms on quantum gate systems requires a transformation to an optimization problem (see Subsect. 2.2)). Thus in these cases, we are solving a generalization of the satisfiability problem, the *MAX-SAT* problem. In the MAX-SAT problem, we are given a Boolean formula ϕ consisting of m clauses. The task is to find an assignment of truth values to the variables of ϕ such that as many clauses as possible are satisfied. Finding an assignment in the MAX-SAT problem that satisfies m clauses is thus equivalent to solving the corresponding satisfiability problem (i.e., determining whether ϕ is satisfiable). MAX-SAT is thus also NP-hard. Throughout this paper, we will call instances of satisfiability problems (SAT and MAX-SAT alike) *satisfiability instances* or *SAT instances*

2.2   Quadratic Unconstrained Binary Optimization (QUBO)

To solve satisfiability problems on a quantum annealer or a quantum gate computer using the quantum approximate optimization algorithm, they must be transformed into an instance of QUBO first.

A QUBO instance is defined as follows: [12]:

$$\text{minimize} \quad H(x) = x^T Q x = \sum_i^n Q_{ii} x_i + \sum_{i<j} Q_{ij} x_i x_j \tag{1}$$

The n-dimensional vector $x = (x_1, x_2, ..., x_n) \in \{0, 1\}^n$ represents an assignment of Boolean values to the Boolean variables x_i (for $1 \leq i \leq n$). Furthermore,

$Q \in \mathbb{R}^n \times \mathbb{R}^n$ is a $n \times n$-dimensional upper triangular matrix of constants, which is often also called the *QUBO matrix* [12]. To solve this problem, a vector $x = (x_1, x_2, ..., x_n) \in \{0, 1\}^n$ needs to be found, such that $H(x) = x^T Q x$ is minimal. This problem is NP-hard [12].

3   Related Work

As the field of solving satisfiability problems is already several decades old, a lot of helpful tools for solving these problems and benchmarking new solvers have been created. In this section, we will briefly mention the most important ones.

The first of these tools is SATLIB [14], which provides a collection of satisfiability problems of different types (for example, randomly generated instances or satisfiability instances that stem from graph coloring instances) that can be used to benchmark solvers. However, SATLIB was published in 2000, and according to the project's homepage [14], it has not been updated for over 20 years. We have solved all benchmark problems within the library to assess the difficulty of the provided instances with today's SAT solvers and modern hardware. We found that apart from a few instances that reached a self-imposed timeout of 6 h (i.e., the instances have not been solved within 6 h), all other instances were solved mostly within milliseconds, with some exceptions taking several seconds to a few minutes.

Another resource for finding possibly hard satisfiability instances that can be used for benchmarking is the annual SAT Competition [4]. At this competition, SAT solvers are benchmarked with regard to their capability of solving a set of pre-selected potentially hard-to-solve satisfiability instances within a certain amount of time. Although some of these instances are really hard (i.e., it can take several days to weeks to solve with state-of-the-artSAT solvers on state-of-the-artCPUs), these instances can get very large (i.e., several hundred thousand to millions of clauses). As current quantum hardware only has a limited amount of qubits available, satisfiability instances that consist of more than a couple of hundred clauses cannot be solved directly on these devices. However, the goal of our framework is to provide satisfiability instances that are challenging to state-of-the-artSAT solvers but can also be solved using quantum or quantum-hybrid methods on currently (or nearly) available quantum hardware. Thus, as part of our framework, we provide practically hard instances of different sizes (i.e., number of clauses) that can already be solved on currently available quantum hardware directly (depending on the method) or by using quantum-hybrid methods.

PySAT [15] is an open-source Python toolkit that provides many helpful features, like utility functions for manipulating formulas or creating encodings for pseudo-Boolean constraints into conjunctive normal form (CNF). The easy access to some of the state-of-the-art SAT solvers it provides is especially helpful. Our framework, however, is completely different from PySAT. We do not implement similar features that PySAT has already implemented but rather offer new and additional features that are concerned with the transformation of satisfiability instances into instances of QUBO, which is not in the scope of PySAT.

However, we will use PySAT in our `examples` package to demonstrate how to use state-of-the-art SAT solvers to create benchmark comparisons.

Finally, there is the Python framework PyQUBO [30], whose goal is to aid in the construction of QUBO formulations from given objective functions. It strives to create concepts that make it easy to read and write Python code concerning formulating QUBO problems and efficiently solving combinatorial optimization problems. PyQUBO can be seen as a helpful tool for developing a solution (especially for quantum annealing) for several classes of combinatorial optimization problems. However, because of the breadth of possible applications it offers, it sacrifices depth (i.e., PyQUBO cannot provide every possible QUBO transformation for every possible combinatorial optimization problem). Regarding solving satisfiability problems, PyQUBO offers a (singular) method to transform satisfiability problems into instances of QUBO. However, as shown by recent studies [18,31], it does not suffice to use an arbitrary method of transforming a given satisfiability instance to an instance of QUBO. One should instead evaluate multiple different methods of performing this transformation, as the results can change up to orders of magnitude just by changing the QUBO transformation. Thus, more than PyQUBO's provided functionality concerning the transformation of satisfiability problems to instances of QUBO is required for researchers or practitioners who want to leverage the full capabilities of quantum technologies to solve instances of satisfiability problems specifically.

4   Satqubolib: Creating and Benchmarking (Max-)3SAT Instances

This section explains the core architecture and functionalities of `satqubolib`. An overview of our framework's modules, packages, and features can be seen in Fig. 1. The framework is available via github[1] or as a pip package[2]. As shown in Fig. 1, the `dataset` of practically hard SAT instances (used to develop and benchmark QUBO transformations and quantum and quantum-hybrid algorithms), as well as the `examples` Python package, are only available via GitHub and not part of the pip package. We decided to separate the dataset from the pip installation, as the dataset will take up much space as it grows. Additionally, we decided to include several convenience implementations (e.g., for using SAT solvers via PySAT [15], metaheuristics like simulated annealing and tabu search) that require additional dependencies that are not needed for the core functionalities of `satqubolib`. Thus, we split the framework's core functionality from the benchmarking data and the complementary examples. In the following chapters, we will now demonstrate core usages. As we cannot present or explain every usage scenario, the `examples` package contains additional code examples and comments explaining the relevant concepts.

---

[1] https://github.com/ZielinskiSebastian/satqubolib/.
[2] pip install satqubolib

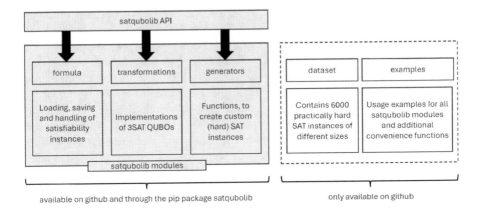

Fig. 1. Core architecture of the satquoblib's Python framework

4.1   Handling SAT Instances: The Satqubolib.formula Module

When using our framework to solve problems, at first, a 3SAT instance is needed. The python class `satquoblib.formula.CNF` within the `satquoblib.formula` module is the class representing a satisfiability instance in `satquoblib`. There are two possibilities for creating a `CNF` instance. The following listing shows these methods in line 2 and line 3.

```
1  from satqubolib.formula import CNF
2  my_formula = CNF([[1,2,3], [-2,-5,7]])
3  my_formula = CNF.from_file("/path/to/file/")
```

The first method, shown in line 2 of the above listing, is to represent the 3SAT instance $(x_1 \vee x_2 \vee x_3) \wedge (\neg x_2 \vee \neg x_5 \vee x_7)$, as a list of lists `[[1,2,3], [-2,-5,7]]`, where each of the inner lists represents a clause. The second method of creating a `CNF` instance, shown in line 3 of the above listing, is to load it directly from a file, in which the formula is specified in the .dimacs file format [1]. The .dimacs file format [1] is the standard format for representing instances of satisfiability problems in CNF form.

Besides the above-shown functionality, the `CNF` object contains several more convenience functions (e.g., to load metadata of the dataset we created for the framework). These usages and explanations can be found in the corresponding `examples` module (see Subsect. 4.5).

4.2   Creating SAT QUBOs: The Satqubolib.transformations Module

The `satqubolib.transformations` module contains all methods for transforming satisfiability instances to instances of QUBO. These transformations create QUBO instances Q that differ in several aspects, like the dimension of Q, the density of Q (i.e., the number of non-zero elements in Q), and the energy spectrum. It has been shown in multiple studies ([18,31]) that the choice of a 3SAT-to-QUBO transformations can significantly impact the solution quality when solving these instances on quantum annealing hardware. Thus, our framework aims to provide implementations of state-of-the-art QUBO transformations for satisfiability problems.

One of the first 3SAT-to-QUBO transformations often used in scientific publications is the transformation by Choi [8]. Because this transformation was one of the first mappings from 3SAT to QUBO, it was also included in the seminal paper by Lucas [19]. Due to its widespread use in many publications of the past decade and to better understand this paper, we want to explain this transformation in more detail.

Choi's Transformation [8] is based on a well known reduction from 3SAT to the maximum independent set (MIS) problem. Let $G = (V, E)$ be an empty graph and $\phi = C_1 \wedge ... \wedge C_m$ be a 3SAT formula consisting of m clauses $C_1, ..., C_m$ over n Boolean variables $x_1, ..., x_n$. We now expand G as follows:

1. Let $y_{i,j}$ be the literal at position i of clause j of ϕ. For each literal we add a new vertex to V. We name this vertex according to the literals they represent, i.e., the vertex corresponding to literal $y_{i,j}$ is called vertex $v_{i,j}$.
2. Let $y_{i,j}$ and $y_{k,j}$ be two literals of the same clause, then we add an edge $(v_{i,j}, v_{k,j})$ to E.
3. Let $y_{i,j}$ and $y_{k,l}$ be two literals representing the same binary variable x_z but with different signs (i.e. $y_{i,j} = \neg y_{k,l}$) then we add an edge $(v_{i,j}, v_{k,l})$ to E.

Solving MIS on G will now also represent a solution to the 3SAT problem for formula ϕ. This transformation results in a QUBO matrix of dimension $3m \times 3m$.

Since the proposal of Choi's transformation, several new QUBO transformations for satisfiability problems have been proposed, e.g. [7,18,21,22,29]. We have explicitly implemented the transformations that result in QUBO matrices of dimension larger than $(n+m) \times (n+m)$. With regard to the transformations that lead to QUBO matrices of dimension $(n+m) \times (n+m)$, we only implemented transformations *explicitly*, if we have found studies using these transformations for practical benchmarking (or comparing). We want to highlight the use of the word *explicitly* here. An explicit implementation in our framework is provided by a dedicated class. There exist many thousand of $(n+m) \times (n+m)$-dimensional transformations. Creating an individual class for all of these transformations is infeasible. However, a method theoretically able to automatically create all $(n+m) \times (n+m)$-dimensional transformations from satisfiability problems to instances of QUBO has been published recently. This method is called the Pattern QUBO method [32]. By implementing this method, our framework provides ready-to-use access to all of these $(n+m) \times (n+m)$-dimensional transformations through a unified interface. Furthermore, `satqubolib` comes with a functionality that can create explicit implementations (i.e., dedicated standalone classes) for all of the transformations the Pattern QUBO method created. Because a deeper understanding of this method is vital for efficiently using our framework, we explain the Pattern QUBO method in depth and demonstrate how to use it.

The **Pattern QUBO** approach was introduced in [32]. It is a meta method capable of automatically identifying thousands of different QUBO transformations for satisfiability problems. QUBO matrices created by this method are all of the dimension $(n + m) \times (n + m)$, where n is the number of variables and m is the number of clauses of a given 3SAT instance. This method can be seen as a generalization of existing QUBO transformations for the 3SAT problem. Manually created QUBO transformations (like the methods proposed by Chancellor [7], or Nüßlein [22]) follow some custom logic to finally arrive at a QUBO representation of a given 3SAT instance. However, all of these methods have in common that 1) all satisfying solutions for the 3SAT instance correspond to the minimum in the created QUBO optimization problem corresponding to the 3SAT instance, and 2) all non-satisfying solutions do not correspond to the minimum of the QUBO optimization problem. As it turns out, it is possible to exploit this property (solutions to a given 3SAT instance corresponds to optimal energy in the corresponding QUBO instance) to create new 3SAT-to-QUBO transformations automatically. Thus, this method provides an easy way to create and use previously published, but also to create and use thousands of previously unknown 3SAT-to-QUBO transformations, without the need to understand all the different logical deductions for these transformations, let alone the effort to implement all of them. By implementing the Pattern QUBO method, our framework provides:

1. Thousands of different ready-to-use $(n + m) \times (n + m)$-dimensional QUBO transformations.
2. Implicit implementations of all existing $(n+m) \times (n+m)$-dimensional QUBO transformations that result from superimposing clause QUBOs (like in the transformations by Nüßlein [22] and Chancellor [7].

Figure 2 shows an illustration of the general idea behind the Pattern QUBO method.

To transform an instance ϕ of 3SAT, consisting of m clauses, to an instance of QUBO, one first starts by sorting the variables of each clause, such that negated variables are always at the end of the clause. This does not change the formula or the difficulty of solving the formula, but it reduces the effort of finding transformations from a clause to QUBO, as only four possible clause types are remaining:

Type 0 - no negations: $(a \lor b \lor c)$
Type 1 - one negation: $(a \lor b \lor \neg c)$
Type 2 - two negations: $(a \lor \neg b \lor \neg c)$
Type 3 - three negations: $(\neg a \lor \neg b \lor \neg c)$

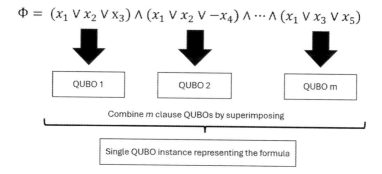

$$\Phi = (x_1 \lor x_2 \lor x_3) \land (x_1 \lor x_2 \lor -x_4) \land \cdots \land (x_1 \lor x_3 \lor x_5)$$

QUBO 1   QUBO 2   QUBO m

Combine m clause QUBOs by superimposing

Single QUBO instance representing the formula

Fig. 2. Schematic representation of the Pattern QUBO method presented in [32]. Each clause of a given 3SAT formula ϕ gets transformed to a QUBO instance representing this clause. Each QUBO matrix one receives by transforming a clause of the 3SAT instance to an instance of QUBO is called a *clause QUBO*. All m of these clause QUBOs get combined into a single QUBO instance representing the formula ϕ.

As a next step, the Pattern QUBO method searches automatically for ways to transform each of these four prototype clauses (type 0 through type 3) to an instance of QUBO. For each of the 4 clauses, the search method starts with an empty (4×4)-dimensional QUBO matrix. The search method can insert a pre-determined set of values specified by the user into the QUBO matrix during its search process. As the search method is an exhaustive search, the running time of this method scales exponentially with the size of the set of values the algorithm is allowed to use. Using a small set, like $\{-1, 0, 1\}$, the search method only needs a few seconds to create 6 pattern QUBOs for clauses of type 0, 7 pattern QUBOs for clauses of type 1, 6 pattern QUBOs for clauses of type 2 and 8 pattern QUBOs for clauses of type 3.

We want to emphasize the following key takeaway of the Pattern QUBO method to fully make use of the benefits of its implementation in our framework: The Pattern QUBO method finds *multiple* ways to transform a clause of a given type (type 0 through type 3) to instances of QUBO (6 ways for clauses of *type 0*, 7 for clauses of *type 1*, 6 for clauses of *type 2* and 8 for clauses of *type 3*). However, we only need one of these pattern QUBOs per clause type. Thus, any 4-tuple (t_0, t_1, t_2, t_3), where t_i is a pattern QUBO for a clause of *type i*, can be seen as a valid transformation for a 3SAT instance to an instance of QUBO. Thus, in the above case, we have $2016 = 6 \cdot 7 \cdot 6 \cdot 8$ valid transformations from 3SAT instances to instances of QUBO. Choosing different combinations of transformations (t_0, t_1, t_2, t_3) from clauses to instances of QUBO leads to different (up to isomorphism) 3SAT-to-QUBO transformations with different properties. These properties have been empirically shown to influence the solution quality of current quantum annealing up to an order of magnitude [31]. Therefore, we encourage a user of this framework to try to combine different transformations from clauses to instances of QUBO, to create different 3SAT-to-QUBO transformations in order to get the most benefit in practical and research applications (i.e., by empirically finding a transformation that is particularly beneficial for the given problems at hand).

We now demonstrate how to use the `satqubolib.transformations` module. The first use case is using an *explicitly* implemented QUBO transformation, like Choi's transformation, for a given 3SAT instance. This can be done as follows:

```
1   from satqubolib.formula import CNF
2   from satqubolib.transformations import ChoiSAT
3   my_formula = CNF([[1,2,3], [-2,-5,7]])
4   choi_model = ChoiSAT(my_formula)
5   choi_model.create_qubo()
6   qubo = choi_model.qubo
7   choi_model.print_qubo()
8   # suppose a QUBO solver gave the following solution:
9   solution = {0: 0, 1: 0, 2: 0, 3: 1, 4: 0, 5: 0}
10  output = choi_model.is_solution(solution)
11  # output in this case is a tuple: (False, 1)
```

We first created a `satquoblib.formula.CNF` object (line 3) in the listing above, as described in Subsect. 4.1. Then a `satqubolib.transformations.ChoiSAT` object, which implements Choi's transformation [8], is created in line 4. To create the QUBO matrix resulting from Choi's transformation applied to the formula we initialized the ChoiSAT object with, the `create_qubo()` function is called in line 5. The created QUBO is saved in the `qubo` variable of the `choi_model` object, which can be accessed as shown in line 6. For convenience, we provide every transformation within the `satqubolib.transformations` module with a visualization method called `print_qubo()` to inspect the created QUBO matrix. An example of the usage of this method is shown in line 7. As a next step, the created QUBO matrix is used as an input for a QUBO solver, like D-Wave's quantum annealing hardware, the QAOA algorithm on quantum gate computers, or classical heuristical methods like simulated annealing or tabu search. The output of these solvers are usually Python dictionaries of the form:

`{variable_1: value, ..., variable_n: value}`.

To check whether a solution given by a QUBO solver does indeed solve the given 3SAT instance, all QUBO transformations in our framework provide the method `is_solution(solution_dictionary)`. This method returns a tuple of the form (boolean, integer). The boolean indicates whether the solution is indeed a solution for the given 3SAT instance. The integer represents the number of satisfied clauses.

We now demonstrate how to use the Pattern QUBO method.

```
1   from satqubolib.transformations import PatternQUBOFinder
2   from transformations import PatternQUBONM
3   from satqubolib.formula import CNF
4   my_formula = CNF([[1,2,3], [-2,-5,7]])
5   pqf = PatternQUBOFinder(8)
```

```
6   clause_qubos = pqf.find({1,0,-1})
7   new_transformation = PatternQUBONM(my_formula)
8   new_transformation.add_clause_qubos(clause_qubos[0][0],
        clause_qubos[1][0], clause_qubos[2][0], clause_qubos
        [3][0])
9   new_transformation.create_qubo()
10  new_transformation.export("/path/to/file")
```

First, an object of satqubolib.transformations.PatternQUBOFinder must be created (line 5 of the above listing). The parameter value 8 in the constructor of the PatternQUBOFinder object in line 5 of the above listing denotes the number of parallel processes the Pattern QUBO search algorithm will use. As this search procedure is an exhaustive search, parallelizing the search is highly beneficial. To search for Pattern QUBOs for all clause types, the find(allowed_values: set) function of the pqf object is called (line 6 of the above listing). As explained previously, the allowed_values parameter of the find(allowed_values: set) function in line 6 of the above listing is the set of values the Pattern QUBO method is allowed to use (i.e., the Pattern QUBO method will examine all possible QUBO matrices that only consists of the values 1, 0 and -1). After the search for Pattern QUBO matrices is completed, a new 3SAT-to-QUBO transformation can be created. This is done in line 7 of the above listing. At this point, the transformation is not yet functional. To make this transformation a fully working 3SAT-to-QUBO transformation, one pattern QUBO for each clause type (clause type 0 through clause type 3) has to be added to the transformation. This is done in line 8 of the above listing. After this step is completed, the transformation can create a QUBO matrix representing the given satisfiability instance.

Finally, we would like to highlight a unique functionality of this implementation, shown in line 10 of the above listing. Each concrete instantiation of an object of type satqubolib.transformations.PatternQUBONM, where the four clause QUBOs have already been added (see line 8 of the above listing), can be exported to a standalone file. That is, if one finds a Pattern QUBO transformation that works particularly well for the given type of 3SAT instances, it can be exported to a file such that it does not require satqubolib as a dependency but instead works as a standalone implementation of a QUBO transformation.

4.3   Generating Hard SAT Instances: The Satqubolib.generators Module

In the satqubolib.generators module, we implemented methods that enable a user of satqubolib to create satisfiability instances of arbitrary parameterization (i.e., an arbitrary number of clauses and variables). Using different parameters for these algorithms will create instances that empirically vary in difficulty (i.e., choosing significantly more variables than clauses almost always results in trivially solvable SAT instances). We used the same methods to create the dataset of practically hard 3SAT instances that satqubolib provides. The algorithm implementations are provided through the classes BalancedSAT and NoTriangleSAT in the `satqubolib.generators` module. The former is an implementation of the method provided by Spence [28] while the latter is an implementation of the method provided by Escamocher et al. [11]. The following listing shows how to use the Balanced SAT method to create new 3SAT instances.

```
1  from satquoblib.generators import BalancedSAT
2
3  balanced_generator = BalancedSAT(3, 10, 20)
4  # generate() returns an object of type satqubolib.formula.
     CNF
5  cnf = balanced_generator.generate()
```

The first parameter (the number 3) of the constructor of the BalancedSAT object in line 3 of the above listing denotes the number of variables in each clause. In this case, each clause consists of precisely three variables. The second parameter (the number 10) refers to how many variables the satisfiability instance possesses. The last parameter (the number 20) denotes the number of clauses of the satisfiability instance. It is known that to create hard satisfiability instances, the number of variables and the number of clauses of a satisfiability instance need to be in a certain ratio [26]. This ratio is different for each method of creating satisfiability instances. To create hard instances, the ratio of clauses to variables was experimentally determined to be around 3.6 (that is, 3.6 times more clauses than variables) for the Balanced SAT [28] method. For the No Triangle SAT method, this ratio seems to be around 4.1 (that is 4.1 more times more clauses than variables) [11]. However, not every instance with this clauses-to-variables ratio is also hard to solve. A modern SAT solver (like Kissat3.1.0 [6]) could be used to determine practical hardness. Suppose a modern SAT solver takes more than a few minutes to solve an instance. This instance is potentially interesting for a benchmark with a quantum, quantum-hybrid, or classical QUBO solver. For the creation of the dataset that is part of `satqubolib`, we found that using a clause-to-variable ratio of approximately 0.3 - 0.5 below the above-mentioned empirically determined hardness ratio yields the best results for creating hard satisfiable instances that take less than multiple hours to solve with Kissat3.1.0.

4.4   Benchmark Dataset of Practically Hard Satisfiability Instances

The goal of the dataset included in `satqubolib` is to enable the following pursuits meaningfully:

1. Benchmarking SAT solvers
2. Benchmarking quantum, quantum-hybrid, and classical QUBO solvers
3. Provide data input for creating non-trivial QUBOs

We will now first explain how we created our dataset before we explain how this dataset enables the endeavors mentioned above.

Our dataset consists of 6000 practically hard, satisfiable SAT instances simultaneously small enough to be solved with current quantum hardware using quantum or quantum-hybrid methods. The 2023 SAT Competition defines satisfiability instances as hard if the Minisat SAT solver cannot solve an instance within one minute on an AMD Ryzen 7 Pro 3700U CPU and 16GB RAM [4]. However, as the solving process is stopped after one minute, it is unclear how long it would take to solve this instance. The instance could be solved within the next minute or within a time frame of many hours. Furthermore, as the solving process is stopped, it is unclear whether the instance is satisfiable or not. For our dataset, we considered SAT instances as *practically hard* if they are satisfiable and if the Kissat3.1.0 SAT [6] solver needs more than 10 min to solve the instance on an AMD Ryzen Threadripper PRO 5965WX 4.5 GHz CPU. We decided to use the Kissat SAT solver instead of the Minisat SAT solver, as the Kissat SAT solver is currently among the best-performing SAT solvers.

Out of the 6000 instances our dataset comprises, 3000 were created randomly using the Balanced SAT method [28], while the other 3000 were created using the No Triangle SAT method [11]. As mentioned earlier in this section, we aim to create small and hard SAT instances. We found that utilizing the Balanced SAT and No Triangle SAT methods, generating satisfiability instances with fewer than 600 clauses proves exceedingly challenging. This difficulty arises from the advanced capabilities of modern SAT solvers and CPUs. Regardless of the algorithm parameterization, a majority of the created instances are solved within seconds. Creating practically hard instances between 600 and 800 clauses with these methods is generally possible but computationally very expensive, as formulas are often either solved within a few minutes or take many hours to be solved (i.e., by trying to create formulas in that range, we often hit a self-imposed solver timeout of 6 h, without a result of the SAT solver). Hence, we started our dataset with instances that consist of 800 clauses. We created 1000 instances for each of the SAT instance sizes *800 clauses*, *900 clauses*, and *1000 clauses* using the Balanced SAT method and repeated this procedure for the No Triangle SAT method. The problem-solving time distribution, for the 3000 instances created with the Balanced SAT method is shown in Fig. 3.

The y-axis of Fig. 3 shows the solution time in seconds. Note that the y-axis is log-scaled. The x-axis displays the instance sizes given by the number of clauses a SAT instance possesses. The least time the Kissat3.1.0 SAT solver needed to solve any of the 3000 SAT instances was slightly above 10 min, while the most time the solver needed to solve a SAT instance was 5 h and 30 min. This information is part of a metadata header that every SAT instance of our dataset possesses. The full header is shown in the following listing:

```
1   c Solution 1 -2 3
2   c Time 600
3   c Solver Kissat3.1.0
4   c CPU AMD_Ryzen_Threadripper_PRO_5965WX_4.5_GHZ
```

As is convention in the Dimacs file format, each line of the above listing starts with the letter *c*, which signals any potential solver that this line is a comment

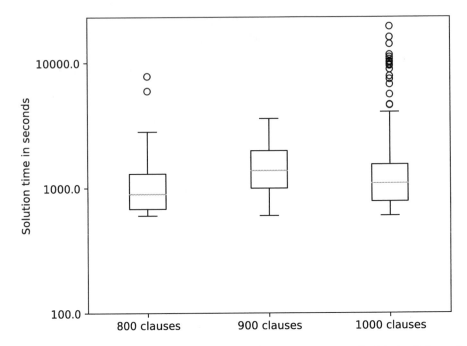

Fig. 3. Problem-solving time distribution for SAT instances created with the Balanced SAT method. Each boxplot consists of the solution times, measured in seconds, of 1000 SAT instances of a fixed instance size (800 clauses, 900 clauses, and 1000 clauses). Note that the y-axis is log-scaled.

and can be skipped. The first information each SAT instance contains is its solution. In line 1 of the above listing, the example solution 1 -2 3 is the short version of $x_1 = True$, $x_2 = False$, $x_3 = True$. Line 2 of the above listing states the exact time needed to solve this instance using the SAT solver shown in line 3 of the above listing with the CPU shown in line 4 of the above listing.

Because of the construction of our dataset, we enable multiple pursuits. First, we enable meaningful benchmarking of new quantum and quantum-hybrid algorithms for QUBO-based solving of SAT instances. QUBO-based SAT solvers, including quantum and quantum-hybrid methods, belong to a class of SAT solvers called *incomplete solvers*. These types of solvers, often including heuristic methods, ideally return a correct answer if the SAT instance is satisfiable. However, if these solvers do not return a correct answer, it does not immediately follow that the given SAT instances are indeed not satisfiable. In this case, the solver may not have found a correct solution yet. Thus, by providing a dataset of only satisfiable instances alongside a satisfying solution for this instance, QUBO-based SAT solvers can be benchmarked by their ability to find answers to solvable problems. Furthermore, our instances are not only challenging for state-of-the-artSAT solvers but also rather small, allowing these instances to be solved by purely quantum or quantum-hybrid methods on currently available hardware. Note that depending on the chosen hardware system and method of modeling SAT instances as instances of QUBO, a pure quantum method might not be possible right now. However, because of the small size of the provided SAT instances, quantum hardware available in the near future should be able to solve these SAT instances by employing pure quantum methods.

As these instances are also challenging for state-of-the-artclassical SAT solvers, this dataset can also be used to benchmark new classical methods of solving satisfiability problems.

Finally, we will aid the development of new QUBO solvers. Hard QUBO instances are needed to benchmark the capabilities of QUBO solvers. Using our dataset of hard SAT instances and applying the 3SAT-to-QUBO transformations provided by our framework to these instances, potentially hard-to-solve (but in any case interesting) QUBO instances can be created. We assume these QUBO instances to be hard, as they represent SAT instances that cannot be efficiently solved using state-of-the-artSAT solvers. If a QUBO solver could solve these QUBO instances efficiently, this QUBO solver would be the preferred method of solving the corresponding SAT instances.

4.5   The Satqubolib.examples Package

We demonstrated the most important usage scenario for each of the modules `satqubolib` provides. However, these explanations do not span the whole range of implemented functionalities. Therefore, `satqubolib` provides the `examples` package: `satqubolib.examples`. This package contains one module for each of satqubolib's base modules (e.g., there is `satqubolib.examples.formula`, `satqubolib.examples.transformations` and `satqubolib.examples.generators`) providing documented examples for various usage scenarios of the respective module. Furthermore, we included convenience functions and usage scenarios, such as using a SAT solver provided by PySAT, to test whether the satisfiability instances created by our `generators` module are hard and satisfiable.

4.6   Framework Maintenance and Community Involvement

By implementing several known 3SAT-to-QUBO transformations and the Pattern QUBO method, our framework provides thousands of QUBO transformations. However, there probably exist interesting 3SAT-to-QUBO transformations that we still need to implement. To increase the reproducibility of scientific studies and the range of possible applications, we encourage contributing to `satqubolib` by providing implementations of QUBO models via pull requests in the framework's GitHub[2], or by hinting us of their existence. We also plan to keep our dataset up to date. As quantum computers' computational capabilities grow, we plan to add new, more challenging-to-solve instances to the benchmark dataset to reflect this change. Therefore, we also encourage submissions of new practically hard satisfiability instances that are at the same time small enough to

---

[2] (https://github.com/ZielinskiSebastian/satqubolib).

be solved by currently available quantum hardware (either directly or through quantum-hybrid methods). The contributed satisfiability instances do not need to be created via the Balanced SAT or No Triangle SAT methods.

5   Conclusion

Satisfiability problems are ubiquitous in practical computer science. For many domains (like planning, dependency resolution, and more), transforming a domain-specific problem into an instance of a satisfiability problem is an effective and maintainable method of solving these problems due to the capabilities of modern SAT solvers. In this paper, we presented `satqubolib`, an open-source Python framework that facilitates scientific publications' reproducibility and the use, development, and benchmarking of QUBO-based quantum and quantum-hybrid methods for solving satisfiability problems. Our framework thus also bridges the gap between quantum (optimization) technologies and researchers or practitioners of these related domains by providing easy-to-use mappings from resulting satisfiability instances to instances of QUBO, which is the input model for several different quantum methods (like quantum annealing or the QAOA algorithm on quantum gate systems).

By implementing several well-known and widespread transformations from satisfiability problems to instances of QUBO and the Pattern QUBO method, our framework provides thousands of ready-to-use 3SAT-to-QUBO transformations. As part of the framework, we also created a dataset containing 6000 practically hard and satisfiable 3SAT instances of different sizes using the Balanced SAT and the No Triangle SAT methods to enable meaningful benchmarking of newly developed quantum and quantum hybrid methods. Each formula within the dataset possesses a metadata header that contains the solution of this formula, the solution time, the processor, and the SAT solver that was used to solve the formula. Finally, we also enable the user to create custom satisfiability instances of arbitrary sizes (and hardness) by implementing and providing the Balanced SAT and No Triangle SAT methods. We hope that `satqubolib` will help to bridge the gap between application domains, in which SAT solvers are a vital part of the solution process, and quantum technologies.

In the future, we plan to include further structurally different satisfiability instances (of equal hardness and size) to enable broader benchmarking of quantum and quantum-hybrid methods and, thus, to identify possibly interesting domains for applying these methods. Furthermore, we want to include harder satisfiability instances of equal size that take even longer (i.e., multiple days), where we do not know whether these instances are satisfiable or not. As the capabilities of modern SAT solvers and hardware systems grow, we will continually update the instance sizes (i.e., the number of clauses of the satisfiability instances) within our dataset to ensure that the dataset remains a viable resource for benchmarking. Finally, we plan to keep track of future publications on transformations from satisfiability problems to instances of QUBO and will provide them in our framework.

Acknowledgments. The partial funding of this paper by the German Federal Ministry of Education and Research through the funding program "quantum technologies — from basic research to market" (contract number: 13N16196) is gratefully acknowledged.

References

1. 2011, S.C.: Sat competition 2011: Benchmark submission guidelines (2011). https://satcompetition.github.io/2023/benchmarks.html. Accessed 9 Feb 2024
2. Abate, P., Di Cosmo, R., Gousios, G., Zacchiroli, S.: Dependency solving is still hard, but we are getting better at it. In: 2020 IEEE 27th International Conference on Software Analysis, Evolution and Reengineering (SANER), pp. 547–551. IEEE (2020)
3. Arora, S., Barak, B.: Computational complexity: a modern approach. Cambrtidge University Press (2009)
4. Balyo, T., Heule, M., Iser, M., Järvisalo, M., Suda, M. (eds.): Proceedings of SAT Competition 2023: Solver, Benchmark and Proof Checker Descriptions. Department of Computer Science Series of Publications B, Department of Computer Science, University of Helsinki, Finland (2023)
5. Barták, R., Salido, M.A., Rossi, F.: Constraint satisfaction techniques in planning and scheduling. J. Intell. Manuf. **21**, 5–15 (2010)
6. Biere, A., Fleury, M.: Kissat homepage (2020). https://fmv.jku.at/kissat/ Accessed Feb 11 2024
7. Chancellor, N., Zohren, S., Warburton, P.A., Benjamin, S.C., Roberts, S.: A direct mapping of max k-sat and high order parity checks to a chimera graph. Sci. Rep. **6**(1), 37107 (2016)
8. Choi, V.: Adiabatic quantum algorithms for the np-complete maximum-weight independent set, exact cover and 3sat problems. arXiv preprint arXiv:1004.2226 (2010)
9. Cook, S.A.: The complexity of theorem-proving procedures. In: Proceedings of the Third Annual ACM Symposium on Theory of Computing, pp. 151–158 (1971)
10. Duan, Q., Al-Haj, S., Al-Shaer, E.: Provable configuration planning for wireless sensor networks. In: 2012 8th International Conference on Network and Service Management (cnsm) and 2012 Workshop on Systems Virtualiztion Management (svm), pp. 316–321. IEEE (2012)
11. Escamocher, G., O'Sullivan, B., Prestwich, S.D.: Generating difficult sat instances by preventing triangles. arXiv preprint arXiv:1903.03592 (2019)
12. Glover, F., Kochenberger, G., Du, Y.: A tutorial on formulating and using qubo models. arXiv preprint arXiv:1811.11538 (2018)
13. Gutin, G., Karapetyan, D.: Constraint branching in workflow satisfiability problem. In: Proceedings of the 25th ACM Symposium on Access Control Models and Technologies, pp. 93–103 (2020)
14. Hoos, H.H., Stützle, T.: Satlib: an online resource for research on sat. Sat **2000**, 283–292 (2000)
15. Ignatiev, A., Morgado, A., Marques-Silva, J.: PySAT: a python toolkit for prototyping with SAT oracles. In: Beyersdorff, O., Wintersteiger, C.M. (eds.) Theory and Applications of Satisfiability Testing – SAT 2018: 21st International Conference, SAT 2018, Held as Part of the Federated Logic Conference, FloC 2018, Oxford, UK, July 9–12, 2018, Proceedings, pp. 428–437. Springer International Publishing, Cham (2018). https://doi.org/10.1007/978-3-319-94144-8_26

16. Jose, M., Majumdar, R.: Cause clue clauses: error localization using maximum satisfiability. ACM SIGPLAN Notices **46**(6), 437–446 (2011)
17. Karapetyan, D., Parkes, A.J., Gutin, G., Gagarin, A.: Pattern-based approach to the workflow satisfiability problem with user-independent constraints. J. Artif. Intell. Res. **66**, 85–122 (2019)
18. Krüger, T., Mauerer, W.: Quantum annealing-based software components: An experimental case study with sat solving. In: Proceedings of the IEEE/ACM 42nd International Conference on Software Engineering Workshops, pp. 445–450 (2020)
19. Lucas, A.: Ising formulations of many np problems. Front. Phys. **2**, 5 (2014)
20. Marques-Silva, J.P., Sakallah, K.A.: Boolean satisfiability in electronic design automation. In: Proceedings of the 37th Annual Design Automation Conference, pp. 675–680 (2000)
21. Nüßlein, J., Gabor, T., Linnhoff-Popien, C., Feld, S.: Algorithmic qubo formulations for k-sat and hamiltonian cycles. In: Proceedings of the Genetic and Evolutionary Computation Conference Companion, pp. 2240–2246 (2022)
22. Nüßlein, J., Zielinski, S., Gabor, T., Linnhoff-Popien, C., Feld, S.: Solving (max) 3-sat via quadratic unconstrained binary optimization. arXiv preprint arXiv:2302.03536 (2023)
23. Radicchi, F., Vilone, D., Yoon, S., Meyer-Ortmanns, H.: Social balance as a satisfiability problem of computer science. Phys. Rev. E **75**(2), 026106 (2007)
24. Rintanen, J.: Planning as satisfiability: Heuristics. Artif. Intell. **193**, 45–86 (2012)
25. Rintanen, J., Heljanko, K., Niemelä, I.: Planning as satisfiability: parallel plans and algorithms for plan search. Artif. Intell. **170**(12–13), 1031–1080 (2006)
26. Selman, B., Mitchell, D.G., Levesque, H.J.: Generating hard satisfiability problems. Artif. Intell. **81**(1–2), 17–29 (1996)
27. Shor, P.W.: Algorithms for quantum computation: discrete logarithms and factoring. In: Proceedings 35th Annual Symposium on Foundations of Computer Science, pp. 124–134. IEEE (1994)
28. Spence, I.: Balanced random sat benchmarks. SAT Competition **2017**, 53 (2017)
29. Verma, A., Lewis, M., Kochenberger, G.: Efficient qubo transformation for higher degree pseudo boolean functions. arXiv preprint arXiv:2107.11695 (2021)
30. Zaman, M., Tanahashi, K., Tanaka, S.: Pyqubo: Python library for mapping combinatorial optimization problems to qubo form. IEEE Trans. Comput. **71**(4), 838–850 (2021)
31. Zielinski, S., Nüßlein, J., Stein, J., Gabor, T., Linnhoff-Popien, C., Feld, S.: Influence of different 3sat-to-qubo transformations on the solution quality of quantum annealing: A benchmark study. In: Proceedings of the Companion Conference on Genetic and Evolutionary Computation, pp. 2263–2271. GECCO '23 Companion, Association for Computing Machinery, New York, NY, USA (2023). https://doi.org/10.1145/3583133.3596330
32. Zielinski, S., Nüßlein, J., Stein, J., Gabor, T., Linnhoff-Popien, C., Feld, S.: Pattern qubos: algorithmic construction of 3sat-to-qubo transformations. Electronics **12**(16) (2023). https://doi.org/10.3390/electronics12163492, https://www.mdpi.com/2079-9292/12/16/3492

Pervasive Computing

Better Together – Empowering Citizen Collectives with Community Learning

Wessel Kraaij[1,2]([⊠]) [iD], Geiske Bouma[2] [iD], Marloes van der Klauw[2] [iD], and Pepijn van Empelen[2] [iD]

[1] Leiden Institute of Advanced Computer Science, Leiden University, Leiden, The Netherlands
`wessel.kraaij@tno.nl`
[2] Netherlands Organisation for Applied Scientific Research (TNO), The Hague, The Netherlands

Abstract. Citizen collectives have the potential to contribute significantly to various societal transitions. Rather than focusing on the individual, collective action improves empowerment and agency, and can contribute to effective collaboration between citizens, policy makers and other institutes. This can be facilitated by enabling efficient monitoring, reflection, and multi-level learning, but an infrastructure is missing to scale bottom-up approaches and bridge the gap with the systems world of government policy makers. We discuss four open problems that need to be addressed in order to create this comprehensive data and learning infrastructure for empowering citizen collectives: 1. Providing value and accessibility for all; 2. Handling privacy, providing trust and autonomy; 3. Enable community learning from observational data; 4. Enabling scaling in order to accelerate and link to the 'systems world'. We conclude with sketching the research methodology that we plan to use to address these challenges.

Keywords: Community learning · Data sovereignty · Positive reinforcement · Data governance · Multi-level learning · Citizen science

1 Introduction

The societal challenges with regard to climate, energy and health/well-being are huge, inter-related and require changes and collaborative action at all levels. Sustainable transitions are currently hampered by increased polarization and low trust in government among citizens. While the digitalisation of government services such as requesting a new ID, a permit or following the city council sessions online has resulted in more efficiency, government is now criticized for missing the human dimension. Still, many citizens are willing to contribute to societal challenges by making lifestyle changes, or by improving their living environment. However, they often do not have sufficient agency since other challenges – such as the harsh reality of dealing with poverty – prevail. Studies have shown that behavioural change interventions directed at individuals are hardly effect, and therefore the focus needs to be redirected to the (social) system [1]. In this multi-crisis, the potential of citizens collectives to help achieving local transitions is under-explored. Many initiatives exist, but these often miss longevity and organizing power.

F. Phillipson et al. (Eds.): I4CS 2024, CCIS 2109, pp. 69–82, 2024.
https://doi.org/10.1007/978-3-031-60433-1_5

Our research programme 'Better Together' aims at rebuilding trust and collaboration between citizens and government by i) improving the agency, value and representativeness of place-based citizen collectives leading to better social cohesion and ii) structurally stimulating engagement of citizen collectives for participatory community-up local policy making, thereby increasing trust, mutual understanding, and support.

In this paper, we describe our approach to address these challenges, with a focus on the data and learning infrastructure that supports the learning and collaboration process. We first elaborate on the complex multi-level stakeholder setting that provides the context for our research (Sect. 2). Next, we present an overview of various (social) mechanisms for learning and developing local transformative solutions to transitions (Sect. 3). The main contribution of our paper is the description of four (socio-)technical open problems that currently prevent scaling up a community approach to societal challenges (Sect. 4). The paper concludes with some reflections on how we can apply co-creation as a means to engage citizen collectives in our research and vice versa. We include a list of terminology definitions to guide the reader below.

Important Concepts

Agency: the capacity, condition, or state of acting or of exerting power.

Citizens' initiatives are 'collective activities by citizens aimed at providing local 'public goods or services' (e.g. regarding the liveability and safety) in their street, neighbourhood or town, in which citizens decide themselves both about the aims and means of their project and in which local authorities have a supporting or facilitating role' [2]. Sometimes also referred to as the group of citizens themselves (Dutch: 'burgerinitiatief').

Citizen science describes participatory research practices and knowledge co-production by/with citizens and societal actors. In our project vision, it is essential that the output of citizen science is directly relevant for the participating citizens.

Coalition an organization of individuals representing diverse organizations, factions or constituencies who agree to work together in order to achieve a common goal. The advantage to work together is to bring about a specific change that can only be achieved collectively [3].

Collectives are groups of people and/or organisations that share or are motivated by at least one common issue or work together to achieve a common objective. Typical legal embodiments of a collective are cooperatives, foundations, or associations, but collectives are not necessarily institutionalized. In our research, we are mainly focused on citizen collectives. A related term is -citizens' initiative-

Communities are groups of individuals sharing one or more social characteristics (e.g. place, religion, values, interests) represented as one social unit. The term community is used in various contexts, with slightly different meanings. We provide the definition by Israel based on Klein and Sarason in the context of community empowerment. 'A community can be characterized by the following elements: (1) membership - a sense of identity and belonging; (2) common symbol systems including similar language, rituals, and ceremonies; (3) shared values and norms; (4) mutual influence between community members; (5) shared needs and commitment to meeting them (this is in fact a property of a coalition); and (6) shared emotional connection including common history, experiences, and mutual support' [4]. Communities differ from coalitions, the former are focused on relations between group members, the latter on achieving a joint goal.

Community learning is a generic term for a learning process at the group level. Various instantiations are possible, depending on the context, with different learning mechanisms, different outcomes (individual/group) and different group compositions (communities, collectives, coalitions, networks of collectives). Rather than a focus on participation and information exchange, the focus is on community engagement, with a dialogue and interaction between different (local) players [5]. A common related term is 'learning community'.

Collective Data hub a repository for collecting and analysing aggregated household data and other relevant data at the level of a collective, controlled by the collective. The hub provides input to various applications and dashboards for learning and feedback.

Disadvantaged refers to marginalised, socially vulnerable groups.

Living Labs are user-centred and co-created open innovation ecosystems integrating research, experimentation and innovation processes in real life communities and settings.

Multi-level learning concerns learning at local level from experiments changes are (not) successful, learning across different local activities to grow, replicate. And accumulate activities, and finally (at macro-) system level learning to link transition to global KPI.

Monitoring Evaluation Learning (MEL) refers to routine monitoring of project activities and results, evaluate to a periodic assessment of goal progress and to reflect on the outcomes and processes in order to learn how outcomes could be improved [6]. Various related concepts exists such as reflective practice and reflexive monitoring.

Personal data locker an individual repository for collecting and analysing data of one household/family., controlled by the individual household.

Place based collective: related to a certain neighbourhood, which defines the challenges and assets of a collective.

Transformative governance: transformative governance concerns the formal and informal (public and private) rules, rulemaking systems and actor networks at all levels of human society that enable transformative change. Transformative governance addresses power asymmetries, stimulates dialogue, learning and reflections, acknowledging diverse values, perspectives and knowledge systems [7].

2   Problem Analysis: Social and Technical Barriers Preventing Progress on Transitions

Citizen collectives addressing local societal challenges such as the energy transition and neighbourhood security are gaining traction. There is solid evidence that citizen neighbourhood engagement interventions can have positive impact on community outcomes [8, 9]. Several fundamental issues need to be addressed to increase value and scale, valorise such an approach and make it accessible for all citizens, no matter their financial or housing situation. We suggest that multi-level monitoring and learning of actions and outcomes within and across communities is the enabler to achieve create systemic changes needed to establish social transitions. This paper articulates several of the technical challenges that need to be addressed before further scaling can be done. The technical challenges are tightly related to the social mechanisms that we intend to support (Sect. 3). In the rest of this section, we motivate our research challenges, linking to the state-of-the-art, and sketch some of our ideas how to solve the challenges. Further details on the technical challenges will be provided in Sect. 4.

Point of departure for understanding critical success factors of citizen communities is the 'asset-based community development' (ABCD) approach, which is a methodology based on strengths and potentials from within a collective (so-called assets). Assets involve individual assets, physical environmental assets, and collective assets, such as the resources, skills, connections. Key functions are 1) to understand existing assets (i.e. asset mapping), 2) build connections between community members and between communities and agencies, 3) share knowledge and resources and identify common interests, 4) create a vision and activity plan [10].

Although citizen collectives are not new, the mechanisms of informal learning and scalable, inclusive and durable collaboration by citizen collectives have hardly been conceptualized and are not well understood in the context of achieving societal transitions [11]. We will address the complexity of transitions by focusing on building trust and relational quality and success experiences, analysing and dividing the work to leverage a diversity of engaged citizens in different fitting roles [12], Sect. 3.

Several stakeholders (cooperatives, NGOs, municipalities), and scholars [13] mention the absence of a trusted and up to date Monitoring & Evaluation infrastructure as a real bottleneck, hampering progress. Such an infrastructure would enable understanding which interventions effectively result in meaningful changes in relation to the social transitions and helps communities to speed up and scale activities. In order to create trust, it is important that local data and findings will be fully owned, controlled and trusted by the citizen collectives. The local information can serve as input for community-up exchange on policy tailoring; mutually, democratic decision making between citizens and policy makers, which will contribute to place-based, locally tailored planning [14].

It will be conditional for the success, financial sustainability, and transferability of citizen collectives to have a reliable link with the 'systems world'. Collaboration, communication, and interaction with stakeholders requires some standardization of procedures, agreement on outcome indicators and a capability to report on impact. Collectives need be able to relate to scaled national level challenges and local government for setting up financial and regulatory conditions to make their initiatives durable and thriving. Transformative governance [15] has been recognized as a means to change socio-ecological systems (e.g. the health deals or green deal), and focusses on self-organization and decentralized decision-making, including citizens. However, the understanding and evaluation of transformative governance is in its infancy. Evidence based policy making is seen as a promising instrument for transformative governance [16] and for monitoring and steering systems changes. However, the required dense, timely, high quality local data is often not available and hard to obtain since citizens are tired of surveys and distrust government/commercial data collection efforts (cf. Subsect. 4.1).

In the following sections in this paper, we will provide a sketch of how we aim to overcome these challenges by building an infrastructure that enables collective collaboration and learning.

3 Multi-Level Approach to Community Learning and Transitions

We propose a multi-level learning approach, to tackle the societal wicked problems and initiate and accelerate transformations. We start from the viewpoint, that collectives and coalitions are generally action-oriented and focus on reducing or preventing a common problem, identifying and implementing solutions and creating social change [3]. Collaboration, collective action, and agency can be stimulated by having a shared vision (including organisation model and funding), setting collective goals, by monitoring progress and providing feedback during the activity and by reflective evaluation on the collaboration process and outcome.

We distinguish multiple levels of learning (cf. Table 1), each with its own feedback loop, starting from learning at the micro-level (household level), learning at the meso level (within and between local collectives) and macro level (society). In our conceptual analysis of learning strategies we align and combine various disciplines related to: behaviour change (e.g., [17]), community and coalition processes (e.g., [3]), system innovation and transition management [11, 18], and transformative innovation policy [19].

First, people may engage in *mastery learning* [17]. This can be at the level of households or collective. Mastery learning is the process of learning from self-set or mutual goals, and to evaluate whether the behaviours or actions initiated, result in the desired outcomes. Reflecting on goal achievement is important for two reasons. First, achieving the desired outcomes could enhance positive reinforcement. This can foster intrinsic motivation, i.e. satisfaction and enjoyment to proceed an activity. Reaching a goal can also contribute to feelings of collective or self-competence. Reaching a particular outcome in itself is not sufficient for sustaining collective actions. Collaboration should also promote collaborative synergy, which could foster citizen engagement and sense of collective identity (i.e., a sense of belonging to a group), social cohesion and social capital (e.g., the resources obtained through social connections such as norms of reciprocity, trust, [20]. Importantly, collective actions could contribute to basic human psychological needs of autonomy, relatedness and competence [21]. Second, in case of not reaching the planned goals or activities, the evaluation enables re-evaluation and adaptation of the originally set goals and activities, i.e. so-called iterative plan-do-check-act cycles.

A second way of learning is based on *social learning within a collective*. Social learning occurs through the observation, imitation and modelling of other people [17]. Hence, community members may learn from the actions of other citizens or households. For instance, understanding how to maintain a healthy lifestyle or understanding how to lower energy consumption can be achieved by understanding what a neighbour is doing, why and how. Social learning in transition research can be defined as a process in which people align, share, and discuss their ideas together. As a result they develop new shared mental models, form new relationships, and develop the capacity to take collective action and manage their environment [22]. At this level, social learning is limited to the learning that occurs within a single project or situation. It, however, is not limited to learning amongst citizens, but focusses on community engagement in broader sense, where also other stakeholders (policy makers, NGOs, and private companies) collaborate on mutual goals. Key element in this context is to move beyond participation

Table 1. Levels of learning

Level	Type	Subjects/Actors	Objectives/Outcomes	Strategies	Inputs
1	Mastery learning	Citizens (households)	Self-/collectively set goals (eat more vegetarian, reduce fossil fuel use, be 30 min active)	Reflection, improve self-efficacy	KPI measurements, (household indicators), process step measurements
2	Social learning	Citizen collective members, and other stakeholders	Shared goals	Dialogue, joint action, monitoring, aggregated KPIs	Data at household level (level 1), goal setting related to national objectives
3	Best practices	Between collectives	Tailor-made best practices (FAIR)	Exchange success and failures. Predictive modelling	FAIR experiment descriptions, input based on level 2
4	Systemic change	Stakeholders, local and national (global)	Systems change	Reflexive monitoring, multi-level learning	System analysis, and actively feeding back learning experiences (based on best practices and inventory of barriers, level 3)

and information exchange, but to focus on dialogue and interaction between the different (local) players [4] which fosters also trust, empowerment and agency.

A third level of learning can occur across collective actions and local experiments (e.g. [23]). This type of learning could be defined as transition learning. Learning across different collective actions enables deepening, broadening, and scaling up. Deepening can be the result of monitoring and evaluating single collective actions which helps to understand barriers and facilitators, and to learn what works, which facilitates social learning and leads to growth of activities. Broadening can be the result of learning across collectives, leading to opportunities for replication.

Finally, a significant scale up of collective actions via replication and extension is likely to induce a system change and hence transformation. Replication enables other collectives to make use of best practices and to understand barriers and facilitators. Extension could mean making connections between initiatives. In our vision, an independent national network organization needs to be set-up to act as a knowledge broker. This organization will aggregate, and curate lessons learned by the associated local collectives. The learning experiences and best practices can be made available to new collectives to have a warm start, e.g. using a predictive model that selects the best practice given local contextual parameters, and also to build new networks, including non-usual (disadvantaged) citizen members.

We acknowledge that learning at different levels as we have discussed so far is often not effective since transitions face systemic barriers. The existing situation often is linked to vested interests of stakeholders. This complex challenge therefore calls for system level learning, which can be viewed as an integrated multi-level learning approach, where coordination is established between the micro, meso and macro levels as discussed above.

The discipline of transition studies proposes various conceptual frameworks. One of the frameworks is the multi-level perspective (MLP) on (e.g. sustainability) transitions [24]. The MLP conceptualization is slightly different from the learning levels we discussed so far. Starting point is the so-called 'regime' the current practices, institutes that make up our societal and economic processes. A possible approach to address transitions in a complex context is to start parallel social experiments [25] in 'niches' (a practice referred to as 'probe-sense-respond' in the Cynefin decision-making framework [26]). When one or more niches become successful, they can be further scaled up when the contextual conditions (e.g. financial/legal) defined by the so-called 'landscape' are favourable. In the complex transition field, monitoring, data and structured observations are conditional for fruitful reflection, collaboration and successful innovation/systemic change by involved stakeholders.

4 Open Challenges for Data and Learning Infrastructure

Our multi-level approach to community learning consists of various social and behavioural processes, at individual, community, network and system level. These stakeholder groups and processes can come into full swing when multi-level monitoring and learning is facilitated. Curated information is a catalyst and can either be qualitative or quantitative. Curated information is the result of planning, monitoring, and evaluation data, which enables reflective learning at the different layers (from household level to systems level). Hence our slogan 'data as a vehicle'. Raw monitoring data and qualitative data are important ingredients for assessing the current situation, setting the agenda, and measuring progress in a learning setting and the ability to re-adapt (via plan-do-check-act cycles). Although experimental design, data collection, cleaning and analysis are commonplace in research and industry, this practice is less common for citizens and government, perhaps with the exception of various citizen science collectives. Various obstacles exist for a reflective learning practice. We now describe four important open challenges.

4.1 Providing Value and Accessibility for All

A significant challenge that we face is to engage citizens beyond a small group of innovators or early adopters (the usual suspects). The reality of many neighbourhoods is that they are heterogeneous. That means not all solutions, services appeal to everybody. Not every person has the same amount of time, each age segment comes with its own challenges and social networks may not be connected. We advocate a research approach that is not 'extractive', but where the direct value ('what is in it for me') is clear to the participants. Several disadvantaged areas and some citizen collectives already suffer from 'overload by research attention', sometimes called 'extractive research'. Often citizens are discouraged because they do not see what is done with the data gathered, how it is of value for them, and participation generally is not facilitated. Key Enabling Methodologies such as co-design and co-creation are suitable instruments for keeping 'direct value' in focus, and so is agile project execution. In the end, neighbourhood communities/coalitions should become more self-guiding in their goal setting and monitoring, so it is important to leave the initiative with the citizen initiatives. A second aspect of heterogeneity that is possibly more important is communication. Differences in socioeconomic position and migration background shape communication, interpretation and cultural elements that determine the success of reaching citizens and interventions. It is important to keep these factors in mind when designing our methods and evaluate accessibility. The move to inclusion and diversity in citizen science and action, requires the need to engage all members of society regardless of their background. This also necessitates making connections between social networks, such as via gatekeepers, key community members/opinion leaders or via place-based approaches connecting issues, networks and relationships [27]. In this way it is possible to create spill-over effects connecting members across neighbourhoods or social networks. Lastly, a related but important factor is 'literacy' and language fluency. This also requires a multi-channel, including offline and online but uniform communication that is understandable by most citizens. We may be able to benefit from insights concerning diffusion of innovations [28]. Specifically, how can we identify 'positive deviants', opinion leaders or change makers in subcommunities that are able to inspire and guide social innovations. There is some evidence that important changes can be achieved in relatively short time, taking advantage of the network effect in complex systems, achieving social tipping points [29].

Challenge 1: *Co-design reciprocal value exchange archetypes, that can serve as starting point for a network of local learning communities. Co-design local missions where all citizens, existing institutions, government, and other private and public partners can join and feel represented. Design methods for quantifying / qualifying inclusivity and representativeness.*

4.2 Handling Privacy, Providing Trust and Autonomy

Since we intend to collect data at individual household level in data lockers and aggregate at the level of collectives in collective data hubs, data privacy is of prime importance. Analysis of personal data has become a very sensitive topic, given the recent misconduct by the Dutch Tax Office. Handling and processing personal data is governed by the Dutch instantiation of the EU General Data Protection Regulation. We choose 'consent' as the legal basis for processing data to compute aggregate KPIs, correlations and other analytics that are a central element in our learning framework. Nonetheless, we think it is important to safeguard privacy at the design level, by employing privacy enhancing technologies such as secure multi-party computation. Citizens must always be able to revoke their consent. We conjecture that privacy safeguards at the deep technical level will help to build the trust level that is an important factor determining the adoption of new technologies involving 'big data'. Such an approach (hiding the data points of individual households) may help to prevent unethical social stigmatizing mechanisms [30] such as 'neighbour shaming' a practice to put the blame on individuals that lag behind. This would also mean that analytics can only be presented for a group with a sufficient number of individuals.

A recent study on trust in data processing systems [31] pointed out that transparency is not a sufficient remedy to rebuild trust in big data processing systems. A more important factor is trust in the organization in charge of and controlling the data processing infrastructure. Recently, some incidents in automatic fraud detection by Dutch tax authorities have significantly diminished trust in the government as an independent organization that acts in the interests of all its citizens. Several alternative data collection, processing and governance infrastructures are in the making (public spaces etc.), stimulated by the EU Data Governance Act. What these initiatives have in common is that they enhance the autonomy of citizens, since they fully control data collection and processing (data sovereignty), that is without waiving permission to commercial entities (data storage often outside EU legislation) that offer 'free' services but in reality, trade aggregated personal data. Autonomy and working together as a group may help to rebalance the existing power inequalities between citizens and governments/corporations. A detailed example of how this could work is provided in [32, 33]. We need data pods, pod providers, data intermediaries that implement the data strategy as laid out by the DGA. The EU will introduce a special register for so-called data altruism organisations, with the aim to increase trust. If privacy and data sovereignty are correctly implemented and the value of participating in the community learning hub outweighs the cost and effort, it will be easy to grow a data backbone for a network of citizen collectives working on joint missions. If such a learning network gets sufficient traction and is a true representation of a certain neighbourhood, we conjecture that it is a good starting position to build sufficient authority and visibility to provide a counterfactor for the current destabilizing effects of personalized social media that are gradually getting more attention of our population. Here individuals are subjected to targeted advertising, influencers, hate speech, conspiracy theories and misinformation.

Challenge 2: *Design and build a (federated) data processing infrastructure which handles consent, is compliant with GDPR, DGA and provides the technical basis for trust and autonomy.*

4.3   Enable Systematic Community Learning from Observational Data Using Open Science Principles

A possible means for community learning is to record repeated measurements of quantitative or qualitative data for analysis. We aim to empower and motivate citizen collectives to contribute to a data panel (longitudinal dataset) for their own collective, making it possible to have a better understanding of needs, interactions, inequalities, impact of interventions and promising solutions. In statistical terms, each citizen collective will control a collective data hub with so-called panel data, that is a longitudinal data collection linked to the households that are linked to the collective. The panel data will include qualitative and quantitative data, which are the basis for further analysis. We envisage various ways to learn from the household level panel data (these ideas are not limitative).

1. Peer group levelling by comparing the KPI score on a certain outcome (e.g. energy use per month) to the average score of similar households in the collective, citizens get feedback on their relative performance.
2. KPI stratification per household attribute: using the KPI scores in combination with e.g. house insulation data, it will be possible to provide recommendations on potential energy use reduction measures based on actual data in the neighbourhood.
3. Citizen collective level feedback and inspiration: The panel data can be used for monitoring progress on a collective mission, problem solving, or celebrate achievements.

Section 3 provides a brief overview of various levels of learning, where learning from observational data and experiences plays a role. An extensive discussion of the interaction between different levels of learning is beyond the scope of this paper. Effective learning obviously involves social, cognitive and governance methodologies. Data and infrastructure are primarily supportive tools, not a means in itself.

Challenge 3: *Design a generic systematic impact measurement methodology that is applicable to citizen collectives, supporting citizen science, which can be instantiated by different collectives whilst keeping interoperability of impact measurements and methodology descriptions. Of particular importance is a FAIR process ontology and data schema* [34–36].

4.4   Enabling Scaling in Order to Accelerate and Link to the 'Systems World'

So far, we have discussed requirements at the level of citizen collectives. Yet, to make real impact, it is critical that a promising approach can be scaled up (just like a start-up needs to transition into scale up phase to remain in business). There are several aspects that we want to mention here. First, we intend to work with network organisations that link citizen collectives at a regional or national level. These network organisations are value driven and not for (shareholder) profit. We envisage that research organisations support accelerated scale up of best practices, using a mix of methods, fit for purpose.

1. Scale up can be accelerated if we can predict which mix of building blocks will be the most appropriate for a new neighbourhood to achieve their goals e.g. the heat transition. We intend to create predictions based on the experiments documented in the citizen collective data panels.
2. Scale up can be even further accelerated when interventions can be based on a causal analysis of the success of interventions. Such an approach may be feasible as soon as some standard approaches have matured and have been tested in similar neighbourhoods. Where data points are either matched on collective or household level using propensity scores. If matching is impossible we could also compare policy actions and resolve this issue using mixed analysis such as Qualitative Comparative Analysis (QCA) which is a useful method to study causal complexity [37].

A second important condition for scaling is linking to the 'system world'. International regulation, national legislation, local policy making, all these contexts require a precise measurement of impact. This is important because government policy regarding e.g. climate change, quality of living environment, health is costly, and evidence-based interventions are becoming the norm. If a certain intervention does not deliver on its intended effect or that the impact cannot be measured on the scale accepted in the 'systems world', it risks not be financially supported by government or investors. Still, an unsuccessful experiment can be a stepping stone to an improved intervention or improve social cohesion. It is therefore important to manage expectations and take sufficient time for learning to collaborate.

Challenge 4: Scaling i) predict the success of interventions given a small set of neighbourhood parameters; ii) design a method to identify the main success factors of interventions, preferably by causal inference; iii) provide guidance towards (networks of) citizen collectives as to how to measure impact (in a co-creation approach).

5   Discussion and Future Work

Societal transitions are urgent, but highly complex because all stakeholders need to agree on the way forward and there are so many dependencies and value chains affected by proposed systemic changes. In the research programme 'Better Together; empowering citizen collectives', we focus on supporting citizen collectives to become players with sufficient agency at the transition planning table while keeping a keen interest to influence the transitions in such a way that they serve the interests of their member citizens (transitions are achievable) and are sustainable (do not postpone the burden/negative impact of current policy and lifestyles on future generations). Collaboration with other stakeholders on an equal level is key.

In this paper we have focused on the technical challenges that need to be addressed to build the approach that we envisage. We do not need to explain that the challenges are primarily social. Transitions ask for changes in behaviour and lifestyle, call on solidarity to align with equity goals, since the level of social inequalities inversely determines social stability. Technology cannot provide a solution alone but can support and facilitate the necessary changes. Since digital technology is now distrusted by many people, a careful step-by-step interdisciplinary co-creation process is needed to make sure that the proposed infrastructure will be adopted by everyone.

We have started to set-up living labs in several neighbourhoods in the Netherlands. The idea is that citizens themselves formulate their objectives and obstacles. By performing Participatory Action Research (PAR), researchers become part of the community teams. In this way, trust can be established leading to deeper insights. On the other hand, PAR has potential drawbacks since it is more difficult to keep an objective distance from the research context. We intend to remedy this potential bias, by structurally involving internal and external reviewers. If we manage to build a successful learning infrastructure, we may be able to build momentum for transitions and reach social tipping points that are instrumental for systemic change.

At the same time, we need to follow, and where possible influence, relevant developments regarding data sharing that are currently being shaped by the EU. Especially in the health domain. Relevant legislation is in the making, that may impact the viability of the transition approach that we envision. Harmonizing data is a good thing, but the value and impact for population and individuals should be balanced [38].

Acknowledgments. This research was funded by the TNO Early Research Programme 'Better Together: Empowering Citizen Collectives'. We acknowledge the inputs and ideas of many individuals that helped to shape the vision of Better Together: Sarah Giest, Jan Willem Erisman, Margaret Gold, Reint Jan Renes, John Verheijden, Moniek Buijzen, Lex Burdorf, Roel Woudstra, Djoera Eerland, Jan Engels, Jurriaan Edelenbos, Mike Duijn, Peter van Daalen, Andre Boorsma, Yvonne Schönbeck ,Ellian Lebbink, Kit Buurman, Hilde van Keulen, Jeroen Pronk, Annelieke van den Berg, Liza van Dam, Suzanne Vugs, Annemarie Mink, Thomas Schuurman Hess, Hade Dorst, Jelle Dijkstra, Suzan van Kempen, Willem Datema, Anne Fleur van Veenstra, Antonella Maiello, Henk Rosendal, Thijs Bouman, Teije Terhorst, Barteld Braaksma, Henri de Ruiter. The coalition website https:/better-together.dev/ provides more information on our associated partners.

Disclosure of Interests. The authors have no competing interests to declare that are relevant to the content of this article.

References

1. Chater, N., Loewenstein, G.: The i-Frame and the s-Frame: how focusing on individual-level solutions has led behavioral public policy astray (2022). https://doi.org/10.2139/ssrn. 4046264. https://papers.ssrn.com/abstract=4046264
2. Bakker, J., Denters, B., Oude Vrielink, M., Klok, P.-J.: Citizens' initiatives: how local governments fill their facilitative role. Local Gov. Stud. **38**, 395–414 (2012). https://doi.org/10. 1080/03003930.2012.698240
3. Butterfoss, F.D., Kegler, M.C.: 17. A coalition model for community action. In: 17. A Coalition Model for Community Action, pp. 309–328. Rutgers University Press (2012). https://doi.org/ 10.36019/9780813553146-019
4. Israel, B.A., Checkoway, B., Schulz, A., Zimmerman, M.: Health education and community empowerment: conceptualizing and measuring perceptions of individual, organizational, and community control. Health Educ. Q. **21**, 149–170 (1994). https://doi.org/10.1177/109019819 402100203
5. Dobos, Á., Jenei, Á.: Citizen engagement as a learning experience. Procedia Soc. Behav. Sci.a Soc. Behav. Sci. **93**, 1085–1089 (2013). https://doi.org/10.1016/j.sbspro.2013.09.335
6. Macnamara, J.: Measurement, evaluation + learning (MEL): new approaches for insights, outcomes, and impact. In: The Routledge Companion to Public Relations. Routledge (2022)
7. Visseren-Hamakers, I.J., et al.: Transformative governance of biodiversity: insights for sustainable development. Curr. Opin. Environ. Sustain. **53**, 20–28 (2021). https://doi.org/10. 1016/j.cosust.2021.06.002
8. O'Mara-Eves, A., Brunton, G., Oliver, S., Kavanagh, J., Jamal, F., Thomas, J.: The effectiveness of community engagement in public health interventions for disadvantaged groups: a meta-analysis. BMC Public Health **15**, 129 (2015). https://doi.org/10.1186/s12889-015-1352-y
9. Cyril, S., Smith, B.J., Possamai-Inesedy, A., Renzaho, A.M.N.: Exploring the role of community engagement in improving the health of disadvantaged populations: a systematic review. Glob. Health Action **8**, 29842 (2015). https://doi.org/10.3402/gha.v8.29842

10. Harrison, R., Blickem, C., Lamb, J., Kirk, S., Vassilev, I.: Asset-based community development: narratives, practice, and conditions of possibility—a qualitative study with community practitioners. SAGE Open **9**, 215824401882308 (2019). https://doi.org/10.1177/215824401 8823081
11. van Mierlo, B., Beers, P.J.: Understanding and governing learning in sustainability transitions: a review. Environ. Innov. Soc. Transit. **34**, 255–269 (2020). https://doi.org/10.1016/j.eist. 2018.08.002
12. Wittmayer, J.M., Schäpke, N.: Action, research and participation: roles of researchers in sustainability transitions. Sustain. Sci. **9**, 483–496 (2014). https://doi.org/10.1007/s11625-014-0258-4
13. Paskaleva, K., Cooper, I.: Are living labs effective? Exploring the evidence. Technovation **106**, 102311 (2021). https://doi.org/10.1016/j.technovation.2021.102311
14. Porto de Albuquerque, J., et al.: The role of data in transformations to sustainability: a critical research agenda. Curr. Opin. Environ. Sustain. **49**, 153–163 (2021). https://doi.org/10.1016/j.cosust.2021.06.009
15. Chaffin, B.C., et al.: Transformative environmental governance. Annu. Rev. Environ. Resour. **41**, 399–423 (2016). https://doi.org/10.1146/annurev-environ-110615-085817
16. Sanderson, I.: Evaluation, policy learning and evidence-based policy making. Public Adm. **80**, 1–22 (2002). https://doi.org/10.1111/1467-9299.00292
17. Bandura, A.: An agentic perspective on positive psychology. In: Positive Psychology: Exploring the Best in People, Vol 1: Discovering Human Strengths, pp. 167–196. Praeger Publishers/Greenwood Publishing Group, Westport, CT, US (2008).
18. Schot, J., Geels, F.W.: Strategic niche management and sustainable innovation journeys: theory, findings, research agenda, and policy. Technol. Anal. Strateg. Manag. **20**, 537–554 (2008). https://doi.org/10.1080/09537320802292651
19. Diercks, G., Larsen, H., Steward, F.: Transformative innovation policy: addressing variety in an emerging policy paradigm. Res. Policy **48**, 880–894 (2019). https://doi.org/10.1016/j.respol.2018.10.028
20. Mackenbach, J.D., et al.: Neighbourhood social capital: measurement issues and associations with health outcomes. Obes. Rev. **17**, 96–107 (2016). https://doi.org/10.1111/obr.12373
21. Ryan, R.M., Deci, E.L.: Self-determination theory and the facilitation of intrinsic motivation, social development, and well-being. Am. Psychol. **55**, 68–78 (2000). https://doi.org/10.1037/0003-066X.55.1.68
22. Pieter, J., Beers, F.H., Veldkamp, T., Hinssen, J.: Social learning inside and outside transition projects: Playing free jazz for a heavy metal audience. NJAS: Wageningen J. Life Sci. **69**(1), 5–13 (2014). https://doi.org/10.1016/j.njas.2013.10.001
23. Holmes, A.J.: Transformative Learning, Affect, and Reciprocal Care in Community Engagement. Community Lit. J. (2015)
24. Geels, F.W., Schot, J.: Typology of sociotechnical transition pathways. Res. Policy **36**, 399–417 (2007). https://doi.org/10.1016/j.respol.2007.01.003
25. Van den Bosch, S.: Transitie-experimenten. Praktijkexperimenten met de potentie om bij te dragen aan transities (in Dutch) (2006)
26. Snowden, D.J., Boone, M.E.: A Leader's Framework for Decision Making (2007). https://hbr.org/2007/11/a-leaders-framework-for-decision-making
27. The Place Principle | Our Place. https://www.ourplace.scot/about-place/place-principle. Accessed 19 Feb 2024
28. Rogers, E.M.: Diffusion of Innovations, 5th Edition. Simon and Schuster (2003)
29. Juhola, S., Filatova, T., Hochrainer-Stigler, S., Mechler, R., Scheffran, J., Schweizer, P.-J.: Social tipping points and adaptation limits in the context of systemic risk: concepts, models and governance. Front. Clim. 4, (2022)

30. Safari, B.T.: Azar: on the effectiveness and legitimacy of 'shaming' as a strategy for combatting climate change 1. In: The Routledge Handbook of Applied Climate Change Ethics. Routledge (2023)
31. Kennedy, H.: ACM TechBrief: The Data Trust Deficit. Association for Computing Machinery, New York, NY, USA (2023)
32. Micheli, M., Farrell, E., Carballa, S.B., Posada, S.M., Signorelli, S., Vespe, M.: Mapping the landscape of data intermediaries. https://publications.jrc.ec.europa.eu/repository/handle/JRC 133988. Accessed 05 Feb 2024. https://doi.org/10.2760/261724
33. Stefanija, A.P., Buelens, B., Goesaert, E., Lenaerts, T., Pierson, J., Van den Bussche, J.: Toward a solid acceptance of the decentralized web of personal data: societal and technological convergence. https://m-cacm.acm.org/magazines/2024/1/278882-toward-a-solid-acceptance-of-the-decentralized-web-of-personal-data-societal-and-technological-convergence/fulltext. Accessed 19 Feb 2024
34. Dumontier, M., et al.: The semanticscience integrated ontology (SIO) for biomedical research and knowledge discovery. J. Biomed. Semant. **5**, 14 (2014). https://doi.org/10.1186/2041-1480-5-14
35. Kaliyaperumal, R., et al.: Semantic modelling of common data elements for rare disease registries, and a prototype workflow for their deployment over registry data. J. Biomed. Semant. **13**, 9 (2022). https://doi.org/10.1186/s13326-022-00264-6
36. Wilkinson, M.D., et al.: The FAIR guiding principles for scientific data management and stewardship. Sci. Data. **3**, 160018 (2016). https://doi.org/10.1038/sdata.2016.18
37. Marx, A., Rihoux, B., Ragin, C.: The origins, development, and application of qualitative comparative analysis: the first 25 years. Eur. Polit. Sci. Rev. **6**, 115–142 (2014). https://doi.org/10.1017/S1755773912000318
38. EU Health Data Space must be individual-centric to benefit all stakeholders, https://mydata.org/2023/12/13/eu-health-data-space-must-be-individual-centric-to-benefit-all-stakeholders/. Accessed 19 Feb 2024

The Future of Ageing: The Impact of Smart Home Technologies on Ageing in Place

Lucie Schmidt[✉] and Christian Erfurth

University of Applied Sciences Jena, Jena, Germany
lucie.schmidt@eah-jena.com

Abstract. This paper presents a comprehensive analysis of the development and potential of smart home technologies to address the challenges of aging at home. By examining current trends, technologies, and their acceptance among the elderly population, the study aims to gain insights into the preferences and needs of seniors regarding intelligent living solutions. Considering a literature review, factors such as usability, security, and privacy are evaluated. The paper identifies key areas where smart home innovations can enhance the independence and quality of life for older individuals and discusses implications for future research and development. The goal is to contribute to the design of age-appropriate smart homes that are not only technologically advanced but also tailored to the specific requirements and desires of this growing user group.

Keywords: Smart home innovations · Living and ageing in place · Technology acceptance

1 Introduction

The demographic trend towards an ageing population poses new challenges for societies worldwide. According to statistics from the German Federal Statistical Office, the urgency of this challenge is clear, as the number of people aged 65 and over in Germany has already risen by 50% to 17.9 million between 1990 and 2018. Forecasts show that this figure will grow to at least 22.7 million in the next 20 years [35]. Against this backdrop, there is a growing desire among older people to live independently in their familiar homes for as long as possible. The relevance of smart home technologies arises not only from their potential to make everyday life easier through automation and remote monitoring, but also from their ability to improve quality of life through individual customization and support. Smart home technologies, which offer innovative solutions for comfortable and safe ageing at home, are therefore increasingly becoming the focus of research and development.

Despite impressive progress in this area, the question remains as to what extent these technologies are specifically geared towards the needs and challenges of ageing at home and what role acceptance and the importance of social relationships play, among other factors.

F. Phillipson et al. (Eds.): I4CS 2024, CCIS 2109, pp. 83–101, 2024.
https://doi.org/10.1007/978-3-031-60433-1_6

In this context, this paper examines smart home technologies in the categories of "health", "safety" and "comfort" to present an analysis of their development and potential. By analyzing current trends and technologies as well as their acceptance among the elderly population, this study aims to gain insights into the preferences and needs of seniors regarding smart home solutions. Implications for future research and development are also discussed. The aim is to design age-appropriate smart homes that are not only technologically advanced, but also specifically tailored to the requirements and wishes of this growing user group.

To achieve these goals, the paper focuses on the central research question: "How can current smart home technologies help to support and improve independent living for older people at home?".

By addressing this question, this paper strives to contribute to shaping the future of ageing at home, focusing on the needs and preferences of older people.

2 Basics and Methodological Approach

This section opens with a detailed account of the methodological approach of this study and explores in depth the importance of the concept of 'ageing in place' for older people, with a particular focus on the role that smart home technologies play in this. This section sets out the foundations and practical considerations necessary to understand the interaction between older residents and smart home technology. It demonstrates how smart home technologies have the potential to enhance the quality of life of older people by promoting their independence and safety by enabling adaptations in the home environment that support them to remain in their familiar surroundings for longer.

2.1 Smart Home Technologies and Independent Living in Older Age

Smart home technologies offer an integrated ecosystem of connected devices that aim to increase living comfort, improve energy efficiency, ensure security, and improve the overall quality of life for residents. These technologies enable the automation and remote control of lighting, temperature, security, access control and household appliances. By integrating information and communication technologies (ICT), smart homes can consider the individual preferences and needs of residents, which is particularly relevant in the context of supporting ageing at home. A smart home is a networked home in which various devices and systems can be automated and controlled centrally or decentrally. These technologies include, but are not limited to, systems for controlling lighting, temperature, security, and access control, as well as household appliances [3].

The demographic development in Germany (as well as in Europe) is characterized by a continuously ageing population, which is the result of increasing life expectancy and low birth rates (Federal Statistical Office). This development represents one of the greatest challenges for society, particularly regarding the health and social system. At the center of this challenge is the concept of "ageing in place", which emphasizes the importance of enabling older people to live in their familiar surroundings for as long as possible and maintain a high degree of independence.

According to the Federal Statistical Office, around one in three people in Germany is expected to be aged 65 or over by 2060. This projected demographic shift illustrates the urgency of developing effective strategies and measures to support ageing in place. "Aging in place", as described by Wiles et al. [41], refers to the phenomenon of older people wishing to remain in their familiar home environment for as long as possible rather than moving into specialized facilities. This approach supports the autonomy and independence of the older population by utilizing technology and adaptations in the home to meet individual needs as they age.

The concept of Aging in Place is not only favored from the perspective of the individual quality of life of older people, but also from a socio-economic point of view. The field of Ambient Assisted Living (AAL) technologies is significant in many respects and economically, as it not only reduces the need for care, but also specifically addresses the needs of older people. However, technological developments in the living environments of older people encompass more than just AAL technologies. Structural changes brought about by digitalization, such as the switch to digital services (e.g., online banking, telemedicine, digital government forms), often affect older people indirectly. They must deal with such changes, which challenges their possibilities and abilities and at the same time represents both solutions to problems and new challenges [33]. There is a consensus in research that the potential of age-appropriate assisting systems is still at the project stage. There are considerable challenges in implementing these systems in the everyday lives of older people. In terms of the sociology of technology, reference is made to the difficulties of using hybrid systems, which can be seen, for example, in assistance technology for independent living in old age. Comprehensive support measures are therefore required to enable ageing in place. These include structural adaptations to homes to make them age-appropriate and barrier-free, as well as the provision of outpatient care services and technological aids. Technologies such as emergency call systems, automated household aids and telemedical services can help older people to live safely and independently for longer.

The realization of "Aging in Place" requires a comprehensive approach that encompasses both the building infrastructure and social and health support systems. Investment in the adaptation of housing and the development of innovative technologies are just as important as the creation of social support networks and the promotion of community activities that enable older people to participate in social life.

In conclusion, it can be said that the promotion of "ageing in place" offers an opportunity to improve the quality of life of older people and at the same time reduce the burden on the health and social system. The demographic development in Germany requires a rethink and the development of sustainable concepts that enable older people to live in their familiar surroundings for as long as possible. Appropriate measures and the integration of assistive technologies can make it possible to overcome the challenges of an ageing society and enable older people to lead independent and fulfilling lives.

2.2 Methodological Approach

In this literature review, the focus was on analyzing the needs, requirements, and barriers of older people in the context of smart home technologies as well as researching current smart home technologies and products in the areas of health, comfort, and safety. Another key aspect of this work was to analyze future developments in the smart home sector within these three categories. The aim was to paint a comprehensive picture of the current state, future directions and potential of these technologies that could support and improve the lives of older people.

The search for relevant literature and product information was supplemented by a broad search of academic databases such as Google Scholar, PubMed, IEEE Xplore and Scopus, supported by information from technology developers. The search terms used included general terms such as "smart home" and "ageing in place" as well as specific keywords such as "future of smart home technologies", "innovative living solutions" and "trend analyses in the smart home sector".

Sources that explicitly address future developments and innovations in the areas of health, comfort and security were selected for inclusion in the analysis. This included scientific studies that present novel approaches and technologies and address future market trends and product innovations. This approach enabled the current state of research and development as well as predicted trends and challenges for the integration of smart home technologies into the lives of older people to be captured.

Following the careful selection of relevant literature sources and information on future developments, a detailed analysis was conducted with the aim of gaining insights into the directions in which smart home technologies could develop. Particular attention was paid to the potential arising from the use of innovative technologies and concepts to promote living and ageing in place. Both the technological possibilities and the associated challenges were considered.

The synthesis of these findings made it possible to draw a comprehensive picture of future development paths in the field of smart home technologies and to analyze their potential impact on the quality of life of older people. The results of this work provide valuable insights for researchers, developers and decision-makers involved in the design of future smart home solutions and help to lay the foundations for technologies that meet the needs and requirements of older people.

3   Overview of Smart Home Technologies

Smart home technologies have become an integral part of modern living, especially in the context of ageing at home. These technologies can be divided into various categories, each of which is designed to address and improve specific aspects of domesticity. The categories selected for the study include health, safety, and comfort. Each of these categories encompasses a range of technological developments that aim to improve the well-being and quality of life of older people in their homes.

3.1   Health

Smart home technologies in the healthcare sector encompass a wide range of applications and devices that aim to optimize health management, prevention, and the detection of health risks. They range from wearables that monitor vital data to complex systems that can intelligently adapt the living environment to the needs of their users. The core idea behind the use of these technologies is to promote the independence and safety of users through continuous monitoring and automated assistance systems.

Specific smart home technologies from the health sector are described (Table 1):

Table 1. Smart home technologies in the "Health" category

Smart-Home-Technology	Description
Wearables	Devices such as fitness trackers and smartwatches that monitor vital signs such as heart rate, step count, sleep quality and sometimes even blood oxygen levels. Well-known examples are the Apple Watch, Fitbit devices and Samsung Galaxy Watches
Smart Health Monitors	This category includes blood pressure monitors, blood glucose meters and thermometers that are connected to the internet. They allow users to track their health data and share it with their healthcare provider if necessary. Examples include the Withings blood pressure monitor[1] and the smart thermometer from Kinsa[2]
Medication dispensers	Smart medication dispensers can help to monitor medication intake and send reminders to ensure adherence to the medication schedule. One example is the Hero[3] medication dispenser
Fall detection systems	Some smartwatches and specialized wearables are equipped with fall detection systems[4] that can automatically make an emergency call if the wearer falls and is unable to call for help themselves. The Apple Watch Series 4 and newer, for example, offers this function
Smart home assistants	Voice-controlled assistants such as Amazon Echo and Google Home can be used for health monitoring by sending medication reminders, suggesting fitness routines, or providing quick access to emergency services
Telemedicine and virtual consultations	Some smart home platforms offer integrations with telemedicine services that allow users to conduct virtual doctor visits directly from home

The integration of smart home technologies in the healthcare sector, particularly to support older people, has gained considerable attention in recent years.

---

[1] https://www.withings.com/it/en/blood-pressure-monitors.

[2] https://www.home.kinsahealth.com/shop.

[3] https://www.herohealth.com/our-product/.

[4] https://www.support.apple.com/en-us/108896.

Wearables and **smart health monitors** are crucial for the continuous monitoring of vital signs and offer the possibility of recognizing health anomalies at an early stage. These devices, ranging from fitness wristbands to specialized medical monitoring devices, collect important data such as heart rate, blood pressure or blood sugar levels, which are essential for preventive healthcare. However, their development and use in the context of smart homes requires careful consideration of user-friendliness and data protection aspects in order to ensure broad acceptance [40].

Medication dispensers help to improve medication adherence by reminding users to take their medication on time. This technology is particularly beneficial for older people who may be faced with managing multiple medications. The challenge is to make these systems intuitive and accessible to ensure they can be used effectively [25].

Fall detection systems provide a critical safety function by detecting falls and automatically calling for help. This technology can be lifesaving, especially for elderly people living alone [17]. However, it must be integrated into smart home systems in such a way that false alarms are minimized, and user privacy is protected.

Smart home assistants, such as Amazon Echo or Google Home, facilitate interaction with the smart home through voice commands and can be used for health monitoring, for example by sending reminders to take medication or providing quick access to emergency services. The challenge here is to ensure that voice recognition is precise and accessible to users of all ages [32].

Telemedicine and **virtual consultations** have proven to be particularly valuable in enabling older people to access medical advice directly from their homes. These technologies reduce the need for physical visits to the doctor while providing access to a wide range of healthcare services [21]. However, implementation must consider the technological capabilities and preferences of end users to ensure effective utilization.

The role of smart home technologies in healthcare for older people is invaluable, but also brings challenges that need to be addressed. Data protection, user-friendliness and integration into existing healthcare systems are crucial factors for the success of these technologies. Careful and user-centered development and implementation are required to fully realize the potential of smart home technologies and achieve an elevated level of user acceptance and satisfaction. Further development and research in this area must continue to develop innovative solutions that meet the requirements of an ageing society.

3.2 Security

Smart home technologies are transforming the way we live by bringing increased security to our living spaces. By integrating intelligent devices and systems, residents can monitor, control, and automate their homes in innovative ways. These technologies not only offer the convenience of remote control of household functions, but also play a crucial role in ensuring the safety and security of residents. Below we take a detailed look at various smart home security technology devices.

Specific smart home technologies from the security sector are described (Table 2):

Table 2. Smart home technologies in the "Security" category

Smart-Home-Technology	Description
Smart Locks	Smart locks allow residents to lock and unlock their doors remotely via a smartphone app. Many models offer additional security features such as access logs that show who have entered or left the house and when, and the ability to create temporary access codes for visitors or service providers
Video doorbells	Video doorbells are equipped with cameras that allow residents to see and communicate with visitors at the front door, even when they are not at home. Some models offer motion detection and send notifications to the resident's smartphone when someone approaches the door
Surveillance cameras	Modern indoor and outdoor surveillance cameras offer live streaming, motion detection, night vision and sometimes even facial recognition. The recorded videos can be stored in the cloud so that residents can access them at any time
Sensors for water leaks	Water leakage sensors can monitor vulnerable areas in the home and alert residents immediately if a leak is detected to prevent water damage. Some systems can even switch off the main water valve automatically
Smoke and carbon monoxide detectors	Smart smoke and carbon monoxide detectors can not only trigger loud alarms, but also send notifications to residents' smartphones. This enables a quick response, even if the occupants are not at home
Motion sensors	Motion sensors can help monitor unattended areas in and around the home. They can be integrated with other smart home systems to trigger actions such as switching on lights or sending alarms when motion is detected
Emergency call systems	Emergency call systems specially designed for older people or people with health restrictions enable users to call for help quickly in an emergency. These systems can be designed as wearable devices (e.g. bracelets or necklaces) and often have a direct link to emergency services or family members

Smart locks and **video doorbells** improve access convenience and enable effective monitoring of the entrance area. However, dependence on such technologies can lead to problems if the internet connection fails or in the event of technical faults. There is also a risk of hackers gaining access to these systems and compromising the security of the building.

Surveillance cameras make an important contribution to deterring potential burglars and monitoring the domestic environment. However, permanent surveillance and data storage raise questions about data protection and personal freedom. The balance between security and privacy is an essential aspect that needs to be carefully considered [12].

While **water leakage sensors** and **smoke and carbon monoxide detectors** offer an elevated level of protection against domestic hazards, their effectiveness depends heavily on the reliability of the systems and regular maintenance. False alarms or the absence of alarms due to technical faults can be both an inconvenience and a potential risk.

Motion sensors and **emergency call systems** are particularly useful for older people or people with health restrictions. Nevertheless, it is crucial that these technologies are easy to use and do not create additional complexity or stress factors in users' everyday lives.

Smart home technologies in the security sector undoubtedly offer numerous advantages by simplifying the monitoring and control of home security. However, it is essential to be aware of the associated risks and challenges. The development of future smart home systems requires a balanced approach that considers both security and privacy. Ongoing research and improvement of security standards are crucial to fully exploit the potential of these technologies without jeopardizing the rights and well-being of users.

3.3 Comfort

Smart home technologies have the potential to significantly simplify everyday life through automation and remote control of household functions. While these technologies undoubtedly bring convenience and efficiency to living spaces, it is equally crucial to recognize potential challenges and limitations. Below, we discuss both the benefits and drawbacks of key technologies such as smart thermostats, smart lighting systems or smart curtains and blinds.

Specific smart home technologies from the comfort sector are described (Table 3):

Table 3. Smart home technologies in the "Comfort" category

Smart-Home-Technology	Description
Intelligent thermostats	These devices learn the temperature preferences of the occupants and automatically adjust the heating or cooling to ensure optimum room temperatures. They can also be controlled on the move via an app, allowing users to adjust the temperature of their home before they arrive
Smart lighting systems	Smart lighting solutions allow users to personalize the lighting in their home by adjusting the brightness and color temperature of the lights via smartphone apps or voice commands. Some systems can also be automatically adjusted according to daylight or occupant activity

(continued)

Table 3. (*continued*)

Smart-Home-Technology	Description
Voice assistants	These devices allow users to interact with their smart home through voice commands. They can be used to control lights, thermostats, media playback and other connected devices, allowing easy and intuitive control of the smart home
Smart sockets and switches	These products can transform conventional household appliances into smart devices by providing the ability to remotely switch appliances on and off or create schedules for their operation
Robot hoovers and mops	These autonomous cleaning devices keep the home clean without the residents having to clean it themselves. They can be programmed to clean at specific times and some models can even be controlled via an app
Smart curtains and blinds	These products can be automatically opened or closed according to the time of day or light conditions to improve energy efficiency and increase living comfort

Intelligent thermostats and **smart lighting systems** improve access comfort by enabling effective control of room temperature and lighting. However, their dependence on technology can lead to problems if the internet connection fails or in the event of technical faults. There is also a risk that the collection of user data could compromise privacy. Research shows that smart thermostats and lighting systems can significantly increase energy efficiency, but privacy concerns must be carefully addressed [31].

Voice assistants make an important contribution to simplifying the control of the smart home. However, constant monitoring and data collection raise questions about data protection and personal freedom. The balance between convenience and privacy is a key aspect that needs to be carefully weighed up. Research has shown that voice assistants such as Amazon Echo and Google Home have the potential to make everyday life much easier but raise concerns about constant listening and data storage [27].

While **smart sockets, switches,** and **robotic hoovers** offer a high level of convenience by automating everyday tasks, their effectiveness depends heavily on the reliability of the systems and regular maintenance. Malfunctions or failure to function due to technical faults can be both an inconvenience and a potential risk. A study by Cheng & Lee [9] shows that smart sockets and switches can improve energy management in households but require a robust network infrastructure.

Smart curtains and blinds are particularly useful for automated adjustment to time of day or temperature. However, it is crucial that these technologies are easy to use and do not create additional complexity or stress factors in users' daily lives. Researchers have found that smart curtains and blinds increase home comfort, but the initial cost and installation effort is a barrier for some households [3].

4   User-Centered: Needs and Preferences of the Older Generation

The integration of smart home technologies into the lives of older adults represents a significant opportunity to improve their quality of life, independence, and safety in their own homes. However, a sound consideration of the needs and preferences of this user group is essential to design and implement the technologies accordingly. The research literature offers valuable insights into the factors that influence the adoption and acceptance of such technologies. By critically analyzing these studies, it is possible to draw a comprehensive picture of the specific requirements and barriers that need to be considered during development.

The research literature, such as the studies by Lou et al. [23] and Bušatlić et al. [5], shows that older people are open to innovative technologies in principle, but that the decision to adopt them depends largely on their perceived usefulness, user-friendliness, and recognizable added value in everyday life. These findings emphasize the importance of designing technologies in such a way that they are intuitive to use and offer clear added value. This perspective is complemented by the study by Harris et al. [18], which examines the use and learning preferences of older adults regarding smartphones and digital home assistants. Their findings shed light on current adoption rates and provide important insights for the design of these technologies, specifically for older adults.

The specific requirements of older users primarily include safety, comfort, and support for independence, as studies by Nicholls & Strengers [26] and Putrada et al. [29] show. These requirements reflect the desire to be able to live independently in their own home for as long as possible. At the same time, the literature also addresses barriers such as physical limitations, data protection and security concerns and technology anxiety [5].

Research by Lou et al. [23] highlights how smart thermostats can use machine learning to enable individual adjustment of room temperature to optimize comfort and energy efficiency without overwhelming users with complex settings. Similarly, Putrada et al. [29] show that intelligent lighting systems that adapt to the time of day and activities of residents can not only increase living comfort but also contribute to energy savings. Nicholls and Strengers [26] also point out the potential impact of robotic hoovers on household management and discuss how such devices can make everyday life easier.

A critical analysis of the research findings by Arthanat et al. [2] and Cao et al. [6] shows that the successful adoption of smart home technologies by older people depends on a complex interplay of several factors. These include technology familiarity, security and privacy concerns, ease of use, cultural values, and the availability of support. According to Cao et al. [6], it is training and a staunch support system that can empower older adults in their decision to adopt technology. Pirzada et al. [28] discuss ethical and acceptance challenges that lead to low adoption of health technologies, especially in relation to smart homes for older people. They emphasize that technologies must be personalized to protect their dignity and independence [28].

Table 4 summarizes the key barriers and specific challenges faced by older people that influence the adoption of smart home technologies:

Table 4. Key barriers and specific requirements of older smart home users

Key barriers	Specific requirements
Technology anxiety and lack of confidence	Safety, comfort, and support of independence
Physical and cognitive limitations	Simplicity, user-friendliness, and non-invasiveness
Lack of knowledge and support	Personalization and adaptation to individual needs
Lack of customization to individual needs and data protection concerns	Cultural sensitivity and social support

Overcoming these barriers requires the development of smart home technologies that are not only user-friendly and easy to learn, but also customizable. Transparent communication about data protection and security is essential to build trust and reduce concerns. A multidisciplinary approach that integrates these dimensions is therefore essential for the design of successful technologies.

The key findings can be summarized as follows:

- Technology design must prioritize perceived usefulness and ease of use to encourage wider adoption.
- Security and privacy concerns require transparent communication strategies and the integration of robust security features.
- Personalization and adaptability of technologies are critical to meet the diverse needs and abilities of older users.

This results in the following practical recommendations:

- Develop interfaces that are intuitive to use even without extensive technical knowledge.
- Strengthen trust in smart home technologies through clear data protection guidelines and security guarantees.
- Implement customization options that allow technologies to be personalized according to individual preferences.

Taking the needs and preferences of the older generation into account when developing and introducing smart home technologies is crucial. By focusing on user-centricity and overcoming barriers, technologies can be created that not only improve the quality of life of older people, but also promote their independence and safety in their own homes. A critical analysis of the research findings suggests that a deep understanding of the specific requirements and barriers is essential for the design of successful and accepted smart home solutions.

5   Future Developments in the Smart Home Sector

5.1   Smart Home Developments

Future developments in the smart home sector, particularly in the categories of health, comfort, and safety, promise a significant improvement in the quality of life of older people from a technical perspective. The integration of innovative technologies such as artificial intelligence (AI), the Internet of Things (IoT) and wearables opens new possibilities for independent and safe living in one's own home.

Health. Health monitoring in smart homes is a dynamic and fast-growing field of research that has the potential to revolutionize the way older people receive medical care and support. The integration of technologies such as IoT devices, wearables and artificial intelligence offers unprecedented opportunities for continuous monitoring and initiative-taking healthcare in the home [16]. However, with these advances come challenges and critical considerations that are both technical and ethical in nature.

The benefits of improved health monitoring through smart home technologies are manifold. By continuously recording vital data such as heart rate, blood pressure and activity levels, abnormalities can be recognized early, and preventative measures can be initiated before serious health problems occur. This promises not only to improve the quality of life for the individual, but also to reduce the burden on the healthcare system by reducing hospital stays and optimizing medical care.

Despite these benefits, the implementation of health monitoring technologies in smart homes raises important questions regarding privacy, data security and user autonomy [37]. The collection and analysis of personal health data requires strict data protection measures to ensure that this information is protected from misuse. In addition, acceptance of such technologies among older people is often a challenge due to concerns about ease of use, trust in the technology and fear of surveillance and loss of privacy.

Another critical aspect of health monitoring in smart homes is the need to design these technologies in a way that not only monitors but also empowers users. Smart systems should be designed to provide users with understandable feedback and recommendations to help them actively manage their health and improve their wellbeing. This requires careful tailoring of the technology to the individual needs and preferences of users to ensure that the systems are perceived as supportive and not intrusive.

Future developments in the field of health monitoring in smart homes are likely to increasingly rely on the integration of AI-based analytics tools. Research is focused on improving interoperability between different devices and systems to enable comprehensive and seamless health monitoring. A multidisciplinary approach that combines expertise from the fields of technology, medicine, ethics, and design is crucial to develop solutions that are effective, safe, trustworthy and user-friendly [24].

The discussion on health monitoring in smart homes shows that the key to a successful implementation of these technologies lies in the balance between technological innovations and the ethical, social, and personal needs of users. A multidisciplinary approach that combines expertise from the fields of technology, medicine, ethics, and design is crucial in order to develop solutions that are not only effective, but also safe, trustworthy and user-friendly.

Security. Security in smart homes is a crucial aspect that is increasingly at the center of research and development, especially in the context of ageing at home. The integration of security technologies in smart homes not only offers protection against external threats such as burglaries, but also addresses internal risks, for example through the early detection of health emergencies or the prevention of accidents in the home. These technologies range from simple alarm and monitoring systems to advanced sensor networks and artificial intelligence that offer a comprehensive security solution [4].

A critical point of discussion in smart home security concerns the balance between effective surveillance and privacy protection. While technologies such as cameras and motion sensors have the potential to significantly improve security, they also raise questions about data collection and use. The key lies in developing systems that collect minimal data to fulfil their function while implementing strong encryption and privacy measures to protect residents' information [7, 13].

Another important aspect is the user-friendliness of the security systems. For older people, it is particularly important that technologies are not only effective but also easy to use. Complex systems can function as a deterrent and reduce their acceptance. Future developments should therefore focus on intuitive user interfaces and automated systems that require little to no manual interaction [11].

The role of artificial intelligence (AI) in the security of smart homes is also an area of intensive research. AI systems can learn behavioral patterns and distinguish normal activities from potential dangers. This enables more precise detection of anomalies and minimizes false alarms, resulting in more efficient and less intrusive monitoring. However, the use of AI also requires careful consideration of ethical aspects, especially regarding decisions made automatically based on behavioral data [13].

Interdisciplinary collaboration between technology developers, security experts, ethicists and end-users is critical to developing smart home security systems that are both effective and respectful of the needs and rights of residents. The future of smart home security lies in solutions that are not only technologically advanced, but also ethically defensible and user-centered [28].

In summary, ensuring security in smart homes requires a careful balance between implementing effective security measures and protecting the privacy and autonomy of residents. Developing security technologies that achieve this balance is both a key challenge and a significant opportunity for the future of housing, particularly for older people and other vulnerable groups who can benefit from the possibilities of a safe and supportive living environment.

Comfort. The future of comfort in smart homes is on the cusp of significant technological advances that have the potential to fundamentally change the way older people and residents in broad experience their home environment. Three principal areas are emerging that are receiving particular attention in scientific research: the further development of technologies to improve living conditions, the integration of security systems to ensure well-being and the use of IoT technologies to create a seamless and intuitive living experience.

A central aspect of future comfort in smart homes is the personalized adaptation of living conditions to the individual needs and preferences of residents. The development of intelligent thermostats and lighting systems based on machine learning and semantic technologies already shows how far the possibilities in this area extend. Such systems can not only optimally regulate temperature and lighting, but also control air quality and humidity to create an ideal living environment [34]. The challenge is to further develop these technologies so that they can intuitively understand and implement the complex and often unspoken needs of residents.

Security in smart homes is intricately linked to the comfort of the residents. Advances in sensor technology and artificial intelligence make it possible not only to recognize potential break-ins, but also to identify and respond to health emergencies at an early stage. The critical discussion here centers on the balance between security and privacy. While technological capabilities to monitor and protect residents are constantly growing, it is crucial that these technologies follow ethical guidelines and respect the autonomy and privacy of users [8].

The Internet of Things (IoT) plays a key role in the development of smart homes that take comfort to a new level. The networking of various devices and systems in the home creates opportunities for a highly personalized and responsive living environment. However, we also face challenges here: The interoperability between devices from different manufacturers, the security of the networked systems and the user-friendliness of the control elements are decisive factors that will determine the success of these technologies [1].

A critical examination of future developments in comfort in smart homes makes it clear that the key to successful innovations lies in the careful balancing of technological possibilities and the needs of users. Close collaboration between technology developers, architects, healthcare professionals and the occupants themselves is essential to create solutions that are not only technically sophisticated, but also useful and desirable in real-world applications [15]. The future of home comfort in smart homes therefore depends not only on technological advances, but also on our ability to use these technologies responsibly and for the benefit of users.

5.2   Assessment of the Future of Ageing at Home

The future of ageing at home, decisively influenced by advances in smart home technologies, harbors a complex interplay of opportunities and challenges. These technologies promise to significantly improve the quality of life of older people by providing support in the areas of health monitoring, safety, and comfort. At the same time, we must face up to the associated social, ethical, and technical challenges.

Sociological perspectives emphasize the potential of smart home technologies to strengthen the autonomy and safety of older people by enabling longer-term independence in their own homes. The implementation of environmental and wearable sensors that can monitor health data, recognize emergencies, and facilitate everyday tasks is a key factor in promoting a self-determined life in old age [24]. However, these technological advances also raise critical questions. Data protection and data security are of crucial importance, as the collection and processing of sensitive data entails risks to the privacy and autonomy of users. The design of human-technology interaction requires careful consideration to ensure that technologies are user-friendly and accessible without promoting social isolation or overburdening users [28].

The positive aspects of smart home technologies are manifold. They range from improving health monitoring and increasing safety to promoting social contacts through technologically supported means of communication. These aspects make a significant contribution to enabling older people to remain in their familiar surroundings for longer, which both supports their desire for independence and contributes to their mental and physical health. Nevertheless, the negative aspects should not be underestimated. The risk of social isolation, being overwhelmed by complex technologies and the potential stigmatization of older people as technologically incompetent are serious problems [8]. These aspects require careful consideration and the development of strategies that both promote the technological competence of older people and ensure that technologies support rather than replace their social needs.

The future challenges and opportunities lie in developing a balanced approach that maximizes the benefits of smart home technologies while minimizing the risks. This requires a multidisciplinary approach that integrates the perspectives of technology developers, social scientists, ethicists, and older people themselves. The future of ageing at home should foster an environment that is not only technologically advanced but also socially inclusive, recognizing older people as active participants and shapers of their own living space [13]. Meeting this challenge will not only change the way we age, but also redefine the role of technology in our lives.

6 Reflection and Outlook

As part of this paper, which was guided by the central research question "How can current smart home technologies help to support and improve independent living for older people at home?", the potential and limitations of smart home technologies in the areas of health, safety, and comfort in the context of ageing at home were analyzed in detail. By critically analyzing empirical studies it was possible to develop a detailed understanding of the complex interplay between technological innovation and the needs of older people. This reflection makes it possible to draw well-founded conclusions about the potential applications and challenges of smart home technologies in the context of ageing.

The analysis makes it clear that a multidimensional approach is essential to utilize the full potential of smart home technologies to support independent living for older people. In the healthcare sector in particular, technologies such as IoT devices and wearables offer innovative opportunities for initiative-taking health management. At the same time, however, they raise important questions regarding data protection, autonomy, and user acceptance. Security technologies that protect against external and internal risks need to balance privacy protection with effective monitoring capabilities. In the area of comfort, intelligent thermostats and lighting systems show the potential to significantly improve the quality of living but pose challenges in terms of user-friendliness and adaptability to individual needs.

A central result of this work is the realization that the design of smart home technologies that meet the requirements of older people requires a pronounced user-centric approach. This should prioritize the autonomy, dignity, and data protection of users. The development of future technologies must therefore pursue a comprehensive approach that harmonizes technical innovations with ethical considerations and the preferences of end users.

The further development of smart home technologies faces the challenge of developing innovative solutions that are both ethically justifiable and technologically advanced. The ongoing integration of artificial intelligence and machine learning offers promising prospects for adaptive and intuitive smart home environments but requires careful consideration of data protection and ethical aspects. Interdisciplinary research that combines technology, gerontology, and ethics is crucial to develop solutions that meet the needs of older people and sustainably improve their quality of life.

The involvement of municipalities is a possible starting point for the successful further development and implementation of smart home technologies to enable older people to live independently. As an interface between technology providers, older users, and social services, communities can play a key role in increasing acceptance and confidence in these technologies. By providing information resources and organizing training programs, they help to break down barriers. In addition, pilot projects and model homes, such as the smart neighborhood in Jena-Lobeda ("Smartes Quartier Jena-Lobeda") as part of Smart City Jena, provide insights into the practical application and illustrate the benefits of these technologies. Such initiatives not only provide valuable feedback from users but also serve as a model for further implementations on the municipal side. It is therefore important that the projects are not only focused on short-term goals but also take sustainability and scalability into account. The continuous review and adaptation of the measures, based on user feedback and technological developments, ensures that the solutions also meet the needs of older people in the long term and can be applied beyond individual neighborhoods.

In the context of the research results, future studies should be based on quantitative data. This should serve to validate and deepen the insights gained. Theoretical models such as the Technology Acceptance Model (TAM) [10] and the Unified Theory of Acceptance and Use of Technology (UTAUT) [39] appear to be particularly important here. These provide a sound framework for analyzing the acceptance factors of these technologies among older user groups in more detail. These models' emphasis on perceived usefulness, ease of use, social influence and supporting conditions is critical to understanding the complex mechanisms behind technology acceptance among older people.

Future work should also pay particular attention to the cost and maintenance burden of smart home technologies. The financial and practical challenges associated with purchase, installation, customization, and ongoing maintenance are major barriers to the acceptance and use of these technologies. An in-depth study of cost structures, customization and maintenance could be crucial in developing solutions that are not only cost-effective and minimal maintenance, but also consider the financial and practical realities of older people.

To summarize, smart home technologies have the potential to support and improve independent living for older people by providing innovative solutions in the areas of health, safety, and comfort. The active involvement of communities and the development of user-centered, ethically sound smart home solutions are essential for promoting the autonomy and well-being of older people in their own homes. Ongoing research and development in this area must consider the dynamic demands of an ageing society and produce innovative technologies that bridge the gap between technological advances and individual needs.

Acknowledgments. This study is part of the project Multi-Generation Smart Community (mGeSCo). The project is funded by the Carl Zeiss Foundation.

Disclosure of Interests. The authors have no competing interests to declare that are relevant to the content of this article.

References

1. Alonazi, W., Hamdi, H., Azim, N., El-aziz, A.: SDN architecture for smart homes security with machine learning and deep learning. Int. J. Adv. Comput. Sci. Appl. **13** (2022)
2. Arthanat, S., Wilcox, J., Macuch, M.: Profiles and predictors of smart home technology adoption by older adults. OTJR (Thorofare N J) **39**, 247–256 (2018)
3. Balta-Ozkan, N., Davidson, R., Bicket, M., Whitmarsh, L.: Social barriers to the adoption of smart homes. Energy Policy **63**, 363–374 (2013)
4. Batalla, J., Vasilakos, A., Gajewski, M.: Secure smart homes. ACM Comput. Surv. (CSUR) **50**, 1–32 (2017)
5. Bušatlić, S., et al.: Smart homes and voice activated systems for disabled people. Convergence: The International Journal of Research into New Media Technologies (2017)
6. Cao, Y., Erdt, M., Robert, C., Naharudin, N., Lee, S., Theng, Y.: Decision-Making Factors towards Adoption of Smart Home Sensors by Older Adults: An Intervention Study in Singapore (Preprint). JMIR Aging (2021)
7. Chakravorty, A., Wlodarczyk, T., Rong, C.: Privacy preserving data analytics for smart homes. In: 2013 IEEE Security and Privacy Workshops, pp. 23–27 (2013)
8. Chan, M., Estève, D., Escriba, C., Campo, E.: A review of smart homes - present state and future challenges. Comput. Methods Programs Biomed. **91**(1), 55–81 (2008)
9. Cheng, C., Lee, D.: Enabling smart air conditioning by sensor development: a review. Sensors (Basel, Switzerland) **16**, 2028 (2016)
10. Davis, F.D.: Perceived usefulness, perceived ease of use, and user acceptance of information technology. MIS Q. **13**(3), 319–340 (1989)
11. Demiris, G., Hensel, B., Skubic, M., Rantz, M.: Senior residents' perceived need of and preferences for "smart home" sensor technologies. Int. J. Technol. Assess. Health Care **24**, 120–124 (2008)
12. Fleck, S., Straßer, W.: Smart camera based monitoring system and its application to assisted living. Proc. IEEE **96**, 1698–1714 (2008)
13. Gochoo, M., Alnajjar, F.S., Tan, T., Khalid, S.: Towards privacy-preserved aging in place: a systematic review. Sensors (Basel, Switzerland) **21**, 3082 (2021)
14. Guan, K., Shao, M., Wu, S.: A remote health monitoring system for the elderly based on smart home gateway. J. Healthcare Eng. **2017**, 1 (2017)
15. Gubbi, J., Buyya, R., Marusic, S., Palaniswami, M.: Internet of Things (IoT): a vision, architectural elements, and future directions. ArXiv, abs/1207.0203 (2012)
16. Guizani, K., Guizani, S.: IoT healthcare monitoring systems overview for elderly population. Int. Wirel. Commun. Mob. Comput. (IWCMC) **2020**, 2005–2009 (2020)

17. Haghi, M., Spicher, N., Wang, J., Deserno, T.: Integrated sensing devices for disease prevention and health alerts in smart homes. Stud. Health Technol. Inform. **291**, 39–61 (2022)
18. Harris, M.T., Blocker, K.A., Rogers, W.A.: Older adults and smart technology: facilitators and barriers to use. Front. Comp. Sci. **4**, 835927 (2022)
19. Hossain, M.: Patient status monitoring for smart home healthcare. In: 2016 IEEE International Conference on Multimedia & Expo Workshops (ICMEW), pp. 1–6 (2016)
20. Jarvis, M., Sartorius, B., Chipps, J.: Technology acceptance of older persons living in residential care. Inf. Dev. **36**(3), 339–353 (2020)
21. Jung, Y.: Hybrid-aware model for senior wellness service in smart home. Sensors (Basel, Switzerland), 17, 1182 (2017)
22. Lee, C., Coughlin, J.: PERSPECTIVE: older adults' adoption of technology: an integrated approach to identifying determinants and barriers. J. Prod. Innov. Manag. **32**(5), 747–759 (2015)
23. Lou, R., Hallinan, K.P., Huang, K., Reissman, T.: Smart wifi thermostat-enabled thermal comfort control in residences. Sustainability **2020**, 12 (1919)
24. Majumder, S., et al.: Smart homes for elderly healthcare-recent advances and research challenges. Sensors (Basel, Switzerland) **17**(11), 2496 (2017)
25. Nath, R., Thapliyal, H.: Wearable health monitoring system for older adults in a smart home environment. In: 2021 IEEE Computer Society Annual Symposium on VLSI (ISVLSI), pp. 390–395 (2021)
26. Nicholls, L., Strengers, Y.: Do robotic vacuum cleaners save energy? Raising cleanliness conventions and energy demand in Australian households with smart home technologies. Energy Research & Social Science (2019)
27. Perez, A., Zeadally, S., Cochran, J.: A review and an empirical analysis of privacy policy and notices for consumer Internet of things. Secur. Priv. **1**, e15 (2018)
28. Pirzada, P., Wilde, A., Doherty, G., Harris-Birtill, D.: Ethics and acceptance of smart homes for older adults. Inform. Health Soc. Care **47**, 10–37 (2021)
29. Putrada, A.G., Abdurohman, M., Perdana, D., Nuha, H.H.: Machine learning methods in smart lighting toward achieving user comfort: a survey. IEEE Access **10**, 45137–45178 (2022). https://doi.org/10.1109/ACCESS.2022.3169765
30. Salman, L., et al.: Energy efficient IoT-based smart home. In: 2016 IEEE 3rd World Forum on Internet of Things (WF-IoT), pp. 526–529 (2016)
31. Soheilian, M., Fischl, G., Aries, M.: Smart lighting application for energy saving and user well-being in the residential environment. Sustainability **13**, 6198 (2021)
32. Sokullu, R., Akkaş, M., Demir, E.: IoT supported smart home for the elderly. Internet Things **11**, 100239 (2020)
33. Suden, W.: Digitale Teilhabe im Alter: Aktivierung oder Diskriminierung? In: Stadelbacher, S., Schneider, W. (eds.) Lebenswirklichkeiten des Alter(n)s, pp. 267–289. Springer, Wiesbaden (2020). https://doi.org/10.1007/978-3-658-29073-3_9
34. Spoladore, D., Mahroo, A., Sacco, M.: Leveraging ontology to enable indoor comfort customization in the smart home. In: Cuzzocrea, A., Greco, S., Larsen, H.L., Saccà, D., Andreasen, T., Christiansen, H. (eds.) FQAS 2019. LNCS (LNAI), vol. 11529, pp. 63–74. Springer, Cham (2019). https://doi.org/10.1007/978-3-030-27629-4_9
35. Statistisches Bundesamt. https://www.destatis.de/DE/Themen/Querschnitt/Demografischer-Wandel/Aeltere-Menschen/anstieg-aeltere.html. Accessed 28 Feb 2024
36. Tang, S., Kalavally, V., Ng, K., Parkkinen, J.: Development of a prototype smart home intelligent lighting control architecture using sensors onboard a mobile computing system. Energy Build. **138**, 368–376 (2017)
37. Townsend, D., Knoefel, F., Goubran, R.: Privacy versus autonomy: a tradeoff model for smart home monitoring technologies. In: 2011 Annual International Conference of the IEEE Engineering in Medicine and Biology Society, pp. 4749–4752 (2011)

38. Vaportzis, E., Giatsi Clausen, M., Gow, A.: Older adults perceptions of technology and barriers to interacting with tablet computers: a focus group study. Front. Psychol. **8**, 1687 (2017)
39. Venkatesh, V., Morris, M.G., Davis, G.B., Davis, F.D.: User acceptance of information technology: toward a unified view. MIS Q. **27**(3), 425–478 (2003)
40. Wang, Z., Yang, Z., Dong, T.: A review of wearable technologies for elderly care that can accurately track indoor position, recognize physical activities and monitor vital signs in real time. Sensors (Basel, Switzerland) **17**, 341 (2017)
41. Wiles, J.L., Leibing, A., Guberman, N., Reeve, J., Allen, R.E.S.: The meaning of "aging in place" to older people. Gerontologist **52**(3), 357–366 (2012)

Examining Smart Neighborhood Platforms: A Qualitative Exploration of Features and Applications

Sabrina Hölzer[(✉)] and Christian Erfurth

University of Applied Sciences Jena, Jena, Germany
Sabrina.hoelzer@eahjena.com

Abstract. Smart neighborhood platforms have emerged as innovative solutions to address the challenges of urbanization and as smart living approaches to create sustainable, interconnected communities. This study aims to provide a qualitative exploration of multiple smart neighborhood platform initiatives in the German speaking region. The research examines the diverse characteristics, features and capabilities offered by these platforms, as well as their potential application in various aspects of smart community living. Qualitative research methods are employed to identify key parameters. Additionally, the study investigates the practical application of these platforms, ranging from optimizing resource consumption and improving quality of life to enhancing social interactions and fostering social cohesion and sustainable behaviors. The findings contribute to a deeper understanding of the design and applications of smart neighborhood platforms, providing valuable insights for further research as well as urban planners, policymakers, and technology developers seeking to create smarter and more livable communities.

Keywords: Smart neighborhood · Smart community · Neighborhood platforms · Platform analysis · Sustainable urban development

1 Introduction

Nebenan.de, Nextdoors.com, BeUnity.app, and Nachbarschafts.net are just examples on digital platforms that have emerged in the German-speaking region to facilitate various forms of neighborhood engagement. These platforms adopt the principles of social media networks but differ in that they focus on hybrid networking and offer exchange, and other features based on geographical proximity [1]. In discussions related to the subject of community living and aging, these platforms have sparked considerable debate. Neighborhood platforms are particularly significant because they provide individuals with a valuable opportunity to share their experiences and perspectives, thereby promoting empathy and understanding among users. Moreover, these platforms empower individuals to actively participate in collective or social actions, fostering a sense of community and shared purpose [2–4].

© The Author(s), under exclusive license to Springer Nature Switzerland AG 2024
F. Phillipson et al. (Eds.): I4CS 2024, CCIS 2109, pp. 102–117, 2024.
https://doi.org/10.1007/978-3-031-60433-1_7

The growing interest in digital platforms for neighborhood networking can be attributed to the significance of neighborhood development. The concept of neighborhood development has a universal appeal and is reflected in various terms used in different countries. In Germany, the term Quartier is commonly used, while in neighboring countries like Switzerland and Austria, Quartier or Siedlung are used. In France, the terms quartier or cartier are used, and the concept can also be found under the notion of urban villages or district in some cases [5]. Neighborhood itself plays a crucial role as it has proven to be an important approach in addressing societal challenges at the community level [6]. This has also sparked political debates surrounding the topic.

The concept of neighborhood development is intricately linked to the digitalization of communities. However, it extends beyond that and encompasses the notions of active living and aging in place, where the concept of smart living, characterized by the intelligent interconnection of people, services, and communities, anchored in extensive information and data usage plays a crucial role [7].

Supported by initiatives such as the "New Leipzig Charta" [8], which was adopted by the EU on November 30, 2020, and position papers like the "Economic Initiative Smart Living Germany," [9] efforts are being made to promote and advance the concept of intelligent neighborhood development and living. These initiatives provide guidance and frameworks for sustainable urban development, emphasizing the integration of digital technologies and innovative solutions in improving the quality of life and well-being in communities.

The new challenges in the field such as energy efficiency, integrated healthcare, and integrated mobility concepts require both cross-sector value creation networks and a strong focus on neighborhood development. To address this phenomenon, a diverse range of interest groups have collaborated to initiate the development of a DIN standard, the DIN SPEC 91397:2022–03 [10]. The primary goal is to establish a standardized framework and guidelines for implementing digital systems in neighborhood management. This initiative seeks to provide a comprehensive set of recommendations, including defined responsibilities and performance indicators, to ensure the efficient and effective utilization of digital technologies in enhancing and optimizing neighborhood management processes.

Given this context, the pertinent issue shifts from whether a platform should be implemented to support neighborhood activities, to a matter of determining the optimal timing and functionalities for such an implementation. In conclusion, a reorientation towards neighborhood dynamics unveils new opportunities and challenges. This necessitates a strategic selection of appropriate platforms that are equipped to effectively address these multifaceted challenges.

The purpose of this contribution is to outline this diversity and identify new application domains for this specific use. More important than providing a conclusive representation is to develop a concept that is suitable for various disciplines, both in academia and practice, while still conveying a tangible understanding of smart neighborhood platforms that is precise enough to work with. Therefore, the aim of this paper is to provide an initial overview. In summary, potential options for digital platforms that can be utilized in a socio-digital urban neighborhood context, with a trend towards digitizing the living conditions.

The objectives of this contribution are to:

- Capture the landscape and potential domains of neighborhood platforms in the German-speaking region, providing a detailed characterization and assessing their development.
- Analyze and summarize the platforms based on various criteria.
- Determine key factors for the success of such platforms and provide practical recommendations for their establishment at the local level.

While the research on this topic is still limited, there are existing insights from the domain of online neighborhood social networks that will be explored in more detail later. To expand the scope of the study, platforms with a networking purpose from the smart living or data-driven platform domain, as well as platforms from the real estate industry, will also be examined. This broader approach aims to provide a comprehensive understanding of the subject matter.

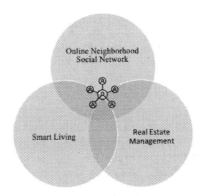

Fig. 1. Investigation of digital platforms with the intention of networking in various domains

These diverse types of platforms need to be differentiated, and the degree of networking they offer should be assessed. Therefore, a fundamental understanding of how digital neighborhood platforms differ from each other is necessary (Fig. 1).

2   Related Work

2.1   Defining Neighborhood and Neighborhood Platforms

To establish a shared foundation, the following section provides a closer examination of the concepts of neighborhood ("Nachbarschaft" and "Quartier"), as well as the neighborhood platform ("Quartiersplattform") and its functions. This clarification aims to ensure a mutual understanding of these terms before delving further into the topic.

In this paper neighborhood is defined as: "a collection of people and institutions occupying a subsection of a larger community" [11].

As evident from the Eighth Elderly Report of the German Federal Government [12], neighborhood and initiatives, has been supporting since 2018 and promoting the "Tag der Nachbarn" (Day of Neighbors) initiative, which was originally initiated by nebenan.de. This initiative has the primary goal of enhancing social cohesion across Germany. The Day of Neighbors serves as a platform to raise awareness about the significance of neighborly relationships and encourages individuals to actively participate in the development of more resilient and close-knit communities.

An approximation of the concept of neighborhood ("Quartier") is provided by Olaf Schnur [4], where he defines "Quartier" as a contextually embedded, socially constructed space that is delineated by external and internal actions, yet with blurred boundaries. It encompasses manageable everyday living and working environments, particularly the place of residence. A neighborhood is significantly smaller in size compared to a city and is primarily determined by its spatial and architectural context, which can reflect the intersections of individual social spheres and shape the identification of acting individuals with this space. This understanding aligns with the definitions presented in the Seventh Elderly Report of the German Federal Government [13], emphasizing the socially produced and transformative nature of neighborhoods, their diverse social functions, their influence on residents' perceptions and actions, and the potential for fostering identification and a sense of community.

The definition of neighborhood platform "Quartiersplattform" is not yet universally established, but an initial approximation can be found in the yet-to-be-finalized DIN SPEC 91397:2022–03 with reference to DIN SPEC 91357 and DIN SPEC 91387 [10]. This standard describes elements of the definition as follows: A neighborhood platform is an integrated infrastructure that incorporates digital systems from various vertical application areas within different fields of action in a municipality. These fields of action encompass mobility, social affairs, health, environment, energy, supply, construction and housing, water, waste/recycling, and other application examples. The focus is on residents, operators, users, and owners within a neighborhood. The neighborhood platform serves as a platform for coordinating and integrating digital solutions across these diverse domains to enhance the functionality and efficiency of neighborhood services and improve the overall quality of life for the individuals and stakeholders involved. Figure 2 illustrates the set of tasks associated with a neighborhood platform.

Considering Fig. 2, it becomes apparent that the human being is at the forefront, and technology is meant to empower them. This emphasizes the complexity of the phenomenon, as highlighted by Chourabi et al. [7]. Smart living, facilitated by intelligent networking among individuals, services, and communities, and relying on immersive information and data, is a multifaceted phenomenon that may not be equally accessible to all citizens.

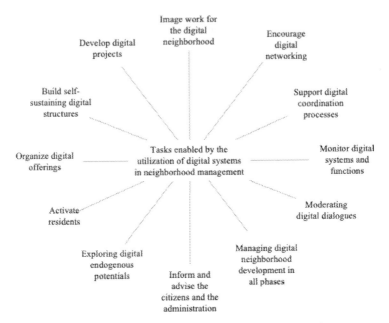

Fig. 2. Tasks enabled by the utilization of digital systems in neighborhood management - based on DIN SPEC 91397:2022–03 [10]

2.2 Exploring Digital Neighborhood Platforms: Networking Dynamics and Emerging Trends in Community Engagement

This research paper examines the networking aspects of different domains of neighborhood platforms. When examining the market for neighborhood-oriented platforms, there is a varying emphasis placed on networking. Despite the increasing availability of digital platforms for communication and participation at the neighborhood or community level, there is limited research on this topic. Existing studies have focused on platforms targeting specific user groups or broader neighborhoods, with fewer platforms specifically tailored to technologically enhanced residential settings and multigenerational site-based neighborhoods.

These platforms encompass a wide range of formats, from volunteer-run neighborhood blogs and local discussion groups on social media (e.g., Facebook or WhatsApp) to region-specific initiatives (e.g., Quartiersleben Neuhegi [14], meinenachbarn.hamburg) and target-oriented networks (e.g., Unser-Quartier.de, Digitale-Dörfer.de, or Crossiety.ch). Some country-specific networks include fürenand.ch and hoplr.com, while there are also commercially managed platforms like nebenan.de or nextdoor.com that cater specifically to neighborhood communities.

Vogel et al. [15] proposed a taxonomy and archetype framework for categorizing online neighborhood social networks, focusing on fostering social connections. However, there is potential to integrate neighborhood-specific requirements, such as smart living and services, into platform designs to create unique features tailored to residents' living situations [16]. Certain neighborhood platforms, including Animus, Casavi, and

Allthings [17–19], prioritize property management but also offer networking and communication features such as messaging, directories, event calendars, and feedback/rating functions for residents. However, an excessive emphasis on property management may overshadow other crucial functions for neighborhood development, such as addressing resident needs and facilitating interaction between residents and the local community. Emerging concepts such as data-driven open-source platforms, like the one developed by the Urban Institute, have made their mark in the field through various applications. One notable example is the collaboration between the Urban Institute and the city of Rüsselsheim [20], where a neighborhood network has been integrated into the open urban platform. This integration demonstrates the commitment to enhance community engagement and to foster connections among residents within the urban context.

Decision-makers in the field of neighborhood development face the challenge of developing a suitable digitalization strategy. Depending on the context and existing infrastructure, diverse types of platforms are utilized, such as social networks for communication, information platforms for content provision, transaction platforms, IoT platforms, or a combination. Emerging concepts like the ForeSight Initiative with the SmartLivingNext [21] platforms are being explored, primarily from a technical perspective, aiming to integrate intelligent solutions into residential settings. However, a noticeable lack of participatory networking among residents is observed. Moreover, there is a limited presence of open data platforms that offer comprehensive networking opportunities for tenants with appealing designs. The current market for neighborhood platforms is not yet clearly defined but the construction of new neighborhoods or the modernization of existing ones is a highly relevant and current topic. There is an understanding that the selection and utilization of platforms depend on various factors [10]. To provide an initial overview of potential application areas, it is essential to analyze existing possibilities and challenges.

3 Methodology and Research Design

To gain comprehensive insights into the topic, the following steps were undertaken in the first phase. Further steps, such as expert interviews, focus groups, and case studies, are planned. Table 1 provides an overview:

The initial literature search aimed to provide a general overview of the various manifestations of platforms that can be used within a neighborhood or community setting. Different keywords were identified for this purpose. Due to linguistic variations, as explained earlier, where the term "neighborhood" or "neighborhood platform" may be referred to differently in the German-speaking context as "Quartier" or "Quartiersplattform" both German and English keywords were searched to ensure comprehensive coverage. To exclude irrelevant articles from the search, secondary keywords were added, and the search was conducted in various combinations. The outcome is presented as a keyword list, listed in Table 2.

The keyword search was conducted in metadata databases (Scopus, Google Scholar, Web of Science) as well as in literature databases (IEEE Xplore, AISeL, EBSCOhost, ScienceDirect). A specific focus was placed on projects from the German-speaking region for the platform analysis.

Table 1. Research process and methodologies

Research Process	Methods	Research Outcome
Identification of the research purpose and definitions	Literature and Media review	Analysis of relevant definitions, debates, and conceptual foundations (Part of Sect. 2)
Research on digital neighborhood platforms	Qualitative content analysis based on Kuckartz and Rädiker [22]	Overview of the landscape of digital neighborhood platforms and characterization criteria
Preparation of practical examples	Desktop analysis and platform observations	Comparison of practical examples on selected characteristics, features, and possible applications of neighborhood platforms

Table 2. Keyword list and combinations

German	English
Primary Keywords	
Quartiersplattform	Neighborhood platform
Nachbarschaftsplattform	Community platform
Digitale Nachbarschaft	Digital Neighborhood
Nachbarschaftsnetzwerk	Online Neighborhood Social Network
Mobile Quartiersapp	Digital Neighborhood Application
Smarte Community/ Smarte Digitale Quartiere	Smart community/smart neighborhood
Quartiersentwicklung	Digital Neighborhood Development
Zukunft Wohnen	Future Living
x	Community informatics
Secondary Keywords	
Nachbarschaft	Neighborhood
(Smartes) Quartier	(Smart) City District
Kümmerer Smart/Intelligent/Nachhaltig	Community Management Smart / Intelligent/Sustainable

To adequately handle the collected data material, a qualitative content analysis following the approach developed by Kuckartz and Rädiker [22] is conducted for the evaluation. Within this analysis method, categories were initially formed deductively based on existing derived theories after an initial review of the material. The resulting category system was then expanded inductively with additional categories through further application to the material.

The foundation for the evaluation of neighborhood platforms is derived from the DIN SPEC 91397:2022–03 [10] standard. This standard has been expanded to incorporate additional content and guidelines from various sources, since there is limited existing literature available for the classification and comparison of neighborhood platforms. For example, the reference framework for IoT platforms developed by the Fraunhofer Institute [23] and "The Digital Media Readiness Framework" from the World Economic Forum [24] were examined. In the context of online social neighborhood networks, Vogel et al. [15] developed a taxonomy for these types of platforms, which also served as a basis for further development in this study. The study also draws upon the taxonomy development approach by Nickerson et al. [25], which was also consulted. In addition, criteria were added that were deemed relevant for assessing the features such as level of participation based on [26] and characteristics of the variety of platforms for a potential use for further analysis. These criteria were included to gain insights that may not have been apparent previously and to uncover new findings throughout the study.

The provided information was examined and classified. Various sources such as platform or project websites, studies, whitepapers, self-tests available on the platform, and informal interviews with platform employees were utilized to gather details about the features and attributes. Additionally, targeted searches were conducted to explore how these platforms are applied in diverse areas, with a particular focus on their usage within specific neighborhoods.

4 Exploring the Results

4.1 Exploring Characteristics and Features

In the German-speaking region, initial approaches and initiatives of neighborhood platforms have emerged since approximately 2011. Building upon the principles of social media, these platforms have limited their scope to the neighborhood or various groups. These types of platforms have also gained momentum in the scientific community, as evidenced by several funding projects. However, it is notable that most developed platforms from these funding projects are currently inactive or discontinued after the project ended. In some cases, there is a lack of scientific publications explaining the reasons, there are only indications, such as in the case of SONIAnetz [27]. Despite being designed with participatory principles, the app was not adopted, leading to a significant user base not being established.

62 different platforms were evaluated based on initial characteristics and their thematic relevance, with a focus on their potential use in a neighborhood. Out of these, 23 platforms were specifically selected for a more detailed examination of their key features. Figure 3 provides an initial overview.

As evident from Fig. 3, more professionally oriented platforms have evolved over the past decade. It should be noted that there were also partial, non-scalable websites, blogs, or forums that emerged much earlier but are not relevant in this context due to their limited scope.

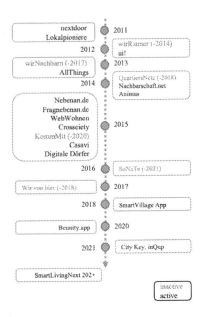

Fig. 3. Founding years and status of selected digital platforms for neighborhood networking at the neighborhood level in the German-speaking region

During the analysis of the examined platforms, it was observed that there was a significant surge in platform introductions in 2015 after a gradual increase. Interestingly, the emergence of the first well-known neighborhood platforms and open data platforms occurred around the same time, but the demand for a unified application of these platforms only emerged many years later. This further emphasizes the trend towards the digitalization of neighborhood development.[1]

After the initial analysis and considering the goal of comparing the current situation and trends, inactive, highly targeted, and non-scalable platforms were excluded for this analysis. However, these inactive platforms still provide value in terms of insights, design, and features, which could potentially be useful for future developments. For a more detailed analysis of specific functions to assess their utility at a later stage, they were included in a criteria catalog but not considered in this context. Based on this, the following platforms were summarized in their original application areas as follows (Fig. 4):

- Platform Type A - **Online Neighborhood Social Network** (ONSN): This platform emerged from the domain of social networking, with a strong emphasis on fostering

---

[1] Many websites had to be accessed through web archiving due to their current inactivity. It was also noticed that there was a pre-existing forum under the URL nebenan.de (likely serving as a local portal for the city Bremen) with features such as forum discussions, neighborhood photo contests, emergency calls, facility, and business directories. Screenshots from 2001 to 2005 are available, after which the domain was reserved, and the forum ceased its operations.

Fig. 4. Analyzed platforms categorized based on their respective domains of origin

communication and interaction among neighborhood residents. They serve as a centralized hub for providing relevant content, such as local news, events, and services, to keep residents informed and connected.

- Platform Type B - **Smart Living** (SL): With its roots in the Internet of Things (IoT) domain, the platforms incorporate smart home devices and services into the neighborhood infrastructure. It provides functionalities such as remote home monitoring, energy management, and automated systems, emphasizing the utilization of open-source applications to fulfill the requirements in this field.
- Platform Type C - **Real Estate Management** (RE): The platforms focus on the efficient management of properties within the neighborhood. It offers features such as property listings, tenant management, maintenance requests, and financial transactions. This platform aims to streamline the processes related to real estate operations and enhance the overall management of properties in the neighborhood. It provides channels and tools for effective communication, such as messaging systems, notifications, and feedback mechanisms.

By understanding the origins of these platforms, stakeholders can gain insights into their core functionalities, target audience, and underlying principles, which can inform decision-making processes regarding their implementation and suitability for specific neighborhood contexts.

The following two tables illustrate the selected criteria, distinguishing between social and smart features. The social features are further divided into levels of participation. The platforms from the different domains were aggregated, and the average values are presented in Table 3.

Following the provision of an overview of the diverse functionalities across platform types by the tables, attention is directed towards a horizontal comparison of feature groups, including aspects like Customizability and Usability. This approach facilitates an analysis of the strengths and weaknesses inherent to the platforms with regard to social interaction and smart technology integration, spanning various types (Table 4).

Table 3. Analysis of social features

	Design principles	Criteria	A	B	C
Social	Information	Newsfeed, Digital Bulletin Boards	●	●	●
		Local businesses, services etc.	●	●	●
		Events	●	●	●
		Neighborhood Directory	●	●	●
		Open Street Map (interactive - location based)	◑	○	●
		Search (location-based)	○	●	●
		Newsletter, Weekly Summary etc.	●	◑	●
		District Homepage	●	●	◑
		Data Storage, Gallery etc.	◑	●	◑
		Official Information and (Safety) Alerts	◑	●	●
	Consultation	Polls and Voting	●	○	●
		Integration of digital assistant / live options	○	●	◑
		Communication to local facilities (e.g. Communitymanagement, welfare station)	◑	●	●
	Communication	Private chats	●	●	●
		Community / Group chat	●	●	●
		Integration of Video etc.	○	◑	◍
	Participation	Issue Reporting System	○	●	●
		Profile Page (e.g. interest, about me)	●	●	●
		Campaigns, Planning tool for initiatives and Events	●	○	●
		Groups & group directory	●	○	●
		Calender	●	○	●
		Reviews and Feedback (e.g. for services, local facilities)	◑	○	◍
		Feature for neighborhood support (looking for and offering help)	●	●	●
		Sharing, Rental Booking- Neighborhood Level	●	●	◑
		Online Marketplace	●	●	●
		Fundraising	○	○	◑
		Games and Entertainment	○	○	○
	Support	FAQ, Videos etc.	◑	●	●
	Statistics	Analysis Tool, Reporting	◑	◑	●
	Trust & Identity	Role Based Concept	◑	●	●
		Identity Verification	◑	●	●
		Invitation Mechanism (possibility to limit entry / views)	◑	●	●
		Real-name policy	●	●	●

● possible   ◑ partially possible   ◍ not actively used   ○ not possible

(A) Online Neighborhood Social Network (B) Smart Living) (C) Real Estate Management

Social Features: In relation to the social features such as messaging, news/feed, events, directory, etc., it is evident that a significant number of platforms already cover these functionalities. Therefore, future development should be built upon and consider them as a foundation. However, a notable difference can be observed in the platforms from the real estate sector, which lack solutions for participation features. This is partially compensated for by platforms from the SL sector, where open integration makes such features possible.

Smart Features: When examining the provided criteria, it is evident that the real estate platforms and smart living platforms have a clear advantage in terms of integration possibilities and adaptability. These platforms offer greater flexibility in integrating smart technologies and adapting to changing needs and preferences. This advantage allows them to provide advanced features and functionalities that enhance the overall smart living experience for users.

Table 4. Analysis of smart features

Design principles		Criteria	Type		
			A	B	C
Smart	Knowledge & Education	Online Learning, Sustainability concepts or integration possibilites	O	◐	◉
		(Intelligent) Information modules	O	●	◉
	Integration	Real Estate Management (Contracts etc.)	O	●	◉
		Health (e.g. Wearables)	O	◐	●
		Mobility (e.g. Board, Mobility Booking, Sharing System, Public Transformation	O	◐	●
		Facility Bookings, Resource Reservation and Calendar	◐	O	◐
		Services Booking (e.g. Household services, health and care services)	O	◐	●
		Integration of local (security) management and statistics	O	O	●
		Energy (e.g. Smart Metering)	O	◐	●
		Water, Waster etc.	O	O	●
		Integration of other 3rd Party Applications and Services (reffered to DIN SPEC 91397:2022-03)	O	◐	●
	Innovation	Technical innovations (AR, VR, XR - community building)	O	O	O
		Open Source Concept	O	◐	●
		Applied machine-learning algorithms to enhance decision-making and tasks	O	◐	◐
		Innovative reward and payment models	O	O	O
		(Serious) Gamifikation Approaches	◐	O	O
	Fair Involvement Concepts	e.g. Mulit-Language, simple language, interactive help text	◐	O	◐
Other	Others	Multi tenancy	◐	◐	◐
		Modular structure and displayable	O	●	●
		DSGVO	●	●	●
		Consulting Concept	●	●	●

● possible	◐ partially possible	◉ not actively used	O not possible

(A) Online Neighborhood Social Network **(B)** Smart Living **(C)** Real Estate Management

Innovations: While neighborhood platforms share many similarities in terms of social features, the landscape looks different when it comes to innovative concepts such as serious gamification approaches for learning, specifically for energy-saving measures or social networking. The implementation of these innovative concepts is not yet foreseeable across the platforms. Only a few solutions exist, mostly tailored to specific use cases, where a greater emphasis is placed on health and active living. Similarly, innovative learning concepts and reward models, potentially involving tokens specific to the neighborhood, are not widely known. These areas should continue to be monitored for further developments.

Customizability: In general, it can be observed that online neighborhood social network platforms have limited customization options, while real estate platforms offer partial opportunities for further development in this aspect. Smart living platforms, which are based on open standards, exhibit much greater flexibility in terms of customization. This flexibility allows SL platforms to adapt and evolve according to the specific needs and preferences of users, providing a more tailored and personalized experience.

User Design: It is worth noting that despite the flexibility to customize the design of the platforms, ONSNs clearly prioritize the larger user group of neighbors. On the other hand, platforms in the real estate sector and some smart living platforms still appear quite technical in their design.

4.2 Exploring Practical Applications

While the study conducted by the Federal Association for Housing and Urban Development (vhw-Bundesverband Wohnen und Stadtentwicklung) [1] provides insights into the application of various neighborhood platforms in different regions, it is worth mentioning the specific areas of application for real estate platforms and smart living platforms as well.

As an example within the ONSN domain, the smart city district EnStadt:Pfaff can be mentioned, which has developed its own mock platform based on digitale-dörfer.de, along with additional modules for health, mobility and energy. They have also implemented a game to raise awareness about mobility topics. Although digitale-dörfer.de were originally designed for rural regions, their application in an urban neighborhood like in the Pfaff project demonstrates the potential for their use beyond their initial scope [28].

Within the real estate platform applications, the Living Smart Project [29] stands out. It has been further developed based on the Animus platform and offers integrated services beyond its core functionalities. This includes the provision of critical and welfare services, as well as communication with local social services. The Living Smart Project demonstrates the potential of leveraging technology to provide comprehensive solutions within the real estate sector and active (assistance) aging in place.

The "Quartier der Zukunft" (Neighborhood of the future) [20] project in the city of Rüsselsheim, in collaboration with the Urban Institute, is an excellent example of utilizing an open data platform. The neighborhood platform serves as a central artifact for equipping the neighborhood and can be flexibly expanded. This project demonstrates the importance of using open data platforms as a foundation for digitalization and innovation in neighborhood development.

5 Conclusion and Future Research Directions

This study embarked on a qualitative exploration of smart neighborhood platforms within the German-speaking region, uncovering the vast landscape and potential of digital platforms designed for enhancing community engagement and smart living. Our analysis delved into a broad spectrum of platforms, including those rooted in social networking principles and those that extend to smart living and real estate management functionalities. The diversity observed among these platforms reflects a rich ecosystem where digital solutions cater to various facets of neighborhood life, from fostering social interactions and community spirit to integrating smart technologies for efficient resource management and sustainable living.

Through our research, we discovered a notable trend towards the digitalization of neighborhood interactions and operations. This shift is driven by a growing recognition of the role that digital platforms can play in addressing contemporary challenges of urban living, such as the need for sustainable development, energy efficiency, and enhanced quality of life. The platforms evaluated in this study display innovative approaches to community engagement, offering features that facilitate communication, participation, and access to local resources and services. Moreover, the adoption of smart technologies within these platforms underscores a commitment to leveraging digital innovations for the betterment of community living spaces. However, our findings also highlight the challenges and limitations inherent in the current landscape of smart neighborhood platforms. Despite the advancements made, there remains a gap in fully realizing the potential of these digital solutions to foster inclusive, participatory, and sustainable neighborhood ecosystems. Challenges such as the integration of innovative features like gamification for social engagement, customization options for diverse user needs, and the accessibility of smart functionalities for all community members, are areas that warrant further exploration and development.

The analysis has also underscored the importance of selecting or developing platforms that align with specific community needs and existing infrastructural setups, incorporating an understanding of emerging trends in the field. The consideration of existing solutions is crucial to mitigate risks associated with media discontinuity and potential non-acceptance by the community. Additionally, the maturity level of the neighborhood should be considered when offering appropriate solutions that can be effectively utilized. An initial approach in this regard has been proposed by Renyi et al. [30]. Furthermore, the sustainability and viability of the operating model of these platforms are paramount, as evidenced by the discontinuation of numerous pilot projects. The operating model should consider long-term management, maintenance, interoperability, and scalability in response to evolving community needs and technological advancements.

Future research should delve into validating and broadening the criteria, trends, and implications identified in smart neighborhood platforms, employing expert interviews to refine insights and extend the scope to include a broader range of applications such as smart health and active living. The exploration of platform interoperability, with an emphasis on module-based and open standards, is vital for enhancing their adaptability to meet the varied needs of different communities. Addressing the technological, socioeconomic, and privacy challenges, alongside promoting digital literacy, is crucial to mitigate resistance and ensure all community members have equitable access to these platforms. Additionally, determining the suitability of specific platforms for different neighborhoods based on their unique characteristics and needs will be a key area of focus, aiming to match each community with the most appropriate and beneficial smart neighborhood platform.

This analysis has revealed a landscape of various platforms with potential for use in a neighborhood, considering the criteria and potential applications. The central aim was to investigate how these platforms can promote social interactions among residents and, at the same time, align with the growing trend of smart living. This required a thorough analysis of the design and functionality of these digital platforms, focusing on their ability to simultaneously boost community involvement and incorporate smart living technologies within the framework of real estate management. In the next step, it is necessary to validate the described criteria, trends, and implications. Subsequently, additional use cases will be identified, and the current overview will be expanded.

In conclusion, it is important to understand that there are different smart neighborhood platforms with different focuses, and realistic selections should be made based on requirements and existing infrastructures, considering trends and demands. The requirements from the user community should be given attention. When further developing existing solutions, a greater emphasis should be placed on knowledge generation and fair involvement, with a particular focus on ensuring that technical implementations do not become hurdles (digital divide), especially in the areas of languages, learning, and gamification. Additionally, technological barriers, socioeconomic factors, privacy concerns, resistance to change, and the promotion of digital literacy must be considered as critical introduction barriers. By addressing these barriers, smart neighborhood platforms can be more effectively designed and implemented to foster social interactions and enable smart living, ensuring broad acceptance and sustainable use.

References

1. Schreiber, F., Göppert, H.: Wandel von Nachbarschaft in Zeiten digitaler Vernetzung: Endbericht. vhw - Bundesverband für Wohnen und Stadtentwicklung e.V, Berlin (2018)
2. Bellogín, A., Castells, P.: A performance prediction approach to enhance collaborative filtering performance. In: Gurrin, C., He, Y., Kazai, G., Kruschwitz, U., Little, S., Roelleke, T., Rüger, S., van Rijsbergen, K. (eds.) ECIR 2010. LNCS, vol. 5993, pp. 382–393. Springer, Heidelberg (2010). https://doi.org/10.1007/978-3-642-12275-0_34
3. Boyd, D.: It's Complicated: The Social Lives of Networked Teens. Yale University Press, New Haven London (2014)
4. Schnur, O.: Quartiersforschung: zwischen Theorie und Praxis. Springer VS, Wiesbaden (2014). https://doi.org/10.1007/978-3-531-19963-4
5. Neal, P. (ed.): Urban Villages and The Making of Communities. Spon Press, London (2003)
6. Michell-Auli, P., Kremer-Preiß, U.: Quartiersentwicklung: KDA-Ansatz und kommunale Praxis. Medhochzwei Verlag, Heidelberg (2013)
7. Chourabi, H., et al.: Understanding smart cities: an integrative framework. In: 2012 45th Hawaii International Conference on System Sciences, pp. 2289–2297. IEEE, Maui, HI, USA (2012). https://doi.org/10.1109/HICSS.2012.615
8. Neue Leipzig Charta (2020). https://www.nationale-stadtentwicklungspolitik.de/NSPWeb/SharedDocs/Publikationen/DE/Publikationen/die_neue_leipzig_charta.pdf;jsessionid=1BB80025F96B3F232F27AD10578E82F1.live21302?__blob=publicationFile&v=7
9. Wirtschaftsinitiative Smart Living, S.: Wohnen in Gebäuden der Zukunft – Aanforderungen an eine digitale Infrastruktur (2021). https://www.smartliving-germany.de/wp-content/uploads/2022/04/WISL_Positionspapier_Infrastruktur_210126.pdf
10. DIN e.V.: DIN SPEC 91397:2022–03, Leitfaden für die Implementierung von digitalen Systemen des Quartiersmanagements. Beuth Verlag GmbH (2022). https://doi.org/10.31030/3332314
11. Sampson, R.J., Raudenbush, S.W., Earls, F.: Neighborhoods and violent crime: a multilevel study of collective efficacy. Science **277**, 918–924 (1997). https://doi.org/10.1126/science.277.5328.918
12. BMFSFJ: Ältere Menschen und Digitalisierung : Achter Bericht zur Lage der älteren Generation in der Bundesrepublik Deutschland und Stellungnahme der Bundesregierung : Achter Altenbericht : Achter Altersbericht (2020)
13. BMFSFJ: Siebter Altenbericht zur Lage der älteren Generation in der Bundesrepublik Deutschland: Sorge und Mitverantwortung in der Kommune - Aufbau und Sicherung zukunftsfähiger Gemeinschaften und Stellungnahme der Bundesregierung. Berlin (2016)
14. Quartierleben Neuhegi. https://neuhegi.mopage.ch. Accessed 25 Apr 2023
15. Vogel, P., Grotherr, C., Kurtz, C., Böhmann, T.: Conceptualizing design parameters of online neighborhood social networks. In: Proceedings der 15. Internationalen Tagung Wirtschaftsinformatik 2020. GITO Verlag, Berlin (2020). https://doi.org/10.30844/wi_2020_o5-vogel

16. Hölzer, S., Honner, L., Preßler, W., Schulz, A., Erfurth, C.: Towards designing a user-centered local community platform to foster social cohesion in a multi-generational smart community. In: Krieger, U.R., Eichler, G., Erfurth, C., Fahrnberger, G. (eds.) Innovations for Community Services, pp. 277–291. Springer Nature Switzerland, Cham (2023). https://doi.org/10.1007/978-3-031-40852-6_15

17. Allthings. https://www.allthings.me/de. Accessed 24 Apr 2023

18. Animus. https://animus.de. Accessed 26 Apr 2023

19. Casavi. https://casavi.com/de/. Accessed 24 Apr 2023

20. Stadtwerke Rüsselsheim: Quartier der Zukunft. https://www.quartier-der-zukunft.de/de/Die-Projektergebnisse/. Accessed 24 Apr 2023

21. Smart Living Germany: SmartLivingNext. https://www.smartliving-germany.de/aktuelles/foerderaufruf-smartlivingnext-veroeffentlicht/. Accessed 06 Jan 2023

22. Kuckartz, U., Rädiker, S.: Qualitative Inhaltsanalyse: Methoden, Praxis, Computerunterstützung: Grundlagentexte Methoden. Beltz Juventa, Weinheim Basel (2022)

23. Krause, T., Strauß, O., Scheffler, G., Kett, H., Schaefer, K., Renner, T.: IT-Plattformen für das Internet der Dinge (IoT): Basis intelligenter Produkte und Services. Fraunhofer Verlag, Stuttgart (2017)

24. World Economic Forum: The Digital Media Readiness Framework (2016). https://www3.weforum.org/docs/WEF_WhitePaper_GAC_Digital_Media_Readiness_Framework.pdf

25. Nickerson, R.C., Varshney, U., Muntermann, J., Isaac, H.: Taxonomy development in information systems: developing a taxonomy of mobile applications. In: 17th European Conference on Information Systems, ECIS 2009, Verona, Italy, 2009, pp. 1138–1149 (2009)

26. Arnstein, S.R.: A ladder of citizen participation. J. Am. Plann. Assoc. **85**, 24–34 (2019). https://doi.org/10.1080/01944363.2018.1559388

27. Renyi, M., Gündogdu, R., Kunze, C., Gaugisch, P., Teuteberg, F.: The Networked Neighborhood – A User-Centered Design Study. IEEE, Piscataway, NJ (2018)

28. Elberzhager, F., Mennig, P., Polst, S., Scherr, S., Stüpfert, P.: Towards a digital ecosystem for a smart city district: procedure, results, and lessons learned. Smart Cities. **4**, 686–716 (2021). https://doi.org/10.3390/smartcities4020035

29. Brauer, C., et al.: LivingSmart: Wohnquartiere neu gedacht – Service-gesteuert: lebensnah, integrativ, intelligent, innovativ. In: Lattemann, C. and Robra-Bissantz, S. (eds.) Personennahe Dienstleistungen der Zukunft, pp. 201–218. Springer Fachmedien Wiesbaden, Wiesbaden (2023). https://doi.org/10.1007/978-3-658-38813-3_12

30. Renyi, M., Hegedüs, A., Maier, E., Teuteberg, F., Kunze, C.: Toward sustainable ICT-supported neighborhood development—a maturity model. Sustainability. **12**, 9319 (2020). https://doi.org/10.3390/su12229319

Information Analysis

WebMap - Large Language Model-assisted Semantic Link Induction in the Web

Shiraj Pokharel[1]([✉]) [ID], Georg P. Roßrucker[2] [ID], and Mario M. Kubek[1] [ID]

[1] Georgia State University, Atlanta, GA, USA
{spokhare13,mkubek}@gsu.edu
[2] FernUniversität in Hagen, Hagen, Germany

Abstract. Carrying out research tasks is only inadequately supported, if not hindered, by current web search engines. This paper therefore proposes functional extensions of *WebMap*, a semantically induced overlay linking structure on the web to inherently facilitate research activities. These add-ons support the dynamic determination and regrouping of document clusters, the creation of a semantic signpost in the web, and the interactive tracing of topics back to their origins.

Keywords: Web search · Semantic link induction · Sequential clustering · Large language models · WebMap

1 Initial Situation

Web search engines exploit the explicit linking structure of the World Wide Web (WWW) to determine the relationships between web documents and assess the relevance and authority of content. Typically, hyperlinks are intentionally created and strategically placed by human efforts. However, it would be beneficial to also use semantically induced links between web documents and their content fragments to indicate topical relations and topically group potentially relevant web search results. This approach could facilitate labor-intensive research processes by automating the identification of relevant connections and topics.

Furthermore, as web search engines do not topically group potentially relevant web search results, conducting research using them constitutes a labor-intensive task as it involves having to manually inspect and evaluate the returned results. Therefore, it might be beneficial to return clusters of conceptually similar and related documents that match a query's intent, too.

To this end, in [1], we introduced the *WebMap*, a novel solution to extending the existing linking structure of a hyperlinked network of text documents such as the WWW by a peer-to-peer-based semantic overlay, which induces and represents a distributed graph structure.

The paper's remainder introduces conceptual extensions to *WebMap*, aimed at enhancing support for research tasks. These extensions, though still in

© The Author(s), under exclusive license to Springer Nature Switzerland AG 2024
F. Phillipson et al. (Eds.): I4CS 2024, CCIS 2109, pp. 121–131, 2024.
https://doi.org/10.1007/978-3-031-60433-1_8

development, are providing functionalities such as dynamic determination and regrouping of document clusters, creation of semantic signposts, and interactive tracing of topics. By conceptualizing these advancements, the paper lays the groundwork for future development and implementation within *WebMap* to better facilitate research activities on the Web.

2   WebMap's Architecture

The main idea of *WebMap* is to embed a semantic and meaningful linking mechanism into the existing Web to make navigation and search independent of the existing – rather chronologically evolved – link structure. This is crucial because classical hyperlinks typically point to existing (older) content, putting new content at a disadvantage in terms of discoverability.

To achieve this, the global overlay linking structure is designed as a network of so called *Cluster Files*, generated and provided by the participating peers (web servers). Cluster files are identified by meaningful terms (text-representing centroids, TRCs [2]) and consist of two sets of hyperlinks:

- a set of links referring to documents (leaves) that are related within the given cluster's *context*, and
- a set of links pointing to semantically related clusters, realizing traversable, bi-directional edges.

Figure 1 illustrates how the overlaying linking structure of the *WebMap* extends the present linking structure of the underlying Web.

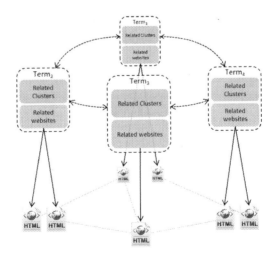

Fig. 1. WebMap's architecture

3   Improving WebMap

3.1   Language Modeling and Large Language Models (LLMs)

Let's take a representative sentence - "A German Shepherd is a [blank]". Most likely, our guess for [blank] is "dog", which means that the context provided does not refer to a "human shepherd with German nationality". Similarly, assigning a guess or probability to every possible word via mathematical reasoning and computation is called language modeling. Further, language models developed via deep neural networks and the Transformer [13] architecture with possibly hundreds of billions of programmable connections (called "parameters") are referred to as Large Language Models (LLMs). Below, we briefly touch upon two of the most successful LLM-families recently.

Generative Pre-trained Transformers (GPT). Released by OpenAI, GPTs are types of decoder-only Transformer [13]-based language models. GPT-1 and GPT-2 are open source while GPT-3 [15] and GPT-4 [16] are closed source models [14]. GPT-3 is the model which excels in tasks that can be provided in natural human language like translation. GPT-4 is a multi-model which can produce text-based outputs from image or text-based inputs.

LLaMA. Released by Meta, LLaMA [17] uses the transformer architecture of GPT-3 [15], with some modifications in the activation function, positional embeddings and layer-normalization. The latest release is LLaMA-2 [18]. Thus far, LLaMA models are open-sourced by Meta where the model weights are made publicly available for non-commercial study and research purposes.

3.2   Neural Induction of Local Term Proximity Graphs

To derive the globally valid cluster assignment for documents and the necessary relations between clusters, peers of the *WebMap* make use of individual co-occurrence graphs [3] that are induced by local text documents and capture simple syntagmatic term relations [4]. Extracting *significant* term relations and *meaningful* topical connections between documents and cluster files therefore greatly depends on the available number, quality, and context of the individual peers' documents.

To obtain more meaningful document assignments and cluster associations in a harmonized manner that is commonly accepted and verifiable, we propose to change the underlying mechanism from using co-occurrence graphs to local term proximity graphs induced by LLMs such as BERT [5] and its variants, GPT-3 [15], GPT-4 [16], LLaMA-1 [17], LLaMA-2 [18], Mistral 7B [19], etc. Following the principle of distributional semantics [4], LLMs are able to convert input words into (sub)tokens and then into contextualized vector embeddings (high-dimensional real-valued vectors) that capture the words' meanings in context.

To induce the required local term proximity graphs, we hence propose to generally compare the word embeddings of selected and meaningful textual elements such as nouns and proper nouns that appeared together in the local documents using the cosine similarity measure. We will refer to them as terms in the following considerations. The following two approaches to determining the degree of term similarity make sense here:

- In the first approach, we compute the embeddings for each occurrence of a selected term in a document. Then, we average these embeddings to create a single term representation for the entire document. After that, we compare the averaged embeddings of each pair of terms using the cosine similarity measure to find out how similar they are in meaning. This method helps us understand their overall semantic relationships within the document.
- In the second approach, we compute embeddings for each selected term in the document and compare these embeddings with the embeddings of neighboring terms within each sentence. To address variations in similarity values due to different contexts, we aggregate similarity values for each term pair across multiple occurrences in various contexts. By averaging these similarity values, we obtain a more stable measure of the semantic relationship between terms, which helps capture their general semantic similarity across diverse contexts.

In both cases, if the cosine similarity between two elements is higher than a predefined threshold value s, nodes are created for these elements in the local proximity graph and an edge is created between them. The edge weight will be set to s correspondingly. Thus, the hyperparameter s regulates the growth of the term graph. This way, the used LLM acts as a reference resource.

When updating the graph with a new document, a nuanced approach is adopted to account for potential overlaps with existing term pairs. Each term pair from the new document is compared with those already in the graph. If a term pair overlaps, its overall similarity value is updated as follows: The edge's weight for that term pair is updated by averaging the existing similarity value(s), which need to be retained, with the new similarity. Here, it should be noted that the updated edge weight can be less than the threshold value s. This approach can also be adapted so that only the maximum t previously occurring term pair similarity values are included in this calculation in order to take into account the possibly important topicality and time dependency of the local documents. For non-overlapping term pairs, if their similarity surpasses the threshold s, they are added to the graph as laid out before. This method balances retaining meaningful edges while accommodating new semantic associations, ensuring the graph's relevance and accuracy with continuously updated information.

We also would like to point out that the partaking peers do not necessarily have to agree upon a common LLM. On the contrary, depending on the individual web servers' content, domain-specific models such as SciBERT [6], and FinBERT [7] might be better suited to capture domain-specific characteristics and nuances.

To incorporate new documents and cluster files into the *WebMap* and establish links between documents and their corresponding cluster files, the following procedures in Algorithm 1 must be executed:

Algorithm 1. Link induction and cluster assignment in the *WebMap*

1: <START>
2: Create local term proximity graph based on chosen LLM
3: Cluster assignment: for all local documents, derive TRCs (cluster identification) based on local term proximity graph
4: **for** all local documents **do**
5:　　**if** respective cluster exists on the *WebMap* **then**
6:　　　　Attach document link to cluster
7:　　**else**
8:　　　　Create cluster file locally and attach document link to cluster file
9:　　　　Derive the shortest path from the set of existing cluster files represented in the local term proximity graph to the new cluster file
10:　　　　Create cluster files and bi-directional links among them for all nodes on the path
11:　　**end if**
12: **end for**
13: <END>

The updated methodology, leveraging LLMs for inducing local term proximity graphs described before, is evident in steps 2 and 3.

3.3　Towards a Semantic Signpost

The assignment of individual documents to the global clusters is done by calculating their TRC terms using the local term proximity graphs just discussed. Within the global cluster files, it is now possible to organize the documents based on their similarity as well as in relation to incoming search queries, which are assigned TRCs, too. However, documents within a cluster will not only exhibit (flat, horizontal) semantic similarities, but topical (hierarchical) dependencies as well. For instance, a document on the main topic *earthquake* could refer to contents that predominantly discuss its important subtopics such as *seismic waves* and *movement of plate boundaries.*

The establishment of this intra-cluster linking structure yields a semantic signpost aiming to facilitate the targeted navigation to a topical direction of interest by lexically and semantically chaining documents. The mentioned topical dependencies can be uncovered by creating a cluster's directed and document-specific term associations graphs and applying for instance an extended variant [8] of the HITS algorithm [9] on them that takes into account the term association strengths *Assn*, too. For this purpose, the formulae for the update rules of the HITS algorithm must be extended. The authority value of a node x can then be determined using formula 1:

$$a(x) = \sum_{v \to x} h(v) \cdot Assn(v \to x) \tag{1}$$

The hub value of a node x can be calculated using formula 2:

$$h(x) = \sum_{x \to w} a(w) \cdot Assn(x \to w) \tag{2}$$

This way, a document's main (authorities) and source topics (hubs) can be identified. Figure 2 illustrates this approach.

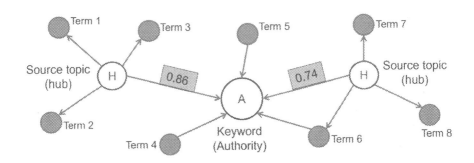

Fig. 2. Determining authorities (keywords) and hubs (source topics) in directed term association graphs

Table 1 shows that the main topic "Android" (mobile operating system) is greatly influenced by the subtopics "source code", "development", and "platform", which makes sense.

Table 1. Terms with high authority and hub scores of the English Wikipedia article "Android" (mobile operating system)

Term	Authority Score	Term	Hub Score
Android	0.32	source code	0.19
Google	0.31	development	0.18
application	0.27	platform	0.14

Based on the resulting lists of keywords and source topics per document, directed edges between the documents can now be induced as follows: If a document A primarily addresses the source topics of another document B, a link from A to B can be established. This exploits the fact that the source topics of documents are often the authorities of other documents, creating a chain of documents that are actually thematically dependent. This way, the herein described approach to obtain directed term associations is modified to gain the same effect at the document level, thereby generating recommendations for specific documents. In doing so, *WebMap* incrementally learns new document relationships. Consequently, new search results can include links not only to similar documents but also to those primarily dealing with their source topics. This approach provides users access to background information on a topic of interest and allows them to follow related topics across multiple documents. The concept behind this approach is that the identified source topics, particularly, can guide users to documents covering important aspects of the analyzed search results, offering a novel method for discovering related documents.

3.4   Detecting Subclusters and Handling Outliers

The described cluster assignment process works in a sequential manner and the number of cluster files does not need to be specified beforehand. However, this number is constrained by the finite set of terms in a natural language.

Each cluster file is associated with a potentially large set of documents, which in turn can be associated with a set of subtopics and, in addition to the thematic dependencies described in the previous section, can provide important clues for vertical navigation within a global cluster file. Therefore, it is advisable to regularly run an iterative and density-based clustering algorithm to identify those meaningful and disjoint subclusters. In the following considerations, we will simply refer to them as clusters.

In order to model the intrinsic characteristics of given sets of feature vectors with as low redundancy as possible, model-constituting clusters should be rather densely filled with data points – our assigned documents – and should have clear boundaries. An approach to do so is based on a probabilistic interpretation, which considers feature vectors of items (here: the documents) as observations of a mixed population constituted by several overlapping populations, the sum of whose single unimodal distribution densities is a multimodal distribution density, which has several local maxima (cf. Fig. 3). Under the condition, that the single populations are sufficiently separated, it is assumed, that the local maxima characterize the regions in feature space where the single populations are concentrated, i.e. where clusters are expected.

Based on this interpretation, the method proposed in [11] and its faster variant [12] that replaces Gaussian functions by other bell-shaped and very similar looking curves, namely B-splines, are both able to detect clusters of complex shapes. According to the methods, those locations in feature space are searched, where a given data set exhibits local point concentrations with higher densities than in the respective vicinities. The search works by iteratively translating with a small step-size all feature vectors towards regions of higher point density. By this process, the vectors gradually approach the local maxima. Merging into a single cluster all feature vectors thus arriving in the neighbourhood of a certain location, an exhaustive and disjoint clustering of the data set is produced, with the number of these clusters derived from the characteristics of the data set, but not specified a priori. This also facilitates the detection of outliers by identifying clusters with low point density after the algorithm's execution.

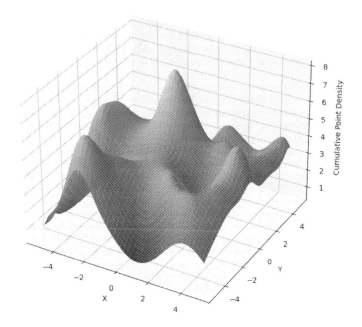

Fig. 3. Multimodal distribution density (according to [10])

In the context of *WebMap*, documents in subclusters with a low point density can thus be regarded as outliers and as candidates for re-clustering. This could either mean that those documents will need to be assigned a different cluster file instead, or that they must be taken into account for a future subcluster assignment attempt. In any case, the described approach ensures that the subclusters obtained do not include any documents that are potentially semantically dissimilar within a cluster file. Likewise, a new management structure must be added to the cluster files that points to the subclusters and the documents contained in them.

4   Discussion, Limitations, and Future Directions

The proposed enhancements to *WebMap* introduce significant improvements to the existing framework, aiming to address key challenges in web-based research activities. By leveraging LLMs, *WebMap* seeks to enhance the semantic understanding of web content, thereby improving the accuracy and relevance of search results. The transition from co-occurrence graphs to local term proximity graphs induced by LLMs represents a paradigm shift in how document clusters are determined, enabling a more nuanced analysis of semantic relationships between terms and documents.

However, while the adoption of LLMs holds great promise for enhancing the effectiveness of *WebMap*, several limitations and challenges need to be addressed.

Firstly, the reliance on textual content restricts the applicability of *WebMap* to domains where multimedia content plays a significant role. Future iterations of the system may need to explore methods for integrating and analyzing diverse media types to ensure comprehensive coverage of web-based information.

Moreover, the current implementation of intra-cluster signposts, while facilitating navigation within clusters, may hinder the exploration of cross-cluster relationships and thematic connections. Enhancements to the linking structure, possibly through the incorporation of semantic similarity measures or thematic analysis algorithms, could improve the discoverability of related content across different clusters.

To maximize the effectiveness of utilizing *WebMap*, it is essential to dedicate effort towards analyzing ideal use cases. This involves examining how current user workflows, such as enhancing search capabilities for specific topics, implementing targeted navigation features, and optimizing content crawling and discovery processes to focus on relevant information, can be enhanced further.

In the context of developing innovative use cases through the utilization of *WebMap's* technology, the newly devised approaches for sustainable research support can play a pivotal role. For instance, the herein discussed method of identifying sources discussing a given topic X, which exhibit high relevance, either hierarchically as subordinates or superordinates, or present contradictory perspectives, makes thematic dependencies explicit. *WebMap* may also serve as a foundational search index for the development of novel search agents, especially those Artificial Intelligence (AI) tools aimed at the research synthesis process of identifying, organizing, extracting, and combining studies. This is particularly significant as researchers often struggle to keep up with new findings, especially within their specific fields. This challenge is exacerbated by disciplinary silos, especially in interdisciplinary areas like STEM education research. For example, cognitive psychologists may miss relevant work in math education research, and vice versa. Therefore, AI tools need to be developed to help accelerate, transform and reimagine the practice of research synthesis while being user-friendly, reliable, trustworthy, ethical and possibly freely available. Such tools can be suitably backed by *WebMap's* search infrastructure.

Additionally, the reliance on cooperative peers for providing cluster files introduces challenges related to data redundancy, reliability, and distribution. Ensuring equitable access to cluster files and maintaining data integrity across distributed networks will be crucial for the scalability and robustness of *WebMap* in real-world settings. To cope with the sheer mass of online text resources, it therefore seems to make the most sense to apply *WebMap* and its herein discussed extensions to closed networks such as enterprise networks and intranets first.

Overall, while the proposed enhancements represent a significant step forward in enhancing web-based research capabilities, ongoing research and development efforts are needed to address the aforementioned limitations and ensure the effectiveness and usability of *WebMap* across diverse use cases and environments. Collaborative efforts from the research community will be essential in advancing the state of the art in web-based information retrieval and knowledge discovery.

5   Conclusion

The proposed extensions to *WebMap* aim to support web-based research activities by leveraging advanced natural language processing techniques. By integrating LLMs and refining clustering algorithms, *WebMap* aims to provide users with more accurate, relevant, and comprehensive search results, ultimately enhancing their ability to navigate and explore complex information spaces on the web.

However, to fully realize the potential of *WebMap*, it is imperative to address the existing limitations and challenges, including the restriction to textual content, the need for improved cross-cluster navigation, and the complexities associated with distributed data management. Through continued research and innovation, *WebMap* has the potential to become a valuable tool for researchers, educators, and information seekers, facilitating seamless access to knowledge and insights across the vast expanse of the World Wide Web. These aspects will be addressed in future research works.

References

1. Roßrucker, G.: A Concept for a distributed Webmap. In: Supporting Web Search and Navigation by an Overlay Linking Structure. Studies in Big Data, vol. 142. Springer, Cham (2024). https://doi.org/10.1007/978-3-031-48393-6_3
2. Kubek, M., Unger, H.: Centroid terms as text representatives. In: Proceedings of the 2016 ACM Symposium on Document Engineering, pp. 99–102, ACM, New York, NY, USA (2016)
3. Jin, W., Srihari, R.K.: Graph-based text representation and knowledge discovery. In: Proceedings of the 2007 ACM Symposium on Applied Computing, ACM, New York, NY, USA (2007)
4. Biemann, C., Heyer, G., uasthoff, U.: Wissensrohstoff Text: Eine Einführung in das Text Mining. 2nd Edition, Springer Fachmedien Wiesbaden (2022)
5. Devlin, J., Chang, M., Lee, K., Toutanova, K.: BERT: pre-training of deep bidirectional transformers for language understanding (2019)
6. Beltagy, I., Lo, K., Cohan, A.: SciBERT: a pretrained language model for scientific text (2019)
7. Araci, D.: Finbert: Financial sentiment analysis with pre-trained language models (2019)
8. Kubek, M.: Concepts and Methods for a Librarian of the Web. In: Studies in Big Data, Vol. 62, Springer, Cham (2020)
9. Kleinberg, J.M.: Authoritative sources in a hyperlinked environment. J. ACM **46**, 604–632 (1999) ACM, New York, NY, USA
10. Bock, H.H.: Automatische Klassifkation. Vandenhoeck & Ruprecht, Göttingen (1974)
11. Schnell, P.: Eine Methode zur Auffindung von Gruppen. Biometrische Zeitschrift, **6**, 47–48 (1964)
12. Komkhao, M., Kubek, M., Halang, W.A.: Sequential clustering and condensing the meaning of texts into centroid terms. Inf. Technol. J. **14**, 1–10 (2018)
13. Vaswani, A., et al.: Attention Is All You Need. arXiv:1706.03762v7 [cs.CL] (2017)
14. Minaee, S., Mikolov, T., et al.: Large Language Models: a survey. arXiv:2402.06196v2 [cs.CL] (2024)

15. Brown, T., et al.: Language models are few-shot learners. Adv. Neural. Inf. Process. Syst. **33**, 1877–1901 (2020)
16. OpenAI: GPT-4 Technical Report (2023). https://arxiv.org/pdf/2303.08774v3.pdf
17. Touvron, H., et al.: LLaMA: open and efficient foundation language models. arXiv:2302.13971 [cs.CL] (2023)
18. Touvron, H., Martin, L., et al.: Llama2: open foundation and fine-tuned chat models. arXiv:2307.09288 [cs.CL] (2023)
19. Jiang, A.Q., Sablayrolles, A., et al.: Mistral 7B. arXiv:2310.06825v1 [cs.CL] (2023)

Development and Validation of AI-Driven NLP Algorithms for Chatbots in Requirement Engineering

Patrick Seidel[1]([✉]) and Steffen Späthe[2]

[1] Navimatix GmbH, 07743 Jena, Germany
Patrick.0512@hotmail.de
[2] Friedrich Schiller University Jena, 07743 Jena, Germany
steffen.spaethe@uni-jena.de

Abstract. The present research focused on the use of artificial intelligence (AI) and natural language processing (NLP) techniques in the field of requirements engineering within software development. The primary challenge is the prevention of miscommunication between the customer and the development team. In the worst-case scenario, it might lead to the premature termination of the project. The aim of this project is to develop a prototype of a chatbot able to evaluate consumer needs and suggest potential requests. The first step comprised a thorough evaluation of the chatbot's requirements, followed by the development of a prototype. Two transformer models have been developed to classify customer input, and an additional model has been established to generate suitable requests. The classification was obtained by assessing the level of detail of the provided user input using a classification model, as well as classifying them based on ISO 25010 (quality criteria for software). Both versions utilized the DistilBERT models as their foundation. A GPT-2 model was trained to generate the inquiry. This approach utilized ambiguous user inputs and generated inquiries to get further information. To determine the user's intention, it was decided to use RASA software to train an intention module. This module will be able to differentiate between a user's question and their intention to proceed with the acceptance procedure. The initial classification model achieved an accuracy of 0.7033, whereas the second model had an accuracy of 0.2784. Moreover, the output generated by the GPT model varies only to a limited degree. The quality of the model is directly influenced by the quality of the training data. Increasing the number of data points and balancing the classes can help enhance the model quality. Nevertheless, this scientific work presents a fundamental basis for the possible utilization of transformer models in the field of requirement engineering. Further exploration of the application of NLP approaches using transformer models to understand customer requirements has the potential to reduce the failure rate of software development projects.

F. Phillipson et al. (Eds.): I4CS 2024, CCIS 2109, pp. 132–149, 2024.
https://doi.org/10.1007/978-3-031-60433-1_9

Keywords: Artificial intelligence · Software engineering ·
Requirement engineering · Natural language processing · Natural
language understanding · Chatbots

1 Introduction

In recent years, the potential of artificial intelligence (AI) has significantly
increased. Currently, several techniques of AI may be utilized in diverse domains
to enhance the efficiency of everyday operations [21]. In the field of software
engineering, the phrase ai-oriented software engineering (AIOSE) is utilized to
explore the integration of AI with the software development life cycle (SDLC)
and assess the level of support AI can provide in this context [17].

The issue of communication difficulties in software development was previously examined by Thorsten Spitta in 1989 [32]. Agile methodologies like Scrum
and Kanban can mitigate the risk of misconceptions related to client needs,
however, they cannot entirely eradicate them. Customer-generated user stories
can enhance specification accuracy [11]. In the worst-case scenario, the software
that is created fails to fulfill the customer's specifications, resulting in the client
having the option to terminate the project early.

A further risk involves the inadequate prioritization or validation of client
needs by the project management [13]. The customer's understanding of this
matter is clear; hence the project manager must independently determine the priority. Consequently, if the requirements are incorrectly prioritized, it can result
in issues.

Moreover, the process of organizing the recording of customer needs requires a
significant amount of time [13]. Throughout this process, there may be language
difficulties between customers and developers, which might impact the ability to
accurately capture and comprehend the needs of customers. One of the imped-
iments is the customer's usage of vocabulary that is not comprehended by the
software team, leading to misinterpretation. Nevertheless, a similar situation can
arise when the developer team employs technical terms that the client may not
possess a complete comprehension of. In both situations, there is a potential for
communication issues that could be evident in the outcome and affect consumer
satisfaction.

Thus, it is imperative to establish precise customer requirements from the
onset of a project to ensure comprehensive understanding by the customer and
precise guidance for the developers. Alternatively, the project's conclusion may
be accompanied by substantial issues. The current research aims to illustrate
how the utilization of AI and natural language processing (NLP) techniques can
enhance the process of requirement engineering, thereby facilitating the effective
completion of projects.

The primary aim of this research is to assess the capacity of chatbots to mitigate communication challenges between clients and developers in the field of software development. The primary objective is to create a chatbot prototype that effectively captures client requirements and assesses them using suitable technology. Various techniques from the fields of AI, NLP, and natural language understanding (NLU) are employed. Furthermore, transformer models are being evaluated for examination because of their novel approach to addressing issues within the realm of NLP.

The results of the evaluation can be used to identify areas for optimization and develop relevant improvements and additions for the chatbot prototypes. The emphasis can be placed on modifying the algorithms, expanding the training data set, or incorporating supplementary AI and machine learning (ML) techniques.

2   Related Work

To carry out the systematic literature study, the following keyword string is utilized, which accurately defines and restricts the scope of the subject area:

1. ('"Software Development Life Cycle"' OR '"Software Development"') AND
2. ('"Artificial Intelligence"' OR "Machine Learning"' OR '"Deep Learning"' OR "Natural Language Processing"' OR '"Natural Language Understanding"') AND
3. ('"Requirement Engineering"') AND
4. ('"Chatbot"')

The initial segment relates to the domain of software development. The second clamp encompasses the topic domains of AI and NLP. To emphasize the significance of Requirement Engineering, this topic area is also included in a clamp. In conclusion, the term 'chatbot' is employed to delineate the subject matter. To maintain the research's currency, the year 2015 is selected as the earliest publication date. The research utilized the following scientific databases:

- Google Scholar
- Research Gate
- IEEE Xplore
- ScienceDirect
- ACM Digital Library
- arXiv

The provided conceptual matrix condenses the collected literature sources into a concise and organized format, facilitating further investigation.

Table 1. Concept matrix by Webster and Watson

Source	Software development	AI	NLP/NLU	Requirement Engineering	Chatbot
[5]	X	X	X	X	X
[22]	X	X	X	X	
[28]	X	X	X	X	X
[23]	X	X		X	
[33]		X	X	X	
[6]			X	X	
[29]		X	X		X
[26]	X	X			
[3]	X	X		X	
[4]	X	X		X	
[31]	X	X			
[18]	X	X			
[27]	X	X			
[14]		X		X	
[12]	X			X	
[8]	X		X	X	
[17]	X	X			
[2]		X			X
[25]		X	X		X
[10]		X	X		
[24]		X	X		
[20]		X	X		
[16]	X		X	X	
[30]		X	X		
[9]	X	X	X	X	
[7]			X	X	
[34]	X		X	X	
[26]	X	X			
[1]			X	X	
[19]		X	X	X	
Results:	17	23	18	17	5

Based on the current conceptual matrix (Table 1), we can derive some relevant results for the present research. Initially, it is evident that the prevalence of AI has expanded across several domains. Specifically, we will discuss the techniques of ML, deep learning (DL), and the transformer architecture. Furthermore, it is apparent that there is a significant amount of study being conducted on Requirement Engineering. Considering the significance of this stage in the software development process, it is advisable to pursue this research effort in the future. In addition, techniques of NLP and NLU have been experimented with in software development across different domains to facilitate the process and enhance the outcome's quality. A notable discovery about the subject matter of this study is the limited amount of research conducted on the advancement of chatbots and their incorporation into software development and requirement engineering. Furthermore, a few two additional scientific works comprehensively cover all five thematic areas concurrently [5,28]. This implies that the combination of these themes is new and should be investigated further in light of the advancing development of AI.

3   Theory

3.1   Stakeholder Identification

The chatbot was created to assist in the initial requirement analysis phase of software development. During this stage, the customer's needs are documented and analyzed. The system aims to condense and disclose customer requirements following a thorough study. The project manager receives a summary of customer requirements that has been thoroughly examined for misunderstandings or discrepancies. The project manager can analyze the outcome and convey it to the software development team. The client request is currently being transferred from the project manager to the software engineers. The direct stakeholders are the client, project managers, and software developers. Indirect stakeholders encompass all other interest groups that may seek information from the requirements. The interests of the direct stakeholders are further elucidated in the order mentioned above.

3.2   Stakeholder Requirements

The customer is aware of his requirements for the software solution to be developed. He is cognizant of the issue he aims to solve with the software. Furthermore, he possesses suitable quality standards and a hierarchy of requirements that he needs to convey to the project team. Failure to transmit or errors in transmission may lead to information asymmetries that could negatively impact the quality of software development. Common issues with requirements involve imprecise targeting, low requirement quality, and frequent objective changes. Hence, it is important for a customer to precisely characterize the problem, clearly explain the software's goal, and establish the necessary framework requirements. Financial and temporal considerations are crucial for customers and should be established early in a project. Furthermore, the chatbot's user interface should be highly intuitive. Overly intricate design, leading to input errors, might negatively impact software quality. After a client request is documented, the customer should have the ability to examine it to prevent duplications or misinterpretations. To enhance the chatbot's operation, it must autonomously approach customers to maintain an ongoing conversation and provide guidance. This establishes a setting where the customer can articulate their software solution and inquire about any relevant details. Once the customer outlines the proposed software solution, the chatbot will generate a summary to be forwarded to the project manager for additional project planning.

The chatbot must undergo consistency verification of customer requirements and create a summary for the project manager to review. It is crucial for the criteria to have a well-organized structure and be free of inconsistencies. The last aspect can impact the end product's quality, thus influencing consumer happiness. It is beneficial to rank the requirements based on the customer's preferences. This is crucial for accurately evaluating the significance of the functions for the client. Improper prioritization of requirements by the project manager might negatively impact client satisfaction.

Precise instructions aligned with the customer's requirements are crucial for software developers to effectively carry out the implementation process. Consider the software's technical information and specifications. The project manager must extract these facts from the customer's needs. Next, proceed with designing the software component. During implementation, the developer team might benefit from asking the client any questions that may arise. This can decrease the probability of misinterpretations and mistakes during the development process.

Finally, the client's focus is to clearly convey his ideas and desires to the project team. Concise articulation and proper prioritization of client requirements are more advantageous for the project manager and the software team. Adhering to these principles enhances the probability of creating software that effectively assists the consumer in resolving their issue.

3.3   Chatbot Requirements

After the needs of the parties have been analyzed, the requirements for the chatbot can be determined in the next stage. The functions are detailed following the Volere Requirements Specification Template, with points including description, justification, author, pass criterion, and requirement priority.

This assignment involves creating a prototype of a chatbot. This encompasses all pertinent functions but is restricted in its possibilities. This chatbot uses the transformer architecture and is specifically designed to understand and address customer needs for software development projects, setting it apart from other chatbots. The goal is to minimize communication challenges between customers and developers to provide a product that aligns with customer preferences. The subsequent features could be crucial for the examination and recording of conversations.

Record Customer Requirements. The chatbot is specifically programmed to gather and store user requirements for future reference. The system should appropriately record the requirements, which specify the required characteristics of the customer's software solution. The customer should have the capability to input his ideas into the system in order to transmit them to the project team for the purpose of software development. Once the chatbots restart, it's crucial to permanently store consumer requests. This function is crucial and has immense significance.

Manage Customer Requirements. Having the ability to change customers' written requirements proves to be beneficial. The consumer should have the ability to make bug repairs or additions, thereby influencing the quality of the final output. If there are any inaccurate entries, it should be feasible to take the appropriate actions to correct them. Therefore, the goal is to possess the capacity to modify the demands of customers in a manner that is sustainable and persistent. While changes in client demand are significant, they are of lesser importance when it comes to capturing and analyzing software requirements.

Analyze Customer Requests. The examination of customer requirements is thorough to detect any weaknesses and prepared them for following processing stages. Custom specifications possess diverse attributes that could have an extended impact on the end result. Identifying these traits is crucial for accurately classifying them for future applications. Analyzing customer requirements and identifying deficiencies assist the project team in creating an appropriate software solution. The customer specifications are thoroughly studied and then included into the current process. This analysis is of greatest significance and should be accorded top priority.

Identify User Intention. The chatbot requires the capability to analyze the user's intention in order to provide an appropriate response to its input. The user is driven by a certain objective, which he aims to achieve through his input. The chatbot's objective is to precisely discern the user's intention and deliver a suitable response. This function holds significant importance, as it requires the chatbot to determine the objective before initiating a suitable action.

Generate Requests. The chatbot should have the capability to generate responses by analyzing the specific attributes of the customer's inquiry. In order to more accurately discern the requirements of users, the chatbot must possess the capability to generate suitable questions. If the project team misunderstands the inaccurate specifications, it can negatively affect the quality of the software. The chatbot is capable of formulating requests to gather additional information regarding the specific software requirements of the customer. Integrating this can enhance the quality of the software.

Create Summary. The chatbot should possess the capability to concisely clarify the documented requirements of the customers with sufficient accuracy. Customer requests will persist in the system without any specific order and will need to be analyzed by the project manager at the beginning. A summary can help prevent any misinterpretations. The utilization of automatically generated written documentation enables the project team to expedite the development of the software project. The chatbot compiles and presents all the client requirements that have been supplied in a single text. The client requirements lack proper organization within the system. This can result in possible errors, which is why it is imperative to assign adequate importance to this condition.

This list is not complete and should be updated as the chatbot continues to improve. The functions listed above will be implemented and integrated into the chatbot as the work progresses.

4   Concept

This chapter explains the theoretical framework of the chatbot prototype. Initially, the distinct elements are elucidated, followed by a subsequent explication of their respective functionalities. The system incorporates the following components: the user, the Graphic User Interface, the Dialog Manager, the Intent module, the Transformer model, and the database. The components are thoroughly explained in the Table 2. These components communicate by exchanging messages. The objective is to generate a comprehensive summary of customer requirements and improve the accuracy of these requirements through requests. The process can be seen in the Fig. 1 and expanded upon in the subsequent paragraph.

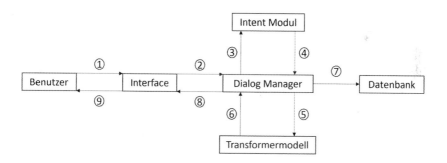

Fig. 1. Concept of the chatbot

1. At this stage, the user enters the message using natural language into the Graphic User Interface.
2. The Graphic User Interface transmits the message without any modifications to the Dialog Manager.
3. The message is sent to the Intent module to determine the user's intention. Furthermore, throughout this stage, the message remains unaltered and is analyzed by the module.

Table 2. Components explanation

Component	Explanation
User	The user submits his development requests to the chatbot system and responds to any inquiries
Graphic User Interface	Acts as a mediator between the user and the chatbot. The system acquires consumer input through a text box and subsequently transmits it. Furthermore, this component offers the chatbot's chat history to the customer
Dialog Manager	Operates as the central control unit of the chatbot. The system receives and assesses the input provided by the customer, and then transmits it to the appropriate modules. Furthermore, the consumer input is transmitted to the database
Intent Module	Module for determining intention and purpose. This module categorizes consumer inputs based on their intentions. From this classification, an appropriate response is deduced
Transformer models	These models are specifically developed to categorize customer requirements according to distinct attributes (DistilBERT model) and create requests (generative pre-training (GPT)-2 model). This facilitates the further processing of the client requirements entered the system
Database	Serves the purpose of persistently keeping all crucial information pertaining to the current session

4. The Intent module transmits the intention, typically in the form of a singular string, to the Dialog Manager. According to this analysis, it can react appropriately.
5. The customer request is sent to the appropriate transformer model, based on the relevant classification. The message is written in natural language.
6. During this stage, the output produced by a transformer model is transmitted on to the Dialog Manager. The message can be presented in several formats, including numerical representation or statements in plain language. The response format is contingent upon the specific transformer model employed.
7. To ensure effective and lasting storage of consumer input, it is kept in a database.
8. In order to enhance the precision of customer requirements, it is possible to request specific requirements from the user. These outputs are produced using a transformer model and transmitted to the Graphic User Interface using the Dialog Manager.
9. Finally, the generated queries are shown to the user in the Graphic User Interface, allowing them to respond to the requests. This allows it to specifically tailor information about its software preferences to the system.

This process demonstrates a singular procedure in which a consumer request is received and subsequently transmitted by the chatbot. In order to maintain a smooth and logical conversation, the various strategies outlined before are combined into an infinite number. However, demand creation only takes place when the customer's inquiry is classified as neutral or imprecise, leading to the acquisition of more precise information regarding the demand. It may be observed that the aforementioned functions have been effectively executed. The chatbot has the capability to receive requests from customers and accurately understand the user's intention. In addition, additional analysis is conducted, and the request is processed accordingly. Lastly, there is the option to inquire with the user in order to acquire supplementary information. In this case, the associated database is responsible for the permanent storage of the data.

The prototypes utilize a rule-based chatbot that operates on a set of predefined questions, which the chatbot asks the consumer. The questions are derived from the quality criteria outlined in ISO 25010 [15], which can be used as a foundation for efficient requirement engineering in software development. Each of the eight primary categories is accompanied by a concise question and an explanation. Regarding the functioning category, the user is presented with the following question:

- Functionality:
- What are the core functions you expect the software to perform?
- This category focuses on the functions that software provides to meet users' needs.
- Are there any secondary features or functionalities you'd like the software to have?

Initially, the user is informed about the specific category they are currently in. The second piece of information comprises an inquiry regarding the category, accompanied by a concise explanation to prevent any potential confusion. The conversation comprises a grand total of eight categories, which will be systematically completed one after another. To expedite the availability of inquiries, a data structure known as a stack structure (Request Stack) is utilized. It encompasses every request to be posed to the user. The stack data structure was intentionally selected because of its ability to efficiently store and retrieve created queries, allowing for prompt delivery to the user. Furthermore, it may be inferred that when the request stack is devoid of any requests, all the topics have been fully addressed and the interaction with the customer can be concluded. Therefore, all relevant information is accessible based on the quality standards outlined in ISO 25010 for the system.

To summarize, this approach aims to conduct a thorough requirement engineering process that particularly detects vulnerabilities in client needs. The purpose of this is to detect and prevent errors and misconceptions prior to the commencement of the active development process.

Following the explanation of the chatbot method, the subsequent discussion will center on the utilized technology and tools. The technologies encompassed are the Python programming language, the Intent Module RASA, the Hugging Face Library, and the NoSQL database technology MongoDB.

Python was used as the foundational programming language for the creation of the chatbot. Python's notable attribute is its exceptional flexibility in comparison to other programming languages, making it particularly suitable for prototyping. Furthermore, Python offers comprehensive standard libraries that facilitate quick program development. The subsequent libraries can be utilized to fabricate the prototype (Table 3):

Table 3. Explanation Python libraries

Library	Explanation
Tkinter/CustomTkinter	Tkinter is a package utilized for rapid generation of graphical user interface. CustomTkinter is a derivative of Tkinter that facilitates the rapid development of sophisticated graphical user interfaces
Requests	The library enables you to transmit HTTP requests. This library is used to establish a local RASA server in the prototypes
Pymongo	This module serves the purpose of enabling communication with the MongoDB database
Transformers	The library provides access to pre-trained transformer models through a Hugging Face API. These models can be trained on a local dataset
Dataset	This is a library designed to optimize the loading and preparation of data records. The software was created by Hugging Face and is utilized by the corresponding transformers
Huggingface_Hub	This function is employed to upload the trained transformers to the Hugging Face platform
PyTorch	This library encompasses a diverse range of techniques derived from the domain of deep learning, making it suitable for training neural networks on a computer. Furthermore, it has the capability to utilize the graphics processing unit for enhanced processing efficiency

The chosen libraries have expertise in implementing the functions that are listed. Furthermore, the Hugging Face library offers an evaluator that may assess the language models developed, as elaborated in the subsequent section.

5   Evaluation

The subsequent models will undergo evaluation to determine their quality. The quality of the classification models is assessed using suitable evaluation metrics, which are elaborated on in the Table 4 provided below. These metrics are extracted from the Hugging Face library and can be established prior to training the model. In this instance, the dataset employed was partitioned into a training dataset and a test dataset. The assessment was conducted subsequent to the model training.

Table 4. Explanation of evaluation metrics

Quality metrics	Explanation
Accuracy	The formula expresses the ratio of accurately identified data to the total amount of data: $Accuracy = \frac{Number of correct predictions}{Total number of predictions}$
Precision	Denotes the accuracy rate of accurately identifying positive-classed examples out of all positively categorized instances
Recall	Denotes the accuracy rate of positive examples with respect to the true positive instances
F-Score	This statistic is a combination of precision and recall, with equal weight given to both. $F1 = \frac{Precision x Recall}{Precision + Recall}$

First, we discuss the precision classification model, followed by the ISO 25010 model. Table 5 displays the relevant quality metrics of the first model. The values suggest an average quality. Modifying the training parameters or increasing the size of the training dataset can achieve model optimization.

Table 5. Quality metrics of the precision

Quality metrics	Value
Accuracy	0.7033
Precision	0.7215
Recall	0.7033
F1-Score	0.6945

The model's values for the ISO 25010 categorization do not yield satisfactory results. The goal is to enhance the quality of the model before implementing it into a functional system. Several variables can influence this attribute. It may be essential to invest more time in training to achieve a significant shift in values. Simultaneously, this raises the likelihood of overfitting. Furthermore, the quality of training data used throughout the training process may have an impact. These potential options need to be considered throughout the subsequent development phase to enhance the model's quality. However, it is crucial to thoroughly consider the software that will be built in a qualitative manner (Table 6).

Table 6. Quality metrics of the ISO 25010 model

Quality metrics	Value
Accuracy	0.2784
Precision	0.1854
Recall	0.2784
F1-Score	0.1894

The Table 7 displays ten client requests. The trained transformer model processed them and created related requests, which are displayed in the table. Some requests are clearly duplicated. The reason for this may be traced back to the training data, which needs to be modified as the process continues. The model fulfills fundamental functionality.

Table 7. Quality of the GPT-2 model

Requirement	Request
1. I want it to look good on mobile	What specific aspects or functionalities are you referring to in this requirement?
2. Something with notifications would be cool	What changes or improvements do you envision for the user interface?
3. Integration with Google Calendar is required	What specific aspects or functionalities are you referring to in this requirement?
4. The software should be compatible with both Windows and Mac	What specific aspects or functionalities are you emphasizing?
5. Maybe a feature for video?	What changes or improvements do you envision for the user interface?
6. I'd like a dashboard to see user activity	What specific aspects or functionalities are you referring to in this requirement?
7. I'd like a search feature to easily find records	What specific aspects or functionalities are you referring to in this requirement?
8. It would be great to have a dark mode option	What specific aspects or functionalities are you referring to in this requirement?
9. An offline mode would be beneficial	What specific aspects or functionalities are you referring to in this requirement?
10. I've heard about cloud, maybe we can use that?	What specific aspects or functionalities are you referring to in this requirement?

The model's size should be regarded as an additional criterion. The Bidirectional Encoder Representations from Transformers (BERT) models have a size of 3.49 gigabytes and 1.99 gigabytes, respectively. The generative pre-training (GPT)-2 model has a capacity of 3.71 gigabytes. The RASA module has a model size of 35.7 megabytes. There are noticeable disparities in size between the transformer models and the intent module. Nevertheless, it is possible to enhance the training of these models, which can subsequently impact both the size and quality of the models.

Three distinct models have been created to specialize in certain jobs. Nevertheless, they do not now reach the necessary standard to be deemed suitable for practical application. Upon assessing the progress of various transformer models utilized in these domains, it becomes evident that enhanced model training can improve outcomes. Hence, enhancing and expanding the training data is crucial for the chatbot's future advancement.

6   Discussion

This chapter critically examines the study's results. It helps uncover more opportunities for enhancement in the research field.

The literary research has supplied relevant information to explore the research theme of this work. Furthermore, it emphasized the originality of this subject and provided reasoning for its importance. Additional sources may have been considered in the analysis. The purpose of this work was not to conduct a comprehensive literary study but to create a summary of the originality of the subject.

The requirement analysis concentrated on assessing the needs of the demographics of the target audience and ranking the features to be integrated into the chatbot. It is recommended to confirm the demands of the target groups by conducting practical surveys like interviews or questionnaires. By using this method, additional requirements can be recognized and should be considered during the chatbot's development. Moreover, the target groups could be broadened by including other stakeholders. The demand analysis in this study complements the research process; however, it has potential for additional expansion.

Several models have successfully produced satisfactory results for developing a prototype. In the future, the models should be trained using higher-quality training data, and the trainer arguments should be fine-tuned. Increasing the epochs can impact both training time and memory use. Care should be taken to prevent overfitting the training data.

Additional stages in the advancement of this chatbot involve integrating diverse NLP methods, which might be accomplished through the use of transformer models. Furthermore, it is possible to train several transformer models that can perform additional jobs in semantic analysis. These possibilities possess the capacity to mitigate the likelihood of failure in a software development project and to enhance requirements engineering.

An overview of the use of chatbots in requirement engineering was generated, and the research objective was accomplished. Further research is required in this area because demand analysis plays a crucial role in different software projects, and the subject areas together show new insights.

7   Conclusion

The major objective of this study was to create the fundamental framework of an AI-driven chatbot focused on requirement engineering. An analysis of how this can help reduce communication problems between developers and customers should be conducted. A prototype and a concept were developed using transformer models to analyze customer needs in order to achieve the goal. Moreover, the chatbot might ask about incorrect user inputs. This can improve transparency in the software development process, increasing the likelihood of successfully finishing a project. The talk will include a detailed analysis of the quality standards specified in ISO 25010 to ensure a comprehensive evaluation of software quality. These chatbots can do demand surveys and analyses, thereby increasing the probability of project success.

Previous research shows a lack of investigation into the use of chatbots in requirement engineering. On the other hand, AI technology is commonly used in software development. NLP has the potential to be utilized in requirement engineering to automate processes and minimize errors.

The demand research results reveal the target groups' specific needs. The chatbot should take those factors into account and support them. Expand the prototype's functional range through iterative research. This can improve demand analysis, making the process faster and higher quality.

Furthermore, the assessment of the records produced by AI was conducted to evaluate their quality. The training data for this prototype was generated by the GPT-4 model and possesses sufficient quality to accurately represent the fundamental concept. Hence, these data is adequate for pursuing a novel avenue of investigation, although necessitating manual verification.

Academic studies should investigate the potential uses of chatbots in conjunction with technologists' studies. These facilitate communication between the computer and real people. By integrating language input and processing, specialized AI-driven assistants can be developed for many applications. Applications are varied and hold great potential, but achieving proficiency in these technologies requires a significant amount of dedication.

A model should be established in requirement engineering to evaluate client requirements for vulnerabilities, transform them into system requirements, and logically depict them in software development. In this situation, sequence-to-sequence models that can interpret needs and translate them into system requirements that software engineers can easily comprehend could be crucial.

Additional research is needed to explore the recommended issue further, building upon the current work and thoughts that have been provided. This can assist in the requirement analysis process in software development, thereby decreasing project failures.

References

1. Abdelnabi, E.A., Maatuk, A.M., Hagal, M.: Generating UML class diagram from natural language requirements: a survey of approaches and techniques. In: 2021 IEEE 1st International Maghreb Meeting of the Conference on Sciences and Techniques of Automatic Control and Computer Engineering MI-STA, pp. 288–293 (2021)
2. Adamopoulou, E., Moussiades, L.: An overview of chatbot technology. In: Maglogiannis, I., Iliadis, L., Pimenidis, E. (eds.) AIAI 2020. IFIP Advances in Information and Communication Technology, vol. 584, pp. 373–383. Springer, Cham (2020). https://doi.org/10.1007/978-3-030-49186-4_31
3. Ahmad, K., Abdelrazek, M., Arora, C., Bano, M., Grundy, J.: Requirements engineering for artificial intelligence systems: a systematic mapping study. Inf. Softw. Technol. **158**, 107176 (2023)
4. Ahmad, K., Abdelrazek, M., Arora, C., Bano, M., Grundy, J.: Requirements practices and gaps when engineering human-centered artificial intelligence systems. Appl. Soft Comput. **143**, 110421 (2023)
5. Ahmed, M.: Knowledge Base Enhanced & User-centric Dialogue Design for OTF Computing (2022)
6. Alzayed, A., Al-Hunaiyyan, A.: A bird's eye view of natural language processing and requirements engineering. Int. J. Adv. Comput. Sci. Appl. **12**(5) (2021)
7. Arora, C., Sabetzadeh, M., Briand, L., Zimmer, F.: Automated checking of conformance to requirements templates using natural language processing. IEEE Trans. Softw. Eng. **41**(10), 944–968 (2015)
8. Calle Gallego, J.M., Zapata Jaramillo, C.M.: QUARE: towards a question-answering model for requirements elicitation. Autom. Softw. Eng. **30**(2), 25 (2023)
9. Cevik, M., Yildirim, S., Başar, A.: Natural language processing for software requirement specifications. In: Proceedings of the 31st Annual International Conference on Computer Science and Software Engineering. CASCON 2021, pp. 308–309, USA, IBM Corp. (2021)
10. Chai, J., Li, A.: Deep learning in natural language processing: a state-of-the-art survey. In: 2019 International Conference on Machine Learning and Cybernetics (ICMLC), pp. 1–6 (2019). ISSN 2160-1348
11. Cohn, M.: User Stories: Für die agile Software-Entwicklung mit Scrum, XP u.a. BoD - Books on Demand (2021). Google-Books-ID: AT4qEAAAQBAJ
12. Daun, M., Grubb, A.M., Tenbergen, B.: A survey of instructional approaches in the requirements engineering education literature. In: 2021 IEEE 29th International Requirements Engineering Conference (RE), pp. 257–268 (2021). ISSN 2332-6441
13. Demant, C.: Prozesse für die Softwareentwicklung. In: Demant, C. (ed.) Software Due Diligence: Softwareentwicklung als Asset bewertet, pp. 161–243. Springer, Heidelberg (2018)
14. Guizzardi, R., Amaral, G., Guizzardi, G., Mylopoulos, J.: An ontology-based approach to engineering ethicality requirements. Softw. Syst. Model. (2023)
15. Haoues, M., Sellami, A., Ben-Abdallah, H., Cheikhi, L.: A guideline for software architecture selection based on ISO 25010 quality related characteristics. Int. J. Syst. Assur. Eng. Manag. **8**(2), 886–909 (2017)
16. Haris, M.S., Kurniawan, T.A.: Automated requirement sentences extraction from software requirement specification document. In: Proceedings of the 5th International Conference on Sustainable Information Engineering and Technology. SIET 2020, pp. 142–147. Association for Computing Machinery, New York (2021)

17. Hossain Faruk, M.J., Pournaghshband, H., Shahriar, H.: AI-oriented software engineering (AIOSE): challenges, opportunities, and new directions. In: Mejía, J., Muñoz, M., Rocha, A., Hernández-Nava, V. (eds.) CIMPS 2022. LNNS, vol. 576, pp. 3–19. Springer, Cham (2023). https://doi.org/10.1007/978-3-031-20322-0_1

18. Hou, X., et al.: Large Language Models for Software Engineering: A Systematic Literature Review arXiv:2308.10620 (2023)

19. Kolahdouz-Rahimi, S., Lano, K., Lin, C.: Requirement Formalisation using Natural Language Processing and Machine Learning: A Systematic Review arXiv:2303.13365 (2023)

20. Kotei, E., Thirunavukarasu, R.: A systematic review of transformer-based pretrained language models through self-supervised learning. Information **14**(3), 187 (2023)

21. Liang, W., et al.: Advances, challenges and opportunities in creating data for trustworthy AI. Nat. Mach. Intell. **4**(8), 669–677 (2022)

22. Liu, K., Reddivari, S., Reddivari, K.: Artificial intelligence in software requirements engineering: state-of-the-art. In: 2022 IEEE 23rd International Conference on Information Reuse and Integration for Data Science (IRI), pp. 106–111 (2022)

23. Magableh, A.A.: Towards leveraging explainable artificial intelligent (XAI) in requirements engineering (RE) to identify aspect (crosscutting concern): a systematic literature review (SLR) and bibliometric analysis. In: 2023 International Conference on Information Technology (ICIT), pp. 319–326 (2023). ISSN 2831-3399

24. Mathew, L., Bindu, V.R.: A review of natural language processing techniques for sentiment analysis using pre-trained models. In: 2020 Fourth International Conference on Computing Methodologies and Communication (ICCMC), pp. 340–345 (2020)

25. Narynov, S., Zhumanov, Z., Gumar, A., Khassanova, M., Omarov, B.: Development of chatbot psychologist applying natural language understanding techniques. In: 2021 21st International Conference on Control, Automation and Systems (ICCAS), pp. 636–641 (2021). ISSN 2642-3901

26. Nascimento, E.D.S., Ahmed, I., Oliveira, E., Palheta, M.P., Steinmacher, I., Conte, T.: Understanding development process of machine learning systems: challenges and solutions. In: 2019 ACM/IEEE International Symposium on Empirical Software Engineering and Measurement (ESEM), pp. 1–6 (2019). ISSN 1949-3789

27. Parikh, N.A.: Empowering Business Transformation: The Positive Impact and Ethical Considerations of Generative AI in Software Product Management – A Systematic Literature Review arXiv:2306.04605 (2023)

28. Rajender Kumar Surana, C.S., Shriya, Gupta, D.B., Shankar, S.P.: Intelligent chatbot for requirements elicitation and classification. In: 2019 4th International Conference on Recent Trends on Electronics, Information, Communication & Technology (RTEICT), pp. 866–870 (2019)

29. Rawat, B., Bist, A.S., Rahardja, U., Aini, Q., Ayu Sanjaya, Y.P.: Recent deep learning based NLP techniques for chatbot development: an exhaustive survey. In: 2022 10th International Conference on Cyber and IT Service Management (CITSM), pp. 1–4 (2022). ISSN 2770-159X

30. Schomacker, T., Tropmann-Frick, M.: Language representation models: an overview. Entropy **23**(11), 1422 (2021)

31. Siebert, J., et al.: Construction of a quality model for machine learning systems. Software Qual. J. **30**(2), 307–335 (2022)

32. Spitta, T.: Kommunikation, Lernprozesse und Prototyping. In: Spitta, T. (ed.) Software Engineering und Prototyping: Eine Konstruktionslehre für administrative Softwaresysteme. Springer Compass, pp. 147–157. Springer, Heidelberg (1989)
33. Yadav, A., Patel, A., Shah, M.: A comprehensive review on resolving ambiguities in natural language processing. AI Open **2**, 85–92 (2021)
34. Zhao, L., et al.: Natural language processing for requirements engineering: a systematic mapping study. ACM Comput. Surv. **54**(3), 55:1–55:41 (2021)

Structured Knowledge Extraction for Digital Twins: Leveraging LLMs to Analyze Tweets

Sergej Schultenkämper[✉] and Frederik Simon Bäumer

Bielefeld University of Applied Sciences and Arts, Bielefeld, Germany
{sergej.schultenkaemper,frederik.baeumer}@hsbi.de

Abstract. This paper concentrates on the extraction of pertinent information from unstructured data, specifically analyzing textual content disseminated by users on X/Twitter. The objective is to construct an exhaustive knowledge graph by discerning implicit personal data from tweets. The gleaned information serves to instantiate a digital counterpart and establish a tailored alert mechanism aimed at shielding users from threats such as social engineering or doxing. The study assesses the efficacy of fine-tuning cutting-edge open source large language models for extracting pertinent triples from tweets. Additionally, it delves into the concept of digital counterparts within the realm of cyber threats and presents relevant works in information extraction. The methodology encompasses data acquisition, relational triple extraction, large language model fine-tuning, and subsequent result evaluation. Leveraging a X/Twitter dataset, the study scrutinizes the challenges inherent in user-generated data. The outcomes underscore the precision of the extracted triples and the discernible personal traits gleaned from tweets.

Keywords: Privacy · Information extraction · Knowledge graph

1 Introduction

In the realm of online activities, individuals consistently leave behind digital footprints. These traces encompass various forms of shared content. Moreover, individuals often struggle to oversee the information concealed within the texts and images they disseminate, often oblivious to the potential repercussions. The potency of this information has been exemplified through numerous instances, including the utilization of social media to ascertain vacant homes based on vacation-related posts. These methodologies have been employed for diverse purposes, ranging from scoping out unoccupied residences for potential burglaries [10] to pinpointing locations of military installations by scrutinizing soldiers' jogging routes shared on fitness applications [5]. Even seemingly inconsequential data fragments, when correlated with supplementary information, present notable privacy threats, as corroborated by previous research [3].

In this study, our focus lies in analyzing the textual content shared by individuals on X/Twitter, with the aim of distilling pertinent insights from the chaotic

F. Phillipson et al. (Eds.): I4CS 2024, CCIS 2109, pp. 150–165, 2024.
https://doi.org/10.1007/978-3-031-60433-1_10

and unstructured deluge of data streams. The term "deluge of data streams" accurately characterizes the situation, especially considering that over 500 million tweets flood the platform daily, serving diverse purposes ranging from personal expression to news dissemination and contemporary discourse [11]. In this landscape, data analysis techniques play a pivotal role in sifting through both overt and covert personal information [15]. Consequently, the objective of this research is to scrutinize tweets across several dimensions, such as encompassing geographic locations, mentioned peers/users, and marital status. The overarching objective is to construct a comprehensive knowledge graph by harnessing information extracted from these unstructured data sources. This graph serves as the foundation for developing a digital twin (DT), which plays a central role in crafting a bespoke early warning system. In order to surmount the challenges associated with data extraction from tweets, we explore the suitability of contemporary, state-of-the-art (SOTA) open source large language models (LLMs). This study endeavors to ascertain the efficacy of open source LLMs in information extraction endeavors, given that existing proprietary LLMs pose constraints for our comprehensive analysis objectives, owing to the substantial effort required for processing the unstructured and often scantily informative X/Twitter data of varying lengths [1]. The development and refinement of LLMs, including GPT-4 and LLaMA-2 [20], have markedly transformed the landscape of information extraction, transitioning from unstructured to structured data with unprecedented efficiency and accuracy. This study is dedicated to assessing the proficiency of cutting-edge open source LLMs in executing triple extraction from tweets – a process that entails the identification of entities and their interrelations within the confines of unstructured textual data. Guiding this exploration are several pivotal research questions (RQs):

RQ1: Reliability of Structured Output Generation

How reliable are open source LLMs in generating structured outputs, such as JSON, suitable for further processing? This RQ assesses the adaptability and reliability of LLMs in producing structured outputs that facilitate the integration with modern technologies and the construction of knowledge graphs from unstructured data, comparing the original and fine-tuned models' output structuring capabilities.

RQ2: Effectiveness and Fine-Tuning of Models for RTE from Tweets

How do current SOTA models perform in extracting relational triples from tweets, and what impact does fine-tuning have on their efficiency, especially compared to proprietary models such as GPT-4? This research question aims to thoroughly evaluate the ability of SOTA models for relational triple extraction (RTE) from tweets using the precision metric for evaluation. Furthermore, it investigates the impact of fine-tuning open source LLMs on their performance on triple extraction tasks, analyzing the improvements achieved and how these improvements compare to the performance of closed-source models such as GPT-4.

RQ3: GPT-4 as Evaluator for Triple Extraction

Can LLMs serve as effective evaluators for the analysis of triples extracted by both the original and the fine-tuned models? This RQ explores the potential of LLMs to function as evaluators for assessing the quality of the extracted triples. It aims to provide a comparative analysis of traditional manual evaluation techniques in terms of accuracy. Additionally, it investigates how well GPT-4 can score the quality of the extracted triples.

The ADRIAN research project is dedicated to exploring and developing machine learning-driven methodologies for detecting potential risks to individuals within online data repositories. The background and related research for this study are thoroughly outlined in Sect. 2, while the data collection and methodological framework are elaborated in Sect. 3. The modeling strategies employed and the results obtained are meticulously described in Sect. 4. Finally, our are discussed in Sect. 5, and our overarching conclusions are succinctly summarized in Sect. 6.

2   Related Work

In this section, we delve into the concept of DTs within the realm of cybersecurity threats, examining the role and potential applications of DTs in forecasting, mitigating, and understanding cyber vulnerabilities (Subsect. 2.1). Additionally, we explore existing research related to information extraction (Subsect. 2.2), focusing on how LLMs are utilized and fine-tuned for enhanced performance in extracting valuable insights from vast datasets (Subsect. 2.3).

2.1   Navigating Cyber Threats Through Digital Twin Technology

The concept of DTs encompasses a wide range of applications across different fields, including medicine, computer science, and beyond, reflecting its multifaceted nature and adaptability [2,5,17]. With the evolution of artificial intelligence, the definition of DTs has expanded, now commonly referring to digital entities that simulate, replicate, or act as counterparts to real-world objects, processes, or beings. This broad definition allows DTs to serve as a bridge between the physical and digital realms, offering a dynamic tool for analysis, prediction, and optimization in various domains [2].

Within the scope of our research, we categorize DTs into three levels of integration based on their interaction with the physical world: the digital model, digital shadow, and DT [2]. The digital model represents a static virtual depiction requiring manual updates to reflect changes in its physical counterpart. Progressing from this, the digital shadow allows for a unidirectional flow of information from the physical entity to its digital representation, facilitated by sensors that transmit real-world data to the virtual model. The pinnacle of this hierarchy, the DT, achieves a symbiotic relationship through bidirectional communication, enabling the digital entity to mirror the real-time status and evolution of its physical counterpart accurately. The discussion extends to the emerging concept of the human digital twin, which, despite its significance, lacks a universally accepted definition [8,9,17]. This concept extends the idea of DTs to encompass digital representations of individuals, often derived from their digital footprints or digital shadows. These representations focus on capturing relevant personal characteristics such as demographic information, health status, or behavior patterns, aiming to provide a comprehensive yet individualized digital reflection of a person [8,17].

In the context of the ADRIANX project, we adopt a focused definition of a DT as a digital representation of an individual, created using publicly accessible web information [4,5]. It is crucial to recognize that while a DT attempts to replicate certain aspects of an individual's identity and potential vulnerabilities, it inherently cannot encompass the full complexity of a human being. Instead, it highlights specific attributes that, in isolation or conjunction with others, may expose the individual to various risks [3]. This nuanced understanding of DTs underscores their potential as a powerful tool in identifying and mitigating potential threats to individuals in the digital age, particularly within the ambit of cybersecurity and privacy protection.

2.2   Few-Shot Information Extraction

Relation extraction (RE) is the identification of pairs of entities and their relations, expressed as (HEAD, RELATION, TAIL), from unstructured text. Traditional approaches to RE are divided into two separate tasks: named entity recognition (NER) and relationship classification (RC) [6,23]. To mitigate the problem of error propagation that plagues conventional methods, recent research efforts have focused on developing integrated models for directly extracting relational triples in a comprehensive manner. Therefore, recent studies have aimed to overcome this problem by exploring common models for extracting relational triples in an end-to-end manner [19]. A prominent example of this new direction is the adoption of text generation strategies that consider a relational triple as a sequence of tokens. The work of Zeng [24,25] explains how this method uses an encoder-decoder architecture, similar to that used in machine translation, to generate the parts of a triple in a planned way.

With the advent of transformer-based text generation models, especially for GPT-3.5 [16] and GPT-4 [16], in-context learning (ICL) has become more important. Two studies by Wan et al. [21] and Xu et al. [22] have shown how these models use ICL to adapt quickly to new tasks by using context cues in inference prompts. This approach eliminates the need for task-specific training datasets. Few-shot ICL allows already trained LLMs to perform new tasks without the need for further gradient-based training. This is done by adding a small number of example inputs to the model's inference mechanism. This ability to adapt contextually allows a wide variety of tasks to be performed without the need for custom fine-tuning. Xu et al. [22] investigate the use of ICL to improve Few-Shot RE with LLMs. Their research distinguishes between two different types of prompts: basic text prompts, which contain only the elements necessary for RE, and more complex instructional prompts, which contain both these elements and explicit task-related instructions. Her results show that adding task-related instructions to prompts makes a big difference to how well LLMs can perform RE tasks. This shows the importance of including detailed instructions in prompts when trying to get the best results from LLMs on difficult tasks such as RE.

Wan et al. (2023) [21] present GPT-RE, an innovative approach that exploits the ICL capabilities of GPT-3 for relational extraction tasks. This method combines two main techniques: entity-aware demonstration retrieval and inferential demonstration. Entity-aware demonstration retrieval uses specific entity pair information to improve context reconstruction, and inferential demonstration uses correct relational labels to make inferences that improve demonstrations. Their results show that the quality of demonstrations greatly affects on how well GPT-3 performs in RE tasks and that demonstrations improved by reasoned inference outperform traditional fine-tuning approaches. This suggests not only that the quality of demonstrations is more important than their quantity, but also that the strategic use of inference in demonstrations can significantly improve ICL performance, underscoring the importance of well-designed demonstrations and the power of inference in advancing the use of LLMs for RE.

2.3   Fine-Tuning for Large Language Models

In the area of parameter-efficient fine-tuning (PEFT) strategies [14], our research focuses on evaluating the effectiveness of parameter-efficient fine-tuning (QLoRA) methods [7] for efficient fine-tuning of the Miqu-1-70B model on a specific dataset. Derived from the foundational work on low-rank adaption (LoRA) [13], QLoRA represents an advancement in PEFT by significantly reducing memory requirements. This reduction facilitates the fine-tuning of LLMs on devices with limited computational resources.

As a technique, adapter tuning, incorporates small, trainable modules into the interstices of an LLM's layers [12]. LoRA, on the other hand, focuses on modifying a selective subset of the model's weights through a low-rank decomposition approach. This method allows precise fine-tuning of LLMs by adjusting a limited number of task-specific parameters, thereby preserving the integrity of the model's extensive pre-trained weights. QLoRA extends this approach by integrating quantization techniques with LoRA's basic strategy, allowing efficient manipulation of gradients by a quantized, pre-trained language model without compromising task-specific performance.

Significant innovations in QLoRA include the introduction of NormalFloat, a breakthrough 4-bit data type designed to optimize memory usage while maintaining computational accuracy. QLoRA also incorporates dual quantization for constants and introduces page optimizers, a sophisticated mechanism for dynamic memory allocation during training phases. Taken together, these advances contribute to QLoRA's ability to fine-tune LLMs such as Miqu-1-70B on hardware platforms with limited memory resources, exemplifying a significant leap forward in the field of parameter-efficient fine-tuning.

3 From Dataset Construction to Extraction Evaluation

In this section, we outline the comprehensive methodology employed in our study (see Fig. 1), structured into three critical phases: (1) dataset creation in Subsect. 3.1, where we detail the processes involved in compiling and preparing the data; (2) modeling in Subsect. 3.2, in which we describe the development and application of computational models designed to perform the task at hand; and (3) evaluation in Sect. 4, where we assess the effectiveness and accuracy of the extraction process facilitated by our models.

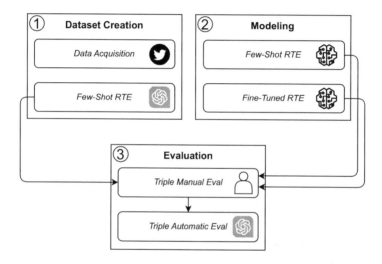

Fig. 1. Proposed approach for relational triple extraction

3.1 Dataset Creation

The data collection phase was carried out through X/Twitter, a prominent online social network (OSN), which served as a crucial source for modeling DTs and conducting threat analysis within the ADRIAN project. The dataset encompasses tweets spanning from October 5, 2015, to February 3, 2023, providing a broad temporal range for analysis. During this period, the OSN API was employed to facilitate the acquisition of detailed and expansive datasets, despite encountering challenges inherent to the platform's design.

One of the primary obstacles faced was the inherent character limit imposed on tweets, which, while fostering succinct communication, often necessitated the condensation of complex ideas into a constrained format. This brevity, coupled with the frequent inclusion of hashtags, user mentions, URLs, and emoticons, introduced a considerable amount of noise into the data. Such elements, while enriching the tweets with context and connectivity, also complicated the process of extracting clean, reliable information for substantive analysis.

To manage the vast dataset and ensure a focused approach, we randomly selected 300 users from our extensive database. Among these, 246 users were identified as active, having contributed tweets during the collection period. For the purposes of our analysis, the study was narrowed to focus exclusively on tweets crafted in English, aiming to maintain consistency and reliability in the evaluation of the extracted data (see Table 1). This deliberate selection process and targeted approach allowed for a more controlled examination of the data, facilitating the identification and analysis of potential threats within the digital discourse captured through X/Twitter.

Table 1. Overview of descriptive statistics for the data collection

Dataset Feature	Count
No. of Users	246
Avg. Tweets/User	3,532
Median Tweets/User	546
Min. Tweets/User	1
Max. Tweets/User	80,689
Top Languages	English, German, French
Total Tweets	869,069

In our preceding study [18], we delved into the realm of few-shot RTE leveraging GPT-4, scrutinizing a corpus of 5,000 tweets from 100 distinct users. Extensive manual inspection was added to this project with the goal of being able to assess the extracted relational triples' precision. This rigorous process culminated in the assembly of a dataset encompassing 1,288 relational triples. In our ongoing research, we are dedicated to expanding this dataset, thereby enriching both its comprehensiveness and scope. To this end, we analyzed an additional 5,000 tweets, during which we elected to omit the "*s:interest*" predicate class owing to its inherently vague nature. We used Label Studio[1] to check the accuracy of the extracted subjects, predicates, and objects. This allowed for a thorough evaluation based on the accuracy of each triple's component parts. Through this methodical evaluation, we were able to collect a dataset with 2,054 entries. The distribution of these entries is shown in Fig. 2. This expansion and refinement of our dataset underscore our commitment to enhancing the depth and breadth of our analysis in the domain of RTE.

The diagram (Fig. 2) illustrates a distinct contrast in the depiction of various predicates, with "*s:location*", "*s:attendee*", and "*s:spouse*" being particularly prominent. This suggests that, e.g., geographic and relational information are heavily emphasized in the dataset, indicating their significance or relevance to the intended application or type of data collected. Conversely, other categories

---

[1] https://labelstud.io/, accessed: 2024-02-16.

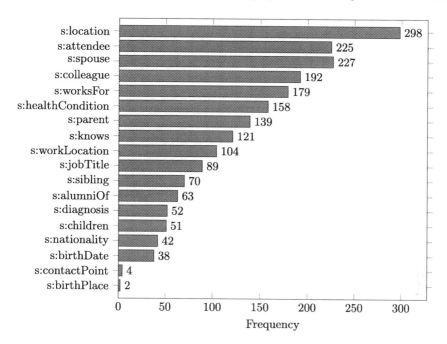

Fig. 2. Distribution analysis of predicate classes

are underrepresented and require further expansion in the future. The dataset's usefulness for certain analyses, particularly those requiring detailed biographical or contact information, could be limited due to the under-representation of predicates such as "*s:birthPlace*", "*s:contactPoint*", and "*s:birthDate*".

3.2 Modeling

For our study, we use the Miqu-1-70B model[2], accessible via HuggingFace[3]. Our initial comparative analysis contrasting the performance of LLaMA-2 and Mixtral 8x7B showed that Miqu-1-70B outperformed the others in terms of efficiency metrics. The model, a creation of Mistral.ai, is equipped with advanced natural language processing capabilities. Initially, our approach adopted few-shot learning techniques akin to those applied in GPT-4, utilizing OpenAI's capability for function calling to generate structured outputs for GPT models. With the Miqu-1-70B model, we crafted few-shot prompts in JSON format, intricately detailing the author and text of a tweet as input and the anticipated relational triple

---

[2] The selection of the Miqu-1-70B model for our study is based on its availability as an open-sourced resource, despite its origins in a leak. It's important to note that, due to these circumstances, there are no official publications or documented references that can be cited. Our choice to utilize this model is rooted in its potential for advancing research objectives, acknowledging the unconventional nature of its dissemination.

[3] https://huggingface.co/miqudev/Miqu-1-70B, accessed: 2024-02-16.

in JSON format as output. This method refined the learning process, markedly enhancing the precision and efficiency of extracting relational triples from tweets. Next, we used QLoRA to fine-tune the Miqu-1-70B model to improve the efficiency of the model for our task (see Fig. 3).

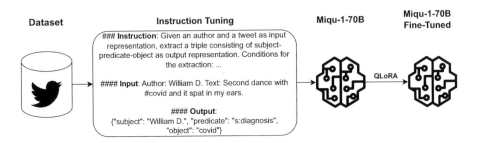

Fig. 3. Overview of the components required for the fine-tuning process

In configuring the training environment for our model, we meticulously optimized performance by setting specific parameters. Each device processed a training batch size of four, balancing computational efficiency with memory constraints. Our training strategy extended over 700 steps, with a carefully selected learning rate of 2×10^{-4}. This was complemented by a weight decay factor of 0.01 to mitigate overfitting risks. Optimization was further enhanced using the Paged AdamW optimizer, notable for its 8-bit precision capability, optimizing computational efficiency without compromising learning capacity. Furthermore, the integration of LoRA into our model tuning involved precise parameter adjustments. The rank of low-rank factorization, denoted as $lora\_r$, was set to 64. This setting aimed to maintain a manageable yet complex model structure. The scaling factor for this rank, $lora\_alpha$, was selected as 16, balancing the impact of low-rank factorization within the model's architecture. Additionally, we implemented a LoRA dropout rate of 0.1 to prevent overfitting and ensure robust model generalization. Next, we specifically targeted key modules within the transformer architecture for LoRA adjustments to enhance model performance. These modules, including "q_proj", "k_proj", "v_proj", "o_proj", "$gate\_proj$", "up_proj", "$down\_proj$", and "lm_head", are integral to the self-attention mechanism, a cornerstone of transformer models. By focusing on these components, we aimed to refine the model's attention mechanism, making it more adept at handling the nuances of language processing tasks.

The model's vast architecture comprises 35,582,074,880 parameters, of which 830,947,328 are trainable. This subset of trainable parameters represents 2.34% of the total parameter count, highlighting our targeted approach to model tuning. Such precision in fine-tuning allows for significant improvements in model performance without the need to adjust the entirety of the model's parameters.

One Nvidia A6000 GPU with 48 GB of memory powered our training infrastructure. This setup provided the necessary computational resources to handle the intensive demands of training a model of this scale. The fine-tuning process is crucial for tailoring LLMs to specific instructional goals. By training the model on carefully selected instruction-output pairs, we ensure that it is not only more controllable but also more adept at adapting to specific domains. This approach enhances the model's practical applicability, ensuring it performs efficiently on targeted tasks while optimizing computational resources.

4   Results and Evaluation

In this section, we delve into the comprehensive outcomes of our study, emphasizing both the qualitative and quantitative evaluation of the RTE capabilities of our model. The analysis presented herein spans manual and automatic evaluation methodologies to offer a holistic view of the model's performance. These evaluations serve to validate the the model's effectiveness in extracting relational triples with high precision. Initially, we embark on a meticulous manual evaluation of the RTE process. This phase is pivotal, for it provides an in-depth look at the model's precision in identifying and extracting relational triples from a curated dataset. Through this lens, we scrutinize the model's ability to discern and accurately represent the nuanced relationships present in natural language, offering insights into its practical applicability in real-world scenarios.

RQ1: Reliability of Structured Output Generation

To generate structured outputs, we adopted a novel approach distinct from our previous methodology involving GPT-4. This time, instead of relying on function calls, we utilized direct prompts paired with few-shot examples formatted in JSON. This strategy proved to be efficient in yielding structured outputs directly in JSON format, thereby negating the necessity for external libraries such as lmql[4] and guidance[5]. Across the spectrum of 1,015 texts analyzed, the outputs conformed to the requested format – either JSON or *None* – demonstrating precision in adherence to the provided prompts. Despite this accuracy, both models exhibited instances of deviation from the set extraction conditions, leading to the creation of hallucinations. Notably, the original model generated 17 such predicates, while the fine-tuned version limited this to just 7, including but not limited to *"s:acquiredBy"*, *"s:feeling"*, *"s:worksWith"*, and *"s:burialPlace"*, all of which were inaccuracies. Impressively, the model's fidelity to the instructions and its capability in structured in data extraction were commendable. The fine-tuning process, in particular, played a pivotal role in significantly diminishing the occurrence of hallucinated predicates, enhancing the model's performance and reliability.

RQ2: Effectiveness and Fine-Tuning of Models for RTE from Tweets

Manual evaluation is necessary because our approach aims to extract only one triple, and a tweet may contain multiple triples, as shown in Table 2.

---

[4] https://github.com/eth-sri/lmql, accessed: 2024-02-16.
[5] https://github.com/guidance-ai/guidance, accessed: 2024-02-16.

Table 2. Examples of triples extracted from tweets

Example 1

Author: *Lyle Povah* **Text:** *Earlier today Luke displays his baking* *@SixEightKafe #bakerboy:* http://t.co/7grEEekQ

Triple 1: *(Luke; s:jobTitle; baker)*

Triple 2: *(Luke; s:worksFor; @SixEightKafe)*

Example 2

Author: *Jim Thijs* **Text:** *From 1 island to another. Just when my friends from BEL arrived for the World Cup in Sardegna I'm leaving for Lanza!*

Triple 1: *(Jim Thijs; s:attendee; World Cup in Sardegna)*

Triple 2: *(Jim Thijs; s:location; Sardegna)*

Table 3 compares the performance of the model Miqu-1-70B in its quantized (q4_k_m) version before and after fine-tuning.

Table 3. Performance analysis before and after fine-tuning

Predicate Class	Miqu-1-70B				Miqu-1-70B-FT			
	Subj.	Pred.	Obj.	Support	Subj.	Pred.	Obj.	Support
s:alumniOf	1.0000	0.5273	0.8182	55	1.0000	0.5556	0.8667	45
s:attendee	1.0000	0.9231	0.9231	26	1.0000	0.9565	0.9855	69
s:birthDate	0.9231	0.8462	0.7692	26	1.0000	0.9333	0.8667	15
s:birthPlace	1.0000	0.6667	0.6667	3	1.0000	1.0000	1.0000	4
s:children	1.0000	0.8929	0.8571	28	1.0000	0.9459	0.9189	37
s:colleague	1.0000	0.9412	0.9118	34	1.0000	0.8992	0.8992	119
s:contactPoint	1.0000	0.2000	0.2000	10	1.0000	0.3333	0.6667	3
s:diagnosis	1.0000	1.0000	1.0000	9	1.0000	1.0000	1.0000	11
s:healthCondition	0.9891	1.0000	1.0000	92	1.0000	0.9897	0.9588	97
s:jobTitle	0.8889	0.8889	0.8889	9	0.9565	0.8261	0.8261	23
s:knows	1.0000	0.7740	0.9231	208	1.0000	0.8716	0.9324	148
s:location	0.9834	0.8729	0.9282	181	1.0000	0.9318	0.9545	132
s:nationality	1.0000	0.8889	0.8889	9	1.0000	0.9167	0.9167	12
s:parent	1.0000	0.9722	0.9167	36	0.9811	0.9811	0.9623	53
s:sibling	1.0000	1.0000	1.0000	12	1.0000	0.9615	0.9231	26
s:spouse	1.0000	0.9853	0.9412	68	1.0000	0.9535	0.9302	86
s:workLocation	1.0000	0.7755	0.8367	49	0.9818	0.8727	0.9455	55
s:worksFor	0.9692	0.7077	0.6923	65	1.0000	0.8704	0.9074	54
Micro Avg	0.9902	0.8370	0.8913	920	**0.9970**	**0.9050**	**0.9312**	989
Macro Avg	0.9863	0.8257	0.8423	920	**0.9955**	**0.8777**	**0.9145**	989

The results focus on different predicate classes, assessing metrics such as subject, predicate, and object accuracy, along with the number of supporting instances. *None* entries predicated by the model were excluded; the eval dataset has a total of 1015 entries. The original model extracted 95 times *None*, while the fine-tuned model extracted only 26 times *None*. Fine-tuning significantly improved performance in all metrics, with the micro and macro averages showing significant increases in accuracy for subject, predicate and object. *None* entries predicated by the model were excluded; the eval dataset has a total of 1015 entries. The original model extracted 95 times *None*, while the fine-tuned model extracted only 26 times *None*. Fine-tuning significantly improved performance in all metrics, with the micro and macro averages showing significant increases in accuracy for subject, predicate and object. In particular, individual predicate classes such as "*s:attendee*", "*s:birthPlace*" and "*s:children*" showed considerable improvements in predicate and object accuracy. The fine-tuning process also led to changes in the number of supporting instances for some classes, indicating a rebalancing of the dataset. For example, the "*s:colleague*" class saw a significant increase in support, while the "*s:jobTitle*" class saw a decrease. Notable improvements in accuracy were seen in areas such as "*s:contactPoint*" and "*s:healthCondition*", indicating the effectiveness of the fine-tuning process in improving the semantic understanding and relationship extraction capabilities of the model. Furthermore, we are also measuring the precision in regards to the annotations of GPT-4:

$$\text{Precision} = \frac{\text{True Positives (TP)}}{\text{True Positives (TP)} + \text{False Positives (FP)}} \tag{1}$$

$$\text{Precision}_{\text{miqu}} = \frac{399}{399 + 555} \approx 0.418 \tag{2}$$

$$\text{Precision}_{\text{miqu-ft}} = \frac{591}{591 + 398} \approx 0.598 \tag{3}$$

RQ3: GPT-4 as Evaluator for Triple Extraction

After manual assessment, we conduct initial tests to explore the possibility of automating this process using LLMs in the future. This will aid in pre-filtering and prioritizing information for the graph. For this purpose, we perform a small analysis with 100 tweets (50 correct and 50 incorrect) to evaluate the ability of GPT-4 to identify correct and incorrect extractions of the Miqu-1-70B-FT model. For prioritization purposes, we extract 50 samples from both the original and fine-tuned models to evaluate their ability to recognize tweets with more information content. Additionally, we analyze the model annotations to assess the potential of this approach for future use. For this approach, results are generated using the pairwise string comparison approach from Langchain[6].

Pre-filtering: The objective is to filter out noise and irrelevant data and only keep the triples that are relevant for further analysis. In this context, precise

---

[6] https://python.langchain.com/docs/guides/evaluation, accessed: 2024-02-16.

descriptions of the classes and statements are included in the prompt so that, for example, classes such as "*s:parent*" and "*s:children*" are not confused, as happens when classifying without the few-shot approach. GPT-4 is able to classify the triples in relation to the tweets very reliably, with an accuracy of 0.96.

Prioritizing: The For this approach, results are of the prioritization phase is to further refine the analysis by distinguishing between different types of information content and focusing on those that are most relevant in the context of user privacy analysis. GPT-4 has shown that it is able to accurately distinguish between different types of information content, which is crucial for the creation of knowledge graphs for user privacy analysis. After a manual evaluation, 47 of 50 examples would also receive human consent. An illustrative example involves a tweet that mentions "*Mother/daughter selfies! #selfie #frenchie #frenchbulldog #friday #instafrenchie @ Hamburg, Europa Passage.*" Here, the model identified two key predicates: "*s:location*" and "*s:children*". It prioritized the "*s:location*" predicate as it provided explicit information about the author's whereabouts, showcasing the model's ability to distinguish between direct and more implicitly conveyed information. This revision keeps the focus on the specific predicates and the model's prioritization decision without detailing the entire triples, making the explanation more concise and to the point.

5   Discussion

This approach highlights the dynamic development in the field of LLMs and the broad applicability of current open source models to a wide range of individual tasks. A major advantage is the ability to run these models in a quantized version (q4_k_m) on a 48 GB graphics card with only minimal performance loss compared to the original version. Hosting the models locally enables comprehensive analysis of large amounts of data at a lower cost. This approach enables the creation of a comprehensive knowledge graph from unstructured information, such as tweets, which can be used to analyze privacy-sensitive features. The Miqu-1-70B model has already proven its ability to extract important information from unstructured text. Through fine-tuning, the model has improved its accuracy in identifying triples (subject, predicate, object), which increases its effectiveness in extracting relevant information. These improvements are particularly evident in the consistent extraction of objects, even with slight variations such as "Hamburg" and "HH, Hamburg".

Although this approach has advantages, it also has weaknesses. One challenge is extracting triples from tweets, particularly in precisely identifying predicates and objects. Normalizing objects is essential for building a comprehensive knowledge graph, which requires various techniques such as geocoding for location information or resolving links in tweets for additional information. Another issue is the repetition of tweets on similar topics by the same users, which causes information redundancy. Future improvements should take into account the timing of tweets for tracking specific events or analyzing changes over time. The initial approach focused on extracting a single triple per tweet, assuming that tweets provide limited information density. However, the objective should be to identify all potential triples within a tweet to maximize the analysis possibilities and deepen the understanding of content on social media.

The paper's approach and outcomes offer several benefits for the ADRI-ANX project, particularly in improving its ability to identify and address risks related to profiling individuals and institutions in Web 2.0 environments. The precision required to extract structured information, such as relational triples, from noisy data characterized by slang, misspellings, abbreviations, and mixed languages is crucial in accurately identifying personal and sensitive information disseminated online. This precision is vital for ADRIAN's objectives as it enables the accurate mapping of an individual's digital footprint across heterogeneous online data repositories. By improving these extraction techniques, the project can more effectively identify subtle, implicit data points that may not be overtly personal but can become sensitive when aggregated. With a more accurate and detailed extraction of information, the ADRIAN project can customize its alert mechanisms to be more specific and relevant to the individual or institution at risk. By comprehending the precise nature of the extracted data and its potential implications, the project can offer more personalized and actionable advice on mitigating the risks associated with online profiling and attacks.

6 Conclusion

In conclusion, this study presents valuable insights into the field of RTE using advanced language models. The study demonstrates the robustness, efficiency, and adaptability of the Miqu-1-70B model in understanding and extracting complex relational data from natural language texts through a comprehensive set of evaluations, including manual and automatic analysis. The evaluation shows that the model enables the possibility of extracting triples from tweets with high accuracy, achieving micro-average scores of 0.9970 for subjects, 0.9050 for predicates, and 0.9312 for objects.

Our manual and automatic evaluations of RTE show that the model achieves high precision in extracting relational triples and is efficient across a diverse dataset. The model's ability to quickly analyze tweets in the quantized version allows it to process and analyze large-scale, rich, and dynamic social media data, demonstrating its potential for real-world applications in social media analytics, intelligence gathering, and beyond. In the context of our research project, the processing of large volumes of data is crucial. Additionally, the fine-tuning process, which leverages QLoRA, has been instrumental in enhancing the model's training efficiency and adaptability to specific domains. This approach to model optimization enables the extraction of high-quality relational triples with minimal computational resources, demonstrating the practicality of deploying such models in various operational environments.

Upon reflection of our study, it is evident that integrating few-shot RTE with advanced language models such as Miqu-1-70B presents a promising approach for extracting and analyzing relational data on a large scale. The knowledge gained from this research not only contributes to academic discourse but also facilitates innovative applications in natural language processing and beyond. The discussion has highlighted weaknesses and disadvantages that need to be addressed in further work. Moving forward, we anticipate exploring the optimization of RTE methodologies, expanding model capabilities to encompass a broader range of languages and domains, and developing more sophisticated models that can navigate the complexities of language with unprecedented accuracy and efficiency.

Acknowledgments. This research is funded by dtec.bw – Digitalization and Technology Research Center of the Bundeswehr. dtec.bw is funded by the European Union – NextGenerationEU.

References

1. Ahmed, W., Bath, P.A., Demartini, G.: Using Twitter as a data source: an overview of ethical, legal, and methodological challenges. Ethics Online Res. **2**, 79–107 (2017)
2. Barricelli, B.R., Casiraghi, E., Fogli, D.: A survey on digital twin: definitions, characteristics, applications, and design implications. IEEE Access **7**, 167653–167671 (2019). https://doi.org/10.1109/ACCESS.2019.2953499
3. Bäumer, F.S., Grote, N., Kersting, J., Geierhos, M.: Privacy matters: detecting nocuous patient data exposure in online physician reviews. In: Damaševičius, R., Mikašytė, V. (eds.) ICIST 2017. CCIS, vol. 756, pp. 77–89. Springer, Cham (2017). https://doi.org/10.1007/978-3-319-67642-5_7
4. Bäumer, F.S., Kersting, J., Orlikowski, M., Geierhos, M.: Towards a multi-stage approach to detect privacy breaches in physician reviews. In: SEMANTICS Posters&Demos (2018)
5. Bäumer, F.S., Denisov, S., Su Lee, Y., Geierhos, M.: Towards authority-dependent risk identification and analysis in online networks. In: Halimi, A., Ayday, E. (eds.) Proceedings of the IST-190 Research Symposium (RSY) on AI, ML and BD for Hybrid Military Operations (AI4HMO) (2021)
6. Chan, Y.S., Roth, D.: Exploiting syntactico-semantic structures for relation extraction. In: Proceedings of the 49th Annual Meeting of the Association for Computational Linguistics: Human Language Technologies, pp. 551–560 (2011)
7. Dettmers, T., Pagnoni, A., Holtzman, A., Zettlemoyer, L.: QLoRA: efficient fine-tuning of quantized LLMs. In: Advances in Neural Information Processing Systems, vol. 36 (2024)
8. Engels, G.: Der digitale Fußabdruck, Schatten oder Zwilling von Maschinen und Menschen. Gruppe. Interaktion. Organisation. Zeitschrift für Angewandte Organisationspsychologie (GIO) **51**(3), 363–370 (2020). https://doi.org/10.1007/s11612-020-00527-9
9. Feher, K.: Digital identity and the online self: footprint strategies-an exploratory and comparative research study. J. Inf. Sci. **47**(2), 192–205 (2021)
10. Flinn, M.B., Teodorski, C.J., Paullet, K.L.: Raising awareness: an examination of embedded GPS data in images posted to the social networking site twitter. Issues Inf. Syst. **11**(1), 432–438 (2010)
11. Gopi, A.P., Jyothi, R.N.S., Narayana, V.L., Sandeep, K.S.: Classification of tweets data based on polarity using improved RBF kernel of SVM. Int. J. Inf. Technol. **15**(2), 965–980 (2020). https://doi.org/10.1007/s41870-019-00409-4

12. Houlsby, N., et al.: Parameter-efficient transfer learning for NLP. In: International Conference on Machine Learning, pp. 2790–2799. PMLR (2019)
13. Hu, E.J., et al.: LoRA: low-rank adaptation of large language models. In: International Conference on Learning Representations (2022). https://openreview.net/forum?id=nZeVKeeFYf9
14. Liu, H., et al.: Few-shot parameter-efficient fine-tuning is better and cheaper than in-context learning. Adv. Neural. Inf. Process. Syst. **35**, 1950–1965 (2022)
15. Mazza, M., Cola, G., Tesconi, M.: Ready-to-(ab)use: from fake account trafficking to coordinated inauthentic behavior on Twitter. Online Soc. Netw. Media **31**, 100224 (2022). https://doi.org/10.1016/j.osnem.2022.100224
16. OpenAI: ChatGPT: Optimizing Language Models for Dialogue (2022). https://openai.com/blog/. Accessed 02 Oct 2023
17. Schultenkämper, S., Bäumer, F.S.: Privacy risks in German patient forums: a NER-based approach to enrich digital twins. In: Lopata, A., Gudonienė, D., Butkienė, R. (eds.) ICIST 2023. CCIS, vol. 1979, pp. 113–123. Springer, Cham (2024). https://doi.org/10.1007/978-3-031-48981-5_9
18. Schultenkämper, S., Bäumer, F., Geierhos, M., Lee, Y.S.: From unstructured data to digital twins: from tweets to structured knowledge. In: Proceedings of the Thirteenth International Conference on Social Media Technologies, Communication, and Informatics, SOTICS 2023, pp. 6–11. IARIA (2023)
19. Shang, Y.M., Huang, H., Sun, X., Wei, W., Mao, X.L.: Relational triple extraction: one step is enough. In: Raedt, L.D. (ed.) Proceedings of the Thirty-First International Joint Conference on Artificial Intelligence, IJCAI 2022, pp. 4360–4366. International Joint Conferences on Artificial Intelligence Organization (2022). https://doi.org/10.24963/ijcai.2022/605
20. Touvron, H., et al.: Llama 2: Open Foundation and Fine-Tuned Chat Models (2023)
21. Wan, Z., et al.: GPT-RE: In-context Learning for Relation Extraction using Large Language Models (2023)
22. Xu, X., Zhu, Y., Wang, X., Zhang, N.: How to Unleash the Power of Large Language Models for Few-shot Relation Extraction? (2023)
23. Zelenko, D., Aone, C., Richardella, A.: Kernel methods for relation extraction. J. Mach. Learn. Res. **3**, 1083–1106 (2003)
24. Zeng, D., Zhang, H., Liu, Q.: Copymtl: copy mechanism for joint extraction of entities and relations with multi-task learning. In: The Thirty-Fourth AAAI Conference on Artificial Intelligence, pp. 9507–9514 (2020)
25. Zeng, X., Zeng, D., He, S., Liu, K., Zhao, J.: Extracting relational facts by an end-to-end neural model with copy mechanism. In: Proceedings of the 56th Annual Meeting of the Association for Computational Linguistics, pp. 506–514 (2018)

Graphs and Routing

Oblivious Graph Algorithms for Solving TSP and VRP Using FHE and MPC

Sam Leder[1,2(✉)] and Thijs Laarhoven[2,3]

[1] TU/e, Eindhoven, The Netherlands
[2] TNO, The Hague, The Netherlands
sam.leder@tno.nl, mail@thijs.com
[3] NXP, Eindhoven, The Netherlands

Abstract. As the world is starting to realize the necessity and potential of privacy-friendly data processing, various questions need to be answered regarding potential solutions. Especially for the developing field of fully homomorphic encryption (FHE), which aims to offer the best privacy protection at a high computational cost, there are big expectations for future applications, but the question of practicability remains a major issue. Can this technology compete with more mature and efficient technologies like multiparty computation (MPC)? Can current state-of-the-art FHE schemes and libraries be deployed in realistic applications? In this paper we attempt to gain further insights into the current status of FHE as a privacy-enhancing technology, by studying a use case related to route planning in transport and logistics. In this application, a central computing server is tasked with (obliviously) computing a short tour along various destinations (known as the traveling salesman problem, or TSP), without seeing the privacy-sensitive input data of the user, namely which destinations the user wishes to visit. We also study a generalization of this problem with multiple tours being planned, each departing from the same central depot (known as the vehicle routing problem, or VRP). Finally, we aim to assess how solutions for TSP and VRP using FHE compare to solutions using MPC.

Keywords: Traveling Salesman Problem (TSP) · Vehicle Routing Problem (VRP) · Fully Homomorphic Encryption (FHE) · Multiparty Computation (MPC) · Privacy-enhancing technologies

1 Introduction

Ever since Gentry's breakthrough in 2009 [15], it has been known that it is possible to construct so-called fully homomorphic encryption (FHE) schemes: encryption schemes which allow evaluating arbitrary circuits under encryption, without having to decrypt in between. This new technology has the potential to make a large impact on our society, allowing more privacy-friendly data processing. One major drawback of this technology is the enormous computational

© The Author(s), under exclusive license to Springer Nature Switzerland AG 2024
F. Phillipson et al. (Eds.): I4CS 2024, CCIS 2109, pp. 169–196, 2024.
https://doi.org/10.1007/978-3-031-60433-1_11

overhead – even after various improvements since then [5–7, 10, 13, 14], the technology is struggling to compete with computationally cheaper technologies such as multiparty computation (MPC). With a lot of work being done on FHE however, this technology is gradually evolving from a theoretical novelty to a practical and mature privacy-enhancing solution.

1.1 Related Work

Over the past decade, a lot of work has been done to improve various aspects of FHE and make it usable in practical applications. This includes the development of various FHE libraries, such as Concrete [33], HEaaN [17], HElib [16], Lattigo [19], OpenFHE [12], and SEAL [22]. Applications of FHE have also been studied, such as those involving private information retrieval [1, 21] and privately using health data [3, 25, 31], and a few online demos have been publicly released [4, 18, 32]. Users can further benchmark various FHE implementations with HEBench [23], and some high-level comparisons between FHE and techniques like MPC have been described [8, 24, 28]. For practitioners however, various open questions still remain: How big is the computational overhead of FHE in various applications? How easy is FHE to use with existing libraries, and how does it compare to MPC in practice?

We note that a lot of research exists on solving logistical problems such as TSP and VRP, and also on secure computation methods such as FHE and MPC, but so far no paper has been published on the combination of both. For this reason, this work is possibly the first on this specific combination of topics and does not build on earlier work that is similar, but rather aims to combines ideas and approaches from logistical research on the one side and cryptographic research on the other side.

1.2 Contributions

In this work, we study a concrete use case in transport and logistics, where the use of privacy-enhancing solutions can be beneficial: letting a cloud service do route planning for a client, without the cloud service learning the sensitive input data. Specifically, we study methods for two well-known graph problems, the traveling salesman problem (TSP) and its generalization, the vehicle routing problem (VRP), using either FHE or MPC to guarantee data privacy to the client. Our implementations of algorithms for TSP and VRP were done using two Python libraries: the FHE library Concrete [33] and the MPC library MPyC [26].

The purpose of this case study is twofold. First, route planning is a generic problem appearing in various contexts, both in actual route planning involving vehicles visiting several physical locations [30], but also in other problems where a number of nodes must be visited in a graph. For a more concrete example of a use case, consider the situation where multiple parcel delivery companies operate in the same area. While cooperating with each other can make their delivery routes much more efficient in total, these companies normally do not want to share all of their delivery data with their competitors. Therefore, studying the applicability of privacy-sensitive solutions to this problem can help shed light on possible solutions for securely computing short routes.

Secondly, we believe that this problem is a good example of a problem one might encounter in practice when studying the use of privacy-enhancing technologies, and studying the feasibility of FHE and MPC for this use case may help give insights to other use cases as well. Various lessons and conclusions we draw therefore apply more broadly to FHE and how it compares to MPC.

1.3 Lessons Learned

Regarding the practicality of FHE (Concrete), and how it compares with MPC (MPyC) for these graph problems, we have both good and bad news for FHE.

The good news for FHE in our case study is that we indeed managed to implement the selected algorithms in Concrete. Despite the large key sizes and the number of table lookups, the algorithm runs in a reasonable amount of time for small to moderate parameters. With optimized hardware, more optimized implementations, and addressing some of the issues we faced when using Concrete, one may be able to run these algorithms under FHE for moderately-sized parameters in a reasonable amount of time. Moreover, if one can amortize the setup costs (compilation, key generation, sending the keys) over many runs with the same parameters, then in this case study FHE can be competitive with MPC.

The bad news for FHE in our study is that, compared to MPC, the overhead is still enormous, with key sizes/communication complexities which are higher by a factor between 1000–10000, and total time complexities which are commonly a factor 100–1000 higher when comparing our implementation in Concrete with our implementation in MPyC. Moreover, we ran into various usability issues when trying to run these algorithms in Concrete, which made implementing these algorithms in FHE significantly more challenging than when using MPC.

Overall, our main conclusions may be summarized as that although FHE clearly has potential, and conceptually it has clear advantages over MPC, in practice we currently observe between two and four orders of magnitude difference in efficiency between our (non-optimized) implementations of these algorithms in FHE and MPC, which severely limits the practicability of FHE for real-world settings where deep computations are needed. In terms of usability, there is still a way to go to make FHE as easy to use as MPC, let alone as easy to use as a baseline implementation without privacy-enhancing technologies.

1.4 Outline

The remainder of this paper is organized as follows. In Sect. 2 we cover notation and preliminaries regarding graph theory and cryptography. Section 3 covers how we model the desired functionality of our solutions. Section 4 describes how we amended these graph algorithms in a privacy-sensitive manner, and Sect. 5 contains experimental results from our implementations, and discusses how to interpret these results.

2   Preliminaries

Below we first introduce notation and recall definitions from graph theory (Subsect. 2.1), covering the traveling salesman problem and the vehicle routing problem. Then we cover the graph algorithms studied in this paper (Subsect. 2.2); here we differentiate between construction algorithms and enhancement algorithms. This is followed by cryptographic methods used for executing these algorithms in a secure manner (Subsect. 2.3). Finally we discuss some basic techniques for making algorithms run in a manner which is oblivious to the secret input (Subsect. 2.4).

2.1   Graph Problems

Throughout the paper we write $G = (V, E)$ for undirected graphs, with V denoting the set of $|V| = n$ nodes, and $E \subseteq V \times V$ denoting the set of (undirected) edges. Unless stated otherwise, we assume the graph is the complete graph on V, i.e., $E = V \times V$.

The Traveling Salesman Problem (TSP). For finding "short" tours through a graph, to the edges we first associate a distance or weight function $d : E \to \mathbb{N}$, and with abuse of notation we will write $d(v, w)$ for the function d applied to the edge $\{v, w\}$. We assume this distance function is symmetric, i.e. $d(v, w) = d(w, v)$ for all $v, w \in V$, and we assume that $d(v, v) = 0$.

Definition 1 (Hamiltonian tour). *Given a graph $G = (V, E)$, a Hamiltonian tour is a tuple $\mathbf{r} = (r_0, r_1, \ldots, r_{n-1})$ such that the vertices in $\mathbf{r}$ form a partition of V. We write $\mathcal{H}(G)$ for the set of all Hamiltonian cycles of the graph G. The length of a Hamiltonian tours $\mathbf{r} \in \mathcal{H}(G)$ is defined as:*

$$d(\mathbf{r}) := d(r_0, r_1) + d(r_1, r_2) + \cdots + d(r_{n-1}, r_0). \tag{1}$$

Definition 2 (Traveling salesman problem). *Given a graph $G = (V, E)$, the traveling salesman problem (TSP) asks to find a Hamiltonian tour $\mathbf{r} \in \mathcal{H}(G)$ such that:*

$$d(\mathbf{r}) = \min_{\mathbf{r}' \in \mathcal{H}(G)} d(\mathbf{r}'). \tag{2}$$

The Vehicle Routing Problem (VRP). For the generalization to computing multiple tours starting from a central depot (the vehicle routing problem), we assume that the distance function d is extended to a depot v^*, and we can therefore also compute distances $d(v^*, w) = d(w, v^*)$ for $w \in V$.

Definition 3 (Depot route). *Given a graph $G = (V, E)$ and a depot v^*, a depot route is a tuple $\mathbf{r} = (v^*, r_0, r_1, \ldots, r_{k-1})$ such that the nodes $r_0, \ldots, r_{k-1}$ are (distinct) vertices of V. We denote its length as:*

$$d(\mathbf{r}) := d(v^*, r_0) + d(r_0, r_1) + \cdots + d(r_{k-1}, v^*). \tag{3}$$

Below we define vehicle schedules and the vehicle routing problem with and without a constraint function Q, which defines if a solution is valid or not.

Definition 4 (Vehicle schedule with/without constraints). *Given a graph* $G = (V, E)$ *and an integer* $m \geq 1$, *we define a vehicle schedule without constraints with* m *vehicles as a tuple of* m *depot routes* $\mathbf{s} = (\mathbf{r}_0, \ldots, \mathbf{r}_{m-1})$ *such that the (non-depot) nodes of these* m *routes together form a partition of* V. *We define* $\mathcal{S}_m(G)$ *as the set of all vehicle schedules on* G *with* m *vehicles. Given a function* $Q : \mathcal{S}_m(G) \rightarrow \{true, false\}$, *we further define* $\mathcal{S}_m(G; Q) \subseteq \mathcal{S}_m(G)$ *as the set of vehicle schedules* $\mathbf{s} \in \mathcal{S}_m(G)$ *such that* $Q(\mathbf{s}) \equiv true$. *For a vehicle schedule* $\mathbf{s} = (\mathbf{r}_0, \ldots, \mathbf{r}_{m-1}) \in \mathcal{S}_m(G)$, *we define its length as:*

$$d(\mathbf{s}) := \sum_{i=0}^{m-1} d(\mathbf{r}_i). \tag{4}$$

Definition 5 (Vehicle routing problem without constraints). *Given a graph* $G = (V, E)$ *and an integer* $m \geq 1$, *the vehicle routing problem (VRP) without constraints with* m *vehicles asks to find a vehicle schedule* $\mathbf{s} \in \mathcal{S}_m(G)$ *such that:*

$$d(\mathbf{s}) = \min_{\mathbf{s}' \in \mathcal{S}_m(G)} d(\mathbf{s}'). \tag{5}$$

Definition 6 (Vehicle routing problem). *Given a graph* $G = (V, E)$, *an integer* $m \geq 1$, *and a function* $Q : \mathcal{S}_m(G) \rightarrow \{true, false\}$, *the vehicle routing problem (VRP) with* m *vehicles asks to find a vehicle schedule* $\mathbf{s} \in \mathcal{S}_m(G; Q)$ *such that:*

$$d(\mathbf{s}) = \min_{\mathbf{s}' \in \mathcal{S}_m(G;Q)} d(\mathbf{s}'). \tag{6}$$

The Role of the Constraint Function Q. One might wonder why one would need the constraint function Q above, i.e. why the above definition without constraints is not sufficient to define the vehicle routing problem in a clean way. This is because without constraints (i.e. defining $Q(\mathbf{s}) \equiv true$ for all $\mathbf{s} \in \mathcal{S}_m(G)$), and assuming the triangle inequality on $d(\cdot, \cdot)$, the solution to the vehicle routing problem without constraints will always involve one vehicle going through all nodes in V (so $|\mathbf{r}_0| = n + 1$), and all other vehicles having the trivial route $\mathbf{r}_1 = \cdots = \mathbf{r}_{m-1} = (v^*)$. The point of the generalization from TSP to VRP is to somehow achieve a balance between minimizing the total distance traveled, while also making sure that the work load is balanced between the different vehicles. This could for instance manifest in constraints in Q of the form $|\mathbf{r}_i| \approx n/m$ for all i, or $d(\mathbf{r}_i) \approx d(\mathbf{s})/m$ for all i. The precise shape of Q will depend on the application, but it is clear that a constraint function Q is needed to make sure that the problem does not trivially reduce to the traveling salesman problem.

The Distribution of Problem Instances. To study different algorithms and their performance for solving the above problems, we first define how we generate TSP and VRP problem instances. We will focus on graphs with nodes corresponding to coordinates distributed uniformly at random in a (discretized) square, and with distances corresponding to (rounded) Euclidean distances between the node coordinates. The continuous version of this problem is defined below.

Definition 7 (Uniformly random Euclidean graphs). *Let $n \geq 1$ be given. To sample a uniformly random Euclidean graph $G = (V, E)$ on n nodes, for each node $v_i \in V$, $0 \leq i < n$, we first sample uniformly random coordinate vectors $(X_i, Y_i) \in [0, 1]^2$. The graph consists of the vertices $V = \{v_0, \dots, v_{n-1}\}$, and to each edge $\{v_i, v_j\}$ we associate the distance:*

$$d(v_i, v_j) := \sqrt{(X_i - X_j)^2 + (Y_i - Y_j)^2}. \tag{7}$$

In practice, and especially when dealing with FHE, one needs to specify the precision and bitlength of different values. While coordinates are only used to generate the distance matrix, the distances are also used in the algorithm, and are now in the (continuous) interval $[0, \sqrt{2}]$. Throughout we will work with discretized distances, using a parameter T to define the precision used in the distances:

$$d_T(v_i, v_j) := \frac{1}{T} \left\lfloor T\sqrt{(X_i - X_j)^2 + (Y_i - Y_j)^2} \right\rceil.$$

Note that as $T \to \infty$, we have $d_T(v_i, v_j) \to d(v_i, v_j)$ for all vertices v_i and v_j. With the above discretized distances, $T \cdot d(v_i, v_j) \in \{0, \dots, \lfloor T\sqrt{2} \rceil\}$, e.g. with $T = 100$ one distance can be represented in a single byte. Note that, unlike when using exact Euclidean distances, this approximate distance function only approximately satisfies the triangle inequality: due to the rounding, for $T = 2$ the distances between the nodes $v_0 = (1/3, 0)$, $v_1 = (1/2, 0)$, and $v_2 = (2/3, 0)$ satisfy $1/2 = d_2(v_0, v_2) > d_2(v_0, v_1) + d_2(v_1, v_2) = 0$.

Throughout the paper, we will work with the above definition of random graphs, corresponding to nodes distributed independently and uniformly at random from a square. In practical applications, e.g. route planning problems with real-world data, the data might be more clustered, or distances might behave differently (e.g. Manhattan distances may more accurately model distances in real-world road networks in cities). The above distribution of random problem instances has the advantage of being parameterless (apart from the precision parameter T, which will always be needed for implementations). Moreover, for the continuous version of the above distribution, we know quite well how long a shortest Hamiltonian tour will roughly be.

Lemma 1 (Expected optimal tour length for uniformly random Euclidean graphs [2]). *There exists a constant $\beta > 0$ such that, as $n \to \infty$,* *the length $d(\mathbf{r})$ of a shortest Hamiltonian tour in a uniformly random Euclidean graphs on n nodes satisfies:*

$$\lim_{n \to \infty} \frac{d(\mathbf{r})}{\sqrt{n}} = \beta. \tag{8}$$

The best proven bounds on β are $0.62 < \beta < 0.93$ (see e.g. [29]), while Monte Carlo experiments suggest that $0.70 \leq \beta \leq 0.72$, with [20] estimating the constant as $\beta \approx 0.7124$. For this distribution of problem instances, this therefore gives us a good idea about the length of an exact TSP solution, so that we can see how far algorithms are from the optimum. Concretely, we expect the length of a TSP solution $\mathbf{r}_{\text{TSP}}$ to scale proportional to $\mathbf{n}$, and a VRP solution to scale proportional to $\mathbf{n} + \mathbf{m}$ roughly as:

$$d(\mathbf{r}_{\text{TSP}}) \approx 0.71\sqrt{n}, \qquad d(\mathbf{r}_{\text{VRP}}) \approx 0.71\sqrt{n + m}. \tag{9}$$

Note that for the vehicle routing problem without constraints, one would expect the same scaling, but with typical constraints the leading constant may go up slightly, depending on the constraints. The above scaling for VRP may serve more as a heuristic lower bound for VRP. For both problems, this means that given an approximate solution $\mathbf{r}$, we can define the expected approximation ratio as the ratio between the actual length and the expected optimal length:

$$\text{EAR}(\mathbf{r}_{\text{TSP}}) = \frac{d(\mathbf{r}_{\text{TSP}})}{0.71\sqrt{n}}, \qquad \text{EAR}(\mathbf{r}_{\text{VRP}}) = \frac{d(\mathbf{r}_{\text{VRP}})}{0.71\sqrt{n + m}}. \tag{10}$$

For TSP this ratio is more accurate depiction of the approximation factor of the solution than for VRP, but note that in both cases $\text{EAR}(\mathbf{r})$ may be less than 1, depending on the sampled graph.

2.2 Graph Algorithms

As the aforementioned graph problems are NP-complete, no efficient algorithms exist for finding exact solutions. In this paper we will focus on efficient heuristic algorithms which attempt to find approximate solutions to the above problems within a reasonable amount of time – as we will see later, even these elementary algorithms will already be quite costly to run in an oblivious manner on medium-sized graphs.

Below, we will consider two types of algorithms: algorithms for generating an initial solution (for TSP or VRP) from scratch, and algorithms that take an existing solution and make (local) improvements to it.

Tour Construction. For constructing initial solutions for TSP and VRP, we describe three different algorithms below:

- A trivial construction;
- A greedy nearest neighbor approach;

– A divide-and-conquer approach via clustering.

First, for constructing an initial solution to the above graph problems, for both TSP and VRP we can easily construct trivial algorithms running in essentially constant time. Given a graph $G = (V, E)$ with nodes $V = \{v_0, v_1, \ldots, v_{n-1}\}$, for TSP the trivial algorithm outputs a tour $\mathbf{r} = (v_0, v_1, \ldots, v_{n-1})$. For VRP with m trucks (and assuming $m|n$ for simplicity), a trivial algorithm simply outputs the vehicle schedule $\mathbf{s} = (\mathbf{r}_0, \ldots, \mathbf{r}_{m-1})$ with $\mathbf{r}_i = (v^*, v_{in/m}, \ldots, v_{(i+1)n/m-1})$.

For the traveling salesman problem, besides the trivial algorithm we consider the greedy nearest neighbor approach outlined in Algorithm 1. Given a starting vertex of the tour, the algorithm iteratively looks for the nearest vertex to connect to from the end of the chain, until finally the last remaining vertex is assigned and the loop is closed by connecting the last vertex with the initial vertex. This algorithm is deterministic and runs in time $O(n^2)$, but the quality of the output may heavily depend on the choice of initial vertex v_0. A randomized version of this algorithm may involve running the algorithm several times with different starting vertices, and outputting the shortest of the tours found in this process.

Algorithm 1. Greedy(V, v_0)

Input: A set of n vertices V, and a starting vertex $v_0 \in V$
Output: An initial solution $\mathbf{r} \in \mathcal{H}(G)$ with $r_0 = v_0$
1: $(\mathbf{r}, V') \leftarrow ((v_0), V \setminus \{v_0\})$
2: **for** i from 1 to $n - 1$ **do**
3: $\quad v \leftarrow \arg\min_{w \in V'} d(r_{i-1}, w)$
4: $\quad (\mathbf{r}, V') \leftarrow ((\mathbf{r}, v), V' \setminus \{v\})$
5: **return** $\mathbf{r}$

For the vehicle routing problem, the crucial difference with the traveling salesman problem (and the main challenge) is how to assign nodes to different vehicles. This is important to do well from the start, since it is hard to update the assignment of nodes to vehicles while still making progress: small inaccuracies in the edge selection within a route can be addressed quite efficiently with tour improvement algorithms, but changing the node assignment will often ruin the solution found so far.

For finding a suitable assignment of nodes to vehicles, we consider the clustering algorithm described in Algorithm 2. This algorithm first creates a set of centers C which are as far spread out as possible, by iteratively computing a new center vertex as the vertex which is the furthest from the existing set of center vertices. Once a set of m centers $c_0, \ldots, c_{m-1}$ has been constructed, the assignment of the remaining vertices to the clusters is again done in a greedy manner by letting each center in turn pick the vertex closest to them from the remaining set of vertices. Ultimately the algorithm returns a partition of V into subsets

$V_0, \ldots, V_{m-1}$. The clustering can be done in time $O(n^2)$ similar to the nearest neighbor approach, with a larger leading constant than the nearest neighbor approach.

Algorithm 2. Clustering(V, m)

Input: A set of n vertices V, a number of clusters m
Output: A clustering partition $(V_0, \ldots, V_{m-1}$ of V)
 1: $(V_0, \ldots, V_{m-1}) \leftarrow (\emptyset, \ldots, \emptyset)$
 2: $c \leftarrow v^*$ ▷ dummy center: depot v^*
 3: $(C, V') \leftarrow (\{c\}, V)$
 4: **for** j **from** 0 **to** $m - 1$ **do**
 5:      $c_j \leftarrow \underset{w \in V'}{\arg\max} \left(\underset{c \in C}{\min} d(w, c) \right)$ ▷ find center far from C
 6:      $(C, V') \leftarrow (C \cup \{c_j\}, V' \setminus \{c_j\})$
 7: **while** $V' \neq \emptyset$ **do**
 8:      **for** j **from** 0 **to** $m - 1$ **do**
 9:          $v \leftarrow \arg\min_{w \in V} d(c_j, w)$ ▷ find closest vertex to c_j
10:          $(V_j, V') \leftarrow (V_j \cup \{v\}, V' \setminus \{v\})$
11: **return** $(V_0, \ldots, V_{m-1})$

The output of the clustering algorithm can subsequently be used as input for, e.g., the greedy approach to create a TSP solution for each subset of vertices $V_0, \ldots, V_{m-1}$, to ultimately obtain a balanced (initial) VRP solution. Alternatively, one can combine the assignment of nodes to clusters with the generation of an initial tour for each subset by dividing nodes differently over the clusters: for each cluster, we find the closest node to the latest node added to this cluster, rather than to the center representing this cluster. This way, after the clustering is done, each cluster already contains a short solution, saving some time later to generate a good tour.

Note that the clustering approach could also be used for TSP directly, to save time, by partitioning the graph into smaller graphs, running the nearest neighbor approach on the subgraphs, and then tying the chains together to form one big tour. If a TSP algorithm has a complexity scaling as αn^2 for n nodes, then such an algorithm would have complexity $m \cdot (\alpha(n/m))^2 = (\alpha n^2)/m$, i.e., saving a factor m in the time complexity. In this paper we will only consider the clustering approach in the context of VRP with m vehicles.

Tour Enhancement. Given an existing solution to TSP or VRP, we can also try to build a better solution from this solution by making small, local updates. We will consider a number of algorithms which are related to the 2-opt algorithm:

- Performing a single local swap;
- A full round over all potential swaps;
- Generalizations to VRP and randomizations.

The basic local improvement that lies at the foundation of all these algorithms is the local update described in Algorithm 3. Given a tour $\mathbf{r} = (r_0, r_1, \ldots, r_{n-1})$, we see if there is a pair of edges $\{r_i, r_{i+1}\}$ and $\{r_j, r_{j+1}\}$ that could be improved by replacing these two edges with $\{r_i, r_j\}$ and $\{r_{i+1}, r_{j+1}\}$. If these two replacement edges together are shorter than the edges currently in the tour, then we can indeed decrease the length of the tour by replacing the tour $\mathbf{r}$ by a tour $\mathbf{r}'$ as follows:

$$\mathbf{r} = (\ldots, r_{i-1}, r_i, r_{i+1}, r_{i+2}, \ldots, r_{j-1}, r_j, r_{j+1}, r_{j+2}, \ldots) \qquad (11)$$

$$\big\downarrow \quad \text{TwoSwap}(\mathbf{r}, i, j)$$

$$\mathbf{r}' = (\ldots, r_{i-1}, r_i, r_j, r_{j-1}, \ldots, r_{i+2}, r_{i+1}, r_{j+1}, r_{j+2}, \ldots) \qquad (12)$$

Here the black nodes in the tour remain untouched from $\mathbf{r}$ to $\mathbf{r}'$; the edges between the red nodes decide whether to swap or not, and impact the potential decrease from $d(\mathbf{r})$ to $d(\mathbf{r}')$; and the blue nodes are part of the tour that needs to be reversed, to make sure that only the two red edges are changed. Figure 1 illustrates this same example visually.

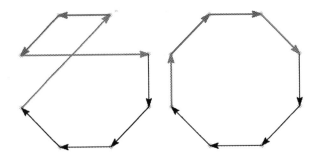

Fig. 1. Example of an application of the TwoSwap algorithm to the tour $\mathbf{r}$ on the left, resulting in the tour $\mathbf{r}'$ on the right

Algorithm 3 describes this swapping procedure in pseudocode. For large n, the complexity of one potential swap is already $O(n)$, due to the bookkeeping of the blue part of the tour which generally has length $O(n)$ for random indices i and j[1].

Applying the swapping algorithm for all candidate pairs of indices i, j, and repeating these (potential) swaps until no more progress is made is known in the literature as an algorithm due to Croes [11]. A single round of this algorithm, where all pairs i, j are considered once, is sketched in Algorithm 4 and will be denoted as one round of the 2-opt algorithm. In practice one might have to run

---

[1] More precisely, the algorithm has a complexity scaling as $O((|i - j| \bmod n))$, which for random i, j will be $O(n)$, but which for near-adjacent indices i, j may be $o(n)$.

Algorithm 3. TwoSwap($\mathbf{r}$, i, j)

Input: A TSP solution $\mathbf{r}$, and two indices $0 \leq i, j \leq n - 1$
Output: A TSP solution $\mathbf{r}'$ with $d(\mathbf{r}') \leq d(\mathbf{r})$
1: $\mathbf{r}' \leftarrow \mathbf{r}$
2: $d_{\text{cur}} \leftarrow d(r_i, r_{i+1}) + d(r_j, r_{j+1})$
3: $d_{\text{new}} \leftarrow d(r_i, r_j) + d(r_{i+1}, r_{j+1})$
4: **if** $d_{\text{new}} < d_{\text{cur}}$ **then**   ▷-swapping i, j improves tour
5:     **for** k from 0 to $\lfloor \frac{j-i}{2} \rfloor$ **do**
6:        swap($(\mathbf{r}')_{i+k+1}$, $(\mathbf{r}')_{j-k}$)   ▷ reverse tour between i, j
7: **return** $\mathbf{r}'$

---

several full rounds over all pairs of indices to make sure a local minimum in the solution space is reached, and no more progress with these simple updates can be found. As a single swap already takes time $O(n)$ due to the bookkeeping and reversing part of the tour, a full iteration over all pairs takes $O(n^3)$ operations. Experiments with randomly generated graphs further suggest that the number of rounds t until convergence scales as $t \propto \log n$ as n grows[2], suggesting that running the 2-opt algorithm until no more improvements can be made requires $O(n^3 \log n)$ operations.

Algorithm 4. TwoOpt($\mathbf{r}$)

Input: A TSP solution $\mathbf{r}$
Output: A TSP solution $\mathbf{r}'$ with $d(\mathbf{r}') \leq d(\mathbf{r})$
1: $\mathbf{r}' \leftarrow \mathbf{r}$
2: **for** i from 0 to $n - 2$ **do**
3:     **for** j from $i + 2$ to $n - 1$ **do**   ▷ skip adjacent edges
4:        $\mathbf{r}' \leftarrow$ TwoSwap($\mathbf{r}'$, i, j)
5: **return** $\mathbf{r}'$

Apart from the 2-opt algorithm, various generalizations can be constructed. As the 2-opt algorithm ultimately ends up in a local minimum, and this local minimum may not be a global minimum, one might also attempt to obtain a better solution by randomizing this algorithm and running it several times from different starting tours. When reaching a local minimum in the space of 2-opt solutions, one might further attempt to make further progress with more involved updates, such as 3-opt steps (or more generally k-opt steps) where larger tuples of edges are considered for replacement by another tuple of edges, otherwise keeping the tour intact.

In this paper we will focus on the "plain" 2-opt algorithm, as this algorithm will already be costly enough to run under encryption, and because it gives decent solutions for small to moderate graph sizes. In practical settings, one can

---

[2] More precisely: a least-squares fit for data collected for n up to 100 suggests the number of rounds r scales roughly as $r \approx 0.6 + 1.05 \ln n$.

always choose to run more iterations of 2-opt, randomize the algorithm, or run more advanced algorithms to achieve a different time–quality trade-off.

2.3   Cryptographic Methods

In this paper, we consider two main cryptographic methods for achieving additional privacy guarantees: fully homomorphic encryption (FHE), and multiparty computation (MPC). In this section, we describe both in more detail.

Fully Homomorphic Encryption (FHE). Homomorphic encryption is a method to encrypt data so that functions f can be computed under encryption, without having to decrypt: besides the encryption and decryption functions satisfying $\text{Dec}(\text{Enc}(x)) = x$, we have $\text{Dec}(\text{Eval}(f, \text{Enc}(x))) = f(x)$ for some (public) evaluation method Eval to evaluate f on a ciphertext $c = \text{Enc}(x)$. This means that a user can encrypt their data, send it to a computing server, after which the server can evaluate a function f on the encrypted data, send back the modified ciphertext to the user, and the user can finally decrypt this ciphertext to recover f evaluated on their private input. The computing server does not see the private data inside the encryption, but can still perform function evaluation for the user.

Various encryption schemes satisfying certain homomorphic properties have been described over the years, where e.g. f is limited to only additive or only multiplicative operations. In 2009 Gentry [15] solved the long-standing open problem of constructing a scheme which is able to evaluate arbitrary functions f under the encryption, based on lattice-based cryptography. Although for some applications, a low multiplicative depth may suffice and "partial" homomorphic encryption may suffice, the algorithms considered in this paper have a too high depth that one really needs (one of) these FHE schemes to be able to evaluate e.g. 2-opt under encryption.

Bootstrapping. FHE schemes work with noisy ciphertexts, and performing operations on encrypted data increases the noise in these ciphertexts. To guarantee correct decryption after many operations, for all FHE schemes it is necessary to implement a *bootstrapping* procedure, which can be seen as a washing machine: at a relatively high computational cost, bootstrapping takes a ciphertext with high noise and "cleans" it to produce a ciphertext of the same value but with less noise, so that it can then be used again for further computations.

Over the last decade, various improvements to the initial scheme of Gentry have been described, with the main popular schemes currently being BFV [5,14], BGV [6], CKKS [7], DM [13], and TFHE [10]. These offer different trade-offs in terms of e.g. the costs of a bootstrapping step, the ability to perform additional computation steps during the bootstrapping procedure, the possibility of packing larger amounts of data in a single ciphertext, and the guarantee that the final result will be exact or approximate.

Choice of Scheme/Library: TFHE and Concrete. As all schemes have their own merits, it is hard to predict exactly which scheme, and which FHE implementation will work best for a given application. In this paper we chose to work with TFHE [10], and specifically the implementation in Zama's Concrete library [33]. Reasons for this choice include the speed of the bootstrapping step, which will need to be performed often for the algorithms considered here; the maturity of the implementation, with a large team at Zama working on it; the ability to perform table lookups during the bootstrapping step; and the ease of use, with a high-level Python library for implementing these graph algorithms.

Multiparty Computation (MPC). Besides the setting of outsourcing the computation to a single compute server, one can also consider methods where several parties perform the computations together. Assuming these computing parties do not collude to extract the user's private input data (e.g. if the user is one of the computing parties), this solution information-theoretically guarantees the privacy of the input data.

Unlike FHE, MPC has a long history, with the main building block of Shamir secret sharing dating as far back as 1979 [27]. To share a private input s, the user creates a degree-m polynomial $p(x)$ with constant term $p(0) = s$, and shares evaluations $p(x_0), \ldots, p(x_{k-1})$ with the k computing parties. As the polynomial, and hence the evaluation at 0 can only be constructed with at least $m + 1$ polynomial evaluations, the user is guaranteed to keep s secure as long as no $m + 1$ parties collude to open this sharing. Additions of multiple secrets can be done easily by adding individual shares, while for multiplications some additional communication between all parties is needed to create a proper sharing.

Choice of Scheme/Library: MPyC. Similar to the field of FHE, various implementations and variations of MPC have been studied and implemented. In this paper we will work with Schoenmakers' MPyC library [26], which is particularly easy to use, offers a lot of functionality, and has a good performance. Just like Concrete, this library is written in Python, making it easy to implement the aforementioned graph algorithms in MPyC.

Comparison Between FHE and MPC. Compared to FHE, one may argue that MPC has the drawback of requiring multiple compute parties, and security is only guaranteed if these computing parties do not (all) collude to reveal the secret input data of the user. Moreover, ciphertext multiplications require communication between the computing parties, whereas in FHE the single compute server can perform the whole function evaluation without further interaction with the user after they provided the input data. On the other hand, MPC is generally considered significantly more efficient, both in terms of computation times and key sizes, and if the computing parties in MPC do not collude one gets very strong (information-theoretic) security guarantees that the input data remains private – in the setting of FHE, the data remains private only under the assumption that the lattice problems underpinning the security of the lattice-based cryptography of FHE are actually hard to solve, classically and/or quantumly.

2.4   Oblivious Computation

To be able to perform the considered graph algorithms under encryption, with the computing party oblivious to the data and the decisions it is making, we use standard techniques from oblivious computation to modify these algorithms accordingly. These techniques are often used to make code execution constant-time as well, in order to make sure that the branching of the algorithm does not leak any information about private data.

As an example, to deal with conditional if-statements, the following branched code depends on whether a boolean b is equal to true (1) or false (0):

   if b **then**
      $x \leftarrow x_1$
   else
      $x \leftarrow x_0$

For private input data b, we cannot branch based on the value b. However, we can use the encryption of the bit b in our computations as follows to do the "conditional" assignment directly:

$$x \leftarrow x_0 + b \cdot (x_1 - x_0)$$

These computations can be done under encryption to get an encryption of x equaling x_0 if $b \equiv 0$ and x_1 if $b \equiv 1$. Similarly, conditional pairwise swaps are an integral part of the above graph algorithms, and these would normally be performed as:

   if b **then**
      swap(x, y)

This can be made branchless with the following code, requiring only one cipher-text multiplication:

$$\delta \leftarrow b \cdot (y - x)$$
$$x \leftarrow x + \delta$$
$$y \leftarrow y - \delta$$

For data structures it is further necessary that e.g. lists/arrays have a fixed length, independent of the private input data. For the vehicle routing problem, dividing the graph into parts which may or may not contain an equal number of nodes would complicate implementations, which is why we mainly focus on methods where the division of nodes across vehicles is perfectly balanced.

3   Model

The goal of this paper is to describe how someone can let one or more computing parties calculate (approximate) solutions to their TSP or VRP instance, without the computing parties learning specifics about the input. The nodes in the problem instance are therefore provided in encrypted form, and the computing parties should be unable to ever learn anything about these locations.

To model this situation, we assume that there is a public graph $G = (V, E)$ with a large number N of locations, and a public distance function/table describing all pairwise distances in this complete graph on N nodes. For instance, the public graph could be all cities within some country with a sufficiently large population, and the distances are public information. The private input, provided by the client, is a subset $S \subseteq V$ of $n \leq N$ of these nodes, for which they would like to find a short Hamiltonian tour. These nodes may correspond to customers or clients, and their identities and locations must remain private and unknown to the computing parties. After providing S in encrypted form (denoted $[\![S]\!]$), the computing parties apply a TSP or VRP algorithm $\mathcal{A} : G \to \mathcal{H}(G)$ to the private input $[\![S]\!]$, computing an encrypted tour $[\![\mathbf{r}]\!] = [\![\mathcal{A}(S)]\!]$. The client then receives this encrypted tour, and decrypts it to recover the solution $\mathbf{r}$. This functionality (with a single server doing the computations) is sketched in Fig. 2. Here the subset of nodes $S \subseteq V$ for the routing problem remains private to the client, while the algorithm $\mathcal{A}$ used to compute a TSP/VRP solution on the nodes S can potentially remain private to the server.

In this paper, we assume that the data is provided by the user as an encrypted list of node indices, e.g. the complete graph has nodes $V = \{0, 1, \ldots, N-1\}$, and the private input is a list of encryptions of $S = \{i_0, i_1, \ldots, i_{n-1}\} \subseteq V$ describing the indices of the nodes which must be included in the tour. If the number of nodes in the tour n is close to the total number of nodes N in the graph, there is not much privacy; in practical settings, one may assume that $N \gg n$. This model is not perfect, as it leaks how many nodes are in the set S. Future work may focus on ways to deal with this leakage without incurring a large overhead in the computation time. Furthermore, in the FHE setting, there is only one computing party. In practical applications, this constitutes a single point of failure, meaning the process could be vulnerable to attacks targeted at the computing party. A detailed resilience analysis could also be covered in further research.

Multiple Input Parties. Although in this paper we focus on the setting where a single party provides the secret input, this functionality can be extended to the setting where multiple parties each provide part of the secret input. First, the parties set up a shared public/secret key pair together, such that only together they can decrypt any encrypted data (e.g. using techniques from threshold cryptography). Then, they all encrypt their data with the shared public key, and all this data is provided to the server(s). The functionality in Fig. 2 is then executed, and once $[\![\mathbf{r}]\!]$ gets sent back to the input parties, they run a threshold decryption procedure to recover $\mathbf{r}$ together. In other words: the protocol described in Fig. 2 and studied in this paper can be extended to the setting with multiple input parties with standard techniques.

Multiple Computation Parties. Apart from having multiple input parties, in the setting of MPC one would also work with multiple computation parties. This either corresponds to the client cooperating with the computations, or the input data being split into secret shares which are divided over multiple computation parties, who are assumed not to collude. In Fig. 2, the latter instantiation would correspond to the encryption being replaced by several secret shares, and the server would consist of multiple parties running the algorithm $\mathcal{A}$ together on their shares to construct shares of $\mathcal{A}(S)$.

Client	$(G = (V, E))$	**Server**
$(S \subseteq V)$		$(\mathcal{A} : G \to \mathcal{H}(G))$
$(sk, pk, ek) \leftarrow \text{Init}(\lambda)$		
$[\![S]\!] \leftarrow \text{Enc}_{pk}(S)$		
	$\xrightarrow{\;[\![S]\!],\; ek\;}$	
		$[\![\mathbf{r}]\!] \leftarrow \text{Eval}_{ek}(\mathcal{A}, [\![S]\!])$
	$\xleftarrow{\;[\![\mathbf{r}]\!]\;}$	
$\mathbf{r} \leftarrow \text{Dec}_{sk}([\![\mathbf{r}]\!])$		

Fig. 2. The ideal functionality in the setting of an outsourced TSP/VRP computation, where $[\![x]\!]$ denotes an encryption of x

4　Oblivious Graph Algorithms

With the cryptographic tools described in the preliminaries, we are ready to convert the graph algorithms from the preliminaries into oblivious variants, adhering to the aforementioned model: the server receives only the encrypted data, evaluates the graph algorithm under encryption, and sends back the encrypted result to the client without ever learning anything about the input data.

4.1　Tour Construction

Trivial Construction. For the tour construction algorithms, we first note that the trivial construction can be done obliviously without any effort: one can always initialize a random tour for TSP, and insert depot locations at every n/m nodes to turn it into a VRP solution.

Greedy Construction. Recall that in the greedy construction method, one starts from an arbitrary (random) node and iteratively selects the nearest remaining node to be the next one in the tour, until all nodes are selected. Obliviously, this algorithm works well *in place*, where rather than finding the index of the next nearest neighbor and swapping, we do conditional swaps for every pair of indices i and j: if the current node is v_{i-1}, then v_i is the current

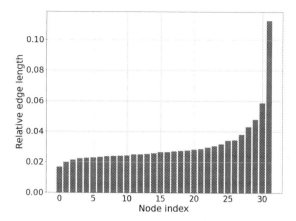

Fig. 3. Relative edge length after NN versus index corresponding to edge, $n = 32$, average of $10,000$ samples

nearest node in the graph, and we swap v_i and v_j if v_j lies closer to v_{i-1}. This needs to be done obliviously, as outlined in Algorithm 5.

Algorithm 5. SecureGreedy(V, v_0)

Input: A set of n vertices V, and a starting vertex $v_0 \in V$
Output: An initial solution $\mathbf{r} \in \mathcal{H}(G)$ with $r_0 = v_0$
1: $\mathbf{r} \leftarrow (v_0, v_1, \ldots, v_{n-1})$
2: **for** i **from** 1 **to** $n - 1$ **do**
3:      **for** j **from** $i + 1$ **to** $n - 1$ **do**
4:          $b \leftarrow (d(v_{i-1}, v_j) < d(v_{i-1}, v_i))$
5:          $\delta \leftarrow b \cdot (v_j - v_i)$
6:          $(v_i, v_j) \leftarrow (v_i + \delta, v_j - \delta)$
7: **return** r

Greedy Extra. Note that, as the greedy algorithm assigns more nodes to the tour, the number of remaining nearby nodes becomes smaller, and therefore the final nodes will be further away from their neighbor than at the start of the tour. Moreover, the algorithm may well start and finish at random location in the square $[0, 1]^2$, and since we need to build a tour, the last edge connecting the final vertex to the start will likely be long. Figure 3 illustrates this phenomenon for random graphs on $n = 32$ nodes, clearly showing the increase in length towards the end and a spike at the last edge.

Normally, when presented with a tour under encryption, we have no idea where to start looking for improvements to augment the tour to a better tour. For the greedy algorithm however we know exactly where to look for improvements: at the end of the tour. We therefore also consider the "greedy extra" algorithm as the greedy nearest neighbor approach, where at the end we run 2-swaps with

j fixed as $n - 1$ and i iterating over 1 to $n - 3$. Asymptotically the costs of one such extra step are negligible compared to either a full round of 2-opt or a full greedy run, but this may help improve the performance when running these algorithms obliviously.

Clustering. For the clustering variant of the above algorithm, tailored for solving VRP, we applied similar techniques – rather than finding the right index of the best center or the closest vertex and then swapping, we always do conditional swaps, so that everything can be done in place with pairwise swaps which may or may not take place, depending on bits/booleans which are computed under encryption. This can be done both for the clustering variant where new nodes are chosen by their distance from the centers, and for the clustering variant where a greedy approach is used to immediately form a somewhat short tour in each cluster.

4.2   Tour Augmentation

TwoSwap. The simplest tour augmentation algorithm is a single 2-swap, given indices i and j. The pseudocode of Algorithm 3 can easily be adjusted to the oblivious setting by replacing the pairwise, and then replacing the conditional if-statement depending on $\delta > 0$ by computing a boolean/bit $b \equiv (\delta > 0)$ and then using the bit b in assignments. One can easily verify that this leads to the correct outcome that is identical to the approach taken in Algorithm 3. This leads to the branchless code as outlined in Algorithm 6.

Algorithm 6. SecureTwoSwap($\mathbf{r}$, i, j)

Input: A TSP solution $\mathbf{r}$, and two indices $0 \leq i, j \leq n - 1$
Output: A TSP solution $\mathbf{r}'$ with $d(\mathbf{r}') \leq d(\mathbf{r})$
1: $\mathbf{r}' \leftarrow \mathbf{r}$
2: $d_{\mathrm{cur}} \leftarrow d(r_i, r_{i+1}) + d(r_j, r_{j+1})$
3: $d_{\mathrm{new}} \leftarrow d(r_i, r_j) + d(r_{i+1}, r_{j+1})$
4: $b \leftarrow (d_{\mathrm{new}} < d_{\mathrm{cur}})$ $\triangleright\ b \equiv d(\mathbf{r}_{\mathrm{new}}) < d(\mathbf{r}_{\mathrm{cur}})$
5: **for** k from 0 to $\lfloor \frac{j-i}{2} \rfloor$ **do**
6:      $\delta \leftarrow b \cdot ((\mathbf{r}')_{j-k} - (\mathbf{r}')_{i+k+1})$
7:      $(\mathbf{r}')_{i+k+1} \leftarrow (\mathbf{r}')_{i+k+1} + \delta$
8:      $(\mathbf{r}')_{j-k} \leftarrow (\mathbf{r}')_{j-k} - \delta$
9: **return** $\mathbf{r}'$

Note that for the "bookkeeping" step of (potentially) reversing all nodes between i and j, naively the average cost (iterating over all pairs between i and j) is to consider $n/6 + o(n)$ pairs which need to be swapped. This cost can be reduced to $n/8 + o(n)$ by considering which "half" of the tour (between i and j or between j and i) is the shortest to reverse, saving 25% in the overall costs. Since the pairs i and j are chosen/precomputed in the clear, the shortest half can be precomputed as well, and this is just as efficient when doing the computations obliviously.

TwoOpt. For converting the 2-swap algorithm to a full round of the 2-opt algorithm, we simply call the 2-swap algorithm for all pairs $0 \leq i < j \leq n-1$, and to reach a local optimum we can execute $O(\log n)$ full rounds of this algorithm. Note that, unlike when running the algorithm in the clear, we need to specify in advance how many full rounds we run, and we cannot (easily) tell how much progress we have made. In our experiments we will focus on the costs of a single full round over all pairs.

TwoOpt with Constraints. When adapting the 2-opt algorithm to the vehicle routing problem, we need to take into account additional constraints, such as that each vehicle visits roughly the same number of vertices. To deal with this in an oblivious manner, we keep track of the locations of the depots (under encryption), and use penalty scores to make sure swaps do not happen if the tour becomes too imbalanced. So rather than computing $\delta = d(\mathbf{r}_{\text{new}}) - d(\mathbf{r}_{\text{old}})$ and using the boolean $b \equiv (\delta > 0)$, we compute $\delta = \text{penalty} + d(\mathbf{r}_{\text{new}}) - d(\mathbf{r}_{\text{old}})$ and compute $b \equiv (\delta > 0)$. With a suitable penalty function, this guarantees that tours always stay somewhat balanced.

4.3   Comparison

To get an idea of the performance of the different algorithms, running without any branching, Fig. 4 shows a violin plot of three approaches for solving TSP: one full round of 2-opt (starting from a random initial solution); a greedy initialization; and a greedy initialization with an additional 2-opt step to augment only the last edge in the tour (greedy extra).

In Fig. 5 we further see the average tour lengths for approaches for TSP and VRP when running two full rounds of algorithms, as a function of the graph size n. In both plots, the y-axis shows the ratio between the route length and its expected value, scaling as $0.71\sqrt{n}$. In both plots, after an initial round of either 2-opt, greedy, clustering (from the centers or in a greedy nearest neighbor fashion), or constrained 2-opt, we follow up with a round of (constrained) 2-opt. Note that the dip for TSP around $n = 20$ is due to the approximation $0.71\sqrt{n}$ for the best solution not being accurate for small n.

5   Experimental Results

We finally proceed with the results of implementing the algorithms described in the previous sections in an oblivious manner with FHE and MPC. All implementations and experiments were done on an HP EliteBook 830 G6 with an i58356U CPU @ 1.60GHz, with 4 cores, and with 8 GB RAM. The timing results should

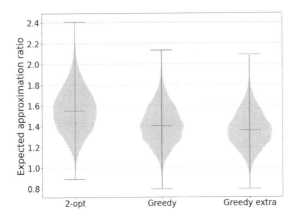

Fig. 4. Route lengths after one round, $n = 16$, average of $10,000$ samples. 2-opt corresponds to starting with a random initialization and running a full round of 2-opt, while greedy and greedy extra correspond to the greedy nearest neighbor approach without/with an attempt to augment the last edge of the tour.

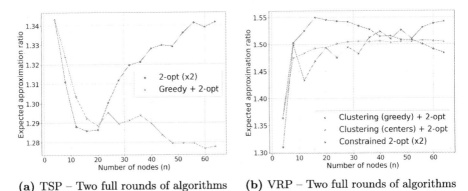

(a) TSP – Two full rounds of algorithms   (b) VRP – Two full rounds of algorithms

Fig. 5. Comparisons between average route lengths of two of the TSP algorithms (left) and three of the discussed VRP algorithms for $m = 2$ (right), based on two full rounds of algorithms. Each data point is based on 1000 samples.

therefore be taken with a grain of salt – both the FHE and MPC algorithms would be faster on better or optimized hardware.

We describe the used libraries and their strengths and weaknesses Concrete and MPyC as well as their strengths and weaknesses in Subsects. 5.1 and 5.2 respectively. Then we give and summarize the results on time and space complexity of the considered implementations in Subsect. 5.3.

5.1   FHE Implementation – Concrete

Concrete Python is a library aiming to simplify the use of FHE, developed by Zama and based on the TFHE scheme [33]. It compiles Python code into FHE code, something which most FHE libraries do not offer. However, there are some issues we ran into when using it. We describe some of these issues here.

Supported Operations. Multivariate operations were not supported at the time of implementing, including multiplications of two ciphertexts. This is unfortunate, as it is an integral part of fully homomorphic encryption. A workaround was possible, requiring one (oblivious) table lookup (TLU). For instance, to compute $b \cdot \delta$ for an encrypted bit b and a value $\delta \in \{0, \ldots, M-1\}$, we can use a table of length $2M$ of the form $T = [0, \ldots, 0, 0, \ldots, M-1]$. Here looking up the index $u = b \cdot M + \delta$ guarantees that $T[u] = b \cdot \delta$. Apart from efficiency, a lack of support for, e.g., ciphertext multiplications may hinder ease of use for more complex use cases.

Input Set. Concrete uses input sets provided by the user to measure and predict the necessary bit width of every variable. However, the input set only gives a sample of possible intermediate values, which may not cover edge cases not considered in the input set. For instance, if the input set encounters intermediate values v which are always positive, the compiler will make this an unsigned integer. Then, if in a run of the algorithm one actually encounters $v < 0$, the unsigned integer will return an incorrect value. Implementing the algorithm correctly and robustly would have been easier if one could specify the range of each intermediate value, but this is currently not supported.

Compilation. Compiling the circuit can take a very long time. In the case of the 2-opt algorithm, we essentially repeat the same instructions many times, albeit with different indices each time. When going from $n = 8$ to $n = 16$ in the 2-opt algorithm for TSP, the number of operations increases by a factor of 7. However, the compilation time roughly goes from $5\,\mathrm{s}$ to $55\,\mathrm{min}$, an increase by a factor of 650. This while the calculation time only increases by a factor 9. This causes compilation to dominate the timings. Fortunately, it is possible to save a compiled circuit to avoid recompilation, but it is not yet possible to manually generate the list of operations and provide this directly to the compiler, a change that could save quite a lot of time. Moreover, one might be able to improve the efficiency if one could tell the compiler that the circuit is essentially a concatenation of a large number of identical subcircuits which may well be compiled separately, but this is currently not supported.

Public LUTs. Currently lookup tables (LUTs) are not encrypted, even though the indices and outputs both are. From a cryptographic standpoint, this functionality could be added to achieve function hiding [9].

5.2   MPC Implementation – MPyC

MPyC is a Python library that can be used to run MPC protocols, developed by Schoenmakers [26]. It enables multiple parties to use the library simultaneously to perform computations in a secure manner. One user can also simulate multiple users, for which the library uses multiple processes.

Compared to Concrete, the mentioned issues are not present here. MPyC supports all necessary operations, does not require an input set and has negligible compilation times. Furthermore, it supports *barriers* that can be used to split up the circuit into smaller parts that can be compiled more efficiently. For these reasons, MPyC was considerably easier to use for our purposes than Concrete. In our experiments, we always used 3 computing parties, running as different processes on the same laptop.

5.3   Results

The results of the experiments for various values of N (the total graph size) and n (the secret set of nodes to include in the tour) are given in Tables 1, 2 (FHE only), and 3 (comparison of FHE and MPC).

FHE Results. In Table 1 we see that for FHE, the compilation, key generation, and calculation times all grow quickly with the size of the problem instance. For the VRP instances we further were not able to run the algorithms for large N and n at all, as the compilation terminated without result or the calculation had a memory overflow. We further stress that the memory entries are given in MBs – even for tiny problem instances, the bootstrapping and key switching keys are already hundreds of MBs. Note that the dips in the time complexity for $(N, n) = (8, 8)$ compared to $(N, n) = (6, 6)$ for VRP are not an experimental error; the keys generated for these larger instances were actually smaller, resulting in smaller time complexities.

FHE and MPC Results In Table 3 we compare the accumulated FHE complexities with implementations of these algorithms in MPC. For FHE we added up all the time and space complexities (key sizes). For MPC, the time complexity counts the time between the start and end of the protocol, when running all MPC parties on the same machine, and the space complexity counts the total size of the messages sent between the parties during the computation.

Table 1. Experimental results of running the secure TSP algorithms with FHE. The timings are the compilation, key generation, and circuit execution times. The memory covers the bootstrapping and key switch keys.

(a) TSP – FHE – Construction (Greedy)

		Time (s)			Circuit size		Memory (MB)	
N	n	Compil.	KeyGen.	Calc.	Depth	TLU	Bootstrap	KeySwitch
4	4	1	85	4	56	8	235	294
8	4	1	83	3	56	8	235	294
6	6	1	306	20	252	36	235	294
12	6	1	306	21	252	36	227	510
8	8	3	304	47	560	80	227	510
16	8	3	306	49	560	80	227	510
12	12	21	306	134	1512	216	227	511
24	12	21	324	142	1512	216	231	519
16	16	150	329	270	2912	416	229	516
32	16	152	2213	654	2912	416	1431	716

(b) TSP – FHE – Augmentation (2-opt)

		Time (s)			Circuit size		Memory (MB)	
N	n	Compil.	KeyGen.	Calc.	Depth	TLU	Bootstrap	KeySwitch
4	4	1	331	4	90	12	235	294
8	4	1	304	6	90	12	235	294
6	6	2	302	27	405	54	235	294
12	6	2	304	29	405	54	227	510
8	8	5	306	60	968	124	227	510
16	8	5	310	61	968	124	227	510
12	12	110	309	170	3042	360	228	512
24	12	110	456	201	3042	360	340	510
16	16	3331	454	523	6720	744	340	510
32	16	3345	2229	1111	6720	744	1431	716

Table 2. Experimental results of running the secure VRP algorithms with $m = 2$ with FHE. The timings are the compilation, key generation, and circuit execution times. The memory covers the bootstrapping and key switch keys. Dashes correspond to experiments which did not successfully terminate despite multiple attempts.

(a) VRP – FHE – Construction (Clustering)

		Time (s)			Circuit size		Memory (MB)	
N	n	Compil.	KeyGen	Calc.	Depth	TLU	Bootstrap	KeySwitch
4	4	1	23	6	192	33	235	294
8	4	1	22	16	192	33	227	510
6	6	2	309	77	447	73	954	716
12	6	2	309	45	447	73	955	716
8	8	4	24	59	810	129	227	510
16	8	4	1974	-	810	129	3045	1776
12	12	17	313	254	1860	289	963	722
24	12	20	-	-	1860	289	-	-
16	16	118	2045	-	3342	513	3051	1780
32	16	-	-	-	3342	513	-	-

(b) VRP – FHE – Augmentation (2-opt with constraints)

		Time (s)			Circuit size		Memory (MB)	
N	n	Compil.	KeyGen	Calc.	Depth	TLU	Bootstrap	KeySwitch
4	4	2	309	71	531	99	953	715
8	4	2	24	33	531	99	227	510
6	6	6	309	168	1251	224	954	716
12	6	6	311	167	1251	224	956	717
8	8	19	310	295	2316	400	956	717
16	8	20	1971	-	2316	400	3048	1778
12	12	564	318	704	5661	917	983	737
24	12	574	-	-	5661	917	-	-
16	16	11979	2630	-	10926	1674	3067	1789
32	16	-	-	-	10926	1674	-	-

Table 3. A comparison of the time and space complexities of FHE (Concrete) and MPC (MPyC with 3 parties) for various algorithms

		TSP								VRP							
		Constr. (Greedy)				Augment. (2-opt)				Constr. (Clustering)				Augment. (2-opt)			
		Time (s)		Space (MB)		Time (s)		Space (MB)		Time (s)		Space (MB)		Time (s)		Space (MB)	
N	n	FHE	MPC	FHE	MPC	FHE	MPC	FHE	MPC	FHE	MPC	FHE	MPC	FHE	MPC	FHE	MPC
4	4	90	0.1	529	0.01	336	0.1	529	0.01	30	0.3	529	0.02	382	0.3	1668	0.03
8	4	87	0.2	529	0.01	311	0.1	529	0.01	39	0.2	737	0.02	59	0.4	737	0.04
6	6	328	0.2	529	0.03	330	0.5	529	0.03	388	0.5	1670	0.04	483	0.4	1670	0.06
12	6	328	0.3	737	0.03	335	0.3	737	0.03	356	0.6	1671	0.06	484	0.7	1673	0.08
8	8	354	0.5	737	0.05	371	0.3	737	0.05	87	1.0	737	0.11	624	1.0	1673	0.16
16	8	358	0.7	737	0.06	376	0.7	737	0.07	-	1.2	4821	0.13	-	1.2	4826	0.19
12	12	461	1.8	738	0.17	589	2.0	738	0.19	584	2.1	1685	0.23	1586	2.0	1720	0.31
24	12	487	2.0	750	0.21	767	2.4	850	0.25	-	2.6	-	0.30	-	2.6	-	0.41
16	16	749	2.7	745	0.31	4308	3.3	850	0.36	-	4.8	4831	0.56	-	5.9	4856	0.74
32	16	3019	3.3	2147	0.40	6685	4.4	2147	0.48	-	6.0	-	0.71	-	8.4	-	0.97

6   Conclusion

We have investigated several aspects of solving TSP and VRP with FHE and MPC. Mainly, we can conclude that (time) efficiency is the largest hurdle to overcome for FHE when compared to MPC and even more so compared to unencrypted solutions. We refer to the results of Tables 1, 2 and 3.

In terms of practicability, note that the values of N and n in these tables are small. Additional experiments showed that the time and memory do not grow quickly with N for fixed n, but one can see from these results that all complexities grow quickly with n, making e.g. planning a tour among $n = 100$ locations infeasible in the current setting. With better hardware and further optimized implementations one can get closer to realistic parameters, but together with the issues faced when implementing these algorithms, there is still a gap to overcome to make FHE practical.

From these results, it is clear that FHE performed significantly worse than MPC for all four algorithms: the time complexities are often 100 to 1000 times larger than for MPC, while the overall space complexity is 1000 to 10000 times larger. As both implementations are on the same machine, it is unlikely that optimized hardware will close the gap; both FHE and MPC may be expected to benefit from specialized hardware or larger clusters, and the above gaps may remain similar when both implementations are further optimized.

To put these results into context and explain the gap with, e.g., more favorable demonstrations of FHE, we note that demos such as [4,18,32] often involve use cases where more data is processed, but the circuit under consideration has a low multiplicative depth, and a lot can be done in parallel. In contrast, the algorithms we consider here have a highly sequential nature, with a small number of operations being performed before another bootstrapping operation needs to be performed. For these sequential algorithms, it may take longer for techniques like FHE (and MPC) to become practical.

For the comparison between FHE and MPC, and assessing the practicability of FHE, we note that the FHE results in Table 3 are based on adding all time and space complexities. One might imagine however that in a practical context, the problem data does not change much. If plannings need to be made every day with the same parameters, then many costs can be amortized: (1) circuit compilation only needs to be done once; (2) key generation can ideally be done only once; and (3) the large bootstrapping and key switching keys can be sent once to the server to be reused.

With such an amortization over multiple runs, we remark that the memory complexity of FHE drops *enormously*, from gigabytes to kilobytes (!), while the time complexity may decrease by one order of magnitude. The time complexity would still be significantly higher than MPC, but the communication complexity would be competitive. With the lower level of trust required for FHE compared to MPC, this may render FHE a competitive solution. This however heavily relies on being able to reuse keys and circuits, as otherwise the costs of FHE are still prohibitively large.

References

1. Angel, S., Chen, H., Laine, K., Setty, S.: PIR with compressed queries and amortized query processing. In: 2018 IEEE Symposium on Security and Privacy (S&P), San Francisco, CA, USA, pp. 962–979. IEEE (2018). https://doi.org/10.1109/SP.2018.00062
2. Beardwood, J., Halton, J.H., Hammersley, J.M.: The shortest path through many points. Math. Proc. Cambridge Philos. Soc. **55**(4), 299–327 (1959). https://doi.org/10.1017/S0305004100034095
3. Blatt, M., Gusev, A., Polyakov, Y., Goldwasser, S.: Secure large-scale genome-wide association studies using homomorphic encryption. Proc. Natl. Acad. Sci. **117**(21), 11608–11613 (2020). https://doi.org/10.1073/pnas.1918257117. https://www.pnas.org/doi/abs/10.1073/pnas.1918257117
4. Blyss: Private access to 6gb (30%) of English Wikipedia (2022). https://spiralwiki.com/
5. Brakerski, Z.: Fully homomorphic encryption without modulus switching from classical GapSVP. In: Safavi-Naini, R., Canetti, R. (eds.) CRYPTO 2012. LNCS, vol. 7417, pp. 868–886. Springer, Heidelberg (2012). https://doi.org/10.1007/978-3-642-32009-5_50
6. Brakerski, Z., Gentry, C., Vaikuntanathan, V.: (leveled) fully homomorphic encryption without bootstrapping. In: Proceedings of the 3rd Innovations in Theoretical Computer Science Conference, ITCS 2012, pp. 309–325. Association for Computing Machinery, New York (2012). https://doi.org/10.1145/2090236.2090262
7. Cheon, J.H., Kim, A., Kim, M., Song, Y.: Homomorphic encryption for arithmetic of approximate numbers. In: Takagi, T., Peyrin, T. (eds.) ASIACRYPT 2017. LNCS, vol. 10624, pp. 409–437. Springer, Cham (2017). https://doi.org/10.1007/978-3-319-70694-8_15

8. Chillotti, I.: The three musketeers of secure computation: MPC, FHE and FE. COSIC Cryptography Blog (2019). https://www.esat.kuleuven.be/cosic/blog/the-three-musketeers-of-secure-computation-mpc-fhe-and-fe/
9. Chillotti, I.: TFHE deep dive (part 1). Zama Blog (2022). https://www.zama.ai/post/tfhe-deep-dive-part-1
10. Chillotti, I., Gama, N., Georgieva, M., Izabachène, M.: Faster fully homomorphic encryption: bootstrapping in less than 0.1 seconds. In: Cheon, J.H., Takagi, T. (eds.) ASIACRYPT 2016. LNCS, vol. 10031, pp. 3–33. Springer, Heidelberg (2016). https://doi.org/10.1007/978-3-662-53887-6_1
11. Croes, G.A.: A method for solving traveling-salesman problems. Oper. Res. **6**(6), 791–812 (1958). http://www.jstor.org/stable/167074
12. OpenFHE: Lattigo – open-source fully homomorphic encryption library (2023). https://www.openfhe.org/
13. Ducas, L., Micciancio, D.: FHEW: bootstrapping homomorphic encryption in less than a second. In: Oswald, E., Fischlin, M. (eds.) EUROCRYPT 2015. LNCS, vol. 9056, pp. 617–640. Springer, Heidelberg (2015). https://doi.org/10.1007/978-3-662-46800-5_24
14. Fan, J., Vercauteren, F.: Somewhat practical fully homomorphic encryption (2012). https://eprint.iacr.org/2012/144
15. Gentry, C.: Fully homomorphic encryption using ideal lattices. In: Proceedings of the Forty-First Annual ACM Symposium on Theory of Computing, pp. 169–178. Association for Computing Machinery, New York (2009). https://doi.org/10.1145/1536414.1536440
16. Halevi, S., Shoup, V.: Helib – an open source software library that implements homomorphic encryption (2023). https://homenc.github.io/HElib/
17. HEaaN – fully homomorphic encryption with CKKS scheme [SIC] (2023). https://heaan.it/
18. Insight: Lattigo polls demo – scheduling meetings with FHE (2020). https://github.com/ldsec/lattigo-polls-demo
19. Insight: Lattigo – a library for lattice-based multiparty homomorphic encryption in go (2023). https://github.com/tuneinsight/lattigo
20. Johnson, D.S., McGeoch, L.A., Rothberg, E.E.: Asymptotic experimental analysis for the held-karp traveling salesman bound. In: Proceedings of the Seventh Annual ACM-SIAM Symposium on Discrete Algorithms, SODA 1996, pp. 341–350. Society for Industrial and Applied Mathematics, USA (1996)
21. Menon, S.J., Wu, D.J.: Spiral: fast, high-rate single-server PIR via FHE composition. In: 2022 IEEE Symposium on Security and Privacy (S&P), San Francisco, CA, USA, pp. 930–947. IEEE (2022). https://doi.org/10.1109/SP46214.2022.9833700
22. Microsoft: Microsoft seal – an easy-to-use and powerful homomorphic encryption library (2023). https://github.com/microsoft/SEAL
23. The HEBench Organization: Hebench – homomorphic encryption benchmarking framework (2023). https://hebench.org/
24. Privacy-Preserving Computation Techniques: Un handbook on privacy-preserving computation techniques (2023). https://unstats.un.org/bigdata/task-teams/training/catalog/Details?id=285
25. Scheibner, J., Ienca, M., Vayena, E.: Health data privacy through homomorphic encryption and distributed ledger computing: an ethical-legal qualitative expert assessment study. BMC Med. Ethics **23**(1), 1–13 (2022). https://doi.org/10.1186/s12910-022-00852-2
26. Schoenmakers, B.: MPyC – multiparty computation in python (2023). https://github.com/lschoe/mpyc

27. Shamir, A.: How to share a secret. Commun. ACM **22**(11), 612–613 (1979). https://doi.org/10.1145/359168.359176
28. Society, T.R.: From privacy to partnership: the role of privacy enhancing technologies in data governance and collaborative analysis (2023). https://royalsociety.org/topics-policy/projects/privacy-enhancing-technologies/
29. Steinerberger, S.: New bounds for the traveling salesman constant. Adv. Appl. Probab. **47**(1), 27–36 (2015). https://doi.org/10.1239/aap/1427814579
30. Vigo, D., Toth, P. (eds.): Vehicle Routing. Society for Industrial and Applied Mathematics, Philadelphia (2014). https://doi.org/10.1137/1.9781611973594. https://epubs.siam.org/doi/abs/10.1137/1.9781611973594
31. Weng, H., Hettiarachchi, C., Nolan, C., Suominen, H., Lenskiy, A.: Ensuring security of artificial pancreas device system using homomorphic encryption. Biomed. Signal Process. Control **79**, 104044 (2023). https://doi.org/10.1016/j.bspc.2022.104044. https://www.sciencedirect.com/science/article/pii/S174680942200516X
32. Zama: Sentiment analysis on encrypted data using homomorphic encryption (2022). https://huggingface.co/spaces/zama-fhe/encrypted_sentiment_analysis
33. Zama: Concrete – an open-source FHE framework based on TFHE (2023). https://docs.zama.ai/concrete

Route Optimization of an Unmanned Aerial Vehicle Beyond Visual Line of Sight

Florian Blauensteiner[1] and Günter Fahrnberger[2]([⊠])

[1] Vienna University of Technology, Vienna, Austria
[2] University of Hagen, Hagen, North Rhine-Westphalia, Germany
guenter.fahrnberger@studium.fernuni-hagen.de

Abstract. Undoubtedly, Unmanned Aerial Vehicles (UAVs), also known as drones, have experienced significant growth in recent decades and will continue their increase. Presently, drone operators view the endurance of their devices' flights as one of the most challenging obstacles. This challenge becomes even more pronounced when UAVs must remain airborne for extended periods without ground contact for recharging or refueling. This contribution further addresses autonomous Beyond Visual Line Of Sight (BVLOS) flight, hydrogen propulsion, and optimized joined wing design, considering both demands and constraints. However, as no recent scientific work adequately addresses all these challenges, this disquisition aims to provide mitigation strategies by proposing prudent routing for an already constructed drone prototype. Findings from an experimental test flight substantiate the intended improvements.

Keywords: Beyond Visual Line Of Sight (BVLOS) · Route optimization · Unmanned Aerial Vehicle (UAV)

1 Introduction

Like other technologies, drones' initial use cases originated from the military domain. Unlike manned aircraft, UAVs achieve notable results without risking the well-being of their pilots. Nowadays, drones also deliver parcels and have even made their way into private homes as toys. While leisure activities with UAVs exhilarate hobby pilots, governmental interests in drones take precedence over any recreational use. UAVs particularly suit well for autonomous or supervised patrols along predetermined routes. Night-vision-equipped drones enable patrols around the clock, along long fronts, borders, or fences, without requiring labor-intensive efforts. Personnel planners can then allocate staff as reserve forces to respond to incidents identified by UAVs.

Occasionally, the Austrian government feels compelled to suspend the Schengen Treaty and impose partial border control to combat immigrant smuggling. The ministries of the interior and the defense lack sufficient troops for continuous, long-term border surveillance without leaving spatial gaps. Therefore, drones offer them an appropriate tool to achieve their objectives despite man-power constraints. Unfortunately, the batteries of UAVs do not provide sufficient power for long-range flights. Consequently, this paper presents a route optimization method for a novel hydrogen-powered, long-range drone prototype. In addition to endurance through energy efficiency, several other requirements have influenced both the construction and the route calculation.

- autonomous BVLOS flying
- Hydrogen and Fuel cell based Electric (HFE) propulsion
- optimized joined wing design
- advanced manufacturing techniques, such as Carbon Fiber-Reinforced Plastics (CFRP), Glass Fiber-Reinforced Plastics (GFRP), and 3D-printing

The consideration of all requirements has resulted in a UAV with a Maximum Take-Off Mass (MTOM) of ten kilograms and a wingspan of 1.6 m. The hydrogen-powered fuel cell delivers a continuous power output of 650 W, with a peak performance of one kilowatt over 30 s. In case of an emergency, such as the loss of 868 megahertz telemetry and all redundant systems, the flight terminates by triggering an embedded parachute. The drone incorporates a Global Positioning System (GPS) module and Real-Time Kinematics (RTK) to ensure redundancy [25]. Additionally, it features an Automatic Dependent Surveillance-Broadcast (ADS-B) transmitter to make it traceable via Flightradar24 [11] and ADS-B exchange [9]. ADS-B can be utilized for air conflict management [14]. Figure 1 provides a glimpse of the prototype design.

Fig. 1. Prototype (Final version will be twin-engined.) [17]

Section 2 elucidates a couple of constraints that complicated the development of the depicted UAV. Section 3 surveys related literature that contributes but does not entirely meet the requirements established in Sect. 1 and aggravated by the constraints in Sect. 2. The routing optimization in Sect. 4 ensures efficient energy consumption by the drone. Section 5 delves into empiric insights of the prototype. A recapitulation and forecast of future work in Sect. 6 completes this treatise.

2   Constraints

In particular, several limitations justify the existence of this disquisition as they have necessitated the engineering of a novel drone, including routing, rather than utilizing or adapting existing hardware and software.

2.1   Regulatory Constraints

UAVs fall under the category *Specific* of the European Union Aviation Safety Agency's (EASA) regulatory framework for drone operations [5]. This framework only allows cruising altitudes of up to 120 m Above Ground Level (AGL) with an additional contingency height of 30 m. Hence, the 3D flight path must never exceed 150 m AGL in total. Additionally, drones must respect all other restricted airspaces, such as Airport Control Zones (ACZs), Temporary Flight Restrictions (TFRs), and other types of Notices to Airmen (NOTAM). Moreover, the Austrian airspace controller *Austro Control* prohibits crossing motorways with UAVs, further complicating flight route optimization.

2.2   Technical Constraints

Flight Controller Constraints. In the absence of viable alternatives, a Cube Orange flight controller with a triple-redundant Inertial Measurement Unit (IMU) system has to support the prototype's navigation [22]. It comprises gyroscopes, accelerometers, two barometers, one magnetometer, and runs ArduPlane and ArduPilot software [12]. The latter limits a flight route to 724 waypoints, 50 emergency landing spots, and 84 possible fence points. This represents a strong limitation for flight paths because a route through a country usually contains several thousand coordinate pairs. Hence, route planning necessitates an efficient cartographic generalization algorithm that minimizes the number of waypoints.

Computational Constraints. Austria's Federal Statistical Office provides files in Geo-Tagged Image File Format (TIFF) of the Austrian elevation profile with resolutions down to ten square meters. Not all programs can inherently process these files, and, for this reason, they must be costly converted beforehand to make them machine-readable. The computational effort overproportionally scales with higher resolution, which leads to immense calculating time for the aforementioned granularity of ten square meters. Usability of a drone in the field mandates running a route optimization algorithm on a high-end, consumer-grade personal computer rather than on a scientific supercomputer or in the cloud. This shortage of computing power resources exacts efficiency of the applied algorithm.

2.3   Aeronautical Constraints

Topographical Constraints. A hydrogen-powered fuel cell requires significantly more power when a UAV's slope exceeds roughly ±10°. A computation for this treatise's underlying drone deduces a maximum flight path angle of ±14.80° while maintaining a safety margin. Therefore, the height profile must be as flat as possible to save a maximum of energy during air maneuvers, e.g., when crossing mountains [4]. For instance, when a UAV descends too quickly, it wastes energy because its wing layout does not support high speed and, thus, entails higher air resistance. It goes without saying that the topography plays a very important role in route optimization.

Physical Constraints. The devised drone's hull weighs ten kilograms. It endures a maximum velocity of 33 m per second ($\frac{m}{s}$), a stall speed of 15 $\frac{m}{s}$, and a maximal load of five times the gravitational force (5g). Route calculation requires the minimal curve radius r. Equating the centripetal force in (1) with the centrifugal force in (2) yields an approximate r of 22.13 m in (3).

$$F_P = m \cdot F_g \tag{1}$$

$$F_C = \frac{m \cdot v^2}{r} \tag{2}$$

$$F_P = F_C \Rightarrow r = \frac{m \cdot v^2}{m \cdot F_g} = \frac{v^2}{F_g} = \frac{(33\frac{m}{s})^2}{5 \cdot 9.81\frac{m}{s^2}} = \frac{1089\,m}{49.05} \approx 22.13\,m \tag{3}$$

Consequently, the prototype must avoid curves with radii below 22.13 m to stay within the maximal g-load. Fortunately, the limited number of waypoints makes this restriction negligible and, therefore, out of scope.

Network Coverage. The UAV should primarily operate autonomously; however, in emergencies, manual control may be required [19]. Some valleys in Austria have poor network coverage, posing a risk of communication loss and potential flight termination. To mitigate this risk, the drone should avoid these areas, selecting paths with sufficient network availability using the AirborneRF airspace measurement analytics tool [3]. If telemetry fails but a potential observer or chase plane can confirm the drone's controllability, the flight stops, and the UAV lands at the next available predetermined fail-safe spot. In the event of a complete connection interruption, the flight terminates by deploying a parachute within two seconds or as soon as the UAV reaches free space, allowing for a safe landing via parachute.

Wind and Weather. Depending on the weather situation, the wind has slightly different directions and intensities that can be exploited to increase the drone's range [21]. Due to the diverting force caused by the earth's rotation (Coriolis force), the wind most of the time blows from the west or northwest in Austria.

The route options depend differently on spontaneous local weather events. Due to the difficulty of predicting such conditions, it befits to evaluate them on the day of flight. However, methods exist to deal with effects of wind turbulence, gusts, and other uncertainties or disturbances [1].

2.4   Population Density

The UAV must not fly over densely populated areas. According to the Specific Operations Risk Assessment (SORA), a drone has to maintain a safe distance to prevent entering settlements in case of an emergency, such as loss of connection and deployment of its parachute. Just to reiterate, the UAV ejects the parachute either two seconds after losing connection or upon entering free space. The drone moves up to 66 m during this period and descends at five meters per second upon parachute deployment. Equation 4 displays the maximal duration from flight termination until landing.

$$t_p = \frac{h_{max}}{v_p} = \frac{120\,m}{5\frac{m}{s}} = 24\,s \qquad (4)$$

With horizontal wind speeds v_w of up to ten meters per second, the UAV can still travel 240 m after flight termination. Equation 5 shows the total possible range after connection disruption.

$$x_{reserve} = t_f \cdot v_{UAV} + t_p \cdot v_w = 2\,s \cdot 33\frac{m}{s} + 24\,s \cdot 10\frac{m}{s} = 66\,m + 240\,m = 306\,m \quad (5)$$

The drone should be unconditionally kept away from densely populated areas by a reserve distance $x_{reserve}$. Austria's Federal Statistical Office and the above-mentioned AirborneRF provide such location data. The program counts the cellphones in a specific area in collaboration with domestic mobile operators [3].

2.5   Other Constraints

Other restricted locations, such as hospitals, military installations, power plants, prisons, crowds of people, conservation areas, and special venues for activities like paragliding, also restrict overflyable regions. These areas get excluded from civil navigation maps, such as regulatory airspace limitations, prior to flight path optimization.

3   Related Work

There exist myriad strategies that address vehicle routing and path optimization. Subsection 3.1 specifies an appropriate pick. Additionally, Subsect. 3.2 refers to Evolutionary Algorithms (EAs) and Genetic Algorithms (GAs) as practicable options for routing. Subsection 3.3, with a digest on Machine Learning (ML), perfects this section.

3.1   Routing and Path Optimization

The model of Niu et al. utilizes the physical structure of motorway networks, resembling the Traveling Salesman Problem (TSP), and focuses solely on minimizing total cruise time and distance [15].

To mitigate the impact of agricultural UAV spraying drift in challenging terrain, Zhu, Xu, and Wang developed a method featuring Gauss Legendre pseudospectral calculation. They discretize optimal control problem variables into optimal ones at Legendre-Gauss points [28]. The Lagrange interpolation polynomial approximates state and control variables using these discrete points. It determines the terminal state by integrating the initial state and the right function throughout the process.

Zhang recommends path optimization through fuzzy control methods, involving leveraging fuzzy logic to enhance decision-making and trajectory planning [27]. By integrating fuzzy control techniques, UAVs can adaptively adjust their flight paths based on real-time environmental data and mission objectives. Fuzzy logic allows for the incorporation of imprecise or uncertain information. This enables UAVs navigating through dynamic and complex environments to autonomously assess factors such as changing weather conditions and terrain variations, as well as to dynamically optimize their paths while ensuring safety and efficiency.

According to Makhanov et al., other sophisticated quantum-enhanced Dijkstra algorithms and even more advanced Grover's unstructured search algorithms exploit the quadratic asymptotic advantage of large unsorted databases [13]. Such quantum-optimized path calculation holds great promise for the future. Unfortunately, its efficiency relies on the available superconducting qubit-architecture. This dependency occurs since the experimentally observed gate operating time of neutral atoms and ion traps succumb to superconductors by being two to four orders of magnitude slower.

3.2   Evolutionary and Genetic Algorithms

EAs and GAs utilize genetic programming to emulate an evolutionary process aimed at developing a viable solution to a significant problem.

Inspired by the principles of natural selection and evolution, GAs iteratively refine potential solutions to reach an optimal path. Initially, they generate a population of potential paths, each represented as a set of waypoints or coordinates. These paths undergo a series of genetic operations such as selection, crossover, and mutation to simulate natural evolutionary processes. Fitness functions evaluate each path's suitability based on predefined criteria. In accordance with Brabazon and McGarraghy, they can also be used to develop a foraging strategy that represents the optimal route and still works in changing environments [2].

In accordance with Novak et al., Fig. 2 delineates how EAs enhance fitness in terms of properties like route quality [17].

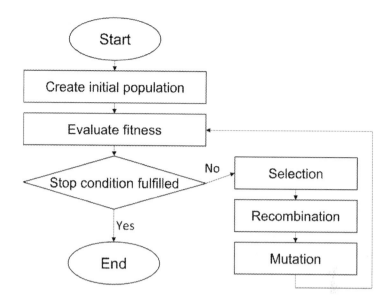

Fig. 2. Common scheme of EAs

3.3 Machine Learning

ML approaches implement abstract models of biological neural network synapses as illustrated in Fig. 3 [24]. Here, x_i denotes the set of input values, w_{ij} represents their corresponding weights, σ signifies the transmission function, ϕ denotes the activation function respecting the threshold value, and o_j stands for the final output, which serves as input for the next layers.

Nouacer et al. as well as Raj generally classify ML into four main groups [16,23].

– **Dimension Reduction Techniques:** Principal Component Analysis, Singular Value Decomposition
– **Unsupervised Learning-based Clustering Algorithms:** Gaussian Mixture Model, k-means, k-nodes
– **Supervised Learning-based Regression Algorithms:** Linear Regression, Decision Trees, Neural Networks, Deep Reinforcement Learning [8, 26]
– **Unsupervised Learning-based Classification Algorithms:** Logistic Regression, Random Forest, Support Vector Machines

Figure 4 depicts a basic artificial neural network model for reinforcement or deep learning, often comprising multiple layers [23]. In feedforward networks,

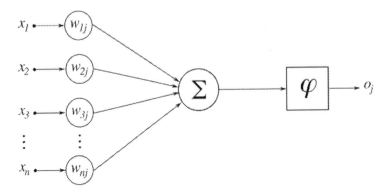

Fig. 3. Synaptic model of artificial neural networks [24]

connections between neurons of one layer solely extend to those of the next layer, and signals only propagate forward. In recurrent networks, the output of a neuron can also be fed back into the previous layer (indirect feedback shown as a blue arrow), to the same neuron (direct feedback shown as a red arrow), or to another neuron of the same layer (lateral feedback shown as a green arrow).

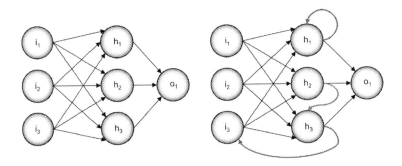

Fig. 4. Models of feedforward (left) and recurrent (right) artificial neural networks (Color figure online)

Every citation in this section fails to meet all the requirements outlined in Sect. 1 and the constraints specified in Sect. 2 due to the introduction of a completely new routing case. Furthermore, most existing publications only examine the situation in two dimensions rather than three, and they aim to minimize the total distance instead of the required energy. This circumstance justifies the problem-oriented heuristic discussed in the following section.

4   Routing Optimization

The compilation of an optimal route occurs in three stages. This section addresses each of them in separate subsections.

4.1   Route Initialization

The initial route stems from a basic A*-algorithm, an extension of Dijkstra's shortest path algorithm [6]. Algorithm 1 provides an outline of the process for constructing the initial route.

Algorithm 1. Route Initialization

1: **procedure** A*$(start, goal)$
2:      $cameFrom[start] = \{\}, fScore[start] = h(start, goal)$
3:      $gScore[start] = 0, openSet = \{start\}$
4:      **while** $openSet \neq \{\}$ **do**
5:          $current = node \in openSet$ with lowest $fScore$
6:          **if** $current = goal$ **then return** $reconstructPath(cameFrom, goal)$
7:          **end if**
8:          $openSet = openSet \setminus \{current\}$
9:          **for** each $neighbor$ of $current$ **do**
10:             $gScore[tentative] = gScore[current] + dist(current, neighbor)$
11:             **if** $gScore[tentative] < gScore[neighbor]$ **then**
12:                 $cameFrom[neighbor] = current$
13:                 $gScore[neighbor] = gScore[tentative]$
14:                 $fScore[neighbor] = gScore[neighbor] + h(goal)$
15:                 **if** $neighbor \notin openSet$ **then**
16:                     $openSet = openSet \cup \{neighbor\}$.
17:                 **end if**
18:             **end if**
19:         **end for**
20:     **end while**
21:     **return** no path found
22: **end procedure**

The heuristic function h in implemented Algorithm 1 simply corresponds to the Euclidean distance, as depicted in (6).

$$h = \sqrt{(n_1[0] - n_2[0])^2 + (n_1[1] - n_2[1])^2} \tag{6}$$

The potential connections within a map link the immediate neighbors N_1 as well as the extended ones N_2. Equations 7 and 8 illustrate the normalized unit vectors of N_1 and N_2, respectively, in the configuration space.

$$N_1 = \left\{ \frac{1}{\sqrt{2}} \begin{pmatrix} 1 \\ 1 \end{pmatrix} ; \begin{pmatrix} 1 \\ 0 \end{pmatrix} ; \frac{1}{\sqrt{2}} \begin{pmatrix} 1 \\ -1 \end{pmatrix} ; \begin{pmatrix} 0 \\ -1 \end{pmatrix} ; \frac{1}{\sqrt{2}} \begin{pmatrix} -1 \\ -1 \end{pmatrix} ; \begin{pmatrix} -1 \\ 0 \end{pmatrix} ; \frac{1}{\sqrt{2}} \begin{pmatrix} -1 \\ 1 \end{pmatrix} ; \begin{pmatrix} 0 \\ 1 \end{pmatrix} \right\} \tag{7}$$

$$N_2 = \left\{ \begin{array}{cccccc} \frac{1}{\sqrt{5}}\begin{pmatrix} 1 \\ 2 \end{pmatrix}; & \frac{1}{\sqrt{5}}\begin{pmatrix} 2 \\ 1 \end{pmatrix}; & \begin{pmatrix} 2 \\ 0 \end{pmatrix}; & \frac{1}{\sqrt{5}}\begin{pmatrix} 2 \\ -1 \end{pmatrix}; & \frac{1}{\sqrt{5}}\begin{pmatrix} 1 \\ -2 \end{pmatrix}; & \begin{pmatrix} 0 \\ -2 \end{pmatrix} \\ \frac{1}{\sqrt{5}}\begin{pmatrix} -1 \\ -2 \end{pmatrix}; & \frac{1}{\sqrt{5}}\begin{pmatrix} -2 \\ -1 \end{pmatrix}; & \begin{pmatrix} -2 \\ -0 \end{pmatrix}; & \frac{1}{\sqrt{5}}\begin{pmatrix} -2 \\ 1 \end{pmatrix}; & \frac{1}{\sqrt{5}}\begin{pmatrix} -1 \\ 2 \end{pmatrix}; & \begin{pmatrix} 0 \\ 2 \end{pmatrix} \end{array} \right\} \quad (8)$$

Furthermore, Fig. 5 illustrates N_1 and N_2 along with their respective normalization denominators.

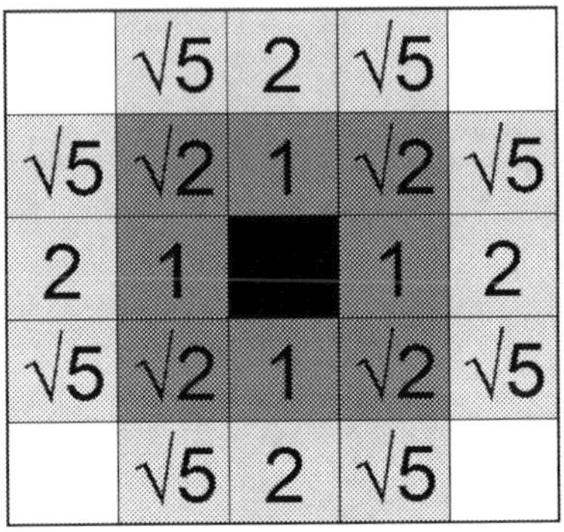

Fig. 5. N_1 and N_2 with their respective normalization denominators

Subsect. 2.1 stipulates the exclusion of non-accessible areas such as motorways or densely populated areas according to the map, thereby requiring routing to automatically avoid them. The output of the first stage includes graphic files in the formats Portable Network Graphics (PNG), Scalable Vector Graphics (SVG), and Keyhole Markup Language (KML) depicting the initial path, as well as a visual representation of the height profile.

4.2   Route Optimization

All of the approaches listed in Sect. 3 solely focus on optimizing travel efficiency in two-dimensional space and do not consider variations in terrain elevation. This limitation has led to the development of a new approach, such as Algorithm 2, which not only minimizes the total path length but also flattens the height profile of the three-dimensional flight path, even if it increases the total length.

The penalty can be adjusted by altering the weight of *slope* from an exponential function to alternatives such as *slope*^{1}, *slope*^{2}, *slope*^{3}, or *slope*^{4}. A shorter and steeper route results from each decrease in the slope penalty factor. Conversely, increasing the latter leads to a longer and flatter route.

4.3   Route Simplification

The Ramer-Douglas-Peucker (RDP) Algorithm 3 exemplifies a widely used technique in the field of computational geometry and data compression [18,20]. It

---

Algorithm 2. Route Optimization (e.g. with e^{slope})

1: **procedure** OPTIMIZATION($start, goal$)
2:     $g[current] = 0$ ▷ Initialization of current g-score
3:     $x[current] = start$ ▷ Initialization of current position
4:     $dist = x[neighbor] - x[current]$▷ Calculation of 2D-distance from current node
to its neighbors
5:     $h[diff] = h[neighbor] - h[current]$ ▷ Calculation of height difference from
current node to its neighbors
6:     $slope = |\frac{h[diff]}{dist}|$ ▷ Calculation of resulting slope
7:     **if** $\arctan(slope) < 14.8°$ **then**
8:         $g[new] = g[current] + dist \cdot (1 + e^{slope})$ ▷ Calculation of penalty $g[new]$
from 2D-distance and slope if $\arctan(slope) < 14.8°$
9:     **end if**
10:    **if** $g[neighbor]$ undefined **or** $g[new] < g[neighbor]$ **then**
11:        $g[neighbor] = g[new]$ ▷ Update of neighbor entries if new g-score better
than current one in conjunction with f-heap data structure
12:    **else**
13:        **if** $x[current] = goal$ **then return** optimized route
14:        **else**
15:            Repetition of process with next neighbor
16:        **end if**
17:    **end if**
18: **end procedure**

---

simplifies an input path while preserving its essential shape to fulfill the efficacy claimed in Subsect. 2.2.

The adjustable tolerance parameter or compression factor ϵ correlates with the level of route simplification. A smaller ϵ results in fewer eliminated waypoints and a more detailed representation, while a larger ϵ yields less attention to detail with fewer waypoints.

5   Results

The literature exploration in Sect. 3 evidently does not yield a perfectly suitable solution that addresses the challenges described in Sect. 1 and the constraints in Sect. 2. Hence, Sect. 4 presents a series of successive routing processes as a much-needed resort. Upon their application, this section reveals experimental setup details and demonstrates the relevant outcomes through four subsections.

5.1   Flight Route

A later comparison of this paper's routing model necessitates fixed starting and endpoint locations. Both venues should offer acceptable takeoff and landing possibilities and be as far apart from each other as possible. The landing point should be close to Vienna to garner significant public attention during and after

---

Algorithm 3. Route Simplification

1: **procedure** SIMPLIFICATION(Original path W, tolerance ϵ)
2:     Selection of first and last waypoint in W as initial line segment
3:     **for** each $w \in W$ **do**
4:         Identification of waypoint w_{max} farthest from line segment
5:         **if** w_{max} significant, i.e. maximum deviation $> \epsilon$) **then**
6:             $S = S \cup \{w_{max}\}$
7:                 Recursive application of algorithm for subsets of waypoints on either side
    of w_{max}
8:         **end if**
9:     **end for**
10: **return** simplified path S
11: **end procedure**

---

the drone's arrival. Table 1 provides location parameters for the test flight's departure in Zell am Ziller in Tyrol and arrival in Guntramsdorf in Lower Austria (15 km south of Vienna) in both the *European Petroleum Survey Group (EPSG):3857 World Geodetic System (WGS)* and *EPSG:4326 WGS 84* formats.

Table 1. Flight route

	EPSG:3857 WGS 84	EPSG:4326 WGS 84
Departure	47°13'32.27"N 11°53'58.44"E	1324653.700182,5978980.789495
Arrival	48°2'57.834"N 16°20'2.124"E	1818284.028848,6115076.918357

The route covered a straight-line distance of approximately 350 km and traversed four Austrian states. It capitalized on the prevailing west-east wind direction in the country and encompassed a vertical elevation change of around 450 m. The ground map initialization included all Airspace Control Zones (ACZs) and Temporary Flight Restrictions (TFRs), and integration with the Austrian elevation profile considered topography for route optimization.

5.2   Penalty Functions

At first glance, it seems that e^{slope} provides the best (lowest) altitude/path length ratio among all penalty functions. This assumption arises from the fact that e^x always increases more rapidly than x, x^2, and x^3. However, a look at Fig. 6 disproves this assumption because x^3 surpasses e^x between $x \approx 2$ and $x \approx 4.5$.

Two-dimensional route calculations typically conclude within a few milliseconds [10]. However, the slope-enhanced Algorithm 1 takes significantly longer, requiring over ten minutes due to its worst-case time complexity of $O(b^d)$. Here, b denotes the average branching factor and d represents the depth of the optimal solution. Figure 7 illustrates five different routes resulting from alternate executions of Algorithm 2 with the penalty functions $slope^1$, $slope^2$, $slope^3$, $slope^4$, and e^{slope}.

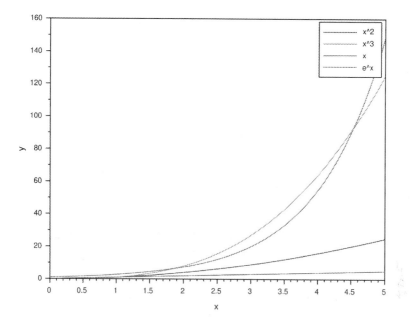

Fig. 6. Penalty functions x, x^2, x^3, and e^x ($x^3 > e^x$ between $x \approx 2$ and $x \approx 4.5$)

The textual and graphical route characteristics in Table 2 and Fig. 8, respectively, demonstrate that increasing the weight of the slope results in longer path lengths and lower altitude/path length ratios. The optimal route achieves minimal values for path length and total covered altitude. With these considerations in mind, $slope^2$ emerges as the optimal penalty function in this case.

Table 2. Route characteristics depending on penalty function

	$slope^1$	$slope^2$	$slope^3$	$slope^4$	e^{slope}
Waypoints	3,166	3,641	4,526	5,943	6,749
Path Length [km]	374.21	421.20	524.44	718.58	797.29
Altitude Gain [m]	12,880.29	4,973.89	5,128.29	6,786.61	9,459.28
Altitude Loss [m]	13,224.05	5,402.45	5,589.27	7,148.38	9,788.79
Total Covered Altitude [m]	26,124.33	10,376.34	10,717.56	13,934.99	19,248.07
Total Covered Altitude/ Path Length Ratio $[\frac{m}{km}]$	69.81	24.64	20.44	19.39	24.14
Energy Consumption [kJ]	2,873.77	3,234.61	4,027.49	5,518.37	6,122.86
Steepest Climb Rate [°]	14.78	13.31	9.05	7.03	6.45

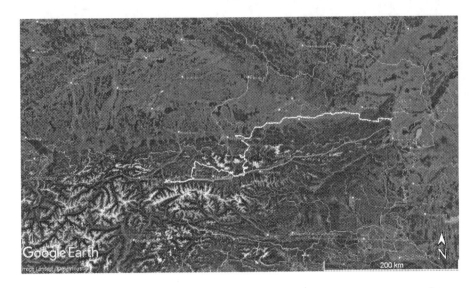

Fig. 7. Slope-optimized routes depending on penalty functions (yellow: $slope^1$, red: $slope^2$, green: $slope^3$, blue: $slope^4$, white: e^{slope}) (Color figure online)

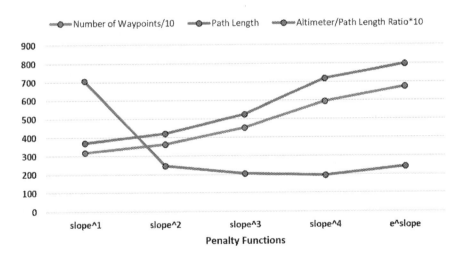

Fig. 8. Route characteristics depending on penalty function

The choice of $slope^2$ as the optimum proves to be true, as it emerges as the weakest penalty function that combines the second shortest path length of 421.20 km with the lowest total covered altitude of 10,376.34 m. All penalty functions, including the weaker $slope^1$, do not exceed the maximum climb rate of 14.80°. As mentioned in Subsect. 2.3, climb rates exceeding 10° lead to immense energy consumption of the hydrogen-powered fuel cell. For clarification, the steepest slope must be lower than 14.80° but may exceed 10° at one point of the route to maximize overall route efficiency and minimize total altimeter change. Nonetheless, the total covered altitude of $slope^1$ unacceptably surpasses that of $slope^2$ by more than twice as much. Figures 9, 10, 11, 12 and 13 visualize the height profiles of the five routes. A glimpse of them immediately reveals their differently scaled y-axes. The routes of $slope^1$ in Fig. 9 and e^{slope} in Fig. 13 peak hundreds of meters higher than those of $slope^2$ in Fig. 10, $slope^3$ in Fig. 11, and $slope^4$ in Fig. 12 at roughly 1,500 m.

Overly strong penalty functions such as $slope^3$, $slope^4$, and e^{slope} result in very long total paths as they prioritize avoiding height differences at almost any cost. Figure 14 depicts a portion of the e^{slope}-route in a steep environment where Algorithm 2 attempts to circumvent strong local gradients by meandering, albeit at the expense of increased path distance.

Avoiding meandering necessitates dismissing $slope^3$, $slope^4$, and e^{slope} as suitable penalty functions, thereby reaffirming $slope^2$ as the best choice.

5.3   Traversing Austria Without Crossing Motorways

As Austro Control prohibits EASA flights of the *Specific* category over motorways, drones must safely cross them via sufficiently long tunnels. Algorithm 2 automatically selects the most suitable tunnels for computed routes. Table 3 lists the selected tunnels, and Fig. 15 indicates their positions on the Austrian map.

Table 4 displays the tunnels crossed by the five different flight routes. Each path passes over two tunnels during the journey across Austria.

Table 3. Relevant tunnels

Tunnel	Location	Motorway	Length of shorter side [m]
Flachau	Salzburg	A10	492
Ofenau	Salzburg	A10	1,320
Selzthal	Styria	A9	940
Wartberg I	Upper Austria	A9	527

Figure 16 zooms in on the tunnel *Wartberg I*, which all routes traverse except for the $slope^1$-route.

5.4   Route Streamlining and Reduction of Waypoints

While Algorithm 3 has a time complexity of $O(n^2)$, it operates more efficiently with $O(n \cdot log(n))$ when utilizing dynamic convex hull data structures [7]. During field testing for this study, Algorithm 3 consumed approximately five times more computing time than Algorithm 2 (over 50 min), rendering it too slow for commercial routing solutions. However, Algorithm 3 yielded very good results for $slope^1$, $slope^2$, $slope^3$, and $slope^4$. It failed to effectively reduce the penalty

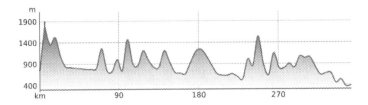

Fig. 9. Height profile of route obtained with penalty function e^{slope^1}

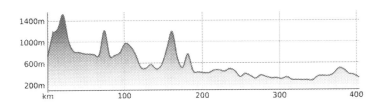

Fig. 10. Height profile of route obtained with penalty function e^{slope^2}

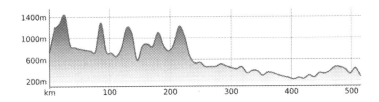

Fig. 11. Height profile of route obtained with penalty function e^{slope^3}

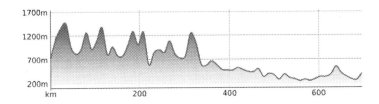

Fig. 12. Height profile of route obtained with penalty function e^{slope^4}

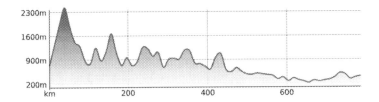

Fig. 13. Height profile of route obtained with penalty function e^{slope}

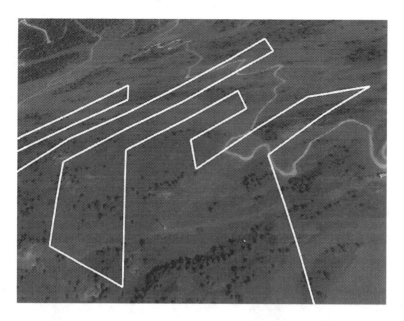

Fig. 14. Meandering in case of too strong penalty function

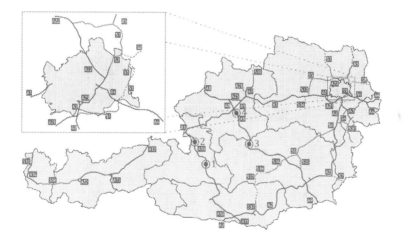

Fig. 15. Relevant tunnels (1. Flachau, 2. Ofenau, 3. Selzthal, 4. Wartberg I)

Table 4. Tunnels depending on penalty function

Penalty function	Tunnel #1	Tunnel #2
$slope^1$	Flachau	Selzthal
$slope^2$	Ofenau	Wartberg I
$slope^3$	Flachau	Wartberg I
$slope^4$	Flachau	Wartberg I
e^{slope}	Flachau	Wartberg I

Fig. 16. Routes crossing motorway A9 at tunnel Wartberg I in Upper Austria

function e^{slope} due to exceeding the maximum recursion depth of the employed programming language, Python. Manually adjusting the recursion limit alleviated this issue but still resulted in excessive program runtime. Currently available technology cannot offer feasible processing times, leaving room for potential improvement. Table 5 refines the data presented in Table 2 by applying Algorithm 3.

Table 5. Route characteristics depending on penalty function and RDP-optimization

	$slope^1$	$slope^2$	$slope^3$	$slope^4$
Waypoints	1,343	1,222	1,412	1,710
Path Length [km]	367.54	401.33	450.20	537.67
Altitude Gain [m]	11,020.66	3,796.25	4,067.37	5,983.67
Altitude Loss [m]	11,873.09	4,648.69	4,919.80	6,410.65
Total Covered Altitude [m]	22,893.75	8,444.94	8,987.17	12,394.32
Total Covered Altitude/Path Length Ratio $[\frac{m}{km}]$	62.29	21.04	19.96	23.05
Energy Consumption [kJ]	2,822.54	3,082.02	3,457.32	4,129.05
Steepest Climb Rate [°]	14.75	9.63	9.36	8.46

Figure 17 more impressively illustrates the reduction in the number of waypoints by factors ranging between two and four with the assistance of Algorithm 3. It also indicates that the preferred $slope^2$-route comprises the smallest number of waypoints after simplification. This reduction holds significance because less complex paths align with the constraints of flight controllers, which have a limited capacity for programmable coordinates (see Subsect. 2.2). By adjusting the compression factor of Algorithm 3, the number of waypoints can be easily modified without sacrificing too much data quality, thereby maintaining flight path resolution.

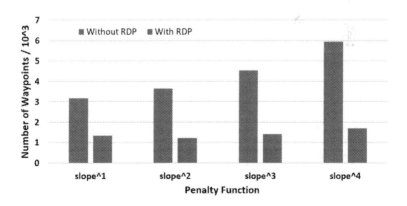

Fig. 17. Route simplification and waypoint reduction of RDP algorithm

6   Conclusion

This scholarly piece proposes a set of algorithms to calculate the best route for traversing Austria with a hydrogen-powered UAV. The optimization process considers various factors, such as airspace regulations, wind patterns, terrain conditions, and refueling locations (even if not needed in the present case).

Careful analysis and evaluation determine the route optimized with the aid of the penalty function $slope^2$ as the best candidate. By incorporating the $slope^2$ criterion, Algorithm 2 prioritizes minimizing the impact of slopes along the route. Steeper inclines significantly affect energy consumption and efficiency of a drone. Algorithm 2, with $slope^2$ as the penalty function, successfully identifies a route that minimizes energy expenditure, maximizes flight efficiency, and ensures a safe and efficient traversal through Austria.

Diminishing the number of waypoints by means of Algorithm 3 plays a crucial role in meeting the flight controller constraints and limited programmable coordinates. Algorithm 3 successfully reduces the number of waypoints by factors between two and four while still upholding acceptable data quality and flight path resolution.

The optimized route identified with the support of this work holds great promise for future BVLOS UAV missions. It serves as a reference for similar projects that aim to accomplish long-distance flights with energy-efficient drones. Furthermore, the insights gained from this project contribute to the growing body of knowledge in UAV route optimization, paving the way for more sustainable and effective applications in the field.

Acknowledgments. Many thanks to Bettina Baumgartner from the University of Vienna for proofreading this paper.

References

1. Berning, A.W., Girard, A., Kolmanovsky, I., D'Souza, S.N.: Rapid uncertainty propagation and chance-constrained path planning for small unmanned aerial vehicles. Adv. Control Appl. **2**(1), 1–17 (2020). https://doi.org/10.1002/adc2.23
2. Brabazon, A., McGarraghy, S.: Evolving foraging algorithms. In: Foraging-Inspired Optimisation Algorithms. NCS, pp. 409–419. Springer, Cham (2018). https://doi.org/10.1007/978-3-319-59156-8_18
3. Dimetor: AirborneRF Fact Sheet (2018). https://www.dimetor.com/downloads/AirborneRF_Fact_Sheet.pdf
4. Federal Aviation Administration: Remote Pilot – Small Unmanned Aircraft Systems Study Guide (2016). https://www.faa.gov/sites/faa.gov/files/regulations_policies/handbooks_manuals/aviation/remote_pilot_study_guide.pdf
5. Goyal, R., et al.: Urban Air Mobility (UAM) Market Study. Tech. rep. (2018). https://ntrs.nasa.gov/api/citations/20190001472/downloads/20190001472.pdf
6. Hart, P.E., Nilsson, N.J., Raphael, B.: A formal basis for the heuristic determination of minimum cost paths. IEEE Trans. Syst. Sci. Cybern. **4**(2), 100–107 (1968). https://doi.org/10.1109/TSSC.1968.300136

7. Hershberger, J., Snoeyink, J.: Speeding Up the Douglas-Peucker Line-Simplification Algorithm. Tech. rep. (1992). https://www.cs.ubc.ca/sites/default/files/tr/1992/TR-92-07_0.pdf

8. Hu, J., Yang, X., Wang, W., Wei, P., Ying, L., Liu, Y.: Obstacle Avoidance for UAS in continuous action space using deep reinforcement learning. IEEE Access **10**, 90623–90634 (2022). https://doi.org/10.1109/ACCESS.2022.3201962

9. JETNET: ADS-B Exchange (2016). https://www.adsbexchange.com/

10. Jin, Z., et al.: Simulation of real-time routing for UAS traffic management with communication and airspace safety considerations. In: 2019 IEEE/AIAA 38th Digital Avionics Systems Conference (DASC), pp. 1–10. IEEE (2019). https://doi.org/10.1109/DASC43569.2019.9081675

11. Kalagireva, K., Radkov, V.: Displaying the air situation through the collection and processing of flight information on Flightradar24 Project. In: Scientific Research and Education in the Air Force (AFASES 2016), 267–272 (2016). https://doi.org/10.19062/2247-3173.2016.18.1.36

12. Li, P., Liu, D., Xia, X., Baldi, S.: Embedding adaptive features in the ArduPilot control architecture for unmanned aerial vehicles. In: 2022 IEEE 61st Conference on Decision and Control (CDC), pp. 3773–3780. IEEE, Cancún, Quintana Roo, Mexico (2022). https://doi.org/10.1109/CDC51059.2022.9993292

13. Makhanov, H., Setia, K., Liu, J., Gomez-Gonzalez, V., Jenaro-Rabadan, G.: Quantum Computing Applications for Flight Trajectory Optimization, pp. 1–11 (2023). https://doi.org/10.48550/arXiv.2304.14445

14. Minucci, F., Vinogradov, E., Pollin, S.: Avoiding collisions at any (Low) cost: ads-b like position broadcast for UAVs. IEEE Access **8**, 121843–121857 (2020). https://doi.org/10.1109/ACCESS.2020.3007315

15. Niu, S., Zhang, J., Zhang, F., Li, H.: A method of UAVs route optimization based on the structure of the highway network. Int. J. Distrib. Sens. Netw. **11**(12), 1–7 (2015). https://doi.org/10.1155/2015/359657

16. Nouacer, R., Hussein, M., Espinoza, H., Ouhammou, Y., Ladeira, M., Castiñeira, R.: Towards a framework of key technologies for drones. Microprocess. Microsyst. **77**, 1–13 (2020). https://doi.org/10.1016/j.micpro.2020.103142

17. Novak, M., Galffy, A., Berens, M., Reichl, C.: Joined wing unmanned aerial vehicle surrogate-based aerodynamic optimization of maximum range. In: 56th 3AF International Conference on Applied Aerodynamics, pp. 48–67 (2022). https://www.3af-aerodynamics.com/

18. Olsson, J., Yberg, V.: Log Data Filtering in Embedded Sensor Devices (2015). https://www.diva-portal.org/smash/get/diva2:860578/FULLTEXT01.pdf

19. Politi, E., Panagiotopoulos, I., Varlamis, I., Dimitrakopoulos, G.: A survey of UAS technologies to enable beyond visual line of sight (BVLOS) operations. In: Proceedings of the 7th International Conference on Vehicle Technology and Intelligent Transport Systems – VEHITS, pp. 505–512. SciTePress (2021). https://doi.org/10.5220/0010446905050512

20. Prasad, D.K., Leung, M.K.H., Quek, C., Cho, S.Y.: A novel framework for making dominant point detection methods non-parametric. Image Vis. Comput. **30**(11), 843–859 (2012). https://doi.org/10.1016/j.imavis.2012.06.010

21. Radzki, G., Thibbotuwama, A., Bocewicz, G.: UAVs flight routes optimization in changing weather conditions – constraint programming approach. Appl. Comput. Sci. **15**(3), 5–20 (2019). https://doi.org/10.23743/acs-2019-17

22. Ragbir, P., et al.: UAV-based wildland fire air toxics data collection and analysis. Sensors **23**(7), 1–17 (2023). https://doi.org/10.3390/s23073561

23. Fantin Irudaya Raj, E.: Implementation of machine learning techniques in unmanned aerial vehicle control and its various applications. In: Ouaissa, M., Khan, I.U., Ouaissa, M., Boulouard, Z., Hussain Shah, S.B. (eds.) Computational Intelligence for Unmanned Aerial Vehicles Communication Networks. SCI, vol. 1033, pp. 17–33. Springer, Cham (2022). https://doi.org/10.1007/978-3-030-97113-7_2
24. Russell, S., Norvig, P.: Artificial Intelligence: A Modern Approach. Pearson, 4th edn. (2020). https://aima.cs.berkeley.edu/
25. Schüttler, T.: Satellitennavigation – Wie sie funktioniert und wie sie unseren Alltag beeinflusst. Springer Berlin Heidelberg, 2nd edn. (2023). https://doi.org/10.1007/978-3-662-58051-6
26. Wang, C., Wang, J., Shen, Y., Zhang, X.: Autonomous navigation of UAVs in large-scale complex environments: a deep reinforcement learning approach. IEEE Trans. Veh. Technol. **68**(3), 2124–2136 (2019). https://doi.org/10.1109/TVT.2018.2890773
27. Zhang, H.: Research on UAV route optimization method based on double target of confidence and ambiguity. Front. Neurorobotics **15**, 1–8 (2021). https://doi.org/10.3389/fnbot.2021.694899
28. Zhu, L., Xu, Z., Wang, Y.: Research on UAV route optimization in complex terrains. In: 2021 IEEE/AIAA 40th Digital Avionics Systems Conference (DASC), pp. 1–6. IEEE, San Antonio, TX, USA (2021). https://doi.org/10.1109/DASC52595.2021.9594471

Spanning Thread: A Multidimensional Classification Method for Efficient Data Center Management

Laurent Hussenet[1], Chérifa Boucetta[2(✉)], and Michel Herbin[1,2]

[1] CReSTIC EA 3804, 51097, Université de Reims Champagne-Ardenne,
Reims, France
{frederic.blanchard,laurent.hussenet}@univ-reims.fr
[2] LIGM CNRS-UMR 8049, Université Gustave Eiffel, Champs-sur-Marne, France
cherifa.boucetta@univ-eiffel.fr

Abstract. Data originating from diverse sources, including relational and NoSQL databases, web pages, texts, images, recordings, and videos, are expanding in both size and complexity. Navigating through these vast datasets poses significant challenges. As the volume of data grows, the complexity of analysis intensifies. Multidimensional data analysis requires effective organization of the data, and different ranking methods can help achieve this goal. Ranking is a way to create a linear order of the data items that reflects their similarity or importance. The essence of ranking lies in providing a systematic way to traverse the entirety of a dataset, from its inception to its conclusion. In this paper, we introduce a novel method named "Spanning Thread" (ST) for classification and ranking multidimensional data. ST aims to establish a meaningful path connecting all data points and starts with a randomly selected data. Additionally, we present OST (Ordered Spanning Thread), which commences with the minimum virtual data and concludes with the maximum virtual data. Both methods are evaluated using an open dataset, wherein we measure the frequency of class changes to assess their effectiveness.

Keywords: Ranking · Data analysis · Multidimensional data · Classification · Virtual machine placement

1 Introduction

Analyzing and exploring multidimensional data pose significant challenges, demanding sophisticated tools to distill extensive datasets with numerous attributes into meaningful insights. Notably, multidimensional projection techniques and data ranking emerge as powerful methodologies for translating multidimensional data into visual representations, leveraging similarity features to enhance comprehension.

The organization of multidimensional data represents a fundamental step in data analysis. Consequently, numerous ranking methods have been developed for various applications, including sports, decision-making, healthcare, and graph mining. These methods are designed to determine the optimal arrangement of data items based on criteria such as performance, cost, risk, or quality. Some approaches leverage dimension reduction techniques like principal component analysis (PCA) [8] while others utilize graph algorithms such as PageRank or rank-by-feature framework [11].

The effectiveness of these ranking methods can vary depending on how objects are assigned to specific groups. In this context, our paper introduces "spanning thread", a classification method designed to assign quantitative multidimensional data to a class by computing the nearest neighbors. The determination of nearest neighbors is a pivotal aspect of various data analysis methods, forming the core of the proposed spanning thread methodology. In most cases, the data set has no classes, only the order of data ranking is important. We need to determine the first data and the last data. In this case, we add two virtual data to our dataset. One of the virtual data will always be the first in the spanning thread. The other one will always be the last in the spanning thread.

The classic "spanning tree" obtained with Prim's algorithm generates a tree that spans the data. We adapt this algorithm to obtain a line or thread that spans the data. This thread is constructed starting from a random piece of data. We propose an improvement to this data arrangement by constructing the thread between a virtual minimum and a virtual maximum, which produces an order in the arrangement.

We applied this method to manage data center operations and virtual machine deployment. Managing virtual machine (VM) placement in cloud environments is a complex task. Dynamic workloads and fluctuating resources constantly challenge optimal placement, potentially leading to inefficient resource utilization and overloaded servers. Load balancing strategies are crucial to tackle this challenge. By effectively distributing network traffic and computational tasks across multiple servers, they enhance resource utilization and prevent server overload.

As part of the DeMETeRE (Deployment of Territorial Micro-Environments for Student Success) project[1], aimed at implementing a virtualization system for workstations catering to both university students and professionals, we focused on optimizing VM placement and resource management. The solution is designed to address techno-pedagogical needs by providing tailored tools and software for each program, while ensuring equitable access regardless of users' workplace or equipment. VMs can be classified into distinct classes, involving the identification of quantitative variables such as memory, CPU, GPU, usage time, and energy consumption to group VMs based on their similarities in requirements and specifications [10]. This allows for more efficient allocation of VMs to servers based on their capabilities.

Evaluation experiments are conducted under multidimensional open datasets. The objective is to validate the method by testing it on several open datasets and then apply it to virtual machine and data center placement. The rest of the paper is organized as follows. Section 2 reviews the related work. In Sect. 3, the spanning

---

[1] https://www.univ-reims.fr/demetere.

thread algorithm is described. Section 4 presents the ordered spanning thread approach and Sect. 5 presents the performance evaluation. Section 6 describes the application of TS and OTS in the management of the data center. Finally, Sect. 7 presents the conclusion and future work.

2   Related Work

Many studies have focused on leveraging dimensionality reduction techniques like Principal Component Analysis (PCA) and t-Distributed Stochastic Neighbor Embedding (t-SNE) to condense high-dimensional data while preserving crucial information for ranking. For example, [12] analyzes and compares PCA and conductes three experiments to show how to apply PCA in the real applications including biometrics, image compression, and visualisation of high-dimensional datasets. [1] presents a Support Vector Machine (SVM) based ranking approach for anomaly detection. Additionally, deep learning models like ranking-optimized neural networks have shown promising results, as seen in [13]. The most classical methods of ranking use the Borda's approach [2]. These methods are based on a model assigning a score to each data. The most usual score is the classical Borda's Count (BC) based on the sum of the ranks assigned by the different variables. The first data corresponds to the lowest score value, while the latest data corresponds to the highest score value [2]. Unfortunately, there is no perfect score, and each application generally builds its own score, making the quality of the score highly subjective. The score depends on the weights of the variables describing multidimensional data. For example, the weighted average of student results obviously depends on the weight of each of the tests taken by the student, thus influencing student ranking [2]. Moreover, when a dataset is partitioned into classes, it is expected that two data from the same class have closer ranks than two data from different classes. However, when the classes have very different meanings, the score approach of ranking does not guarantee this assertion. For instance, considering data classes to which colors are assigned, the ranking of score values may lead to a mixture of colors where data of different classes could have close ranks, thereby "mixing apples and oranges." Several extensions of the Borda method have been proposed in academic literature. For instance, in [14], the authors introduce a quantile-based variant known as the quantile-based Borda Count, which extends and generalizes the original Borda Count. The effectiveness of this generalized ranking approach is demonstrated through case studies conducted on real datasets. Another approach discussed in [7] combines the Borda method with Condorcet's method. This fusion aims to transform a set of rankings, established over a collection of alternatives, into a comprehensive, transitive, and cardinal assessment. This is achieved by computing the average support that each alternative garners when compared with others. In our previous work [3], we proposed a practical and generic approach for multidimensional data ranking. We studied each dimension and we calculated the rank per variable. Finally, we validated the proposed method using open datasets. Despite the reasonable quantity of papers on the areas of classification and clustering and its crescent importance, papers on ranking are rare. Usual solutions are not generic and demand expert knowledge on the specification of the weight of each component and, therefore, the definition of a ranking function. The authors in [6] proposed to build a similarity index based on data rankings called Rank-Based Similarity Index (RBSI). This paper proposes another approach for ranking based on Condorcet's method [5]. Pairwise comparisons of data are performed to obtain the ranking. Although using Condorcet's approach, Kemeny's method could provide an optimal ranking [9], the computation of Kemeny's ranking is NP-hard. Hence, this paper suggests an alternative method based on simpler pairwise comparisons, utilizing a simple distance as a comparison criterion, such as the classical Euclidean distance. Such pairwise comparisons are commonly used in clustering methods, leading us to expect that the proposed ranking (i.e., the spanning thread) respects the classes when ordering the data. However, with this method, the order of classes will be random, meaning that either "apples" come before "oranges" or "oranges" come before "apples." The class order is randomly selected [5].

3   Spanning Thread Algorithm

Let $\Omega = \{X_1, X_2, X_3, ...X_n\}$ be a set of n multidimensional quantitative data. In this paper, a spanning thread of Ω is considered to be a ranking of Ω data. Let us describe the ranking method we propose.

Let X_b be a randomly selected data in Ω to start ranking (i.e. the spanning thread). X_b is called the beginning data. The current ranking then has only one data. So we define the current ranking by $R = (X_b)$.

Then we select a second data following the beginning data. That is the one presenting the lowest dissimilarity (i.e. the closest) with the starting data. In terms of dissimilarity, the following data is optimal within $\Omega - R$ and it is defined by:

$$X_e = \underset{X \in \Omega - R}{\arg \min} \left(dissimilarity(X_b, X) \right)$$

In this paper, the dissimilarity between two data is evaluated using Euclidean distance. The second data X_e ends the current ranking that becomes $R = (X_b, X_e)$.

Let's complete the current ranking (i.e. the current spanning thread) with a new data X. This third data is selected within $\Omega - R$. The data X is the one presenting the lowest dissimilarity with one of the current ranking R. X is placed in R either before X_b or after X_e. There are then two possible cases: either this new data is less dissimilar with X_b or it is less dissimilar with X_e. In the first case, X is placed before X_b and the current ranking becomes $R = (X, X_b, X_e)$. In the second case, X is placed after X_e and the current ranking becomes $R = (X_b, X_e, X)$.

The data in R are ranked data and the data in $\Omega - R$ are unranked data. The complete ranking (i.e. the complete spanning thread) is obtained by adding data one by one in R. We proceed step by step as long as $\Omega - R$ is not empty. Each step consists in:

- select an unranked data from $\Omega - R$,
- add this one to R by ranking into R.

The selected data is the unranked data that is the less dissimilar one with the ranked data. Let X be the selected data that is defined by:

$$X = \arg\min_{X_u \in \Omega - R} \left(\min_{X_r \in R} \left(dissimilarity(X_u, X_r) \right) \right)$$

Now let's explain how we rank X in R. Let C be the ranked data ($C \in R$) with the lowest dissimilarity with X. It is defined by:

$$C = \arg\min_{X_r \in R} \left(dissimilarity(X, X_r) \right)$$

We consider that X is connected to C within R. Then X is ranked into R either before C or after C. We consider three possible cases:

- If C is at the beginning of R, then X is added at the beginning of the ranking and X becomes the new beginning of the current ranking.
- If C is at the end of R, then X is added at the end of the ranking and X becomes the new end of the current ranking.
- If C is neither at the beginning of R nor at the end of R, X is inserted in the current ranking either before C or after C. Let B and A be the ranked data in R that are respectively before C and after C. We compare the dissimilarity of X with B and A.
  - If $dissimilarity(X, B) < dissimilarity(X, A)$, then X is inserted between B and C in the current ranking.
  - Otherwise X is inserted between C and A in the current ranking.

The ranking method described above is summarized in the Algorithm 1. The result we obtain is a spanning thread of $\Omega - R_S$. We suppose that $R_S = U_{x_i \in R} X_i$ for the list $R = (X1 = Xb, ..., Xe = Xn)$ of n elements in the ranking of the objects.

Figure 1 displays some steps making the spanning thread with simulated data. First we show 20 simulated data with 3 classes and we display the starting data with a bold circle. We then show the first steps making the spanning thread with 4, 5, 14 and 16 steps respectively. Note that a new data integrating the thread could distort it. Because of this new data, the near data might not be successive data in the thread. Finally we display the complete spanning thread. A dotted line indicates a class change in the spanning thread. This example gives three class changes in the spanning thread.

4   Ordered Spanning Thread

A spanning thread depend on two elements. First, randomly selecting a data to start a spanning thread can affect the resulting thread. Second, the second

Algorithm 1. Constructing spanning threads

Require: Ω a set of n multidimensional data
$\quad$ X first ranked data: $X \in \Omega$
$\quad$ R current ranking: $R = (X)$
$\quad$ X_b at the beginning of R: $X_b = X$
$\quad$ X_e at the end of R: $X_e = X$
$\quad$ U set of unranked data: $U = \Omega - R$
$\quad$ **while** $(U \neq \emptyset)$ **do**
$$X = \underset{X_u \in U}{\arg \min} \left(\underset{X_r \in R}{\min} \left(dissimilarity(X_u, X_r) \right) \right) \{$$
$\quad\quad$ C is the insertion point of X into R:}
$$C = \underset{X_r \in R}{\arg \min} \left(dissimilarity(X, X_r) \right)$$
$\quad\quad$ **if** $C == X_b$ **then**
$\quad\quad\quad$ X is inserted before X_b at the beginning of R
$\quad\quad\quad$ $X_b = X$
$\quad\quad$ **else if** $C == X_e$ **then**
$\quad\quad\quad$ X is inserted after X_e at the end of R
$\quad\quad\quad$ $X_e = X$
$\quad\quad$ **else**
$\quad\quad\quad$ B is before C within R
$\quad\quad\quad$ A is after C within R
$\quad\quad\quad$ **if** $dissimilarity(X, B) < dissimilarity(X, A)$ **then**
$\quad\quad\quad\quad$ X is inserted between B and C into R
$\quad\quad\quad$ **else**
$\quad\quad\quad\quad$ X is inserted between C and A into R
$\quad\quad\quad$ **end if**
$\quad\quad$ **end if**
$\quad\quad$ $U = U - X$
$\quad$ **end while**
$\quad$ return R

---

data we add to the spanning thread gives a direction to the thread. In a one-dimensional data space, this direction corresponds to increasing order or decreasing order. In the previous algorithm, this second data X_b is placed in front of the starting data X_e. So a spanning thread depends on the selection of X_b and X_e (i.e. the two data beginning and ending the ranking).

This section proposes to determine a single spanning thread by setting X_b and X_e. We define X_{min} which is a virtual data that has minimal value for each variable. Let $(x_{.1}, x_{.2}, x_{.3}, ...x_{.p})$ be the p variables describing data. The data X_i of Ω where $1 \leq i \leq n$ is defined with $X_i = (x_{i1}, x_{i2}, x_{i3}, ...x_{ip})$. Then X_{min} is defined by $X_{min} = (x_{min_1}, x_{min_2}, x_{min_3}, ...x_{min_p})$ where $x_{min_j} = \underset{1 \leq i \leq n}{min} (x_{ij})$. With the same way we define X_{max} which is a virtual data that has maximal value for each variable. The ordered spanning thread is the one which takes X_{min} and X_{max} as beginning data and ending data respectively. We build the ordered

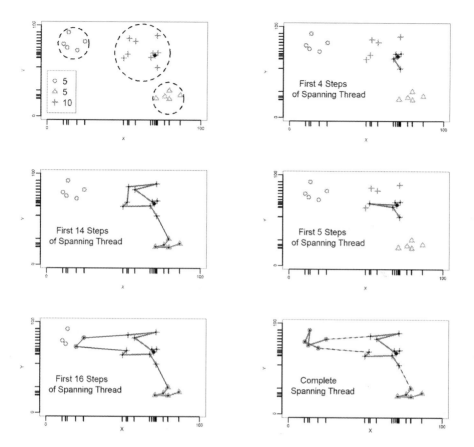

Fig. 1. Some steps to make the spanning thread: first the simulated data with 3 classes, the starting data is a bold circle, then the thread with respectively 4, 5, 14 and 16 steps, finally the complete spanning thread

spanning thread by maintaining $X_b = X_{min}$ and $X_e = X_{max}$. The Algorithm 2 describes how to obtain the ordered spanning thread of Ω R_S.

5   Assessment of the Spanning Thread Method

The purpose of this section is to evaluate the method we use to span a multidimensional dataset. There is no ground truth to validate a spanning thread in a multidimensional dataset. Despite the lack of ground truth, this paper proposes an heuristic method to assess a spanning thread when the dataset has several classes.

We consider that the data belonging to the same class must be successive in a spanning thread. In other words, the number of Class Changes (CC) should be minimal when traversing the dataset from the beginning to the end of the thread.

Algorithm 2. Constructing ordered spanning threads

Require: Ω a set of multidimensional data

$\Omega = \{X_1, X_2, X_3, ...X_n\}$ where $X_i = (x_{i1}, x_{i2}...x_{ip})$

$X_{min} = (min_1, min_2...min_p,)$ with $min_j = \min_{1 \leq i \leq n}(x_{ij})$

$X_{max} = (max_1, max_2...max_p,)$ with $max_j = \max_{1 \leq i \leq n}(x_{ij})$

R current ranking: $R = (X_{min}, X_{max})$

U set of unranked data: $U = \Omega$

while $(U \neq \emptyset)$ **do**

   $X = \underset{X_u \in U}{\arg\min}\left(\min_{X_r \in R}(dissimilarity(X_u, X_r))\right)$ $\{C$ is the insertion point of X into $R\}$

   $C = \underset{X_r \in R}{\arg\min}\left(dissimilarity(X, X_r)\right)$

   if $C == X_{min}$ **then**

      X is inserted into R just after X_{min}

   else if $C == X_{max}$ **then**

      X is inserted into R just before X_{max}

   else

      B is before C within R

      A is after C within R

      if $dissimilarity(X, B) < dissimilarity(X, A)$ **then**

         X is inserted between B and C into R

      else

         X is inserted between C and A into R

      end if

   end if

   $U = U - X$

end while

remove X_{min} and X_{max} from R

return R

If the dataset contains k classes, the spanning thread becomes optimal when CC equals $k - 1$. Unfortunately this optimal value is not observed with real datasets. We assume that the lesser the number of class changes, the better the spanning thread. So we assess our spanning thread method with CC using classical data sets with classes that the reader can find on UCI Machine Learning Repository or Kaggle. We compute the number of Class Changes (CC) using nine datasets called IRIS, WINE, ECOLI, GLASS, SEGMENTATION, SEEDS, BANKNOTE, SOCIAL NETWORK and WIFI LOCALIZATION. In the following n, p and k are respectively the number of data, the number of variables and the number of classes in a dataset (see Table 1).

To validate our approach we will compare our Spanning Thread (ST) with the ranking obtained with the ranking method of Borda [2] using the classical Borda's Count (BC). In a recent work [4], we proposed another score different from BC. This score is called Principal Rank (PR). The PR score is given by the first principal component of the rankings obtained with the different variables.

Generally ranking with PR gives better ranking than the one obtain with BC score values. We compare the number of class changes when using ranking with Borda's Count (BC), Principal Rank (PR), and Spanning Thread (ST). Table 1 shows the results that we obtain with the nine datasets cited above. With ST, the improvement in results is generally very clear except for the IRIS data. This improvement is even spectacular as for the BANKNOTE data.

Table 1. Number of class changes when traversing a dataset through ranking using Borda's Count (BC), Principal Rank (PR), Spanning Thread (ST), and Ordered Spanning Thread (OST). n is the number of data, p is the number of variables, and k is the number of classes.

dataset	n	p	k	BC	PR	ST	OST
IRIS	150	4	3	20	14	14	13
WINE	178	13	3	62	38	20	18
ECOLI	336	7	8	196	185	71	71
GLASS	214	9	6	145	135	85	85
SEGMENTATION	210	19	7	140	119	48	47
SEEDS	210	7	3	48	44	24	24
BANKNOTE	1372	4	2	469	485	6	6
SOCIAL NETWORK	400	2	2	119	111	60	61
WIFI LOCALIZATION	2000	7	4	967	703	58	58
SIMUL	20	2	3	4	4	3	3

Spanning Thread (ST) and Ordered Spanning Thread (OST) differ in start and end data. ST starts with randomly selected data. But OST requires starting with the minimum virtual data and ending with the maximum virtual data. If the virtual minima and maxima are meaningless, then OST provides no improvement to the thread. Figure 2 displays ST and OTS using 20 simulated data with 3 classes (see Fig. 1). OST does not give any improvement in terms of number of class changes. An optimal number of class changes should be 2. But both ST and OST give 3 class changes.

Table 1 shows the number of class changes when using real data. The differences between ST and OST are not significant. If the virtual minima and maxima have meaning, then the ordering object makes sense and OST should be preferred to ST. In this case OST is considered as a ranking method. In other case OST is only a deterministic spanning thread relatively to ST which is a random starting spanning thread. Figure 3 presents the three distinct classes of the iris dataset: Iris Setosa, Iris Versicolor, and Iris Virginica. Each class is represented by a different color in the figure. Black lines separate the classes and presents the classes change based on the OST.

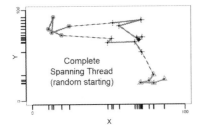
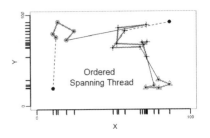

Fig. 2. Using simulated data (see Fig. 1), Spanning Thread obtained with a random starting point (bold circle) and Ordered Spanning Thread ranking between minima and maxima virtual data (bold circles)

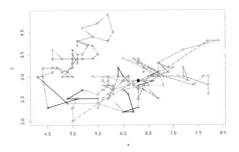

Fig. 3. Number of class changes for iris dataset

6   VM Placement on the Management of the Data Center

Testing the Spanning Thread method for VM placement leverages the university's pedagogical data center, managed by the IT department. This center houses two distinct clusters: one dedicated to administrative tasks (stable workloads) and another dedicated to student needs (dynamic workloads). The administrative cluster features Dell PowerEdge R630 servers with 2.4GHz CPUs and 128GB RAM, ideal for stable workloads. In contrast, the pedagogical cluster utilizes more powerful R630 servers with 2.5GHz CPUs and 512GB RAM to handle student demands. Both clusters connect through two Cisco Nexus 5548UP switches with 2×10 Gbps Ethernet links, and access a shared SAN for storage (see Fig. 4 for the data center architecture).

The data center contains 8 ESXi hypervisors and 15 data stores. The hypervisors enable multiple virtual machines to run concurrently by abstracting the physical hardware resources and allocating them among the virtual machines. They provide isolation between VMs, ensuring that each VM operates independently of others and has its own virtualized set of resources, including CPU, memory, storage, and networking. Data stores serve as repositories for virtual machine files, including virtual disks (VMDK files), configuration files, and snapshots.

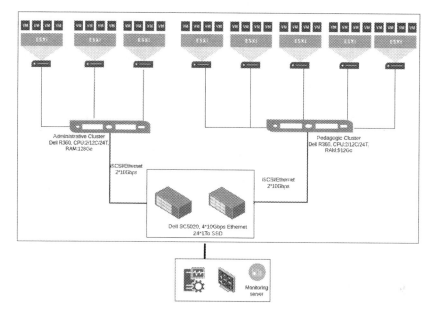

Fig. 4. Architecture of the pedagogic data center (IT department)

We also implemented a comprehensive monitoring system to track various parameters: server performance, network activity, VM activity, and resource utilization. This allows us to identify potential issues, optimize resource allocation, and ensure overall data center health and stability. Real-time data analysis provides insights into operational efficiency, enabling adjustments and improvements as needed.

We present hereafter some graphics from the monitoring dashboard.

Figure 5 shows the statistics of the data stores and the hypervisors. The data stores are used for various purposes within our infrastructure. We define:

- VM Linux Data Store: This data store is dedicated to storing virtual machine images running Linux operating systems. It provides a centralized location for storing and managing VMs based on Linux.
- VM Windows Data Store: Similar to the VM Linux data store, this data store is specifically allocated for virtual machine images running Windows operating systems. It ensures efficient management and storage of VMs running Windows.
- Student Projects Data Store: This data store is allocated for storing project files and resources related to student projects. It serves as a centralized repository for students to access and manage their project materials.
- Local Data Store: The local data store is used for storing files and resources that are accessed and utilized locally within the infrastructure. It facilitates quick access to frequently used data and ensures high-speed data retrieval.

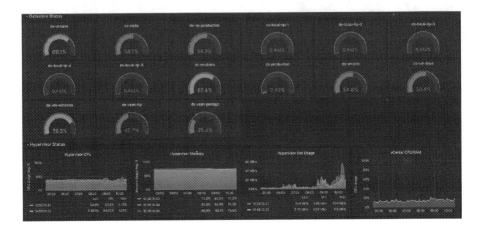

Fig. 5. The statistics of the data-stores and the hypervisors

It allows teachers to share files, documents, and other educational materials easily.

- Intranet Data Store: This data store is specifically used for storing resources and files accessed within the local intranet network. It serves as a centralized storage location for intranet-related data and resources.
- etc.

Each data store serves a specific purpose and contributes to the efficient management and utilization of resources within the infrastructure. Figure 5 illustrates the average utilization of each data store. For instance, the utilization rate for ds-vm-windows is 78.5%, while ds-vm-linux stands at 54.4%.

For hypervisors, the metrics include CPU usage, memory utilization and network usage. The pedagogic cluster dedicated to student's VMs consumes more resources than the production cluster. Figure 6 depicts VM statistics over a duration of 5 h, encompassing metrics such as memory usage, CPU usage, network usage, disk usage, and disk performance. Leveraging these metrics, we extract statistics for both VMs and hypervisors. Subsequently, we utilize this data to apply the TSO classification method. Indeed, resource consumption consisting of CPU, RAM, network usage, disk usage, of each VM are collected and used as an input for the ranking approach. We consider a dataset containing 166 VMs and 3 classes of VMs. The 3 classes correspond to 3 hypervisors in the pedagogic cluster. Figure 7 illustrates the distribution of VMs and classes, along with the number of class changes.

We apply the OST method with the 3 classes. The significant number of class changes obtained with the OST method (97 changes) is due to the arbitrary reference classes (there is no direct link between the variables describing the VMs and the classes used). Indeed, the 3 hypervisors do not correspond to 3 classes of VMs. Therefore, it may be interesting to classify these VMs into 3

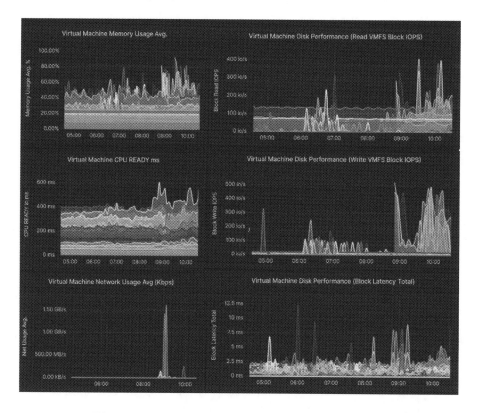

Fig. 6. Statistics of the VMs of the pedagogical cluster

true classes and to place each class of VMs (via migrations) into a hypervisor specialized for that class (redefining the VM classes).

To achieve this, we propose the following approach: When a VM triggers a change of "class" in the OST, we move it to a different class (migration). We migrate the VM to another hypervisor, one that avoids the class change. This approach is likely to reduce the number of class changes as shown in Fig. 8. However, it's important to note that these migrations will eliminate 97 class changes, but they may also create new changes that did not previously exist. Thus, we are moving closer to clustering the VMs with one class of VMs for each hypervisor. Hence, the interest of OST lies in its deterministic nature, as there is no random starting point, ensuring consistency. The objective is to better adapt resources specific to each hypervisor.

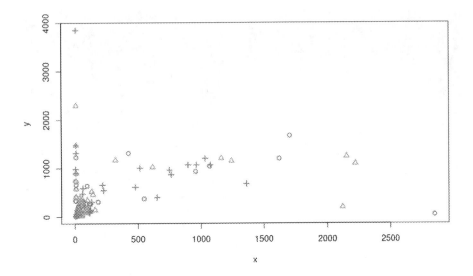

Fig. 7. VM classes

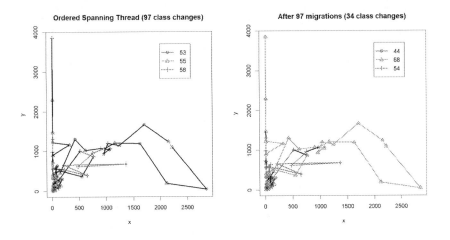

Fig. 8. VM management based on OST

7   Conclusion

In this paper, we introduced a novel ranking approach for multidimensional data known as the spanning thread (ST) method. Initially, a randomly chosen data point is selected to initiate the ranking process, serving as the starting data. Subsequently, we identify a second data point with the lowest dissimilarity to the initial point. Through an iterative process, additional data points are incorporated into the ranking based on their dissimilarity with the already ranked data. We conducted extensive evaluations of the ST method using various open datasets, analyzing the resulting number of class changes. Furthermore, we proposed an enhanced version of the spanning thread, termed the ordered spanning thread (OST), designed for multidimensional datasets. Unlike the ST method, the OST approach commences with predetermined virtual data points representing the minimum and maximum values. This distinction enables the OST algorithm to establish an ordered representation of the data while minimizing class changes. Subsequently, we applied both the ST and OST methods to manage the data center of the department. Our objective was to rank virtual machines (VMs) to aid in the selection of VMs for migration or determining their optimal placement within the data center. In our future work, we will compare through experiments the proposed scheme with other approaches. Moreover, we intend to explore the integration of optimization models for VM migration in geo-distributed cloud systems, considering factors such as migration energy costs. This holistic approach aims to enhance energy management within cloud computing environments.

References

1. Bharadiya, J.: A tutorial on principal component analysis for dimensionality reduction in machine learning. Int. J. Innov. Res. Sci. Eng. Technol. **8**, 2028–2032 (2023)
2. Borda, J.: Mémoire sur les élections au scrutin. Histoire de l'Académie royale des sciences, Paris (1781)
3. Boucetta, C., Hussenet, L., Herbin, M.: Practical method for multidimensional data ranking: Application for virtual machine migration. In: Phillipson, F., Eichler, G., Erfurth, C., Fahrnberger, G. (eds.) I4CS 2022, vol. 1585, pp. 267–277. Springer, Heidelberg (2022). https://doi.org/10.1007/978-3-031-06668-9_19
4. Boucetta, C., Hussenet, L., Herbin, M.: Improved euclidean distance in the k nearest neighbors method. In: Phillipson, F., Eichler, G., Erfurth, C., Fahrnberger, G. (eds.) I4CS 2023, vol. 1876, pp. 315–324. Springer, Heidelberg (2023). https://doi.org/10.1007/978-3-031-40852-6_17
5. Condorcet, N.: Essai sur l'application de l'analyse à la probabilité des décisions rendues à la pluralité des voix. Imprimerie Royale, Paris (1785)
6. Herbin, M., Aït-Younes, A., Blanchard, F., Gillard, D.: Rank-based similarity index (rbsi) in a multidimensional dataset. In: Lüke, K.H., Eichler, G., Erfurth, C., Fahrnberger, G. (eds.) I4CS 2019, vol. 1041, pp. 159–165. Springer, Cham (2019). https://doi.org/10.1007/978-3-030-22482-0_12
7. Herrero, C., Villar, A.: Group decisions from individual rankings: the borda-condorcet rule. Eur. J. Oper. Res. **291**, 757–765 (2020)
8. Jolliffe, I., Cadima, J.: Principal component analysis: a review and recent developments. Phil. Trans. Roy. Soc. A: Math. Phys. Eng. Sci. **374**, 20150202 (2016)
9. Kemeny, J.: Mathematics without numbers. Daedalus **88**(4), 577–591 (1959)
10. Mekala, M.S., Viswanathan, P.: Energy-efficient virtual machine selection based on resource ranking and utilization factor approach in cloud computing for iot. Comput. Electr. Eng. **73**, 227–244 (2019)
11. Seo, J., Shneiderman, B.: A rank-by-feature framework for unsupervised multidimensional data exploration using low dimensional projections. In: IEEE Symposium on Information Visualization, pp. 65–72 (2004)

12. Tharwat, A.: Principal component analysis - a tutorial. Int. J. Appl. Pattern Recogn. **3**, 197 (2016)
13. Wang, H., Lu, H., Sun, J., Safo, S.: Interpretable deep learning methods for multiview learning. BMC Bioinf. **25**, 1–30 (2024)
14. Zhang, Y., Zhang, W., Pei, J., Lin, X., Lin, Q., Li, A.: Consensus-based ranking of multivalued objects: a generalized borda count approach. IEEE Trans. Knowl. Data Eng. **26**, 83–96 (2014)

Secure Applications

Integrating Contextual Integrity in Privacy Requirements Engineering: A Study Case in Personal E-Health Applications

Guntur Budi Herwanto[1,2]($\boxtimes$), Diyah Utami Kusumaning Putri[1,2], Annisa Maulida Ningtyas[1,3], Anis Fuad[1], Gerald Quirchmayr[2], and A Min Tjoa[2,3]

[1] Universitas Gadjah Mada, Yogyakarta, Indonesia
gunturbudi@ugm.ac.id
[2] University of Vienna, Vienna, Austria
[3] Vienna University of Technology, Vienna, Austria

Abstract. The importance of privacy in personal health care has increased due to the widespread use of technology. Therefore, it has become increasingly relevant to incorporate privacy considerations into these socio-technical systems. This has led to the emergence of the use of privacy engineering in the healthcare context, which is based on the principle of privacy by design. The significance of context is emphasized by the diverse norms and principles inherent in each socio-technical system, especially in healthcare information systems. This paper presents a novel approach to privacy engineering by integrating the concept of contextual integrity into a framework for analyzing privacy threats. Contextual integrity, which considers privacy as context-dependent, serves as the theoretical foundation of this approach. The steps of decision heuristics in contextual integrity are aligned with the workflow of privacy threat analysis to increase the tangibility of contextual integrity and incorporate the knowledge of contextual integrity into the privacy threat analysis. A case study in personal e-health application is used to demonstrate the methodology's practical application in the context of privacy protection in healthcare.

Keywords: Privacy engineering · Contextual integrity · Privacy threat analysis · E-health

1 Introduction

In recent years, the importance of protecting privacy in areas where sensitive personal data is processed, such as e-health, has been at the forefront of integrating new technologies with personal health information [24]. The recent COVID-19 pandemic has taught us, that while technology is being used to combat diseases and improve healthcare, it is also crucial to ensure the protection of individuals'

F. Phillipson et al. (Eds.): I4CS 2024, CCIS 2109, pp. 237–256, 2024.
https://doi.org/10.1007/978-3-031-60433-1_14

privacy [1]. This challenge is not only a technological problem but also has political implications, reflecting larger societal concerns about the balance between privacy rights and public health benefits [1]. The rise of technology in healthcare is a double-edged sword. On one hand, it creates new ways to improve health outcomes. On the other hand, it raises serious privacy issues that need to be addressed [24].

To address privacy concerns in building socio-technical systems, researchers have begun to focus on the field of privacy engineering [8]. This emerging field aims to address privacy issues directly during the development of information systems by providing the development team with methods, tools, or frameworks [8]. Privacy engineering is not only about developing technical solutions to privacy problems but also about integrating privacy considerations into the requirements and design of the software development life cycle itself [8]. However, privacy is a concept that often fluctuates between legal, ethical, and political dimensions, making its definition fluid and context-dependent [20]. As a result, developing adaptable and robust methods to deal with these diverse and complex scenarios is a huge challenge.

One of the most important concepts in the privacy discussion is the notion of "contextual integrity". This theoretical framework, developed by Helen Nissenbaum [19], argues that privacy is not a one-dimensional concept but varies depending on the situation. The paper suggests that privacy rules are determined by the types of social situations, activities, and relationships that individuals engage in, which dictate what personal information can be shared and with whom [19]. However, there are insufficient studies that put this theory into practice to be more usable for the development team. Thus, in this research, we aim to answer the following main research question:

> How can we integrate the theoretical concept of contextual integrity into the workflow of privacy requirements engineering?

This study aims to answer the question by incorporating decision heuristics based on contextual integrity [20] into an existing privacy engineering framework, more specifically, a privacy threat analysis framework [5]. Our contribution involves aligning these heuristics to enable their use in a comprehensive process for analyzing privacy threats. This integration aims to enhance the usefulness of decision heuristics and, at the same time, incorporate a contextual understanding of privacy into the privacy threat analysis framework. This approach aims to provide a more sophisticated and practical approach to privacy engineering that caters to the requirements and challenges of different technological environments. A case study on personal health monitoring applications is presented to demonstrate the feasibility of this approach in real-life e-health scenarios.

2   Background and Related Work

This section outlines three key concepts fundamental to our core methodology: (1) the concept of privacy defined as contextual integrity, (2) the framework of nine steps of decision heuristics, and (3) the approach to engineering privacy requirements. Following this, we will briefly review early efforts to apply contextual integrity within the field of privacy engineering, as well as its practical applications in real-world scenarios, which serve as relevant background to this study.

2.1 Privacy as Contextual Integrity

Privacy encompasses more than just an individual's right to solitude and personal space; it also involves a network of laws and regulations. The concept of privacy is also dynamic, changing based on the situation. What might be deemed private in one context may not be regarded as such in another [19]. In computer science, particularly in creating socio-technical systems that manage personal data, this contemporary, context-sensitive perspective is crucial. This idea is exemplified in the theory of Contextual Integrity (CI) [19].

Contextual Integrity emphasizes that various social domains, including healthcare, education, and finance, have their own unique, context-specific norms (often referred to as information norms) that dictate how information should be handled. The transmission of information is influenced not only by the nature of the information itself but also by the roles and expectations of those involved, including senders, receivers, and subjects. Each role has specific expectations for managing and sharing information, and it is important to align information flows with these expectations to maintain privacy. Violations happen when established norms and expectations are ignored, resulting in unexpected or inappropriate information flows that challenge the conventional boundaries of privacy protection [20].

2.2 Decision Heuristics

An essential approach for applying the concept of Contextual Integrity (CI) in evaluating current systems, or as a factor to consider, involves using The "Augmented Contextual Integrity Decision Heuristic" [20]. This method, derived from the concept of contextual integrity, provides a structured way to identify the roots of disputes and to assess the systems or practices being examined. This framework is composed of nine steps:

1. *Describe the New Practice in Terms of Information Flows.* This involves understanding how information is collected, shared, and used in the new system or practice.
2. *Identify the Prevailing Context.* Determine the general context (like healthcare or education) and consider potential impacts from sub-contexts (like personal health monitoring).
3. *Identify Information Subjects, Senders, and Recipients.* Determine who is involved in the information flow, including who the information is about, who is sending it, and who is receiving it.

4. *Identify Transmission Principles.* Understand the principles or rules governing how information is transmitted in the context.
5. *Locate Applicable Entrenched Informational Norms and Identify Significant Points of Departure.* Compare the new practice with existing norms and identify any major differences.
6. *Prima Facie Assessment.* Assess whether the system or practice deviates from entrenched norms, which could indicate a violation of contextual integrity.
7. *Evaluation I - Moral and Political Factors.* Consider the broader moral and political implications of the practice, including potential harms, threats to autonomy and freedom, effects on power structures, justice, fairness, equality, social hierarchy, democracy, etc.
8. *Evaluation II - Contextual Values, Goals, and Ends.* Examine how the system or practice affects the values, goals, and purposes of the context. Consider the significance of moral and political factors in light of these contextual elements.
9. *Final Recommendation.* Based on the above analyses, make a recommendation for or against the system or practice. In rare cases, a practice may be maintained despite negative findings if the practice is deemed essential to the continuation of the context as a viable social unit.

This nine-step heuristic emphasizes that the evaluation of technology is not just about technical specifications but about how it functions in social contexts.

2.3   Privacy Requirements Engineering

Privacy-by-design (PbD) is a crucial concept in developing systems and applications, emphasizing incorporating privacy considerations from the beginning of the design process. This is embodied in two of the seven principles of PbD, which are based on "proactive, not reactive, preventive, not reactive" and "privacy by default" [3]. This means that privacy should be taken into account from the start of development and should be one of the core requirements. The development of privacy requirements aims to achieve this. There are several methods proposed by researchers to identify privacy requirements. Different strategies, such as goal-based, risk-based, or hybrid approaches, are used to elicit privacy requirements [21]. A prominent and mature method in this area is a privacy threat modeling process known as LINDDUN [5], which is primarily risk-based and focuses on identifying privacy threats in data streams across seven categories. LINDDUN is an acronym for its threat categories, which are Linkability, Identifiability, Non-repudiation, Detectability, Disclosure of information, Unawareness, and Non-compliance [5].

The LINDDUN framework for analyzing privacy threats comprises six stages. It starts with defining the data flow diagram (DFD) and mapping threats to data flow elements. The process continues with identifying misuse scenarios, prioritization based on risk, elicitation of data protection requirements, and finally, selecting solutions to fulfill the privacy requirements [5]. This research uses LINDDUN as the reference for the privacy requirements engineering technique.

2.4   Contextual Integrity in Practice

Putting context into the heart of privacy engineering has been presented by Hoel et al. [13]. They propose the concepts of contextual triggers and contextual graphs in privacy engineering, which means creating systems that can automatically adjust their privacy protections in response to changing circumstances. When a context trigger is detected (such as a change in user behavior or environment), the system consults the context graph to decide how best to handle personal data under the new conditions. This approach ensures that privacy management is adaptive, responsive, and always in context.

This concept of contextual integrity finds practical application in several domains, particularly in electronic medical records (EMR) [2]. The research surveys healthcare workers and analyses their responses to hypothetical EMR workaround scenarios, finding that contextual integrity helps explain decisions about information sharing and workarounds. Outside of healthcare, the concepts of CI have also been applied to social networks [23] and Software as a Service (SaaS) [7]. By methodically following the steps outlined in the decision heuristics, one can systematically assess and ultimately determine whether using these systems constitutes an invasion of privacy.

Integrating contextual integrity as the privacy risk analytics framework has been done in previous research, specifically as the foundation to develop a model for open data publishing [9]. It consists of three steps: Explanation, Risk Assessment, and Decision. The Explanation steps involve analyzing datasets, identifying actors, roles, context, and transmission principles, and integrating the first four DHs. Risk Assessment evaluates privacy risks considering norms, values, regulations, disclosure risks, and potential positive impacts, incorporating DHs 5 to 8. The final Decision phase, using the DH 9, involves making informed decisions based on the risk assessment findings.

These current approaches have limitations as many focus on specific domains [2,7,9,23] without providing a general-purpose methodology that could be useful for eliciting privacy requirements. Our work aims not just to stop at the decision but to extend to a full process of eliciting privacy requirements and selecting the technical measure based on the context. We also aim for a general-purpose system, not just a privacy threat analysis framework practice, including a threat analysis framework and data flow diagrams.

3   Application Example: Tuberculosis Patient Monitoring

The example we use for this paper is in a healthcare setting, specifically in the personal monitoring mobile application of multidrug-resistant tuberculosis (MDR-TB) patients in Indonesia. In the usual treatment process, MDR-TB patients visit primary healthcare centers daily for monitored medication intake over 6–24 months. However, this system has limitations, including reliance on manual record-keeping by healthcare staff, which is not accessible to patients, doctors, or case managers [22]. This lack of data accessibility hinders tracking patient compliance. Noncompliance risks reduced treatment effectiveness

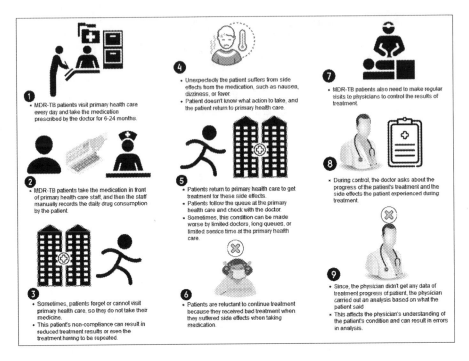

Fig. 1. The scenario of multidrug-resistant tuberculosis treatment in Indonesia

or necessitate treatment repetition. Moreover, handling medication side effects, such as nausea or dizziness, can be inefficient due to limited healthcare resources and long queues, leading to patient reluctance in continuing treatment [22]. Patients with MDR-TB must adhere to long-term daily treatments at health facilities, which often leads to treatment failure due to factors like prolonged therapy duration, patient noncompliance, financial burdens, and adverse drug reactions. Additionally, stigma and boredom pose significant challenges to patient adherence [18,22]. Figure 1 shows the overall scenario of the MDR-TB treatment.

To address these issues, the "TOMO" application was developed in Indonesia [6]. It facilitates communication and coordination among patients, healthcare staff, case managers, and physicians, enhancing patient adherence and side effect management monitoring. The app allows patients to report medication intake and adverse effects, enabling healthcare professionals to respond and adjust treatment as necessary promptly. Furthermore, TOMO aids in tracking patient progress and helps government authorities evaluate healthcare performance and patient adherence rates in specific areas. TOMO offers various features for both patients and healthcare professionals. Patients can log medication intake, report adverse effects, access educational materials, receive appointment reminders, and find healthcare facilities. For healthcare providers, the app supports patient data management, medication assignments, consumption validation, health complaint handling, and event scheduling.

In the following section, we continue with our proposed method of combining contextual integrity with privacy threat analysis and show its application to TOMO.

4 Integrating Contextual Integrity with Privacy Requirements Engineering

We argued that the risk-based approach in privacy requirements engineering, as explained in Subsect. 2.3, aligns well with the nine-step decision heuristics outlined in Subsect. 2.2. This integration transforms contextual integrity into a more tangible and applicable methodology, enhancing its incorporation into privacy by design and privacy engineering frameworks. The integration is depicted in Fig. 2. The knowledge acquired from the decision heuristics can be integrated into the first four steps of the privacy threat analysis framework. This will ultimately aid in the fifth step of the process, which involves extracting privacy requirements and obtaining privacy-enhancing solutions. The resulting privacy requirements can be more contextual, depending on the privacy threats, while also balancing with contextual integrity.

To further elaborate on this integration, we will demonstrate its application within a healthcare setting. This will involve presenting a scenario in Sect. 3, followed by detailed discussions in subsequent sections on how the alignment of decision-heuristics insights with the LINDDUN privacy threat analysis framework enriches the final privacy requirements.

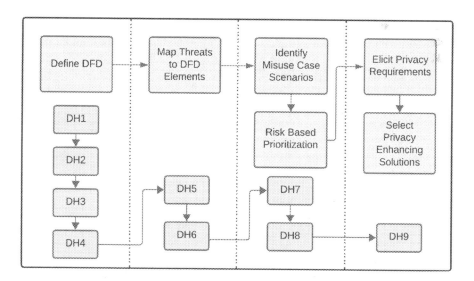

Fig. 2. The integration of the decision heuristics with the LINDDUN privacy threat analysis framework [5]. The LINDDUN process is shown in pink, while the decision heuristics (DH) are shown in yellow. (Color figure online)

4.1   Defining Data Flow Diagram with Contextual Integrity

The first step of LINDDUN is to define a data flow diagram, which essentially characterizes the system to be built regarding how data flows between stakeholders or even third parties. These principles are intuitively consistent with steps 3 and 4 of the CI decision heuristics (DH3, DH4). However, DH1 and DH2 are also important for establishing the context for the elements in the DFD. We will explain this further in this section.

DH1: Describe the New Practice in Terms of Information Flows. The first step of the DH is a detailed examination of how a recent technology, system, or practice will affect the flow of personal information. Identifying the potential personal information from the early stage can make clear whether this subjects to further investigation. From a software development perspective, this may involve a clear system characterization. This phase must be done clearly from a requirement engineering perspective to establish a clear understanding between developers and users. We recommend a user-centric approach to requirements elicitation, such as using user stories.

User stories, often found in the Scrum framework, are a way to express user requirements [4]. Structured in the format "As [role], I want [feature], so that [benefit]," these stories not only outline the need for a feature but also provide a rationale for its inclusion, as indicated by the "so that" segment. This approach not only enriches the subsequent stages of the contextual integrity (CI) process but also facilitates the expression of human values [14], thereby enhancing the understanding of the context, which can be further elaborated in the next step.

DH2: Identify the Prevailing Context. Understanding the role of specific technologies or practices within the broader social and cultural context is critical. This includes understanding the common practices in a given domain, as well as the processes for gathering, sharing, and using information. The goal is to understand the particular environment or situation in which personal information is used and shared. These contexts vary across different domains, such as healthcare, education, or social networking. There may also be subdomains of contextual understanding. For example, within the health domain, the use of personal health monitoring tools to improve medication adherence differs from the use of similar tools for activity tracking or wellness applications.

DH3: Identify Information Subjects, Senders, and Recipients. DH1 identifies the potential personal information circulating in the new system. For a better understanding of the context, it is essential to distinguish three key actors involved in the information exchange: the sender, the recipient, and the subject. The analysis of the user stories suggests the possibility of automatically identifying these privacy-centric entities [10]. These agents, along with the information exchanged between them, form the basis for representation in the DFD.

DH4: Identify Transmission Principles. Visualizing the flow of information helps understand how data moves between different actors. By using DFD, the principles required for each data flow can be more easily identified, allowing application developers to implement clear and effective strategies for handling data. We propose that the data flow between actors in DFD can be enriched [11] with the transmission principles defined in DH4.

Transmission principles are guidelines that dictate how information is exchanged and distributed among various parties within a specific context. Take several examples [20] of these principles: (1) Confidentiality: This principle restricts the sharing of received information with others. (2) Compulsion: It requires certain individuals, usually the subjects of the information, to disclose specific details to others. (3) Notice and Consent: This mandates informing the subject of the information and obtaining their permission. These principles are part of a broader concept of CI.

CI can be formalized further using tuples that contain five key parameters [13]: the actors involved (e.g. data subjects, senders, and recipients), the type of information (attributes), and the conditions under which the information is exchanged (transmission principles). The result of this method is the CI-tuple and the CI-enhanced DFD, which can be seen in Fig. 3.

Application to TOMO. The low adherence and frequent treatment failure of TB in Indonesia led to the idea of providing a digital mobile personal health monitoring application. The decision was made to provide a mobile phone with TOMO installed that enables drug monitoring and provides patient support. This introduces a new context by offering real-time updates on the medication adherence of patients, scheduled reminders, and the ability to report and monitor side effects and health complaints. The initial identification of user stories are the following:

- As an MDR TB patient, I want to track my medication intake, so that I can maintain adherence to my treatment plan.
- As an MDR TB patient, I want to report side effects and health complaints, so that my healthcare team can address any concerns promptly.
- As a primary health care staff member, I want to validate medications, so that patients maintain adherence to their treatment plans.
- As a physician, I want to review health complaints, so that I can address patient concerns promptly and adjust treatment plans as necessary.
- As a government agent, I want to determine the adherence rate of tuberculosis patients in a specific area, so that I can make better decisions about interventions.

The personal health monitoring system TOMO has been deployed in Indonesia as part of the national Zero TB initiative, aimed at eradicating tuberculosis. This involves collecting and potentially sharing personal health data with government agencies engaged in the Zero TB program. In Indonesia, compliance with personal data regulations is mandatory.

Understanding cultural perceptions in Indonesia regarding health data privacy, tuberculosis, and government-led health programs is crucial. The main beneficiaries of this program are low and middle-income patients. The main goal is to increase treatment adherence of TB-MDR patients, which will ultimately lead to the eradication of TB-MDR. However, there might be varying levels of awareness or concern about privacy among these patients, which mostly low and middle-income patients. Consequently, it's essential to safeguard their privacy through ethical frameworks and adherence to data regulations.

Based on the user story of TOMO, we can identify three main actors in the daily information flow: the patient, the primary care staff, and the physician. A fourth actor, government agencies, might receive aggregated adherence report data. We then further divide these actors into three types of subjects, senders and receivers, as recommended by DH3. The details are in Table 1.

Table 1. The result of the identification of information subjects, senders, and recipients in TOMO

Type	Name	Description
Subjects	MDR TB Patients	The primary subjects of the information. Data on their health, treatment adherence, side effects, and personal identifiers are collected and processed
Senders	Patients	They send their health data, treatment adherence information, and side effect reports through the app
	Case Managers and Primary Health Care Staff	They enter patient data, update treatment plans, and communicate with patients through the app
	Physicians	They review patient data, respond to health complaints, and send medical advice or feedback, including feedback on reported side effects
Recipients	Primary Health Care Staff and Physicians	They receive patient health data, adherence information, and reports of side effects for monitoring and decision-making purposes
	Patients	They receive feedback on reported side effects and health complaints, which helps manage their treatment and ensure their concerns are addressed

The data flow diagram in Fig. 3 shows a complete representation of the data flows between the actors, the process, and the data store. Each information flow is subject to strict confidentiality. Each transmission must also be consented to, as shown in the DFD, which guarantees that the use of the data is strictly limited to health-related purposes associated with TB eradication efforts.

The important highlight is that TB-MDR patients are obliged to provide information necessary for the diagnosis and treatment of the disease. This indicates that reporting is compulsory, as indicated by the red color in the data flow between the patient and medication tracking. The patient also voluntarily reports additional side effects through the app, which are not mandatory but may help in her treatment. The voluntary data flow is shown in green (Table 2).

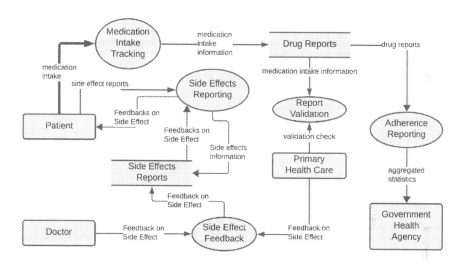

Fig. 3. Data flow diagram of tuberculosis monitoring that focuses only on (1) medication intake tracking, side effect reporting, and adherence reporting. The color in the data flow shows the integration of transmission principles. (Color figure online)

4.2 Mapping Threats Based on Informational Norms

The privacy threat analysis framework uses DFD (Data Flow Diagram) as the basis for analyzing potential privacy threats [5,12]. This aligns with **DH5: Locate Applicable Entrenched Informational Norms and Identify Significant Points of Departure**. Entrenched norms include established practices, widely accepted principles regarding data collection, storage, access, and sharing, as well as local laws and regulations that govern these activities. They serve as a baseline for how information systems have traditionally operated and how stakeholders expect them to function. In addition to understanding these entrenched norms, it is crucial to consider the specific local regulations that apply

Table 2. Transmission principles based on data flow diagrams

No	Subject	Sender	Data Flow Process	Recipient	Transmission Principles
1	Patient	Patient	Drug Reporting, Report Validation	Primary Health Care	Consented, Compulsory
2	Patient	Patient	Side Effect Reporting	Primary Health Care, Doctor	Consented, Voluntary
3	Patient	MDR TB Patient	Medication Intake Tracking	Primary Health Care, Physician	Consented, Voluntary
4	Health Care Staff	Primary Health Care Staff	Medication Validation	MDR TB Patient	Compulsory, Consented
5	Patient	MDR TB Patient	Health Complaint Reporting	Physician	Consented, Voluntary
6	Government	Primary Health Care, Physician	Adherence Rate Reporting	Government Health Agency	Compulsary, Consented

to data handling practices. Local regulations can significantly influence what is considered acceptable or standard practice in a given region or jurisdiction.

This comparison is pivotal because it allows for the identification of "significant points of departure" instances where current practices diverge from what is traditionally expected, accepted, or legally required. These points can be highlighted in the DFD, usually referred to as hotspots [5] or red flags [2].

Following the identification of significant departures from entrenched norms, including local regulations, the next step is **DH6: Prima Facie Assessment**. This initial assessment is aimed at evaluating these departures to determine their potential impact on privacy. It involves a preliminary analysis to assess whether the identified deviations indeed pose a threat to privacy and, if so, the extent of that threat [20].

Application to TOMO. In the Indonesian healthcare context, patient data is typically collected and handled within the confines of healthcare facilities. Traditional norms include confidentiality, direct patient-provider interactions, and manual tracking of treatment adherence. Government involvement in personal health data has generally been limited to aggregated data for public health purposes.

In order to protect patient privacy, Indonesia has implemented several regulations, particularly regarding the handling of personal health information. The primary regulation is Law of the Republic of Indonesia No. 17 of 2023 Concerning Health [17], which contains 458 articles divided into 20 chapters. This law establishes requirements for the development of health, which should be carried out according to the basic principles of humanity: balance, utility, protection, respect for rights and responsibilities, justice, gender, non-discrimination, and religious norms. Chapter Two deals specifically with rights and obligations. Article 4(1)(i) affirms that every individual has the right to confidentiality of his or her private health information. Article 4(4) outlines exceptions to this confidentiality rule. These exceptions include situations involving legal requirements, court orders, consent of the individual concerned, public interest, or the interest of the individual concerned.

The second law is the Law of the Republic of Indonesia No. 11 of 2008 on Electronic Information and Transactions [15]. This law, which contains 54 articles in 13 chapters, aims to protect the rights of individuals in various areas, including the digital domain, electronic transactions, consumer protection, intellectual property rights, and unfair business practices. Chapter Two, Article 4(d) supports the Digital Health Initiative '*Satu Sehat*', which advocates using information technology and electronic transactions to improve the effectiveness and efficiency of public services. In addition, Chapter Seven, Article 27(1) outlines that anyone who knowingly and without authority distributes and/or transmits and/or causes to be accessible electronic information and/or electronic records with contents against propriety is prohibited and may face legal consequences.

The third law, Law of the Republic of Indonesia No. 27 of 2022, concerning to Personal Data Protection [16]. This law, which consists of 76 articles in 16 chapters, aims to protect personal data in the course of processing personal data to guarantee the constitutional rights of personal data subjects. Chapter 1, Article 1 defines personal data as any data that can identify an individual, either directly or indirectly, by electronic or non-electronic means. Chapter Three, in particular Article 4(1), divides personal data into two types: Specific and General. Paragraph 2 elaborates on specific personal data, listing categories such as health data, biometric data, genetic data, criminal records, children's data, personal identity data, and others as provided for by law.

The deployment of TOMO in Indonesia represents a significant shift towards digitization in patient data management, diverging from traditional practices of maintaining data within healthcare facilities. By enabling patients to input their health information into a mobile app for real-time monitoring, TOMO extends data access to healthcare professionals and government entities, aiming to improve healthcare efficiency. However, this innovation also introduces privacy challenges and necessitates stringent data protection measures to align with Indonesia's health, electronic information, and personal data protection laws, ensuring patient privacy is safeguarded.

4.3   Identify Misuse Case Scenarios Based on Contextual Integrity

Having identified the hotspots and red flags in the previous steps, we can further explore the likely threats that may target individual data flow elements. In the LINDDUN framework, these are the leaf nodes of a threat tree within a specific threat category [5]. Our proposed analysis takes an integrated approach, considering both **DH7: Evaluation I - Moral and Political Factors** and **DH8: Evaluation II - Contextual Values, Goals, and Ends**.

In the initial evaluation, we assess the potential impact of each misuse case scenario on personal freedom, autonomy, power structures within society or organizations, and concerns regarding fairness, justice, and democratic principles. This evaluation goes beyond privacy and security considerations and aims to understand the broader societal and ethical landscape of data misuse.

In the second evaluation, we analyze how each misuse case scenario aligns or conflicts with the specific values, goals, and ends relevant to the data flow context. This involves considering the intended purpose of data collection and processing and evaluating how the misuse scenarios deviate from these goals. Secondly, it is necessary to evaluate whether the threats to freedom, autonomy, fairness, justice, or democracy identified in Evaluation I are particularly significant within the context of the specific data flows and the system's overall objectives.

Application to TOMO. Let's consider the workflow of medication intake tracking (MDR TB patient to primary health care physician). We can consider three misuse case scenarios:

- *Linkability in Long-term Monitoring*: In the case of TB-MDR, which requires extended monitoring, there's an increased chance that patient data will be compiled over time to observe treatment adherence and progress. This continuous collection and analysis of medication intake data could be integrated with other health information, resulting in a detailed and comprehensive health profile for each patient.
- *Non-Disclosure in the Treatment*: The use of personal devices in TB treatment introduces risks associated with data security. These devices, which patients use to report medication intake or monitor health parameters, could potentially be accessed by unauthorized individuals or entities. The risk lies in the possibility of exposing or misusing sensitive health information if these devices fall into the wrong hands or are compromised. This scenario underscores the need for robust security measures to protect patient data from unauthorized access and ensure confidentiality.
- *Non-repudiation and Public Health Monitoring*: Non-repudiation is crucial in a public health setting to ensure precise tracking of medication intake. However, this can become problematic if patients perceive that their data is being misused. The system's design, which likely includes strong mechanisms for accurate tracking, means that patients are not able to dispute their recorded medication intake patterns.

Integrating DH7: Moral and Political Factors: In managing multi-drug resistant tuberculosis, patients are required to adhere to specific protocols, such as regularly reporting their medication usage to ensure effective treatment. If primary health care staff do not receive reports, they may contact the patient to investigate the issue. However, this approach could potentially violate patient privacy and autonomy in the effort to eliminate MDR-TB. There is also a concern that the data gathered could be misused to exert inappropriate control or influence over patients.

The design of such monitoring systems, which focuses on accurate and indisputable tracking, might leave little room for patients to contest their recorded medication patterns. Non-repudiation can be perceived as a breach of autonomy and may raise ethical concerns, especially if patients believe their privacy is being compromised or their data is not being handled appropriately. In addition, the inability of patients to challenge their medication intake records could have significant legal repercussions.

Integrating DH8: Contextual Values, Goals, and Ends: The primary objective in treating MDR-TB is to ensure patient health and prevent the disease's spread. Tracking medication usage is key to this objective, as it helps guarantee adherence to the treatment. In the context of public health, especially when managing communicable diseases like MDR-TB, there's a need to consider the broader benefits to society. This involves balancing the importance of personal health against public health needs. Additionally, it's crucial to maintain a balance between individual privacy rights and the prevention of stigmatization.

4.4 Eliciting Privacy Requirements and Selecting Privacy Enhancing Solutions

The **DH9: Final Recommendation** serves as a final evaluation point, determining whether a system under consideration respects privacy within its given context. We argue that this recommendation should extend beyond a mere yes-or-no decision about the system's viability. It acts as a pivotal step in the broader process of identifying specific privacy requirements that the system must meet. These requirements are derived from a thorough understanding of potential privacy threats identified earlier in the development process, as well as from a detailed evaluation of the decision heuristic evaluations.

To ensure that privacy requirements are both comprehensive and understandable, we advocate for the utilization of user stories supplemented by acceptance criteria. User stories offer a narrative-based approach to requirement specification, making it easier to capture the diverse privacy expectations and needs of users in various scenarios. By incorporating acceptance criteria into these stories, developers can set clear, measurable goals for privacy protection, facilitating the transition from abstract requirements to practical solutions.

These requirements, in turn, should guide the selection of appropriate countermeasures, which are privacy-enhancing solutions. These solutions should encompass both technical and organizational measures to ensure a comprehensive approach to privacy.

Given the evolving nature of social norms and technological capabilities, it's vital to continuously monitor and reassess the system's alignment with the principles of contextual integrity. This ongoing evaluation process ensures that the system remains responsive to changes in societal expectations, regulatory landscapes, and technological advancements, thereby maintaining the trust and confidence of users and stakeholders.

Application to TOMO. We have identified Linkability, Non-Disclosure, and Non-Repudiation as potential threats to the user story:

> "As an MDR TB patient, I wish to track my medication intake to adhere to my treatment plan."

After assessing the system using the moral and political factors (DH7) and contextual values, goals, and ends (DH8), we conclude that while addressing Linkability and Non-Disclosure threats aligns with our objectives, the Non-Repudiation requirement might raise privacy concerns, despite its practical benefits. Our primary focus is on mitigating Linkability threats by implementing an Unlinkability requirement [5]. Unlinkability guarantees that individual medication intake records cannot be linked together to form a comprehensive patient health profile. Considering the sensitive nature of tuberculosis and the associated stigma, maintaining the confidentiality of patient profiles is crucial.

Monitoring medication adherence in real-time is crucial for the effective treatment of MDR TB. However, this tracking process must prioritize the security of patient data, safeguarding it from unauthorized access and potential breaches. To ensure the integrity and confidentiality of patient information, it is essential to implement strong encryption techniques and secure communication protocols during data transmission.

Thus, we formulate the user story as the following:

> "As an MDR TB patient, I want to track my medication intake in a way that safeguards my privacy and minimizes the risk of stigmatization, ensuring I can adhere to my treatment plan confidently and without fear of social prejudice."

Given our threat analysis and decision-heuristics process, we establish the following **Acceptance Criteria**:

– **Selective Information Sharing:** Implement a system that allows selective sharing of patient information with authorized healthcare providers. This system should enable healthcare staff to identify and follow up with patients as necessary while limiting access to sensitive information to those directly involved in the patient's care.

- **Encrypted Communication Channels:** Ensure all communications between patients and healthcare providers regarding medication intake and treatment adherence occur over encrypted channels, protecting the confidentiality of the exchange.
- **Audit Trails for Accountability:** Maintain detailed audit trails of who accesses patient information and for what purpose, ensuring accountability and the ability to review access patterns for any potential misuse or overreach.

Obtaining explicit patient consent for sharing aggregated data with government health agencies is mandatory. As an **organizational measure**, conducting regular training for healthcare providers on privacy importance, ethical patient information handling, and stigma-minimizing engagement techniques is crucial.

It is important to note that pseudonymization or anonymization is not performed due to the need to balance healthcare providers' need to monitor patient adherence with the implementation of stringent privacy protections and stigma reduction. This balance ultimately aims to create a supportive, confidential, and respectful atmosphere. This environment promotes patient compliance with their treatment plans, with the assurance that their privacy and dignity are prioritized.

This comprehensive approach not only focuses on assessing the system's compliance with privacy requirements but also emphasizes eliciting specific privacy needs and implementing technical and organizational measures to address them.

5 Discussion

This exploration examines the alignment between contextual integrity and privacy requirements engineering, providing new perspectives for both the practical application of CI and the theoretical framework of privacy requirements engineering. The description of systems in privacy requirements engineering frameworks shares similarities with how contextual integrity identifies contexts by understanding the roles of participants and transmission principles. Applying contextual integrity principles provides a detailed comprehension of privacy that surpasses traditional binary recommendations. It also elicits privacy requirements contextualized by values, morals, and political factors. This enables the elicitation of privacy requirements that are not only technically sound but also socially and ethically informed.

This alignment primarily utilizes the LINDDUN framework. However, the alignment might differ when considering other perspectives. Goal-based frameworks, for example, could provide insights into how privacy objectives align with broader organizational or societal goals. Its effectiveness relies heavily on a thorough understanding of the social context and norms surrounding the system, which may require extensive stakeholder engagement and domain expertise. Additionally, balancing the sometimes-competing demands of contextual integrity and practical system design can be challenging, requiring careful trade-offs and prioritization. The actual usefulness of contextual integrity in eliciting requirements warrants further empirical investigation.

This study focuses on a mobile health application to support adherence among low-income patients with communicable diseases. With its extensive connectivity and wealth of information, the healthcare environment poses unique challenges for managing privacy [2]. Situated within a legal context, public health concerns exemplify the intricate balance between legal requirements and ethical obligations toward patient care. The initial version of the TOMO system was deployed in Indonesia. Our study will inform future versions of this system, particularly regarding integrating privacy requirements.

6   Conclusion and Future Work

This paper presents a novel approach to privacy engineering by embedding the concept of contextual integrity within the established LINDDUN privacy threat analysis framework [5]. The essence of this integration lies in addressing the nuanced and context-dependent nature of privacy, which is especially crucial in e-health applications where sensitive personal data and technology intersect.

Central to this approach is the integration of decision heuristics [20], based on the theory of contextual integrity, with the stages of the LINDDUN framework. This alignment enriches the traditional risk-based model of LINDDUN, enabling a more context-aware analysis and handling of privacy issues. By adopting this integrated approach, the paper demonstrates how privacy engineering can be transformed from a largely technical exercise into a more holistic, socio-technical practice that recognizes privacy's ethical, legal, and societal dimensions.

The practicality and effectiveness of this integrated approach are illustrated through a case study on TOMO, a personal health monitoring system in Indonesia. This application validates the approach in a real-world setting and underscores the need for contextually informed privacy practices in e-health technologies. The paper shows that privacy concerns in such technologies are not merely technical challenges but are deeply embedded in the broader social, cultural, and regulatory fabrics. The alignment proposed in this study also suggests its potential applicability across various domains where privacy is a concern.

Future work in this area can extend in several directions. It is worth investigating the empirical testing of this approach in real-world situations, such as obtaining the development team's perceptions about integrating contextual integrity into the development lifecycle. Additionally, looking at the integration from different perspectives, such as privacy impact assessment, is an open problem. Testing the adaptability and effectiveness of this integrated approach in various domains beyond e-health will broaden its scope. Developing accessible tools and frameworks to facilitate the implementation of this approach can make it more practical for privacy engineering practitioners.

Acknowledgment. The authors acknowledge the scholarship granted by the Indonesia Endowment Fund for Education (IEFE/LPDP), Ministry of Finance, Republic of Indonesia, and the support received from the University of Vienna, Faculty of Computer Science and Universitas Gadjah Mada.

References

1. Al-Anezi, F.M.: Factors influencing decision making for implementing e-health in light of the covid-19 outbreak in gulf cooperation council countries. Int. Health **14**(1), 53–63 (2022)
2. Burns, A., Young, J., Roberts, T.L., Courtney, J.F., Ellis, T.S.: Exploring the role of contextual integrity in electronic medical record (EMR) system workaround decisions: an information security and privacy perspective. AIS Trans. Hum.-Comput. Interact. **7**(3), 142–165 (2015)
3. Cavoukian, A.: Privacy by design (2009)
4. Cohn, M.: User Stories Applied: For Agile Software Development. Addison-Wesley Professional, Boston (2004)
5. Deng, M., Wuyts, K., Scandariato, R., Preneel, B., Joosen, W.: A privacy threat analysis framework: supporting the elicitation and fulfillment of privacy requirements. Requir. Eng. **16**(1), 3–32 (2011)
6. Fuad, A., et al.: Design and prototype of tomo: an app for improving drug resistant tb treatment adherence. F1000Research **10**, 983 (2021)
7. Grodzinsky, F.S., Tavani, H.T.: Privacy in "the cloud" applying nissenbaum's theory of contextual integrity. Acm Sigcas Comput. Soc. **41**(1), 38–47 (2011)
8. Gürses, S., Del Alamo, J.M.: Privacy engineering: shaping an emerging field of research and practice. IEEE Secur. Priv. **14**(2), 40–46 (2016)
9. Henriksen-Bulmer, J., Faily, S., Jeary, S.: Privacy risk assessment in context: a meta-model based on contextual integrity. Comput. Secur. **82**, 270–283 (2019)
10. Herwanto, G.B., Quirchmayr, G., Tjoa, A.M.: A named entity recognition based approach for privacy requirements engineering. In: 2021 IEEE 29th International Requirements Engineering Conference Workshops (REW), pp. 406–411. IEEE (2021)
11. Herwanto, G.B., Quirchmayr, G., Tjoa, A.M.: From user stories to data flow diagrams for privacy awareness: a research preview. In: Gervasi, V., Vogelsang, A. (eds.) REFSQ 2022. LNCS, vol. 13216, pp. 148–155. Springer, Heidelberg (2022). https://doi.org/10.1007/978-3-030-98464-9_12
12. Herwanto, G.B., Quirchmayr, G., Tjoa, A.M.: Leveraging NLP techniques for privacy requirements engineering in user stories. IEEE Access **12**, 22167–22189 (2024). https://doi.org/10.1109/ACCESS.2024.3364533
13. Hoel, T., Chen, W., Pawlowski, J.M.: Making context the central concept in privacy engineering. Res. Pract. Technol. Enhanc. Learn. **15**(1), 1–26 (2020)
14. Hussain, W., et al.: How can human values be addressed in agile methods? a case study on safe. IEEE Trans. Softw. Eng. **48**(12), 5158–5175 (2022)
15. Indonesia, D.P.R.R.: Law of the republic of Indonesia no. 11 of 2008 on electronic information and transactions (2008). https://peraturan.bpk.go.id/Details/37589/uu-no-11-tahun-2008. Accessed 26 Jan 2024
16. Indonesia, D.P.R.R.: Law of the republic of indonesia no. 27 of 2022, concerning to personal data protection (2022). https://peraturan.bpk.go.id/Details/229798/uu-no-27-tahun-2022. Accessed 26 Jan 2024
17. Indonesia, D.P.R.R.: Law of the republic of indonesia no. 17 of 2023 concerning health (2023). https://p2p.kemkes.go.id/undang-undang-republik-indonesia-nomor-17-tahun-2023-tentang-kesehatan/. Accessed 26 Jan 2024
18. Liefooghe, R., Michiels, N., Habib, S., Moran, M., De Muynck, A.: Perception and social consequences of tuberculosis: a focus group study of tuberculosis patients in Sialkot, Pakistan. Social Sci. Med. **41**(12), 1685–1692 (1995)

19. Nissenbaum, H.: Privacy as contextual integrity. Wash. L. Rev. **79**, 119 (2004)
20. Nissenbaum, H.: Privacy in Context: Technology, Policy, and the Integrity of Social Life. Stanford University Press, Stanford (2020)
21. Notario, N., et al.: Pripare: integrating privacy best practices into a privacy engineering methodology. In: 2015 IEEE Security and Privacy Workshops, pp. 151–158. IEEE (2015)
22. Probandari, A., Sanjoto, H., Mahanani, M.R., Azizatunnisa, L., Widayati, S.: Being safe, feeling safe, and stigmatizing attitude among primary health care staff in providing multidrug-resistant tuberculosis care in Bantul district, Yogyakarta province, Indonesia. Hum. Resour. Health **17**(1), 1–10 (2019)
23. Sar, R.K., Al-Saggaf, Y.: Contextual integrity's decision heuristic and the tracking by social network sites. Ethics Inf. Technol. **16**, 15–26 (2014)
24. Tewari, A.: mhealth systems need a privacy-by-design approach: commentary on "federated machine learning, privacy-enhancing technologies, and data protection laws in medical research: scoping review". J. Med. Internet Res. **25**, e46700 (2023)

The System Architecture of a Reliable Telesurgery Service and its Performance Analysis

Manuel Gerwien, Marcel Großmann, and Udo R. Krieger[✉]

Fakultät WIAI, Otto-Friedrich-Universität, An der Weberei 5, 96047 Bamberg,
Germany
udo.krieger@ieee.org

Abstract. Today, new smart e-health applications are enabled by the
very rapid evolution of high-speed networking and cloud computing technologies. This development of new communication and computing techniques as well as the incorporation of machine learning for intelligent
image analysis offer new opportunities for classical medical services like
telesurgery. In our paper we consider the design of a classical telesurgery
system and analyze its architecture. Then we discuss the extension of
its functional modules to support remote surgery based on a reliable
multi-path communication among its components. We provide an investigation of important key performance indices of such a remote-controlled
telesurgery service. To achieve deeper technical insights on the system's
performance of such a distributed architecture and its communication
flows, a telesurgery prototype is studied by GNS3-emulations within a
virtualized test bed. In this way we investigate the fundamental computing and network performance indices of our prototype.

Keywords: e-Health · Telepresence · Telesurgery · Performance
analysis

1 Introduction

Today, new advanced Internet-of-Things services like smart e-health applications
are enabled by the very rapid evolution of high-speed networking technologies
which incorporate 5G and 6G wireless networks, software-defined networking
and network function virtualization as building blocks, cf. [8,9,16]. The latter
communication infrastructure constitutes the basis for cloud computing, fog computing, and multi-access edge computing and offers the opportunity to integrate
blockchain technology for medical applications, cf. [1,3,14]. The fast development of these advanced communication and cloud computing techniques and
the incorporation of new machine learning methodologies for intelligent image
analysis also offer new opportunities to improve classical medical services such
as telesurgery and neurosurgery, cf. [12,15,16].

In our paper we consider first the technical architecture of a classical
telesurgery system. Then we discuss the extension of its components to support

F. Phillipson et al. (Eds.): I4CS 2024, CCIS 2109, pp. 257–274, 2024.
https://doi.org/10.1007/978-3-031-60433-1_15

remote-controlled surgery based on advanced communication networks. We are interested in investigating the impact of distortions within such a network onto the system performance and study important key performance indices (KPIs) of the telesurgery system. To achieve such deep technical insights, the architecture and communication infrastructure of a prototypical telesurgery system is emulated by a virtualized test bed using a GNS3 network simulator. By these means we investigate the computing and network performance indices of our prototypical telesurgery architecture and identify its weaknesses.

The paper is organized as follows. In Sect. 2 we discuss the system architecture and networking functionality of a distributed, remote-controlled telesurgery infrastructure. Then we describe the emulation of a virtualized prototype using the GNS3 network simulator in Sect. 3. We also present experimental results on the penetration of major performance metrics due to distortions in the underlying communication network of our telesurgery system. Finally, some conclusions are presented in Sect. 4.

2   System Architecture of a Remote-Controlled Telesurgery Infrastructure

In this section we analyze the HW/SW-architecture of a classical telesurgery system and identify its basic building blocks. The study is inspired by existing telepresence systems and remote-controlled neurosurgery infrastructures. In particular, we look at the architecture of modern angiography systems like Artis, that are employed for tele-imaging during neurosurgery processes in advanced e-health scenarios, cf. [18]. Our study also reflects on related studies of remote-controlled telesurgery, cf. [2,15,17,19,20].

From a general perspective, a remote-controlled telesurgery system can be divided into three basic building blocks shown in Fig. 1. At the *patient side* on the lhs of Fig. 1, the system comprises *local components* for the medical imaging and treatment of a patient. The patient lies in the center on a patient table. The local staff can move the table by a local control panel. The system includes medical robot functionalities and X-ray arms for tele-imaging, e.g., to provide fluoroscopy images. The X-ray arms can be moved and radiation can be triggered by the same control panel. As soon as an X-ray beam has been triggered, the creation of a fluoroscopy image is initiated. A detector unit captures the X-rays and

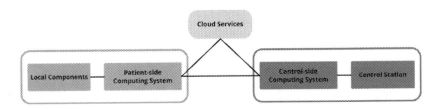

Fig. 1. Basic components of a remote-controlled telesurgery system

imaging algorithms reconstruct the patient's vessel structures. Then the medical images can be viewed on a local screen. If images are frequently triggered in a short amount of time, a related video can be generated and used, for instance, to analyze the function of a heart or other organs. In addition a telepresence system as a user interface for the local medical staff can be incorporated. The *patient-side computing system* also provides the logical endpoint to compute the required control actions for the actuators of the telesurgery units such as the robot arms for a coronary artery treatment, for instance, or the X-ray arms of medical imaging units. These components can execute commands which are triggered by control messages sent from the *remote-control side* on the rhs of Fig. 1.

At this *remote-control side* a *control station* and the *control-side computing system* are the basic functional blocks of the system architecture. They provide the user interfaces for tele-imaging, telepresence, the patient's table movement, and the robotic actuators' control in a joystick like fashion.

In a classical medical treatment the medical operation takes place locally and the physician is near the patient. In the remote-controlled scenario an additional physician resides in a separate location outside the patient's site and controls the telesurgery system by her remote actions after an imaging analysis. In such a scenario the incorporated medical images such as fluoroscopy images depict the patient's status on a remote display.

The *cloud services* are employed to manage the connectivity and the synchronization between both parts of the telesurgery system and its related functional blocks during medical actions. When a logical and physical connections between both sides of the distributed system have been established, the system status, logging messages, and network management information are exchanged. For this purpose a communication system with a TCP/UDP/IP protocol stack including security functionality based on TLS/DTLS and VPN protocols is employed.

The resulting technical structure and the information flows of such a remote-controlled telesurgery infrastructure are illustrated in Fig. 2.

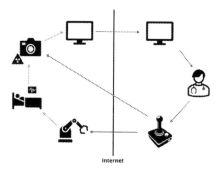

Fig. 2. Technical structure of a remote-controlled telesurgery system and the information flows between its functional components

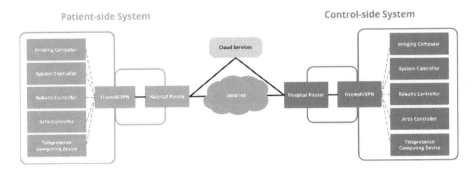

Fig. 3. Basic functional blocks of a prototypical telesurgery system

2.1   Basic Functional Modules of a Prototypical Telesurgery System and Its Information Flows

Now we identify the basic functional modules and information flows within a prototypical telesurgery system shown in Fig. 1. Regarding the patient side, the incorporated technical components of the telepresence and neurosurgery units work independently when a physician is locally available as decision maker at the patient's table. If the remote control via a network connection is instantiated, then all functional components available locally must also be offered remotely. The related data must be transferred between the patient side and the control side, too.

The basic functional modules of a prototypical telesurgery architecture and the required communication units between them is illustrated in Fig. 3, cf. [18]. Considering the green boxes at the patient side on lhs of Fig. 3, the associated local components consist of all the equipment that is necessary for a local treatment. It includes the robotic units, the medical imaging system, a telepresence system and a user interface (UI) for the local staff to control the system. In our prototype we focus on the Artis-system [18] with fluoroscopy images as tele-imaging system. Then this patient's table unit together with the associated computing system can be divided into six subcategories:

- The *imaging computer* preprocesses the captured medical images of the patient, e.g., fluoroscopy images during an angiography operation. In the latter case desired tissue features are highlighted on the local screen and the physician can navigate a guidewire cleanly within the vessel walls of the patient. The latter image data are encoded, compressed and transferred to the remote side by IP-packet streams.
- The *system controller* is the central computational unit. It provides the link between the neurosurgery system and the medical expert via the UI. It also manages the system configuration, the fault handling, the logging of system states and actions as well as the local communication of the system and the connections both to the remote side and to the cloud. To communicate with the remote side, the system controller obtains address information and configuration settings from the cloud services. All data transmitted to a remote side runs along this unit at first.

- The *robotic controller* represents the robot unit of the system. It executes the commands received from the remote side. It consist of a robotic actuator component mounted on the patient's table and a controller for processing incoming control signals and the actuation of the robotic motors as well as for the required local calculations of steering tasks.

  The system and robotic controllers form a unified technical unit in a locally controlled system. Regarding a remote operation, they are expanded by a communication management system and two separated communicating blocks to create a patient side and a remote side system.

- In our setup the employed X-ray arms can be navigated by an *Artis controller*. Depending on the used neurosurgery system, there can be two arms, one in horizontal direction and one in vertical direction. A physician can move these arms to his favorite position and start with the fluoroscopy imaging of a patient. In an angiography scenario, for instance, these resulting images are very important for the physician because she safely navigates a guidewire along the patient's vessel walls based on these medical images.

- The staff's communication between the patient and control side can be established by means of *telepresence computing devices* at both sides. They provides a bi-directional connection. At the patient side one or more room cameras are used normally to have different views on the patient-side system. It must be possible for the medical doctor to see which person is located at what place in the treatment room and where the patient-side operators are. This view is very important for the steering of X-ray beams and the movement of the X-ray arms since X-rays are harmful to humans. Hence, verbal communication must be supported in addition to the video transmission. Then physicians at both sides can exchange information about the current status and the planning of further treatment steps.

- The telesurgery system is supported by a *communication system* which carries IP-encapsulated data traffic along the Internet. It has two building blocks, namely the *hospital routers* and the *hospital network infrastructure*.

The *cloud services* provides three major functions to manage the entire family of devices, their users and the connections between the patient and control side:

- First, a *service for device and user management* is used to manage all users of the system and their privileges, to keep track of all active devices, to configure the robotic networks, to support remote servicing, and to perform software updates. When a new patient-side system is going online, the device management service has to register the status of these devices and their availability for the control-side systems.

- The second task is given by a *session management service*. It is responsible for establishing and managing a control-signal connection between the patient side and the remote side.

- The third task concerns a *network management service* which monitors all systems and their status. When an active connection between a patient side and a control side is established, it controls the availability of both systems, monitors the Quality-of-Service (QoS) of the connections, and collects related usage and performance data. It should also be possible to perform diagnostic network and system tests.

2.2 Communication Infrastructure of a Reliable Telesurgery Service

In this section we briefly describe in more the network architecture and communication structures of our reliable telesurgery system. The communication architecture comprising the hospital routers and the hospital network infrastructure toward the cloud services has been depicted in Fig. 3. In our work we will not focus on the hospital routers and their IP-network in detail since the network infrastructure is set up differently in each hospital and managed by different service providers. Therefore, it is not possible to make a general statement about the error behavior and security issues due to DDoS penetration. Here we assume that the related firewall/VPN unit is directly connected with the Internet. Therefore, we distinguish the following components:

- A *firewall/Virtual Private Network (VPN) controller* constitutes the security interface of the patient side and control side toward the hospital routers. It shall protect the system from cyberattacks and other malicious packet traffic and can establish dedicated connections by a VPN controller. It also creates authorized, encrypted end-to-end IP-connections between the patient side and the remote side or to a cloud services system for management and maintenance purposes.
- The *hospital routers* establish the IP-paths within the distributed telesurgery system and toward the cloud computing infrastructure. They also provide standardized network and traffic management functionalities for IPv4- and IPv6-packet flows.

From a network perspective the entry point into each part of the telesurgery system at the patient side and control side is provided by a router with firewall functionality. To guarantee a high availability of the connections between the patient- and control-side systems, a multi-path concept should be supported among these sides. Therefore, we have employed Fortinet's FortiGate-60E routers with firewall and SD-WAN functionalities in our prototype, cf. [4]. The latter communication system also supports the establishment of a primary and a secondary path among the routers within an SD-WAN zone shown in Fig. 4.

Here the physical network interfaces are represented as black boxes within the two different data paths shown as pipelines. These connections are defined as SD-WAN members. The task of an SD-WAN zone is to evaluate availability checks at each member of the zone. During the evaluation phase the latency, packet loss and jitter of each member are measured. The result of those checks are used in appropriate SD-WAN rules. In this way, the system can monitor and manage the status of the instantiated physical transport connections. Then it can select the best path for the data transmission to satisfy the required QoS/QoE specifications. To ensure a secure transport of the information between both FortiGate routers a VPN tunnel is created along each network path and the data are encrypted by an IPsec tunnel mode, cf. [7].

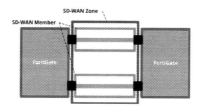

Fig. 4. Interconnection of two FortiGate routers within a single SD-WAN zone

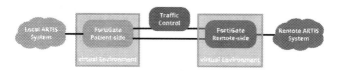

Fig. 5. Communication architecture of two virtualized FortiGate routers embedded into the local and remote Artis system

In our developed prototype these FortiGate routers are integrated into the Artis system as virtualized entities by means of virtual machines, see Fig. 5. To support the manipulation of transferred IP-packet streams during our experiments, e.g., by delaying or dropping packets, a traffic control block has been realized along the first IP-path employing the Linux traffic control function *tc*, see [11].

As the telesurgery system acts in a closed loop mode, the required information flows must be realized in real-time. At the patient side of an angiography action, for instance, the Artis system acquires fluoroscopy images from the patient's body in a specified frequency between one to sixty frames per second. In the remote-controlled setup the release of a X-ray beam to acquire new fluoroscopic images is started by the physician at the remote-control side. The captured images are first computed locally and the resulting video stream of successive fluoroscopy images is shown as a stream on the local display. Then the video signal of the display is captured, encoded as H.265 data set of tele-images and transmitted to the control-side system. There it is decompressed and displayed. Then the remotely acting physician can see the live X-ray images at her control-side display. Based on these images she can control the movement of the robot arms at the patient side with a special console. When she steers one joystick into a direction the associated signal of this movement command is transmitted to the patient-side system. Then the local robot can perform the specified action, e.g., move a used guidewire forward within the vessel walls of the operated patients or rotate the guidewire. Then the movement of the guidewire is captured again by new fluoroscopy images. The latter are transmitted back to the physician at the remote-control side. Such a prototypical workflow with its related information flows between the basic building blocks of the telesurgery system is depicted in Figs. 2 and 6.

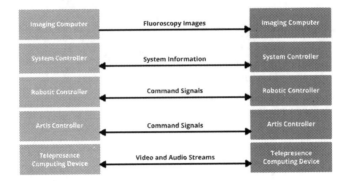

Fig. 6. Information flows between the basic components of the telesurgery system

Using the classical Diffserv QoS-model of IP-networks, cf. [9], the system's information flows and the command-signal flows can then be mapped to the real-time priority QoS-traffic class Expedited Forwarding whereas the tele-imaging and telepresence data streams may be assigned to the high priority QoS-traffic class Assured Forwarding. In our current study we have not been focusing on these assignment issues of optimal QoS-traffic classes.

2.3   Performance Requirements of the Communication Architecture

Regarding the performance requirements of a prototypical telesurgery system we first consider the required bandwidth of the tele-imaging and telepresence system along the logical transport channels between the patient and the remote-control side on the uplink and on the opposite downlink path. Inspired by the Artis system [19] we suppose that three different cameras at the patient-side with 3 Mbps per camera generate a capacity demand of the UDP/IP-stack of 9 Mbps along the uplink. Assuming one camera at the remote-side generates a demand of 3 Mbps along the downlink.

Based on the analysis of typical tele-imaging system we assume that the demanded uplink capacity demand is given about 40 Mbps and the downlink capacity demand is about 4 Mbps. Practical studies reveal that robotic- and system-control traffic demands a symmetric capacity of about 5 kbps, whereas a typical Artis controller needs 200 kbps. In summary, the complete bandwidth requirements of all logical channels of our five components shown in Fig. 6 are summarized in Table 1.

Considering the packet delay from the patient side towards the remote-control side and its associated jitter between the transferred IP-packets, one can assume that jitter values below 700 ms are not vulnerable to a proper operation of the distributed tele-imaging, telepresence and robotic-control components of the systems. Regarding the end-to-end (E2E) delay T_l between the critical tele-imaging or telepresence modules in the distributed telesurgery system, one has to take into account the transmission delay and signal propagation delay along

Table 1. Typical bandwidth requirements of each functional component

Functional Component	Uplink	Downlink
Imaging Computer	40 Mbps	4 Mbps
System Controller	5 kbps	5 kbps
Robotic Controller	5 kbps	5 kbps
Artis Controller	200 kbps	200 kbps
Telepresence Device	9 Mbps	3 Mbps

an IP-path between the routers and their firewalls T_t, and the processing and computing latency in the related functional blocks on top of the IP-layer at the patient and remote-control side T_{ap} and T_{ar}, in total $T_a = T_{ap} + T_{ar}$. If an additional random delay T_i is occurring along the IP-path and if other random effects are ignored, one gets the following E2E-latency formula:

$$T_l = T_a + T_N = T_a + T_t + T_i = T_{ap} + T_{ar} + T_t + T_i$$

Previous studies [10,12,13] have shown that the network induced latency component $T_N = T_t + T_i$ should not exceed 300 ms to guarantee a proper remote-controlled operation of a telesurgery system.

Considering the tele-imaging system, we expect that it encodes medical images by the H.265 standard. Then we can assume that 2% IP-packet loss can be tolerated, see [6,21]. If this value is guaranteed by the communication system along the IP-connections, the required QoS-guarantee of telepresence is also not affected.

3 Emulation of a Virtualized Prototype Offering a Reliable Telesurgery Service

In this section we discuss the emulation of a virtualized prototype offering a reliable remote-controlled telesurgery service based on the system architecture sketched in Sect. 2. The SD-WAN network architecture shown in Subsect. 2.2 is emulated by means of a virtualized test bed applying the tool GNS3, see [5].

3.1 Network Architecture of the GNS3-Prototype

The system architecture of our investigated telesurgery prototype is depicted in Fig. 7. The emulated network architecture of the distributed telesurgery system is directly integrated into the employed Artis-controllers using virtual machines. Using a router virtualization, the related network structure between both sides is depicted in Fig. 8.

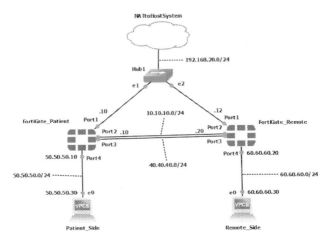

Fig. 7. GNS3-prototype of an emulated telesurgery service with two virtualized Forti-Gate routers

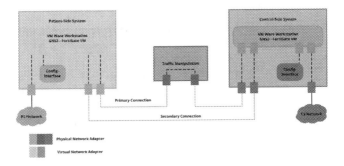

Fig. 8. Integration of virtualized FortiGate routers into the Artis-controller system

The study of our prototype has three objectives. First, the functionality of the Artis-controller which gets access to the session and connection management functionality to steer the SD-WAN IP-network will be tested. Secondly, QoS-requirements on the network connectivity shall be determined that guarantee a proper and reliable operation of the remote-side functionality of the Artis-controller. It has to guarantee the robustness of the system against network distortions. In particular, we want to analyze the performance impact if an additional latency component, a packet loss or a reduced bandwidth is imposed along the used data transport paths. In this manner it is possible to use the prototype for other user studies and one can derive threshold values for KPIs of the system more precisely and gain additional QoE-feedback by potential users. It is the third objective to evaluate the SD-WAN functionality of the FortiGate routers and to analyze how the path redundancy affects the functionality of the system when a switching from the primary to the secondary connection occurs.

In a further experimental step the virtualized FortiGate routers may be replaced by real hardware routers.

For the manipulation of the transmitted data traffic and to test a decreased network quality in the Artis-controller at the remote side a computer running LINUX is introduced in the primary path between both FortiGate routers. On this system two physical network interfaces are bridged to forward network traffic. This traffic stream can be manipulated by the Linux traffic-control functionality of tc [11].

Our virtualized test bed comprises two virtual machines which emulate the medical tele-imaging system and the Artis-control system at the patient side and the remote-control system at the opposite remote side as well as an additional virtualized host as cloud computing side. Both building blocks at the patient and remote-control side are interconnected by two virtualized SD-WAN routers which incorporate traditional TCP/IP-based connectivity and VPN functionalities of commerical high-speed routers for secure cloud communication such as the FortiNet SD-WAN multi-WAN-router FortiGate-60E, cf. [4].

In our prototype the latter routers establish a secure multi-path connection between the virtualized computer systems at the remote-control side and the patient side. To simplify the communication test bed, a primary connection and only one secondary connection as backbone path have been established. Furthermore, they are used to interconnect both computing systems to a centralized cloud. The latter block provides the basic remote control and orchestration functionalities within the emulated telesurgery system. In our virtualized test bed each deployed FortiGate-60E incorporates a web server. It is used to handle the required configuration tasks of the system architecture.

The cloud computing system on the top of the realized communication network in Fig. 7 provides a global API interface to the network interfaces of the SD-WAN routers. Its configuration tasks are handled by a virtual machine management system applying VMware [22].

In our prototype the cloud infrastructure of the organisation offering the telesurgery service is bound to a hub router interconnecting it to both SD-WAN routers within a local address space given by *192.168.20.0/24*. The latter is configured by a NAT functionality. Both FortiGate routers are connected to this hub and the associated local NAT network. In this way both FortiGate router are inside the NAT network to host the cloud system as management system for the configuration of both FortiGate routers and their integrated web servers. They are able to send Internet-Control-Message-Protocol (ICMP) ping messages to a specified destination for availability testing.

The network *50.50.50.0/24* represents the network on the patient-side system. *60.60.60.0/24* represents the network for the remote-side system. Both virtual machines are configured according to their associated network addresses. This means, for example, that the *Patient_Sides* network interface has the configured IP address *50.50.50.30*. Both FortiGate routers have four configured network interfaces. The first one on *Port1* represents the interface to the NAT network to reach the host system. *Port2* is the primary connection between both

FortiGate routers with *10.10.10.0/24* as network address and *Port3* is the secondary connection with *40.40.40.0/24* as network address. The last one, *Port4*, is the network interface for the hospital network. This prototype architecture is able to show that both virtual computers can reach each other with ICMP messages. Both FortiGate routers can supervise the primary and the secondary connection between each other. They can also determine if they prefer to route the whole traffic over the primary IP-path. When the primary connection reveals a bad QoS-quality or the link is completely down then the traffic shall be routed via the secondary network connection based on a trigger by the VPN-controller.

3.2   The Impact of Operational Distortions in the Communication Network on the System's Performance

By our emulation of a prototypical telesurgery architecture we want to investigate the impact of operational distortions in its communication network on the system's performance. For this purpose we focus on major key performance issues that are related to the network specification and the related service-level objectives of the telesurgery service.

The executed experiments are concerned with the performance impact of following effects on three a priori specified key performance indices (KPIs):

– Limiting the available bandwidth of logical channels transferring the user data and signaling traffic
  A logical channel for the user traffic carries video streams uplink between the local tele-imaging system and the remote-control system. Along the downlink path in the reverse direction signaling traffic is transported. We investigate the effect of bounding the required bandwidths of those channels to less than 100% of their available capacity. In our measurement study the reduction of the granted channel bandwidth will be downgraded in steps of 10 kbps. As the data rates of the telepresence streams are lower in both directions, we will focus on the tele-imaging component.
– Changing the latency along the transport channels between the SD-WAN routers
  Following the line of reasing in [13], we investigate the impact of an increasing latency along the transport channels on the end-to-end delay and the performance of the emulated telesurgery system. For this purpose we incorporate additional transport delays in the router network in the range $[0, 1000]$ ms in discrete steps of 0, 150, 250, 400, 600 and 1000 ms. It is the objective of these tests to find out the maximal tolerable end-to-end delay such that the Artis remote-control system is still operating in a proper way and the additional latency is not perceived at the video-decoder side. In our future research those tests may be repeated to monitor the quality-of-experience realized by physicians.
– Evaluation of the SD-WAN multi-path functionality
  The SD-WAN functionality of the FortiGate routers offers a countermeasure to cope with a failure of an instantiated IP-path and the related routers

between the medical imaging source and the remote-control unit. Offering the possibility to integrate a redundant second IP-path triggered by measurements, the availability of the telesurgery service can be increased and the identified path with the better KPIs may be used for the data transport. In our experiments we evaluate how this functionality behaves when the connection is switched over from the primary to the secondary IP-path. We are interested whether this switching process can be noticed by a working physicians and how long it takes until a decreased quality level of an IP-connection is detected.

These performance issue of the SD-WAN functionality will be evaluated on the emulated prototypes by our following measurement studies.

3.3   Performance Results of the GNS3-Experiments

We have performed three different series of experiments to investigate the distortion effects when the data traffic is delivered along the first IP-path based on a connection in our test bed between the functional modules of the Artis-controller at the patient side and the remote-control side.

In the first setting of the GNS3-experiments we study the performance impact when the channel bandwidth of the Artis-command signaling from the remote-controller toward the patient side is limited at the IP-layer. An encryption by IPSec has been disregarded in these experiments. It can be seen that limiting the throughput at the intermediate tc-controller to 180 kbps can guarantee a proper teleservice operation while a limit of 160 kbps induces at freezing effect at the controlled Artis-actuators at the patient side.

The experiments illustrate that a traffic priority concept using a Diffserv QoS-model along the IP-path must be realized to guarantee a proper interaction of the distributed telesurgery service infrastructure.

When the bandwidth of the logical channel of the Artis-controller from the patient side to the remote side is reduced between the related Fortigate routers, the behavior of the telesurgery service is different. The bandwidth can be reduced to 50 kbps without any effect on the controllability of the actuator. At 40 and 30 kbps an activity of the Artis components is strongly disturbed and at 20 kbps the proper operation of the system has stopped.

In the second setting of the GNS3-experiments we look at the end-to-end delay between the patient side and the remote side components and monitor the induced round-trip delay in the test bed. For this purpose the time between a deflection of the joystick at the remote side and a detection of this movement within collected fluoroscopy images at the remote side is determined. In addition, it is estimated how long it takes until the command of the joystick set the Artis actuators in motion. For this purpose an external camera has been used which filmed the control panel, the patient's Artis actuator components and the transmitted video on the display at a rate of 240 frames per second. The transmission delay between the display of the local fluoroscopy image and the display on the remote side was 50 ms. In the setup 10 test runs have been

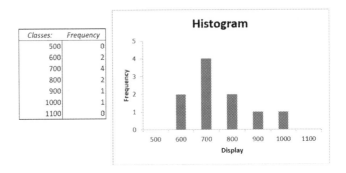

Classes:	Frequency
500	0
600	2
700	4
800	2
900	1
1000	1
1100	0

Fig. 9. Evaluated latency in ms between deflecting the joystick until the resulting movement effect is seen on the remote-side display

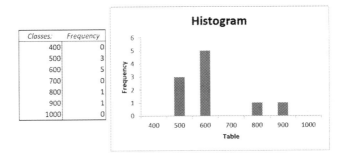

Classes:	Frequency
400	0
500	3
600	5
700	0
800	1
900	1
1000	0

Fig. 10. Evaluated latency in ms between deflecting the joystick until the patient's table starts moving

performed. The resulting average time until an object motion has been seen on the fluoroscopy image is 705 ms with a standard deviation of 106 ms. The standard deviation is that high because a fluoroscopy image has been generated only every 100 ms, i.e., at 10 frames per second. Therefore, a change in the fluoroscopy image on the recorded video can only be determined with an accuracy of 100 ms. The evaluation of the latency measurements is depicted by a histogram in Fig. 9.

It has been harder to evaluate the duration until the Artis-actuator with the related patient's table starts moving because it is moving slowly and its very small movement cannot be detected properly by our video recording. Related experiments with 10 test runs have generated an average delay of 561 ms regarding that action. The standard deviation is given by 114 ms. These measurement results can be seen by the histogram in Fig. 10.

In Fig. 11 we illustrate the monitored latency profile of an Artis-controlled teleservice interaction between the joystick at the remote-control side, the start of a movement of the patient's table, and the aggregated latency along the whole control path. The duration of an image transfer from the local display at the patient's side to the display at the remote-control side is given by 50 ms

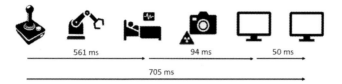

Fig. 11. Monitored latency profile of an Artis-controlled teleservice interaction

if an additional transport delay among the related routers is disregarded. The delay for a triggerd acquisition of a new fluoroscopy image at the patient's side is calculated as 94 ms. It yields an E2E-delay starting with the trigger signal of the remote joystick until the recorded image shows the new status of the moved Artis actuators on the remote display within a round-trip time of 705 ms. Disregarding the distance-based transport delays of the control messages within the underlying IP-network, an average activation of $T_a = 700$ ms can be used as reference value of the studied telesurgery service from a start of the action by a physician, e.g., by deflecting the joystick, until the verification of this activity on the remote display.

In the third setting of the GNS3-experiments we have studied the impact of an induced transport delay along the IP-connection between the FortiGate routers at the patient side and the remote side. Both directions are considered separately in these latency tests. Regarding the downlink path from the remote side toward the patient side an additionally transport delay of 150 ms could not disturb the controllability of the Artis subsystem. A latency value of 250 ms could already be properly perceived, but it did not destroy the controllability requirements of the telesurgery system. At a delay value of 400 ms the patient's control-table setting was noticeably affected, whereas the table movement became uncontrollable for latency values of 600 ms, when the joystick is deflected sharply.

Regarding the uplink connection from the patient side toward the control side, an operational deterioration of the system could not be perceived if a transport delay in the range [0, 1000] ms has been introduced. The reason is that in our current Artis-prototype only the TCP-acknowledgment messages arising from the control signals of the Artis-system are transmitted uplink via the FortiGate routers. This message transfer is not so much penetrated by the induced delay impairments along the downlink path. Based on these experiments we may conclude that a transport delay along the communication network of the Fortigate routers can be tolerated up to 250 ms which is achieved in normal situations within Germany.

The reconfiguration tests on the FortiGate router's capability to switch a specified IP-network path within the SD-WAN zone has shown very poor performance results so far. In our preliminary tests more than 3 sec were required to detect a malfunctioning of the working path and to switch over to the secondary one. In our future research more detailed investigations on the network management are required to solve the related availability issues.

4   Conclusions

Nowadays, new advanced Internet-of-Things applications are enabled by high-speed communication and cloud computing technologies. The latter can support the effective processing of smart e-health services such as telesurgery, cf. [1,8]. In our paper we consider the system architecture of a classical telesurgery system. We have discussed the extension of its functional modules to support remote surgery based on a reliable multi-path communication among its components. We have also provided an investigation of important key performance parameters of such remote-controlled telesurgery services. To achieve deeper technical insights on the system's performance of such a distributed architecture and its inherent communication flows, a telesurgery prototype with its major control components that are inspired by the well-known Artis system has been emulated within a virtualized test bed by several GNS3-experiments. In this way we have investigated fundamental computing and network performance indices of our prototype.

Based on these experiments we may conclude that a transport delay within the incorporated communication network of the prototypical telesurgery infrastructure can be tolerated up to 250 ms. Assuming a symmetric transfer delay, we conclude that a maximal transport delay of 125 ms in each direction can be tolerated to assure a proper remote-controlled telesurgery service in our setting. We have also illustrated that a multi-path concept has to be employed to guarantee a high availability level of the remote-controlled telesurgery service.

Furthermore, these GNS3-experiments illustrate that an intensive training of remotely operating physicians is needed to handle such a complex telesurgery infrastructure. Moveover, additional measurement-based QoE-studies are needed to elaborate on those complex treatment scenarios. The latter insight can indicate some feasible ways to realize advanced system architectures including a secure distributed data processing and communication architecture based on 5G/6G technology and its service category ultra-reliable low latency (URLL).

Acknowledgment. This feasibility study was done while Mr. Gerwien was working as master student in the Computer Networks group at the University of Bamberg. The other authors are very much indebted to his efforts in implementing a first virtualized prototype of the telesurgery architecture by means of the GNS3 emulator.
Furthermore, the authors are indebted to the staff of Siemens Healthineers AG, Germany, who provided on request substantial technical insights for the described research on the design and operation of modern telesurgery systems.

References

1. Al-Fuqaha, A., et al.: Internet of Things: a survey on enabling technologies, protocols, and applications. IEEE Commun. Surv. Tutor. **17**(4), 2347–2376 (2015)
2. Barba, P., et al.: Remote telesurgery in humans: a systematic review. Surg. Endosc. **36**, 2771–777 (2022)
3. Cech, H.L., Großmann, M., Krieger, U.R.: A fog computing architecture to share sensor data by means of blockchain functionality. In: IEEE International Conference on Fog Computing (ICFC) 2019, pp. 31–40 (2019)
4. Fortinet: Fortinet - Next-Generation Firewall (2024). https://www.fortinet.com/products/next-generation-firewall
5. GNS3: Getting Started with GNS3 (2024). https://docs.gns3.com/docs/
6. Hoßfeld, T., et al.: QoE of YouTube Video Streaming for Current Internet Transport Protocols. In: Fischbach, K., Krieger, U.R. (eds.) MMB & DFT 2014. LNCS, vol. 8376, pp. 136–150. Springer, Heidelberg (2014)
7. Internet Engineering Task Force: Security Architecture for the Internet Protocol (2024). https://datatracker.ietf.org/doc/html/rfc2401
8. Islam, S.M.R., Kwak, D., Kabir, M.H., Hossain, M., Kwak, K.S.: The Internet of Things for health care: a comprehensive survey. IEEE Access **3**, 678–708 (2015)
9. Kreutz, D., et al.: Software-defined networking: a comprehensive survey. Proc. IEEE **103**(1), 14–76 (2015)
10. Legeza, P., et al.: Impact of network performance on remote robotic-assisted endovascular interventions in porcine model. J. Rob. Surg. **16**(1), 29–35 (2022)
11. Linux man-pages project: tc(8) - Linux manual page (2024). https://man7.org/linux/man-pages/man8/tc.8.htmll
12. Madder, R.D., et al.: Robotic telestenting performance in transcontinental and regional pre-clinical models. Catheter. Cardiovasc. Interv. **97**(3), E327–E332 (2021)
13. Madder, R.D., et al.: Network latency and long distance robotic telestenting: exploring the potential impact of network delays on telestenting performance. Catheter. Cardiovasc. Interv. **95**(5), 914–919 (2020)
14. McGhin, T., Choo, K.-K.R., Liu, C.Z., He, D.: Blockchain in healthcare applications: research challenges and opportunities. J. Netw. Comput. Appl. **135**, 62–75 (2019)
15. Navarro, E.M., et al.: A new telesurgery generation supported by 5G technology: benefits and future trends. Procedia Comput. Sci. **200**, 31–38 (2022)
16. Penn, J.W., et al.: Fifth generation cellular networks and neurosurgery: a narrative review. World Neurosurg. **156**, 96–102 (2021)
17. Philips: Philips announces new augmented-reality surgical navigation technology designed for image-guided spine, cranial and trauma surgery. https://www.philips.com/a-w/about/news/archive/standard/news/press/2017/%20170112-philips-announces-new-augmented-reality-surgical-navigation-technology-designed-for-image-guided-spine-cranial-and-trauma-surgery.html. Accessed 12 Jan (2017)
18. Siemens Healthcare AG. Artis - Systems for interventional angiography (2024). https://www.siemens-healthineers.com/de/angio/artis-interventional-angiography-systems
19. Siemens Healthineers AG. ARTIS icono (2024). https://www.siemens-healthineers.com/de/angio/artis-interventional-angiography-systems/artis-icono
20. Thompson, J.M., et al.: Human factors in telesurgery: effects of time delay and asynchrony in video and control feedback with local manipulative assistance. Telemed. J. **5**(2), 127–221 (1999)

21. Uhl, T., et al.: H.264/AVC and H.265/HEVC codecs in the IP environment: a comparison study of QoE, QoS and UX. In : 2021 International Conference on Software, Telecommunications and Computer Networks (SoftCOM), pp. 1–6 (2021)
22. VMWare (2024). https://www.vmware.com/

Emulation of Denial-of-Service Attacks for Software Defined Networks
Accessible on Commodity Hardware with Kathará

Marcel Großmann[(✉)] [iD] and Noelle Weinmann

Fakultät WIAI, Otto-Friedrich-Universität, An der Weberei 5, 96047 Bamberg,
Germany
marcel.grossmann@uni-bamberg.de

Abstract. In the present era, networks have become intricate and may
not be comprehensible to passionate freshman. Fortunately, virtualization simplifies access for individuals interested in learning about network
challenges. Nevertheless, replicating numerous variations of Distributed
Denial-of-Service (DDoS) attacks remains a tough endeavor. Thus, we
suggest employing widely recognized attack techniques utilized through
virtualization. Our paper uses the network emulator Kathará as the foundation for constructing networks, and we leverage customized Docker
images as network nodes. Additionally, we set up a service called Kathará
as a Service (KaaS) to facilitate access for all users of the network emulator. As an example, we create a network by applying a Software-Defined
Network (SDN) and by conducting DDoS attacks against it. Our goal
is to improve the accessibility of network assaults on next-generation
networks for a diverse group of users.

Keywords: Emulation · Virtualization · DDoS · SDN

1 Introduction

The driving force behind our research is the observation that there appears to
be a lack of comprehensive research on the topic in a broad sense. It is either
focused on a singular attack with a particular execution, or it is very broad
without a precise implementation. Frequently, a comparison is not made. We
attempt to address a wider range of DDoS attack types, where we develop a
readily deployable and highly scalable emulation of a SDN that offers ample
illustrative possibilities, making it suitable for educational purposes. The emulator will encompass all the necessary components to simulate and actively monitor
various sorts of DDoS attacks, the latter both in real-time for demonstration purposes and offline for more extensive analysis. Additionally, the testing will not
be conducted with real-world applications, as this would go beyond the intended
focus of this work. The paper provides a thorough examination of a wide range
of DDoS assaults in a specified scenario. Our solution is primarily lightweight
and low-cost, while also being scalable and adaptable enough to suit various

F. Phillipson et al. (Eds.): I4CS 2024, CCIS 2109, pp. 275–285, 2024.
https://doi.org/10.1007/978-3-031-60433-1_16

security requirements. We want to consider several forms of DDoS attacks, such as *volumetric, protocol,* and *application* layer DDoS attacks.

DDoS assaults present significant risks to both traditional and emerging networks, including Internet of Things (IoT), cloud computing [20], 5G communication networks [32], and SDN [14]. There is a notable deficiency in research about the reduction of DDoS attacks, with little emphasis on their prevention. Numerous studies examine the aspect of mitigating DDoS attacks, however preventing DDoS attacks is rarely mentioned [21]. Our objective is to provide a versatile playground that allows students to fill the aforementioned knowledge gaps.

For effective DDoS attack security solutions a real-time monitoring system is required [14,15]. Therefore, our approach integrates the real-time monitoring tool sFlow-RT [11]. This will establish the basis for detecting anomalies and allowing automatically triggered alerts in future developments.

Research on SDN typically prioritizes focus on network performance rather than addressing security issues that arise from implementing programmable networks [21]. Several studies focus in how the deployment of SDN can help improve security problems in networking [17,27]. Ahmad and Mir [12] provide a comparison of different SDN controllers based on their scalability, consistency, reliability, and security. The literature on SDN security and DDoS attacks primarily concentrates on certain types of DDoS attacks, mainly volumetric attacks. Following Dayal and Srivastava [19], we aim to compare different types of DDoS attacks, demonstrating the impact that each attack has on the SDN infrastructure.

Many studies have focused on applying Machine Learning (ML) approaches to detect DDoS attacks, e. g. [13,24,28]. Different DDoS attack datasets for ML detection approaches are compared in [14], whereas different mitigation practices are summarized in surveys like [15,30].

We currently lack easily deployable, highly configurable, lightweight frameworks for evaluating and learning about DDoS attacks on SDN networks on commodity hardware. Research on DDoS assaults and hands-on activities generally neglect SDN networks. A software platform designed by Fuertes et al. [22] teaches and analyzes DDoS attack security and life-cycle build upon virtual networks. Among others, Das and Sarac [18] implement a lab in a Virtual Machine (VM) using Open vSwitch [10], Open Network Operating System (ONOS) [9], Mininet [8], and Docker [2]. With it, students can learn about SDN security and configure networks securely. Another report [16] highlights SDN security challenges in 5G networks and emphasizes comprehensive student security training.

Predominantly, the Mininet emulator is used to mimic testbeds for SDN networks, however it has fewer configuration capabilities compared to Kathará [5]. Mininet's user-friendly nature and widespread utilization aid students in their early learning about SDN. We suggest KaaS [6], a novel strategy, to promote Kathará usage. We believe that fine-grained settings enhance students' knowledge of the SDN network, node interactions, and attack scenarios.

2   Foundation for the Demonstration

2.1   Software Defined Networks

SDN has emerged as a widely accepted method for managing extensive networks. Given the increasing effectiveness of mitigation solutions for DDoS assaults and other security concerns offered by SDN, our study will specifically concentrate on this technology. In literature, the architecture of SDN is commonly divided into three layers: (1) infrastructure layer, also known as data plane, (2) control layer or control plane, and (3) application layer or application plane [31]. The data plane comprises of forwarding devices and physical switches, while the control plane includes the SDN controllers and the interfaces that enable communication within the SDN architecture. The application plane is responsible for end-user applications, such as network monitoring tools and security applications.

SDN offers a multitude of advantages in the field of networking. The purpose of this design is to support the creation of efficient and adaptable networks, while also simplifying their management. Key benefits encompass adjustable flow abstraction, dynamic networking, and centralized administration of extensive networks, enabled by the separation of data and control planes. Flow abstraction allows the uniform behavior of network devices, while flow programming enables unparalleled flexibility [25]. The adaptable framework permits dynamic reconfiguration of routing rules in network devices, facilitating in-line and network-based attack detection [32]. SDN technology offers a comprehensive perspective of large-scale networks by virtue of its ability to control and monitor them effectively. In this scenario, to overcome scalability and control latency issues, a physically distributed but logically centralized control plane is used [12].

Logical centralization of the control plane and global network state knowledge offer the benefits of decreased errors, automated response to changes, and simplified development of advanced network functions [25]. The programmable control plane is tasked with distributing network and security functions across network instances [17, 26, 32]. It encompasses the logical mechanisms responsible for managing the forwarding behavior, such as routing protocols. The data plane is responsible for carrying out the traffic forwarding, such as Internet Protocol (IP) forwarding and Layer 2 switching, based on the logic provided by the control plane. This functionality can be implemented using either hardware or software routers. The division of responsibilities is a valuable characteristic that serves as a safeguard against Denial-of-Service (DoS) or other malicious assaults. A notable illustration is the preference for well-known paths over unknown and suspect paths, a feature that is currently challenging to integrate into conventional interdomain routing protocols like the Border Gateway Protocol (BGP). The separation of the control and data plane offers additional advantages, such as a more extensive range of policies for route selection [29]. This is feasible because the route controller has the capability to directly modify the state, irrespective of the software, technology, or hardware of the network nodes. In contrast, the current interdomain routing protocol BGP restricts routes based on a fixed set of steps.

Data centers also get advantages from this segregation, not only because it allows for more efficient administration, but also because it leads to reduced expenses. The reason for this is that standard switches can support extensive software and network control, eliminating the need for proprietary switches. Additionally, fewer switches are usually needed in this scenario. Furthermore, the addressing of hosts can be enhanced by employing topology-specific addresses for Layer 2 addressing. This approach often involves less administration and configuration compared to Layer 3 addressing, although it has poor scalability.

While other advantages and applications of programmable networks exist, elaborating on them would exceed the scope of this paper.

2.2   Kathará as a Service

Reproducing trials in network research might be difficult because of complex configurations or devices that are exclusive to certain manufacturers. Emulators aim to address these challenges, but using them effectively demands significant time and a thorough comprehension of how they work. KaaS [23] explains the implementation of a user-friendly emulator that can function as a Network Emulator as a Service (NEaaS).

Various programmable emulators such as GNS3 [4], Mininet [8], and Kathará [5] offer advantages and disadvantages for prototyping network topologies. GNS3 offers a wide range of network experiments by using numerous VMs to simulate switches, routers, and hosts, connecting them through virtual interfaces. Mininet employs Container-based Emulation (CBE) by leveraging lightweight, Operating System (OS)-level virtualization methods to replace VMs as simulated network components. However, each tool requires particular hardware, software, and OS setups, and operates on a single workstation, limiting the testing possibilities because of local resource limitations. For example, Mininet is nimble and efficient, although it has drawbacks including restricted resource limitations and lack of compatibility with Docker [2] containers as hosts. Kathará, the successor of Netkit, enables Docker containers as emulated hosts and utilizes network scenarios to conceal the real implementation of network devices and links.

KaaS is proposed as a cloud-based, multi-tenancy NEaaS platform by incorporating existing technologies into an open-source network emulator. This platform enables users to easily create and test various network configurations. The initial version of this platform can be accessed on Github under the repository uniba-ktr/KaaS [6]. In particular, the new Kathará Representational State Transfer (REST) API is a supplementary interface that enables remote control of Kathará from another service, specifically the Kathará UI. The cornerstone of Kathará REST is built upon the fastAPI [3] framework, chosen for its robustness, agility, and compatibility with advanced libraries such as Pydantic and type hints. Additionally, new Python wrapper classes are created to simplify interactions with the core libraries. The new Kathará REST API offers a dedicated API endpoint for every command in Kathará.

The Kathará-in-Docker concept is integrated into a unified Docker image, facilitating deployment and scalability with container orchestrators such as

Docker Swarm or Kubernetes. The platform's goal is to meet the demand for replicability of proposals within the academic community and facilitate networking across research groups. The platform should possess scalability, flexibility, extensibility, Quality of Experience (QoE), realism, and cost-effectiveness.

The prototype is incomplete and needs a new user administration module to offer additional capabilities to users, like registration, and authentication. A container orchestrator, such as Kubernetes, is required to efficiently schedule and allocate multiple containers requested by various users.

3   Attacks in Software Defined Networks

Attacks in the SDN paradigm can be classified into the traditional architecture levels or planes specific to SDN: the application plane, the control plane, and the data plane.

Attacks in the application plane may target one or several SDN apps and the north-bound API [21]. A targeted attack on a specific SDN application could affect or compromise other apps, increasing the effect of the attack and potentially causing genuine security breaches in SDN.

While centralized control in SDN offers overall advantages, it also presents a significant risk, particularly when targeted attacks are directed at the control plane [12,29]. If an attacker successfully overwhelms the network to a point where the controller is unable to manage the load, it could lead to a complete disruption of the network for legitimate users [12]. In this scenario, we would refer to a Single Point of Failure (SPoF).

Possible attack tactics to cause the network to collapse include flooding the north-bound APIs, the south-bound APIs, or the controller itself [21]. Within distributed control plane implementations, additional security issues arise, making robust authentication protocols essential for validating and verifying controller instances [12]. Hence, the control plane is considered the most vulnerable aspect of the SDN architecture in terms of DDoS attacks. An example of such an attack involves transmitting a large number of newly produced data flows from devices with falsified IP addresses. Switches typically send a header-only packet to the controller when they encounter flows without an entry in their local flow table, as they are unable to manage such flows independently. A DDoS attack involves sending a large number of packet-in messages to the controller, which leads to the use of bandwidth, memory, and CPU in both the control and data planes [21]. OpenFlow switches store packet-in messages in a buffer before transmitting them to the controller [21]. When a packet is received and no flow rules match the existing flow information, it is either delivered entirely to the controller or merely a portion of the packet header. When multiple packets arrive simultaneously and the buffer reaches its maximum capacity, the switch will send complete packets to the controller instead of just sending header-only ones. This situation would lead to the utilization of the control plane bandwidth, causing the network to collapse completely and become inaccessible to valid traffic. In another situation, large incoming packets from the assault may cause the forwarding table of the OpenFlow switch to fill up, preventing the controller from

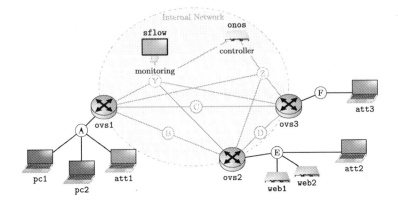

Fig. 1. SDN network topology deployed for DDoS trials

installing new flow rules, which are then refused by the switch. Additionally, the switch will not be able to route packets until memory space is available in the forwarding table, resulting in delays and the rejection of inbound valid traffic. Distinctive apps can generate conflicting flow rules, resulting in DDoS attacks on the control layer [12].

Attacks targeting the data plane and communication channel may result in packet loss, thereby causing network unavailability [21]. In SDN, data plane devices should not be allowed to change stream rules, as this might lead to DDoS attacks.

Possible solutions to aforementioned issues include establishing secure communication channels between data and control planes, implementing traffic scheduling and queuing mechanisms, ensuring isolation and monitoring of shared resources, leveraging throughput confidence intervals, and employing Deep Packet Inspection (DPI), among other approaches. Each of these solutions exhibits its own set advantages and disadvantages [21].

4   Emulation of an Attack Scenario

4.1   Structure of the Example Network

The initial concept for the design of the first rudimentary implementation aimed to create a network that is straightforward, with a manageable number of components, in order to expedite the process of development and testing. Hence, the resolution was to establish a unified network controller based on ONOS [9] called `controller` alongside three Open vSwitches [10], namely ovs1, ovs2, and ovs3. Additionally, the network consists of four "benign" devices, namely pc1, pc2, web1, and web2, as well as three "malicious" devices named att1, att2, and att3. Lastly, a network node is included to house the real-time monitoring tool sFlow-RT [11], referred to as `sflow`. Custom images are utilized for the network nodes and their build instructions are available on Github [7].

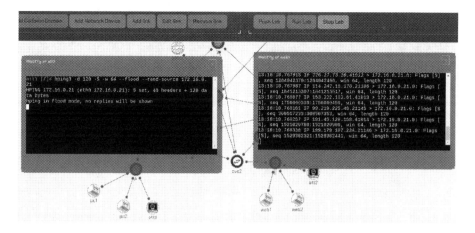

Fig. 2. Deployment of the DDoS demonstration on KaaS

4.2 Generation and Evaluation of DDoS Attacks

Figure 2 illustrates a DoS flood attack, in particular a demonstration of a TCP SYN attack, referred to as *tcp_syn* henceforth. The topology depicted in Fig. 1 was initialized in KaaS, and access was obtained to the nodes att1 and web1. On att1 we executed the *tcp_syn* flood attack to web1 by:

hping3 −d 120 −S −w 64 —flood —rand−**source** 172.16.0.21

The incoming DoS assault on web1 can be detected via the tcpdump tool, which reveals numerous random IP addresses transmitting SYN packets. In the subsequent phase, targets are randomly chosen from all potential attackers in our emulated network to carry out a DDoS attack. In this particular scenario, it is not possible to capture the traffic with tcpdump. Thus, we utilize the sflow monitoring feature of our prototype configuration. The sflow component detects and categorizes all randomly transmitted flows to a certain destination. Currently, it is evident that emulating attacks on network nodes is simply controllable and can be tailored to individual preferences using self-created programs, as long as they are compatible with a container environment.

With the help of cAdvisor [1] we successfully gathered statistics from several nodes in the topology of Fig. 1. We conducted multiple experiments on a Ryzen9 processor equipped with 16 physical cores, which double to 32 threads thanks to Simultaneous Multithreading (SMT), and 128GB of memory, collecting statistical data from a five minute trial.

As a baseline, we collected the statistics of a *regular* traffic mode, where the topology was set up to replicate randomized "benign" web traffic. By extending the *regular* traffic mode, we establish a distributed *http* attack mode by executing curl to retrieve the web pages. All other attack modes involve creating randomized DDoS attacks employing various protocols from the "malicious" devices, which use random source IP addresses to overwhelm all "benign" devices

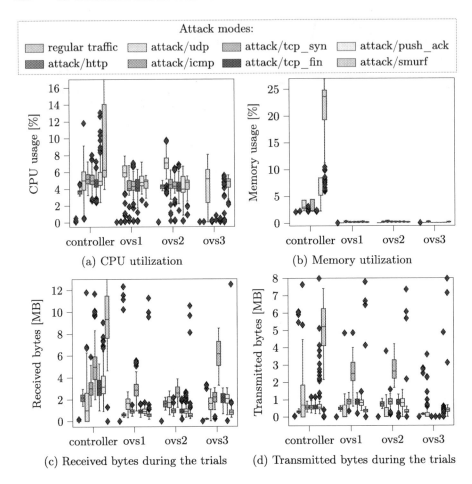

Fig. 3. Utilization statistics for the networking nodes of the trial topology of Fig. 1

through flooding. They use the tool `hping3` on all "malicious" devices to target everyone else in a distributed manner. Our DDoS attacks can be classified into

- *volumetric* attacks, namely *icmp* and *udp*,
- *protocol* attacks, namely *smurf*, *tcp_syn*, *tcp_fin*, and *push_ack*,
- *application* attacks, namely *http*.

For the evaluation shown in Fig. 3 we excluded a few outliers of the box plots to improve the clarity and readability of the remaining boxes. The graphic depicted in Fig. 3a illustrates the CPU consumption with the "benign" mode exhibiting a negligible footprint. This fact is also evident in the memory usage of Fig. 3b. In Fig. 3c the received bytes on the interfaces connecting *ovs1* to *ovs3* with the external networks (*A*, *E*, and *F*) and the *controller*'s interface to *Z* are analyzed. When comparing the attack modes, it is evident that broadcast *smurf* and UDP attacks have a greater demand for CPU and memory resources compared to other attack modes. The controller is primarily concerned with the traffic caused by the *smurf* broadcast messages, followed by the *tcp_syn* attacks, while the Open vSwitch nodes experience a significant amount of traffic due to the *tcp_syn* assaults.

5   Conclusion and Future Work

We demonstrated how emulating attack scenarios on mimicked networks is achievable for any enthusiastic newcomer. We used KaaS as a service-oriented platform that can be accessed using a web browser. The platform provides convenient access to the Kathará network emulator, which can incorporate custom nodes in the form of Docker containers. We constructed modified images for our DDoS example that can either launch attacks with `hping3` or observe network flows by `sflow-rt`. Sflow agents were incorporated into the Open vSwitches to collect and send statistics to the monitoring node.

We choose SDN for the emulation, with both "benign" and "malicious" nodes connected to it. A trial topology is created in KaaS to demonstrate its functionality. Each node in the topology is accessible and can execute installed programs. We utilized this behavior to carry out attacks from the "malicious" nodes and recorded the flows by a monitoring node. The initial results indicate that KaaS can effectively simulate a DDoS assault. Subsequently, we have examined the CPU and memory usage rates from outside of the network. We were able to visualize and compare the impact of different DDoS attacks on the nodes relevant for traffic routing and traffic management in the control and data planes. The results suggest that a different protection mechanism may be required for each attack. This insight is intended to underpin the work to come.

In the future, we aim to enhance our example with automated detection mechanisms in real-time. We are interested in looking at different techniques, which explore how malicious flows can be identified and stopped, particularly utilizing the control plane of SDN. We aim to examine how the feedback from our monitoring node can influence the controller to execute the appropriate action on the network. Finally, our goal is to verify whether our solution is capable of preventing several kinds of DDoS attacks.

Acknowledgments. The work on the KaaS prototype was supported by Mr. Le, who is working with the Computer Networks group at the University of Bamberg.

References

1. cadvisor. https://github.com/google/cadvisor
2. Docker. https://www.docker.com/
3. FastAPI. https://fastapi.tiangolo.com/
4. GNS3 The software that empowers network professionals. https://www.gns3.com/
5. Kathará. https://www.kathara.org/
6. Kathará as a Service. https://github.com/uniba-ktr/KaaS

7. Kathará Images. https://github.com/uniba-ktr/kathara_images

8. Mininet. https://mininet.org/

9. ONOS Open Network Operating System. https://opennetworking.org/onos/

10. Open vSwitch. https://www.openvswitch.org/

11. sFlow-RT. https://sflow-rt.com/

12. Ahmad, S., Mir, A.H.: Scalability, consistency, reliability and security in SDN controllers: a survey of diverse SDN controllers. J. Netw. Syst. Manag. **29**(1), 9 (2021). ISSN 1064-7570, 1573-7705, https://doi.org/10.1007/s10922-020-09575-4

13. Ahuja, N., Singal, G., Mukhopadhyay, D., Kumar, N.: Automated DDOS attack detection in software defined networking. J. Netw. Comput. Appl. **187**, 103108 (2021). ISSN 10848045, https://doi.org/10.1016/j.jnca.2021.103108

14. Aslam, N., Srivastava, S., Gore, M.M.: ONOS flood defender: an intelligent approach to mitigate DDoS attack in SDN. Trans. Emerg. Telecommun. Technol. **33**(9), e4534 (2022). ISSN 2161-3915, https://doi.org/10.1002/ett.4534

15. Bawany, N.Z., Shamsi, J.A., Salah, K.: DDoS attack detection and mitigation using SDN: methods, practices, and solutions. Arab. J. Sci. Eng. **42**(2), 425–441 (2017). ISSN 2193-567X, 2191-4281, https://doi.org/10.1007/s13369-017-2414-5

16. Bouras, C., Kollia, A., Papazois, A.: Teaching network security in mobile 5G using ONOS SDN controller. In: 2017 Ninth International Conference on Ubiquitous and Future Networks (ICUFN), pp. 465–470, IEEE, Milan (2017). ISBN 978-1-5090-4749-9, https://doi.org/10.1109/ICUFN.2017.7993828

17. Dantas Silva, F.S., Silva, E., Neto, E.P., Lemos, M., Venancio Neto, A.J., Esposito, F.: A taxonomy of DDoS attack mitigation approaches featured by SDN technologies in IoT scenarios. Sensors **20**(11), 3078 (2020). ISSN 1424-8220, https://doi.org/10.3390/s20113078

18. Das, S., Sarac, K.: Practical labs for teaching SDN security. J. Colloquium Inf. Syst. Secur. Educ. **10**(1), 7 (Mar 2023), ISSN 2641-4554, 2641-4546, https://doi.org/10.53735/cisse.v10i1.166

19. Dayal, N., Srivastava, S.: Analyzing behavior of DDoS attacks to identify DDoS detection features in SDN. In: 2017 9th International Conference on Communication Systems and Networks (COMSNETS), pp. 274–281, IEEE, Bengaluru, India (2017), ISBN 978-1-5090-4250-0, https://doi.org/10.1109/COMSNETS.2017.7945387

20. Dong, S., Abbas, K., Jain, R.: A survey on distributed denial of service (DDoS) attacks in SDN and cloud computing environments. IEEE Access **7**, 80813–80828 (2019). ISSN 2169-3536, https://doi.org/10.1109/ACCESS.2019.2922196

21. Eliyan, L.F., Di Pietro, R.: DoS and DDoS attacks in software defined networks: a survey of existing solutions and research challenges. Future Gener. Comput. Syst. **122**, 149–171 (2021). ISSN 0167739X, https://doi.org/10.1016/j.future.2021.03.011

22. Fuertes, W., Tunala, A., Moncayo, R., Meneses, F., Toulkeridis, T.: Software-based platform for education and training of DDoS attacks using virtual networks. In: 2017 International Conference on Software Security and Assurance (ICSSA), pp. 94–99, IEEE, Altoona, PA (2017). ISBN 978-1-5386-4808-7, https://doi.org/10.1109/ICSSA.2017.19

23. Großmann, M., Le, D.T.: Visualization of Network Emulation Enabled by Kathará. https://doi.org/10.25972/OPUS-32218

24. Hamarshe, A., Ashqar, H.I., Hamarsheh, M.: Detection of DDoS Attacks in Software Defined Networking Using Machine Learning Models (2023). https://doi.org/10.48550/ARXIV.2303.06513, publisher: arXiv Version Number: 1

25. Kreutz, D., Ramos, F.M.V., Esteves Verissimo, P., Esteve Rothenberg, C., Azodol-molky, S., Uhlig, S.: Software-defined networking: a comprehensive survey. Proc. IEEE **103**(1), 14–76 (2015). ISSN 0018-9219, 1558-2256, https://doi.org/10.1109/JPROC.2014.2371999, http://ieeexplore.ieee.org/document/6994333/

26. Myneni, S., Chowdhary, A., Huang, D., Alshamrani, A.: SmartDefense: a distributed deep defense against DDoS attacks with edge computing. Comput. Netw. **209**, 108874 (2022). ISSN 13891286, https://doi.org/10.1016/j.comnet.2022.108874

27. Rahman, A., Islam, M.J., Band, S.S., Muhammad, G., Hasan, K., Tiwari, P.: Towards a blockchain-SDN-based secure architecture for cloud computing in smart industrial IoT. Digital Commun. Netw. **9**(2), 411–421 (2023). ISSN 23528648, https://doi.org/10.1016/j.dcan.2022.11.003

28. Sahoo, K.S., et al.: An evolutionary SVM model for DDOS attack detection in software defined networks. IEEE Access **8**, 132502–132513 (2020). ISSN 2169-3536, https://doi.org/10.1109/ACCESS.2020.3009733

29. Scott-Hayward, S., Natarajan, S., Sezer, S.: A survey of security in software defined networks. IEEE Commun. Surv. Tutorials **18**(1), 623–654 (2016). ISSN 1553-877X, https://doi.org/10.1109/COMST.2015.2453114

30. Singh, J., Behal, S.: Detection and mitigation of DDoS attacks in SDN: a comprehensive review, research challenges and future directions. Comput. Sci. Rev. **37**, 100279 (2020). ISSN 15740137, https://doi.org/10.1016/j.cosrev.2020.100279

31. Sultana, N., Chilamkurti, N., Peng, W., Alhadad, R.: Survey on SDN based network intrusion detection system using machine learning approaches. Peer-to-Peer Netw. Appl. **12**(2), 493–501 (2019). ISSN 1936-6442, 1936-6450, https://doi.org/10.1007/s12083-017-0630-0

32. Yungaicela-Naula, N.M., Vargas-Rosales, C., Perez-Diaz, J.A.: SDN-based architecture for transport and application layer DDoS attack detection by using machine and deep learning. IEEE Access **9**, 108495–108512 (2021). ISSN 2169-3536, https://doi.org/10.1109/ACCESS.2021.3101650

Information Security in Supply Chains

Scared? Prepared? Toward a Ransomware Incident Response Scenario

Maximilian Greiner[1]([✉])(ID), Judith Strussenberg[3](ID), Andreas Seiler[1,2,3,4,5](ID),
Stefan Hofbauer[1,2,3,4,5](ID), Michael Schuster[1,2,3,4,5](ID), Damian Stano[1,2,3,4,5](ID),
Günter Fahrnberger[4](ID), Stefan Schauer[5](ID), and Ulrike Lechner[3](ID)

[1] University of the Bundeswehr Munich, Neubiberg, Germany
maximilian.greiner@unibw.de
[2] SBCF Cie, Munich, Germany
[3] Lechwerke AG, Augsburg, Germany
[4] University of Hagen, Hagen, Germany
[5] AIT, Vienna, Austria

Abstract. Individuals, organizations, and supply chains must increase
the level of preparedness in response to a cyber incident. This article
is part of a larger research initiative that designs a process framework,
playbooks, serious games, and simulations to prepare for a ransomware
incident with the scenario being common ground. Drawing on a Design
Science Research approach, we use 11 interviews, short cases, four real-
world cases, and cross-case analysis to design a logistics domain scenario
highlighting the business, actor, infrastructure, and threat view. A discussion of the design rationale and the next steps concludes the article.

Keywords: Cybersecurity · Incident response · Ransomware ·
Scenario analysis

1 Introduction

A ransomware sends its notice. The alarm bell rings. What now? Typically, this
stage is considered a point beyond which intervention may be too late. The
increasing prevalence of ransomware attacks has focused on the critical importance of effective incident response, particularly in the context of community
services and critical infrastructure [33]. As these essential sectors, encompassing
healthcare, education, public administration, or logistics, increasingly cross digital borders, integrating more deeply with technology, their susceptibility to such
cyber threats increases [5,27]. The ability of ransomware to disrupt services and
critical infrastructures can have dire consequences on the availability of products and services, the risk to lives, and long-term consequences on privacy or on
financial stability and reputation of companies [37].

Ransomware, a type of malware, incapacitates a user's personal devices, computer, or data. Criminals progressively use it to generate income through extortion or for geopolitical purposes [26]. Statistics show an increase in attacks by

F. Phillipson et al. (Eds.): I4CS 2024, CCIS 2109, pp. 289–320, 2024.
https://doi.org/10.1007/978-3-031-60433-1_17

73% in 2023 [6]. Over the next few years, the threat of ransomware is going to persist. Increasing the level of preparedness helps prevent ransomware attacks or mitigate the consequences. In 2020, a German municipal drinking water and energy supplier fell victim to a hacker attack. Around 500 GB of customer and employee data was stolen and the ransom demand was in the tens of millions. The attack was not even targeted, but resulted from a widespread phishing campaign: an employee opened an email with a malicious attachment, in non-compliance with internal guidelines. Investigations revealed that the attack was only possible because the IT infrastructure was configured so that all employees could open executable macros [24]. As a second example, we refer to an incident in 2023. A ransomware encrypted internal systems at a municipal IT service provider in Germany. More than 100 municipalities could no longer operate their IT systems and special processes hosted by this service provider for months [4]. An unpatched vulnerability in the VPN solution in conjunction with a lack of two-factor authentication (2FA) is a probable gateway for attackers[35]. These two examples illustrate that technical measures and an effective incident response might have mitigated the impact to customers and society as a whole. These two examples illustrate that small vulnerabilities might have intense consequences. This illustrates a demand for immediate and effective incident response mechanisms and a forward-thinking approach that prepares organizations.

This article aims to define a scenario to facilitate the design of serious games, playbooks, simulations, and process frameworks for incident response, specifically incident response in the case of ransomware. The key to such instruments is understanding business models, risks, IT security and incident response capabilities, and the willingness to adopt industrial standards as much as possible. We did 11 interviews, condensed them into 11 short cases, compiled an additional four short cases on ransomware incidents from the literature, and did a cross-case analysis. This is the empirical basis for a reference scenario in the logistics sector. We develop a novel scenario format and analyze its options for further design activities toward serious games and process frameworks.

The article is organized as follows. Our theoretical background, consisting of an analysis of the state of the art in ransomware foundations and incident response frameworks is delineated in Sect. 2. Section 3 presents our research design. Section 4 introduces the investigated organizations and their experiences with ransomware attacks. Section 5 presents the cross-case analysis, giving an impression of what to expect in the event of an incident. Section 6 presents our scenario outline taking into account the initial situation in the event of a ransomware attack, the personas, and possible attack vectors. In Sect. 7, we outline our short cases on ransomware incidents. Finally, Sect. 8 summarizes the main findings and provides an outlook for future work.

2   Theoretical Background and State of the Art

This study aims to provide scenarios to guide the development of serious games and process frameworks that specifically address the needs of small and medium companies and other organizations to prepare for a ransomware attack. Our approach is to use established frameworks, techniques, and technologies in the field for uptake of our results and compatibility with existing cybersecurity structures. With this strategy, we rely on previous experience in creating Serious Games for cybersecurity for practitioners [38].

2.1 Ransomware

Ransomware has evolved from simply encrypting files and demanding a ransom to now posing more threats, as stated in the annual report of the Bundesamt für Sicherheit in der Informationstechnik (BSI) from 2021 [19]. In addition to encrypting digital assets, ransomware threats to exfiltrate data, including business information that can be sold or used for extortion, as well as sensitive personal information that can be used for other criminal purposes. There are examples where malware rather destroys than encrypts data, making assets unrecoverable even when a ransom is paid [19].

Victims of ransomware attacks can be categorized as targeted or opportunistic victims. Targeted victims are often attacked through spear phishing or supply chain attacks, while opportunistic victims are mainly compromised through exploits of unknown or recently discovered vulnerabilities or broader phishing campaigns [34].

2.2 Incident Response

The landscape of information security and threats changed over the last three to two decades. Whereas the primal goal in the past was to build up barriers to prevent intrusions, the information security community shifted to the Paradigm of /"Prevention is ideal, but detection is a must./".

The SANS Institute defines the incident response process as a cycle between the phases of preparation, identification, containment, elimination, recovery, and lessons learned [21]. Another commonly used model for incident response by the National Institute of Standards and Technology (NIST) describes the four phases. Preparation, detection and analysis, removal and recovery of contaminants and post-incident activity. Within the NIST SP800-61r2 Computer Security Handling Guide [14], the definition of Roles, Policies, and Procedures for incident response is advised. In addition, different stakeholders such as legal, communication, data protection, and others should be taken into account.

In addition to organizational readiness and trained staff, incident response requires extensive technical preparation. The setup of a log infrastructure and the use of EDR, IDS, and SIEM systems are just a few important examples of security measures that provide valuable information in incident response.

Other de facto standards or frameworks are the Cyber Kill Chain and MITRE ATT&CK framework. These describe the different intrusion steps and adversary tactics, tools, techniques, and procedures used by the attackers.

The MITRE ATT&CK framework [23] is the de facto standard for structuring attack vectors and the techniques, tools and procedures of each step. It is regularly updated. BSI provides guidelines that focus on security measures to prevent ransomware and emphasizes technology to support the containment and eradication of malware [11].

The incident response in the ransomware case may have to deal with many actors and impact on business and society. Therefore, in the ransomware case, the incident response can take advantage of cybersecurity, crisis management, and business continuity. The ÜBIT framework defines three types of exercises to prepare for a crisis situation: training, testing, and experimentation [15]. ÜBIT borrows several concepts from and tailors them to scenario-based command post-exercises. Several larger exercises have targeted cyber-incidents. Among them are Lükex 2023 and 2011 [10] or Cyber Coalition as NATO's cyber exercise series [25]. These exercises represent a huge effort and require resources and capabilities. For the more mundane cases of incidents in smaller- or medium-sized companies or organizations, there is a lack of guidance and instruments that can be used "out of the box" or adapted to a specific case relatively easily.

There is an understanding of what is desirable, feasible, and necessary in incident response. Attribution to specific threat actors is not the main focus when dealing with ransomware, as prosecution is often not feasible. Using Cyber Threat Intelligence information of ransomware groups/personas like their used tools, techniques, and procedures (TTPs) and indicators of compromise (IOCs) is helpful to tailor incident response to a specific case. Some criminal groups work in organized teams, with different groups responsible for compromising networks, maintaining access, and delivering the ransomware [8].

3   Research Design

The Design Science Research (DSR) framework, according to Hevner et al. [16] guides our research. Following DSR, we incorporate business needs (people, organizations, and technology) and applicable knowledge (foundations and methodologies from theory) in an iterative cycle for the design of our artifact, the scenario. For the analysis part, we employ the informed argument method [16] and use the expertise of the authors team and the project consortium. The justification of the design is done through various empirical methods: an analysis of the state-of-the-art, case studies based on interviews, and a cross-case analysis.

The first element of the research design is the state-of-the-art analysis of ransomware incidents with an identification of the main resources for incident response. The second element is a series of 11 short cases on organizations with their experiences with ransomware, the expectations on incident response in case of a cyber incident, and the security measures in place. We compile from the literature 4 cases on ransomware. A cross case analysis short cases from the interview study and the cases from the literature provides insight into preparedness and expectations. We conducted an interview study (n = 11) between June 2023 and December 2023 with Chief Execution Officers (CEOs) and IT security experts (see Table 1). The interviews took between 45 and 90 min. The interviews were conducted under strict anonymity. The transcribed interviews were analyzed according to Strauss and Corbin [32]. The codes were based on experiences with a ransomware incident, important IT security measures, and expectations toward a response in a cyber incident.

Table 1. Interview partners at a glance

Role	Industry	Time
Consultant	System House 1	June 2023
Board Member	Security Solutions Company	July 2023
Department Head	Pharmaceutical Company	July 2023
SIRT-Team Member	Energy Supplier	August 2023
CEO	Logistics Company 4	August 2023
CEO	Logistics Company 1	September 2023
CEO	Logistics Company 3	September 2023
CEO	Logistics Company 2	October 2023
Security Manager	Austrian Bank	October 2023
CIO	System House 2	December 2023
Director	Defense and Space Company	December 2023

The review of the state-of-the-art, interviews with short cases, real-world cases, and cross-case analysis are the basis for designing the scenario. This scenario is validated by the research consortium and by the authors themselves. The scenario is a fictional scenario composed of four views: business view, actor view, infrastructure view, and threat view. This scenario structure borrows from the eXperience method [36], the KRITIS case study series [22] and guidance on the Case Study Method [9]. For the design of the scenario, we use techniques from reference modeling according to Fettke and Loos [12]. The claim is that the scenario represents a typical business model with the main elements of the IT and physical infrastructure, the relevant actors, and a typical threat vector. Logistics was decided as the domain for this first scenario. The strategy we follow is to have reference models with typical elements. Case analysis demonstrates that more efforts are needed in incident response, even for average ransomware attack vectors. Although the ransomware vector is "typical", the actor view provides all relevant roles in incident response with the goal of demonstrating what is necessary in incident response.

Throughout the research process, we adhere to industrial standards in cyber incidents as much as possible, as previous work in the cybersecurity domain to raise awareness indicates that this is crucial for the relevance of our research on cybersecurity concepts and technologies to practitioners [22,38].

4   Organizations and Their Experiences with Ransomware

This section presents a brief description of our interview partners, a summary of the important security measures, experiences with ransomware or other cyber incidents, and expectations of what would happen in such an event (Table 2).

Table 2. Interview cases and abbreviations

Abbreviation	Interview Partner
SH1	System House 1
SH2	System House 2
AB1	Austrian Bank
SS1	Security Solutions Company
ES1	Energy Supplier
DS1	Defense and Space Company
CP1	Pharmaceutical Company
LO1	Logistics Company 1
LO2	Logistics Company 2
LO3	Logistics Company 3
LO4	Logistics Company 4

4.1 System House 1 (SH1)

The organization is a modern system house that designs and develops software to facilitate digital change. Data-driven solutions and omnichannel business describe some aspects of the business model. Particular to this organization is a high level of transparency. Each organizational unit has a limited number of employees and a high level of independence of these organizational units. Although they have one cloud infrastructure in common, all units are independent regarding financial and IT security implementations. High professional standards of employees and a high level of individual responsibility distinguish the organization's culture.

The interview partner is a consultant, and it seems that incident response would be very individual - depending on the skills and knowledge of individuals and units. His concerns are that newly established units need to step up the security levels to take out insurance policies and that IT security and incident response are not a priority at the global level. The external cloud service provider is responsible for the security of the cloud, albeit it is unknown to the interview partner what measures are being implemented. The employees themselves handle cybersecurity of personal devices, and they decide which software they install and use. There is no defined end-point security.

The interview partner expects that if ransomware affects a laptop, a new laptop will be procured immediately, and all accounts and data of current projects will be installed within one day. In case a customer has a ransomware incident, all interaction with the partner would be stopped, assuming that the customer would not prioritize the development of new solutions in such a case.

4.2 Security Solutions Company (SS1)

The German company, with around 50 employees, creates security solutions and sells innovative software products focusing on endpoint security. Its customers are companies in the private sector, small and medium enterprises (SMEs), large companies, KRITIS companies, public authorities, and, above all, public authorities with security tasks. All products are available worldwide and are offered in multiple languages. All software products are developed and produced in-house in Germany without the need for acquisitions. The company's software is used on over one million workstations daily. Our interview partner, the CEO and owner of the company is active in the security industry in various roles as a spokesperson for security and digital sovereignty. The company is active in research and very active in public relations. It makes an active contribution to placing the topic of IT security on the political agenda and interacts with important authorities.

The company has a strict separation between the daily application and the development environment. The usable applications are limited. A virtual environment must be used for video conferencing or other non-approved applications. Several backups with different solutions are in the company, and a specially secured network for central backups. Further backups are georedundant at various locations in Germany. Recruitment is also viewed from a security perspective: There are no job advertisements, but the company actively searches for suitable candidates in order to rule out risks. These hand-picked candidates are also subjected to a security check. The development environments used are at least five years or older, assuming all vulnerabilities have been identified and less patches are necessary.

The security solutions company has not yet had a ransomware incident in its own company. There was one suspected case, which was identified within minutes and the device was isolated. However, the company has been asked in the past to support a customer with a ransomware incident and to analyze whether executable, potentially infected code can be found in the data that was affected by the ransomware.

4.3   System House 2 (SH2)

The IT system house has been active in Austria for over 20 years and is one of the leading e-commerce providers. Represented in all regions, it supports its customers locally with over 550 IT experts. In addition to traditional system house topics, the company also has expertise in IoT, cloud computing, blockchain data engineering and data science with machine learning.

Regarding its security, the ISO-certified IT system house is increasingly focusing on preventive measures. These include up-to-date emergency manuals and comprehensive risk management, including risk analysis, in order to be prepared for failures and be able to react appropriately. Preventive measures also include comprehensive monitoring and tracking to detect attacks as early as possible.

There is an emergency team that is trained to respond appropriately to ransomware incidents. This has also proven to be relatively effective in stopping attacks at an early stage and minimizing their impact. The IT infrastructure is considered in a differentiated manner for each specialist area, and the selection of on-premise, cloud or hybrid solutions is based on various factors, including an individual risk analysis. In order to stay informed about cyber threats, a platform has been developed that collects, consolidates and prioritizes information from numerous sources. This includes reports from around 6.000–7.000 system manufacturers and daily information from CERT.

4.4   Chemical and Pharmaceutical Company (CP1)

The interview partner leads an incident response team with several years of cybersecurity experience in the defense and telecommunications sectors. The organization operates internationally and produces chemicals, pharmaceuticals, and agricultural products. The interview partner has some experience in incidents, such as an insider attack by a system administrator who took hard disks out of a server home. No personal data has been involved, and there have been no interruptions of mission-critical services. The company has not yet had any experience with ransomware itself. However, a partner company was attacked by ransomware, and large parts of its infrastructure were encrypted. This partner company manages two warehouse management systems at the company's sites. Due to the cyberattack, support was unavailable for weeks, meaning that maintenance would only have been possible to a limited extent. Until then, the company did not have administrator rights to these systems and this was subsequently changed so that it could now administer the systems itself in an emergency.

The company attaches great importance to information security and preventive information security is a high priority. The central element of security in preparation for a cyber incident is a consistent backup strategy. In addition, the level of security is constantly being increased: whitelisting of applications and Secure DNS, endpoint security, an active SIEM, and physical sovereignty over the data are key concepts in information security within the group. As a result, there is also a preference for on-premise solutions over cloud solutions, as long as these are offered by the manufacturers.

Measures of modern information security management such as risk management, training concepts adapted to requirements, separation and virtualization, monitoring, and single sign-on continue to be implemented. The loyal employees in IT security, who contribute to improving corporate security with their own ideas, are also praised in this context. To make employees more aware of the topic in general, consideration is being given to adding the topic of information security to the annual occupational safety training courses.

4.5   Energy Supplier (ES1)

Electricity, heat, solar energy, and e-mobility are key topics for the company. The company is part of an energy supply group. It is a medium-sized company in this sector with a regional focus. With the current situation in the energy market, the price fluctuations, and the new offers for climate neutrality and an ecologically sustainable supply of energy, the company's business model is changing, which is not unusual for this sector. The company is active in research and is also represented in industry associations and UPKRITIS. As a company classified as a critical infrastructure, the energy supplier implements the requirements of the IT Security Act and the IT Security Act 2.0. In organizational terms, it has an information security department and an incident response team. As part of a group, it can use a cyberrange for training and draw on the expertise of the group-wide SIRT team and CERT. In addition, all employees undergo training and there are penetration tests. Overall, the measures are at a high, industry-standard level and are constantly being expanded. IT and OT are separated to protect the networks, with the help of data diodes for particularly critical networks. There are also data hubs for transferring data between the networks and two active directories: one for IT and one for the OT area of the company. There is a group-wide backup concept. The backups are separated from the network, are continuously monitored and are stored georedundantly. There are backup hard disks for all OT clients, which would be used to restore the configuration from the backup in the event of a ransomware incident.

The energy supplier has no experience with major ransomware incidents. Malware, including ransomware, sometimes occurs on a workstation. Such incidents are treated as a standard case in the company's incident response process.

4.6 Austrian Bank (AB1)

The regional bank is organized as a cooperative with a wide catchment area. The bank focuses on the core areas of deposits, loans and payment transactions. In the service business, the bank's portfolio consists of consumer loans, insurance, securities, leasing, building society savings, and other business areas. The bank sees itself as the principal bank for customers in the region and therefore places a strong focus on the branch network as a central sales channel. Advice and relationship orientation play a major role here. The bank has already received several awards for this in the past. In its digital offering, the bank attaches great importance to ease of use and high performance. The bank has decided to outsource the computing center to an internationally renowned service provider, and the bank itself has a team for strategic decisions in all questions related to security and in increasing the security posture.

Among the important security measures that the bank has taken to protect itself from ransomware attacks are solid backups that are regularly created and separated from the main systems. Also important are up-to-date patch management and actively managing the detection of ransomware attacks. As a bank, there is also a focus on the security of the customer side. A phishing takedown service is used here, as well as monitoring the bank's own logos in the major app stores and analyzing bank logs, especially for larger amounts of money. Overall, it can be observed that attackers are constantly developing new fraud methods and so the challenge for the bank is to keep pace with these methods. In 2022, for example, many activation codes for two-factor authentication sent by post were intercepted. This led to a change in this procedure.

The bank states that a service provider that operates banks' alarm systems has fallen victim to a cyber attack. A professional hacker group had encrypted its IT systems. Thanks to backups, the data could be restored and there was no data loss. Operations were restored. The service provider reacted to the incident as follows: There was a password change, updating of the security software, regular checks of the computers and complete re-installation of the computers. Since then, there has been increased organizational vigilance concerning the service provider's communication, especially in connection with invoices, but also with visits by the service provider's service technicians.

4.7   Logistics Company 3 (LO3)

Logistics company 3 is active throughout Germany in transporting part and full loads. The forwarding company has approximately 100 employees and an annual turnover of 10 million euros. It also offers procurement and distribution logistics, transportation of hazardous goods, and empties logistics.

The logistics company relies on an IT infrastructure that includes central servers that are redundantly mirrored to ensure high availability. The security measures include a firewall at the network and application level as well as a web-based IT architecture based on virtual machines. However, it should be noted that there is currently no cyber insurance in place, which indicates a need for optimization in IT security, particularly regarding protection against ransomware and other cyber threats. The logistics company has outsourced all IT services to an external service provider. A contact person is available around the clock. The freight forwarder also obtains information about current threats from the external service provider.

The logistics company has had no experience with ransomware to date. In the last five years, one computer had to be reinstalled due to a spam email being clicked on. However, this had no impact on business operations or partners. In response to the incident, a firewall was implemented, and employees were given training on how to deal with potential threats.

4.8   Logistics Company 2 (LO2)

Logistics Company 2 focuses on procurement and distribution logistics as well as national and international network and cargo transportation. In addition, the company offers consulting, planning, and implementation of inbound processes, as well as the realization of warehouse and logistics projects. Process-optimized IT system landscapes as in-house solutions are just as much a part of the business as the range of telematics solutions for shipment monitoring.

Logistics Company 2 always tries to compare itself with the industry in its security measures. It has a mixture of in-house IT specialists and external IT service providers. The IT for operations and accounting systems are both located on separate servers in an external data center. The company has cyber insurance with corresponding support measures, including backup systems for data protection, for example. The insurer also provides service providers as a process plan in the event of a cyber attack. An action plan or scenario plan is available in the event of a crisis, but this has not yet been rehearsed with the employees. The most drastic effect of an attack would be on the warehouse management systems in logistics, as they rely on IT to track where something has been stored. For this reason, manual options have been set up here and the worst-case scenario has been played out.

The company also states that it has no experience with ransomware, but a virus-related system failure eight to ten years ago triggered a security discussion that continues to impact today. Among other things, the company switched from its own servers to a data center, involved an IT service provider, trained its employees and tried to keep abreast of current threats and the state of the art in its own industry in various ways.

4.9   Logistics Company 1 (LO1)

With an annual turnover of around EUR 20 million, Logistics Company 1 specializes in transport management, network logistics, and warehousing. The company offers Europe-wide general cargo shipments, part and full loads, with a focus on Italy. In addition to overland trucking and logistics outsourcing as core competencies, Logistics Company 1 handles sea and air freight shipments. As an external partner, the company also offers the individual implementation and optimization of customers' logistics processes.

For Logistics Company 1, access control and data mirroring are particularly important in defending against ransomware attacks. By applying these measures, the company hopes to minimize the impact of a ransomware attack and restore data more quickly. The company's IT is independent and forms a stand-alone solution within the Group; data storage is also decentralized. The company is considering taking out cyber insurance, although it should be noted that the insurer does not offer any supportive measures to mitigate losses in the event of an attack. There are no specific catalogs of measures for emergencies and BCM or crisis management plans.

The Logistics Company 1 states that it has no experience with ransomware. There have been a few incidents where suspicious emails that may have contained ransomware were detected, but these were blocked by the firewall and did not affect the company.

4.10   Logistics Company 4 (LO4)

Logistics Company 4, with nine sites and an annual turnover of around 60 million euros, offers its customers part and full loads as a comprehensive full service in national and international transport. The company offers transportation, project planning, handling, and trading of bulk goods and for the handling of tippers and silos, inland waterway transshipment with rail connection and storage areas. It offers also warehouse logistics from goods acceptance to warehousing and goods maintenance.

The company is taking various measures to increase its security level: There is a great awareness of the threat situation and the constant need to improve. An in-house IT company was purchased to implement this. The company operates three independent servers that are geographically decentralized. The data is mirrored daily. Cloud solutions are avoided as far as possible and regular employee training is carried out. In addition, measurements of various factors, such as the utilization of firewalls, data streams and email traffic are used to detect and ward off attacks in good time. So far, two cyber attacks have been successfully fended off in this way. As a further protective measure, the IT infrastructure is only familiar to a small circle of people.

The plan to improve the company's technical infrastructure envisages setting up a redundant IT structure over the next six years to be able to react more quickly to incidents.

Logistics Company 4 cites its own experience with ransomware: in the 2017 incident, a phishing email was received that led to the encryption of an employee's notebook. The attackers demanded a ransom of around €500. After careful consideration, it was decided to dispose of the affected notebook as purchasing a new notebook proved to be the more economical solution to restore business continuity.

4.11   Defense and Space (DS1)

The interview partner is a high-ranked manager of defense and space. The organization works in the defense sector and provides security solutions and services for its customers. Products include communication infrastructure certified for classified communications. The organization adheres to the highest security standards as it can be expected from such an organization. The organization has little experience with ransomware. The few cases that did occur were very limited and could not spread within the organisation thanks to the measures taken. Other company departments would have expertise in incident response and support customers in incident response. The organization follows competitors with similar profiles who have experience with incidents to improve their security. Elements of the security measures include endpoint security, backup strategies, and strict separation of networks, particularly for product developments. The interview partner recently had an incident with a laptop. Endpoint security locked the computer on a business trip—as if someone would have tried to break into the computer. The forensics and security team in the organization was able to determine that this locking of the computer was due to a software glitch. Given, the security levels of the company, it is acceptable not to be able to work on the laptop for a couple of days until such an incident is resolved and the cause of the incident is identified and resolved.

5   Real-World Cases on Ransomware Incidents

Ransomware incidents, vulnerabilities, attack vectors and incident response are the topics of four short case studies that are compiled from open sources. Note that all these cases have been discussed publicly. These cases are meant to give an impression on what to expect.

Table 3. Real-world cases and abbreviations

Abbreviation	Interview Partner
AS1	Aluminum Supplier
CS1	Container Shipping Company
CC1	Computer Company
OD1	Original Design Manufacturer

5.1 Aluminum Supplier (AS1)

In March 2019, one of the world's largest aluminum suppliers was hit by the LockerGoga ransomware both in the company's corporate and control system networks. Although the ransomware attack did not directly affect the control systems, the incident still serves as a case study for the impact a ransomware attack can have on industrial companies as they rely on IT systems.

The ransomware rendered all IT systems unusable by encrypting user data, disabling network adapters, and changing login credentials. No ransom was paid. The company hired cybersecurity consultants to redesign and restore their networks. To maintain operations, the company worked manually and was transparent throughout recovery. This had a positive impact on its reputation.

Operational staff at the company's facilities were the first to notice the cyberattack, as their computer systems were rendered unusable. Frontline staff informed headquarters of their system outages. The company assessed the extent to which its internal networks were infected and decided to shut down and isolate its entire IT infrastructure to prevent access by the attackers and prevent further damage. The company then switched to running operations manually and without IT system support, which slowed down or even brought operations to a halt. Staff began pulling reference guides, manuals, and documentation out of filing cabinets, calling in retired employees, and working everything by hand for weeks before they were able to gradually get the IT equipment back up and running. It took the company several months to be fully operational again.

5.2 Container Shipping Company (CS1)

A large container shipping company was hit: Unknown people used encryption software to temporarily paralyze computer systems. The shipping company was one of the victims of a large-scale hacker attack that hit several companies in different countries. The campaign was aimed mainly at targets in Ukraine, as it spread through the Ukrainian accounting software MeDoc.

The Trojan, deliberately called NotPetya, is classified as significantly more dangerous than WannaCry by the BSI. It disguises itself as blackmail software and it deletes data instead of merely encrypting data. IT experts suspected that the attackers were probably not after a ransom but rather sabotage. This was supported by the observation that the payment process was relatively complicated and insecure, untypical for ransomware [31].

The company announced on Twitter that it had been the victim of an attack. The operations were slowed and came to a standstill mainly until all data was restored, which took weeks [17]. It took several months for the company to fully be operational again. The company recovered from the NotPetya ransomware incident by reinstalling more than 4000 servers, 45000 PCs, and 2500 applications over the course of ten days [1]. The cyber attack caused disruptions to container shipping for weeks, and the company announced that it expects the damage to be between 200 and 300 million dollars.

This case illustrates that data may not be recoverable, and again the magnitude of resources a recovery from an incident takes. Note that this incident could have been prevented with a PAM solution and micro-segmentation.

5.3   Computer Company (CC1)

In March 2021, a ransomware group announced on their data leak website that they had infiltrated a computer company and published some images of stolen files (financial spreadsheets, bank balance sheets, and bank communications) as proof.

The first ransomware claim was $50 million, and the ransomware group presented a link to the data, which at that time was secret. The attackers offered a 20% discount if payment was made quickly. In return, the ransomware group would provide a decryptor, a vulnerability report, and deletion of the extracted data [3]. The group announced that the claim would increase to 100 million USD after a couple of days [13]. It seems that the group targeted a Microsoft Exchange Server [3] and Microsoft rolled out critical security patches to fix exchange vulnerabilities. The exploitation of these vulnerabilities is attributed to many groups, including those located in China.

This case concerns the height of ransomware claims, the number of potential targets when mainstream IT technology is used, extortion methods, and the attribution challenge.

5.4   Original Design Manufacturer (OD1)

In April 2021, a ransomware group launched an attack on an Original Design Manufacturer (ODM), a supplier for Apple, followed by a demand for 50 million USD by the deadline, or USD 100 million after the deadline. ODM is located in Taiwan and is one of the 200 major Apple suppliers. Apple is a huge target for ransomware operators, as is any company with which they work [28].

The ransomware operators threaten Apple by releasing the company's future product designs, coinciding with the Spring Loaded event, at which Apple announces new products. The manufacturer officially confirmed the incident on its website and stated that it had no material impact on company operations [18]. The company stated that only a few internal servers have been affected.

In parallel, the Biden administration announced plans to protect the country's critical infrastructure from cyberattacks and launched a 100-day initiative as a collaboration between government agencies and private companies.

This case is about the vulnerability of supply chains, particularly the vulnerabilities of the digital ecosystem and the difficulties of securing it. Apple was the target, while the incident targeted a supplier.

5.5   Summary and Analysis

The four short cases have been compiled from open sources. They illustrate what to expect: All kinds of organization can be victimized and exemplify the magnitude of interruptions in production and service provisioning. They show how aligned geopolitical questions, economic issues, the political agenda, and IT security measures must be. They demonstrate the range of vulnerabilities exploited and that paying the ransom is potentially not the biggest economic threat: data can be lost, business damage might be huge, and organizations and supply chains need to be secured. The magnitude of potential damage to the IT infrastructure, interruptions and damage, vulnerabilities exploited, and resources differ from the short cases from the interviews.

6   Case Analysis: Expectations, Innovations, and Questions

This section presents an analysis of the cases from three perspectives. The first analysis compares expectations regarding ransomware incidents and their impact. We analyze the impact in terms of assets and the impact on assets. We look forward to innovations, that is, innovative concepts and technologies, and here we analyze the cases based on the project expertise.

The graphic outlined in Fig. 1 provides an overview of the different industries across our interview partners as well as short cases. The majority of short cases (both from interviews and open sources) belong to logistics (5 appearances), followed by system house companies (3 appearances), industry (2 appearances), security solutions (1 appearance), energy suppliers (1 appearance), defense and space (1 appearance) and pharmaceuticals (1 appearance).

6.1   Expectations

This section captures the topics our interview partners associate with ransomware or other cyber incidents. We asked the interview partners about their expectations of a ransomware attack. What would be the vulnerability to be exploited, what would the damage be, and how long would it take to recover? Note that none of the respondents fears a long-term outage.

Differences can be observed above all between production and logistics and purely operational areas. In the worst-case scenario, Logistics Company 3 (LO3) anticipates a day of data loss for logistics data. It would also be necessary to rebuild the entire infrastructure. The CEO concludes, based on the mix of cloud and on-premise solutions in his systems, that the cloud infrastructure does not depend on on-premise IT. "In the event of an incident, partner companies that

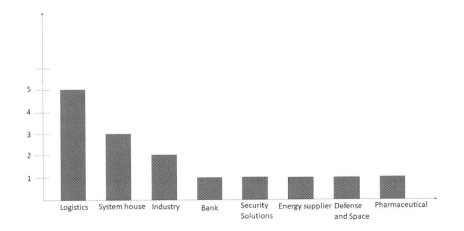

Fig. 1. Short cases across industries

have experienced something similar would need about a day to get back to normal," says the CEO of logistics company 1 (LO1).

"In the worst-case scenario, there would be no access to the systems," says the Managing Director of Logistics Company 2 (LO2) for his company in the event of a ransomware incident. He also sees that the different IT systems are affected to varying degrees. Contingency plans are in place for the forwarding software systems, which amount to manual control of orders. "An attack on warehouse management systems in logistics would be the most drastic, as they rely on IT to track where something has been stored. It is important to have backup solutions in place that can be implemented in good time."

In the event of a successful attack on a laptop as personal IT, the IT service provider's strategy (SH1) focuses on a quick and successful restart. "Burning the laptop" is favored here, that is, buying a new laptop on the market, installing it, and restoring access. As all company data is stored in the cloud, the employee expects to be fully operational after one working day.

The worst-case scenario for the Energy Supplier (ES1) would be a so-called "blackout," an uncontrolled and unforeseen power grid failure. The company does not consider this to be particularly critical. In the OT area, the machines can also be controlled manually or the operation can be started up. Although the operation is inefficient, it would supply its customers in the region with energy, as can be expected from a critical infrastructure. In the event of a large-scale ransomware incident, an external service company would step in, bring its IT, and set up a new, secure network. There is a contract for this.

The IT system house, which operates throughout Europe (SH2) assumes that it will not be able to directly fend off targeted attacks that are well-prepared and take a long time. "Instead, we rely on countermeasures to mitigate the effects. It is crucial to detect attacks at an early stage. That is why we carry out comprehensive monitoring and take irregularities seriously," says the company's CIO.

Expectations vary, and the interview partners do hardly have "first hand ransomware experience". They, however, have experiences from dealing with partners or observing competitors.

6.2   Innovations in Incident Response

This section deals with innovative measures observed among the respondents about cyberattacks. In addition to the known risks, this circumstance also allows companies to diversify their portfolio or to develop new market segments to help affected companies quickly, for example.

Table 4. Innovations and good practices in incident response

Interview	Description
SS1	Supporting a customer, who has been fallen a victim of ransomware with their own experience regarding ransomware.
SH2	Having its own emergency team that is trained to respond fast and effectively to ransomware incidents.
SH2	Development of a platform that collects, consolidates and prioritizes information from numerous sources, such as reports from system manufacturers and information from CERT.
ES1	Using a cyberrange for training on simulated ransomware attacks.
ES1	Separation of IT and OT network using data diodes so that a lateral movement from IT to OT is impossible.
ES1	Having backups separated from the network, continuously monitored and stored georedundant.
ES1	Backup hard disks for all OT clients used to restore the configuration from the backup in the event of a ransomware incident.
AB1	Phishing takedown service to take down phishing sites and social media brand infringements as well as fraud detection systems.
AB1	Password change, update of the security software, multiple scans on the computers as well as re-installation of computers, which have fallen victim of ransomware.
LO3	Obtaining information from current threats (IoC) from external service providers.
LO2	Mixture of in-house IT specialists and an external IT service provider.
LO2	Using a cyber insurance with corresponding support measures, which includes backup systems for data protection.
LO2	An action plan or scenario plan is available during a crisis.
LO4	Utilization of firewalls, analyzing data streams and E-Mail traffic to detect and ward of attacks.

Table 5. Use cases regarding innovations and good practices in incident response

Use case	Description
AB1	A service for online communication and for all relevant contact information online.
AB1	A service for proactive crisis management and alerting in emergency and crisis cases.
AB1	Offline emergency plans for different scenarios that can be pulled from the drawer.
LO1	Redundant telephone lines by different phone providers for up-and-running business.
LO1	Outsourced SIEM/SOC system that is supporting in case of a critical security incident.
LO1	Frequent Table Top exercises, crisis management exercises, and cybercrime resilience.
CC1	Outsourced Incident Response Retainer service with support in case of Ransomware.
CC1	Forensic support is needed to collect, analyze, and archive evidence in case of ransomware.
CC1	Clear attribution of cyberattacks based on IoCs from Threat Intelligence providers.
AS1	Escalation of security incidents based on security incident priority and urgency.
AS1	Separation of 1st Line and 2nd Line of Defense activities as a supervisory requirement.
AS1	Segmentation of IT & OT networks based on the Purdue model across different locations.

An example of this is Logistics Company 4 (LO4). It has a "task force" that could intervene immediately in a cyberattack and supply affected companies with software and hardware. However, according to the managing director, this offer is currently not being taken up, as customers would call specialized partners in the event of a crisis and not the freight forwarder. According to the managing director, some possible ways to support affected companies exist. However, he sees liability issues for his company as a factor inhibiting innovation, which is why such offers are not made. Nevertheless, the company is considering corresponding offers, such as supply chain assurance for the coming years, even if the concept is not yet clear and there is no marketable use case.

Overall, it can be observed that the actual crisis is not making companies more innovative, but rather causing them to fall back on conservative solutions, such as the use of pen and paper for order processing. This is offered by Logistics Companies 1 (LO1) and 3 (LO3), for example. This is despite the knowledge that this solution can only be used temporarily at best and requires human and financial resources to update the digital systems. Logistics Company 2 (LO2) points out that this is not even an option for certain areas of logistics, such as the just-in-time segment, due to its structure.

Several hypotheses can be put forward as to why, despite the apparent threat situation, the companies surveyed are only partially pushing ahead with innovations: A possible answer can certainly be seen in the low assessment of the impact of cyber attacks such as ransomware. Respondents tend to rate the impact of an attack much lower than statistics, the experience of practitioners in this field would suggest. Security gaps are therefore not ascribed to the existence-threatening effect they can have. As a result, many companies see little need for action. The measures taken are seen more as an undoubted cost factor than as a market advantage or even an innovative factor. At the same time, security is something that customers expect from companies and, therefore, cannot be sold as innovation unless it results in a new product.

6.3 The Questions

"The ransomware sends its notice. What now?" is the question that motivates this article and the research in the larger project context. This question is refined based on the analysis of the cases against the backdrop of the project participants' and authors' expertise as well as preliminary findings from serious game design [30]. This section is an analysis to identify questions to ask in preparation for a cyber incident—covering the whole spectrum of cybersecurity, detection, contain & eradication and recovery.

What preparations and resources are necessary for recovery in a given time frame? In interviews and short cases, we see a difference between expectations of how long identification, containment, eradication, and recovery take and the time frames published in the literature and the real-world cases. One day for a personal device, a couple of days for an organization. We state that an informed estimation of the resources is necessary: the time and computing power to decrypt data the ransomware has encrypted, the resources necessary to set up a new infrastructure and preserve the old one for forensic analysis, the resources necessary to set up new infrastructure to be sure that it is ransomware-free and safe to use, and the time necessary to recover all devices in the control systems and OT from their backup files. One question to ask is, "What needs to be prepared?" What resources in terms of computing power, storage capacity, and people are necessary in the case of an event to recover within a given time frame?

What are the criteria of done? This question came from other research activities and interviews for the cases. The topic was notably absent in most interviews: for the Defense and Space company and for the System house it was natural to identify the root cause of an incident—for the rest of the organizations resuming business seems to be the first priority. We argue that without identifying the root cause, the vulnerability persists and can be exploited at any time by the same actor or other actors. Note that (as described in Sect. 2) some actors would provide a vulnerability analysis once the ransom is paid. The ways a ransomware disguises and the way from the initial attack to persistence are manifold. It seems possible that ransomware can hardly be deleted or that it resides in backups. In the public discussion, it seems that ransomware waits for years after initial access before it becomes active or activated. In one of our cases mentioned, the laptop" was mentioned—a laptop that is infected can never be a trusted device, and the interviewee would not use it anymore and would rather destroy it than donate it to a charity. Searching for indicators of compromise can be tedious, and forensic analysis to certify that a network is safe takes months to complete and be handed over to partners and insurance companies, according to recent experiences from the author team. The ransomware notice is evidence, the absence of ransomware is more difficult to prove, and expectations of what can be done, say in a smaller case that is about to become routine, is difficult - the daily workload is in conflict with incident response and the extra time it takes, understanding of indicators of compromise may develop throughout actions and searching for indicators of compromise takes tooling, efforts, and capable incident responders. Clarifying the "criteria of ransomware-free again", the "criteria of done" is valuable: It takes burden and mental load from the immediate team of incident handlers and responders. It allows for the resume of business as usual with partners in the value chain.

What are the decisions to be made in incident response? The context of other research and state-of-the-art frameworks detail what needs to be done at a technical level: identification, containment, eradication, and recovery. All these are tasks at the technical level of incident response. Decisions need to be made about when to block the communication of malware with a Command-and-Control Server [29], whether to separate networks to block propagation into critical parts of the network, whether and what evidence needs to be secured for forensics, when to use the backup and discard the encrypted data and eventually if ransom needs to be paid and how far authorities, partners, and customers need to be informed. These decisions have consequences: blocking ransomware from its server might trigger encryption, warn the attackers, and trigger the ransomware to use "Plan B"—a new way to communicate with the C2 server and a higher ransom claim. Eventually, going for fast recovery could mean destroying forensic evidence, making it unlikely to prosecute the attackers. Beyond the technical tasks, the questions are: "What decisions need to be made?" What impact and risks do the decisions imply? Who will make the decisions?

7   Logistics Scenario

A scenario to facilitate the development of a serious game to explore the incident response of a framework with incident response processes is the next step in the design. Interviews, short cases, and real-world cases delineate the state of preparedness and allow us to understand the capabilities and needs of organizations in Germany and Austria. In the last part of the article, we design the scenario. Reference modeling, Design science, and the eXperience method on case studies, refined in the KRITIS series on Cybersecurity of Critical Infrastructures, inform the process of designing the scenario. The strategy in the definition of the scenario is to have a standard infrastructure, integrating the supply chain and the

IT partners into the scenario as this has been referenced frequently in the short cases, have a full set of roles of actors as the multitude of responsibilities and the work load with resources necessary is not so clear in our interviews and have a standard ransomware vector in order not to have too much attention on the attacker in the discussion of the scenario.

For the description of the scenario, we propose a structure with four views (cf. Fig. 2).

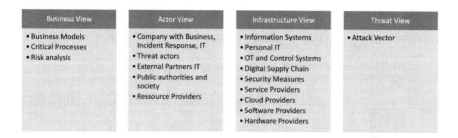

Fig. 2. The four views of a scenario

Logistics is the domain, and the central actor is a logistics company. We decided to move in for logistics for several reasons. Logistics is crucial and disruptions in transport and logistics easily disrupt other sectors. Based on previous work on the resilience of logistics providers and critical infrastructure security and the partners of this project, we understand the business, its role, and the high level of resilience expected in this sector. We also understand from the interviews how differentiated the business models are and that they need instruments to tailor the incident response individually. The four interviews in Subsects. 4.7 to 4.10 manifest the importance of the logistics sector for our daily life, the role of IT partners, and other partners for these companies. Also, a plethora of publicly available information on the DP World incident in November 2023 serves as template for the business view, the actor view, the infrastructure view, and last, the threat view in Subsects. 7.4 and 7.5 deliberates on the preceding subsections by incorporating the interviewees' opinions of Sect. 4.

7.1   Business View and Risk Analysis

The business processes in Fig. 3 provide a basis for the whole section.

Customers immediately perceive disturbances of the order fulfillment process in Fig. 4 once it fails. Therefore, it behooves us to emphasize it as a critical business process. Its characterization follows in Subsect. 7.3. Actors, assets, and threat vectors can be derived from it.

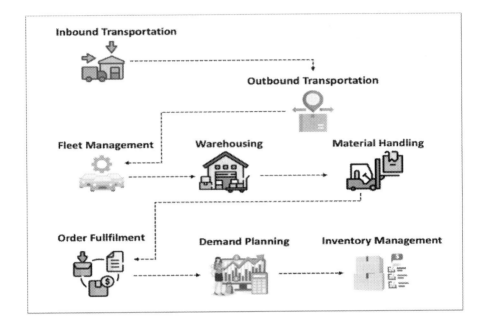

Fig. 3. Business model with activities

Transport and logistics are considered critical infrastructure in Germany, Austria and Europe. Disruption of services would toly risk for society when food or pharmaceutical goods are unavailable or when material is not delivered. Figure 3 shows the elements of business models in logistics. Inbound transportation, outbound transportation, fleet management, warehousing, material handling, order fulfillment, demand planning, and inventory management are important and value-creating business processes in this domain.

From the business model elements we select an internal function, an external IT-Service provider, as our focus points. Figure 4 depicts a critical end-to-end business process from the call center that takes an order to deliver to the door. The call center takes the order, and the manager adds additional information, such as shipment, storage at a warehouse, assorting, weighing, loading, and the necessary supervision, transportation, and delivery, to the business process. Two critical business processes are selected for our scenario: Disposition—when this function is interrupted, e.g., by a malware in its specialized systems, then rather sooner or later the whole company comes to a standstill. We choose a second element of the scenario, a label printer provided by a specialized small company with an on-premise solution administered by the software-hardware provider. In case the provider has malware, no changes in the service can be made: label templates cannot be changed, new users cannot get access rights, software/hardware problems cannot be diagnosed, and a reboot cannot be done.

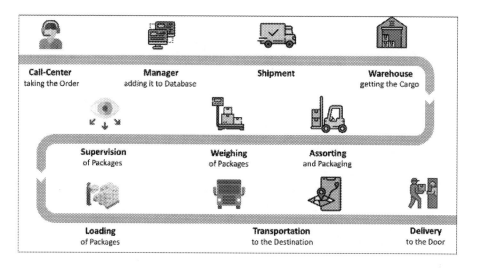

Fig. 4. Critical business process

7.2 Actor View

An analysis of typical commercial organizations under attack reveals the following acting parties and roles.

The left-hand side of Fig. 5 depicts the external partners. The **threat actor** refers to an individual, group, or entity that performs malicious activities against the imaginary enterprise or poses a threat to its assets. In the case of the logistics company, we have threat actors with primary financial or primarily political interests. That is, the threat actor may seek to get money or a maximum disruption of services with damage to the logistics company and mainly to its customers and society as a whole. **Customers and business partners** in this scenario include companies in production and manufacturing, end consumers, other freight forwarders, and warehouses. The **IT partners** include providers of security solutions such as Anti-Virus-Software for the ERP system, the systems used in disposition, warehousing, and the onboard units for drivers, and GPS-tracking of vehicles.

The middle column represents the company, in our case, a logistics company with business level for decisions (CEO, CIO, CFO), the roles responsible for incident response, namely incident handlers, incident responders, and the CERT with its team. The IT organization is responsible for operations and includes CISO, Data Center, Service Desk, IT administration, and IT sourcing. The **management level** takes responsibility for strategy and decision-making during and after a security incident, for example, with regard to resources or escalated. The **legal department and compliance officers** take care of the legal aspects of incidents. Furthermore, they cooperate with law enforcement authorities and report to relevant bodies, such as state data protection officers. **Communications** accounts for initiating and staying in touch with internal

Fig. 5. Actor view

and external stakeholders, including management, if necessary. Team members inform employees, customers, suppliers, and the public about notifiable security incidents. The **Computer Emergency Response Team (CERT)** carries out identification, forensic investigation, and remediation of cyber incidents. Usually, internal and external CERTs cooperate to bring severe incidents under control. The task of the **incident handler** is to contain and mitigate the security incident. To this end, he plans, manages, coordinates, and communicates with other security experts and employees.

The right-hand side of Fig. 5 represents **public authorities** relevant to the incident response and external resources helpful in the incident response. This includes MITRE, yarn for information on attack techniques, actors and their activities, and public authorities that provide support, information about indicators of compromise, and CERT teams or capabilities in forensics. Depending on organizational structures, **external service providers** (such as insurers, lawyers, or consultants) may be invoked for mitigating and recovering an attack.

Regulations require collaboration with several **public authorities**—depending on the status of the company and the kind of impact expected. This embraces federal offices for information security, such as the German BSI and law enforcement authorities, like police forces, public prosecutors, and courts. During a cybersecurity incident, these stakeholders may collaborate closely with affected organizations to contain the breach, mitigate its impact, and restore normal operations. They provide expertise, resources, and support to assist in investigation, recovery, and response efforts. After an incident, they continue to play a vital role in conducting post-incident analysis to understand vulnerabilities and improve resilience against future threats. They may also participate in legal proceedings against perpetrators and contribute to developing policies and regulations aimed at enhancing cybersecurity at both national and international levels.

7.3   Infrastructure View

The infrastructure contains IT elements such as the network, information systems and operational technology, including control systems and physical infrastructure. It contains partners, in particular IT partners that are essential for the information systems and that provide services on-premise or on cloud.

In the logistics scenario, we have headquarters and several warehouses, each with its own IT infrastructure for some smaller information systems. There are services, e.g., a labeling service on-premise provided by a smaller IT company that does troubleshooting, a system in the cloud, and a small IT department that eventually does smaller but mission-critical programming tasks. The systems for physical access control are provided by a specialized company.

We consider the exemplary critical business process *order fulfillment* that commonly takes place in the headquarters of a logistics group. Figure 4 briefly depicts the workflow of the process. Order fulfillment includes all phases of truck selection, as well as communication with truck drivers through short message service (SMS), phone or instant messages, and calls to the destination of the delivered goods. A scheduling system processes all information about orders.

Scheduling requires the following applications: active directory, development system, document management, order and customer management, presentation, print service, spreadsheet (with Macros), virtual desktop infrastructure, word processing, and telecommunication.

7.4   Threat View

The attack with its techniques and impact is the topic of the fourth view, the "Threat View" of the scenario. Similar to the first views, we aim for an attack vector that is relevant for small and medium sized companies and that is utilized by actors with financial interests (ransom) and that is frequently used. The attack phases use techniques and technologies that are fairly common.

Our attack vector is inspired by LockBit. LockBit typifies a typical ransomware [2]. The LockBit group has published different versions since 2020 [7]. The software encrypts the data to provide the code for decryption in return for ransom. The group also makes its software usable for others, such as Ransomware-as-a-Service (RaaS). This means that not every attack carried out with LockBit automatically originates from this group (Fig. 6).

Attackers using this method typically take ransom to unlock data and network connections and abstain from disclosure of sensitive company data. The initial access for this kind of attack is based on social engineering, that is, by purposefully sending a phishing email to an employee of the logistics group who also administers the active directory (AD). The AD stores information on group memberships, rights, and authentication features for all its users on its domain controllers. We define the attack vector for our scenario as follows:

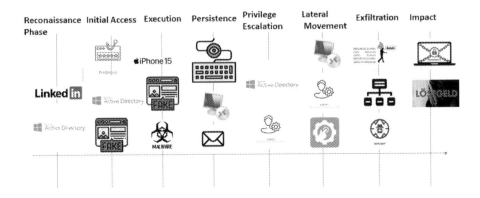

Fig. 6. Attack phases

- **Reconnaissance Phase:** LinkedIn is used to figure out the e-mail address of an employee of the logistics group (MITRE ATT&CK Technique T1591 - Gather Victim Org Information) who also administrates the AD.
- **Initial Access:** Attackers manage to gain access to the employee's AD account by sending them a phishing e-mail. The employee enters his credentials in a fake web-mail input window and unintentionally betrays them to the offenders.
- **Execution:** Despite the captured credentials, the attackers still need to gain complete control over the employee's computer. On this account, they send another email to the employee with the pretended opportunity of winning a new iPhone in a competition. The employee opens another fake website with his click on this link where he enters his personal data (MITRE ATT&CK Technique T1204 - User Execution). Everything looks harmless to the employee, but clicking on the link has downloaded malware onto his computer. This malware can automatically install itself on the employee's computer using the previously phished credentials.
- **Persistence:** The malware makes it possible to control the computer remotely. However, the attacker still wants to log all of the employee's keystrokes to obtain administrative privileges. The already installed malware makes it possible to install a keylogger that sends all keystrokes to the attacker (MITRE ATT&CK Technique T1543 - Create or Modify System Process). The employee connects to the AD via remote desktop for administrative purposes and enters the data for his administrative account. The keylogger captures the administrative account's credentials and conveys them to the attacker.
- **Privilege Escalation:** Subsequently, the attacker takes advantage of the employee's administrative account and creates a new administrative account to persist possible password changes of the employee (MITRE ATT&CK Technique T1098 - Account Manipulation).

- **Lateral Movement:** The attacker can now access the order and customer management asset via remote desktop (MITRE ATT&CK Technique T1021 - Remote Services).
- **Exfiltration:** The attacker succeeds in stealing sensitive data from the corporate network and uploads it to the darknet via his Command & Control (C2) servers (MITRE ATT&CK Technique T1020 - Automated Exfiltration).
- **Impact:** Finally, the attacker succeeds in encrypting the files in the order and customer management system using ransomware like LockBit (MITRE ATT&CK Technique T1486 - Data Encrypted for Impact). Subsequently, they block data and network connections to the servers responsible for order and customer management. The attacker now confronts the company with a ransom demand to unlock the data, release the network connections, and not disclose the stolen sensitive data.

This attack vector allows for various relevant entry points for an analysis.

7.5   Upshot

The scenario explained in this section aims to reproduce a cybersecurity incident in a logistics company as realistically as possible. Interest grew before and during the interviews regarding whether the interviewees reported similar incidents. They indeed had experience with various incidents involving either specific components of their infrastructure or (those of) partners. The scenario draws from these experiences.

One of them reported fear of failures at their label printing service. It belongs to a critical business process, as storing and shipping of goods requires labels for traceability. The label printer in question runs at a specialized service provider on-premises. Considered as a highly specialized appliance, only its vendor may service it. In the event of a ransomware incident at this service provider, no changes in the labels can be made. This would alter their critical business process and, of course, their environmental supply chain sooner or later.

Although the four interview partners in the logistics industry endeavored to contribute with case examples, they deemed their own security posture as high and sufficient. Throughout all interviews and cases, social engineering and phishing were considered the most likely initial attack followed by a movement to the business information systems before the OT and control systems would be tackled. This perception of likelihood is reflected in the Threat View and aims to prepare for the kind of incident that is expected from the interview partners. We asked them about the partners and experiences shared with customers in the logistics industry, providers of physical access control systems, and highly specialized systems, represented in the scenario. It seems worthwhile to prepare equally for incidents in the own organization and in partners of all kinds. We argue that this is closer to reality than separate scenarios of individual organizations and whole supply chains.

The attack vector covers three levels of analysis: ransomware on a personal device, ransomware in an organization, and ransomware with impact on the whole supply chain. The logistics case "ensures" an impact on many partners once such an organization is affected by an incident.

The scenario allows for manifold analysis for various stakeholder groups. In this scenario, we consider the IT outage of a partner in the supply chain of a company based on a Ransomware infection. In such a case, it has to be determined which data have been compromised, if data from the client has been compromised or stolen, and if the attackers have access to the client via the compromised partner. Therefore, forensic experts must gather detailed information from the available logs to be able to comment on it. The partner in the supply chain has to inform all affected clients that he has been compromised. In a written document, the partner must disclose which information and IT systems have been affected by the cyberattack. Also, if the data has been stolen or if the partner has been able to restore the data from its backup systems. The report must also state if an external access is possible via the compromised IT systems of the partner towards the client. More information about the information stored on compromised IT systems, whether it is sensitive information or personal information, is needed. The information if passwords are stored on affected IT systems, how passwords are stored, and how access to passwords is secured is mandatory. It has to be explained how the attackers have been able to compromise the affected IT systems and to which other IT systems these affected IT systems have access. Finally, the report needs information if the information on affected IT systems is encrypted at rest and in transit, if regular vulnerability scans are carried out and security patches are applied, and if affected IT systems have been reinstalled from scratch and scanned for Malware several times.

The client of the partner in the supply chain itself can correspond to the partner in terms of inquiries, as well as security measures that the client can take to mitigate the risk of unauthorized access of cyber criminals to the client's IT systems. As well a schema of the IT architecture can be requested at the partner and sent to the client, for better understanding. If there are still remaining questions, these should be clarified between the Head of IT or security department of the partner together with the security responsible person at the client side, during a meeting.

The four views are close to reality and resemble the resources and capabilities found in many organizations. In the next step, the views will be combined in a game board. In principle, there can be two possible scenarios within the logistics scenario. Either the logistics company itself gets infected with Ransomware or the service provider/external IT-provider gets infected with ransomware.

8   Discussion and Outlook

The result of this work is a scenario entitled "The ransomware reports - what now?", which was analyzed from various perspectives. The technical and organizational measures the companies surveyed took to prepare for a corresponding attack were examined. It turns out that there are certain measures that the respondents have in common, such as the use of virus scanners or backups.

All respondents are aware of the need to prepare for cyber attacks, and phishing emails are seen as an important attack vector. This aligns with the BSI's 2023 situation report, which confirms that ransomware poses an "outstanding potential threat" [20]. At the same time, however, it is also clear that the surveyed sample of eleven companies alone shows such a wide range of technical and organizational measures that it is impossible to make universally valid statements here. In contrast, for the development of awareness measures such as serious games, an individual approach is recommended to meet the requirements of the individual organizations. Companies were also asked about the expected impact of an attack. Here, the assessments are strikingly positive and therefore differ greatly from the average downtime determined in practice. Issues such as ransomware are developing very quickly and effectively due to the increasing professionalization, specialization, and division of labor of the relevant groups and providers. Cybercrime-as-a-Service (CaaS) is now a service that can be easily purchased and used without the corresponding technical expertise. This makes it all the more important to counteract this on the defense side with innovative measures. In reality, however, conservative means, such as the use of pen and paper for order processing, tend to be resorted to in the event of an attack. In the Analysis chapter, questions are developed from the observations made to help improve preparation for cyber attacks. The aforementioned positivity bias (What impact does a ransomware attack really have on my company?) is addressed, as is the question of when a ransomware attack can really be considered complete or how an organization should deal with the possibility of its own IT service provider being hit by a cyber attack.

The database for this work was collected empirically through interviews. The observations in this work are limited by the number of eleven interview partners from a limited number of sectors (logistics, chemicals, IT, energy, and finance). One limitation of this paper is the different functions of the interviewees, who may not be able to provide full information on technical issues. A quantitative research approach is suitable for validating the observations made and developing further recommendations.

The knowledge gained from the scenario analysis is fed back into the CONTAIN project in various ways. The overall aim of the project is to increase the effectiveness and efficiency in the management of IT security incidents. The knowledge gained from the interviews and their analysis is therefore fed back into the development of the serious games. It helps to formulate questions more specifically and adapt the design of the games accordingly in order to ensure the greatest possible practical relevance. Furthermore, the knowledge gained here will be incorporated into the development of a further questionnaire, which should provide a more comprehensive picture of the situation regarding preparation for a cyber attack in Germany and Austria.

Acknowledgments. Project CONTAIN is a bilateral German-Austrian research project. We acknowledge funding for CONTAIN by the Bundesministerium für Bildung und Forschung (BMBF) (grant number 13N16581-13N16587) as part of the

SIFO program and the Austrian Research Promotion Agency (FFG) (grant number FO999902707).

The authors have contributed to this article in various ways. Contributions can be attributed to co-authors as described below.

– Maximilian Greiner contributed to the case analysis and his contributions to the article include introduction, research design and outlook.

– Judith Strussenberg mainly wrote the short cases with ransomware, the case study analysis, and contributed to the real-world cases on ransomware incidents.

– Andreas Seiler wrote the theoretical background and contributed to the case and security analysis.

– Stefan Hofbauer wrote the real-world cases and contributed to the analysis and the logistics scenario.

– Michael Schuster contributed to the short cases and the logistics scenario, and he contributed domain knowledge on logistics and the requirements of SMEs.

– Damian Stano contributed to data collection, interview study, case analysis, and short cases.

– Günter Fahrnberger contributed to the logistics scenario, the article layout, and the article's revisions.

– Stefan Schauer contributed to the security analysis and the scenario analysis.

– Ulrike Lechner contributed to the research design, data collection, interpretation, and revisions of the articles.

References

1. Maersk Reinstalled 45,000 PCs and 4,000 Servers to Recover From Not-Petya Attack. https://www.bleepingcomputer.com/news/security/maersk%2Dreinstalled%2D45%2D000%2Dpcs%2Dand%2D4%2D000%2Dservers%2Dto%2Drecover%2Dfrom%2Dnotpetya%2Dattack/,urldate=2018-01-25, author=Bleepingcomputer,month=jan,year=2018

2. Beaumont, K.: LockBit ransomware group assemble strike team to breach banks, law firms and governments, November 2023. https://www.databreaches.net/lockbit%2Dransomware%2Dgroup%2Dassemble%2Dstrike%2Dteam%2Dto%2Dbreach%2Dbanks%2Dlaw%2Dfirms%2Dand%2Dgovernments/

3. Bleepingcomputer: Computer giant Acer hit by $50 million ransomware attack, March 2021. https://www.bleepingcomputer.com/news/security/computer-giant-acer-hit-by-50-million-ransomware-attack/

4. Born, G.: Vertraulicher Forensik-Bericht offenbart viele Versäumnisse, January 2024. https://www.golem.de/news/ransomwarebefall%2Dbei%2Dsuedwestfalen%2Dit%2Dvertraulicher%2Dforensik%2Dbericht%2Doffenbart%2Dviele%2Dversaeumnisse%2D2401%2D181636%2Ehtml

5. Butt, U., Dauda, Y., Shaheer, B.: ransomware attack on the educational sector. In: Jahankhani, H., Jamal, A., Brown, G., Sainidis, E., Fong, R., Butt, U.J. (eds.) AI, Blockchain and Self-Sovereign Identity in Higher Education. Advanced Sciences and Technologies for Security Applications, pp. 279–313. Springer, Cham (2023). https://doi.org/10.1007/978-3-031-33627-0_11

6. Chapmann, R.: Ransomware Cases Increased Greatly in 2023—SANS, January 2024. https://www.sans.org/blog/ransomware-cases-increased-greatly-in-2023/

7. CISA: Understanding Ransomware Threat Actors: LockBit, January 2023. https://www.cisa.gov/news-events/cybersecurity-advisories/aa23-165a

8. Crowdstrike: 2023 Global Threat Report (2023). https://www.crowdstrike.de/ressourcen/reports/global-threat-report-executive-summary-2023/
9. Eisenhardt, K.M.: Building theories from case study research. Acad. Manag. Rev. **14**(4), 532–550 (1989)
10. Federal Office of Civil Protection and Disaster Assistance: How to prepare for disasters (2023). https://www.bbk.bund.de/EN/Home/home_node.html. Accessed 19 Feb 2024
11. Federal Office of Information Security: Ransomware – Facts and defensive strategies (2022). https://www.bsi.bund.de/EN/Themen/Unternehmen-und-Organisationen/Cyber-Sicherheitslage/Analysen-und-Prognosen/Ransomware-Angriffe/ransomware-angriffe_node.html. Accessed 19 Feb 2024
12. Fettke, P., Loos, P.: Reference Modeling for Business Systems Analysis. IGI Global, Hershey (2006)
13. Forbes: Acer Faced With Ransom Up To \$100 Million After Hackers Breach Network, March 2021. https://www.forbes.com/sites/leemathews/2021/03/21/acer-faced-with-ransom-up-to-100-million-after-hackers-breach-network/
14. Grance, T., Kent, K., Kim, B.: NIST Computer Security Incident Handling Guide. Special Publication (NIST SP), Gaithersburg, MD, USA (2004)
15. Heumüller, E.: ÜBIT: Referenzmodell zur Anlage ziel-und auswertungsorientierter, szenarbasierter Übungen. Edition Dr. Stein, WiKu Verlag (2016)
16. Hevner, A.R.: A three cycle view of design science research. Scand. J. Inf. Syst. **19**(2), 4 (2007)
17. Horchert, J.: Maersk—Schaden durch Hackerangriff, January 2017. https://www.containerbasis.de/blog/branche/maersk-hackerangriff/
18. Incibe: Quanta Computer, victim of REvil ransomware threatening Apple, April 2021. https://www.incibe.es/en/incibe-cert/publications/cybersecurity-highlights/quanta-computer-victim-revil-ransomware-threatening-apple
19. für Sicherheit in der Informationstechnik, B.: Die Lage der IT-Sicherheit in Deutschland 2021, October 2021. https://www.bsi.bund.de/SharedDocs/Downloads/DE/BSI/Publikationen/Lageberichte/Lagebericht2021.html
20. für Sicherheit in der Informationstechnik, B.: Die Lage der IT-Sicherheit in Deutschland 2023, November 2023. https://www.bsi.bund.de/SharedDocs/Downloads/DE/BSI/Publikationen/Lageberichte/Lagebericht2023.html
21. Kral, P.: Incident Handler's Handbook, February 2024. https://www.sans.org/white-papers/33901/
22. Lechner, U., Dännart, S., Rieb, A., Rudel, S.: Case Kritis-Fallstudien zur IT-Sicherheit in Kritischen Infrastrukturen. Logos Verlag Berlin (2018)
23. MITRE: MITRE ATT&CK, February 2024. https://attack.mitre.org/
24. Mutzbauer, J.: Wir waren uns einig, dass wir das Lösegeld auf keinen Fall zahlen, September 2023. https://www.csoonline.com/de/a/wir-waren-uns-einig-dass-wir-das-loesegeld-auf-keinen-fall-zahlen,3674197
25. North Atlantic Treaty Organization: NATO's flagship cyber exercise concludes in Estonia (2023). https://www.nato.int/cps/en/natohq/news_220993.htm?selectedLocale=en. Accessed 19 Feb 2024
26. O'Kane, P., Sezer, S., Carlin, D.: Evolution of ransomware. IET Netw. **7**(5), 321–327 (2018)
27. Rege, A., Bleiman, R.: Ransomware attacks against critical infrastructure. In: Proceedings of 20th European Conference on Cyber Warfare Security, p. 324 (2020)

28. Sangfor: Sangfor Ransomware Protection — Learn from Quanta Computer & Apple Attacked by REvil Ransomware, April 2021. https://www.sangfor.com/blog/cybersecurity/sangfor%2Dransomware%2Dprotection%2Dlearn%2Dquanta%2Dcomputer%2Dapple%2Dattacked%2Drevil/
29. Seiler, A., Lechner, U.: Operation Raven - Design of a Cyber Security Incident Response Game. In preparation (2024)
30. Seiler, A., Lechner, U.: Operation Raven—Towards a Cyber Security Incident Response Game. Poster at GameFin 2024 (2024, to appear)
31. Spiegel: Moller-Maersk: Hackerangriff kostet Reederei Hunderte Millionen, August 2017. https://www.spiegel.de/netzwelt/netzpolitik/moller%2Dm%2Drsk%2Dcyberangriff%2Dkostet%2Dreederei%2Dhunderte%2Dmillionen%2Da%2D1163111%2Ehtml
32. Strauss, A., Corbin, J.: Basics of qualitative research techniques (1998)
33. Thakur, K., Ali, M.L., Jiang, N., Qiu, M.: Impact of cyber-attacks on critical infrastructure. In: 2016 IEEE 2nd International Conference on Big Data Security on Cloud (BigDataSecurity), IEEE International Conference on High Performance and Smart Computing (HPSC), and IEEE International Conference on Intelligent Data and Security (IDS), pp. 183–186. IEEE (2016)
34. unit42, P.A.: Ransomware and extortion report 2023 (2023). https://start.paloaltonetworks.com/2023-unit42-ransomware-extortion-report
35. Wermelskirchen, F.: Südwestfalen-IT: Forensik-Bericht zu Ransomware-Angriff, January 2024. https://forumwk.de/2024/01/25/suedwestfalen%2Dit%2Dforensik%2Dbericht%2Dmit%2Derkenntnissen%2Dzu%2Dransomware%2Dangriff/
36. Wölfe, R., Schubert, P.: Dauerhafter Erfolg mit Business Software: 10 Jahre Fallstudien nach der eXperience Methodik. Carl Hanser Verlag, Germany (2009)
37. Yuryna Connolly, L., Wall, D.S., Lang, M., Oddson, B.: An empirical study of ransomware attacks on organizations: an assessment of severity and salient factors affecting vulnerability. J. Cybersecur. 6(1), tyaa023 (2020)
38. Zhao, T., Gasiba, T., Lechner, U., Pinto-Albuquerque, M.: Thriving in the era of hybrid work: raising cybersecurity awareness using serious games in industry trainings. J. Syst. Softw. 210, 111946 (2024). https://doi.org/10.1016/j.jss.2023.111946, https://www.sciencedirect.com/science/article/pii/S0164121223003412

COPYCAT: Applying Serious Games in Industry for Defending Supply Chain Attack

Tiange Zhao[1,2](✉) ⓘ, Tiago Gasiba[1] ⓘ, Ulrike Lechner[2] ⓘ,
Maria Pinto-Albuquerque[3] ⓘ, and Didem Ongu[1] ⓘ

[1] Siemens AG, Otto-Hahn-Ring 6, 81739 Munich, Germany
zhaotiange123@gmail.com
[2] University of the Bundeswehr Munich, Werner-Heisenberg-Weg 39,
85579 Neubiberg, Germany
[3] Instituto Universitário de Lisboa (ISCTE-IUL), ISTAR, Av. das Forças Armadas,
1649–026 Lisboa, Portugal

Abstract. Serious games have found their application in many cases
for improving cybersecurity; one of those cases is for building a successful strategy for defending against potential attacks. Our research tries
to simulate supply chain attacks involving cloud data by adapting serious game frameworks. In this paper, we present the usage of a serious
game called COPYCAT to help the participants raise awareness of supply chain attack threats and build a valid defense strategy against them.
COPYCAT is an abbreviation of **CONTAIN** su**P**pl**Y** **C**hain **AT**tack
and CONTAIN is the name of the project that is the larger context
of this study. The game originates from CATS (Cloud of Assets and
Threats), designed to raise cloud security awareness. In this work, CATS
is adapted to the new attack scenarios specifically for data-related supply
chain attacks, and the adaption is verified in two game events conducted
with practitioners from the industry. This paper marks a milestone in
positioning a new game dedicated to incident response. In this paper, we
share the design of our serious game and the results we collected during
the game events and provide insight into the topic of serious game application for training purposes to raise awareness on data-related supply
chain attacks.

Keywords: Serious game · Cloud security · Supply chain attack ·
Industry · Training

1 Introduction

Cloud computing is an innovative technology being applied in the main business functions in the supply chain [27]. The size and number of cloud-based
applications have risen significantly in the industry, providing great efficiency to
the supply chain. The global cloud computing market size was valued at USD

F. Phillipson et al. (Eds.): I4CS 2024, CCIS 2109, pp. 321–336, 2024.
https://doi.org/10.1007/978-3-031-60433-1_18

483.98 billion in 2022 and is expected to grow at a compound annual growth rate (CAGR) of 14.1% from 2023 to 2030 [16]. Nearly half (45%) of all security incidents target cloud-based services and threaten the supply chain's robustness. Moreover, 80% of business organizations experienced at least one cloud security breach incident in 2022 [30]. Cloud deployments' great flexibility and convenience contribute to development efficiency and business success. However, cloud assets are prone to various cyber-security threats [2] and increasing attack surface for the supply chain. Due to the broad network exposure and architecture that involves cloud service providers and customers, the attack surface increases compared to on-premise and other service provisioning models. Also, there are security topics that are specific to the cloud. The Cloud Security Alliance (CSA) provides a ranking table of the top 11 threats in cloud computing security [8]. In the table of top 11, threats such as Misconfiguration and Inadequate Change Control, Lack of Cloud Security Architecture Strategy, and Insecure Software Development are listed. Among the list, the threat of Metastructure & Applistructure Failures takes the ninth place. It can be mitigated by conducting regular security assessments on the application and checking the 3rd-party software supply chain.

Various standards, best practices, and whitepapers listed below define and regulate how the practitioner should properly secure assets in the industry. The controls are listed and mapped to industry-accepted standards in Cloud Control Matrix [3] (CCM) from CSA. Those standard regulations and control frameworks include but are not limited to ISO 27001/27002/27017/27018 [23–26], NIST SP 800-53 [29], AICPA TSC [34], German BSI C5 [6], PCI DSS [10], ISACA COBIT [22], NERC CIP [7], FedRamp [1], CIS [20]. The study of Gleeson [15] has shown the complexity of those standards. In all three service models, infrastructure as a service (IaaS), platform as a service (PaaS), and software as a service (SaaS), it is the cloud service customers' responsibility to configure the cloud service securely.

In the work of Iosif et al. [21], we examined the quality of infrastructure as code (IaC) in open code repositories in terms of security and found almost 300,000 security violations from over 8000 code repositories, noting that those IaC can be a part of the 3rd-party software supply chain. Our study concludes that many IaCs miss basic concepts of cloud security and that we need to improve awareness about certain issues on cloud deployment and supply chain attacks in an industrial environment.

In recent years, serious games have been increasingly applied for education in the industry and academic world. The game COPYCAT that we present in this work is adapted from CATS, which we developed to raise awareness for cloud security among practitioners in the industry. More details regarding CATS are introduced in our previous work [36]. Therefore, we decided to adapt CATS to a serious game that assists the learning of how to build a defense strategy that cuts the kill chain, improves the supply chain's robustness with cloud assets, and raises awareness about supply chain attacks among the group of practitioners in the industry. In this paper, we aim to provide our answers to the research question:

RQ: What strategies can be employed to adapt the existing serious game framework to address the theme of cloud data-relevant supply chain attacks in the industry?

The paper is structured as follows. Section 2 shows an overview of the related work that inspired our study. Section 3 describes our methodology and research design. Section 4 presents details of the COPYCAT game design. Section 5 introduces the evaluation method. Section 6 shares the results we collected in the evaluation phase. Last but not least, in Sect. 7, we conclude our work and answer the research question.

2   Related Work

This section presents related work that has helped and inspired our research, mainly in three parts: information technology awareness, serious games, and supply chain attacks.

2.1   Information Security Awareness

The work of Hänsch et al. on IT security awareness [17] and its refinement by Gasiba [14] is a theoretical foundation for our research. In their work, Hänsch et al. define three dimensions of IT security awareness: perception, protection, and behavior. According to Hänsch et al., perception is related to knowledge about IT security, protection is related to knowledge of how to protect IT assets, and behavior is related to the intention to protect IT assets actively. Gasiba refines these three dimensions of secure coding: perception-knowing about software security vulnerabilities; protection-knowing how to protect against these software vulnerabilities; and behavior-intention to write secure code.

Kruger et al. proposed a prototype for assessing information security awareness. In their prototype, information security awareness is measured in three dimensions: what does a person know (knowledge); how do they feel about the topic (attitude); and what do they do (behavior) [28], known as the KAB model. The KAB model shares great similarities with the work of Hänsch et al. Perception is a combination of knowledge and attitude; both models have the same definition of behavior. The model of Hänsch et al. emphasizes the idea of "protection," which overlaps with the idea of "knowledge" to some extent in the model of Kruger et al. In this work, a combination of both models is used to understand how serious games affect the participants' cybersecurity awareness level.

2.2   Serious Games Framework

There are various serious games designed and implemented to raise awareness of cybersecurity. Shostack maintains a list of security tabletop games on his website [31]. An early example of a video game with cyber security simulation is CyberCIEGE [33], where players purchase and configure workstations, servers, operating systems, applications, and network devices. They make trade-offs as they struggle to balance budget, productivity, and security. CyberCIEGE is mainly targeted at students in schools and institutes, and it successfully avoids the fear of failing by allowing students to explore simulated scenarios. The video game succeeded in simulating the attack scenarios and the constraints while implementing cybersecurity mitigation. However, the target group is school students who need work experience, and a mapping of the real-world cybersecurity standards and defense mechanisms needs to be included.

The work of Valdemar et al. [32] shows another possibility of applying serious games in university teaching. They found that creating serious games contributes to fostering adversary thinking. Their study lasted over three semesters, and the game's purpose was to teach undergraduate students about network attack and defense by creating educational games in a cyber range environment. The students report that they had a unique opportunity to understand the topic deeply. Their work shows exciting results in the academic environment in that the game created is played by their college mates, who rated the quality and educational value of the games overwhelmingly positively. Unfortunately, due to the constraint in effort and resources, such an approach is not feasible in an industry setting.

Different from CyberCIEGE and the work of Valdemar, another example in the company setting is the game Riskio of Hart et al. [18]. Riskio is dedicated to people without technical backgrounds and successfully increases cybersecurity awareness for people working in organizations. Riskio is a tabletop game focusing on defensive and offensive skills in general IT security. It provides important insights into the impact of such serious games. Riskio manages to raise cybersecurity awareness within an industry setting, but it addresses the cybersecurity issue in general, which needs to be improved for the focus on cloud data-driven supply chain attacks.

Another Week at the Office (AWATO) [13] by Ferro et al. is another serious game developed based on a systematic literature review. The game focuses on the human factor by raising awareness of phishing attacks. The evaluation of the game shows that it is an effective tool for improving users' awareness of cybersecurity best practices. Their work further proves that serious games could be a useful approach to solving awareness issues. Nevertheless, it is still worthwhile to mention that phishing is not the only possible attack through which the attacker gains access to the system.

2.3 Supply Chain Attack

Supply chain compromises are common attacks in industry. In a case, the hacker managed to infect the node.js package to steal from Bitcoin wallets [9]. Once the supply chain is comprised, it can cause significant domestic and international effects, like in the SolarWinds supply chain attack [35]. As described in the MITRE ATT&CK framework [4], in the supply chain compromise tactic, the attacker aims to manipulate products or product delivery mechanisms before receipt by a final consumer for data or system compromise. Examples of supply chain compromise include manipulation of development tools, source code repository, infected system images (e.g., via removable media infected at the factory), and shipment interdiction.

In our work, we derive the COPYCAT game element according to the MITRE ATT&CK framework. The attacker's goal is to cause data destruction, encryption, manipulation, or denial of service. We chose these attack techniques as our game element because they best reflect the different supply chain compromises.

3 Research Design

This work describes how we adapted the existing game, CATS, to the new use cases. CATS went through 3 design iterations as shown in our paper [38], including adapting and extending the ontology from Fenz et al. [12] and including the common vulnerability scoring system (CVSS) in the conditional probability calculation in the core simulator. In this work, we show the details of one full design cycle of the COPYCAT game.

This work is an instantiation of design science research (DSR), following the design science paradigm proposed by Hevner et al. [19]. Their work describes the core of design science research as the cycle of Design & Implement and Justify & Evaluate. Our research contribution is the novel approach of designing COPYCATS to raise awareness of cloud data-driven supply chain attacks and the useful design artifact.

The Design & Implement phase of this work extends the existing implementation of CATS with the Cybersecurity Challenges platform. This phase shifts the game's focus from shared responsibility in cloud security to cloud security in the supply chain and incident response. The attack scenarios use the MITRE ATT&CK industrial control system matrix [5] structure. The matrix describes the kill chain of an attacker, how to cause a security incident, and the relevant mitigation for every attack technique.

The Justify & Evaluate phase of this work is accomplished by two game events in the industry: one organized in China with 40 participants and one organized in Germany with 22 participants. The serious game was deployed as a category of Cyber-security Challenge event [14]. The game's dynamic data is captured in the backend, and the player's performance is the base of the evaluation.

4 Game Design

In this chapter, we introduce the COPYCAT game design in detail, including the game process, the design of the game interface, and the twelve attack scenarios. A serious game is a type of game with purposes other than entertainment [11]. COPYCATS is a serious game with a learning objective. The player learns about different organizational roles and responsibilities in implementing mitigation mechanisms by playing COPYCATS. The players benefit from the discussion during the game event with their teammates. The game participants gain a first impression of how various defense actions can mitigate cloud data-driven supply chain attacks and raise awareness about cloud data-driven supply chain attacks and the associated defense actions while exercising their skills in building a successful defense strategy.

4.1 Game Process

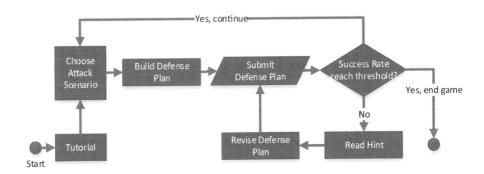

Fig. 1. The game process from player perspective

The flowchart in Fig. 1 shows the game process. As the game starts, the players follow a tutorial to learn about the rules and game elements as the first part of the game. The players are free to choose from the available attack scenarios. During the game event, we show the players one attack scenario for the tutorials, and the rest of the eleven attack scenarios remain yet to be solved. We will introduce the details of attack scenarios in the next section.

The game aims for players to build a defense plan by assigning defense cards to the correct responsibility. When the defense plan is ready, players submit it to the back end by clicking a "submit" button. The back end then evaluates the chances of the cloud deployment being attacked based on the scenario, the players' selected cards, and their positions. The evaluator calculates a success rate: the probability that the submitted defense plan withstands the attack scenario. The game is pre-configured with a threshold visible to the player in the game interface. If the calculated success rate is bigger or equal to the given threshold, the player successfully solves the scenario and can move on to the next one. Hints are automatically generated and returned to the player if the success rate does not reach the threshold. These hints justify to the player why the card selection did or did not work. The player can further adjust the defense plan based on the received hints at this stage. The player can change the defense plan and submit the new plan to the back end until the game scenario is solved.

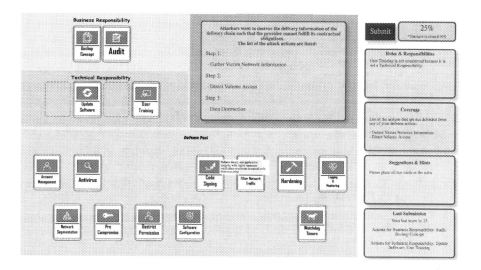

Fig. 2. The game interface

4.2   Game Interface

The interface of the COPYCAT game (in Fig. 2) borrows from the CATS interface. It is designed to provide players with a comprehensive and intuitive platform for enhancing their understanding of cybersecurity's business and technical aspects. In the top-left section of the game, players are presented with two distinct areas for defenses. The first area is for business responsibilities with two defenses, while the second addresses technical responsibilities with four defenses. This segmentation allows players to strategically allocate their defense cards below from the defense pool based on the specific nature of the cyber threats they encounter.

At the top-middle of the interface, the game scenario unfolds with a three-step process, each presenting a unique attack action. Players must navigate these steps, deploying appropriate defenses to inhibit potential threats. The bottom section of the interface houses the defense pool, where players can select defense cards to place in the solution area. A key feature is the ability to gain insights into each defense card through mouseover actions, as shown on the "Code Signing" card, triggering tooltips that provide concise explanations of the defense mechanisms, empowering players with valuable information for decision-making.

On the right side of the game interface, an information area displays tips for the players. Players can submit their solutions with the click of a "Submit" button, after which a success rate is revealed at the top. The target success rate for each scenario is communicated underneath, guiding players towards achieving optimal results.

The lower part of the information area is dedicated to the roles and responsibilities of defenses in the solution. Any misplaced defense cards trigger a warning in the first box, emphasizing the importance of proper placement. The second box focuses on coverage information, ensuring players know of undefended attacks that may compromise their success. In the third box, players receive valuable suggestions and hints. If the success rate is insufficient despite a correct solution, the hint system suggests increasing the success rate, guiding players toward a more effective defense strategy. The play can only solve the attack scenario if the submitted strategy reaches the threshold, has no error in the responsibility assignment, and covers all presented attack actions.

Finally, a log of the players' last submissions and their respective scores is presented at the bottom of the information area, allowing for reflection and learning from previous attempts. This comprehensive and interactive game interface serves as a dynamic tool for cybersecurity training, fostering experiential learning and skill development.

4.3   Attack Scenarios

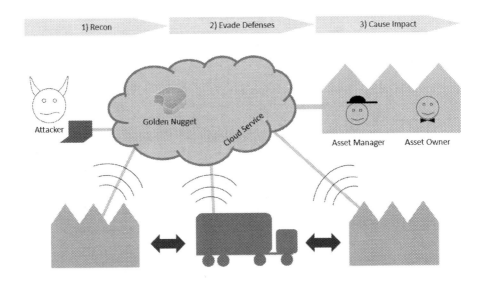

Fig. 3. The set up of an attack scenario

The attack scenarios in this work consist of three steps: 1) Recon; 2) Evade defense; 3) Cause impact. The simplified kill chain is derived from MITRE ATT&CK Matrix for industrial control systems (ICS). In the original matrix, twelve tactics describe the adversary's tactical goal: the reason for acting [5]. In the first step of reconnaissance, the attacker's goal is to collect useful information, e.g., about the infrastructure, network, and existing vulnerabilities, to pave the way for steps two and three. Compared to the CATS game [37], the number of possible attack actions in each step is reduced. In the COPYCAT game, there is only one attack action in each step, and the player needs to defend all the attack actions in the scenario. In the second step of evading defenses, the attacker tries to bypass the defenses in place and reach the final goal. In the last step, the attacker tries to make an impact with the attack by manipulating data or causing a denial of service. All the attack actions in the last step are targeted at data stored in the cloud: data destruction, data encryption, data manipulation, or denial of service when the cloud data is unavailable.

Figure 3 depicts the delivery chain composed of parties and delivery mechanisms. Parties deliver and accept goods. One party can be the owner of a delivery chain, or a delivery chain can be independently owned. The cloud instance contains important information necessary for the functioning of the delivery chain, which is highlighted as "Golden Nugget" in Fig. 3. Essential communication to the delivery chain goes through the cloud instance. The stakeholders from the defender side are the asset owners, who take responsibility for critical business decisions, and the asset managers, who take responsibility for implementing the protection measures. On the left side is the attacker, who is intended to affect the delivery of goods.

Table 1. An overview of twelve attack scenarios in a three-step kill chain

	Recon Technique	Defense Evasion	Impact
S1.1	Gather Victim Network Information	Direct Volume Access	Data Destruction
S1.2	Phishing for Information	Access Token Manipulation	
S1.3	Active Scanning	Abuse Elevation Control Mechanism	
S2.1	Gather Victim Network Information	Direct Volume Access	Data Encryption
S2.2	Active Scanning	Access Token Manipulation	
S2.3	Search Open Technical Databases	Abuse Elevation Control Mechanism	
S3.1	Gather Victim Network Information	Direct Volume Access	Data Manipulation
S3.2	Search Open Technical Databases	Access Token Manipulation	
S3.3	Active Scanning	Indirect Command Execution	
S4.1	Gather Victim Network Information	Masquerading	Denial of Service
S4.2	Search Open Technical Databases	Abuse Elevation Control Mechanism	
S4.3	Active Scanning	Hijack Execution Flow	

We developed twelve attack scenarios listed in Table 1. They are categorized according to the different last steps of the attack. In S1.1, S1.2, and S1.3, the attacker aims to cause the destruction of data, which means the adversaries may destroy data and files on specific systems or in large numbers on a network to interrupt the availability of systems, services, and network resources. In our work, the attackers want to destroy the delivery information of the delivery chain so that the provider cannot fulfill its contractual obligations. In S2.1, S2.2, and S2.3, the attacker aims to encrypt the data and ask for ransom or cause interruption of services. In our work, the attackers hold the delivery information for ransom. They aim to extort money from the delivery company by impeding deliveries or menacing disclosure of sensitive routes and clients. In S3.1, S3.2, and

S3.3, the attacker aims to insert, delete, or manipulate data to influence external outcomes or hide activity, thus threatening the integrity of the data. By manipulating data, adversaries may attempt to affect a business process, organizational understanding, or decision-making. In our work, the attacker wants to divert the delivery of goods. For this, attackers want to manipulate delivery documentation to include non-contractual destinations. In S4.1, S4.2, and S4.3, the attacker aims to cause a denial of service to degrade or block users' availability of targeted resources. In our game, attackers want to make it difficult or impossible for the delivery company to fulfill its contractual obligations using a denial of service, e.g., delivery drivers cannot access delivery information and, therefore, cannot deliver goods.

Table 2. The motivation of the attacker in different threat scenarios

Threat	Motivation	How
Service disruption	- Cause financial or reputation damage to parties involved in the delivery chain. - Cause a sudden increase of price of materials or goods through manipulation of volume of offering	- Data Encryption - Denial of Service - Data Destruction
Stealing Information	- Disclosure of secret or sensitive delivery plans - Collect information on sourcing of materials or goods - Disclosure of financial information related to the sourcing of materials or goods	- Data Encryption - Data Manipulation
Manipulation of Delivery Chain	- Re-route delivery of materials or goods - Cause delivery of lower quality goods - Steal materials or goods	- Data Manipulation

Table 2 explains the attacker's motivation in different threat scenarios. For example, the attack might cause a service disruption by data encryption, denial of service, or data destruction. The motivation for such could be to cause financial or reputation damage or a sudden price increase.

5   Evaluation Method

We have organized two game events (GE) for evaluation. The game was deployed as a category of challenge in a full-day CyberSecurity Challenge (CSC) event. Each attack scenario was one challenge. The player can choose the order of solving the challenges. Players could choose from COPYCAT and other challenges in the CSC. By solving the attack scenario, the player wins points, and at the end of CSC, the team with the highest number of points wins the game.

Table 3. General information about the two game events organized for evaluation

Game Event	Date	No. of players	No. of teams	No. of players per team	Country	Mode
GE1	08.12.2023	40	7	5∼8	China	Onsite
GE2	26.01.2024	22	5	3∼6	Germany	Hybrid

We present the details about the game events in Table 3. The first game event was organized in China, with 40 participants joining onsite. They worked together in teams in a meeting room. During the game, they can ask questions to the coach for hints or help if there are any questions. The second game event was organized in Germany, with 22 participants. Six players joined onsite, forming two teams. Sixteen players joined online, forming three teams. They can also turn to the coaches for help during the game, as in the previous game event.

The players' activities were captured in the backend for game dynamics analysis during the game events. The game dynamic data were the primary source of the evaluation, and additionally, the players gave feedback during and after the game events. These are the two main parts of the evaluation.

6   Result

According to our collected feedback, the players agreed with the COPYCAT game logic and solved the scenarios with an explanation before the game event. They found the game playful and meaningful. The winning conditions are explained before the game event: 1) The player should have a defense plan with a higher threshold success rate. 2) All the applied cards should be assigned to the correct responsibility. 3) All the attacks in the attack scenario should be defended by at least one card. The player will solve the attack scenario only when all three conditions are fulfilled. However, there were still questions about them during the game. It should be explained more thoroughly in future game events with an adaptation of the game interface. Those conditions are addressed in the last three lines of Table 4 on the dynamics statistics.

Apart from the direct feedback, we captured the game dynamic data and applied statistical analysis based on the collected data. The result is presented in Table 4.

The Table 4 provides a comprehensive overview of the game dynamics data, starting from the second line. The "Number of captured submissions" reflects the total data entries captured throughout the game event. The "Overall" column aggregates the data from GE 1 and GE 2.

Table 4. Game dynamic statistic during the game event

	GE 1	GE 2	Overall
Number of captured submissions	1024	84	1108
Submission per scenario per team	7.99	8.08	8.04
Time per scenario (minutes: seconds)	3:47	2:57	3:22
Number of submissions with incorrect responsibilities per scenario	3.78	0.38	2.08
Number of submissions with undefended cards per scenario	11.93	1.91	6.92
Number of submissions with low success rate per scenario	10.22	1.75	5.99

"Submission per scenario per team" illustrates the average number of submissions required to solve a scenario successfully. This metric is derived by dividing the total number of submissions made to a scenario before solving it by the number of teams that have both played and solved it. This process generates twelve values corresponding to the twelve scenarios, with 7.99 in Table 4 representing their average. It is calculated because not all teams have played and solved all the scenarios. The "overall" column presents the average of GE 1 and GE 2. In GE 1, the total captured submissions are significantly higher than in GE2. However, the submission per scenario per term is almost the same as in GE2 since the teams in GE1 made many submissions after solving the scenario. Those submissions are valid for "Number of captured submissions" but not for "Submission per scenario per team." The data show that the team solves the scenario at around eight tries. We could imply that the game logic is valid and the difficulty level is proper. In GE 1, numerous submissions were made to the platform event after successfully solving the game scenario. This fact showed that the players were still interested in understanding the attack and defense mapping and the responsibility assignment even after getting the points.

"Time per scenario" denotes the average duration for a team to resolve a scenario successfully. In the backend, we track when a team first accesses a scenario and when the scenario is solved. The difference in time shows the time it took for the team to solve the scenario. The "overall" column shows the average case. On average, the players spent 3 min 22 s for one scenario.

"Number of submissions with incorrect responsibilities per scenario" quantifies erroneous submissions due to misassigned responsibilities. This value is calculated by dividing the total number of such submissions across all scenarios by the number of scenarios and teams participating in each scenario. For GE2, the value is smaller than one since, in some scenarios, the participating team made no mistake in the responsibility assignment. Similar calculation principles apply to the subsequent lines in the table.

In total, the players in GE 2 performed better than those in GE 1. In GE 1, the total number of players is almost twice as much as in GE 2. There were two trainers in both game events. The difference in the number of participants contributes to the fact that in GE 2, the players are better supported and instructed. Another factor contributing to the result might be the size of teams. In GE 1, the largest team had eight players. However, the team size in GE 2 was smaller, which might enable more efficient communication within the team.

During the game events, we also observed the whole process. Assistance was provided in case of needed help. The discussion within a group regarding the solving of an attack scenario was heated and informative. In the feedback round, the players often mentioned they enjoyed the game and found it helpful. Some even asked if a longer-term deployment is possible.

7 Conclusion

The article presents a new game called COPYCAT to prepare for a cyber incident in a data-related supply chain attack. This work is based on the experience we gathered with CATS. With CATS, we developed a successful serious game design and a method to tailor games to further cyber security scenarios. We also developed challenges for the domain of supply chain attacks and resilience of cloud infrastructures. This paper marks a milestone in positioning a new game dedicated to incident response. Our research question is answered:

RQ: What strategies can be employed to adapt the existing serious game framework to address the theme of cloud data-relevant supply chain attacks in the industry?

In our work, we follow the design science research methodology and identify the elements that need to be reflected in the game design. The game is adapted based on elements derived from real-world problems, and it suits the organizational setting. In the evaluation cycle, we collect data and feedback, which directly or indirectly show the usefulness of the designed artifact.

Based on the data collected and the analysis in the result section, we conclude that our adaptation to the CATS game is valid. The players understand the logic of the COPYCAT game and enjoy the game. With the hints we provided during the game, the majority solved the attack scenarios and took notes of the necessary know-how for solving the attack scenario.

However, the current game interface and the missing explanation of the game's winning condition caused some confusion, according to the questions asked to the trainer during the game event. We plan to address this in the next design iteration of COPYCAT.

COPYCAT is a useful artifact designed and implemented following the design science research (DSR) methodology. It contributes to the existing body of knowledge in instantiating the DSR theory and inspires similar research in this field. The adaption process we made to the game element is novel. In the future, we would like to introduce more incident response scenarios in the story setting and develop more data-related supply chain attack scenarios based on our experiences in the first design iteration. We look forward to organizing more game events and marching into the next design iteration.

Acknowledgments. This research task was partially supported by Fundação para a Ciência e a Tecnologia, I.P. (FCT) [ISTAR Projects: UIDB/04466/2020 and UIDP/04466/2020]. Ulrike Lechner acknowledges funding for project CONTAIN by the Bundesministerium für Bildung und Forschung (FKZ 13N16581). Tiange Zhao and Tiago Gasiba acknowledge the funding provided by the Bundesministerium für Bildung und Forschung (BMBF) for the project CONTAIN (FKZ 13N16585).

References

1. Administration, G.S.: Fedramp (federal risk and authorization management program). Program, General Services Administration, Washington, D.C. (2019). https://www.fedramp.gov
2. Al Nafea, R., Almaiah, M.A.: Cyber security threats in cloud: literature review. In: 2021 International Conference on Information Technology (ICIT), pp. 779–786. IEEE (2021)
3. Alliance, C.S.: Cloud controls matrix v4 (2021). https://cloudsecurityalliance.org/artifact-s/cloud-controls-matrix-v4/
4. ATT&CK, M.: Supply Chain Compromise. https://attack.mitre.org/techniques/T1-195/
5. ATT&CK, M.: Techniques (2017). https://attack.mitre.org/techniques/
6. BSI: Cloud computing C5 criteria catalogue (2020). http://tinyurl.com/5665jp8y
7. Corporation, N.A.E.R.: Cip (critical infrastructure protection) reliability standards. Standards, North American Electric Reliability Corporation, Atlanta, GA (2020). https://www.nerc.com/pa/Stand/Pages/CIPStandards.aspx
8. CSA: Top threats to cloud computing: The egregious 11. BLACKHAT2019 (2019)
9. Cybercrime & Digital Threats, C.M.: Hacker Infects Node.js Package to Steal from Bitcoin Wallets). https://www.trendmicro.com/vinfo/dk/security/news/cybercrime-and-digital-threats/hacker-infects-node-js-package-to-steal-from-bitcoin-wallets
10. PCI DSS: PCI Security Standards Council (PCI SSC) (2022). https://www.pcisecuritystandards.org/
11. Dörner, R., Göbel, S., Effelsberg, W., Wiemeyer, J.: Serious Games: Foundations, Concepts and Practice. Springer, Cham (2016). https://doi.org/10.1007/978-3-319-40612-1
12. Fenz, S., Ekelhart, A.: Formalizing information security knowledge. In: Proceedings of the 4th international Symposium on Information, Computer, and Communications Security, pp. 183–194 (2009)
13. Ferro, L.S., Marrella, A., Catarci, T., Sapio, F., Parenti, A., De Santis, M.: AWATO: a serious game to improve cybersecurity awareness. In: Fang, X. (ed.) HCI in Games, pp. 508–529. Springer, Cham (2022). https://doi.org/10.1007/978-3-031-05637-6_33. http://tinyurl.com/ykfjph4x
14. Gasiba, T.: Raising Awareness on Secure Coding in the Industry through Cyber-Security Challenges. Ph.D. thesis, Universität der Bundeswehr München (2021)
15. Gleeson, N., Walden, I.: 'It's a jungle out there'?: cloud computing, standards and the law. SSRN Electron. J. (2014). https://doi.org/10.2139/ssrn.2441182
16. GVR-4-68038-210-5: Market Analysis Report: Cloud Computing Market Size, Share & Trends Analysis Report By Service (SaaS, IaaS), By Deployment, By Enterprise Size, By End-use, By Region, And Segment Forecasts, 2023–2030. https://www.grandviewresearch.com/industry-analysis/cloud-computing-industry

17. Hänsch, N., Benenson, Z.: Specifying IT security awareness. In: 25th International Workshop on Database and Expert Systems Applications, pp. 326–330. IEEE (2014). https://doi.org/10.1109/DEXA.2014.71

18. Hart, S., Margheri, A., Paci, F., Sassone, V.: Riskio: a serious game for cyber security awareness and education. Comput. Secur. **95**, 101827 (2020). https://doi.org/10.1016/j.cose.2020.101827

19. Hevner, A.: A three cycle view of design science research. Scandinavian J. Inf. Syst. **19**, 1–6 (2007). http://aisel.aisnet.org/sjis/vol19/iss2/4

20. for Internet Security, C.: Cis (center for internet security) controls. Standards, Center for Internet Security, East Greenbush, NY (2020). https://www.cisecurity.org/controls

21. Iosif, A.C., Gasiba, T.E., Zhao, T., Lechner, U., Pinto-Albuquerque, M.: A large-scale study on the security vulnerabilities of cloud deployments. In: Wang, G., Choo, K.K.R., Ko, R.K.L., Xu, Y., Crispo, B. (eds.) Ubiquitous Security (UbiSec 2021), pp. 171–188. Springer, Singapore (2022). https://doi.org/10.1007/978-981-19-0468-4_13

22. ISACA: Cobit (control objectives for information and related technologies). Framework, ISACA, Rolling Meadows, IL (2019). https://www.isaca.org/resources/cobit

23. ISO27001: ISO/IEC 27001 Information Security Management (2017). https://www.iso.org/isoiec-27001-information-security.html

24. ISO27002: ISO/IEC 27002:2013Information technology - Security techniques - Code of practice for information security controls (2013). https://www.iso.org/standard/54533.html

25. ISO27017: ISO/IEC 27017:2015 Information technology - Security techniques - Code of practice for information security controls based on ISO/IEC 27002 for cloud services (2015). https://www.iso.org/standard/43757.html

26. ISO27018: ISO/IEC 27018:2019Information technology - Security techniques - Code of practice for protection of personally identifiable information (PII) in public clouds acting as PII processors (2019). https://www.iso.org/standard/76559.html

27. Manuel Maqueira, J., Moyano-Fuentes, J., Bruque, S.: Drivers and consequences of an innovative technology assimilation in the supply chain: cloud computing and supply chain integration. Int. J. Prod. Res. **57**(7), 2083–2103 (2019). https://doi.org/10.1080/00207543.2018.1530473

28. Kruger, H., Kearney, W.: A prototype for assessing information security awareness. Comput. Secur. **25**(4), 289–296 (2006). https://doi.org/10.1016/j.cose.2006.02.008. https://www.sciencedirect.com/science/article/pii/S0167404806000563

29. NIST: NIST SP 800-53 Rev. 5 Security and Privacy Controls for Information Systems and Organizations (2020). https://csrc.nist.gov/pubs/sp/800/53/r5/upd1/final

30. Raza, M.: The Shared Responsibility Model for Security in The Cloud (IaaS, PaaS & SaaS). http://tinyurl.com/3aez4epc

31. Shostack, A.: Tabletop security games & cards (2021). https://shostack.org/games.html

32. Švábenský, V., Vykopal, J., Cermak, M., Laštovička, M.: Enhancing cybersecurity skills by creating serious games. In: Proceedings of the 23rd Annual ACM Conference on Innovation and Technology in Computer Science Education, pp. 194–199 (2018). https://doi.org/10.48550/arXiv.1804.03567

33. Thompson, M., Irvine, C.: Active learning with the cyberciege video game. In: Proceedings of the 4th Conference on Cyber Security Experimentation and Test. p. 10. CSET'11, USENIX Association, USA (2011)

34. TSC, A.: 2017 Trust Services Criteria (With Revised Points of Focus - 2022) (2017). https://www.aicpa-cima.com/resources/download/2017-trust-services-criteria-with-revised-points-of-focus-2022

35. Wolff, E.D., Growley, K., Gruden, M., et al.: Navigating the solarwinds supply chain attack. Procurement Lawyer **56**(2), 3–10 (2021)

36. Zhao, T., Gasiba, T., Lechner, U., Pinto-Albuquerque, M.: Thriving in the era of hybrid work: raising cybersecurity awareness using serious games in industry trainings. J. Syst. Software **210**, 111946 (2024). https://doi.org/10.1016/j.jss.2023.111946. https://www.sciencedirect.com/science/article/pii/S0164121223003412

37. Zhao, T., Lechner, U., Pinto-Albuquerque, M., Ata, E., Gasiba, T.: Cats: a serious game in industry towards stronger cloud security. In: Wang, G., Choo, K.K.R., Wu, J., Damiani, E. (eds.) Ubiquitous Security, pp. 64–82. Springer, Singapore (2023). https://doi.org/10.1007/978-981-99-0272-9_5

38. Zhao, T., Lechner, U., Pinto-Albuquerque, M., Ongu, D.: An ontology-based model for evaluating cloud attack scenarios in cats - a serious game in cloud security. In: 2023 IEEE International Conference on Engineering, Technology and Innovation (ICE/ITMC), pp. 1–9 (2023). https://doi.org/10.1109/ICE/ITMC58018.2023.10332371

Operation Raven
Design of a Cyber Security Incident Response Game

Andreas Seiler[1,2]([📧]) [ID], Ulrike Lechner[2] [ID], Judith Strussenberg[2] [ID],
and Stefan Hofbauer[2] [ID]

[1] Lechwerke AG, Augsburg, Germany
[2] University of the Bundeswehr Munich, Neubiberg, Germany
{andreas.seiler,ulrike.lechner,judith.strussenberg,
stefan.hofbauer}@unibw.de

Abstract. Envisioning a major ransomware incident with its potential consequences might be unpleasant, and preparing for such an incident takes quite an effort. Operation Raven is a serious game designed to facilitate discussion about processes and decisions to detect, contain, and eradicate ransomware. This paper presents the game idea and game material of Operation Raven and the results after two game events. The article reflects on the next steps.

Keywords: Incident response · Serious game · Tabletop exercise · Adversary emulation · Cyber threat intelligence · Ransomware

1 Introduction

"A ransomware sends its message. What now?" The serious game "Operation Raven" is designed to answer this question. Consequences of a ransomware incident include disruption of production and service delivery, blackmailing, personal and organizational liabilities for a data breach or negligence, and the need to notify public authorities. Ransomware is a threat to individuals, organizations, and supply chains. Preparing for a ransomware incident is challenging: Thinking about such an event is not a pleasure, and preparation takes effort and resources. Operation Raven facilitates discussions about processes, communication, and decisions to detect, contain, and eradicate the malware. It is meant to increase effectiveness and efficiency in incident response.

In its current version, Operation Raven is designed for an energy provider's infrastructure and ransomware capable of encrypting and exfiltrating data. In our game setting, we assume that the organization is a critical infrastructure in Germany and that the regulatory frameworks of NIS II, Informationssicherheitsgesetz 2.0, and DSGVO apply. Operation Raven is a serious game played by one or several groups as a tabletop exercise (TTX) to simulate the incident response to ransomware. A game master simulates the course of action of a ransomware attack. The gaming material includes a game board depicting the organization's infrastructure under attack, incident cards representing

F. Phillipson et al. (Eds.): I4CS 2024, CCIS 2109, pp. 337–347, 2024.
https://doi.org/10.1007/978-3-031-60433-1_19

the ransomware and incident response actions, and a structured way to model the response on a response board, typically on a whiteboard. The game board also displays the relationship between the critical infrastructure provider and its external IT providers. The ransomware makes its move (simulated by the game master), the players define their incident response actions and note them on the incident response board, and the game master evaluates the effectiveness of these actions and determines the next move of the simulated ransomware. A highly modular game design allows customization for specific IT and OT infrastructure and organization designs, industries, and incident scenarios.

The first two game events were done with researchers and technical staff from CERTs and SOCs. Results from these first two games are promising—the game contributes to better preparedness, and participants enjoy the gaming experience. This article reports on the design to gamify incident response in the serious game Operation Raven and the first two games being played to validate the gamification idea. The article is organized as follows. Research design (Sect. 2) and a discussion of Background and Related Work (Sect. 3) set the stage for the presentation of the Game Design (Sect. 4) and a discussion of the evaluation results (Sect. 5) and next steps (Sect. 6).

2   Research Design

The Design Science paradigm by Hevner [5] guides our research, and we take inspiration from Action Design Research [12] to solve a specific organizational problem in a collaboration between practitioners and researchers. In design and evaluation activities, we follow an iterative approach.

The research design involves establishing an agreement between researchers and organizations through a successfully evaluated joint research proposal, an analysis of concepts and technologies to increase proficiency in cyber incident response, an initial game design, and two game events meant for testing the game idea. The two events were conducted in July and August 2023. Experts in cyber security games and academic experts played the first game. The second game was performed with practitioners from Security Operations Centers (SOCs), the Computer Emergency Response Team (CERT), and one researcher. The first author of this article acted as a game master and directed Operation Raven in both games.

3   Background and Related Work

We aim to empower incident responders, such as the staff from SOCs and CERTs, to react effectively to cyber threats. This section reviews the state of the art in serious cybersecurity games, frameworks, and standards in incident response, training, and exercise support.

3.1   Frameworks, Norms, and Standards in Incident Response

This subsection outlines frameworks used in incident response that are either standards or de facto standards. We use these standards to ensure the relevance of our game in the industry and straightforward playability by teams.

The Bundesamt für Sicherheit in der Informationstechnik (BSI) provides with the BSI-Standard 100-4 Notfallmanagement a guideline to prepare for business continuity in case of a cyber incident [1]. NIST provides a structured Incident Response Life Cycle to identify and deal with cyber security incidents. The activities are (1) Preparation, (2) Detection and Analysis, (3) Containment, Eradication and Recovery, and (4) Post-Incident Activities [10]. This guideline describes what "is necessary for rapidly detecting incidents, minimizing loss and destruction, mitigating the exploited weaknesses, and restoring IT services." The NIST report describes that organizations must create, provision, and operate a formal incident response capability. The required activities include creating an incident response policy and plan, developing procedures for performing incident handling and reporting, setting guidelines for communicating with internal and external stakeholders and regularly train these activities.

The Mitre ATT&CK Matrix for Enterprise is a globally accessible knowledge base of adversary tactics and techniques based on real-world observations [14]. It captures the steps and techniques of an attack.

These norms, standards and frameworks mainly define what organizations need to do to be able to react to security incidents, but not how to implement it in your ecosystem. Operation Raven is designed as a modular tool to customize and adapt given best practices to your organization, teams an resources (staff, tools, know-how). The modularity of the game allows it to be adapted to different scenarios, employee qualification levels and company maturity levels.

3.2   Training in Incident Response: Cyber Ranges and Serious Games

A cyber range is a simulated environment designed to train cyber security personnel in technical skills and tools in cyber security in general and attack detection, incident handling, or forensics in particular. Red teaming, blue teaming, Capture-the-Flag games, and forensics simulation or competitive genres can be facilitated in a cyber range. [9,17] provides an overview of cyber ranges, the technology, and the concepts. In our experience, exercises in cyber ranges are valuable in training technical skills. However, documentation of hypotheses, decisions, and processes falls short during the precious time on the cyber range, and the learnings are not solidified into unified, organization-wide coordinated processes after the training.

Serious games address awareness of security topics. Shostack maintains a list of serious games in cyber security online [13]. Most of the games listed aim to raise awareness, particularly for topics such as social engineering, or lean more towards the red-teaming side. Incident response is hardly represented in this list. A notable incident response game listed by Shostack is the game

Backdoors&Breaches. Backdoors&Breaches is a card game for incident response developed by Black Hills Information Security in 2019, focusing on awareness. Capture-the-flag is a competitive game genre in which players earn flags for successfully solving cyber security tasks and puzzles [7,8]. Tasks include cyber defense techniques and red teaming capabilities. There are also Capture-the-flag games available for digital forensics and incident response from SANS Institute [11] or providers like Hack The Box [3]. These serious games focus on developing and training personal skills. The escape room game format [2,16] has several puzzles to be solved under time pressure to escape a room. Tasks include solving puzzles, decryption, and (basic) forensic skills of analyzing documents and encryption/decryption. These games train awareness and red teaming or forensic skills. Escape room games do typically not address the strategic dimensions of planning a complex endeavor. Increasing IT security awareness is good and important, but not enough. Learned behavior must also be practiced to be quickly available in an emergency. With its highly customizable setting, Operation Raven creates a training environment tailored to your company.

4 Game Design: Operation Raven

This section presents the game design and gaming material of Operation Raven and the core design decisions made in formulating the first game ideas. Operation Raven is designed to raise the level of preparedness for a cyber incident. The setting of Operation Raven in the initial version is an energy provider, and it is designed primarily for technical personnel from CERTs and SOCs as game participants in the initial design iteration.

The design ideas were to use a tabletop setting for several groups of two to five players that can be played several times, a game master leading the game, and a time frame from three to four hours for the game experience. The main takeaways from the game are processes and decisions made in incident response. The results from the game will—in forthcoming design iterations—be refined to playbooks for incident response.

4.1 Game Design Process

Inspired by the Backdoors & Breaches card game, we decided to evolve the game idea of revealing the different steps an attacker takes and how to react to them, based on the Mitre ATT&CK Matrix for Enterprise. Our primary focus for improvement was realism and authentic details concerning the attack and the defensive side. So, for the game design process, our three main pillars are industry and infrastructure analysis, cyber threat intelligence (CTI), and adversary emulation.

To ensure a realistic gaming experience, the first design activity is the industry and infrastructure analysis. It considers the industry the participants are working in, interested parties, the infrastructure they are running, roles and responsibilities, and the detection and reaction capabilities established.

The game board results from analyzing the relevant IT infrastructure and its abstraction to make the infrastructure suitable for the game and a tailoring step to the potential audience. Another crucial aspect concerns the stakeholders involved or required in responding to a cyber security incident. In addition to authorities, the press, customers, and business partners, internal interfaces such as the business, management, communications department, and legal department must also be considered. These are represented as interchangeable entities in the stakeholder part of the game board. Furthermore, the experience of SOC and CERT staff in the industry has influenced the creation of IOC and Inject cards, as well as the design of the response board.

The use of Cyber Threat Intelligence (CTI) answers the question: from whom do we want to protect us, and what do we have to be able to react to? For that, we leverage core concepts of CTI: threat modeling, open source intelligence (OSINT), and intrusion analysis. Extensive CTI research is the foundation of good, serious game content. First, a threat model was created for a given use case. For the prototype of our game, a threat that has a broad application was chosen: a criminal group using ransomware droppers introduced by phishing attacks on enterprises. Using the MITRE ATT&CK framework [14], groups of relevant APTs can be identified, as well as their used tools, techniques, and procedures (TTPs). To flesh out our threat model, we use OSINT to create game material based on real threats, such as the BlackBasta group [4] and the Qakbot malware family [15]. Besides that, technical malware analysis reports and write-ups of actual incidents were used as sources of information for this task.

Once a specific threat is chosen, a sequence of adversary actions can be defined. We utilize MITRE ATT&CK tactics and the Cyber Kill Chain as de-facto standards for categorizing adversary actions within the sequence. The results of the CTI phase can be used to choose which tools, techniques, and procedures should be part of the incident phases. With this information, a master scenario event list (MSEL) is created, which documents the courses of action of the adversary, the relation to the game board assets, resulting IOCs, and linking to the MITRE ATT&CK tactics and techniques. Based on the MSEL TTP, IOC and inject cards are created, depicting the technical details of the incident from the attackers' and defenders' perspectives.

The outcome of our game design process is five game content elements:

1. game board
2. master scenario event list (MSEL)
3. incident cards - representing TTPs, IOCs, and injects
4. response board
5. response cards (color-coded cards for documentation of hypotheses and incident response actions)

4.2 Game Material

The game material includes a game board (cf. Fig. 1) that is structured in three main sections: an infrastructure diagram, a round marker, and the attack phases.

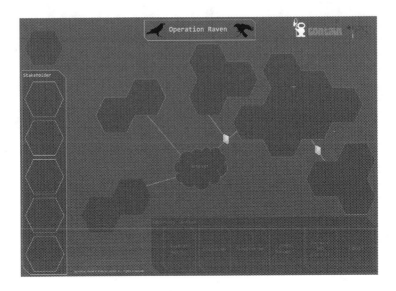

Fig. 1. Operation Raven game board

The infrastructure diagram depicts an abstract model of the IT network of an energy provider. It results from an industry and infrastructure identification analysis based on organizations in the energy sector in Germany. This infrastructure diagram contains network elements of particular interest in a ransomware attack: critical assets (business applications, central IT systems), supporting IT (Active Directory, mail systems, servers), network segmentation, and security systems as, e.g., firewalls IDS/IPS, VPN, monitoring, SIEM. Further elements to include in other use cases could also consider external service providers and cloud services. The game board is a reference for the players, which provides them a unified view for discussions concerning attack vectors, affected assets, containment possibilities, and consequences of their actions.

The principal place where the incident response actions of the players are documented is the response board (cf. Fig. 2). The response board is structured into various areas. On the top is a section where the players are supposed to document their hypothesis at the start of each game round based on the incident information. Below that, the board provides a structure according to the SANS/NIST incident response phases: identification, containment, eradication, and recovery. On the response board, the players document their defined IR actions on colorized post-its within their respective before-mentioned IR phases. The Courses of Action defined by Lockheed Martin [6] can be used as a guide for the player's defined IR actions: discover, detect, deny, disrupt, degrade, deceive, or destroy the adversary's TTPs and infrastructure. Those actions are sorted into four categories, which are identified by respectively colored cards called response cards: immediate measures (red), incident response tasks (blue), communication & organization (yellow), and decisions (green).

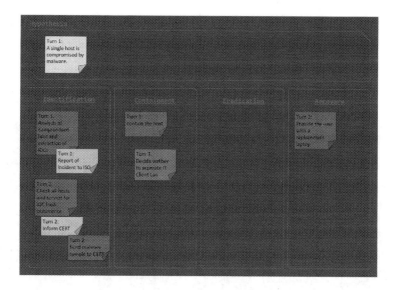

Fig. 2. Illustrative example of the response board (Color figure online)

- Immediate measures describe priority tasks in the incident response process that are ideally defined beforehand. This includes functions like network separation or system shutdown. These actions are typically identification and containment activities.
- Incident response tasks capture steps to be taken within the phases of identification, containment, eradication, and recovery. This includes, e.g., checks of systems for indicators of compromise.
- Communication defines who needs to inform whom, what, and when. These kinds of tasks require the involvement of different stakeholders and reporting and reporting channels. Communication and organization tasks include, e.g., interaction with stakeholders beyond the team enacted by the players. Typical actions include interaction with legal experts, technical experts within the organization, experts in crisis management, media representatives, public administration, insurance companies, or the C-level in the organization.
- Decisions show the points in time in a response effort where the incident responders need to obtain decisions on alternative tasks at a given time with given information on the incident. It mostly comes down to business decisions beyond the IR team's responsibility.

All adversary actions (of the ransomware and the attackers), defined in the CTI part of the game design process, are documented in the master scenario event list (MSEL). Each entry in the MSEL represents the adversary's step in the Cyber Kill Chain to progress in the attack. The documentation briefly describes the action, the targeted assets, IOCs, detection possibilities, the ATT&CK tactic, technique, sub-technique, and ID.

The game provides three decks of cards (cf. Fig. 3). Adversary actions are written down in the Tactics, Techniques, and Procedures (TTP) cards. External and internal events that influence the IR efforts are represented by "Inject" cards. The "IOC" deck contains cards with information on evidence and indicators of compromise (IOCs).

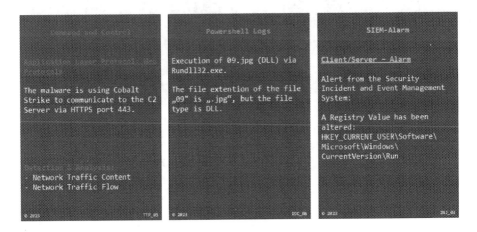

Fig. 3. Operation Raven TTP, IOC, and inject cards

4.3   Gameplay Operation Raven

Operation Raven is played in several rounds. The game master manages the game flow through a round-based game flow. Initially, the setup for the game is as follows: players get the game board that depicts the infrastructure, a set of empty color-coded task cards, and a dice to mark the round. Players can access the Incident Response Board - a whiteboard with a template to document the actions per round structured in identification, containment, eradication, or recovery. Players also receive the initial inject cards. Then the game starts with several rounds, and each round has four steps:

1. players formulate a hypothesis for the current game round based on the inject cards, identify TTPs, and document it in the hypothesis section on the Incident Response Board
2. players define actions in four different categories (immediate measures, incident response tasks, communications, decisions) and document them on the color-coded task cards
3. players put the task cards on the Incident Response board in their respective IR Phase (identification, containment, eradication, or recovery)
4. the game master evaluates the task cards, compares them with the MSEL and TTP Cards, and decides, based on the defined task cards in that round, which TTP cards will be revealed to the players and which IOC or inject cards the players get for the next round

After the fourth step, the game master assesses the situation and selects the next inject cards from his deck. At this moment, the game master emulates the ransomware attack. The game lasts until the players reveal all the TTP cards.

5   Test Games and First Results

The first game was played with cyber security experts and experts in cyber security gamification at the university's premises.

The players enjoyed the gaming experience and played the game as one group. They were also able to handle the game material, and it seems that the Mitre ATT&CK framework and the game board are sound bases for the decisions.

Discussions in the game were meant to identify potential attacks and detection and containment activities. Notable points in the debate were: When to cut off the ransomware from its command&control server. A ransomware that cannot reach its server might turn to a second alternative to perform its task, adding to the risk. Professionals in the group would instead observe what the ransomware does; the less experienced academic participants would be more eager to stop the communication of ransomware with the C2 server. Similar discussion topics involved proactively searching the network and IT infrastructure for ransomware samples. At the same time, the CERT members would argue that they would wait for indicators of compromise to happen and would rather not disturb the daily operations. The event list started with an employee clicking on a phishing email and the spread of the ransomware in the organization. In the discussion following the gaming phase, concerns were raised about the fun factor and the possibility of winning the game and defeating the ransomware. For the players, seeing step after step of the ransomware and needing to react seemed to be rather serious with little fun factor. Players did not challenge the transferability of learning and documentation results to the real-world setting.

The second game took place on the premises of an energy provider. Two groups of SOC and CERT members and one researcher played the game in groups of three and four. Again, ransomware was entered via phishing and gradually entered the infrastructure. The discussions in the game centered on whether to search proactively or wait for indicators of compromise, about the need to make sure that ransomware is eradicated and that the efforts expected from them are high—given the actual workload and the frequency of minor phishing attacks in the organization. Discussions were about whether to disrupt the communication of the ransomware with its command and control server (C2 server), and it turns out that security experts from the OT and the IT department would do it differently, with the OT cutting off much earlier than the IT experts. The IT security experts would only close the ports if the data loss prevention system would detect a significant amount of data. Players agreed that having mixed teams, senior management, and other roles would be valuable in raising mutual understanding in incident response and crisis management.

In both games, players relied on their infrastructure and knowledge and remained within the realm of what an energy provider has in terms of infrastructure and IT security controls. This is again an indicator that tentative actions in the game would transfer into real-life settings.

6 Conclusions and Next Steps

Effective response to cyber threats depends on trained staff, processes, and communication. Serious games, like the presented tabletop exercise Operation Raven, can be an important tool to achieve this goal. This paper presents the game idea and results from the first design iteration. The feedback and experience of the first iteration and the first game events of the game showed that the game material and analog nature of Operation Raven inspired discussions and supported creative problem-solving. The developed game design process of analyzing the industry and infrastructure, conducting tailored cyber threat intelligence, and using adversary emulation ensures realistic technical details for the game materials, the relevance and usefulness of the game results, and how the game can be adapted to participants' and organizations' needs.

The next steps include designs of Operation Raven for more target groups, such as managers and decision-makers, and designs for different maturity levels of cybersecurity organizations. The next steps include analyzing what is necessary to create valid playbooks for the organization out of the game results and how to review and refine them. Other next steps include the design of more professional game material to enter the next phase in the design and evaluation setup. More game boards for other critical infrastructures and other scenarios and variations of ransomware incidents will also be created, and the skills to adapt the game to specific organizations and stakeholder groups will develop over time with more games being played. Another open challenge is the dependence on the game master. We will try to incorporate more intelligence and mechanisms into the game so that the demands on the game master are reduced. Once the game ideas have matured, we will consider designing and developing a digital game platform for Operation Raven.

Acknowledgments. We gratefully acknowledge funding for Project CONTAIN by the Bundesministerium für Bildung und Forschung (BMBF) (grant number 13N16581) as part of the SIFO program. We thank all game participants and all the partners in the German and Austrian research consortium of CONTAIN for contributing and validating our research.

Disclosure of Interests. The authors have no competing interests to declare that are relevant to the content of this article.

References

1. Bundesamt für Sicherheit in der Informationstechnik: BSI-Standard 100-4 Notfall-management. Technical report, Bundesamt für Sicherheit in der Informationstechnik (2008). www.bsi.bund.de/gshb
2. Costa, G., Ribaudo, M.: Designing a serious game for cybersecurity education. In: Cooper, K.M.L., Bucchiarone, A. (eds.) Software Engineering for Games in Serious Contexts: Theories, Methods, Tools, and Experiences, pp. 265–290. Springer, Cham (2023). https://doi.org/10.1007/978-3-031-33338-5_12
3. Hack The Box: Enhance digital forensics and incident response (dfir) skills with sherlocks (2023). www.hackthebox.com/blog/sherlocks
4. Health Sector Cybersecurity Coordination Center (HC3): Threat profile: Black basta. Tech. rep., U.S. Department of Health & Human Services (2023). https://www.hhs.gov/sites/default/files/black-basta-threat-profile.pdf
5. Hevner, A., March, S., Park, J.: Design science in information systems research. MIS Q. 75–105 (2004). https://doi.org/10.2307/25148625
6. Hutchins, E.M., Cloppert, M.J., Amin, R.M., et al.: Intelligence-driven computer network defense informed by analysis of adversary campaigns and intrusion kill chains. Leading Issues Inf. Warfare Secur. Res. **1**, 80 (2011)
7. Karagiannis, S., Maragkos-Belmpas, E., Magkos, E.: An analysis and evaluation of open source capture the flag platforms as cybersecurity e-learning tools. In: Drevin, L., Von Solms, S., Theocharidou, M. (eds.) WISE 2020. IAICT, vol. 579, pp. 61–77. Springer, Cham (2020). https://doi.org/10.1007/978-3-030-59291-2_5
8. Kucek, S., Leitner, M.: An empirical survey of functions and configurations of open-source capture the flag (CTF) environments. J. Network Comput. Appl. **151**, 102470 (2020). https://doi.org/10.1016/j.jnca.2019.102470, www.sciencedirect.com/science/article/pii/S1084804519303303
9. Late, I., Boja, C.: Cyber range technology stack review. In: Ciurea, C., Pocatilu, P., Filip, F.G. (eds.) Education, Research and Business Technologies, pp. 25–40. Springer, Singapore (2023). https://doi.org/10.1007/978-981-19-6755-9_3
10. National Institute of Standards and Technology: NIST cybersecurity framework (2023). www.nist.gov/cyberframework
11. SANS Institute: Netwars dfir tournament & continuous (2023). www.sans.org/cyber-ranges/
12. Sein, M.K., Henfridsson, O., Purao, S., Rossi, M., Lindgren, R.: Action design research. MIS Quart. **35**(1), 37–56 (2011). https://doi.org/10.2307/23043488
13. Shostack, A.: Games for security (2023). https://shostack.org/games.html
14. The MITRE Cooporation: MITRE ATT&CK cloud matrix (2020). https://attack.mitre.org/versions/v8/matrices/enterprise/cloud/
15. The MITRE Corporation: Qakbot (2023). https://attack.mitre.org/software/S0650/
16. Williams, T., El-Gayar, O.: Design of a virtual cybersecurity escape room. In: Choo, K.-K.R., Morris, T., Peterson, G., Imsand, E. (eds.) NCS 2021. LNNS, vol. 310, pp. 60–73. Springer, Cham (2022). https://doi.org/10.1007/978-3-030-84614-5_6
17. Yamin, M.M., Katt, B., Gkioulos, V.: Cyber ranges and security testbeds: scenarios, functions, tools and architecture. Comput. Secur. 101636 (2020). https://doi.org/10.1016/j.cose.2019.101636

Blockchain and Digital Sovereignty

Greenhouse Gas Emissions as Commons: A Community Service Approach with Blockchain on the Edge

Karl Seidenfad[(⊠)] [iD], Maximilian Greiner [iD], Jan Biermann,
David Dannenberg, Sven Keineke, and Ulrike Lechner [iD]

Computer Science Department, University of the Bundeswehr Munich,
Neubiberg, Germany
{karl.seidenfad,maximilian.greiner,jan.biermann,david.dannenberg,
sven.keineke,ulrike.lechner}@unibw.de

Abstract. Designing distributed infrastructures for the common good
becomes a driver of decarbonization as one of the significant endeavors
of this time. This article explores the design principles for a community
service approach in developing resilient infrastructure, as well as secure
tools for managing greenhouse gas emissions. We introduce the prototype of an information system that utilizes blockchain technology and
edge computing for collaborative automation of measuring, reporting,
and verifying (MRV) greenhouse gas (GHG) emissions. In addition, the
paper discusses the concept and early results of a field trial conducted
with industry partners.

Keywords: Blockchain · Edge computing · Commons · Governance

1 Introduction

Designing distributed infrastructures for the common good becomes a driver of
decarbonization as one of the significant endeavors of this time. Exemplifying
the bottom-up approach of the Paris Agreement [51], which outlines the importance of contributions of non-state actors [42] to decarbonization [60] and the
European Emissions Trading System (EU ETS) as a concrete implementation
of a co-responding information system, which governs greenhouse gas (GHG)
emissions as a common. In 2023 the EU ETS has covered approximately 40% of
the European GHG emissions, while the remaining 60% are caused by non-ETS
sectors (e.g., agriculture and residential), and holding non-state actors accountable by a sectoral expansion of the EU ETS is intensely discussed [60]. In this
regard, the European Union's (EU) Effort Sharing Regulation (ESR) serves as
a complementary information system to address non-ETS emissions by market
mechanisms at the national level.

Tackling the challenge of holding non-state actors accountable on international carbon markets, this article lightens the limitations of *market regulation*

F. Phillipson et al. (Eds.): I4CS 2024, CCIS 2109, pp. 351–376, 2024.
https://doi.org/10.1007/978-3-031-60433-1_20

and *governmental regulations* exemplifying the EU ETS and ESR, and proposes advanced automation and an approach of Governing the Commons inspired by Nobel laureate Elinor Ostrom [40] as a third way to organize human cooperation on climate action, backed as a *community service*. Therefore, we propose to complement the Paris Agreement's bottom-up approach of measuring, reporting and verification (MRV) [36] of GHG emissions by designing a new technological interaction layer, which may serve as a community service on climate action for non-state actors.

Our scenario-driven research employs the Design Science methodology of Hevner et al. [21] and the scenario illustrates a coffee roaster consortium that jointly implements MRV of GHG emissions. Therefore, this article extends the work of two previous design cycles [55,58], and presents Design Cycle 3. Especially, the questions of how to reduce transaction costs on MRV, how to raise ambitions on climate action in the spirit of the Paris Agreement, and tokenization as a risk management measure are in the scope of our proposal. To address these challenges, we combine the approach of up-scaled crediting [43] and the allocation of GHG emissions as a common pool resource (CPR), referring to Ostrom's eight design principles on self-governance of communities [40]. We propose a blockchain-based information system with edge computing capabilities, which allows the interaction of non-state actors inside a consortium on MRV. Therefore, the prototype of an edge installation serves as a gateway to the consortium blockchain, and we present the prototype node and evaluate it in a field installation with industry partners.

The remainder of the article is structured as follows. Section 2 presents the state-of-the-art of our research domain. Section 3 describes the problem. Section 4 presents the general solution approach and Sect. 5 illustrates a concrete scenario. Section 6 documents the implementation and Sect. 7 its evaluation. Finally, Sect. 8 concludes our findings from three design cycles in a draft of four design principles on blockchain-based MRV of GHG emissions. Finally, we outline future research activities.

2   State of the Art

The state of the art is shaped by knowledge in the domains: design and operation of blockchain technology, blockchain for climate action, and complementary work in the fields of socioeconomics and regulatory on MRV.

2.1   Design and Operation of Blockchain Technology

Addressing the design and operation of blockchain-based solutions, Lamken et al. [31] introduce a *design pattern* for blockchain-based information systems in supply chain management (SCM), and Hoiss et al. [24] describe a *taxonomy to orchestrate operations* inside a consortium blockchain. Labazova [29] analyzes the evaluation of blockchain implementations and presents an analytical framework that includes factors that need to be considered before starting blockchain projects. Ziolkowski, Miscione, and Schwabe [70] argue that the initial design of a blockchain is proposed by a core group of stakeholders, which have a major influence on the blockchain system. This might hamper the growth of the blockchain while reaching a critical mass. Therefore, the configuration and setting of a blockchain should be able to change or at least adapt to the new needs of the growing community. Sato and Himura [49] propose a solution based on native blockchain functionalities. Using smart contract functionality and consensus protocols, they suggest defining operations as smart contracts in the blockchain network. Gorski and Bednarski [15] developed a model-driven method based on UML to deploy distributed ledger networks. They implemented a model-to-code transformation for the R3 Corda framework. In the model, services are introduced for several tasks: provisioning TLS certificates, enforcing participating nodes, ordering, and time stamping of transactions, providing oracle data, controlling admissions in the Corda network, and resolving inquiries and incidents as stereotypes. These services are run by and hosted on the nodes.

Realizing the *business potential of blockchain* is crucially dependent on advanced design and engineering methods. Laurier et al. [33] discuss blockchain as a new accounting technology and, in general, the systematic analysis of economic value created by blockchain [32]. In Falazi et al. [12] business processes access the blockchain as a communication infrastructure. The Caterpillar framework [35] provides a business process execution engine that can be deployed entirely on a blockchain platform in such a way that once a process is deployed, no off-chain component is required to execute and monitor instances of the process. Ladleif et al. [30] approach the challenges of organizations to introduce blockchain into their business process management systems from a business process perspective. They analyze the core components of state-of-the-art blockchain-based business process management systems before rearranging them into a multi-chain choreography context.

Advanced features such as business process coordination and monitoring in blockchain are presented by Weber et al. [67]: data from business processes are encrypted and private and public keys are exchanged off-chain. The relation of which functionalities should be on-chain versus off-chain is discussed by Ladleif et al. [30]. Federated architectures are proposed by Adams et al. [1]. The topics considered include blockchain design, advanced methods, and tools for chaincode or blockchain orchestration. Although many approaches look at the blockchain and its support of business processes, blockchain operations are hardly considered. Beck et al. [5] proposed a research agenda by investigating blockchain governance in the light of IT Governance using the dimensions (decisions, accountabilities, and incentives) provided by Weill and Ross [48]. Greiner et al. [18] take up this approach and suggest design principles for the governance of blockchain-based consortia.

Blockchain technology is progressing toward technological maturity through the introduction of design patterns [31], taxonomies [24], and a growing number of projects in practice. Popular applications are supply chain management (SCM) projects such as IBM's TradeLens [28], BMW's PartChain [37], and

SiGREEN by SIEMENS for accounting product carbon footprints along the value-chain on a blockchain [59]. Furthermore, projects in the field of healthcare [50], education [16], identity management [34], voting [62], tokenization of real estate [69] or art works [66] etc. are known. In this regard, Monrat et al. [38] provides a survey from the perspectives of applications, challenges, and opportunities for blockchain technology.

2.2   Blockchain for Climate Action

Blockchain technology has gained recognition for its potential to support climate action and address environmental challenges. This chapter exemplifies use cases from the field of: carbon crediting, supply chain management (SCM), grid management, climate finance, and climate research.

Carbon Credits and Offset Market. One of the primary ways blockchain technology can contribute to climate action is improving the transparency, security, and efficiency of carbon credit markets. Carbon credits are tradable permits that represent the right to emit a specific amount of GHGs. Blockchain can be used to: First, to verify emissions reductions by allowing transparent and immutable tracking of emissions reductions. Each carbon credit can be associated with a unique digital token on a blockchain, making it easy to verify the authenticity of carbon offsets. Second, improve accessibility by making carbon credit markets with tokenization more accessible to small-scale projects and individuals, allowing a broader range of participants to contribute to emissions reductions. The discussion about *blockchain-based carbon markets* is lively [2,4,11]. International carbon markets employ a cap-and-trade schema that allows monetizing emissions reductions, and Richardson and Xu [47] present the model of a private permissioned blockchain for the EU ETS and discuss potential advantages over existing solutions. Furthermore, Braden [6] evaluates Bitcoin, Ethereum, Hyperledger Fabric, and EOS with regard to their applicability to climate policy applications. Schneider et al. [52] compare centralized and decentralized architectures to track international emissions mitigation transfers, and Schletz et al. [51] present a decision framework and architecture to embed the requirements of Article 6.2 in a blockchain-based market model.

Renewable Energy and Grid Management. Blockchain technology can facilitate the integration of renewable energy sources into existing grids and improve energy efficiency [14]. Blockchain-based peer-to-peer energy trading allows households with renewable energy sources, such as solar panels, to sell excess energy directly to their neighbors. This promotes decentralized energy production and reduces dependence on centralized power plants [65].

Climate Finance and Transparency. The transparency and efficiency of climate finance mechanisms, including the allocation and tracking of funds for climate-related projects, can benefit from the use of blockchain technology. Therefore, blockchain-based decentralized finance (DeFi) platforms can streamline climate finance disbursement, reduce administrative costs, and improve transparency in fund allocation [10]. Furthermore, smart contracts on blockchain can automate the release of funds to climate projects when predefined milestones are met, reducing the risk of misallocation or misuse of funds [68].

2.3   The Socioeconomic Background

The socioeconomic background of this article comprises the concept of business web typology according to Tapscott et al. [61], and theory about governing the commons [40].

The Business Web Typology. Tapscott et al. [61] discuss the transformation of the industrial-age corporation into the Business Web (B-Web) in the digital era. They highlight how companies like eBay and Cisco disrupted traditional industries with innovative offerings. These transformative firms relied on partners to move quickly and efficiently. B-Webs, partner networks connecting producers, suppliers, service providers, and customers via digital channels, are revolutionizing wealth creation. Tapscott et al. [61] categorize b-webs into five types: Agoras, Aggregations, Value Chains, Alliances, and Distributive Networks. Through case studies, they provide insight into the innovation of business models. They emphasize that participation in b-webs is essential to meet digital customers' needs, and businesses must lead or partner in these networks.

Governing the Commons. In her influential work, "Governing the Commons" [40] Elinor Ostrom delves into strategies for communities to adeptly oversee shared resources, steering clear of the tragedy of the commons. Through in-depth case studies, Ostrom outlines key principles for effective common-pool resource governance. She emphasizes the importance of local self-organized institutions, well-defined rules, and collaborative decision-making to promote sustainable resource management and prevent depletion. Ostrom's findings offer valuable guidance for policymakers and communities grappling with collective action challenges, aiming to secure the enduring sustainability of shared resources.

Jain et al. [27] explore blockchain governance for SME clusters and references to the *"Tragedy of Commons"* problem, stated in the dissertation of Hardin [19]. Poux et al. [44] analyze the use of blockchain to support the governance of common pool resources (CPR) based on Ostrom's design principles of self-governance for communities [40], and Jain et al. [27] summarize these eight principles as follows:

- `Clearly defined community boundaries`: It defines the rights of access and privileges for stakeholders within the network.
- `Congruence between rules and conditions of common goods`:
  The locus of rules that governs the behaviour of commons may change depending on local conditions.

- **Ensure participation in modifying the rules**: In order to have a collective choice arrangement and modification, people should participate in the network who are affected by rules.
- **Monitoring**: Some individuals in the network are responsible for the rest of the individual due to their role of monitoring of behaviour.
- **Graduated Sanctions for rule violators**: If there is a conflict or change in the behaviour of an individual in the network, other members may find it against the rules.
- **Dispute resolution mechanisms**: Access to spaces for low-cost conflict resolution.
- **Local enforcement of local rules**: Enforcement of rules in the network with the approval of higher authorities.
- **Multiple layers of nested enterprises**: The layer of an organisation to address the issues that may affect resource management in the network.

3   Problem Description

Article 6 of the Paris Agreement encourages the design of new mechanisms for climate action, in contrast to traditional project-based crediting, *up-scaled* crediting aggregates emissions mitigations across a group of sources, using a common baseline emission [43]. The up-scaled crediting of GHG emissions is a promising candidate to tackle the challenge of a sectoral expansion of the Emissions Trading System (ETS). Typically, non-ETS sectors are characterized by numerous emitters with a small individual emissions impact, which makes the accurate and cost-efficient reporting of emissions challenging and poses an attack surface for the issue of fraudulent emissions certificates. In this regard, the literature widely acknowledges the problems of transaction costs and the way to raise ambitions. However, the literature assumes that blockchain technology and process automation (e.g., through Internet of Things applications) could lead to a comprehensive expansion of ETS sectors in the future [6].

Transaction Costs. Transaction costs can be distinguished by costs for upstream and downstream pricing [8]. A carbon tax for fossil fuels represents an upstream approach, and downstream pricing is represented by market-based approaches (e.g., the EU ETS). There is a wide agreement about that regulating upstream (e.g., in the fossil fuel chain) yields lower transaction costs than regulating downstream, since fuel consumption is easier to monitor by existing systems than emissions. Furthermore, the number of emitters is larger than firms importing fossil fuels. However, the upstream approach considers carbon units from a relatively small number of large sources, which does not reflect the total number of GHG emissions, while a downstream approach allows the crediting of GHG emissions from emitters and may lead to a more exact measurement of GHG emissions. Coria and Jaraité [8] present a model for the composition of transaction costs on MRV, which gathers: (1) internal costs, spent on MRV tasks, (2) external costs for consulting, maintenance, and audit to ensure compliance; and (3) capital costs for instruments, software, and infrastructure. Beside the challenge of reducing transaction costs, MRV holds a certain investment risk; e.g., incorrect accounting of emissions can lead to rejection of the complete annual inventory and monetary sanctions by an authority.

Raising Ambitions. The Paris Agreement as a legally binding international treaty propagates the step-wise raising of ambitions on climate action, and the Global Stocktake [63] aims on raising ambitions on international level, where the pricing trajectory of certified emissions inside of carbon markets serves as a tool to raise ambitions on sub-national level. Increasing the price for certified emissions is one way to raise ambitions inside the Paris Agreement and drives the demand of knowledge transfer between non-state actors in implementing cost-efficient MRV and its continuous improvement.

4 Solution Proposal

Anticipating the challenges of reducing transaction costs, raising ambitions, and preventing the monetization of fraudulent emissions certificates, the European Union (EU) decided to manage non-ETS sectors separately within the ESR in 2018 as a complementary system to the EU ETS. The ESR operates a cap-and-trade schema exclusively between member states, and contrasts to the EU ETS which operates cap-and-trade between non-state actors. The ESR and the EU ETS have in common the employment of *market regulation* on the international level, while national registries serve as the database for carbon markets and maintain *governmental regulations* (see Fig. 1).

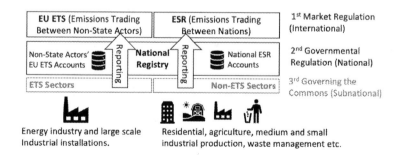

Fig. 1. "Governing the Commons" as the third regulation mechanism

The establishment of the ESR clearly displays an issue regarding the non-ETS sectors and the challenge of holding non-state actors accountable. In this regard, the question arises as to how up-scaled crediting may solve this problem. In her publication on a multi-scale approach to cope with climate action and other collective action problems, Ostrom [41] states that it is easier to design solutions for collective action problems related to smaller-scale CPRs' than for those related to the global commons. In this context, Streck [60] outlines that, according to Ostrom [41] there is potential in involving 'lower-level' or contextually situated actors who are highly specialized and best placed to implement actions that lead to the achievement of defined goals. In this regard, we recognize a *third way* to organize cooperation on MRV within the Paris Agreement. *Governing the commons*, according to Nobel laureate Elinor Ostrom [40] opens the door to the self-governance of CPRs' for communities on subnational level. Ostrom's eight design principles gather considerations such as the definition of actors' boundaries, the monitoring of CPR usage, graduated sanctions, and the setup of nested enterprises.

The following section introduces the scenario, which guides us through the consortium design on this third way to organize cooperation on MRV inside the Paris Agreement.

5   The Coffee Roastery Scenario

This article builds on the findings of two previous scenario-driven design cycles, namely in the field of greenhouse gas management for the coffee supply chain [58], and the use case of MRV within a consortium of biogas plants [55].

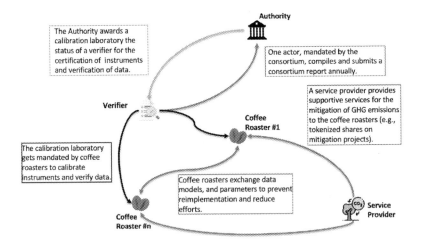

Fig. 2. Actors and relationships of the Coffee Roastery Scenario

The scenario of this article comprises a group of actors (see Fig. 2), which seek for cost-efficient satisfaction of regulations on MRV, and the opportunity to monetize emissions reductions. Therefore, several coffee roasters decide to organize MRV activities as a community and build relationships (see Table 2). For this purpose, coffee roasters mandate a calibration laboratory (known from the classical MRV process) as a verifier in the consortium. Furthermore, the consortium engages a service provider on climate action as a new actor to address the topic of risk reduction by tokenization. Note that the scenario illustrates a minimal setup with two roasters, and the collaborative approach benefits from additional actors (e.g., coffee roaster) in terms of cost reductions by effort sharing. In the following, we introduce the types of actors and the relationships in this scenario.

Coffee Roaster. The process of roasting coffee emits significant GHG emissions, depending on the machinery and process parameters used. The installation owner is responsible for measuring and reporting GHG emissions. Furthermore, a comprehensive set of ambient quality assurance and process documentation (see Fig. 2) is necessary to prove the correctness of the collected data in an annual compliance cycle.

Verifier. A verifier (e.g., an auditor or calibration laboratory) certified by an authority and mandated by a coffee roaster, proceeds quality assurance measures on equipment (e.g., instrument calibration) and verifies the correctness (four-eyes-principle) of emissions data before handing over a joint consortium report to the authority.

Service Provider. This type of actor provides supportive services to contribute directly or indirectly to the mitigation goal of the consortium. In our concrete scenario, this actor offers tokenized emissions reductions from afforestation and reforestation projects (see the Clean Development Mechanism (CDM) method AR-ACM0003 [9]) (Table 1).

Table 1. Actor Relationships within the Coffer Roastery Scenario

Relationship	Description
Verifier-to-Roaster	The roaster appoints the auditor to review the documentation and to calibrate instruments. Furthermore, once a year, the auditor prepares a deduction for the consortium report and sends it to the corresponding authority on behalf of the consortium
Roaster-to-Service Provider	As a measure to reduce financial risks, the roaster may purchase a limited amount of tokenized negative emissions from the service provider if regular certificates are unavailable on the carbon market or are too expensive in the auction
Roaster-to-Roaster	Each roaster maintains an own documentation trail, but data models, business logic, and parameters are exchanged, and hence reused between the roasters in the consortium

6   Implementation

The prototype implementation consists of two parts: The blockchain-based information system as the communication layer, and the edge installation to illustrate a real-world gateway. The architecture in Fig. 3 comprises both artifacts and is structured in three layers: First, the Business Actors layer gathers types of actors and their business relationships. Second, the Information Systems layer displays types of corresponding full or partial node of the peer-to-peer network, and provides further details (e.g., if it is an edge node or a virtual instance). Third, the Distributed Ledger Technology (DLT) Persistence layer depicts how each actor interacts with the consortium blockchain. The following sections elaborate the features of this architecture more in detail.

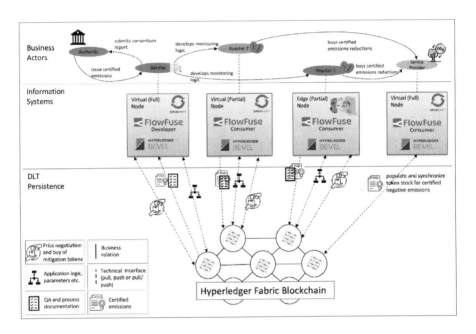

Fig. 3. The consortium's layered architecture with actor's relationships and interfaces

6.1   The Blockchain-Based Information System

The deployment of the consortium blockchain in the DLT persistence layer of Fig. 3 is done with tool Hyperledger Bevel [25] and employs a Hyperledger Fabric blockchain [3], which allows the partition of communication in the so-called channels. A channel defines a subnet for selective data sharing between actors with a corresponding channel membership and is technically represented by a dedicated ledger. Note that the features of our blockchain-based information system refer to the model in Fig. 4, which assigns actors and their data sharing use cases to derive a corresponding channel topology.

Joint Reporting. The joint reporting feature of the scenario is grounded in the non-state actors' annual reporting of GHG emissions to a national registry of the EU ETS and the ESR as downstream platforms. Therefore, the edge installation performs an automated continuous logging of emissions data (see Fig. 5) and the installation owner stores QA documentation throughout the year through invocation of the corresponding smart contracts. To complete the picture, scenario introduces a verifier for the consortium, which is required to annually compile a consortium emissions report (see Fig. 4) from the ledger and manage the submission to the authority. For this purpose, a verifier holds memberships of numerous channels in the consortium (see Fig. 4) and links emissions data and QA reports to a joint report. Additionally, negative emissions from a reforestation project (managed by the Service Provider actor) are assigned to actors who have participated.

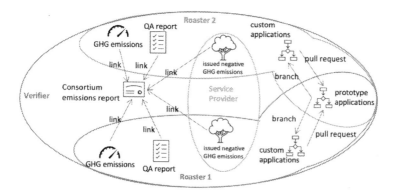

Fig. 4. Channel topology for data sharing inside the consortium

Shared Implementation. Shared implementation of monitoring systems aims to reduce costs by employing the concept of information commons [20] to prevent reimplementation of MRV. The scenario assumes that there are a number of actors with similar activities in MRV that profit from the community service of an information common for MRV. In the scenario, the verifier actor (e.g., a calibration laboratory) has the highest level of knowledge about implementing monitoring system, compliant with regulatory. Therefore, the verifier develops and provides the prototype monitoring logic to the consortium. To do so, the verifier provides two items to the consortium. First, the code for the monitoring logic and second, a corresponding hash of the code to allow the proof of integrity later.

In the prototype, the verifier uses the FlowFuse [13] low-code platform as a "Developer" (see Fig. 3) to deploy the monitoring logic within the consortium. FlowFuse allows the seamless deployment of code between other participants in the same network, and is a commercial spin-off from the node-RED project [39]. It extends node-RED by the mentioned capability of sharing code (the so-called "flows") with other network participants. In the same step of deploying code to the consortium, the verifier employs a corresponding smart contract, which hashes the content of the lightweight JavaScript Object Notation (JSON) based code artifact and stores it on the ledger. Subsequently, other actors start to compare the hash stored on the ledger and the hash which is generated by the code artifact present locally, before employing a new software release.

Furthermore, Fig. 4 illustrates that actors could create branches to customize the application logic for their needs and may create pull requests to provide application improvements. Finally, the verifier maintains the prototype application and decides whether to accept or reject pull requests. Note that this feature is rather conceptual and is part of a future development. The proposed prototype covers only the unidirectional development of the verifier code.

Mitigation Token Trading. Identical to tokenization of real estate [69] or art works [66], tokenization may also be a use case for mitigation projects. Concretely, to implement a certain level of risk management within a carbon market where pricing is dynamic and the amount of certified emissions reductions is highly limited. Due to the annual reduction of the threshold for free allocations within the EU ETS, the EU promotes a clear trend in the pricing trajectory.

In the scenario, a provider of tokenized mitigations sells these as negative emissions within the consortium. Therefore, the provider populates the available tokens and frequently synchronizes the stock on the blockchain. Subsequently, other actors can invoke a smart contract to purchase mitigation tokens to compensate for emissions. However, to secure business value for the service provider and to reach a certain level of automation, the service provider sets a minimum prize, which is recognized by the smart contract. Furthermore, the smart contract limits the amount of purchasable tokens relative to the emissions of the actors, to prevent an unfair use of this supportive service, as a common pool resource (CPR).

The following section presents the edge installation as the real-world embodiment of the described architecture.

6.2   The Edge Installation

The approach of a edge installation [56] builds on the hardware and software stack of two previous design iterations [53,58], and acts as a gateway for production machinery and users on field level to interact with the blockchain consortium. The hardware stack depicted in Fig. 5 is c-rail mounted inside a industrial rack, and consists of a edge controller, a touch display, a 4G router, and a radio-frequency identification (RFID) reader. The 4G router connects the installation with the Internet and acts as an internal network switch to allow the RFID reader and the edge controller to communicate via a Representational State Transfer (REST) interface.

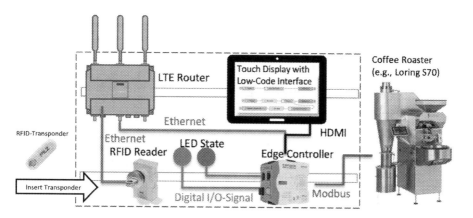

Fig. 5. Hardware-stack for the field test installation

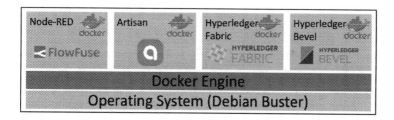

Fig. 6. Software-stack for the field test installation

The edge controller connects to the roasting machine via the Modbus TCP protocol. Therefore, we exploit the implementation of the interface and data models of the Artisan software project [45] as a universal connector to various types of roasting machines and to retrieve relevant emission data. Artisan helps coffee roasters record and control roast profiles, and can automate the creation of roasting metrics to improve the final coffee flavor. We performed modifications on the Artisan software and it became part of our software stack (see Fig. 6). The software stack comprises a containerized setup of Hyperledger Bevel, for Fabric deployment on edge devices, and FlowFuse for low-code development and software deployment.

Furthermore, this design cycle introduces a new rack assembly (see Fig. 9) for edge installation and a graphical user interface (see Fig. 7) to streamline the

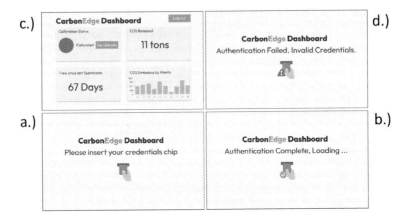

Fig. 7. Overview of the user interface screens

interactions between machine and user. The graphical user interface in Fig. 7 comprises four different screens and integrates the two-step security process of a previous design cycle [55] (to prevent insider threats [22], and enable novel digital signature processes [23]): First, a.) display of an idle mode, where the edge node waits for the insertion of a RFID transponder. Second, b.) succesful authentication after insertion of a RFID transponder by a user. Third, display of the CarbonEdge dashboard, which depicts the current status of the edge node (e.g., calibrated or not calibrated, remaining certification time, past GHG emissions etc.), and lastly, d.) the error state if the chosen transponder does not meet the authentication requirements.

The final tree of interaction for the user interface is shown in Fig. 8. At the time of publication, a visualization of additional performance data from the roasting process is still open and will soon become part of the main project [54].

To conclude, the novelty versus the previous design of an edge computing node [55] relies on three major changes: First, the replacement of node-RED by FlowFuse, which allows the seamless distribution of software between the edge nodes. Second, we modify the Artisan project's software by a new REST API. Third, we introduce a simplistic graphical front-end to ease the use of the proposed edge computing node. From a socioeconomic perspective, this design cycle presents a prototype based on the theory on archetypes of MRV consortia, especially for the ecosystem consortium [58].

7   Evaluation

This section carries out an evaluation of the consortium architecture itself and the edge installation as its real-world embodiment.

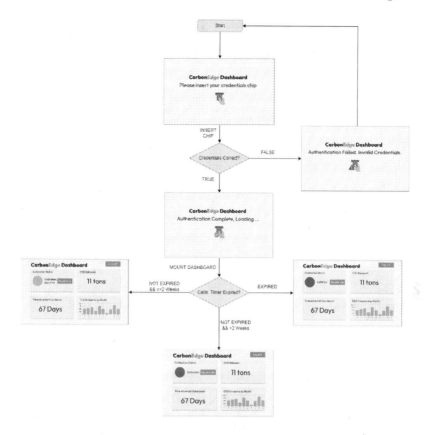

Fig. 8. Overview of user interface interaction flows

7.1   Evaluation of the Consortium Architecture

The proposed features of Design Cycle 3 complement the set of features and concepts of Design Cycle 2 in light of three lenses: First, the lens of IT Governance. Second, the lens of the Business Web Typology. Third, the lens of governing the commons.

The IT Governance Lens. To evaluate that our prototypical set of features illustrates a reasonable simplified scenario with relevant features for a blockchain-based information system on MRV, the relationship model for the four main focus areas of IT Governance of the IT Governance Institute (ITGI) [26] mentioned by Grembergen et al. [64], and Fig. 10 provides a mapping of features and concepts to this relationship model.

Fig. 9. The edge installation as the physical part of the demonstrator concept

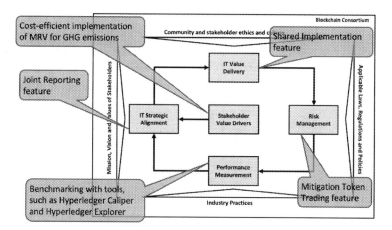

Fig. 10. Mapping of the main focus areas for IT Governance according the ITGI [26, 64], with the features and concepts of Design Cycle 2 and Design Cycle 3

In addition, the governance of our consortium is influenced by external factors such as industry practices or the applicable laws, regulations, and policies within the domain. The ethics and culture of the community and the stakeholders play a decisive role, as heterogeneous companies work together in a global supply chain. Every company has its own functioning business model. Governance must therefore also take into account that the mission, vision, and values of the individual participants flow into a consortial strategy. Successful mapping of the proposed features to all elements in Fig. 10 already involves a certain level of completeness and relevance within the demonstrated scenario. To further analyze the nature of the proposed consortium architecture and evaluate its *stakeholder value drivers*.

The Commons Lens. Although our consortium architecture addresses central aspects of IT Governance [26], and shows high coverage with architectures from the strongly founded Business Web Typology [61], Ostrom et al. [40] provides design principles for self-governance of communities as the third lens of evaluation. Since this work builds on the design of a previous design cycle inspired by Ostrom's theory [55], this paragraph focuses on the advancements in this scenario and neglects a review of all design principles. In this regard, Table 2 summarizes the features and how they recognize the design principles on self-governance for communities.

Table 2. Analysis of the features under the light of Ostrom et al. [40]

Feature	Aspect of Self-Governance for Communities
Joint Reporting	This feature comprises the compilation of a joint consortium report by a single verifier organization, which aims at reducing the overall communication effort between numerous organizations and a authority. Furthermore, the feature empowers the verifier to oversee the consortium and to detect negative behavior, e.g., a strong exceeding of emissions caps by certain actors, and therefor an overexploitation of emissions as a CPR within the consortium. Hence, the feature recognizes the design principle of *Monitoring*. Furthermore, the interaction with the local authority recognizes the principle of *Local Enforcement of Rules* (e.g., for reporting deadlines and standards).
Shared Implementation	This feature manages the monitoring logic in the flavor of modern software development, exemplifying the proposed branching concept and tooling. The establishment of monitoring logic as an information commons [20], where actors contribute and profit from the contributions of other actors, is significant here. Monitoring code contributions and giving advantage to highly active developers (e.g., by the allocation of further mitigation tokens) can facilitate collaborative development. This feature recognizes the design principle of *Monitoring*, where activities on developing monitoring logic are oversight, and the principle of *Graduate Sanctions*, where the helpful behavior of actors is positively sanctioned, and thus an incentive.
Mitigation Token Trading	The feature is associated with the Agora business web [61] and builds a marketplace-like structure within the consortium, which meets the design principle of *Multiple layers of nested enterprises*. Here, the nested layer is the agora itself, where the proposed mitigation token shapes a new CPR, exclusive to a subset of actors

The Business Web Lens. With an eye on the vertical consortium integration of Design Cycle 1 [58] (inspired by the Value-Chain Business Web [61]) and the horizontal consortium integration of Design Cycle 2 [55](inspired by the Alliance Business Web [61]), the question arises whether a consortium with hybrid characteristics, such as in Design Cycle 3 still relates with the Business Webs Typology, and if yes, what are the similarities.

In this regard, Fig. 11 decomposes the consortium into two heterogeneous webs. This hybrid characteristic of the Coffee Roastery Scenario in Design Cycle 3 is grounded in the various nature of relationships between the actors. Exemplifying coffee roasters, which jointly implement monitoring logic in a community-like approach, on the one hand, and on the other hand, the coffee roasters that trade tokenized emissions reductions with a service provider in a buyer-seller relationship. Revisiting the Business Webs Typology according to Tapscott et al. [61], the proposed consortium design holds characteristics of two different b-webs (see Fig. 11): First, the horizontal integration (between each coffee roaster) known from Design Cycle 2. Second, the relationship between the buyer and the seller, identified as a type of Agora business web [61]. Combining these two types of business webs, this Design Cycle employs the term "Ecosystem Consortium" as an archetype of consortium on MRV, which was originally coined by Seidenfad et al. [58].

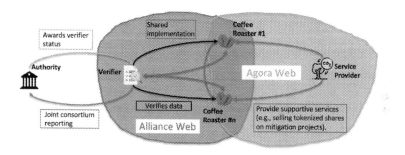

Fig. 11. The Alliance Web and the Agora Web within the Coffee Roastery Consortium

7.2   Evaluation of the Edge Installation

We perform a field test within an industrial site to rigorously evaluate the functionality of the edge installation and the blockchain-based information system. We are interested in two main aspects of operation: First, how well do edge installation and its security features integrate into the infrastructure and existing business processes? Second, how does the system perform under certain conditions, such as a large number of actors and long-term operation in a rough industrial environment? Therefore, the edge installation connects via the 4G router to the consortium, where virtual nodes run on a locally hosted compute cluster with Red Hat's OpenShift [46] and allows us to vary the number of actors to benchmark for different transaction throughputs. The compute cluster consists of seven 19" compute nodes, and each node is equipped with 376GB RAM, 80 cores, and 12TB internal storage.

In our scenario, there are two distinct blockchain node compositions possible, involving three basic components (client, peer, and orderer) defined by the Hyperledger Fabric blockchain. First, a full node operates all three components. Second, a partial node only uses the client and peer components.

Edge installations operate as partial nodes (see Fig. 3), where the client creates and invokes transactions on the consortium blockchain, and the peer synchronizes the local ledger copy. To avoid a bottleneck for edge computations, the ordering service is not intended to run on the edge. Instead, a verifier operates the ordering service on a virtual instance.

Fig. 12. The field test at the Murnauer Kaffeerösterei

At the time of publication, we already performed the integration test where the installation owner performs defined MRV tasks using the edge installation and rates aspects of usability (see Fig. 12). The utilization of personalized RFID transponders led to a stronger anticipation of responsibilities, as all activities are traceable. The combination of a small number of easy-to-understand state indications by light-emitting diode (LED) and the reduction of user interaction to a few event triggers led to increased user acceptance. Furthermore, we focus on a stable and highly automated deployment of the Hyperledger Fabric. Therefore, we employed Hyperledger Bevel as a deployment tool. The highly automated setup of the edge installation minimized training efforts on site, and efforts for remote support remain notable small.

8   Conclusion and Future Work

In this paper, we present the prototype of a blockchain-based information system with edge computing capabilities. We illustrate the scenario of a consortium in the coffee industry that jointly implements and operates MRV of GHG emissions. Therefore, we introduce actors' roles and relationships, present the overall architecture of the information system, and the setup of the edge installation to connect production machines and users with the consortium blockchain. Next, we formalize four design principles, suggesting the exploitation of business webs [61] and *archetypes of consortia* [53,58] to build an MRV consortium, the opportunities of *shared implementation* inspired by CDM and up-scaled MRV [9], the application of *self-governance of communities* [40] for MRV consortia, and the design of *secure oracles* [7]. Following we provide a brief summary about the characteristics of the desired design principles.

Archetypes of Consortia. Building a consortium poses general challenges in the management of stakeholders and the preservation of interests. Identification of archetypes [57] and the exploitation of existing relationships (e.g., Business Webs according to Tapscott et al. [61]) may be an accelerator for the construction of consortia. Therefore, Design Cycle 1 introduced the so-called archetypes on MRV consortia [58], and each of the three design cycles commits to the goal of illustrating realistic scenarios to evaluate the proposed archetypes.

Shared Implementation. Up-scaled crediting proposes collectively established emissions baselines and credits are issued based on aggregated achievements. This may lead to a cost reduction for non-state actors if a corresponding information system serves features for the shared implementation of up-scaled measures. In this regard, blockchain technology acts as an interaction layer for actors with a limited amount of trust.

Self-Governance of Communities. In case of up-scaled MRV for a group of non-state actors, the absence of governmental regulation demands a certain level of self-governance. Therefore, the consideration of GHG emissions as a CPR allows the application of Ostrom's eight design principles as a *meta principle* for self-governance of MRV communities.

Secure Oracles The MRV of GHG emissions relies on trustworthy real world data to serve as a source of certified emissions for carbon markets. The literature widely acknowledges the challenge of implementing blockchain oracles [7], and the principle of secure oracles aims on the design of security measures for oracles in the context of MRV measures. This Design Science project, comprising two previous design cycles [55, 58], and the present Design Cycle 3 illustrated the means to secure blockchain oracles on the network edge (e.g., by introducing a RFID-based access management and management of certificate material).

These four design principles are in the draft stage and reflect our understanding of the current challenges in transitioning GHG management from governmental regulation to a commons solution, and with our experience in designing [31] and operating [24] blockchain-based information systems, we try to elevate the discussion to a *community service* approach. Future work in this regard comprises the further refinement of the proposed design principles by conducting further experiments on the presented infrastructure.

Acknowledgements. We thank Thomas Eckel from the Murnauer Kaffeerösterei for supporting the field test, Benjamin Gröschel from the Münchner Kaffeerösterei for providing datasets, and Rene Hennen from FUND THE PLANET [17] for insides about the tokenization of reforestation projects. We acknowledge funding for Project LIONS as part of dtec.bw. dtec.bw is funded by the European Commission under NextGenerationEU.

References

1. Adams, M., Suriadi, S., Kumar, A., ter Hofstede, A.H.M.: Flexible integration of blockchain with business process automation: a federated architecture. In: Herbaut, N., La Rosa, M. (eds.) CAiSE 2020. LNBIP, vol. 386, pp. 1–13. Springer, Cham (2020). https://doi.org/10.1007/978-3-030-58135-0_1
2. Al Kawasmi, E., Arnautovic, E., Svetinovic, D.: Bitcoin-based decentralized carbon emissions trading infrastructure model. Syst. Eng. **18**(2), 115–130 (2015). https://doi.org/10.1002/sys.21291

3. Androulaki, E., et al.: Hyperledger fabric: a distributed operating system for permissioned blockchains. In: Proceedings of the Thirteenth EuroSys Conference (EuroSys 2018), pp. 1–15 (2018). https://doi.org/10.1145/3190508.3190538
4. Baumann, T.: Blockchain and emerging digital technologies for enhancing post-2020 climate markets (2018). https://doi.org/10.13140/RG.2.2.12242.71368
5. Beck, R., Mueller-Bloch, C., King, J.: Governance in the blockchain economy: a framework and research agenda. J. Assoc. Inform. Syst. **19**, 1020–1034 (2018). https://doi.org/10.17705/1jais.00518
6. Braden, S.: Blockchain potentials and limitations for selected climate policy instruments (2019). https://www.giz.de/en/downloads/giz2019-en-blockchain-potentials-for-climate.pdf
7. Caldarelli, G.: Before ethereum. the origin and evolution of blockchain oracles. IEEE Access **11**, 50899–50917 (2023). https://doi.org/10.1109/ACCESS.2023.3279106
8. Coria, J., Jaraitė, J.: Transaction costs of upstream versus downstream pricing of CO2 emissions. Environ. Resour. Econ. **72**(4), 965–1001 (2019). https://doi.org/10.1007/s10640-018-0235-y
9. Dawson, B., Spannagle, M.: Clean Development Mechanism Methodology Booklet (CDM) (2020). https://cdm.unfccc.int/methodologies/documentation/meth-booklet.pdf
10. Dorfleitner, G., Braun, D.: Fintech, digitalization and blockchain: possible applications for green finance. In: Migliorelli, M., Dessertine, P. (eds.) The Rise of Green Finance in Europe. PSIF, pp. 207–237. Springer, Cham (2019). https://doi.org/10.1007/978-3-030-22510-0_9
11. Eckert, J., López, D., Azevedo, C.L., Farooq, B.: A blockchain-based user-centric emission monitoring and trading system for multi-modal mobility. CoRR **abs/1908.0** (8 2019). http://arxiv.org/abs/1908.05629
12. Falazi, G., et al.: Smart Contract Invocation Protocol (SCIP): a protocol for the uniform integration of heterogeneous blockchain smart contracts. In: Dustdar, S., Yu, E., Salinesi, C., Rieu, D., Pant, V. (eds.) CAiSE 2020. LNCS, vol. 12127, pp. 134–149. Springer, Cham (2020). https://doi.org/10.1007/978-3-030-49435-3_9
13. FlowForge Inc.: FlowFuse (2024). https://flowfuse.com/
14. Gawusu, S., et al.: Renewable energy sources from the perspective of blockchain integration: from theory to application. Sustain. Energy Technol. Assessments **52**, 102108 (2022). https://doi.org/10.1016/j.seta.2022.102108
15. Gorski, T., Bednarski, J.: Applying model-driven engineering to distributed ledger deployment. IEEE Access **8**, 118245–118261 (2020). https://doi.org/10.1109/ACCESS.2020.3005519
16. Gräther, W., Kolvenbach, S., Ruland, R., Schütte, J., Torres, C., Wendland, F.: Blockchain for education: lifelong learning passport. In: Proceedings of 1st ERCIM Blockchain workshop 2018. European Society for Socially Embedded Technologies (EUSSET) (2018). https://dl.eusset.eu/items/b02679a3-7e9b-4b22-8249-009737a0d52d
17. Green token GmbH: About us (2023). https://fundtheplanet.net/
18. Greiner, M., Zeiß, C., Lechner, U., Winkelmann, A.: Towards a governance model design for blockchain-based traceability systems. In: 18th International Conference on Design Science Research in Information Systems and Technology (2023). https://doi.org/10.18726/2023_2
19. Hardin, G.: The tragedy of the commons. Science **162**(3859), 1243–1248 (1968). http://www.jstor.org/stable/1724745

20. Hess, C., Ostrom, E. (eds.): Understanding Knowledge as a Commons. The MIT Press (2006). https://doi.org/10.7551/mitpress/6980.001.0001
21. Hevner, A.R., March, S.T., Park, J., Ram, S.: Design science in information systems research. MIS Q. **28**(1), 75–105 (2004). https://doi.org/10.2307/25148625
22. Hofmeier, M., Seidenfad, K., Rieb, A., Lechner, U.: Risk factors for malicious insider threats - an analysis of attack scenarios. In: Americas Conference on Information Systems (AMCIS) 2023 (in press). Panama City (2023). https://aisel.aisnet.org/amcis2023/sig_sec/sig_sec/3/
23. Hofmeier, M., Seidenfad, K., Hommel, W.: Validating a modified JSON web signature format using the scenario of ammunition issuance for training purposes. In: MILCOM 2023 - 2023 IEEE Military Communications Conference (MILCOM), pp. 237–238 (2023). https://doi.org/10.1109/MILCOM58377.2023.10356342
24. Hoiss, T., Seidenfad, K., Lechner, U.: Blockchain service operations - a structured approach to operate a blockchain solution. In: 2021 IEEE International Conference on Decentralized Applications and Infrastructures (DAPPS), pp. 11–19. IEEE (8 2021). https://doi.org/10.1109/DAPPS52256.2021.00007
25. Hyperledger foundation: hyperledger bevel (2024). https://github.com/hyperledger/bevel
26. ITGI: Board briefing on IT governance (2001). www.itgi.org
27. Jain, G., Shrivastava, A., Paul, J., Batra, R.: Blockchain for SME clusters: an ideation using the framework of ostrom commons governance. Inform. Syst. Front. **24**(4), 1125–1143 (2022). https://doi.org/10.1007/s10796-022-10288-z
28. Jensen, T., Hedman, J., Henningsson, S.: How TradeLens delivers business value with blockchain technology. MIS Q. Executive **18**(4), 221–243 (2019). https://doi.org/10.17705/2msqe.00018
29. Labazova, O.: Towards a framework for evaluation of blockchain implementations. In: 40th International Conference on Information Systems, ICIS 2019 (2019)
30. Ladleif, J., Friedow, C., Weske, M.: An architecture for multi-chain business process choreographies. In: Abramowicz, W., Klein, G. (eds.) BIS 2020. LNBIP, vol. 389, pp. 184–196. Springer, Cham (2020). https://doi.org/10.1007/978-3-030-53337-3_14
31. Lamken, D., et al.: Design patterns and framework for blockchain integration in supply chains. In: 2021 IEEE International Conference on Blockchain and Cryptocurrency (ICBC), pp. 1–3. IEEE (5 2021). https://doi.org/10.1109/ICBC51069.2021.9461062
32. Laurier, W.: Blockchain value networks. In: 2019 IEEE Social Implications of Technology (SIT) and Information Management (SITIM), pp. 1–6 (2019). https://doi.org/10.1109/SITIM.2019.8910187.
33. Laurier, W., Schwaiger, W.S., Polovina, S.: Traditional accounting with decentralised ledger technology. In: CEUR Workshop Proceedings **2574**, 202–208 (2020). https://ceur-ws.org/Vol-2574/short18.pdf
34. Liu, Y., He, D., Obaidat, M.S., Kumar, N., Khan, M.K., Raymond Choo, K.K.: Blockchain-based identity management systems: a review. J. Netw. Comput. Appl. **166**, 102731 (2020). https://doi.org/10.1016/j.jnca.2020.102731
35. López-Pintado, O., García-Bañuelos, L., Dumas, M., Weber, I., Ponomarev, A.: Caterpillar: a business process execution engine on the Ethereum blockchain. Softw. - Pract. Experience **49**(7), 1162–1193 (2019). https://doi.org/10.1002/spe.2702
36. Michaelowa, A., Brescia, D., Wohlgemuth, N., Galt, H., Espelage, A., Maxinez, L.: CDM method transformation: updating and transforming CDM methods for use in an Article 6 context. Tech. rep., University of Zurich, Zurich (2020). https://doi.org/10.5167/uzh-195559

37. Miehle, D., Henze, D., Seitz, A., Luckow, A., Bruegge, B.: PartChain: a decentralized traceability application for multi-tier supply chain networks in the automotive industry. In: 2019 IEEE International Conference on Decentralized Applications and Infrastructures (DAPPCON), pp. 140–145. IEEE, Newark, CA, USA (4 2019). https://doi.org/10.1109/DAPPCON.2019.00027

38. Monrat, A.A., Schelén, O., Andersson, K.: A survey of blockchain from the perspectives of applications, challenges, and opportunities. IEEE Access **7**, 117134–117151 (2019). https://doi.org/10.1109/ACCESS.2019.2936094

39. OpenJS Foundation & Contributors: NODE-RED (2013). https://nodered.org

40. Ostrom, E.: Governing the Commons: The Evolution of Institutions for Collective Action. Political Economy of Institutions and Decisions, Cambridge University Press (1990). https://doi.org/10.1017/CBO9780511807763

41. Ostrom, E.: A multi-scale approach to coping with climate change and other collective action problems. Solutions **1** (2010). http://thesolutionsjournal.com/print/565

42. Oxford University Press: Definition of non-state actor (2021). https://www.lexico.com/definition/non-state_actor

43. Partnership for Market Readiness (PMR): establishing scaled-up crediting program baselines under the Paris agreement : issues and options (2017). https://openknowledge.worldbank.org/handle/10986/28785

44. Poux, P., de Filippi, P., Ramos, S.: Blockchains for the governance of common goods. In: Proceedings of the 1st International Workshop on Distributed Infrastructure for Common Good, pp. 7–12. DICG 2020, ACM, New York, NY, USA (12 2020). https://doi.org/10.1145/3428662.3428793

45. Rafael Cobo: Artisan (2023). https://github.com/artisan-roaster-scope

46. Red Hat Inc.: Red Hat OpenShift (2023). https://docs.openshift.com/

47. Richardson, A., Xu, J.: Carbon Trading with Blockchain. Springer International Publishing, Cham (2020). https://link.springer.com/chapter/10.1007/978-3-030-53356-4-7

48. Ross, J.W., Weill, P.: How top performers manage IT Decisions Rights for Superior Results. No. Harvard Business School Press Boston, Massachusetts, Harvard Business Press (2004). http://www.msu.ac.zw/elearning/material/1300172657060910itgovernancematrix2535p4.pdf

49. Sato, T., Himura, Y., Nemoto, J.: Design and evaluation of smart-contract-based system operations for permissioned blockchain-based systems. arXiv (1 2019). http://arxiv.org/abs/1901.11249

50. Saxena, M., Sanchez, M., Knuszka, R.: Method for providing healthcare-related, blockchain-associated cognitive insights using blockchains (2018). https://patents.google.com/patent/US20180165416A1/en

51. Schletz, M., Franke, L., Salomo, S.: Blockchain application for the Paris agreement carbon market mechanism-a decision framework and architecture. Sustainability (2020). https://doi.org/10.3390/su12125069

52. Schneider, L., et al.: Robust accounting of international transfers under article 6 of the Paris agreement discussion paper (2017). https://www.dehst.de/SharedDocs/downloads/EN/project-mechanisms/discussion-papers/Differences_and_commonalities_paris_agreement2.pdf?__blob=publicationFile&v=4

53. Seidenfad, K., Biermann, J., Lechner, U., Greiner, M., Biermann, J., Lechner, U.: CarbonEdge: demonstrating blockchain-based monitoring, reporting and verification of greenhouse gas emissions on the edge. In: 2023 IEEE International Conference on Blockchain and Cryptocurrency (ICBC), pp. 123–147. Dubai (2023). https://doi.org/10.1109/ICBC56567.2023.10174891, https://link.springer.com/10.1007/978-3-031-40852-6%5C_7

54. Seidenfad, K., Biermann, J., Olzem, P.: CarbonEdge Github repository (2023). https://github.com/KSilkThread/carbonedge

55. Seidenfad, K., Greiner, M., Biermann, J., Lechner, U.: CarbonEdge: collaborative blockchain-based monitoring, reporting, and verification of greenhouse gas emissions on the edge. In: Phillipson, F., Eichler, G., Erfurth, C., Fahrnberger, G. (eds.) Proceedings of the 23rd International Conference on Innovations for Community Services (I4CS 2023), pp. 123–147. Springer International Publishing, Cham (2023). https://doi.org/10.1007/978-3-031-40852-6_7, https://link.springer.com/10.1007/978-3-031-40852-6%5C_7

56. Seidenfad, K., Greiner, M., Biermann, J., Lechner, U.: Blockchain-based monitoring, reporting and verification of ghg emissions on the network edge - a system integration study in the artisan coffee industry. In: 2024 IEEE/SICE International Symposium on System Integration (SII), pp. 1227–1228 (2024). https://doi.org/10.1109/SII58957.2024.10417510

57. Seidenfad, K., Hrestic, R., Wagner, T.: Pull request #322 Create Running-OnArm.md on Minifabric from Hyperledger Labs (2022). https://github.com/hyperledger-labs/minifabric/pull/322

58. Seidenfad, K., Wagner, T., Hrestic, R., Lechner, U.: Demonstrating feasibility of blockchain-driven carbon accounting - a design study and demonstrator. In: Phillipson, F., , Eichler, G., , Erfurth, C., Fahrnberger, G. (eds.) Proceedings of the 22nd International Conference on Innovations for Community Services (I4CS 2022), pp. 28–46. Springer International Publishing, Delft (2022). https://doi.org/10.1007/978-3-031-06668-9_5

59. SIEMENS AG: kick off the carbon countdown (2021). https://new.siemens.com/global/en/company/topic-areas/product-carbon-footprint.html

60. Streck, C.: Strengthening the Paris agreement by holding non-state actors accountable: establishing normative links between transnational partnerships and treaty implementation. Transnational Environ. Law (2021). https://doi.org/10.1017/S2047102521000091

61. Tapscott, D., Ticoll, D., Lowy, A.: Digital capital: harnessing the power of business webs. Ubiquity **2000** (2000). https://doi.org/10.1145/341836.336231

62. Taş, R., Tanrıöver, Ö.Ö.: A systematic review of challenges and opportunities of blockchain for E-voting. Symmetry **12**(8), 1328 (2020). https://doi.org/10.3390/sym12081328

63. United Nations: why the global stocktake is a critical moment for climate action (2023). https://unfccc.int/topics/global-stocktake/about-the-global-stocktake/why-the-global-stocktake-is-a-critical-moment-for-climate-action

64. Van Grembergen, W., De Haes, S., Guldentops, E.: Structures, processes and relational mechanisms for IT governance. In: Strategies for Information Technology Governance, pp. 1–36. IGI Global (2011). https://doi.org/10.4018/978-1-59140-140-7.ch001

65. Wang, Q., Su, M.: Integrating blockchain technology into the energy sector - from theory of blockchain to research and application of energy blockchain. Comput. Sci. Rev. **37**, 100275 (2020). https://doi.org/10.1016/j.cosrev.2020.100275

66. Wang, Z., Yang, L., Wang, Q., Liu, D., Xu, Z., Liu, S.: ArtChain: blockchain-enabled platform for art marketplace. In: 2019 IEEE International Conference on Blockchain (Blockchain), pp. 447–454 (2019). https://doi.org/10.1109/Blockchain.2019.00068

67. Weber, I., Xu, X., Riveret, R., Governatori, G., Ponomarev, A., Mendling, J.: Untrusted business process monitoring and execution using blockchain. In: La Rosa, M., Loos, P., Pastor, O. (eds.) BPM 2016. LNCS, vol. 9850, pp. 329–347. Springer, Cham (2016). https://doi.org/10.1007/978-3-319-45348-4_19

68. Woo, J., Fatima, R., Kibert, C.J., Newman, R.E., Tian, Y., Srinivasan, R.S.: Applying blockchain technology for building energy performance measurement, reporting, and verification (MRV) and the carbon credit market: a review of the literature. Build. Environ. **205**, 108199 (2021). https://doi.org/10.1016/j.buildenv.2021.108199

69. Zheng, M., Sandner, P.: Asset tokenization of real estate in Europe. In: Lacity, M.C., Treiblmaier, H. (eds.) Blockchains and the Token Economy: Theory and Practice, pp. 179–211. Springer International Publishing, Cham (2022). https://doi.org/10.1007/978-3-030-95108-5_7

70. Ziolkowski, R., Miscione, G., Schwabe, G.: Decision problems in blockchain governance: old wine in new bottles or walking in someone else's shoes? J. Manag. Inf. Syst. **37**(2), 316–348 (2020). https://doi.org/10.1080/07421222.2020.1759974

The Digital Product Passport: Enabling Interoperable Information Flows Through Blockchain Consortia for Sustainability

Maximilian Greiner[1]([⊠]) [iD], Karl Seidenfad[1] [iD], Christoph Langewisch[2] [iD], Andreas Hofmann[3] [iD], and Ulrike Lechner[1] [iD]

[1] Computer Science Department, University of the Bundeswehr Munich, Neubiberg, Germany
maximilian.greiner@unibw.de
[2] Digital Business University of Applied Sciences, Berlin, Germany
[3] AFTS GmbH, Berlin, Germany

Abstract. Global supply chains face mounting pressure for collaboration and reliable data exchange in an inter-organizational environment, especially in the pursuit of sustainability. The inherent complexities, driven by intricate multi-layered processes and worldwide connectivity, pose significant challenges. Within this article, we want to present our current research towards a Digital Product Passport enabled by blockchain as a decentralized ecosystem for reliable, traceable, and interoperable data exchange without a central authority. Following a Design Science Research methodology, it explores the convergence of a blockchain consortium and a public blockchain interface, including a discussion of the necessary governance structures. This research promotes a system-independent Digital Product Passport within blockchain-based information systems, ensuring privacy, traceability, transparency, and trust in global supply chains, advancing standardized data structures for a reliable information flow. Additionally, our Digital Product Passport supports companies in providing and verifying sustainability criteria to legislators. Reliable and interoperable information are key aspects to establish governance for successfully managed community resources without the intervention of a central authority enabled by blockchain.

Keywords: Interoperability · Supply chain · Blockchain · Sustainability · Governance

1 Introduction

Inter-organizational collaboration and trusted data exchange are becoming increasingly relevant in global supply chains. These processes are complex due to their multilayered nature and global interrelations, exemplifying privacy concerns and data integrity. Governments are imposing considerable pressure on companies by enacting new laws, such as the Supply Chain Due Diligence Act [5],

© The Author(s), under exclusive license to Springer Nature Switzerland AG 2024
F. Phillipson et al. (Eds.): I4CS 2024, CCIS 2109, pp. 377–396, 2024.
https://doi.org/10.1007/978-3-031-60433-1_21

that concern sustainability. The obligation for verification is pushing companies towards innovative resolutions. Therefore, a continuous product and information flow along global multitier supply chains of various parties involved (such as farmers, logistics, manufacturers, etc.) from the raw material to the end product is a basic requirement for establishing sustainable, compliant, and resilient supply chains. Especially when it comes to information flows, integrity, traceability, availability, and a certain level of privacy are necessary [34]. Innovative technologies, such as blockchain, could play a transformative role not only by increasing the transparency and trustworthiness of data exchange but also by enabling the traceability and documentation of information. Facilitating collaboration and data exchange among diverse stakeholders with disparate digital infrastructures presents a considerable challenge, where the issue of open standards assumes paramount significance. Here, the Digital Product Passport (DPP) comes into play, which has already gained publicity from a political perspective [4].

As part of our research, we designed blockchain systems for food supply chains [13], for Monitoring, Reporting and Verification (MRV) of greenhouse gas (GHG) emissions [29,30] or track and trace solutions for roasted coffee [6]. With this article we go one step further and examine how to enable the interoperability of a consortium blockchain with a public blockchain interface in combination with a DPP on the use case of sustainability in coffee supply chains.

The goal is to design a decentralized ecosystem for the interoperability of blockchain-based information systems, particularly between consortium and public blockchains. This approach ensures tamper-proof data transfer, privacy, traceability, and trust in global supply chains. We introduce a scenario-driven conceptual DPP that is based on a consortium and a public blockchain within a community of predefined stakeholders without a central authority. Based on this approach, a community is established through the development of a consortium that collectively shares and controls digital resources (information throughout the supply chain). To regulate the over-consumption of individual organizations within this self-governing and self-managing ecosystem, a distributed and fair governance structure is needed.

We present the following artifacts: First, a supply chain scenario that includes relevant stakeholders and critical supply chain events. Second, blockchain technology as a decentralized ecosystem that provides tamper-proof stored and exchanged information. Third, a DPP that ensures the handover of data for different stakeholders in a user-friendly way. The main information aspects of the DPP are product information, sustainability criteria, and verification. Fourth, governance structures in the light of Ostrom's design principles [23] to address the absence of a central authority and to provide an alternative to the "winner-takes-all" principle. In this article, we want to contribute to the understanding of standardization of data structures for the realization of an interoperable, trusted information flow along global sustainable supply chains.

The article is structured as follows. Section 2 describes the theoretical background towards blockchain and interoperability, blockchain governance, and the related work towards DPP approaches. Our research design is described in

Sect. 3. Section 4 provides the outline of the scenario by describing the actual coffee supply chain, including the requirements for our system design outlined in Sect. 5. Section 6 presents our governance features. Finally, the paper concludes by discussing the benefits and limitations of our approach (Sect. 7).

2 Theoretical Background

Our theoretical background is outlined by a brief description of blockchain and interoperability, followed by the state-of-the-art of blockchain governance and current DPP approaches.

2.1 Blockchain and Interoperability in Brief

Blockchain refers to the decentralized peer-to-peer management of tamper-proof data through an append-only list known as the ledger. All nodes in a blockchain network maintain a replica of the ledger, and new ledger entries are added through a consensus protocol. The National Institute of Standards and Technology (NIST) presents a comprehensive definition of distributed ledger technologies, with a particular focus on blockchain [41]. Blockchain technologies can be differentiated by their right to participate in the consensus process or by their level of network exposure.

The network structure of blockchains can be customized to suit various scenarios. Public, private and consortium (hybrid) blockchains are decentralized information systems that have different characteristics, uses, and benefits [31]. A public blockchain is accessible to all network users and implemented via a peer-to-peer network with freely given writing and reading rights. A private blockchain provides a closed network that limits participation to a selected group and assigns predefined roles to participants. These roles determine permissions for writing and reading on the blockchain. Consortium blockchains are a hybrid of prior forms, allowing a group of pre-approved participants and assigned read and write permissions based on the number of participants to work together while maintaining some level of decentralization [21].

In practice, the majority of currently active blockchain networks, such as Bitcoin or Ethereum, operate in a standalone environment, isolated from other blockchain networks. This causes a lack of communication and leads to limitations on data transfer, preventing it from freely transmitting to and from various blockchains regardless of the underlying infrastructure [39]. Recognizing the immense potential of blockchain interoperability, researchers have put forth numerous protocols in recent years, and the array of proposed solutions continues to expand. According to Talib et al. [35], blockchain interoperability solutions can be categorized into four main types: sidechain or relay chain solution, blockchain router solution, smart contract-based solutions and industrial solutions.

Within our approach, we use stakeholder wallets and a DPP (see Sect. 4) to provide interoperability between the blockchain consortium and the public blockchain network enabling a trusted and tamper-proof transfer of particular information along the value chain. As we use an independent certifier to validate transactions (trusted data), we classify our approach within industrial solutions.

2.2   Blockchain Governance

Blockchain governance is analyzed through various theories, including platform governance, collaborative economy, and stakeholder theory. It involves on-chain governance, which encodes rules and decision-making processes in blockchain code, and off-chain governance, encompassing non-technical regulations affecting the system's development and operation [28]. Beck et al. [2] explore the dimensions of IT governance, decision rights, responsibilities, and incentives, within the blockchain economy, proposing a research agenda. Hofman et al. [12] developed a framework to understand blockchain's global integration, focusing on its worldwide implications. Katina et al. [17] identify three crucial governance aspects: control, communication, and integration, focusing on direction, oversight, and accountability. Pelt et al. [25] outline blockchain network governance through six dimensions and three layers, including formation, roles, incentives, and decision making, across off-chain and on-chain activities. Lumineau et al. [22] analyze contractual and relational governance roles, while Laatikainen et al. [20] define blockchain governance as a combination of technical and social decision-making tools across various levels and aspects, covering the entire lifecycle of a blockchain network.

These studies mainly concentrate on public blockchain networks that are open for anyone to join and where participants are largely anonymous. However, few researchers have delved into the realms of private and consortial blockchains, where participants are identified and roles can be clearly defined. Success in blockchain consortia hinges on early alignment in both relational and technological aspects. Unlike standard IT projects, blockchain consortia demand the early establishment of collaboration rules among current and future members, ensuring that these rules are integrated into the immutable ledger [7]. Yue et al. [42] suggest a governance framework with six attributes and 13 subattributes, covering decision making, accountability, privacy, trust, and effectiveness. Zavolokina et al. [43,44] illustrate the importance of governance through a blockchain-based car dossier consortium, highlighting its role in enhancing collaboration and value creation among participants. They also note the challenges in consortium management and governance. Viguere et al. [36] examine the dynamics of openness in enterprise blockchains, identifying key archetypes for participant and platform engagement. Furthermore, using a Design Science Research approach, Greiner et al. [6] propose seven design principles for supply chain consortia using a blockchain-based traceability system.

These studies underscore the importance of early rule negotiation and governance in the success of blockchain consortia, showcasing the need for comprehensive integration and collaborative rule-setting from the outset.

2.3   Towards the Digital Product Passport

In this section, we delineate our DPP to existing approaches and use cases. A DPP is a record of the journey of a product through the supply chain that contains information about a product, including its origin, materials, production processes or sustainability [15]. They can be used to provide consumers and organizations with transparent and accurate information about the products they purchase [26].

Various approaches and projects for the integration and use of the DPP have already been established in recent years. The scientific literature is primarily concerned with the circular economy and the construction sector, as well as the automotive and manufacturing industries [37]. In the study by Adisorn et al. [1], the DPP is considered in relation to the circular economy. The transparency of product information through the use of the DPP turns out to be beneficial for reuse in terms of the circular economy.

Walden et al. [38] present two existing DPPs: the Material Passport and the Battery Passport. For the establishment of the DPP, traceability, compliance with laws, and better support of sustainability efforts are stated. As described as part of a working paper from the Wuppertal Institute [15], the Catena-X Project [3] is building a DPP for development, deployment, and collaboration within the automotive value chain. Other approaches, such as a standardized repair protocol, material declarations, or product comparisons for consumers with the DPP, are described by Koopelaar et al. [18]. Furthermore, Panza et al.'s [24] work takes a look at the social and environmental sustainability, which has hardly been considered in the context of the DPP. Jansen et al. [16] explain the high importance of interoperability between information systems and the DPP, as well as the potentials of the DPP. Addressing the trust and sovereignty of stakeholders, Heess et al. [9] propose design principles that provide insight information on how DPPs should be designed to verify the carbon footprint of hydrogen in a reliable way and to ensure the willingness of stakeholders to share their data. A trend towards the use of blockchain technology as an implementation technology of the DPP is also apparent [15].

In summary, existing DPP approaches focus mainly on transparency, standardization, trust, and compliance. Taking these points into account, we go one step further and propose a DPP that focuses on manipulation security and trusted (certified) provision of information along global supply chains.

3   Research Design

Our research approach is guided by the Design Science Research (DSR) framework of Hevner et al. [11]. According to DSR, we integrate a three-phase research process considering the requirements of the environment (people, organizations, technology, business needs) and the knowledge base (foundations, methodologies) within each phase (see Fig. 1). The successive phases of our research design consist of problem identification and environment (1), the technological perspective (2), and the organizational perspective (3), whereby each phase entails its own knowledge base and empirical data collection. Throughout all phases, the iterative refinement suggests a dynamic process where the findings and outputs of each stage are continually revisited, with an emphasis on integrating academic and practical insights to refine the design of our artifacts being developed.

Phase 1. The first phase compromises the problem identification and the environment and lays the foundation for our system design from a technological and organizational perspective. The foundational knowledge base that informs this phase is segmented into three distinct components. First, we viewed literature in the fields of coffee supply chains and collaboration, and second, we used the project environment of the Ledger Innovation and Operation Network for Sovereignty (LIONS) to establish a basis for our scenario outline. Third, an interview study with 11 sustainability and supply chain experts from medium to large companies was conducted to gain insight into the evidence and verifiability of sustainability criteria in supply chains. The interviews conducted were transcribed, coded and analyzed according to the approach of Kuckartz and Rädicker [19]. The resulting artifact of this phase is the coffee supply chain scenario (stakeholder, critical supply chain events), to which the current status and challenges of companies in the implementation of sustainability criteria are attached.

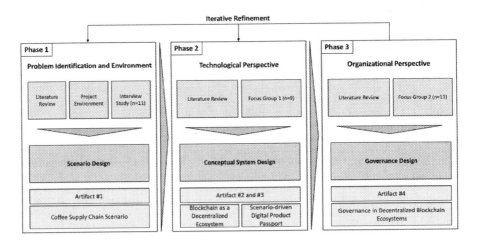

Fig. 1. Three-phase research process

Phase 2. Our second phase provides the technological perspective and draws on the results of our scenario design. Therefore, we reviewed the literature in the fields of blockchain and interoperability, as well as approaches towards DPPs. In addition, we conducted a focus group (n = 9) with experts in supply chain, sustainability, and blockchain. In this workshop, the scenario and a tentative design approach of our system design were introduced. Together with the participants, important tasks and characteristics of the system design and the digital product passport (public data point) were identified. Furthermore, we discussed which interoperabilities are necessary in such an ecosystem. For our analysis, we also used the coding according to the procedure of Strauss and Corbin [33]. The combination of research techniques (literature review, focus group) leads to our conceptual system design compromising two artifacts: blockchain as a decentralized ecosystm (consortium and public) and our scenario-driven DPP.

Phase 3. The last phase of this article goes further and incorporates the organizational (governance) perspective of our ecosystem. The literature in the fields of blockchain governance and consortium governance, as well as an additional focus group (n = 11), serves as a foundational knowledge base. In Workshop 2, we introduced our system design and the DPP to blockchain and supply chain experts. Subsequently, separate groups discussed the responsibilities, decisions, and changes that stakeholders will face when participating in a decentralized blockchain-based consortium. We used a qualitative content analysis according to Strauss and Corbin [33], and our coding procedure follows the dimensions of IT governance (decisions, responsibilities, and incentives) provided by Weill et al. [40]. As a result, a governance design has been designed that leads to our fourth artifact: governance in decentralized ecosystems. The outcomes are discussed in light of Ostrom's [23] design principles within Sect. 6.

This research methodology reflects a rigorous, iterative and scenario-driven DSR approach that aims to bridge theoretical knowledge with practical application.

4 Scenario Outline

Based on our findings from theory and practice, we identified relevant stakeholders, critical supply chain events, and socio-technical challenges with respect to interoperability and data exchange in the context of global supply chains that form the requirements for our proposed system design.

State-of-the-Art and Challenges in Companies. Our research has revealed that the collection of sustainability-related data is a common practice among all the companies surveyed. However, none of the entities have implemented a standardized procedure for data exchange. In addition, the process is characterized by a lack of automation. Data exchange is conducted primarily by email, telephone, and the use of Excel spreadsheets. With regard to reporting sustainability metrics, the codes applied show minimal engagement with governmental institutions, even by large companies. Companies tend to comply with legal requirements by labeling their products accordingly. Furthermore, sustainability performance indicators are typically published on companies' websites and QR codes on products are employed to provide additional information. Our investigation also highlights a limitation: companies have little or no visibility into sustainability data related to their suppliers' supplier. This indicates a lack of transparency within the more complex tiers of supply chains, hindering comprehensive sustainability assessments and reporting.

The analysis of our interviews shows that the integration of sustainability criteria within companies presents a socio-technical set of challenges. Research identifies that initial investment and ongoing costs represent a significant hurdle for organizations that seek to generate a return on investment (ROI) for sustainability initiatives. This requires not only financial investment, but also the cultivation of understanding of sustainability within the company and its resulting processes. Additionally, companies often find themselves in a state of dependence on the practices and cooperation of other entities, compounding the complexity of achieving sustainability goals. The implementation of new technologies adds another layer of complexity and expense. Legislative regulation also plays a pivotal role; they can either drive or deter the adoption of sustainability measures, depending on their design and enforcement. The complexity of supply chains further exacerbates the challenge, with interdependencies and the need for transparency across all stages and actors. Lastly, a particularly notable gap is the lack of inclusion of origin countries in sustainability efforts. This omission can lead to the failure to communicate the added value that sustainability brings, not just to the end consumer, but also to the regions where products are sourced. After describing the findings of our interview study, stakeholders, as well as critical supply chain events, are now outlined to complete the problem space and the requirements of our system design.

Stakeholders. Coffee production involves multiple actors, beginning with *coffee farms* growing coffee plants in various regions, mainly in developing countries. Collectors and cooperatives purchase harvested coffee cherries and deliver them to *processing facilities* or other cooperatives to monitor their quality and processing. After the green coffee has been processed, *exporters* and *importers* become involved, handling transportation and export processing, with importers bringing green coffee to target markets. *Roasters* play a crucial role in the coffee industry by acquiring green coffee from importers and roasting it to create unique flavor profiles. Traders and *distributors* then obtain the roasted coffee from the roasters and supply it to retailers, where it is sold in cafes, supermarkets, and other outlets. Ultimately, *consumers* serve as end users who appreciate coffee and impact the market through their preferences and purchasing choices. The connections between these actors are interrelated and collectively determine the direction and accomplishments of the entire coffee provision network. Throughout a sustainable supply chain, *auditors* are assigned a key role. Both in the physical world (certifications for products, such as the organic seal) and in the digital world (auditing data for handover, see Sect. 5).

Critical Supply Chain Events. In the complex dynamics of global supply chains, certain critical events crystallize that are crucial to the performance of seamless supply chain processes. In this context, we identified five decisive events related to data exchange and communication throughout the supply chain. These critical events include *transactions of product and price flows (1)*, which not only represent the economic settlement, but also mark *transfer of risk in terms of information flow (2)*. Furthermore, *the split and merging batches (3)* is an event in which the integrity and traceability of the product must be maintained. *Verification of sustainability (4)*, including social and environmental aspects, is gaining importance and requires transparent evidence throughout the supply chain.

Similarly, *collecting basic information (5)*, such as weight, quantity, and origin, plays a crucial role in ensuring quality and smooth process operations. Managing these critical events requires close collaboration, standardization, advanced technologies, including system-independent interfaces, and transparent information flows between supply chain actors.

5   System Design

Considering the initial situation and challenges of stakeholders within the coffee supply chain, we introduce a system-independent decentralized ecosystem approach for interoperable blockchain-based information systems to allow for tamper-proof handover of information such as sustainability and visualize this information in a user-friendly way for all relevant stakeholders via a DPP (see Fig. 2).

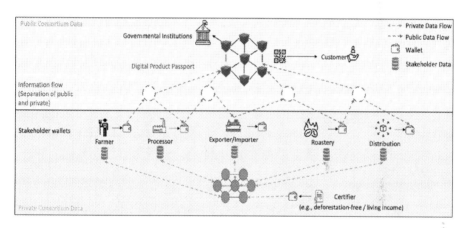

Fig. 2. System design: blockchain-based coffee supply chain consortium

The overall system consists of four main elements: First, the *stakeholder data (1)* including product information together with sustainability criteria (per batch), generated by private systems, such as ERP systems. These data are stored within the consortium level, the blockchain-based data model, and also provide sensible business and company-related data with respect to pricing, personal data, or compliance. This information is not intended for the public and, therefore, is only provided to participating companies as part of the consortium. On the other hand, there is the public blockchain-based data model, which is designed to enable the information flow of the product for public use (reporting and verification of sustainability criteria to the government, product information for customers).

These two components (the consortium and the public blockchain-based information systems) represent our *decentralized ecosystem (2)* network that enables a distributed register to issue, store, and transfer digital tokens. At this point, the *DPP (3)* is introduced (see Fig. 3). Taking into account the requirements of stakeholders, for our first conceptual approach, we draw upon a mobile application that is accessible through a QR code. Within our system, the DPP provides a digital twin of the product in the form of a digital token. It entails the verified product information including the sustainability criteria per batch of production. In addition to product information, a landscape of the coffee journey is depicted, including a unique identifier ID that refers to the batches from which the product was produced. Furthermore, ESG criteria are highlighted that consider the production and carbon footprint of the product. To strengthen trust, certifications for the product (phyisical or digital) can be taken from our DPP.

Fig. 3. Conceptual digital product passport design

Ultimately, to connect participants and the network, a digital twin is required for each stakeholder. Therefore, *stakeholder wallets (4)* are implemented to read and write the transactions of the decentralized ecosystem.

Basically, three parties are required for a transaction (transfer of information). Producer (Seller), Certifier, Verifier (Buyer) (see Fig. 4). Furthermore, we distinguish between outgoing (outbound) and incoming (inbound) transactions. Here, the seller (Wallet A) has the responsibility of creating a transaction. The auditor (Wallet B) signs/confirms the data of the transaction before it can be transferred to the buyer (Wallet C).

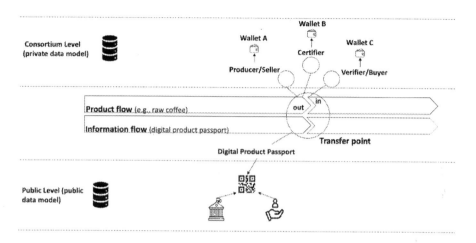

Fig. 4. Point of transfer

One step further, the product and information flow are shaped as follows (see Fig. 5). The prerequisite for the *product flow* out-bound is a produced product that has to be linked and labeled with the stock-label containing all relevant product information. To sell and transfer the product, a respective sales label has to be generated containing all relevant product sales information and be labeled accordingly. At the in-bound procedure, the buyer receives, scans, and verifies the coming good before putting it on stock.

For the *information flow*, parallel to the product flow, the seller has to generate the public product information based on the produced product (e.g., properties, sustainability criteria, quality, date, origin) that is linked to a specific batch. Furthermore, the seller issues a token that equates in number or amount equivalent to the product. The token is linked to the ownership (#-token based on qty. or pcs.) of a product batch, as well as the metadata that contain the information of the public product per batch together with the sustainability criteria. This procedure also addresses the challenge of keeping components transparent while batch merging, as new DPPs are created for each transaction, which in turn link back to previous transactions, respectively. At this point, the product information is verified and signed by the auditor/certifier to ensure the data correctness. Subsequently, the seller issues the DPP by storing the trusted information on the blockchain and links the ownership (# token) with metadata based on the public product information. During the physical in-bound procedure at the the buyer the #-token is transferred into the buyer-wallet. The buyer scans the product

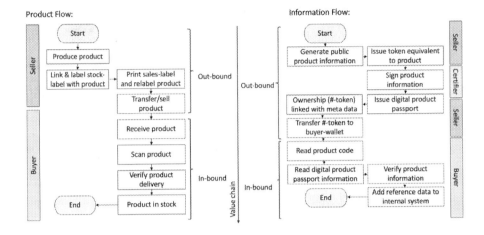

Fig. 5. Flowchart: product and information flow

code and thus also the DPP. He verifies the information (e.g., sustainability criteria) and adds the reference data to his internal system (e.g., ERP). During this process both the physical product and the digital ownership proof represented by the #-token have been transferred into the buyers possession.

6   Towards Governance in Decentralized Blockchain Ecosystems

The previous sections described our system design and the DPP. This section is now about the context of the DPP: the blockchain consortium, i.e., the community that uses the blockchain for business purposes, to collect and retrieve information about the product. Again, our guiding principle is full decentralization. The question is how to govern such a consortium for successful operation and use. Full decentralization has its risks and risks include the thread of the digital commons [23]: freeriding and the fact that costs and benefits might be fairly distributed in this community. Therefore, we first discuss our blockchain consortium with a public interface in the light of Ostrom's design principles of self-governance for communities [23]. In addition, we outline the responsibilities, decisions, and changes that actors face when being part of a blockchain consortium or community that uses a digital product past, as the one we designed.

Elinor Ostrom's concept of Common Pool Resources (CPR) [23] addresses the complexities of managing resources that are collectively used by various groups, where individual actions can significantly impact the collective outcome. She extends this approach by the information commons, emphasizing the need for collective management of data and knowledge [10]. In this regard, Jain et al. [14] investigate blockchain governance for small- and medium-sized enterprise clusters, and references to the "Tragedy of Commons" problem, stated in the dissertation of Hardin [8]. Furthermore, Poux et al. [27] explore the use of blockchain to support the governance of CPR based on Ostrom's design principles of self-governance for communities [23]. Now, we want to use these eight design principles to discuss governance requirements within fully decentralized blockchain consortia.

1. *Boundaries.* This principle refers to the importance of establishing clear and well-defined borders for resources that are collectively managed. In our scenario, CPR, in particular information commons, are general product information (e.g., origin and quality) and sustainability criteria (e.g., deforestation-free supply chains) along the supply chain that affect all participants within the consortium. The focus here should be on ensuring that every stakeholder benefits from these resources, including those who have less technological capacity than others.

2. *Congruence.* In accordance with the principle of congruence, Elinor Ostrom posits that the rules that govern the appropriation and provision of a resource should be in accordance with local conditions and cultural norms, ensuring that the allocation of costs among users is proportional to the benefits received. Global supply chains, such as coffee, are fundamentally different in terms of technological and social factors (heterogeneity of stakeholders). The consortium should consider the requirements of the stakeholders, especially those in the production countries, and collaboratively establish the regulations in this matter.

3. *Collective decisions.* The principle of collective decision-making claims that the majority of individuals affected by a resource system should have the opportunity to participate in decision-making processes that determine and revise the rules of resource use. The characteristic of blockchain requires distributed decision making that includes all stakeholders involved in the management and use of the platform. Here, stakeholders should have a right of co-determination when considering the use of data generated in their field. An important factor is the on-boarding and off-boarding process of participants at the organizational level. During this stage, it is vital to establish mutual agreement on eligibility requirements and exclusion criteria. The technology provides on-chain and off-chain governance, increasing the feasibility of standardization and automation of certain processes through smart contracts.

4. *Monitoring of users and resources.* This principle suggests that there be adequate oversight of resources to prevent rule violations; the individuals assigned with this surveillance, as well as the appropriation of the resource, must be users themselves or responsible to the users. Within a consortium without a central service provider, effective monitoring of activities and the use of collaborative resources are essential. The blockchain network already provides a high level of logging and monitoring, but it is important to ensure how data is processed in companies. So, from a governance perspective, agreements towards data usage have to be negotiated.

5. *Sanctions.* The principle of graduated sanctions refers to penalties for rule violations that should be proportional to the severity of the problem caused.

This approach ensures that punishments are both fair and effective, deterring repeat offenses within the governance system. Our scenario represents a separate ecosystem that is managed and controlled by all participating organizations within a global supply chain. Within such an ecosystem, sanctions are indispensable to punish violations of rules against the management of common goods. Due to the tamper-proof nature of the blockchain, this should be established within the consortium through both deterrence in the form of clearly defined sanctions and incentives for compliance. Particular attention should be paid to differentiating sanctions by stakeholder, as producer countries have different interests than consumer countries.

6. *Conflict resolution mechanisms.* This principle advocates for mechanisms that are swift, cost-effective, and accessible, providing localized areas to resolve disputes between users and between users and authorities, such as mediation. This ensures that conflicts are handled efficiently, maintaining the overall functionality of the system. The participation of various stakeholders requires customized dispute resolution mechanisms. On the one hand, the restriction of specific datasets for certain stakeholders can be enforced through the distribution of read access on-chain. However, from an organizational perspective, it requires a reconciliation of the individual strategy of the participants with the consortium strategy. Nethertheless, in case of a conflict, the consortium needs to define additional concrete processes for resolution.

7. *Recognition.* Recognition underscores the need for a minimum level of governmental acknowledgment of user rights to self-organize and establish their own rules. This is critical in legimiting the autonomy of local governance structures, ensuring their operational effectiveness within the broader legal and societal framework. With the introduction of jointly determined rules and responsibilities, legal contracts are associated with participation in a blockchain-based consortium. These contracts are signed by organizations as part of the on-boarding process. The contents of the contracts are to be individually designed depending on the use case.

8. *Embedded institutions.* This principle highlights that when a CPR is linked to larger resource systems, governance structures must be developed across multiple layers. This multilevel approach facilitates the coordination and coherence necessary to manage resource interdependencies effectively. Our proposed approach serves, on the one hand, the collaborative exchange of information between organizations and, on the other hand, compliance with legal requirements (e.g., due diligence) by passing sustainability criteria to governmental institutions. In addition to handover through the standardized DPP and decentralized environment, communication channels between organizations and authorities must be created in addition to the network.

A community using a blockchain, i.e., the blockchain consortium with its end-customer stakeholder, may experience the "Tragedy of the Commons". A blockchain needs components such as nodes, interfaces, software, resources to maintain the infrastructure and electricity. Benefits can accrue to many while being limited and, above all, unevenly distributed. Within our blockchain-based supply chain consortium, several aspects such as IT infrastructure, participation in the consortium, voting on decisions, changes due to new smart contracts, or heterogeneity of stakeholders considering technological capabilities are affected by a governance structure.

Based on our empirical focus group findings, we want to go one step further and outline the concrete responsibilities and decisions that are necessary to implement and operate a blockchain-based consortium collectively. Furthermore, we outline the changes that actors face when participating in such an ecosystem.

Responsibilities. Our focus group on governance in blockchain-based consortia show four categories of responsibilities for the consortium and the participating actors: supply chain, compliance, technical and organizational responsibilities. As the consortium operates within a global value chain, it must take into account supply chain processes, laws, and standards from various countries. Taking into account the supply chain, it is important to involve independent instances that are trusted by all participants to certify transactions within the information flow of the consortium. From a technical perspective, the consortium must share responsibilities among the organizations to ensure the security and high availability of nodes, peers, and wallets on the blockchain network. The organizations provide tamper-proof data (product certificates and sustainability criteria), and a verification authority for the documentation of assigned certificates restricts the use of the information. From an organizational perspective, the consortium graves for a higher instance that is elected by all participating actors following a proven governance mechanism and is responsible for the decisions to be made.

Decisions. In addition to high-level decisions, for example, on the type of blockchain, the consortium must make further decisions. These also include communication within the consortium, the weighting of votes in decisions, and the governance structure to be used. Here, requirements for the on- and off-boarding process of participants need to be defined. Furthermore, a sanctioning structure must be introduced and constantly reviewed, which is enforced when rules are violated. For the organization, aspects regarding operative integration with the blockchain, data sovereignty, legislation, as well as the utilization of technical components are relevant.

Changes. The changes by stakeholders through participation in a consortium include the acceptance of all stakeholders, the verification of the data, and thus also the level of trust towards other stakeholders. Furthermore, stakeholders must accept shared ownership considering the data of their value chain. This is accompanied by an increased focus on sensitive data that must not be shared, as information on the network is immutable and accessible to all actors. Due to the growing use of digital services, such as certification of information or exchange of the DPP, the scope of the stakeholders' tasks is shifting from the physical to the digital world. Here, the establishment of technological know-how is indispensable and leads to a restructuring or expansion of IT departments in organizations.

7   Conclusion and Further Work

This article proposed a system-independent decentralized ecosystem approach for the interoperability of blockchain-based information systems between a private and a public data model within a supply chain consortium that allows the tamper-proof handover of data through the introduction of a standardized DPP. Furthermore, we investigate the organizational perspective, discussing governance needs in light of Ostrom's eight design principles [23] and proposed with regard to responsibilities, decisions, and changes by stakeholders for a self-governing blockchain consortium.

Our approach aims to ensure privacy, traceability, transparency, as well as trust, and provides an alternative to the "winner-takes-all" platform ecosystem within a shared-resource and self-governing decentralized blockchain consortium in a global supply chain to counteract the "Tragedy of Commons". Our innovative approach is designed to deliver a multifaceted set of benefits, including protecting privacy, ensuring the traceability of transactions, improving transparency in data sharing, and fostering trust among participants. The technical novelty lies in the seamless interaction of a standardized and system-independent DPP between two distinct yet self-organized blockchain platforms. This interaction facilitates the efficient exchange of information, benefiting not only participants and customers but also regulatory bodies and governments. In essence, our approach represents a pivotal step towards achieving a secure data-sharing ecosystem in the context of supply chain management.

In addition to the technical artifacts, we outline responsibilities, decisions, and changes with regard to fully decentralization. Decentralized governance allows us to make the resources private property, to determine self-declared rules and responsibilities, including a transparent decision-making within our ecosystem, and to specifically limit alleged drawbacks of participating organizations from development countries.

This study acknowledges several limitations that warrant consideration. First, from a technological perspective, challenges such as scalability, throughput, latency, and maintaining privacy and confidentiality in public ledgers present significant barriers. As transaction volumes increase, networks can face congestion, leading to delays and increased transaction costs, underscoring the importance of selecting an appropriate blockchain network. Furthermore, while blockchain enhances transparency and immutability, ensuring data privacy and confidentiality poses difficulties, although advances in zero-knowledge proofs and privacy-preserving smart contracts are emerging to tackle these issues. Additionally, the security of smart contracts, vulnerable to exploits due to coding flaws, emphasizes the need for thorough testing and auditing. From the standpoint of stakeholder resistance, various factors contribute to hesitancy towards blockchain adoption. A lack of understanding among stakeholders, particularly those unfamiliar with technology, requires targeted education and awareness efforts. Fear of change and potential disruptions to existing processes and roles, coupled with concerns about job security and changes in organizational power dynamics, further compounds resistance. Moreover, blockchain's challenge to traditional trust models and organizational cultural barriers, including attitudes towards risk and innovation, highlight the complexity of achieving widespread acceptance. Regarding regulatory compliance, the evolving and disparate regulatory landscape across jurisdictions poses additional challenges.

Our next steps can be divided into three categories: First, we want to conclude the design of the proposed Digital Product Passport for appropriate use in practice through a participatory design (PD) with stakeholders and user focus groups [32]. Second, we want to enrich and evaluate our technical ecosystem approach through a real-world field experiment, in which we aim to involve all relevant stakeholders throughout the entire coffee supply chain, from the initial coffee farm to the distribution point within a global value chain. In doing so, we want to outline a demonstrator to consider the functionality and compatibility of requirements within a field test. Third, from an organizational perspective, we aspire to establish the governance procedures that will be based on the outcomes of this experiment. This involves defining the roles, responsibilities, decision-making protocols, and adaptation strategies essential for the effective operation of the consortium, which comprises both private and public network components, along with the standardized and system-independent DPP.

Acknowledgements. We acknowledge funding for Project LIONS as part of dtec.bw. dtec.bw is funded by the European Commission under NextGenerationEU.

References

1. Adisorn, T., Tholen, L., Götz, T.: Towards a digital product passport fit for contributing to a circular economy. Energies **14**(8), 2289 (2021)
2. Beck, R., Müller-Bloch, C., King, J.: Governance in the blockchain economy: a framework and research agenda. J. Assoc. Inform. Syst. (10 2018). https://aisel.aisnet.org/jais/vol19/iss10/1
3. Catena-X: Catena-x: the first open and collaborative data ecosystem (2023). https://catena-x.net/fileadmin/user_upload/01_Vision_und_Ziele/230731_Catena-X_general_presentation.pdf. Accessed 31 Jan 2024
4. Denter, L., Graf, J., Welsch, F.: The digital product passport (2023). www.germanwatch.org/en/88232
5. Federal ministry of labour and social affairs: supply chain act (2021). https://www.bmas.de/EN/Europe-and-the-World/International/Supply-Chain-Act/supply-chain-act.html
6. Greiner, M., Zeiß, C., Lechner, U., Winkelmann, A.: Towards a governance model design for blockchain-based traceability systems. In: 18th International Conference on Design Science Research in Information Systems and Technology (2023). https://doi.org/10.18726/2023_2
7. Hacker, J., Miscione, G., Felder, T., Schwabe, G.: Commit or not? how blockchain consortia form and develop. California Manag. Rev., 110–131 (2023). https://journals.sagepub.com/doi/full/10.1177/00081256231175530
8. Hardin, G.: The Tragedy of the commons. Science 3859 (10 1968). http://www.jstor.org/stable/1724745

9. Heeß, P., et al.: Enhancing trust in global supply chains: conceptualizing digital product passports for a low-carbon hydrogen market. Electron. Markets **34**(1), 1–20 (2024)

10. Hess, C., Ostrom, E.: Understanding Knowledge as a Commons: From Theory to Practice. MIT press PBK (2011)

11. Hevner, A.R., March, S.T., Park, J., Ram, S.: Design science in information systems research. MIS Quarterly (2004). https://doi.org/10.2307/25148625

12. Hofman, D., DuPont, Q., Walch, A., Beschastnikh, I.: Blockchain governance: De facto (X)or designed? Building decentralized trust: multidisciplinary perspectives on the design of blockchains and distributed ledgers, pp. 21–33 (2021). https://doi.org/10.1007/978-3-030-54414-0_2/FIGURES/2

13. Hoiss, T., Seidenfad, K., Lechner, U.: Blockchain service operations - a structured approach to operate a blockchain solution. In: 2021 IEEE International Conference on Decentralized Applications and Infrastructures (DAPPS), pp. 11–19. IEEE (8 2021). https://doi.org/10.1109/DAPPS52256.2021.00007, https://ieeexplore.ieee.org/document/9566184/

14. Jain, G., Shrivastava, A., Paul, J., Batra, R.: Blockchain for SME clusters: an ideation using the framework of ostrom commons governance. Inform. Syst. Front. (2022). https://doi.org/10.1007/s10796-022-10288-z

15. Jansen, M., Gerstenberger, B., Bitter-Krahe, J., Berg, H., Sebestyén, J., Schneider, J.: Current approaches to the digital product passport for a circular economy. Wuppertal Institute (2022)

16. Jansen, M., et al.: Stop guessing in the dark: identified requirements for digital product passport systems. Systems **11**(3), 123 (2023)

17. Katina, P.F., Keating, C.B., Sisti, J.A., Gheorghe, A.V.: Blockchain governance. Int. J. Critical Infrastruct. **2**, 121–135 (2019). https://doi.org/10.1504/IJCIS.2019.098835

18. Koppelaar, R.H.E.M., et al.: A digital product passport for critical raw materials reuse and recycling. Sustainability **15**(2), 1405 (2023)

19. Kuckartz, U.: Qualitative inhaltsanalyse: methoden, praxis, computerunterstützung. Beltz Juventa (2012)

20. Laatikainen, G., Li, M., Abrahamsson, P.: A system-based view of blockchain governance. Inform. Softw. Technol. 107149 (5 2023). https://doi.org/10.1016/J.INFSOF.2023.107149

21. Li, Z., Kang, J., Yu, R., Ye, D., Deng, Q., Zhang, Y.: Consortium blockchain for secure energy trading in industrial internet of things. IEEE Trans. Industr. Inform., 3690–3700 (2017). https://doi.org/10.1109/TII.2017.2786307

22. Lumineau, F., Wang, W., Schilke, O.: Blockchain governance-A new way of organizing collaborations? Organization Science, pp. 500–521 (3 2021). https://pubsonline.informs.org/doi/abs/10.1287/orsc.2020.1379

23. Ostrom, E.: Governing the Commons: The Evolution of Institutions for Collective Action. Political Economy of Institutions and Decisions, Cambridge University Press (1990). https://doi.org/10.1017/CBO9780511807763

24. Panza, L., Bruno, G., Lombardi, F.: Integrating absolute sustainability and social sustainability in the digital product passport to promote industry 5.0. Sustainability **15**(16), 12552 (2023)

25. Pelt, R.v., Jansen, S., Baars, D., Overbeek, S.: Defining blockchain governance: a framework for analysis and comparison. Inform. Syst. Manage. **1**, 21–41 (2021). https://doi.org/10.1080/10580530.2020.1720046

26. Plociennik, C., et al.: Towards a digital lifecycle passport for the circular economy. Procedia CIRP (2022)

27. Poux, P., De Filippi, P., Ramos, S.: Blockchains for the governance of common goods. In: Proceedings of the 1st International Workshop on Distributed Infrastructure for Common Good, pp. 7–12 (2020)
28. Reijers, W., et al.: Now the code runs itself: on-chain and off-chain governance of blockchain technologies. Top, 821–831 (2021). https://doi.org/10.1007/S11245-018-9626-5/METRICS
29. Seidenfad, K., Greiner, M., Biermann, J., Lechner, U.: Carbonedge: collaborative blockchain-based monitoring, reporting, and verification of greenhouse gas emissions on the edge. In: Krieger, U.R., Eichler, G., Erfurth, C., Fahrnberger, G. (eds.) 23rd International Conference on Innovations for Community Service. I4CS 2023, pp. 123–147. Springer, Cham (2023). https://doi.org/10.1007/978-3-031-40852-6_7
30. Seidenfad, K., Greiner, M., Biermann, J., Lechner, U.: Blockchain-based monitoring, reporting and verification of GHG emissions on the network edge-a system integration study in the artisan coffee industry. In: 2024 IEEE/SICE International Symposium on System Integration (SII), pp. 1227–1228. IEEE (2024). https://doi.org/10.1109/SII58957.2024.10417510
31. Shrimali, B., Patel, H.B.: Blockchain state-of-the-art: architecture, use cases, consensus, challenges and opportunities. J. King Saud Univ.-Comput. Inform. Sci. 6793–6807 (2022). https://doi.org/10.1016/j.jksuci.2021.08.005
32. Spinuzzi, C.: The Methodology of participatory design. Tech. Commun. 52(2), 163–174 (2005)
33. Strauss, A., Corbin, J.: Basics of Qualitative Research. Sage publications (1990)
34. Sunyaev, A., et al.: Token economy. Bus. Inf. Syst. Eng. 63(4), 457–478 (2021)
35. Talib, M.A., et al.: Interoperability among heterogeneous blockchains: a systematic literature review. In: Rehman, M.H., Svetinovic, D., Salah, K., Damiani, E. (eds.) Trust Models for Next-Generation Blockchain Ecosystems. EICC, pp. 135–166. Springer, Cham (2021). https://doi.org/10.1007/978-3-030-75107-4_6
36. Viguerie, C., Ciriello, R.F., Zavolokina, L.: Formative archetypes in enterprise blockchain governance: exploring the dynamics of participant dominance and platform openness. In: 57th Hawaii International Conference on System Sciences (2024). https://hdl.handle.net/10125/107173
37. Voulgaridis, K., Lagkas, T., Angelopoulos, C.M., Boulogeorgos, A.A.A., Argyriou, V., Sarigiannidis, P.: Digital product passports as enablers of digital circular economy: a framework based on technological perspective (2023). https://doi.org/10.36227/techrxiv.22309216.v1
38. Walden, J., Steinbrecher, A., Marinkovic, M.: Digital product passports as enabler of the circular economy. Chemie Ingenieur Technik 93, 1717–1727 (2021). https://doi.org/10.1002/cite.202100121
39. Wang, G., Wang, Q., Chen, S.: Exploring blockchains interoperability: a systematic survey. ACM Comput. Surv. (2023). https://doi.org/10.1145/3582882
40. Weill, P., Ross, J.W.: IT Governance: How top performers manage IT decision rights for superior results - Peter Weill, Jeanne W. Ross. https://books.google.de/books?hl=de&lr=&id=xI5KdR21QTAC&oi=fnd&pg=PR7&dq=weill+2004&ots=VFGceZQfnQ&sig=l6dvRRDp6OXL8UJ4kMhMIr_VgpM&redir_esc=y#v=onepage&q=weill%202004&f=false
41. Yaga, D., Mell, P., Roby, N., Scarfone, K.: Blockchain technology overview (2018). https://doi.org/10.6028/NIST.IR.8202, https://nvlpubs.nist.gov/nistpubs/ir/2018/NIST.IR.8202.pdf

42. Yue, K.B., Kallempudi, P., Sha, K., Wei, W., Liu, X.: Governance Attributes of Consortium Blockchain Applications (Conference Paper) | NSF PAGES. https://par.nsf.gov/biblio/10308845

43. Zavolokina, L., Hein, A., Carvalho, .A., Schwabe, .G., Krcmar, H.: Preface to the special issue on "Enterprise and organizational applications of distributed ledger technologies" Electronic Markets **34:1** (1), 1–5 (1 2024). https://doi.org/10.1007/S12525-023-00688-7, https://link.springer.com/article/10.1007/s12525-023-00688-7

44. Zavolokina, L., Ziolkowski, R., Bauer, I., Schwabe, G.: Management, Governance and Value Creation in a Blockchain Consortium. MIS Quarterly Executive (2020). https://doi.org/10.17705/2MSQE.00022

Digital Sovereignty and Open-Source Software - A Discussion Paper

John Bechara and Ulrike Lechner[(✉)]

University of the Bundeswehr Munich, Neubiberg, Germany
{john.bechara,ulrike.lechner}@unibw.de

Abstract. Digital sovereignty is an important goal in Germany's and Europe's political agendas. To achieve this goal, the IT or OT systems' design, the life cycle, and the digital ecosystems must be reconsidered. Our research interest is the potential role of open-source software in strengthening digital sovereignty. This idea paper discusses its risks and potential contribution to digital sovereignty. It presents the research idea and a research design.

Keywords: Open-source · Digital sovereignty · Cybersecurity

1 Introduction and Motivation

The COVID-19 pandemic, the war in Ukraine, the looming crises worldwide, and the resulting economic consequences have highlighted the dependence of Germany and Europe on suppliers and how this shapes and limits the political options of a liberal democracy. For digital products, the value chain is global, products and services are complex, and often, there is only a single supplier for hardware, operating systems, or applications. The license agreements can provide an interesting basis for assessing this situation. E.g., in the year 2021, the license costs of the public sector for Microsoft products in Germany were around €205 million at the federal level alone [42]. This represents an increase of nearly 15% after the jump from €57.2 million in 2019 to €178.5 million in 2020 [31]. This means that in 2021, the licensing costs for proprietary software of a single company exceeded the total budget of the German Federal Office for Information Security (BSI) as one of the central bodies for digitization in Germany (€197.16 million) [9]. This exemplifies the costs for software and the market position of a single non-European vendor. The list of products and goods on which Germany and Europe critically depend is long. It includes personal devices, such as smartphones, tablets, and PCs, core digital technology, such as semiconductors, or digital platforms, such as Amazon, PayPal, Netflix, and gaming platforms.

Recognizing the need to strengthen digital sovereignty and the challenges to more sovereignty, Germany and the EU must set an agenda. Open-source initiatives can be an essential factor in reaching digital sovereignty - as an alternative or a complement to the conventional IT industry. Arguments include freedom of

F. Phillipson et al. (Eds.): I4CS 2024, CCIS 2109, pp. 397–407, 2024.
https://doi.org/10.1007/978-3-031-60433-1_22

choice, cost-effectiveness, empowerment of users, qualification of software developers, transparency, and security. However, striving towards digital sovereignty might result in a higher total cost of ownership.

On the one hand, successful initiatives like the operating system Linux, the Web infrastructure Apache, and Hyperledger as a distributed-ledger infrastructure prove that it is possible to build reliable open-source digital infrastructure. On the other hand, the countless failed open-source projects also show that a successful open-source project is by no means a sure-fire success. Even if an open-source project is successfully developed and maintained, it is not easy to implement it within the organization.

This is where we want to start with this idea article by initiating a discussion about the research idea, goal, and research design, trying to answer the question of what is necessary to successfully implement Open-Source software (OSS), especially under the view of how this OSS contributes to the digital sovereignty. The objective is to design an instrument to analyze the value of sovereignty. Our aim is to understand the source code and the structures, processes, and organization of the OSS and its community before integration to make informed decisions.

2   Digital Sovereignty

Pohle and Theissen describe the genesis of 'Digital sovereignty' as a political concept that relates to the security and safety of critical infrastructure, economic autonomy and competition concerning foreign technology and technology providers, and user autonomy and individual self-determination. Examples of initiatives to increase digital sovereignty include the Gaia-X platform as a European Cloud for data or the initiatives to rebuild the semiconductor industry in Europe [29]. Moerel & Timmers state that "Digital Strategic Autonomy" is more accurate than digital sovereignty [24]. Bürger et al. refer to "active and self-determined digital participation," which requires a minimum of "digital sovereignty" [4]. Fries et al. capture this digital participation in three dimensions, characterized by a constant multidirectional interaction between the state, organizations (e.g., companies), and the individual [12]. According to this model, the individual is pivotal in digital sovereignty as the individual needs to decide and set action towards digital sovereignty.

In our work, we follow the definition of "Digital Sovereignty" by the Kompetenzstelle Öffentliche IT (ÖFIT): *Digital sovereignty is the sum of all individuals and institutions' abilities and possibilities to exercise their role(s) in the digital world in an independent, self-determined, and secure manner* [16].

This definition of digital sovereignty uses independent, self-determined, and secure to capture digital sovereignty. Independent, self-determined, and secure are the three attributes that we begin the endeavor to assess digital sovereignty. Note that security is essential for digital sovereignty. For example, the promotion of data protection, which the GDPR has significantly strengthened, pays off in terms of self-determination, as it enables every EU citizen to decide who has access to their data and how they are used. The promotion of end-to-end encryption promotes security in addition to data protection. Open data, which is the free provision of data generated with the help of taxpayers' money, enables companies and individuals to obtain information independently and even to develop business models based on it. The increased use of OSS, as envisaged in central IT strategies such as the Open-Source Software Strategy, is a further measure to strengthen digital sovereignty [10]. This measure can be equally relevant to all actors since the state, companies, and individuals can benefit from it. However, the increased use of OSS also entails risks for organizations and the state, which must find solutions to address the challenges arising from its use.

3 Open-Source Software

The term OSS is used to describe a variety of models. OSS is often equated with free software. Stallmann, one of the founders of free software, describes that free software is software that gives the user the freedom to share, study, and modify it. We call this free software because the user is free." The distinction between "free beer" and "free software" is being attributed to him. Free software is characterized by the basic idea that source code should constantly be and without restrictions free of charge accessible [15,33], and this is being supported, e.g., by the GNU foundation.

Free software and the Free Software Foundation represent one notion of open software. Open Software is well differentiated regarding license models and the freedom to use as a provider for creating IT systems for professional use and in various business models [7]. OSS and free software have in common that the source code is generally made freely available so that anyone can use, review, and further develop it.

In contrast to free software, OSS may come with many different license models. An example is the widespread GNU General Public License (GNU GPL). It includes a so-called copyleft, which obliges anyone using this software to make it available free of charge and as copyleft software. This is a challenge for commercial use by IT companies [1]. Furthermore, the unrestricted use of an open-source product for commercial purposes may be excluded, which has implications for the service.

In addition to the licensing model, another important factor is the supporting organization [6]. The pure number of maintaining developers and, sometimes more importantly, the affiliation to a foundation can increase the reliability of an OSS. The reason for this is that a foundation can help maintain a certain level of consistency, which goes beyond the purely voluntary contributions of developers. Furthermore, the foundation's reputation can make it more attractive for developers to contribute to the software, affecting the organization's size [38]. Well-known examples are the Firefox Browser, which is maintained by Mozilla, and the Apache HTTP Server, which the Apache Foundation maintains. Especially those foundations can also be very company-driven, like the Hyperledger Project, which is maintained by the Linux Foundation and to which some industry leaders like IBM or Intel contribute.

Another factor in the use of OSS can be the range of functions. In general, the complexity of the software tends to increase with the range of functions. Software limited to providing a single function, such as the Apache HTTP server, must be considered differently than software that offers many different functions, such as LibreOffice. Also relevant is whether the software is at the end of the "usage chain," i.e., it can be used directly by the end-user or a function that may only be used by other products as a dependency. The reason here could be that the more functions are implemented inside the software, the bigger the community must be to provide long-term support, and therefore the harder this community is to manage.

These are some of the significant aspects that need to be considered when determining the value an OSS could have concerning the degree of sovereignty resulting from its use. The decision-making process for selecting software usually involves identifying and weighing decision criteria. This applies to end-user software [3] and to packages in the context of developing your software [20].

4   Three Perspectives for Selection and Decision

But why should the usage of OSS even be considered regarding the caveats described in the previous chapters? A literature review by Johansson, which sought to analyze the reasons for choosing ERP systems, found that the four most important are (1) price, (2) speed of implementation, (3) support, and (4) vendor reliability [21].

A similar picture emerges from the analysis of the Linux in Munich (LiMux) project, one of the largest and most comprehensive projects following the vision to switch a whole governmental administration from proprietary software to OSS. According to Silic, the goal of the Linux initiative was independence from large central providers (in this case, mainly Microsoft) [35]. Grassmuck comes to a similar conclusion extended by a cost consideration, resulting from the dependence [17]. According to Singh et al., these cost savings and flexibility are the most important arguments

Fig. 1. Three dimensions of selection and decision on the use of open-source software

for using OSS [36]. All those aspects come into play in our model depicted in Fig. 1, which will be elaborated in this chapter.

4.1   Cost

Lower costs are probably the most widely used argument in favor of OSS. Even if this is generally true, looking at pure procurement costs in isolation would be too short-sighted.

License Costs. Though license costs are lower for OSS than for proprietary software, applications are not necessarily free. This applies especially for commercial use, where the devil is usually in the detail [26]. A very in-depth analysis of the respective license is essential, which can also be costly.

License Restrictions. Pure Procurement Costs are not the only reason for scrutinizing the license. Some of the licenses come with certain restrictions. Copyleft Licenses, for example, could force every software that uses it to be a free-of-charge OSS [25]. This could be a heavy caveat for the business model.

Personnel Requirements. The use of OSS does not directly lead to higher personnel costs. It is already a mitigation measure for the unclear responsibilities and a direct consequence of using the source code's extensibility and verifiability. A trustful mediator could also meet this requirement, though one must be careful not to replace a dependency on a proprietary software vendor with another.

Free Developer Capacities. The ongoing shortage of skilled workers, at least in Germany, is resulting in higher personnel costs for software development. Software developers were already identified as a bottleneck resource in 2017 [19]. Since OSS is often developed voluntarily in one's spare time, additional unpaid capacities can be drawn on here, such as building software on top of existing OSS and reducing development work.

Extensibility. Even if the extensibility of OSS depends on the corresponding license model, free insight into the source code offers the possibility of adaptations, extensions, and further developments. Compared to proprietary software, that is a clear advantage since a dependency on a closed system arises, which can be easily exploited by the software owner [30]. Closed interfaces are a proven and effective way to lock a customer in their software and prevent migration to alternatives, proprietary or [37]. Usually, this occurs in environments characterized by a lack of standardization [27], which are promoted and used by open-source projects [5]. A recent example of this is Twitter. After the takeover by Elon Musk, interfaces were made interfaces were charged for. Business models built up to that point were endangered by a unilateral decision of the provider [32].

Multi-sourcing Strategy. Open interfaces create the basis for switching between providers, establishing a multi-sourcing strategy, and promoting competition between applications [40]. In this context, reducing dependency on individual providers also reduces the risk of failure and thus increases security [14].

Compliance. Compliance and alignment of the IT strategy with regulations such as accounting, GDPR, NIS, and NIS-directive, or the EU AI-Act are challenging. An open-source community that is large enough to ensure software operation is often international. This can lead to a different knowledge of the regulations, as they can differ in each country.

4.2   Provider

Extensibility was already mentioned as an argument that reduces the risk of a single vendor. However, more topics have to be considered when examining the provider level of the OSS.

Implementation Speed. Fast implementation speed is another widespread argument for OSS. Due to the general availability and usability without overcoming obstacles, OSS is considered to have a fast implementation speed [21]. However, this advantage probably applies mainly to small projects with limited functionality.

Responsibilities. Unclear responsibilities are very much intertwined with the governance aspect and also part of the safety topic. These aspects are expanded here to include legal responsibilities. While in the case of a proprietary software purchase, where the relationships are regulated by contract, there is no such obligation per se in the case of OSS. Instead, there is a dependency on the functionality and willingness of an unknown, intangible community [8].

4.3   Safety

The Safety aspect covers the Security and Resilience Perspective. Cybersecurity and the need to protect critical infrastructures and society from cyberattacks are major drivers of strategic considerations regarding cybersecurity. It covers more than the security topics and considers things like organization and processes.

Verifiability of the Source Code. The verifiability of the source code seems to be the most apparent advantage of OSS. Since the source code is public for reviews, everyone can check whether it does what it is intended for and not more or less. On the other hand, errors can be found and identified better in such a way [39]. BSI code reviews are not without reason, mandatory in Germany for critical applications that require certification [2]. Integrated into a life cycle development process, code reviews are an efficient way to ensure the quality of the source code. This can be a challenge even in industry [13]. We argue that open-source communities and organizations face similar challenges in setting up code review practices. Good examples are studies regarding discussion platforms like Stack Overflow developers used to discuss and solve problems, as they are used for open-source in the same way as for proprietary software. Almost a third of the source code analyzed on Stack Overflow by Zhang et al. had severe flaws, which can lead to problems such as program crashes and resource leaks [41] and almost 15% of the analyzed android applications analyzed by Fisher et al. contained security-related code snippets from Stack Overflow with at least one insecure code snippet [11]. By performing independent code reviews, those errors could be identified before release.

Vulnerability Management. Reliable defect identification requires, above all, appropriate quality assurance processes [23]. In communities, the adherence to processes, if introduced at all, is hardly instructed and even harder to enforce. The governance, especially the leadership in the respective open-source community is of particular interest here. Many successful OSSs, for example, divide very strictly between the general decision-making process, which can be handled very decentralized and community-driven, and the code-level decisions, which is government by a very small subset of the community [28]. Sometimes, this leadership is based on a strict hierarchy, like in the Linux community, or professionalized due to companies' contributions, as in the Hyperledger blockchain case. This can help reduce that risk. A company has many more ways to ensure that development processes are mature, supported by tooling, and, most importantly, applied. That is why it is more likely to find possible vulnerabilities in proprietary software due to continuous and often contractually secured support and recent security incidents, as Log4j and Solarwinds are examples of code weaknesses in OSS that exist and can be propagated.

Bug Fixing. The processes of Bug Fixing aligned in an economically oriented organization for the error removal, together with limited developer capacities, often lead to a faster bug fixing in OSS, a working community presupposed [26].

No Security Through Obscurity. No Security through Obscurity is a dictum emphasizing the big difference between Security and Secrecy. In other words, to address the big question, how can OSS be more secure than Close Source Software when everyone, including possible attackers, can see the Source Code and find potential weak spots? Hoepmann and Jacobs describe the answer to this question as the shift of security topics from the implementation to the design phase of the software lifecycle [18]. A concept that goes back to military studies 150 years ago [22]. If security has already been addressed in the design phase, it does not matter when everyone can see the source code. If security is brought in later in the implementation, the source code needs to be hidden. This kind of security is more than fragile and even "naïve" because it leaves out the fact that attackers will actively work to gain secrets. At the same time, vendors and users are lulled into a false sense of security. Schneier even insists that secrecy leads to non-security [34]. This means an active OSS community where a variety of developers review the design of the software, each maybe with a different point of view, can help increase the security of software.

5 Conclusion and Next Steps

Digital sovereignty is a question of individual stance, whether we are talking about governmental organizations, companies, or individuals. We need to make an effort to further use and develop IT systems. OSS can be one piece of the puzzle, but it must be analyzed well before use, acknowledging that the different aspects can be intertwined.

The advantage of free access to development resources is accompanied by the need to have personnel in place to handle the characteristics of OSS, like unreliable defect identification and unclear responsibilities. It can also be helpful to use extensibility to make the best use of free access to the source code, not only from a security point of view but also to increase its value. But However, is also clear that not only the license costs, which could be limited by license restrictions, but also the accompanying costs should be considered. The advantage of a multi-sourcing strategy and a possible higher implementation speed, especially for smaller projects, comes with the caveat of having to deal with unclear responsibilities. Last but not least, increased security, which is possible with OSS and faster troubleshooting, comes with the price of unreliable fault and security weakness identification.

Putting all the dots together, it seems logical that none of the cost, safety, and provider factors can be considered separately. They do not point strictly in one direction and have interdependencies. That is why every introduction of OSS should be regarded as a whole. The development processes, the OSS community, the features on the one side and the personal resources, the existence of a trustful mediator, and the requirements on the other side must be juggled to decide the usefulness for the company and the impact on the digital sovereignty. This is a very complex and time-consuming task that must be done whenever introducing an OSS is considered. Therefore, the following steps would be to identify and evaluate the right factors that reflect all the criteria mentioned above and find possibilities to support such a process, such as automatic code and commit reviews, as well as testing and analysis of the OSS community. The key questions here will identify and relate appropriate metrics and indicators. Due to unclear data availability, mandatory and optional data should be distinguished. Also, the question of which OSS community data can be used automatically must be answered. If these questions are omitted, OSS can become a risk that can jeopardize entire business models or even society.

Credits

Acknowledgments. We acknowledge funding for Project LIONS as part of dtec.bw. dtec.bw is funded by the European Commission under NextGenerationEU.

Disclosure of Interests. The authors have no competing interests to declare relevant to this article's content.

References

1. Almeida, D.A., Murphy, G.C., Wilson, G., Hoye, M.: Do software developers understand open source licenses? In: 2017 IEEE/ACM 25th International Conference on Program Comprehension (ICPC), pp. 1–11. IEEE, Buenos Aires, Argentina (2017)
2. Bundesamt für Sicherheit in der Informationstechnik: CON.8 Software-Entwicklung (2020)
3. Byrd-Bredbenner, C., Pelican, S.: Software: how do you choose? J. Nutr. Educ. **16**(2), 77–79 (1984)
4. Bürger, T., Grau, A.: Digital Souverän 2021: Aufbruch in die digitale Post-Coronawelt. Bertelsmann Stiftung (2021)
5. Carl Cargill: The Rise and Fall and Rise of Standardization. UniForum's ITSolutions (1996)
6. Crowston, K.: Towards a portfolio of FLOSS project success measures. In: Collaboration, Conflict and Control: The 4th Workshop on Open Source Software Engineering. W8S Workshop - 26th International Conference on Software Engineering, vol. 2004, pp. 29–33. IEE, Edinburgh, Scotland, UK (2004)
7. CTTEC: Open Source License Comparison Grid. https://www.cmu.edu/cttec/forms/opensourcelicensegridv1.pdf
8. Dalle, J.M., Jullien, N.: Open-source vs. proprietary software. Guest lecture at ESSID Summer School, Cargèse (2001)
9. Ehneß, S.: Mehr Geld für moderne IT (2022). https://www.egovernment.de/mehr-geld-fuer-moderne-it-a-1104590/
10. European Commission: Open Source Software Stragey 2020-2023 (2020). https://commission.europa.eu/system/files/2020-10/en_ec_open_source_strategy_2020-2023.pdf
11. Fischer, F., et al.: Stack overflow considered harmful? The impact of copy&paste on android application security. In: 2017 IEEE Symposium on Security and Privacy (SP), pp. 121–136. IEEE, San Jose, CA, USA (2017)
12. Fries, I., Greiner, M., Hofmeier, M., Hrestic, R., Lechner, U., Wendeborn, T.: Towards a layer model for digital sovereignty: a holistic approach. In: Hämmerli, B., Helmbrecht, U., Hommel, W., Kunczik, L., Pickl, S. (eds.) Critical Information Infrastructures Security. CRITIS 2022. LNCS, vol. 13723. Springer, Cham (2023). https://doi.org/10.1007/978-3-031-35190-7_9
13. Gasiba, T.E.: Raising awareness on secure coding in the industry through Cyber-Security challenges. PhD Thesis, Dissertation, Neubiberg, Universität der Bundeswehr München, 2021 (2021)
14. Ghosh, R.: The European Politics of F/OSS Adoption. The Politics of Open Source Adoption, pp. 7–13 (2005). Publisher: New York: Social Science Research Council
15. Ghosh, R.A., Glott, R., Krieger, B., Robles, G.: Free/libre and open source software. Survey and study (2002)
16. Goldacker, G.: Digitale Souveränität (2017). https://www.oeffentliche-it.de/documents/10181/14412/Digitale+Souveränität
17. Grassmuck, V.: LiMux-Free Software for Munich. the politics of open source adoption, pp. 14–36 (2005). Publisher: Citeseer
18. Hoepman, J.H., Jacobs, B.: Increased security through open source. Commun. ACM **50**(1), 79–83 (2007)
19. Jacobs, K., Kuhlmey, A., Greß, S., Klauber, J., Schwinger, A. (eds.): Pflege-Report 2019: Mehr Personal in der Langzeitpflege - aber woher? Springer, Heidelberg (2020). https://doi.org/10.1007/978-3-662-58935-9

20. Jadhav, A.S., Sonar, R.M.: Evaluating and selecting software packages: a review. Inf. Softw. Technol. **51**(3), 555–563 (2009)
21. Johansson, B., Sudzina, F.: Choosing open source ERP systems: what reasons are there for doing so? In: Boldyreff, C., Crowston, K., Lundell, B., Wasserman, A.I. (eds.) OSS 2009. IAICT, vol. 299, pp. 143–155. Springer, Heidelberg (2009). https://doi.org/10.1007/978-3-642-02032-2_14
22. Kerckhoffs, A.: La cryptographie militaire, ou, Des chiffres usités en temps de guerre: avec un nouveau procédé de déchiffrement applicable aux systèmes à double clef. Librairie militaire de L, Baudoin (1883)
23. Kumar, R., Singh, H.: A model for quality assurance of OSS architecture. In: 2012 CSI Sixth International Conference on Software Engineering (CONSEG), pp. 1–6 (2012)
24. Moerel, L., Timmers, P.: Reflections on Digital Sovereignty. Research in Focus **EU Cyber Direct** (2021)
25. Mustonen, M.: Copyleft-the economics of Linux and other open source software. Inf. Econ. Policy **15**(1), 99–121 (2003)
26. O'Hara, K.J., Kay, J.S.: Open source software and computer science education. J. Comput. Sci. Coll. **18**(3), 1–7 (2003)
27. Opara-Martins, J., Sahandi, R., Tian, F.: Critical analysis of vendor lock-in and its impact on cloud computing migration: a business perspective. J. Cloud Comput. **5**(1), 4 (2016)
28. O'Mahony, S.: The governance of open source initiatives: what does it mean to be community managed? J. Manag. Gov. **11**(2), 139–150 (2007)
29. Pohle, J., Thiel, T.: Digital sovereignty. Internet Policy Rev. **9**(4) (2020)
30. Raymond, E.S.: The cathedral and the bazaar: musings on Linux and Open Source by an accidental revolutionary. O'Reilly, Beijing ; Cambridge, Mass, rev. ed edn. (2001)
31. Rosenbach, M.: Microsoft: Bundesministerien kauften Software für 178 Millionen Euro. Der Spiegel (2021)
32. SAN FRANCISCO (awp international): Twitter macht Zugang zu Schnittstellen kostenpflichtig (2023). https://www.finanzen.ch/nachrichten/konjunktur/twitter-macht-zugang-zu-schnittstellen-kostenpflichtig-1032063424
33. Scacchi, W.: Free/open source software development: recent research results and methods. Adv. Comput. **69**, 243–295 (2007). Publisher: Elsevier
34. Schneier, B.: The nonsecurity of secrecy. Commun. ACM **47**(10), 120 (2004)
35. Silic, M., Back, A.: Technological Risks of Open Source Software Adoption in the Organizational Context Linux in Munich (LiMux) Case. SSRN Electronic Journal (2015)
36. Singh, A., Bansal, R., Jha, N.: Open source software vs proprietary software. Int. J. Comput. Appl. **114**(18), 26–31 (2015)
37. Sjoerdstra, B.: Dealing with vendor lock-in. B.S. thesis, University of Twente (2016)
38. Stürmer, M., Myrach, T.: Open source community building. University of Bern, Licentiate (2005)
39. Witten, B., Landwehr, C., Caloyannides, M.: Does open source improve system security? IEEE Softw. **18**(5), 57–61 (2001). conference Name: IEEE Software
40. Yaseen, M., Khan, S.U., Alam, A.U.: Software multi-sourcing risks management from vendor's perspective: a systematic literature review protocol. Gomal Univ. J. Res. **29**(2), 1–8 (2013)
41. Zhang, T., Upadhyaya, G., Reinhardt, A., Rajan, H., Kim, M.: Are code examples on an online Q&A forum reliable?: a study of API misuse on stack overflow. In:

Proceedings of the 40th International Conference on Software Engineering, pp. 886–896. ACM, Gothenburg Sweden (2018)
42. Ziegener, D.: Bundes-IT: 205 Millionen Euro für Windows und Office (2022). https://www.golem.de/news/bundes-it-205-millionen-euro-fuer-windows-und-office-2202-163451.html

Web-Based Protocol Enabling Distributed Identity Information Networks for Greater Sovereignty

Michael Hofmeier$^{(\boxtimes)}$ ⓘ, Karl Seidenfad ⓘ, Manfred Hofmeier ⓘ, and Wolfgang Hommel ⓘ

Computer Science Department, University of the Bundeswehr Munich, Neubiberg, Germany
{michael.hofmeier,karl.seidenfad,manfred.hofmeier, wolfgang.hommel}@unibw.de

Abstract. This paper presents a design for a Distributed Identity Information Network (DistIN) that can manage digital identities in a decentralized manner while aiming for high security, scalability and sovereignty. This novel approach enables the creation and verification of electronic signatures and offers the functionality of a public key infrastructure. Due to its decentralized nature and flexibility, this system is suitable for various types of organizations, including community services. Common web technologies, state-of-the-art cryptographic algorithms as well as blockchain technology are used. This system design is developed on the basis of universal use cases and validated for its applicability, leading to the web-based DistIN protocol as a result.

Keywords: Decentralized identity management · Public key infrastructure · Digital sovereignty · Blockchain application

1 Introduction

This paper presents a novel concept for distributed Identity Management Systems (IDMS) including an alternative approach for Public Key Infrastructures (PKI). Managing authentication and digital identities across multiple services and applications is a frustrating experience for users, thus service owners and the industry have been waiting for a simpler solution [29]. The concept for a Distributed Identity Information Network (DistIN) presented here is based on a web-based protocol that can be implemented in existing web applications, but will also be provided as a standalone reference implementation including installation instructions at a later point in time, so that a fully functional application can be set up and used. The description of the associated Application Programming Interface (API) including the required actions and resource objects as well as future prototype implementations can be found in the project's GitHub repository [12].

ⓒ The Author(s), under exclusive license to Springer Nature Switzerland AG 2024
F. Phillipson et al. (Eds.): I4CS 2024, CCIS 2109, pp. 408–425, 2024.
https://doi.org/10.1007/978-3-031-60433-1_23

1.1 Motivation

The intended system works both in an individual context and for all types of organizations and enable inter-organizational identity and authorization requests. This also applies to voluntary associations, small, medium-sized and large companies, commercial and government organizations. This makes this approach particularly suitable for community services that aim for a high degree of digital sovereignty and security.

Our design focuses on authentication, authorization, verification and signing of data and documents, using state-of-the-art cryptographic mechanisms. In order not to limit the acceptability of the concept, it should be as developer-friendly as possible, which has influence on the selection of protocols, data formats, libraries and frameworks. For a high level of *sovereignty* on the individual and organizational layer defined by Fries et al. [9], each technically competent participant should be able to set up an *own service* and participate in the network. This makes it easier for users to choose a service they *trust*. A high level of trust in the services is to be achieved through a high level of decentralization and *freedom of choice*.

In addition, the system should expose the public key and relevant attributes of the identities to the Internet so that no entire certificates have to be supplied with signed data records. If these signed data records are transferred via Near Field Communication (NFC), the device must be capable of card emulation, and the data size should not exceed 1 kB [18]. Additionally, in favor of *security* and the sovereignty of the individual, his or her key pair should be renewable at any time and as often as desired, without the need to involve a certificate authority.

Figure 1 shows the structure of the attempted network. In an organizational context, each organization would be associated with one DistIN service. In the case of highly segmented organizations, multiple services are also plausible.

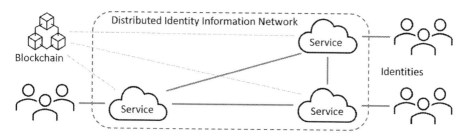

Fig. 1. Distributed identity information network [12]

1.2 Content

This paper is organized as follows. First, Sect. 2 describes the applied research method, and then Sect. 3 discusses related work. Section 5 then describes the core concept of the developed approach. The use cases on which the approach is validated are described in Sect. 4. Subsequently, the developed design is explained in

Sect. 6 and transformed into an API definition in Sect. 7. In Sect. 8 the validation follows and in Sect. 9 differences to existing approaches are highlighted. Finally, Sect. 10 describes the further research steps.

2   Method

First, the core concept and architecture are drafted based on the goals to be achieved. Then, for the development of the concept, the basic technologies are selected and the necessary communication steps are analyzed. For this purpose, various use cases are defined that are to be enabled by this concept. These use cases are analyzed and the methods (including parameters) that are to be implemented for them, as well as the data objects that are returned, are determined.

The design and the associated validation are based on the use cases, that indicate the functional requirements.

This method is based in part on the design science research methodology (DSRM) by Peffers et. al. [22]. Conceptually, a design research artifact can be any designed object in which a research contribution is embedded in the design [10]. In this case, the artifact consists of a defined protocol and at a later point in time of this research of an API specification.

3   Related Work

This section focuses on approaches with a similar focus and objectives, and will be differentiated in a later chapter. One approach with similar objectives is DNS-Based Authentication of Named Entities (DANE). Decentralized Identifiers (DIDs) and Verifiable Credentials (VCs) are used for fully decentralized approaches that bring their own challenges.

3.1   DNS-Based Authentication

DANE offers the option to use the DNS Security Extensions (DNSSEC) infrastructure to store and sign keys and certificates that are used by Transport Layer Security (TLS) [11]. Such an infrastructure makes it possible to access hierarchical and signed identity information via the domain's structure. As [23] describes, ID4me [29], e.g., uses the Automated Certificate Management Environment (ACME) in conjunction with DNSSEC and DANE, which has rarely been used in practice. The role identity agent, which administrates the attributes and is identified by DNS, has to be trusted by the user [23]. In principle, this approach solves the problem of exposed keys and identity information, but it also introduces some inertia in publishing changes. Also, dynamic attribute signatures and their revocation by participants of another domain are difficult to accomplish.

3.2   Decentralized Identities

DIDs and VCs, developed by the World Wide Web Consortia (W3C), are an essential part of most blockchain-based identity approaches [19]. Ownership of a DID, an identifier that can be used for credential exchange and authentication, is proven by demonstrating the possession of the private key associated with the public key bound to the DID [19]. To enable interoperability between different Decentralized identity management solutions, a universal DID resolver, that returns the DID document containing associated data describing the DID subject, is currently in development by the Decentralized Identity Foundation (DIF) [19].

The W3C defined VCs as digital documents issued with digital signatures, that are protected from corruption by asymmetric cryptography [26]. VCs support selective disclosure, so end users can prove claims about their identity without revealing more information than they intend and need for performing a specific action [20]. VCs can express any information that a physical credential contains, but the usage of digital signatures from both the issuer and holder make them tamper-evident and more trustworthy to the verifier [20]. The cryptographic premises are well suited to prove and verify the possession of a DID, however, there is no integrated means of connecting the real-world identity to the DID's owner [3]. While we are able to attach VCs to DIDs and therefore would be able to endorse personal information to a DID, the standard does not describe how the trust in the identity can be established [3].

4   Use Cases

This section explains the different use cases that can occur in the context of this system concept and for which appropriate methods must be built in. These use cases are separated into the tasks of IDM and PKI.

4.1   Identity Management Use Cases

Verify Service (IdmVS). There is a trust relationship between the user and the service of his choice that must be ensured. For this reason, the user must be able to cryptographically verify the authenticity of the service and its responses. This is intended to make Man-in-the-Middle (MITM) attacks more difficult.

Verify Identity (IdmVI). In order to verify the authenticity of other users or identities (devices can be identities as well), it must be possible to retrieve and validate the associated public key.

Sign/Verify Attribute (IdmVA). To make the validity of certain identity information verifiable, it must be possible to sign attributes of the identity and retrieve them together with their signatures. Certificate authorities can play a role in this. In the organizational context, signatures of the organization's administration are relevant in this respect. In addition, it must be possible to revoke attribute signatures.

Sign/Verify Data or Documents (IdmVD). In order to be able to verify the signatures of data records or documents, information must be included with the signature that allows the public key to be retrieved together with a defined set of identity attributes. However, these attributes must remain protected from unauthorized access in all other respects. For signing, a user therefore needs functions to grant such permissions.

4.2 PKI Use Cases

Chain of Trust (PkiCT). For a valid PKI, it must be possible to build a chain of trust up to a trust anchor (TA). This means that it must be possible to build a cryptographically solid validation chain when verifying identity attributes.

Verify Public Key (PkiVK). In order to be able to check the authenticity of an identity, its public key must be verifiable or confirmed by the signature of a higher authority.

Sign/Verify Set of Attributes (PkiVA). An identity confirmed by PKI has verifiable attributes that are closely linked to the identity's public key. Subsection 4.1 (IdmVA) also describes the use case of signature and verification of attributes.

Revoke Set of Attributes (PkiRA). In the conventional PKI, certificates are revoked by revocation lists. More generally, it must be possible to revoke the confirmation of attributes.

5   Core Concept

The ultimate aim is the contribution of a service in the form of a web application that implements this concept and can be installed and configured by any technically competent administrator. The user is free to choose a service. As a consequence, the user must trust this service, but also there is a legally responsible party with whom the user can make an agreement on data protection and usage, which is not easy in completely decentralized concepts, but important.

Figure 2 shows an exemplary system architecture where the dashed lines represent optional linking to a blockchain, the solid lines represent affiliation, and the arrows represent digital signatures as confirmation.

5.1   Service

A service in this concept is a web service that implements the DistIN protocol. In addition to the DistIN resources, the service can or should provide a frontend for users and administrators to manage the data. The protocol can also be

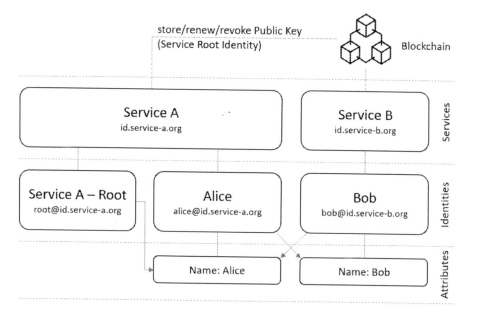

Fig. 2. Network architecture [12]

added to existing web applications. DistIN resources are web requests, and are submitted to the server according to the following Uniform Resource Locator (URL) scheme:

```
https://{SERVICE_DOMAIN}/distin/{Resource}
```

The DistIN resources are derived from Sect. 4 and defined in Sect. 6. To hamper MITM attacks, each service gets its own core identity with its own key pair, so that the service is always uniquely identifiable.

5.2 Identity

An identity can be a real person or, e.g., a device in the Internet of Things (IoT). The identity can be globally identified by its DistIN ID. The ID is structured according to the following scheme:

```
{USER_NAME}@{SERVICE_DOMAIN}
```

From the ID, the service to be addressed can be determined exactly, similar to the Simple Mail Transfer Protocol (SMTP) or the Extensible Messaging and Presence Protocol (XMPP). The identity generates its own key pair and does not pass its private key to the service or other instances. In order to clearly separate the systems, the concept involves an authenticator app that holds the private key and will be used to trigger signatures that either sign objects or serve as proof of identity.

5.3 Attribute

This concept is aimed, in part, at identity exposing, e.g., in the context of electronic signatures, which require verified personal data for legal validity. It should also be able to manage rights and roles within a company. For this reason, we also use an attribute-based approach, in which an attribute can be signed by other, maybe even multiple, identities.

5.4 Blockchain

To be able to uniquely verify a service even though one does not yet know its public key, a public blockchain (e.g., Ethereum) can be used to register, renew, and revoke the public key or key hash of the core identity based on the service domain. This should be **optional** and up to the decision of the service owner, depending on the security needs of the organization. The registration, renewal and revocation of the keys can be managed using so-called Smart Contracts. In addition, hashes can be queried publicly in order to check the authenticity of services.

6 Design

In this section, the system concept is elaborated in a way that it serves for understanding and as a blueprint for implementation.

6.1 Selected Technologies

The first step is to select the required technologies with a focus on developer-friendliness, implementability, security, availability and sovereignty of identities and organizations.

Network Protocol. Due to the ease of implementation and wide availability of libraries, we rely on communication over Hypertext Transfer Protocol Secure (HTTPS) using TLS. However, as [4] has shown, MITM attacks on HTTPS communication are feasible. [30] identified the increasing trend of MITM attacks against HTTPS, and the lack of existing classification systems. To maintain trust between client and service, the service signs all responses with the key of its core identity for an additional trust layer. In particular, the interface is implemented as a Representational State Transfer (REST) interface, since this is well suited for data exchange between applications. REST uses the HTTP methods (CRUD operations) defined in RFC 2616 [2] in an explicit way. Exposing a system's resources through a REST API is a flexible way to provide different kinds of applications with data formatted in a standard way and helps to meet integration requirements that are critical to building systems where data can be easily combined [25].

Data Formats. Generally formats based on Extensible Markup Language (XML) or JavaScript Object Notation (JSON) are the most commonly used ones, although it is clear from the trend of recent years that XML is slowly being replaced by JSON [27]. JSON is particularly performant to be parsed in JavaScript environments [6]. The JSON Web Signature (JWS) developed by the Internet Engineering Task Force (IETF) is a data structure representing a digitally signed message [15]. Since the JWS format is based on JSON, it makes sense to use it in this system in the context of signatures. In terms of direct data exchange between identities, a modified version of the JWS format might be an option [13, 14].

Algorithms. Several public-private key algorithms may be considered with regard to identity management. In order not to overburden application developers, the available set of algorithms should be limited to a few secure algorithms, similar to JWS. RFC-7518 [16] defines a total of 12 combinations of cryptographic algorithm and hash length. For our approach, we rely on Post Quantum Cryptography (PQC) algorithms for higher security. PQC is the field of cryptography where encryption algorithms are developed which are secure from an adversary with quantum computers [1]. The National Institute of Standards and Technology (NIST) plans to standardize either FALCON or CRYSTALS-Dilithium (DILITHIUM), both selected as a finalist for the digital signature schemes [1].

FALCON is a signature scheme that allows compact public key and signature sizes and very fast verification [24], but as [17] demonstrated, some implementations of the FALCON scheme might be vulnerable to side-channel attacks.

DILITHIUM is a lattice-based signature scheme based on the hardness of Module-SIS (short integer solution) and Module-LWE (learning with error) [21]. The scheme incorporates secure implementation against side-channel attacks and has comparable efficiency to the current best lattice-based signature schemes [28].

6.2   System Architecture

The system (Fig. 3) consists of the DistIN web services, the databases associated with each, the users (identities) with their authenticator app, the blockchain, and other services that make use of this system.

The DistIN Services are responsible for storing, managing and providing the public keys, attributes and attribute signatures of the identities. Since the private key of an identity should be under its own control only (not even the service), the use of a separate application on the user's device is proposed. This authenticator application allows signature requests to be retrieved from the chosen DistIN service and, if necessary, a signature to be sent back (e.g., as confirmation/permission). The application is also responsible for key generation. Theoretically, application variants are also conceivable in which the private key is located in the service and other authentication methods are used, e.g., for compatibility reasons, but these are not recommended for security reasons. The

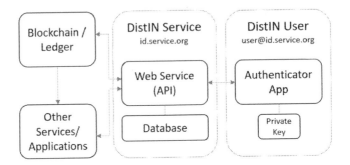

Fig. 3. System communication architecture [12]

blockchain is used to verify the DistIN Services as described in the core concept (Sect. 5). Another role in the system is played by the other services that rely on the system, e.g., for user authentication. The system borrows from the principle of DIDs (Subsect. 3.2) by keeping the private key with the user, keeping the data in the user's sphere of trust, and releasing data or actions individually.

6.3 Trust

One of the main challenges is to verify attributes for correctness even though the associated identities and services are not known. When using conventional X.509 [5] certificates, the certification chain is validated up to the trust anchor, which can be defined application-specifically. With X.509 certificates, the public key is signed together with the identity attributes.

In order to achieve similar trust with our approach, without a key pair change influencing the validity of the certification, the attributes are signed directly in combination with the DistIN ID. In this case, an attribute can be signed by several identities, so that theoretically several (valid) chains of trust can exist for one attribute. To avoid unnecessary queries, a predefined attribute *DistINRole* is used, which can have the values *Identity*, *RootIdentity* and *Authority*. To build chains of trust for validating attributes, the *DistINRole* attribute of the authority can also be signed by a higher authority or trust anchor (Fig. 4). A list of trust anchors must be known at verification and may be predefined depending on the scenario, e.g. a central trust service within a corporation or consortium.

6.4 Privacy

Exposure of identity information must not allow malicious actors to request personal information from the services without being asked. Therefore, an identity can specify for each individual attribute whether it should be public or private. If an attribute is public, it can be queried based on its keyword (e.g., lastName). A non-exhaustive list of common keywords can be found in the documentation [12]. If an attribute is private, it must be queried by its (randomly

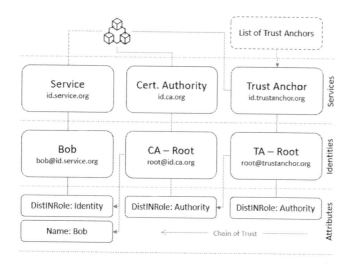

Fig. 4. Chain of trust [12]

generated) ID consisting of at least 32 characters. The necessity of providing an additional ID variant for single-use, i.e., the ID no longer works once the data has been requested by the designated recipient, must still be evaluated.

6.5   Authentication

This subsection explains how a service can check the authenticity of identities using this system (see also Fig. 5). If a Web service wants to authenticate a user based on his DistIN ID, it must perform a simple web request to the user's DistIN service, whose address can be read from the ID. In the request body, a random byte sequence is provided as a challenge to sign. The response body then returns the signature provided by the user. Since this process can take a little longer, the timeout for the web request must be set long enough. Consequently, this is a particularly developer-friendly method of integrating user authentication.

The entire authentication process then proceeds as follows. First, the service or application submits the request, including the challenge, to the DistIN service. The DistIN client/user queries the DistIN service for new signature requests via its authenticator app. In this way, it receives the request on its end device, signs it if necessary, and sends the signature back to its DistIN service. The DistIN service is now able to respond to the service's or application's request with a signature, which the service can then verify cryptographically. The public key required for verification is also retrieved directly from the DistIN Service or from a local database.

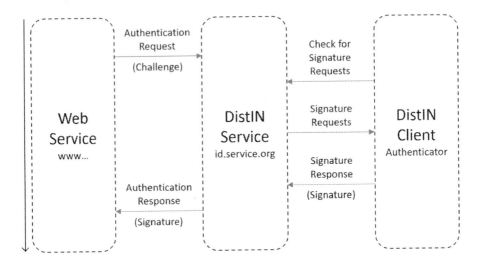

Fig. 5. Authentication process [12]

7   DistIN API

As explained in Subsect. 6.1, the DistIN API is designed as a REST API. The transmitted data objects are serialized as JSON according to Subsect. 6.1.

To be able to identify and authenticate users of the API, the following HTTP(s) **request header** parameters are defined: *DistIN-ID*, *DistIN-Signature* and *DistIN-Token*. The parameter *DistIN-ID* contains the ID of the requesting user and *DistIN-Signature* the requesting identity's signature of the request body. The *DistIN-Token* is intended for authorizing client applications (e.g. Authenticator App) of identities associated with the service. To be able to verify the responding service, it adds its signature of the response body to the **response header** in the *DistIN-Signature* parameter.

7.1   Objects

This section presents the main JSON objects required to verify identities. The associated actions and resources are defined in Subsect. 7.2.

PublicKey. This object can be retrieved for individual identities. It consists of the public key together with the creation date and, if applicable, its signature using the previous key:

```
{
  identity: "alice@id.example.org",
  key: "<---BASE64--->",
  algorithm : "DILITHIUM",
  date: "2023/01/30",
  signature: "<---BASE64--->"
}
```

Attribute. This object is the complete representation of an attribute that can be retrieved for an identity. It contains references to attribute signatures and the value can be of any type specified in the *mimeType* parameter.

```
{
    id: "ndi3xmj...",
    name: "lastName",
    mimeType: "text/plain",
    value: "Peterson",
    identity: "alice@id.example.org",
    signatures: [<AttributeSignatureReference>,..]
}
```

AttributeSignatureReference. Since attribute signatures must remain under the sovereignty of the signer, only a reference to an attribute signature is stored on attributes, providing information about where the full signature can be retrieved:

```
{
    identity: "alice@id.example.org",
    attribute: "ndi3xmj...",
    signer: "bob@id.example.org",
    signature: "hdywbecfxztefwynezuxuevuw"
}
```

AttributeSignature. The full attribute signature can be retrieved from the signer's service, unless the signer has withdrawn it. This object contains the data necessary for verification:

```
{
    id: "hdywbecfxztefwynezuxuevuw",
    identity: "alice@id.example.org",
    attribute: "ndi3xmj...",
    signer: "bob@id.example.org",
    date: "2023/01/30",
    signature: "<---BASE64--->"
}
```

ServiceVerificationState. This object contains the result of a verification of another DistIN service via the requested service. It indicates whether the service responds with the correct key. The *type* parameter specifies whether the verification took place purely via DNS or via a blockchain. Accordingly, this parameter has the values "DNS" or "BLOCKCHAIN":

```
{
    valid: true,
    type: "DNS"
}
```

More object definitions are contained in the full documentation of the DistIN API, available with the DistIN Github repository [12].

7.2   Actions/Resources

DistIN Actions are HTTP(s) methods according to RFC-2616 [2] that are performed on DistIN resources defined by URLs. Table 1 shows the most relevant actions and their input values and response objects. In the case of GET requests, the parameters are passed as URL query parameters, otherwise the input objects are supplied as JSON objects in the request body.

Table 1. DistIN actions

GET	INPUT	RESPONSE
publicKey	id	[PublicKey]
attribute	id, attributeId	[Attribute]
attribute	id, attributeName	[Attribute]
attributeSignature	id	[AttributeSignature]
serviceVerificationState	service	[ServiceVerificationState]
authenticate	id, challenge	[Signature]
signatureRequests	–	[SignatureRequest]
POST	**INPUT**	**RESPONSE**
attribute	[Attribute]	[Attribute]
attributeSignatureReference	[AttributeSignature-Reference]	[AttributeSignature-Reference]
attributeSignature	[AttributeSignature]	[AttributeSignature]
signatureResponse	[Signature]	–
PUT	**INPUT**	**RESPONSE**
publicKey	[PublicKey]	[PublicKey]
attribute	[Attribute]	[Attribute]
attributeSignature	[AttributeSignature]	[AttributeSignature]
DELETE	**INPUT**	**RESPONSE**
attribute	id, attributeId	–
attributeSignature	id, signatureId	–

It depends on the executing identity whether an action can be performed on a resource. Table 2 gives an overview of who may execute which actions and which actions must be implemented at all.

A detailed description of the resources and actions is available with the full DistIN API documentation on Github [12].

Table 2. DistIN resource permissions

RESOURCE	GET	POST	PUT	DELETE
publicKey	all	–	owner	–
attribute	all	owner	owner	owner
attributeSignatureReference	–	all	–	–
attributeSignature	all	owner	owner	owner
serviceVerificationState	all	–	–	–
authenticate	all	–	–	–
signatureRequests	owner	–	-	–
signatureResponse	–	owner	–	–

8 Validation

In this section, the concept is theoretically validated for its functions and applicability using the IDM and PKI use cases.

8.1 Validation on IDM Use Cases

Verify Service (IdmVS). As outlined in Subsect. 5.1, each service signs each response with the private key of its core identity. The hash of the associated public key can be registered in the blockchain for additional security and retrieved from there by others for verification (Subsect. 5.4). The public key can be retrieved using the ID of the core identity.

Verify Identity (IdmVI). To verify the authenticity of an identity, its public key is used analogously to service verification. Here, the same object and API resource are used. Note that the validity of the requested service must also be verified.

Sign/Verify Attribute (IdmVA). To check the validity of attributes, their signatures must be checked. These are provided as a reference object, which contains the necessary information to fetch the attribute signature object from the domain of the signer. The attribute and attribute signature are available for this purpose.

Sign/Verify Data or Documents (IdmVD). In order to verify the signatures of data sets or documents, the cryptographic signature, the DistIN ID of the signer and the time of the signature must be available with the data set. Together with the DistIN ID, the time information allows the public key that was valid at that time to be retrieved (use cases *IdmVS* and *IdmVI*). For a legally valid signature, however, it is necessary to link the digital signature with personal information such as the name of the signer [8,31]. So IDs of the corresponding attributes of the signature of the record or document should also be attached (use case *IdmVA*).

8.2   Validation on PKI Use Cases

Chain of Trust (PkiCT). Using the *DistINRole* attribute, a chain of trust (6.3) can be formed up to a TA to verify the identity and its attributes. Here again, the use cases *IdmVS* and *IdmVI* come into play.

Verify Public Key (PkiVK). In our concept the attributes and the signatures of the authorities are linked to ID of an identity, not to the public key. This means, that the public key must be strongly linked to the ID. The key can be requested from the identity's service using the ID. The service on the other hand can be verified by DNS, Blockchain and the public key of its core identity (use case *IdmVS*).

Sign/Verify Set of Attributes (PkiVA). If the requirements for use case *PkiVK* are fulfilled, only the requirements for use case *IdmVA*, which was validated in Subsect. 8.1, remain for this point.

Revoke Set of Attributes (PkiRA). Since the signatures of the attributes are not stored with the attribute or its identity, but remain in the sphere of the signatory, the signatory can delete or invalidate the signatures at any time, which is equivalent to a revocation.

9   Comparison/Delimitation

In terms of the requirements, both concepts, DANE (Subsect. 3.1) and DistIN, solve the problems of exposing keys and identity information, but in very different ways and with different depth with respect to the application/API layer. Table 3 shows an overview of the most important differences.

DANE relies on X.509 certificates and DNSSEC, while DistIN relies on JSON objects, chained public keys, and blockchain. In addition, DistIN is designed to allow keys, attributes, and signatures to be created, modified, or removed very quickly and with high throughput, even without the involvement of a domain administrator. So the core difference is the speed and nature of system provisioning and identity information alteration. Another difference is that when using DANE according to RFC-7671 [7], the size of the data stored in the DNS record must remain as small as possible, whereas with DistIN entire files or images may be available as verifiable attributes.

When using DIDs and DID wallets, the user himself/herself is the data processing entity within the meaning of the GDPR. This transfers a great amount of responsibility to the user. A loss of the wallet or the device containing it is also

Table 3. Core differences between DANE and DistIN

Characteristic	DANE	DistIN
Underlying protocol	DNS	HTTP(s)
Data format	X.509	JSON
Secured by	DNSSEC	DNS or Blockchain
Get obsolete keys	no	yes
Management features	no	yes
Key renewal intervals	normal	short
Required subdomains	>user count	1

fatal. In our concept, the services are clearly defined as the entity responsible for data processing and data protection. At the same time, the system is designed in a way that a high degree of distribution can be achieved, as only a domain and a small server are required to operate such a service.

10 Conclusion and Future Work

With DistIN, we contribute a new concept that can be used to manage identities, access rights and proofs. At the same time, it enables the creation of chains of trust without having to rely on the existing certificate infrastructure. The concept includes the definition of the API so that not only applications can be developed on this basis, but existing systems can also implement it. For the design, we looked at concepts with a similar target setting, defined general, scenario-independent use cases and developed and validated on this basis. In addition, we focused on sustainable security and usability.

This paper represents the system design. Next, the concept presented in this paper and the results of its **discussion** will be transformed to a final design and **validated** using multiple scenarios. After that an initial **prototype** for a full-scale DistIN identity management web application will be implemented. This includes the development and evaluation of Smart Contracts. The resulting prototype will then be practically validated using a real scenario and later made available as a fully functional application including installation instructions in the DistIN repository [12]. The prototype will then also be tested and optimized on performance and security. The final application will be a productively usable **open source solution** available to everyone.

Acknowledgments. This work originates from the LIONS research project. LIONS is funded by dtec.bw — Digitalization and Technology Research Center of the Bundeswehr, which we gratefully acknowledge. dtec.bw is funded by the European Union — NextGenerationEU.

References

1. Bavdekar, R., Chopde, E.J., Agrawal, A., Bhatia, A., Tiwari, K.: Post quantum cryptography: A review of techniques, challenges and standardizations. In: 2023 International Conference on Information Networking (ICOIN), pp. 146–151. IEEE (2023)
2. Berners-Lee, T., Fielding, R., Frystyk, H.: RFC 2616: Hypertext transfer protocol – HTTP/1.0. Tech. rep. (1996)
3. Brunner, C., Gallersdörfer, U., Knirsch, F., Engel, D., Matthes, F.: Did and vc: Untangling decentralized identifiers and verifiable credentials for the web of trust. In: Proceedings of the 2020 3rd International Conference on Blockchain Technology and Applications, pp. 61–66 (2020)
4. Callegati, F., Cerroni, W., Ramilli, M.: Man-in-the-middle attack to the https protocol. IEEE Secur. Privacy **7**(1), 78–81 (2009)
5. Cooper, D., Santesson, S., Farrell, S., Boeyen, S., Housley, R., Polk, W.: RFC 5280: Internet X. 509 public key infrastructure certificate and certificate revocation list (CRL) profile. Tech. rep. (2008)
6. Dhalla, H.K.: A Performance Analysis of Native JSON Parsers in Java, Python, MS. NET Core, JavaScript, and PHP. In: 2020 16th International Conference on Network and Service Management (CNSM), pp. 1–5. IEEE (2020)
7. Dukhovni, V., Hardaker, W.: RFC 7671: The DNS-based authentication of named entities (DANE) protocol: updates and operational guidance. Tech. rep. (2015)
8. Electronic Signatures in Global and National Commerce Act: 15 U.S.C. Chapter 96 (2000)
9. Fries, I., Greiner, M., Hofmeier, M., Hrestic, R., Lechner, U., Wendeborn, T.: Towards a layer model for digital sovereignty: a holistic approach. In: Hämmerli, B., Helmbrecht, U., Hommel, W., Kunczik, L., Pickl, S. (eds.) Critical Information Infrastructures Security: 17th International Conference, CRITIS 2022, Munich, Germany, September 14–16, 2022, Revised Selected Papers, pp. 119–139. Springer Nature Switzerland, Cham (2023). https://doi.org/10.1007/978-3-031-35190-7_9
10. Hevner, A., Chatterjee, S., Hevner, A., Chatterjee, S.: Design science research in information systems. Design research in information systems: theory and practice, pp. 9–22 (2010)
11. Hoffman, P., Schlyter, J.: RFC 6698: The DNS-based authentication of named entities. DANE) transport layer security (TLS) protocol, TLSA. Tech. rep. (2012)
12. Hofmeier, M.: DistIN Github repository. https://github.com/LIONS-DLT/DistIN (2023)
13. Hofmeier, M., Hommel, W.: Enabling the JSON web signature format to support complex and identity-oriented non-web processes. In: Krieger, U.R., Eichler, G., Erfurth, C., Fahrnberger, G. (eds.) Innovations for Community Services: 23rd International Conference, I4CS 2023, Bamberg, Germany, September 11–13, 2023, Proceedings, pp. 29–47. Springer Nature Switzerland, Cham (2023). https://doi.org/10.1007/978-3-031-40852-6_2
14. Hofmeier, M., Seidenfad, K., Hommel, W.: Validating a Modified JSON web signature format using the scenario of ammunition issuance for training purposes. In: MILCOM 2023 - 2023 IEEE Military Communications Conference (MILCOM), pp. 237–238 (2023). https://doi.org/10.1109/MILCOM58377.2023.10356342
15. Jones, M., Bradley, J., Sakimura, N.: RFC 7515: JSON Web Signature (JWS) (2015)
16. Jones, M.: RFC 7518: JSON web algorithms (JWA). Tech. rep. (2015)

17. Karabulut, E., Aysu, A.: Falcon down: breaking falcon post-quantum signature scheme through side-channel attacks. In: 2021 58th ACM/IEEE Design Automation Conference (DAC), pp. 691–696. IEEE (2021)
18. Karmazín, J., Očenášek, P.: The state of Near-Field Communication (NFC) on the android platform. In: Tryfonas, T. (ed.) HAS 2016. LNCS, vol. 9750, pp. 247–254. Springer, Cham (2016). https://doi.org/10.1007/978-3-319-39381-0_22
19. Kubach, M., Schunck, C.H., Sellung, R., Roßnagel, H.: Self-sovereign and decentralized identity as the future of identity management? Open Identity Summit 2020 (2020)
20. Lux, Z.A., Thatmann, D., Zickau, S., Beierle, F.: Distributed-ledger-based authentication with decentralized identifiers and verifiable credentials. In: 2020 2nd Conference on Blockchain Research and Applications for Innovative Networks and Services (BRAINS), pp. 71–78. IEEE (2020)
21. Lyubashevsky, V., et al.: Crystals-dilithium. Algorithm Specifications and Supporting Documentation (2020)
22. Peffers, K., Tuunanen, T., Rothenberger, M.A., Chatterjee, S.: A design science research methodology for information systems research. J. Manag. Inf. Syst. 24(3), 45–77 (2007)
23. Pöhn, D., Hommel, W.: An overview of limitations and approaches in identity management. In: Proceedings of the 15th International Conference on Availability, Reliability and Security, pp. 1–10 (2020)
24. Prest, T., et al.: Falcon. Post-Quantum Cryptography Project of NIST (2020)
25. Rodriguez, A.: Restful web services: the basics. IBM developerWorks 33(2008), 18 (2008)
26. Sedlmeir, J., Smethurst, R., Rieger, A., Fridgen, G.: Digital identities and verifiable credentials. Business Inform. Syst. Eng. 63(5), 603–613 (2021)
27. Siriwardena, P., Siriwardena, P.: Message-level security with JSON web signature. In: Advanced API Security: OAuth 2.0 and Beyond, pp. 157–184 (2020)
28. Soni, D., et al.: Crystals-dilithium. In: Hardware Architectures for Post-Quantum Digital Signature Schemes, pp. 13–30 (2021)
29. Speck, K.: Independent, Federated Digital Identity Management Solution ID4me Announces Public Beta At CloudFest 2019 (2019). https://id4me.org/independent-federated-digital-identity-management-solution-id4me-announces-public-beta-at-cloudfest-2019/
30. Stricot-Tarboton, S., Chaisiri, S., Ko, R.K.: Taxonomy of man-in-the-middle attacks on https. In: 2016 IEEE Trustcom/Bigdatase/Ispa, pp. 527–534. IEEE (2016)
31. The European Parliament and the Council of the European Union: European Regulation on Electronic Identification and Trust Services for Electronic Transactions in the internal market. Official Journal of the European Union (2014)

Author Index

F. Phillipson et al. (Eds.): I4CS 2024, CCIS 2109, pp. 427–428, 2024.
https://doi.org/10.1007/978-3-031-60433-1

Printed in the United States
by Baker & Taylor Publisher Services